10 ACTUAL, OFFICIAL
LSAT **PREPTESTS**™

A Publication of the Law School Admission Council,
Newtown, PA

ISBN-13: 978-0-9793050-4-7
ISBN-10: 0-9793050-4-7

Print number
12 11 10 9

TABLE OF CONTENTS

INTRODUCTION

The 10 PrepTests in this book are disclosed Law School Admission Tests (LSATs) that were administered between December 1992 and September 1995. Each test in this volume includes actual Logical Reasoning, Reading Comprehension, and Analytical Reasoning items followed by the writing sample, score computation table, and answer key for that test. This publication is designed to be an inexpensive way for you to gain practice and better prepare yourself for taking the LSAT.

The LSAT is a half-day standardized test required for admission to all ABA-approved law schools, most Canadian law schools, and many other law schools. It consists of five 35-minute sections of multiple-choice questions. Four of the five sections contribute to the test taker's score. These sections include one Reading Comprehension section, one Analytical Reasoning section, and two Logical Reasoning sections. The unscored section, commonly referred to as the variable section, typically is used to pretest new test questions or preequate new test forms. The placement of this section in the LSAT will vary.

A 35-minute writing sample is administered at the end of the test. The writing sample is not scored by LSAC, but copies are sent to all law schools to which you apply. The score scale for the LSAT is 120 to 180.

The LSAT is designed to measure skills that are considered essential for success in law school: the reading and comprehension of complex texts with accuracy and insight; the organization and management of information and the ability to draw reasonable inferences from it; the ability to think critically; and the analysis and evaluation of the reasoning and arguments of others.

The LSAT provides a standard measure of acquired reading and verbal reasoning skills that law schools can use as one of several factors in assessing applicants.

For up-to-date information on LSAC's services go to LSAC.org.

SCORING

Your LSAT score is based on the number of questions you answer correctly (the raw score). There is no deduction for incorrect answers, and all questions count equally. In other words, there is no penalty for guessing.

Test Score Accuracy—Reliability and Standard Error of Measurement

Candidates perform at different levels on different occasions for reasons quite unrelated to the characteristics of a test itself. The accuracy of test scores is best described by the use of two related statistical terms: reliability and standard error of measurement.

Reliability is a measure of how consistently a test measures the skills being assessed. The higher the reliability coefficient for a test, the more certain we can be that test takers would get very similar scores if they took the test again.

LSAC reports an internal consistency measure of reliability for every test form. Reliability can vary from 0.00 to 1.00, and a test with no measurement error would have a reliability coefficient of 1.00 (never attained in practice). Reliability coefficients for past LSAT forms have ranged from .90 to .95, indicating a high degree of consistency for these tests. LSAC expects the reliability of the LSAT to continue to fall within the same range.

LSAC also reports the amount of measurement error associated with each test form, a concept known as the standard error of measurement (SEM). The SEM, which is usually about 2.6 points, indicates how close a test taker's observed score is likely to be to his or her true score. True scores are theoretical scores that would be obtained from perfectly reliable tests with no measurement error—scores never known in practice.

Score bands, or ranges of scores that contain a test taker's true score a certain percentage of the time, can be derived using the SEM. LSAT score bands are constructed by adding and subtracting the (rounded) SEM to and from an actual LSAT score (e.g., the LSAT score, plus or minus 3 points). Scores near 120 or 180 have asymmetrical bands. Score bands constructed in this manner will contain an individual's true score approximately 68 percent of the time.

Measurement error also must be taken into account when comparing LSAT scores of two test takers. It is likely that small differences in scores are due to measurement error rather than to meaningful differences in ability. The standard error of score differences provides some guidance as to the importance of differences between two scores. The standard error of score differences is approximately 1.4 times larger than the standard error of measurement for the individual scores.

Thus, a test score should be regarded as a useful but approximate measure of a test taker's abilities as measured by the test, not as an exact determination of his or her abilities. LSAC encourages law schools to examine the range of scores within the interval that probably contains the test taker's true score (e.g., the test taker's score band) rather than solely interpret the reported score alone.

Adjustments for Variation in Test Difficulty

All test forms of the LSAT reported on the same score scale are designed to measure the same abilities, but one test form may be slightly easier or more difficult than another. The scores from different test forms are made comparable through a statistical procedure known as equating. As a result of equating, a given scaled score earned on different test forms reflects the same level of ability.

Research on the LSAT

Summaries of LSAT validity studies and other LSAT research can be found in member law school libraries and at LSAC.org.

To Inquire About Test Questions

If you find what you believe to be an error or ambiguity in a test question that affects your response to the question, contact LSAC by e-mail: LSATTS@LSAC.org, or write to Law School Admission Council, Test Development Group, PO Box 40, Newtown PA 18940-0040.

HOW THESE PREPTESTS DIFFER FROM AN ACTUAL LSAT

These PrepTests are made up of the scored sections and writing samples from the actual disclosed LSATs administered from December 1992 through September 1995. However, in the Analytical Reasoning section the questions are distributed over four pages rather than eight pages as in the more recent versions of the LSAT. Also, the Reading Comprehension sections do not contain a Comparative Reading set (see page 5). These PrepTests do not contain the extra, variable section that is used to pretest new test items of one of the three multiple-choice question types. The three multiple-choice question types may be in a different order in an actual LSAT than in these PrepTests. This is because the order of these question types is intentionally varied for each administration of the test.

THE THREE LSAT MULTIPLE-CHOICE QUESTION TYPES

The multiple-choice questions that make up most of the LSAT reflect a broad range of academic disciplines and are intended to give no advantage to candidates from a particular academic background.

The five sections of the test contain three different question types. The following material presents a general discussion of the nature of each question type and some strategies that can be used in answering them.

Analytical Reasoning Questions

Analytical Reasoning questions are designed to assess the ability to consider a group of facts and rules, and, given those facts and rules, determine what could or must be true. The specific scenarios associated with these questions are usually unrelated to law, since they are intended to be accessible to a wide range of test takers.

However, the skills tested parallel those involved in determining what could or must be the case given a set of regulations, the terms of a contract, or the facts of a legal case in relation to the law. In Analytical Reasoning questions, you are asked to reason deductively from a set of statements and rules or principles that describe relationships among persons, things, or events.

Analytical Reasoning questions appear in sets, with each set based on a single passage. The passage used for each set of questions describes common ordering relationships or grouping relationships, or a combination of both types of relationships. Examples include scheduling employees for work shifts, assigning instructors to class sections, ordering tasks according to priority, and distributing grants for projects.

Analytical Reasoning questions test a range of deductive reasoning skills. These include:

- Comprehending the basic structure of a set of relationships by determining a complete solution to the problem posed (for example, an acceptable seating arrangement of all six diplomats around a table)

- Reasoning with conditional ("if-then") statements and recognizing logically equivalent formulations of such statements

- Inferring what could be true or must be true from given facts and rules

- Inferring what could be true or must be true from given facts and rules together with new information in the form of an additional or substitute fact or rule

- Recognizing when two statements are logically equivalent in context by identifying a condition or rule that could replace one of the original conditions while still resulting in the same possible outcomes

Analytical Reasoning questions reflect the kinds of detailed analyses of relationships and sets of constraints that a law student must perform in legal problem solving. For example, an Analytical Reasoning passage might describe six diplomats being seated around a table, following certain rules of protocol as to who can sit where. You, the test taker, must answer questions about the logical implications of given and new information. For example, you may be asked who can sit between diplomats X and Y, or who cannot sit next to X if W sits next to Y. Similarly, if you were a student in law school, you might be asked to analyze a scenario involving a set of particular circumstances and a set of governing rules in the form of constitutional provisions, statutes, administrative codes, or prior rulings that have been upheld. You might then be asked to determine the legal options in the scenario: what is required given the scenario, what is permissible given the scenario, and what is prohibited given the scenario. Or you might be asked to develop a "theory" for the case: when faced with an incomplete set of facts about the case, you must fill in the picture based on what is implied by the facts that are known. The problem could be elaborated by the addition of new information or hypotheticals. No formal training in logic is required to answer these questions correctly. Analytical Reasoning questions are intended to be answered using knowledge, skills, and reasoning ability generally expected of college students and graduates.

Suggested Approach

Some people may prefer to answer first those questions about a passage that seem less difficult and then those that seem more difficult. In general, it is best to finish one passage before starting on another, because much time can be lost in returning to a passage and reestablishing familiarity with its relationships. However, if you are having great difficulty on one particular set of questions and are spending too much time on them, it may be to your advantage to skip that set of questions and go on to the next passage, returning to the problematic set of questions after you have finished the other questions in the section.

Do not assume that because the conditions for a set of questions look long or complicated, the questions based on those conditions will be especially difficult.

Read the passage carefully. Careful reading and analysis are necessary to determine the exact nature of the relationships involved in an Analytical Reasoning passage. Some relationships are fixed (for example, P and R must always work on the same project). Other relationships are variable (for example, Q must be assigned to either team 1 or team 3). Some relationships that are not stated explicitly in the conditions are implied by and can be deduced from those that are stated (for example, if one condition about paintings in a display specifies that Painting K must be to the left of Painting Y, and another specifies that Painting W must be to the left of Painting K, then it can be deduced that Painting W must be to the left of Painting Y).

In reading the conditions, do not introduce unwarranted assumptions. For instance, in a set of questions establishing relationships of height and weight among the members of a team, do not assume that a person who is taller than another person must weigh more than that person. As another example, suppose a set involves ordering and a question in the set asks what must be true if both X and Y must be earlier than Z; in this case, do not assume that X must be earlier than Y merely because X is mentioned before Y. All the information needed to answer each question is provided in the passage and the question itself.

The conditions are designed to be as clear as possible. Do not interpret the conditions as if they were intended to trick you. For example, if a question asks how many

people could be eligible to serve on a committee, consider only those people named in the passage unless directed otherwise. When in doubt, read the conditions in their most obvious sense. Remember, however, that the language in the conditions is intended to be read for precise meaning. It is essential to pay particular attention to words that describe or limit relationships, such as "only," "exactly," "never," "always," "must be," "cannot be," and the like. The result of this careful reading will be a clear picture of the structure of the relationships involved, including the kinds of relationships permitted, the participants in the relationships, and the range of possible actions or attributes for these participants.

Keep in mind question independence. Each question should be considered separately from the other questions in its set. No information, except what is given in the original conditions, should be carried over from one question to another. In some cases a question will simply ask for conclusions to be drawn from the conditions as originally given. Some questions may, however, add information to the original conditions or temporarily suspend or replace one of the original conditions for the purpose of that question only. For example, if Question 1 adds the supposition "if P is sitting at table 2 ...," this supposition should NOT be carried over to any other question in the set.

Consider highlighting text and using diagrams. Many people find it useful to underline key points in the passage and in each question. In addition, it may prove very helpful to draw a diagram to assist you in finding the solution to the problem. In preparing for the test, you may wish to experiment with different types of diagrams. For a scheduling problem, a simple calendar-like diagram may be helpful. For a grouping problem, an array of labeled columns or rows may be useful. Even though most people find diagrams to be very helpful, some people seldom use them, and for some individual questions no one will need a diagram. There is by no means universal agreement on which kind of diagram is best for which problem or in which cases a diagram is most useful. Do not be concerned if a particular problem in the test seems to be best approached without the use of a diagram.

Logical Reasoning Questions

Arguments are a fundamental part of the law, and analyzing arguments is a key element of legal analysis. Training in the law builds on a foundation of basic reasoning skills. Law students must draw on the skills of analyzing, evaluating, constructing, and refuting arguments. They need to be able to identify what information is relevant to an issue or argument and what impact further evidence might have. They need to be able to reconcile opposing positions and use arguments to persuade others.

Logical Reasoning questions evaluate the ability to analyze, critically evaluate, and complete arguments as they occur in ordinary language. The questions are based on short arguments drawn from a wide variety of sources, including newspapers, general interest magazines, scholarly publications, advertisements, and informal discourse. These arguments mirror legal reasoning in the types of arguments presented and in their complexity, though few of the arguments actually have law as a subject matter.

Each Logical Reasoning question requires you to read and comprehend a short passage, then answer one question (or, rarely, two questions) about it. The questions are designed to assess a wide range of skills involved in thinking critically, with an emphasis on skills that are central to legal reasoning.

These skills include:

- Recognizing the parts of an argument and their relationships

- Recognizing similarities and differences between patterns of reasoning

- Drawing well-supported conclusions

- Reasoning by analogy

- Recognizing misunderstandings or points of disagreement

- Determining how additional evidence affects an argument

- Detecting assumptions made by particular arguments

- Identifying and applying principles or rules

- Identifying flaws in arguments

- Identifying explanations

The questions do not presuppose specialized knowledge of logical terminology. For example, you will not be expected to know the meaning of specialized terms such as "ad hominem" or "syllogism." On the other hand, you will be expected to understand and critique the reasoning contained in arguments. This requires that you possess a university-level understanding of widely used concepts such as argument, premise, assumption, and conclusion.

Suggested Approach

Read each question carefully. Make sure that you understand the meaning of each part of the question. Make sure that you understand the meaning of each answer choice and the ways in which it may or may not relate to the question posed. Do not pick a response simply because it is a true statement. Although true, it may not answer the question posed. Answer each question on the basis of the information that is given, even if you do not agree with it. Work within the context provided by the passage. LSAT questions do not involve any tricks or hidden meanings.

Reading Comprehension Questions

Both law school and the practice of law revolve around extensive reading of highly varied, dense, argumentative, and expository texts (for example, cases, codes, contracts, briefs, decisions, evidence). This reading must be exacting, distinguishing precisely what is said from what is not said. It involves comparison, analysis, synthesis, and application (for example, of principles and rules). It involves drawing appropriate inferences and applying ideas and arguments to new contexts. Law school reading also requires the ability to grasp unfamiliar subject matter and the ability to penetrate difficult and challenging material.

The purpose of LSAT Reading Comprehension questions is to measure the ability to read, with understanding and insight, examples of lengthy and complex materials similar to those commonly encountered in law school. The Reading Comprehension section of the LSAT contains four sets of reading questions, each set consisting of a selection of reading material followed by five to eight questions. The reading selection in three of the four sets consists of a single reading passage; the other set contains two related shorter passages. Sets with two passages are a variant of Reading Comprehension called Comparative Reading, which was introduced in June 2007. (See page 5.)

Reading selections for LSAT Reading Comprehension questions are drawn from a wide range of subjects in the humanities, the social sciences, the biological and physical sciences, and areas related to the law. Generally, the selections are densely written, use high-level vocabulary, and contain sophisticated argument or complex rhetorical structure (for example, multiple points of view). Reading Comprehension questions require you to read carefully and accurately, to determine the relationships among the various parts of the reading selection, and to draw reasonable inferences from the material in the selection. The questions may ask about the following characteristics of a passage or pair of passages:

- The main idea or primary purpose

- Information that is explicitly stated

- Information or ideas that can be inferred

- The meaning or purpose of words or phrases as used in context

- The organization or structure

- The application of information in the selection to a new context

- Principles that function in the selection

- Analogies to claims or arguments in the selection

- An author's attitude as revealed in the tone of a passage or the language used

- The impact of new information on claims or arguments in the selection

Suggested Approach

Since reading selections are drawn from many different disciplines and sources, you should not be discouraged if you encounter material with which you are not familiar. It is important to remember that questions are to be answered exclusively on the basis of the information provided in the selection. There is no particular knowledge that you are expected to bring to the test, and you should not make inferences based on any prior knowledge of a subject that you may have. You may, however, wish to defer working on a set of questions that seems particularly difficult or unfamiliar until after you have dealt with sets you find easier.

Strategies. One question that often arises in connection with Reading Comprehension has to do with the most effective and efficient order in which to read the selections and questions. Possible approaches include:

- reading the selection very closely and then answering the questions;

- reading the questions first, reading the selection closely, and then returning to the questions; or

- skimming the selection and questions very quickly, then rereading the selection closely and answering the questions.

The best strategy for one test taker might not be the best strategy for another. In preparing for the test, therefore, you might want to experiment with the different strategies and decide what works most effectively for you.

Remember that your strategy must be effective under timed conditions. For this reason, the first strategy—reading the selection very closely and then answering the questions—may be the most effective for you. Nonetheless, if you believe that one of the other strategies might be more effective for you, you should try it out and assess your performance using it.

Reading the selection. Whatever strategy you choose, you should give the passage or pair of passages at least one careful reading before answering the questions. Try to distinguish main ideas from supporting ideas, and opinions or attitudes from factual, objective information. Note transitions from one idea to the next and identify the relationships among the different ideas or parts of a passage, or between the two passages in Comparative Reading sets. Consider how and why an author makes points and draws conclusions. Be sensitive to implications of what the passages say.

You may find it helpful to mark key parts of passages. For example, you might underline main ideas or important arguments, and you might circle transitional words— "although," "nevertheless," "correspondingly," and the like—that will help you map the structure of a passage. Also, you might note descriptive words that will help you identify an author's attitude toward a particular idea or person.

Answering the Questions

- Always read all the answer choices before selecting the best answer. The best answer choice is the one that most accurately and completely answers the question.

- Respond to the specific question being asked. Do not pick an answer choice simply because it is a true statement. For example, picking a true statement might yield an incorrect answer to a question in which you are asked to identify an author's position on an issue, since you are not being asked to evaluate the truth of the author's position but only to correctly identify what that position is.

- Answer the questions only on the basis of the information provided in the selection. Your own views, interpretations, or opinions, and those you have heard from others, may sometimes conflict with those expressed in a reading selection; however, you are expected to work within the context provided by the reading selection. You should not expect to agree with everything you encounter in Reading Comprehension passages.

Comparative Reading

Starting with the June 2007 administration, LSAC introduced a new variant of Reading Comprehension, called Comparative Reading, as one of the four sets in the LSAT Reading Comprehension section. In general, Comparative Reading questions are similar to traditional Reading Comprehension questions, except that Comparative Reading questions are based on two shorter passages instead of one longer passage. The two passages together are of roughly the same length as one Reading

Comprehension passage, so the total amount of reading in the Reading Comprehension section will remain essentially the same. A few of the questions that follow a Comparative Reading passage pair might concern only one of the two passages, but most will be about both passages and how they relate to each other.

Comparative Reading questions reflect the nature of some important tasks in law school work, such as understanding arguments from multiple texts by applying skills of comparison, contrast, generalization, and synthesis to the texts. The purpose of comparative reading is to assess this important set of skills directly.

What Comparative Reading Looks Like

The two passages in a Comparative Reading set—labeled "Passage A" and "Passage B"—discuss the same topic or related topics. The topics fall into the same academic categories traditionally used in Reading Comprehension: humanities, natural sciences, social sciences, and issues related to the law. Like traditional Reading Comprehension passages, Comparative Reading passages are complex and generally involve argument. The two passages in a Comparative Reading pair are typically adapted from two different published sources written by two different authors. They are usually independent of each other, with neither author responding directly to the other.

As you read the pair of passages, it is helpful to try to determine what the central idea or main point of each passage is, and to determine how the passages relate to each other. The passage will relate to each other in various ways. In some cases, the authors of the passages will be in general agreement with each other, while in others their views will be directly opposed. Passage pairs may also exhibit more complex types of relationships: for example, one passage might articulate a set of principles, while the other passage applies those or similar principles to a particular situation.

Questions that are concerned with only one of the passages are essentially identical to traditional reading comprehension questions. Questions that address both passages test the same fundamental reading skills as traditional reading comprehension questions, but the skills are applied to two texts instead of one. You may be asked to identify a main purpose shared by both passages, a statement with which both authors would agree, or a similarity or dissimilarity in the structure of the arguments in the two passages. The following are additional examples of comparative reading questions:

- Which one of the following is the central topic of each passage?

- Both passages explicitly mention which one of the following?

- Which one of the following statements is most strongly supported by both passages?

- Which one of the following most accurately describes the attitude expressed by the author of passage B toward the overall argument in passage A?

- The relationship between passage A and passage B is most analogous to the relationship in which one of the following?

This is not a complete list of the sorts of questions you may be asked in a comparative reading set, but it illustrates the range of questions you may be asked.

Eight Sample Comparative Reading Questions and Explanations

The following comparative reading set was administered in field test trials in 2003.

Directions: Each set of questions in this section is based on a single passage or a pair of passages. The questions are to be answered on the basis of what is stated or implied in the passage or pair of passages. For some of the questions, more than one of the choices could conceivably answer the question. However, you are to choose the best answer; that is, the response that most accurately and completely answers the question, and blacken the corresponding space on your answer sheet.

Passage Pair for Questions 1–8

The following passages on freedom of information are adapted from texts published in the United Kingdom.

Passage A
We have made a commitment to openness in government, and now it is essential that we strengthen that commitment with legislation that guarantees public access to government information. This is something
(5) that the previous Government conspicuously failed to do. What resulted was a haphazard approach based largely on nonstatutory arrangements, in particular the Code of Practice on Access to Government Information. Those statutory requirements for openness
(10) that were in place applied only in certain areas, such as environmental information, or were limited to particular sectors of the public service.

We could have scored an early legislative achievement by simply enacting the Code of Practice
(15) into law, but it does not ultimately provide a satisfactory guarantee of openness. Some of its significant drawbacks, which our proposed legislation seeks to remedy, are that:

- it contains too many exemptions—more than
(20) any of the main statutory freedom of
information regimes elsewhere in the world.
This inevitably makes it complex for applicants
to use, and encourages accusations that
Departments "trawl" for possible reasons
(25) for nondisclosure;
- its wording encourages the use of a
"category-based" approach toward exemptions
by which whole classes of information or
records are protected against disclosure,
(30) leaving no scope for partial disclosure of
documents of those types (after deletion of
sensitive material);
- it often requires assessing the relative weights
to be assigned to the harm that a disclosure
(35) could cause and the public interest in
disclosure. But the "public interest" is not
defined, making it difficult for government
staff, as well as for those who may be
unfamiliar with the Code and with effective
(40) disclosure practices, to assess what would
constitute harm to that interest.

Passage B

There is, of course, room for disagreement as to
how best to achieve freedom of information, but
there are a number of features common to all genuinely
(45) successful freedom of information regimes. The statute
(or other legal instrument) creating the regime must
contain a general presumption in favor of disclosure.
There must be a general right of access to information
held by public authorities that relates to their public
(50) functions. This right must be made subject to
exemptions in order to protect specified public interests
such as public health or public safety. These interests
must, however, be narrowly drawn and disclosure refused
only where it can be shown that disclosure of
(55) the particular piece of information withheld would
cause harm to one or more of those interests. Many
advocates of freedom of information would add that
even where there is potential harm to a specified
interest, disclosure should only be refused where the
(60) harm can be shown to outweigh the public's interest in
disclosure of the information in question. Lastly, there
must be the possibility of appeal to an independent
body or official against refusals by public authorities to
disclose information. This body or official must have
(65) the power to redetermine applications
independently and to make binding decisions.

Question 1

Which one of the following most accurately describes a
way in which the two passages are related to each other?

(A) Passage A contains reasoning of a kind that
passage B suggests is fallacious.
(B) Passage B presupposes that information given in
passage A regarding specific events is accurate.
(C) Passage A contains an explanation that, if valid,
helps to resolve a paradox suggested in
passage B.
(D) If all of the claims made in passage A are true,
then some of the claims made in passage B
are false.
(E) If the assertions made in passage B are valid,
they strengthen the position expressed in
passage A.

Explanation for Question 1

This question asks the test taker to identify a way in which
the two passages relate to each other.

The correct response is (E), "If the assertions made in
passage B are valid, they strengthen the position expressed
in passage A." Passage A argues in favor of the new
government's proposed legislation by pointing to alleged
flaws in the previous freedom of information regime and
pledging that the new regime would avoid those
problems. In a nutshell, passage A charges that the
previous freedom of information regime contained too
many exemptions, that it allowed a category-based
approach in which entire classes of information were
protected from disclosure, and that it depended on an
undefined notion of public interest. These criticisms rely
on the presumption that it is good for a freedom of
information regime to limit exemptions, to avoid protecting
entire classes of information, and to define public interest.
Passage B offers general principles that, if valid, justify the
particular presumptions and criticisms made in passage A.
Passage B allows that exemptions may be necessary to
protect other public interests, but states that such
exemptions must be limited to cases in which "disclosure
of the particular piece of information withheld would
cause harm to one or more of those interests" (lines
54–56). Because it permits refusal of disclosure requests
only when it can be shown that harm to a specific public
interest would result from the disclosure, this same
principle also rules out category-based exemptions.
Finally, the author of passage B speaks in terms of
"specified" (lines 51 and 58) and "narrowly drawn" (line
53) public interests, which indicates a belief that "public
interest" can be clearly defined. Thus, if these assertions
from passage B are valid, they do in fact strengthen the
position taken in passage A.

Response (A) is incorrect because passage B does not suggest that the type of reasoning employed in passage A is fallacious. In fact, as noted in the explanation for response (E), the principles articulated in passage B tend to support passage A.

Response (B) is incorrect because none of the particular details mentioned in passage A, for example, the events surrounding the Code of Practice, play any role in passage B. The assertions made in passage B are couched at a very general level; passage B does not presume anything about the accuracy or inaccuracy of any of the particular information in passage A.

Response (C) is incorrect because passage B does not discuss or otherwise give rise to any paradox, nor does passage A offer an explanation that resolves any paradox.

Response (D) is incorrect because the truth of all the claims in passage A does not imply the falsity of any of the claims in passage B. The two passages are not in conflict with each other.

Difficulty Level: Difficult

Question 2

Which one of the following most accurately expresses the main point of passage A?

(A) The current government is fully committed to openness in government, whereas the previous government was not.
(B) The Code of Practice has many weaknesses that the current government's proposed legislation is designed to avoid.
(C) There must be a general right of access to information held by public authorities that relates to public functions.
(D) The previous government was more interested in scoring a legislative victory than in providing a suitable approach to openness in government.
(E) Freedom of information regimes should not depend on nonstatutory arrangements that grant large numbers of exemptions.

Explanation for Question 2

Early in most traditional reading comprehension sets there is a question that asks about the passage's main point or central topic, or the author's main purpose in writing. The same is true of most comparative reading sets. In some cases, these questions might ask about the main point, primary purpose, or central issue of both passages. However, in cases where understanding the main point of one of the passages is particularly important to understanding the broader context of the two passages,

the test taker might be asked about the main point of that individual passage. That is the case here.

The correct response is (B), "The Code of Practice has many weaknesses that the current government's proposed legislation is designed to avoid." Passage A opens with an assertion that it is essential to enact legislative guarantees of public access to government information. The previous government, passage A says, failed to enact such legislative guarantees (note that passage A uses the first person plural pronoun "we" in lines 1, 2, and 13, indicating that its author is affiliated with the current government in the United Kingdom). Because no freedom of information legislation was passed, passage A asserts, the result was a "haphazard approach" to freedom of information that relied on the nonstatutory Code of Practice on Access to Government Information (lines 6–9). The bulk of the passage is then devoted to a description of significant flaws in the Code of Practice, flaws which, the passage says, "our proposed legislation seeks to remedy" (lines 17–18). Thus the main point of the passage is to identify weaknesses in the Code of Practice and to proclaim that the current government's proposed legislation is designed to correct those problems.

Response (A) is incorrect. Although passage A does declare the current government to be committed to openness in government (lines 1–2), it does not claim that the previous government was not committed to openness. Passage A says only that the previous government failed to enact legislation that guarantees public access to government information (lines 4–6). And in any case, the previous government's commitment to openness, or lack thereof, is not the central focus of the passage. The passage is focused on flaws in the Code of Practice and the proposed legislation designed to correct those flaws.

Response (C) is incorrect because passage A does not seek to argue for the principle stated in the response—namely, that there must be a general right of access to information held by public authorities that relates to their public functions. In fact, passage A evidently takes it for granted that this principle—or at least something close to it—is valid, because, rather than seeking to argue for the principle, passage A seeks to show why the current government's proposed legislation offers a better approach to upholding the principle than the Code of Practice does. It is also worth noting that response (C) is taken directly from passage B (lines 48–50). That fact alone is not enough to eliminate response (C) because, though it is unlikely, it is conceivable that a statement from one passage in a comparative reading set could express the main point of the other passage. In this case, response (C) can be eliminated because it fails to accurately state the main point of passage A, not because it is taken from passage B.

Response (D) is incorrect. The phrase "scoring a legislative victory" refers to lines 13–16 in passage A, where it is asserted that the current government "could have scored an early legislative achievement by simply enacting the Code of Practice into law," but did not do so. Passage A does not ascribe this hypothetical goal of seeking a legislative victory to the previous government.

Response (E) is incorrect because it is too narrow in focus to be the main point of passage A. It is true that among the factors identified in passage A as limiting the effectiveness of the Code of Practice are the fact that it is a nonstatutory arrangement (lines 6–9) and that it contains too many exemptions (lines 19–25). But passage A focuses on other flaws in the Code of Practice as well: namely, its "category-based" approach (lines 26–32) and its failure to offer a clear definition for the key term "public interest" (lines 36–41). Because response (E) focuses on the former two flaws while ignoring the latter two, it reflects only part of the main point of passage A.

Difficulty Level: Difficult

Question 3

Which one of the following is identified in passage B, but not in passage A, as a necessary component of an effective guarantee of freedom of information?

(A)   a category-based approach in which certain classes of information are declared exempt from disclosure requirements
(B)   a mechanism for appealing government denials of requests for specific information
(C)   a statutory guarantee of public access to government information
(D)   a government agency devoted solely to the processing of requests for government information
(E)   a limit to the number of exemptions from requirements to release government information

Explanation for Question 3

This question is designed to test the ability to recognize a notable difference in the contents of the two passages. The test taker is asked to identify a feature that is mentioned in passage B, but not in passage A, as necessary for an effective guarantee of freedom of information.

The correct response is (B), "a mechanism for appealing government denials of requests for specific information." This type of mechanism is identified at the end of passage B as necessary for a successful freedom of information regime: "Lastly, there must be the possibility of appeal to an independent body or official against refusals by public authorities to disclose information" (lines 61–64). Passage A, on the other hand, makes no mention of a mechanism for appealing denials of requests for information.

Response (A) is incorrect because, while passage B does argue that the public's right to information must be subject to exemptions, passage B does not call for a "category-based approach" to such exemptions. Passage B states that public access to information must be subject to exemptions to protect interests such as public health and safety, but it also stipulates that these interests must be "narrowly drawn and disclosure refused only where it can be shown that disclosure of the particular piece of information withheld would cause harm to one or more of those interests" (lines 53–56). This approach would evidently allow for fewer exemptions than would a "category-based approach."

Response (C) is incorrect because, while passage A favors a legislative guarantee of public access to information (lines 2–4), passage B does not specifically call for a statutory guarantee. In fact, passage B refers to "the statute (or other legal instrument) creating the regime" (lines 45–46), suggesting that the author of passage B does not regard a statutory guarantee of access to information as necessary. Thus response (C) is identified in passage A, and not passage B, as essential.

Response (D) is incorrect because neither passage identifies an agency devoted solely to the processing of requests for government information as a necessary component of an effective guarantee of freedom of information.

Response (E) is incorrect because both passages argue in favor of limiting exemptions to disclosure (lines 19–25 in passage A; lines 52–56 in passage B). Moreover, passage B does not call specifically for a limit to the *number* of exemptions but rather for balancing the public's interest in disclosure against other public interests, such as health and safety.

Difficulty Level: Medium difficulty

Question 4

Which one of the following most accurately characterizes how the use of the word "regimes" in passage A (line 21) relates to the use of the word "regimes" in passage B (line 45)?

(A)   In passage A it refers to formal hierarchies within a government, whereas in passage B it refers to informal arrangements that evolve over time.
(B)   In passage A it refers to governments that have been in power at particular times, whereas in passage B it refers to statutes that are enacted by those governments.
(C)   In both passage A and passage B it refers to governments that have been in power at particular times.

(D)   In both passage A and passage B it refers to
       sets of laws or other policy mechanisms that
       impose particular duties on governments.
(E)   In both passage A and passage B it refers to
       political ideologies underlying the policies
       followed by various governments.

Explanation for Question 4

In traditional reading comprehension sets, test takers are
sometimes asked to determine the meaning of a particular
word or phrase in the passage based on the surrounding
context. In comparative reading sets, test takers may be
asked to identify how the use of a particular word or
phrase used in one passage compares to the use of that
same word or phrase in the other passage, again based
on the surrounding context. That is the case in this
question, where test takers are asked how the use of the
word "regimes" in passage A relates to the use of the
same word in passage B.

The correct answer is (D), "In both passage A and
passage B it refers to sets of laws or other policy
mechanisms that impose particular duties on
governments." The use of the term "regimes" in passage A
occurs in lines 19–21, where it is asserted that the Code of
Practice contains more exemptions "than any of the main
statutory freedom of information regimes elsewhere in the
world." The word "regime" often refers to a government,
but that is obviously not the case in passage A: it would
make little sense to refer to a freedom of information
regime in that sense of the word. Instead, since these
freedom of information regimes determine how many and
what kinds of exemptions to disclosure are allowable, it
becomes clear from context that these regimes are more
like regulations that set out what obligations governments
have with respect to public access to information.
Meanwhile, passage B opens with the assertion that there
are certain features common "to all genuinely successful
freedom of information regimes" (lines 44–45). Again, the
rest of the passage makes clear that a freedom of
information regime determines a government's obligations
with respect to freedom of information. Thus response (D)
describes how "regimes" is used in both passages.

Responses (A) and (B) are incorrect because they both
say that the two passages use the word "regimes" to mean
different things, whereas, as noted in the explanation for
response (D) above, both passages actually use the term
"regimes" to express the same concept.

Response (C) is incorrect because, as noted in the
explanation for response (D) above, neither passage uses
the term "regimes" to refer to governments.

Response (E) is incorrect because in both passages the
term "regimes" is used to refer to laws or regulations
that govern freedom of information. Nothing in the

context of either passage suggests that "regimes" refers
to ideologies.

Difficulty Level: Very difficult

Question 5

If the author of passage B were to read passage A, he
or she would be most likely to draw which one of the
following conclusions regarding matters addressed in
passage A?

(A)   The Code of Practice did not allow sufficient
       public access to information.
(B)   It would have been premature for the previous
       government to have enacted statutory
       measures to guarantee freedom of information.
(C)   The measures recommended by the current
       government are unnecessarily complex.
(D)   Freedom of information laws ought not to allow
       sensitive material to be deleted from any
       document before disclosure of the document.
(E)   The current government's proposed legislation
       depends too heavily on the questionable
       assumption that "public interest" can be
       clearly defined.

Explanation for Question 5

A significant number of questions for comparative reading
passages require an ability to infer what the authors' views
are and how they compare. In most cases, questions
might ask about points of agreement or disagreement
between the authors; in some cases, however, test takers
will be asked to infer how one author would be likely to
view the other passage or some aspect of the other
passage. Here, the test taker is asked to infer how the
author of passage B would be likely to regard the matters
discussed in passage A.

The correct answer is (A), "The Code of Practice did not
allow sufficient public access to information." The key to
answering this question lies in the fact that passage B presents
a survey of some of the requirements for a successful
freedom of information regime. The Code of Practice, as it
is described in passage A, fails to conform to several of
those requirements. For example, passage B states that
there must be a presumption in favor of disclosure (lines
45–47), whereas the Code of Practice encouraged a
"category-based" approach in which "whole classes of
information or records are protected against disclosure"
(lines 26–29). Similarly, passage B argues that exemptions
should be limited to cases in which "it can be shown that
disclosure of the particular piece of information withheld
would cause harm to one or more [public] interests" (lines
54–56), whereas the Code of Practice "contains too many

exemptions—more than any of the main statutory freedom of information regimes elsewhere in the world" (lines 19–21). Finally, passage B states that the public interests against which possible disclosures are to be weighed must be narrowly drawn (lines 52–53), whereas the Code of Practice does not define "public interest," which makes it difficult "to assess what would constitute harm to that interest" (lines 40–41). All of this evidence supports the conclusion that the author of passage B would regard the Code of Practice as a freedom of information regime that did not allow sufficient public access to government information.

Response (B) is incorrect because there is nothing in either passage to suggest that the previous government's enacting statutory guarantees of freedom of information would have been premature in any way. In fact, since there are grounds for inferring that the author of passage B would regard the Code of Practice as inadequate (see the explanation of response (A)), it seems likely that the author of passage B would view statutory guarantees, had they been enacted by the previous government, as warranted rather than premature.

Response (C) is incorrect because there is no indication that the legislation advocated in passage A is complex in a way that the author of passage B would find objectionable. In fact, there is evidence that the author of passage B would endorse the measures recommended by the current government insofar as they are designed to "remedy" (line 18) shortcomings of the Code of Practice (see the explanation of response (A)).

Response (D) is incorrect because there is no reason to conclude that the author of passage B would object to the idea, stated in passage A (see lines 30–32), that documents can be partially disclosed with sensitive material deleted. Indeed, given that the author of passage B holds that the public's interest in disclosure must be weighed against other public interests (see lines 50–56), the author of passage B might very well endorse the idea of deleting sensitive material before disclosing documents as a way of balancing those competing interests.

Response (E) is incorrect because there is no indication that the author of passage B regards the assumption that "public interest" can be clearly defined as questionable. In fact, the author of passage B speaks in terms of "specified" (lines 51 and 58) and "narrowly drawn" (line 53) public interests, which indicates a belief that "public interest" can be clearly defined.

Difficulty Level: Difficult

Question 6

Passage A differs from passage B in that passage A displays an attitude that is more

(A) partisan
(B) tentative
(C) analytical
(D) circumspect
(E) pessimistic

Explanation for Question 6

Some traditional reading comprehension questions require test takers to identify the attitude displayed by the author, using cues such as tone and word choice. In comparative reading, test takers may be asked to identify and compare, based on the same types of cues, the attitudes displayed in the two passages. This question asks the test taker to select the adjective that accurately describes an attitude displayed in passage A more than in passage B.

The correct response is (A), "partisan." This is based on the fact that passage A argues in favor of proposed legislation and criticizes the freedom of information regime it is meant to replace. In so doing, it also criticizes the previous government. Passage B, in contrast, speaks in fairly abstract terms about the requirements for any successful freedom of information regime. It does not argue in favor of any particular freedom of information regime, legislation, or government.

Response (B) is incorrect because neither passage can be accurately described as "tentative" in its argument.

Response (C) is incorrect because, if anything, it is passage B that is more analytical than passage A. The bulk of passage B is devoted to distinguishing the features possessed by successful freedom of information regimes; this process of identifying the components of a significant phenomenon is the hallmark of an analytical approach. And while it is true that passage A points to three alleged flaws in the Code of Practice, its purpose in doing so is to tout the advantages of the proposed legislation, rather than to analyze the status quo.

Response (D) is incorrect because passage A is quite direct, rather than circumspect, in its assertions.

Response (E) is incorrect because neither passage A nor passage B displays any pessimism with regard to its subject. The author of passage A identifies flaws in the previous freedom of information regime but seems quite optimistic that the proposed legislation will address those problems. Passage B seems equally optimistic about the possibility that the public's right to information can be adequately guaranteed by means of successful freedom of information regimes.

Difficulty Level: Very difficult

Question 7

It can be inferred from the passages that both authors hold which one of the following views?

(A) Freedom of information laws should not compel governments to comply with all requests for disclosure of information.
(B) "Public interest" is too vague a concept to be cited in justifying freedom of information laws.
(C) Freedom of information laws should unequivocally specify the categories to which they apply, so that case-by-case determinations are unnecessary.
(D) Noncompulsory freedom of information policies are often sufficient to guarantee adequate public access to government information.
(E) There should be a presumption in favor of disclosing government information, but only in explicitly specified branches of government.

Explanation for Question 7

A significant number of questions for comparative reading passages require an ability to infer what the authors' views are and how they compare. Some questions ask about points of disagreement between the authors; others, such as this one, ask about points on which the authors are likely to agree.

The correct response is (A), "Freedom of information laws should not compel governments to comply with all requests for disclosure of information." The evidence that the author of passage B holds this view is quite straightforward. The author states that there must be a general right of access to government information, but this assertion is then qualified: "This right must be made subject to exemptions in order to protect specified public interests such as public health or public safety" (lines 50–52). The evidence that the author of passage A holds this view is more indirect; nonetheless, it can be found in the three bulleted statements in the passage. In line 19, the author of passage A charges that the Code of Practice has too many exemptions, and in lines 26–27, the author states that the Code of Practice "encourages the use of a 'category-based' approach towards exemptions." Both of these claims imply that it is appropriate that there be *some* exemptions to the right of access to government information (if that were not the case, the author of passage A would presumably object to the very existence of the exemptions, rather than to their scope). This inference is further supported by the argument in lines 36–41, where the author objects to a lack of clarity in the Code of Practice's requirements for balancing the public's interest in disclosure against other public interests, rather than objecting to the requirement that those interests be balanced at all. Most directly, the author of passage A endorses "*partial* disclosure" (line 30, emphasis added) of government documents.

Response (B) is incorrect because it expresses a view that neither author endorses. The author of passage A does indeed object that "public interest" is not defined in the Code of Practice (lines 36–41), but this does not support the conclusion that, in the author's eyes, the concept is too vague to be cited in justifying freedom of information laws. Indeed, the lack of definition is something the "proposed legislation seeks to remedy" (lines 17–18). Meanwhile, the author of passage B sees no problem in balancing "the public's interest in disclosure of the information" (lines 60–61) with any other "specified interest" (lines 58–59).

Response (C) is incorrect because it expresses a view that neither author would endorse. The principle expressed in response (C) corresponds closely to the "category-based" approach criticized in passage A. Under the category-based approach, information or documents that belong to certain designated categories are automatically exempted from disclosure requirements (lines 26–29). The problem with this approach, according to passage A, is precisely that it leaves "no scope for partial disclosure of documents" (lines 30–31), thereby making case-by-case determinations unnecessary, if not impossible. Likewise, the general presumption in favor of disclosure called for by passage B (line 47), together with the requirement that disclosure be refused only when it can be demonstrated that disclosure would harm certain "narrowly drawn" public interests (lines 52–56), indicates that the author of passage B would favor case-by-case determinations over the broader category-based approach.

Response (D) is incorrect because it expresses a view that neither author would endorse. The author of passage A writes that it is essential that the government strengthen its commitment to openness in government with "legislation that *guarantees* public access to government information" (lines 2–4, emphasis added). The author of passage B presumes that the freedom of information policy would be created by "statute (or other legal instrument)" (lines 45–46) and argues that disclosure should be refused "only where it can be shown that disclosure of the particular piece of information withheld would cause harm to one or more [public] interests" (lines 54–56). Passage B also states that "there must be the possibility of appeal to an independent body or official against refusals by public authorities to disclose information" (lines 61–64). None of these statements is consistent with a view that noncompulsory (i.e., optional or voluntary) freedom of information policies are sufficient to guarantee adequate public access to information.

Response (E) is incorrect because there is no basis for inferring that either author thinks that there should be a presumption in favor of disclosure, but that the presumption should apply only to certain explicitly identified branches of government. To the extent that either author allows exemptions to disclosure requirements, it is to protect other public interests, not certain branches of government. In fact, according to passage A, one of the flaws of the "haphazard approach" to freedom of information that developed over time is that "those statutory requirements for openness that were in place applied only in certain areas, such as environmental information, or were limited to particular sectors of the public service" (lines 9–12).

Difficulty Level: Very difficult

Question 8

Based on what can be inferred from their titles, the relationship between which one of the following pairs of documents is most analogous to the relationship between passage A and passage B?

(A) "What the Previous Management of the Midtown Health Club Left Undone"
"The New Management of the Crescent Restaurant Has Some Bad Policies"

(B) "A List of Grievances by Tenants of Garden Court Apartments"
"Why the Grievances of the Garden Court Apartments Tenants Are Unfounded"

(C) "How We Plan to Improve the Way in Which This Restaurant Is Managed"
"Standards of Good Restaurant Management"

(D) "Three Alternative Proposals for Our New Advertising Campaign"
"Three Principles to Be Followed in Developing an Effective Sales Team"

(E) "Detailed Instructions for Submitting a Formal Grievance to the Committee"
"Procedures for Adjudicating Grievances"

Explanation for Question 8

The response choices in this question consist of the titles of pairs of hypothetical documents. Based on what can be inferred about the contents of those documents from their titles, the test taker is asked to identify the documents that stand in a relationship to each other that is most analogous to the relationship between passage A and passage B. In order to answer this question, the test taker needs to determine, at least in a general way, what the relationship between passage A and passage B is.

As discussed in the explanation for question 1, passage A argues that the previous freedom of information regime in the United Kingdom was flawed in certain ways, and it claims that the freedom of information legislation

proposed by the current government is designed to avoid those flaws. The arguments made in passage A presume certain general principles about what characteristics a freedom of information regime should have. Passage B can be said to support the claims advanced in passage A inasmuch as it articulates those principles directly. The closest analogy to this relationship is found in response (C):

> "How We Plan to Improve the Way in Which This Restaurant Is Managed"
> "Standards of Good Restaurant Management"

Like passage A, the first of these documents describes a plan for improving the administration of a particular enterprise (a restaurant in response (C), the government's freedom of information regime in passage A). And like passage B, the second document in response (C) articulates general standards that ought to govern the administration of such an enterprise.

Response (A) is incorrect because each document describes how the management of a particular enterprise (a health club in the first case, a restaurant in the second) is flawed. Neither document articulates general standards or principles for management that could be applied in the situation addressed in the other document, as is the case with the principles stated in passage B in relation to the situation addressed in passage A.

Response (B) is incorrect because the documents in it appear to concern a dispute between the tenants and owners of an apartment complex, and the two documents appear to be expressing the opposing sides of the dispute. The second document evidently attempts to deny the validity of the claims made in the first document, whereas passage B can be said to support passage A inasmuch as it articulates principles that strengthen the case made in passage A.

Response (D) is incorrect because the first document describes three possible proposals rather than being committed to one, as passage A is. In addition, while the second document evidently expresses some principles, they are not principles that can be applied to the situation addressed in the first document, as is the case with passage B.

Response (E) is incorrect because both documents are evidently procedural documents describing the steps to be followed at different stages in a grievance procedure. Neither document makes any arguments or claims about what should be done in a particular situation, as passage A does, and neither document expresses any principles that could be applied to the discussion in the other document, as passage B does.

Difficulty Level: Medium difficulty

THE WRITING SAMPLE

On the day of the test, you will be asked to write one sample essay. LSAC does not score the writing sample, but copies are sent to all law schools to which you apply. According to a 2015 LSAC survey of 129 United States and Canadian law schools, almost all use the writing sample in evaluating at least some applications for admission. Failure to respond to writing sample prompts and frivolous responses have been used by law schools as grounds for rejection of applications for admission.

In developing and implementing the writing sample portion of the LSAT, LSAC has operated on the following premises: First, law schools and the legal profession value highly the ability to communicate effectively in writing. Second, it is important to encourage potential law students to develop effective writing skills. Third, a sample of an applicant's writing, produced under controlled conditions, is a potentially useful indication of that person's writing ability. Fourth, the writing sample can serve as an independent check on other writing submitted by applicants as part of the admission process. Finally, writing samples may be useful for diagnostic purposes related to improving a candidate's writing.

The writing prompt presents a decision problem. You are asked to make a choice between two positions or courses of action. Both of the choices are defensible, and you are given criteria and facts on which to base your decision. There is no "right" or "wrong" position to take on the topic, so the quality of each test taker's response is a function not of which choice is made, but of how well or poorly the choice is supported and how well or poorly the other choice is criticized.

The LSAT writing prompt was designed and validated by legal education professionals. Since it involves writing based on fact sets and criteria, the writing sample gives applicants the opportunity to demonstrate the type of argumentative writing that is required in law school, although the topics are usually nonlegal.

You will have 35 minutes in which to plan and write an essay on the topic you receive. Read the topic and the accompanying directions carefully. You will probably find it best to spend a few minutes considering the topic and organizing your thoughts before you begin writing. In your essay, be sure to develop your ideas fully, leaving time, if possible, to review what you have written. Do not write on a topic other than the one specified. Writing on a topic of your own choice is not acceptable.

No special knowledge is required or expected for this writing exercise. Law schools are interested in the reasoning, clarity, organization, language usage, and writing mechanics displayed in your essay. How well you write is more important than how much you write. Confine your essay to the blocked, lined area on the front and back of the separate Writing Sample Response Sheet. Only that area will be reproduced for law schools. Be sure that your writing is legible.

TAKING THE PREPTEST UNDER SIMULATED LSAT CONDITIONS

One important way to prepare for the LSAT is to take a practice test under actual time constraints. Doing so will help you estimate the amount of time you can afford to spend on each question in a section and to determine the question types on which you may need additional practice.

Since the LSAT is a timed test, it is important to use your allotted time wisely. During the test, you may work only on the section designated by the test supervisor. You cannot devote extra time to a difficult section and make up that time on a section you find easier. In pacing yourself, and checking your answers, you should think of each section of the test as a separate minitest.

Be sure that you answer every question on the test. When you do not know the correct answer to a question, first eliminate the responses that you know are incorrect, then make your best guess among the remaining choices. Do not be afraid to guess as there is no penalty for incorrect answers.

When you take a practice test, abide by all the requirements specified in the directions and keep strictly within the specified time limits. Work without a rest period. When you take an actual test, you will have only a short break—usually 10–15 minutes—after SECTION III.

When taken under conditions as much like actual testing conditions as possible, a practice test provides very useful preparation for taking the LSAT.

Official directions for the four multiple-choice sections and the writing sample are included in the PrepTests so that you can approximate actual testing conditions as you practice. To take the test:

- Set a timer for 35 minutes. Answer all the questions in SECTION I of the PrepTest. Stop working on that section when the 35 minutes have elapsed.

- Repeat, allowing yourself 35 minutes each for sections II, III, and IV.

- Set the timer again for 35 minutes, then prepare your response to the writing sample topic at the end of the PrepTest.

Refer to "Computing Your Score" for the PrepTest for instruction on evaluating your performance. An answer key is provided for that purpose.

The Official LSAT PrepTest®

7

- February 1993
- Form 3LSS18

The sample test that follows consists of four sections corresponding to the four scored sections of the February 1993 LSAT.

SECTION I

Time—35 minutes

25 Questions

<u>Directions:</u> The questions in this section are based on the reasoning contained in brief statements or passages. For some questions, more than one of the choices could conceivably answer the question. However, you are to choose the <u>best</u> answer; that is, the response that most accurately and completely answers the question. You should not make assumptions that are by commonsense standards implausible, superfluous, or incompatible with the passage. After you have chosen the best answer, blacken the corresponding space on your answer sheet.

1. Before the printing press, books could be purchased only in expensive manuscript copies. The printing press produced books that were significantly less expensive than the manuscript editions. The public's demand for printed books in the first years after the invention of the printing press was many times greater than demand had been for manuscript copies. This increase demonstrates that there was a dramatic jump in the number of people who learned how to read in the years after publishers first started producing books on the printing press.

   Which one of the following statements, if true, casts doubt on the argument?

   (A) During the first years after the invention of the printing press, letter writing by people who wrote without the assistance of scribes or clerks exhibited a dramatic increase.
   (B) Books produced on the printing press are often found with written comments in the margins in the handwriting of the people who owned the books.
   (C) In the first years after the printing press was invented, printed books were purchased primarily by people who had always bought and read expensive manuscripts but could afford a greater number of printed books for the same money.
   (D) Books that were printed on the printing press in the first years after its invention often circulated among friends in informal reading clubs or libraries.
   (E) The first printed books published after the invention of the printing press would have been useless to illiterate people, since the books had virtually no illustrations.

2. Bevex, an artificial sweetener used only in soft drinks, is carcinogenic for mice, but only when it is consumed in very large quantities. To ingest an amount of Bevex equivalent to the amount fed to the mice in the relevant studies, a person would have to drink 25 cans of Bevex-sweetened soft drinks per day. For that reason, Bevex is in fact safe for people.

   In order for the conclusion that Bevex is safe for people to be properly drawn, which one of the following must be true?

   (A) Cancer from carcinogenic substances develops more slowly in mice than it does in people.
   (B) If all food additives that are currently used in foods were tested, some would be found to be carcinogenic for mice.
   (C) People drink fewer than 25 cans of Bevex-sweetened soda per day.
   (D) People can obtain important health benefits by controlling their weight through the use of artificially sweetened soft drinks.
   (E) Some of the studies done on Bevex were not relevant to the question of whether or not Bevex is carcinogenic for people.

3. Harry: Airlines have made it possible for anyone to travel around the world in much less time than was formerly possible.
   Judith: That is not true. Many flights are too expensive for all but the rich.

   Judith's response shows that she interprets Harry's statement to imply that

   (A) the majority of people are rich
   (B) everyone has an equal right to experience world travel
   (C) world travel is only possible via routes serviced by airlines
   (D) most forms of world travel are not affordable for most people
   (E) anyone can afford to travel long distances by air

GO ON TO THE NEXT PAGE.

4. Nutritionists have recommended that people eat more fiber. Advertisements for a new fiber-supplement pill state only that it contains "44 percent fiber."

The advertising claim is misleading in its selection of information on which to focus if which one of the following is true?

(A) There are other products on the market that are advertised as providing fiber as a dietary supplement.
(B) Nutritionists base their recommendation on medical findings that dietary fiber protects against some kinds of cancer.
(C) It is possible to become addicted to some kinds of advertised pills, such as sleeping pills and painkillers.
(D) The label of the advertised product recommends taking 3 pills every day.
(E) The recommended daily intake of fiber is 20 to 30 grams, and the pill contains one-third gram.

5. Many environmentalists have urged environmental awareness on consumers, saying that if we accept moral responsibility for our effects on the environment, then products that directly or indirectly harm the environment ought to be avoided. Unfortunately it is usually impossible for consumers to assess the environmental impact of a product, and thus impossible for them to consciously restrict their purchases to environmentally benign products. Because of this impossibility there can be no moral duty to choose products in the way these environmentalists urge, since _____.

Which one of the following principles provides the most appropriate completion for the argument?

(A) a moral duty to perform an action is never based solely on the effects the action will have on other people
(B) a person cannot possibly have a moral duty to do what he or she is unable to do
(C) moral considerations should not be the sole determinants of what products are made available to consumers
(D) the morally right action is always the one whose effects produce the least total harm
(E) where a moral duty exists, it supersedes any legal duty and any other kind of duty

6. Advertisement: Anyone who exercises knows from firsthand experience that exercise leads to better performance of such physical organs as the heart and the lungs, as well as to improvement in muscle tone. And since your brain is a physical organ, your actions can improve its performance, too. Act now. Subscribe to *Stimulus*: read the magazine that exercises your brain.

The advertisement employs which one of the following argumentative strategies?

(A) It cites experimental evidence that subscribing to the product being advertised has desirable consequences.
(B) It ridicules people who do not subscribe to *Stimulus* by suggesting that they do not believe that exercise will improve brain capacity.
(C) It explains the process by which the product being advertised brings about the result claimed for its use.
(D) It supports its recommendation by a careful analysis of the concept of exercise.
(E) It implies that brains and muscle are similar in one respect because they are similar in another respect.

GO ON TO THE NEXT PAGE.

Questions 7–8

Coherent solutions for the problem of reducing health-care costs cannot be found within the current piecemeal system of paying these costs. The reason is that this system gives health-care providers and insurers every incentive to shift, wherever possible, the costs of treating illness onto each other or any other party, including the patient. That clearly is the lesson of the various reforms of the 1980s: push in on one part of this pliable spending balloon and an equally expensive bulge pops up elsewhere. For example, when the government health-care insurance program for the poor cut costs by disallowing payments for some visits to physicians, patients with advanced illness later presented themselves at hospital emergency rooms in increased numbers.

7. The argument proceeds by

   (A) showing that shifting costs onto the patient contradicts the premise of health-care reimbursement
   (B) attributing without justification fraudulent intent to people
   (C) employing an analogy to characterize interrelationships
   (D) denying the possibility of a solution by disparaging each possible alternative system
   (E) demonstrating that cooperation is feasible by citing an instance

8. The argument provides the most support for which one of the following?

   (A) Under the conditions in which the current system operates, the overall volume of health-care costs could be shrunk, if at all, only by a comprehensive approach.
   (B) Relative to the resources available for health-care funding, the income of the higher-paid health-care professionals is too high.
   (C) Health-care costs are expanding to meet additional funds that have been made available for them.
   (D) Advances in medical technology have raised the expected standards of medical care but have proved expensive.
   (E) Since unfilled hospital beds contribute to overhead charges on each patient's bill, it would be unwise to hold unused hospital capacity in reserve for large-scale emergencies.

9. The commercial news media emphasize exceptional events such as airplane crashes at the expense of those such as automobile accidents, which occur far more frequently and represent a far greater risk to the public. Yet the public tends to interpret the degree of emphasis the news media give to these occurrences as indicating the degree of risk they represent.

If the statements above are true, which one of the following conclusions is most strongly supported by them?

   (A) Print media, such as newspapers and magazines, are a better source of information than are broadcast media.
   (B) The emphasis given in the commercial news media to major catastrophes is dictated by the public's taste for the extraordinary.
   (C) Events over which people feel they have no control are generally perceived as more dangerous than those which people feel they can avert or avoid.
   (D) Where commercial news media constitute the dominant source of information, public perception of risk does not reflect actual risk.
   (E) A massive outbreak of cholera will be covered more extensively by the news media than will the occurrence of a rarer but less serious disease.

10. A large group of hyperactive children whose regular diets included food containing large amounts of additives was observed by researchers trained to assess the presence or absence of behavior problems. The children were then placed on a low-additive diet for several weeks, after which they were observed again. Originally nearly 60 percent of the children exhibited behavior problems; after the change in diet, only 30 percent did so. On the basis of these data, it can be concluded that food additives can contribute to behavior problems in hyperactive children.

The evidence cited fails to establish the conclusion because

   (A) there is no evidence that the reduction in behavior problems was proportionate to the reduction in food-additive intake
   (B) there is no way to know what changes would have occurred without the change of diet, since only children who changed to a low-additive diet were studied
   (C) exactly how many children exhibited behavior problems after the change in diet cannot be determined, since the size of the group studied is not precisely given
   (D) there is no evidence that the behavior of some of the children was unaffected by additives
   (E) the evidence is consistent with the claim that some children exhibit more frequent behavior problems after being on the low-additive diet than they had exhibited when first observed

GO ON TO THE NEXT PAGE.

11. In 1990 major engine repairs were performed on 10 percent of the cars that had been built by the National Motor Company in the 1970s and that were still registered. However, the corresponding figure for the cars that the National Motor Company had manufactured in the 1960s was only five percent.

Which one of the following, if true, most helps to explain the discrepancy?

(A) Government motor vehicle regulations generally require all cars, whether old or new, to be inspected for emission levels prior to registration.

(B) Owners of new cars tend to drive their cars more carefully than do owners of old cars.

(C) The older a car is, the more likely it is to be discarded for scrap rather than repaired when major engine work is needed to keep the car in operation.

(D) The cars that the National Motor Company built in the 1970s incorporated simplified engine designs that made the engines less complicated than those of earlier models.

(E) Many of the repairs that were performed on the cars that the National Motor Company built in the 1960s could have been avoided if periodic routine maintenance had been performed.

12. No mathematician today would flatly refuse to accept the results of an enormous computation as an adequate demonstration of the truth of a theorem. In 1976, however, this was not the case. Some mathematicians at that time refused to accept the results of a complex computer demonstration of a very simple mapping theorem. Although some mathematicians still hold a strong belief that a simple theorem ought to have a short, simple proof, in fact, some simple theorems have required enormous proofs.

If all of the statements in the passage are true, which one of the following must also be true?

(A) Today, some mathematicians who believe that a simple theorem ought to have a simple proof would consider accepting the results of an enormous computation as a demonstration of the truth of a theorem.

(B) Some individuals who believe that a simple theorem ought to have a simple proof are not mathematicians.

(C) Today, some individuals who refuse to accept the results of an enormous computation as a demonstration of the truth of a theorem believe that a simple theorem ought to have a simple proof.

(D) Some individuals who do not believe that a simple theorem ought to have a simple proof would not be willing to accept the results of an enormous computation as proof of a complex theorem.

(E) Some nonmathematicians do not believe that a simple theorem ought to have a simple proof.

13. If you climb mountains, you will not live to a ripe old age. But you will be bored unless you climb mountains. Therefore, if you live to a ripe old age, you will have been bored.

Which one of the following most closely parallels the reasoning in the argument above?

(A) If you do not try to swim, you will not learn how to swim. But you will not be safe in boats if you do not learn how to swim. Therefore, you must try to swim.

(B) If you do not play golf, you will not enjoy the weekend. But you will be tired next week unless you relax during the weekend. Therefore, to enjoy the weekend, you will have to relax by playing golf.

(C) If you work for your candidate, you will not improve your guitar playing. But you will neglect your civic duty unless you work for your candidate. Therefore, if you improve your guitar playing, you will have neglected your civic duty.

(D) If you do not train, you will not be a good athlete. But you will become exhausted easily unless you train. Therefore, if you train, you will not have become exhausted easily.

(E) If you spend all of your money, you will not become wealthy. But you will become hungry unless you spend all of your money. Therefore, if you become wealthy, you will not become hungry.

14. Marine biologists had hypothesized that lobsters kept together in lobster traps eat one another in response to hunger. Periodic checking of lobster traps, however, has revealed instances of lobsters sharing traps together for weeks. Eight lobsters even shared one trap together for two months without eating one another. The marine biologists' hypothesis, therefore, is clearly wrong.

The argument against the marine biologists' hypothesis is based on which one of the following assumptions?

(A) Lobsters not caught in lobster traps have been observed eating one another.

(B) Two months is the longest known period during which eight or more lobsters have been trapped together.

(C) It is unusual to find as many as eight lobsters caught together in one single trap.

(D) Members of other marine species sometimes eat their own kind when no other food sources are available.

(E) Any food that the eight lobsters in the trap might have obtained was not enough to ward off hunger.

GO ON TO THE NEXT PAGE.

15. Eight years ago hunting was banned in Greenfield County on the grounds that hunting endangers public safety. Now the deer population in the county is six times what it was before the ban. Deer are invading residential areas, damaging property and causing motor vehicle accidents that result in serious injury to motorists. Since there were never any hunting-related injuries in the county, clearly the ban was not only unnecessary but has created a danger to public safety that would not otherwise exist.

Which one of the following, if true, provides the strongest additional support for the conclusion above?

(A) In surrounding counties, where hunting is permitted, the size of the deer population has not increased in the last eight years.

(B) Motor vehicle accidents involving deer often result in damage to the vehicle, injury to the motorist, or both.

(C) When deer populations increase beyond optimal size, disease and malnutrition become more widespread among the deer herds.

(D) In residential areas in the county, many residents provide food and salt for deer.

(E) Deer can cause extensive damage to ornamental shrubs and trees by chewing on twigs and saplings.

16. Comets do not give off their own light but reflect light from other sources, such as the Sun. Scientists estimate the mass of comets by their brightness: the greater a comet's mass, the more light that comet will reflect. A satellite probe, however, has revealed that the material of which Halley's comet is composed reflects 60 times less light per unit of mass than had been previously thought.

The statements above, if true, give the most support to which one of the following?

(A) Some comets are composed of material that reflects 60 times more light per unit of mass than the material of which Halley's comet is composed.

(B) Previous estimates of the mass of Halley's comet which were based on its brightness were too low.

(C) The total amount of light reflected from Halley's comet is less than scientists had previously thought.

(D) The reflective properties of the material of which comets are composed vary considerably from comet to comet.

(E) Scientists need more information before they can make a good estimate of the mass of Halley's comet.

17. Office manager: I will not order recycled paper for this office. Our letters to clients must make a good impression, so we cannot print them on inferior paper.

Stationery supplier: Recycled paper is not necessarily inferior. In fact, from the beginning, the finest paper has been made of recycled material. It was only in the 1850s that paper began to be made from wood fiber, and then only because there were no longer enough rags to meet the demand for paper.

In which one of the following ways does the stationer's response fail to address the office manager's objection to recycled paper?

(A) It does not recognize that the office manager's prejudice against recycled paper stems from ignorance.

(B) It uses irrelevant facts to justify a claim about the quality of the disputed product.

(C) It assumes that the office manager is concerned about environmental issues.

(D) It presupposes that the office manager understands the basic technology of paper manufacturing.

(E) It ignores the office manager's legitimate concern about quality.

GO ON TO THE NEXT PAGE.

Questions 18–19

When Alicia Green borrowed a neighbor's car without permission, the police merely gave her a warning. However, when Peter Foster did the same thing, he was charged with automobile theft. Peter came to the attention of the police because the car he was driving was hit by a speeding taxi. Alicia was stopped because the car she was driving had defective taillights. It is true that the car Peter took got damaged and the car Alicia took did not, but since it was the taxi that caused the damage this difference was not due to any difference in the blameworthiness of their behavior. Therefore Alicia should also have been charged with automobile theft.

18. The statement that the car Peter took got damaged and the car Alicia took did not plays which one of the following roles in the argument?

    (A) It presents a reason that directly supports the conclusion.
    (B) It justifies the difference in the actual outcome in the two cases.
    (C) It demonstrates awareness of a fact on which a possible objection might be based.
    (D) It illustrates a general principle on which the argument relies.
    (E) It summarizes a position against which the argument is directed.

19. If all of the claims offered in support of the conclusion are accurate, each of the following could be true EXCEPT:

    (A) The interests of justice would have been better served if the police had released Peter Foster with a warning.
    (B) Alicia Green had never before driven a car belonging to someone else without first securing the owner's permission.
    (C) Peter Foster was hit by the taxi while he was running a red light, whereas Alicia Green drove with extra care to avoid drawing the attention of the police to the car she had taken.
    (D) Alicia Green barely missed hitting a pedestrian when she sped through a red light ten minutes before she was stopped by the police for driving a car that had defective taillights.
    (E) Peter Foster had been cited for speeding twice in the preceding month, whereas Alicia Green had never been cited for a traffic violation.

20. According to sources who can be expected to know, Dr. Maria Esposito is going to run in the mayoral election. But if Dr. Esposito runs, Jerome Krasman will certainly not run against her. Therefore Dr. Esposito will be the only candidate in the election.

The flawed reasoning in the argument above most closely parallels that in which one of the following?

    (A) According to its management, Brown's Stores will move next year. Without Brown's being present, no new large store can be attracted to the downtown area. Therefore the downtown area will no longer be viable as a shopping district.
    (B) The press release says that the rock group Rollercoaster is playing a concert on Saturday. It won't be playing on Friday if it plays on Saturday. So Saturday will be the only day this week on which Rollercoaster will perform.
    (C) Joshua says the interviewing panel was impressed by Marilyn. But if they were impressed by Marilyn, they probably thought less of Sven. Joshua is probably right, and so Sven will probably not get the job.
    (D) An informant says that Rustimann was involved in the bank robbery. If Rustimann was involved, Jones was certainly not involved. Since these two are the only people who could have been involved, Rustimann is the only person the police need to arrest.
    (E) The review said that this book is the best one for beginners at programming. If this book is the best, that other one can't be as good. So this one is the book we should buy.

GO ON TO THE NEXT PAGE.

21. The initial causes of serious accidents at nuclear power plants have not so far been flaws in the advanced-technology portion of the plants. Rather, the initial causes have been attributed to human error, as when a worker at the Browns Mills reactor in the United States dropped a candle and started a fire, or to flaws in the plumbing, exemplified in a recent incident in Japan. Such everyday events cannot be thought unlikely to occur over the long run.

Which one of the following is most strongly supported by the statements above?

(A) Now that nuclear power generation has become a part of everyday life, an ever-increasing yearly incidence of serious accidents at the plants can be expected.

(B) If nuclear power plants continue in operation, a serious accident at such a plant is not improbable.

(C) The likelihood of human error at the operating consoles of nuclear power generators cannot be lessened by thoughtful design of dials, switches, and displays.

(D) The design of nuclear power plants attempts to compensate for possible failures of the materials used in their construction.

(E) No serious accident will be caused in the future by some flaw in the advanced-technology portion of a nuclear power plant.

22. There is a widespread belief that people can predict impending earthquakes from unusual animal behavior. Skeptics claim that this belief is based on selective coincidence: people whose dogs behaved oddly just before an earthquake will be especially likely to remember that fact. At any given time, the skeptics say, some of the world's dogs will be behaving oddly.

Clarification of which one of the following issues would be most important to an evaluation of the skeptics' position?

(A) Which is larger, the number of skeptics or the number of people who believe that animal behavior can foreshadow earthquakes?

(B) Are there means other than the observation of animal behavior that nonscientists can use to predict earthquakes?

(C) Are there animals about whose behavior people know too little to be able to distinguish unusual from everyday behavior?

(D) Are the sorts of behavior supposedly predictive of earthquakes as pronounced in dogs as they are in other animals?

(E) Is the animal behavior supposedly predictive of earthquakes specific to impending earthquakes or can it be any kind of unusual behavior?

23. Defendants who can afford expensive private defense lawyers have a lower conviction rate than those who rely on court-appointed public defenders. This explains why criminals who commit lucrative crimes like embezzlement or insider trading are more successful at avoiding conviction than are street criminals.

The explanation offered above would be more persuasive if which one of the following were true?

(A) Many street crimes, such as drug dealing, are extremely lucrative and those committing them can afford expensive private lawyers.

(B) Most prosecutors are not competent to handle cases involving highly technical financial evidence and have more success in prosecuting cases of robbery or simple assault.

(C) The number of criminals convicted of street crimes is far greater than the number of criminals convicted of embezzlement or insider trading.

(D) The percentage of defendants who actually committed the crimes of which they are accused is no greater for publicly defended than for privately defended defendants.

(E) Juries, out of sympathy for the victims of crimes, are much more likely to convict defendants accused of violent crimes than they are to convict defendants accused of "victimless" crimes or crimes against property.

GO ON TO THE NEXT PAGE.

24. Many major scientific discoveries of the past were the product of serendipity, the chance discovery of valuable findings that investigators had not purposely sought. Now, however, scientific research tends to be so costly that investigators are heavily dependent on large grants to fund their research. Because such grants require investigators to provide the grant sponsors with clear projections of the outcome of the proposed research, investigators ignore anything that does not directly bear on the funded research. Therefore, under the prevailing circumstances, serendipity can no longer play a role in scientific discovery.

Which one of the following is an assumption on which the argument depends?

(A) Only findings that an investigator purposely seeks can directly bear on that investigator's research.

(B) In the past few scientific investigators attempted to make clear predictions of the outcome of their research.

(C) Dependence on large grants is preventing investigators from conducting the type of scientific research that those investigators would personally prefer.

(D) All scientific investigators who provide grant sponsors with clear projections of the outcome of their research receive at least some of the grants for which they apply.

(E) In general the most valuable scientific discoveries are the product of serendipity.

25. Police statistics have shown that automobile antitheft devices reduce the risk of car theft, but a statistical study of automobile theft by the automobile insurance industry claims that cars equipped with antitheft devices are, paradoxically, more likely to be stolen than cars that are not so equipped.

Which one of the following, if true, does the most to resolve the apparent paradox?

(A) Owners of stolen cars almost invariably report the theft immediately to the police but tend to delay notifying their insurance company, in the hope that the vehicle will be recovered.

(B) Most cars that are stolen are not equipped with antitheft devices, and most cars that are equipped with antitheft devices are not stolen.

(C) The most common automobile antitheft devices are audible alarms, which typically produce ten false alarms for every actual attempted theft.

(D) Automobile owners who have particularly theft-prone cars and live in areas of greatest incidence of car theft are those who are most likely to have antitheft devices installed.

(E) Most automobile thefts are the work of professional thieves against whose efforts antitheft devices offer scant protection.

S T O P

**IF YOU FINISH BEFORE TIME IS CALLED, YOU MAY CHECK YOUR WORK ON THIS SECTION ONLY.
DO NOT WORK ON ANY OTHER SECTION IN THE TEST.**

SECTION II

Time—35 minutes

24 Questions

Directions: Each group of questions in this section is based on a set of conditions. In answering some of the questions, it may be useful to draw a rough diagram. Choose the response that most accurately and completely answers each question and blacken the corresponding space on your answer sheet.

Questions 1–7

Seven consecutive time slots for a broadcast, numbered in chronological order 1 through 7, will be filled by six song tapes—G, H, L, O, P, S—and exactly one news tape. Each tape is to be assigned to a different time slot, and no tape is longer than any other tape. The broadcast is subject to the following restrictions:

   L must be played immediately before O.
   The news tape must be played at some time after L.
   There must be exactly two time slots between G and P, regardless of whether G comes before P or whether G comes after P.

1. If G is played second, which one of the following tapes must be played third?

   (A) the news
   (B) H
   (C) L
   (D) O
   (E) S

2. The news tape can be played in any one of the following time slots EXCEPT the

   (A) second
   (B) third
   (C) fourth
   (D) fifth
   (E) sixth

3. If H and S are to be scheduled as far from each other as possible, then the first, the second, and the third time slots could be filled, respectively, by

   (A) G, H, and L
   (B) S, G, and the news
   (C) H, G, and L
   (D) H, L, and O
   (E) L, O, and S

4. If P is played fifth, L must be played

   (A) first
   (B) second
   (C) third
   (D) fourth
   (E) sixth

5. What is the maximum number of tapes that can separate S from the news?

   (A) 1
   (B) 2
   (C) 3
   (D) 4
   (E) 5

6. Which one of the following is the latest time slot in which L can be played?

   (A) the third
   (B) the fourth
   (C) the fifth
   (D) the sixth
   (E) the seventh

7. The time slot in which O must be played is completely determined if G is assigned to which one of the following time slots?

   (A) the first
   (B) the third
   (C) the fourth
   (D) the fifth
   (E) the sixth

GO ON TO THE NEXT PAGE.

Questions 8-12

Doctor Yamata works only on Mondays, Tuesdays, Wednesdays, Fridays, and Saturdays. She performs four different activities—lecturing, operating, treating patients, and conducting research. Each working day she performs exactly one activity in the morning and exactly one activity in the afternoon. During each week her work schedule must satisfy the following restrictions:

    She performs operations on exactly three mornings.
    If she operates on Monday, she does not operate on Tuesday.
    She lectures in the afternoon on exactly two consecutive calendar days.
    She treats patients on exactly one morning and exactly three afternoons.
    She conducts research on exactly one morning.
    On Saturday she neither lectures nor performs operations.

8. Which one of the following must be a day on which Doctor Yamata lectures?

    (A) Monday
    (B) Tuesday
    (C) Wednesday
    (D) Friday
    (E) Saturday

9. On Wednesday Doctor Yamata could be scheduled to

    (A) conduct research in the morning and operate in the afternoon
    (B) lecture in the morning and treat patients in the afternoon
    (C) operate in the morning and lecture in the afternoon
    (D) operate in the morning and conduct research in the afternoon
    (E) treat patients in the morning and treat patients in the afternoon

10. Which one of the following statements must be true?

    (A) There is one day on which the doctor treats patients both in the morning and in the afternoon.
    (B) The doctor conducts research on one of the days on which she lectures.
    (C) The doctor conducts research on one of the days on which she treats patients.
    (D) The doctor lectures on one of the days on which she treats patients.
    (E) The doctor lectures on one of the days on which she operates.

11. If Doctor Yamata operates on Tuesday, then her schedule for treating patients could be

    (A) Monday morning, Monday afternoon, Friday morning, Friday afternoon
    (B) Monday morning, Friday afternoon, Saturday morning, Saturday afternoon
    (C) Monday afternoon, Wednesday morning, Wednesday afternoon, Saturday afternoon
    (D) Wednesday morning, Wednesday afternoon, Friday afternoon, Saturday afternoon
    (E) Wednesday afternoon, Friday afternoon, Saturday morning, Saturday afternoon

12. Which one of the following is a pair of days on both of which Doctor Yamata must treat patients?

    (A) Monday and Tuesday
    (B) Monday and Saturday
    (C) Tuesday and Friday
    (D) Tuesday and Saturday
    (E) Friday and Saturday

GO ON TO THE NEXT PAGE.

Questions 13–18

Each of seven judges voted for or else against granting Datalog Corporation's petition. Each judge is categorized as conservative, moderate, or liberal, and no judge is assigned more than one of those labels. Two judges are conservatives, two are moderates, and three are liberals. The following is known about how the judges voted:

If the two conservatives and at least one liberal voted the same way as each other, then both moderates voted that way.

If the three liberals voted the same way as each other, then no conservative voted that way.

At least two of the judges voted for Datalog, and at least two voted against Datalog.

At least one conservative voted against Datalog.

13. If the two moderates did not vote the same way as each other, then which one of the following could be true?

(A) No conservative and exactly two liberals voted for Datalog.
(B) Exactly one conservative and exactly one liberal voted for Datalog.
(C) Exactly one conservative and all three liberals voted for Datalog.
(D) Exactly two conservatives and exactly one liberal voted for Datalog.
(E) Exactly two conservatives and exactly two liberals voted for Datalog.

14. Which one of the following must be true?

(A) At least one conservative voted for Datalog.
(B) At least one liberal voted against Datalog.
(C) At least one liberal voted for Datalog.
(D) At least one moderate voted against Datalog.
(E) At least one moderate voted for Datalog.

15. If the three liberals all voted the same way as each other, which one of the following must be true?

(A) Both moderates voted for Datalog.
(B) Both moderates voted against Datalog.
(C) One conservative voted for Datalog and one conservative voted against Datalog.
(D) One moderate voted for Datalog and one moderate voted against Datalog.
(E) All three liberals voted for Datalog.

16. If exactly two judges voted against Datalog, then which one of the following must be true?

(A) Both moderates voted for Datalog.
(B) Exactly one conservative voted for Datalog.
(C) No conservative voted for Datalog.
(D) Exactly two liberals voted for Datalog.
(E) Exactly three liberals voted for Datalog.

17. Each of the following could be a complete and accurate list of those judges who voted for Datalog EXCEPT

(A) two liberals
(B) one conservative, one liberal
(C) two moderates, three liberals
(D) one conservative, two moderates, two liberals
(E) one conservative, two moderates, three liberals

18. If the two conservatives voted the same way as each other, but the liberals did not all vote the same way as each other, then each of the following must be true EXCEPT:

(A) Both conservatives voted against Datalog.
(B) Both moderates voted for Datalog.
(C) At least one liberal voted against Datalog.
(D) Exactly two liberals voted for Datalog.
(E) Exactly five of the judges voted against Datalog.

GO ON TO THE NEXT PAGE.

Questions 19–24

An official is assigning five runners—Larry, Ned, Olivia, Patricia, and Sonja—to parallel lanes numbered consecutively 1 through 5. The official will also assign each runner to represent a different charity—F, G, H, J, and K—not necessarily in order of the runner's names as given. The following ordering restrictions apply:

The runner representing K is assigned to lane 4.

Patricia is assigned to the only lane between the lanes of the runners representing F and G.

There are exactly two lanes between Olivia's lane and the lane of the runner representing G.

Sonja is assigned to a higher-numbered lane than the lane to which Ned is assigned.

19. Which one of the following is a possible assignment of runners to lanes by the charity they represent?

     1 2 3 4 5
 (A) F G H K J
 (B) G H J K F
 (C) G K F J H
 (D) H J G K F
 (E) J H F K G

20. The lane to which Patricia is assigned must be a lane that is

 (A) next to the lane to which Larry is assigned
 (B) next to the lane to which Ned is assigned
 (C) separated by exactly one lane from the lane to which Ned is assigned
 (D) separated by exactly one lane from the lane to which Olivia is assigned
 (E) separated by exactly one lane from the lane to which Sonja is assigned

21. If Olivia is assigned to lane 2, which one of the following assignments must be made?

	Charity	Lane
(A)	F	1
(B)	G	5
(C)	H	1
(D)	H	3
(E)	J	5

22. Which one of the following is a complete and accurate list of runners each of whom could be the runner representing F?

 (A) Larry, Ned
 (B) Patricia, Sonja
 (C) Larry, Ned, Olivia
 (D) Larry, Ned, Sonja
 (E) Ned, Patricia, Sonja

23. If Ned is the runner representing J, then it must be true that

 (A) the runner representing G is assigned to lane 1
 (B) the runner representing H is assigned to lane 2
 (C) Larry is the runner representing K
 (D) Olivia is the runner representing F
 (E) Patricia is the runner representing H

24. If Larry represents J, which one of the following could be the assignment of runners to lanes?

	1	2	3	4	5
(A)	Larry	Olivia	Ned	Patricia	Sonja
(B)	Larry	Ned	Olivia	Sonja	Patricia
(C)	Larry	Sonja	Patricia	Ned	Olivia
(D)	Ned	Olivia	Larry	Patricia	Sonja
(E)	Ned	Sonja	Olivia	Patricia	Larry

S T O P

IF YOU FINISH BEFORE TIME IS CALLED, YOU MAY CHECK YOUR WORK ON THIS SECTION ONLY.
DO NOT WORK ON ANY OTHER SECTION IN THE TEST.

SECTION III

Time—35 minutes

27 Questions

<u>Directions:</u> Each passage in this section is followed by a group of questions to be answered on the basis of what is <u>stated</u> or <u>implied</u> in the passage. For some of the questions, more than one of the choices could conceivably answer the question. However, you are to choose the <u>best</u> answer; that is, the response that most accurately and completely answers the question, and blacken the corresponding space on your answer sheet.

The labor force is often organized as if workers had no family responsibilities. Preschool-age children need full-time care; children in primary school need care after school and during school

(5) vacations. Although day-care services can resolve some scheduling conflicts between home and office, workers cannot always find or afford suitable care. Even when they obtain such care, parents must still cope with emergencies, such as illnesses, that keep

(10) children at home. Moreover, children need more than tending; they also need meaningful time with their parents. Conventional full-time workdays, especially when combined with unavoidable household duties, are too inflexible for parents

(15) with primary child-care responsibility.

Although a small but increasing number of working men are single parents, those barriers against successful participation in the labor market that are related to primary child-care

(20) responsibilities mainly disadvantage women. Even in families where both parents work, cultural pressures are traditionally much greater on mothers than on fathers to bear the primary child-rearing responsibilities.

(25) In reconciling child-rearing responsibilities with participation in the labor market, many working mothers are forced to make compromises. For example, approximately one-third of all working mothers are employed only part-time, even though

(30) part-time jobs are dramatically underpaid and often less desirable in comparison to full-time employment. Even though part-time work is usually available only in occupations offering minimal employee responsibility and little

(35) opportunity for advancement or self-enrichment, such employment does allow many women the time and flexibility to fulfill their family duties, but only at the expense of the advantages associated with full-time employment.

(40) Moreover, even mothers with full-time employment must compromise opportunities in order to adjust to barriers against parents in the labor market. Many choose jobs entailing little challenge or responsibility or those offering flexible

(45) scheduling, often available only in poorly paid positions, while other working mothers, although willing and able to assume as much responsibility as people without children, find that their need to spend regular and predictable time with their

(50) children inevitably causes them to lose career

opportunities to those without such demands. Thus, women in education are more likely to become teachers than school administrators, whose more conventional full-time work schedules do not

(55) correspond to the schedules of school-age children, while female lawyers are more likely to practice law in trusts and estates, where they can control their work schedules, than in litigation, where they cannot. Nonprofessional women are concentrated

(60) in secretarial work and department store sales, where their absences can be covered easily by substitutes and where they can enter and leave the work force with little loss, since the jobs offer so little personal gain. Indeed, as long as the labor

(65) market remains hostile to parents, and family roles continue to be allocated on the basis of gender, women will be seriously disadvantaged in that labor market.

1. Which one of the following best summarizes the main idea of the passage?

(A) Current trends in the labor force indicate that working parents, especially women, may not always need to choose between occupational and child-care responsibilities.

(B) In order for mothers to have an equal opportunity for advancement in the labor force, traditional family roles have to be reexamined and revised.

(C) Although single parents who work have to balance parental and career demands, single mothers suffer resulting employment disadvantages that single fathers can almost always avoid.

(D) Although child-care responsibilities disadvantage many women in the labor force, professional women (such as teachers and lawyers) are better able to overcome this problem than are nonprofessional women.

(E) Traditional work schedules are too inflexible to accommodate the child-care responsibilities of many parents, a fact that severely disadvantages women in the labor force.

GO ON TO THE NEXT PAGE.

2. Which one of the following statements about part-time work can be inferred from the information presented in the passage?

    (A) One-third of all part-time workers are working mothers.
    (B) Part-time work generally offers fewer opportunities for advancement to working mothers than to women generally.
    (C) Part-time work, in addition to having relatively poor wages, often requires that employees work during holidays, when their children are out of school.
    (D) Part-time employment, despite its disadvantages, provides working mothers with an opportunity to address some of the demands of caring for children.
    (E) Many mothers with primary child-care responsibility choose part-time jobs in order to better exploit full-time career opportunities after their children are grown.

3. It can be inferred from the passage that the author would be most likely to agree with which one of the following statements about working fathers in two-parent families?

    (A) They are equally burdened by the employment disadvantages placed upon all parents—male and female—in the labor market.
    (B) They are so absorbed in their jobs that they often do not see the injustice going on around them.
    (C) They are shielded by the traditional allocation of family roles from many of the pressures associated with child-rearing responsibilities.
    (D) They help compound the inequities in the labor market by keeping women from competing with men for career opportunities.
    (E) They are responsible for many of the problems of working mothers because of their insistence on traditional roles in the family.

4. Of the following, which one would the author most likely say is the most troublesome barrier facing working parents with primary child-care responsibility?

    (A) the lack of full-time jobs open to women
    (B) the inflexibility of work schedules
    (C) the low wages of part-time employment
    (D) the limited advancement opportunities for nonprofessional employees
    (E) the practice of allocating responsibilities in the workplace on the basis of gender

5. The passage suggests that day care is at best a limited solution to the pressures associated with child rearing for all of the following reasons EXCEPT:

    (A) Even the best day care available cannot guarantee that children will have meaningful time with their parents.
    (B) Some parents cannot afford day-care services.
    (C) Working parents sometimes have difficulty finding suitable day care for their children.
    (D) Parents who send their children to day care still need to provide care for their children during vacations.
    (E) Even children who are in day care may have to stay home when they are sick.

6. According to the passage, many working parents may be forced to make any of the following types of career decisions EXCEPT

    (A) declining professional positions for nonprofessional ones, which typically have less conventional work schedules
    (B) accepting part-time employment rather than full-time employment
    (C) taking jobs with limited responsibility, and thus more limited career opportunities, in order to have a more flexible schedule
    (D) pursuing career specializations that allow them to control their work schedules instead of pursuing a more desirable specialization in the same field
    (E) limiting the career potential of one parent, often the mother, who assumes greater child-care responsibility

7. Which one of the following statements would most appropriately continue the discussion at the end of the passage?

    (A) At the same time, most men will remain better able to enjoy the career and salary opportunities offered by the labor market.
    (B) Of course, men who are married to working mothers know of these employment barriers but seem unwilling to do anything about them.
    (C) On the other hand, salary levels may become more equitable between men and women even if the other career opportunities remain more accessible to men than to women.
    (D) On the contrary, men with primary child-rearing responsibilities will continue to enjoy more advantages in the workplace than their female counterparts.
    (E) Thus, institutions in society that favor men over women will continue to widen the gap between the career opportunities available for men and for women.

GO ON TO THE NEXT PAGE.

Critics have long been puzzled by the inner contradictions of major characters in John Webster's tragedies. In his *The Duchess of Malfi*, for instance, the Duchess is "good" in demonstrating
(5) the obvious tenderness and sincerity of her love for Antonio, but "bad" in ignoring the wishes and welfare of her family and in making religion a "cloak" hiding worldly self-indulgence. Bosola is "bad" in serving Ferdinand, "good" in turning the
(10) Duchess' thoughts toward heaven and in planning to avenge her murder. The ancient Greek philosopher Aristotle implied that such contradictions are virtually essential to the tragic personality, and yet critics keep coming back to this element of
(15) inconsistency as though it were an eccentric feature of Webster's own tragic vision.

The problem is that, as an Elizabethan playwright, Webster has become a prisoner of our critical presuppositions. We have, in recent years, been
(20) dazzled by the way the earlier Renaissance and medieval theater, particularly the morality play, illuminates Elizabethan drama. We now understand how the habit of mind that saw the world as a battleground between good and evil produced the
(25) morality play. Morality plays allegorized that conflict by presenting characters whose actions were defined as the embodiment of good or evil. This model of reality lived on, overlaid by different conventions, in the more sophisticated Elizabethan
(30) works of the following age. Yet Webster seems not to have been as heavily influenced by the morality play's model of reality as were his Elizabethan contemporaries; he was apparently more sensitive to the more morally complicated Italian drama
(35) than to these English sources. Consequently, his characters cannot be evaluated according to reductive formulas of good and evil, which is precisely what modern critics have tried to do. They choose what seem to be the most promising of the
(40) contradictory values that are dramatized in the play, and treat those values as if they were the only basis for analyzing the moral development of the play's major characters, attributing the inconsistencies in a character's behavior to artistic
(45) incompetence on Webster's part. The lack of consistency in Webster's characters can be better understood if we recognize that the ambiguity at the heart of his tragic vision lies not in the external world but in the duality of human nature. Webster
(50) establishes tension in his plays by setting up conflicting systems of value that appear immoral only when one value system is viewed exclusively from the perspective of the other. He presents us not only with characters that we condemn
(55) intellectually or ethically and at the same time impulsively approve of, but also with judgments we must accept as logically sound and yet find emotionally repulsive. The dilemma is not only dramatic: it is tragic, because the conflict is
(60) irreconcilable, and because it is ours as much as that of the characters.

8. The primary purpose of the passage is to

(A) clarify an ambiguous assertion
(B) provide evidence in support of a commonly held view
(C) analyze an unresolved question and propose an answer
(D) offer an alternative to a flawed interpretation
(E) describe and categorize opposing viewpoints

9. The author suggests which one of the following about the dramatic works that most influenced Webster's tragedies?

(A) They were not concerned with dramatizing the conflict between good and evil that was presented in morality plays.
(B) They were not as sophisticated as the Italian sources from which other Elizabethan tragedies were derived.
(C) They have never been adequately understood by critics.
(D) They have only recently been used to illuminate the conventions of Elizabethan drama.
(E) They have been considered by many critics to be the reason for Webster's apparent artistic incompetence.

10. The author's allusion to Aristotle's view of tragedy in lines 11–13 serves which one of the following functions in the passage?

(A) It introduces a commonly held view of Webster's tragedies that the author plans to defend.
(B) It supports the author's suggestion that Webster's conception of tragedy is not idiosyncratic.
(C) It provides an example of an approach to Webster's tragedies that the author criticizes.
(D) It establishes the similarity between classical and modern approaches to tragedy.
(E) It supports the author's assertion that Elizabethan tragedy cannot be fully understood without the help of recent scholarship.

GO ON TO THE NEXT PAGE.

11. It can be inferred from the passage that modern critics' interpretations of Webster's tragedies would be more valid if

(A) the ambiguity inherent in Webster's tragic vision resulted from the duality of human nature

(B) Webster's conception of the tragic personality were similar to that of Aristotle

(C) Webster had been heavily influenced by the morality play

(D) Elizabethan dramatists had been more sensitive to Italian sources of influence

(E) the inner conflicts exhibited by Webster's characters were similar to those of modern audiences

12. With which one of the following statements regarding Elizabethan drama would the author be most likely to agree?

(A) The skill of Elizabethan dramatists has in recent years been overestimated.

(B) The conventions that shaped Elizabethan drama are best exemplified by Webster's drama.

(C) Elizabethan drama, for the most part, can be viewed as being heavily influenced by the morality play.

(D) Only by carefully examining the work of his Elizabethan contemporaries can Webster's achievement as a dramatist be accurately measured.

(E) Elizabethan drama can best be described as influenced by a composite of Italian and classical sources.

13. It can be inferred from the passage that most modern critics assume which one of the following in their interpretation of Webster's tragedies?

(A) Webster's plays tended to allegorize the conflict between good and evil more than did those of his contemporaries.

(B) Webster's plays were derived more from Italian than from English sources.

(C) The artistic flaws in Webster's tragedies were largely the result of his ignorance of the classical definition of tragedy.

(D) Webster's tragedies provide no relevant basis for analyzing the moral development of their characters.

(E) In writing his tragedies, Webster was influenced by the same sources as his contemporaries.

14. The author implies that Webster's conception of tragedy was

(A) artistically flawed

(B) highly conventional

(C) largely derived from the morality play

(D) somewhat different from the conventional Elizabethan conception of tragedy

(E) uninfluenced by the classical conception of tragedy

GO ON TO THE NEXT PAGE.

Cultivation of a single crop on a given tract of land leads eventually to decreased yields. One reason for this is that harmful bacterial phytopathogens, organisms parasitic on plant
(5) hosts, increase in the soil surrounding plant roots. The problem can be cured by crop rotation, denying the pathogens a suitable host for a period of time. However, even if crops are not rotated, the severity of diseases brought on by such
(10) phytopathogens often decreases after a number of years as the microbial population of the soil changes and the soil becomes "suppressive" to those diseases. While there may be many reasons for this phenomenon, it is clear that levels of certain
(15) bacteria, such as *Pseudomonas fluorescens*, a bacterium antagonistic to a number of harmful phytopathogens, are greater in suppressive than in nonsuppressive soil. This suggests that the presence of such bacteria suppresses phytopathogens. There
(20) is now considerable experimental support for this view. Wheat yield increases of 27 percent have been obtained in field trials by treatment of wheat seeds with fluorescent pseudomonads. Similar treatment of sugar beets, cotton, and potatoes has had similar
(25) results.

These improvements in crop yields through the application of *Pseudomonas fluorescens* suggest that agriculture could benefit from the use of bacteria genetically altered for specific purposes. For
(30) example, a form of phytopathogen altered to remove its harmful properties could be released into the environment in quantities favorable to its competing with and eventually excluding the harmful normal strain. Some experiments suggest
(35) that deliberately releasing altered nonpathogenic *Pseudomonas syringae* could crowd out the nonaltered variety that causes frost damage. Opponents of such research have objected that the deliberate and large-scale release of genetically
(40) altered bacteria might have deleterious results. Proponents, on the other hand, argue that this particular strain is altered only by the removal of the gene responsible for the strain's propensity to cause frost damage, thereby rendering it safer than
(45) the phytopathogen from which it was derived.

Some proponents have gone further and suggest that genetic alteration techniques could create organisms with totally new combinations of desirable traits not found in nature. For example,
(50) genes responsible for production of insecticidal compounds have been transposed from other bacteria into pseudomonads that colonize corn roots. Experiments of this kind are difficult and require great care: such bacteria are developed in
(55) highly artificial environments and may not compete well with natural soil bacteria. Nevertheless, proponents contend that the prospects for improved agriculture through such methods seem excellent. These prospects lead many to hope that
(60) current efforts to assess the risks of deliberate

release of altered microorganisms will successfully answer the concerns of opponents and create a climate in which such research can go forward without undue impediment.

15. Which one of the following best summarizes the main idea of the passage?

(A) Recent field experiments with genetically altered *Pseudomonas* bacteria have shown that releasing genetically altered bacteria into the environment would not involve any significant danger.

(B) Encouraged by current research, advocates of agricultural use of genetically altered bacteria are optimistic that such use will eventually result in improved agriculture, though opponents remain wary.

(C) Current research indicates that adding genetically altered *Pseudomonas syringae* bacteria to the soil surrounding crop plant roots will have many beneficial effects, such as the prevention of frost damage in certain crops.

(D) Genetic alteration of a number of harmful phytopathogens has been advocated by many researchers who contend that these techniques will eventually replace such outdated methods as crop rotation.

(E) Genetic alteration of bacteria has been successful in highly artificial laboratory conditions, but opponents of such research have argued that these techniques are unlikely to produce organisms that are able to survive in natural environments.

16. The author discusses naturally occurring *Pseudomonas fluorescens* bacteria in the first paragraph primarily in order to do which one of the following?

(A) prove that increases in the level of such bacteria in the soil are the sole cause of soil suppressivity

(B) explain why yields increased after wheat fields were sprayed with altered *Pseudomonas fluorescens* bacteria

(C) detail the chemical processes that such bacteria use to suppress organisms parasitic to crop plants, such as wheat, sugar beets, and potatoes

(D) provide background information to support the argument that research into the agricultural use of genetically altered bacteria would be fruitful

(E) argue that crop rotation is unnecessary, since diseases brought on by phytopathogens diminish in severity and eventually disappear on their own

GO ON TO THE NEXT PAGE.

17. It can be inferred from the author's discussion of *Pseudomonas fluorescens* bacteria that which one of the following would be true of crops impervious to parasitical organisms?

   (A) *Pseudomonas fluorescens* bacteria would be absent from the soil surrounding their roots.
   (B) They would crowd out and eventually exclude other crop plants if their growth were not carefully regulated.
   (C) Their yield would not be likely to be improved by adding *Pseudomonas fluorescens* bacteria to the soil.
   (D) They would mature more quickly than crop plants that were susceptible to parasitical organisms.
   (E) Levels of phytopathogenic bacteria in the soil surrounding their roots would be higher compared with other crop plants.

18. It can be inferred from the passage that crop rotation can increase yields in part because

   (A) moving crop plants around makes them hardier and more resistant to disease
   (B) the number of *Pseudomonas fluorescens* bacteria in the soil usually increases when crops are rotated
   (C) the roots of many crop plants produce compounds that are antagonistic to phytopathogens harmful to other crop plants
   (D) the presence of phytopathogenic bacteria is responsible for the majority of plant diseases
   (E) phytopathogens typically attack some plant species but find other species to be unsuitable hosts

19. According to the passage, proponents of the use of genetically altered bacteria in agriculture argue that which one of the following is true of the altered bacteria used in the frost-damage experiments?

   (A) The altered bacteria had a genetic constitution differing from that of the normal strain only in that the altered variety had one less gene.
   (B) Although the altered bacteria competed effectively with the nonaltered strain in the laboratory, they were not as viable in natural environments.
   (C) The altered bacteria were much safer and more effective than the naturally occurring *Pseudomonas fluorescens* bacteria used in earlier experiments.
   (D) The altered bacteria were antagonistic to several types of naturally occurring phytopathogens in the soil surrounding the roots of frost-damaged crops.
   (E) The altered bacteria were released into the environment in numbers sufficient to guarantee the validity of experimental results.

20. Which one of the following, if true, would most seriously weaken the proponents' argument regarding the safety of using altered *Pseudomonas syringae* bacteria to control frost damage?

   (A) *Pseudomonas syringae* bacteria are primitive and have a simple genetic constitution.
   (B) The altered bacteria are derived from a strain that is parasitic to plants and can cause damage to crops.
   (C) Current genetic-engineering techniques permit the large-scale commercial production of such bacteria.
   (D) Often genes whose presence is responsible for one harmful characteristic must be present in order to prevent other harmful characteristics.
   (E) The frost-damage experiments with *Pseudomonas syringae* bacteria indicate that the altered variety would only replace the normal strain if released in sufficient numbers.

GO ON TO THE NEXT PAGE.

In 1887 the Dawes Act legislated wide-scale private ownership of reservation lands in the United States for Native Americans. The act allotted plots of 80 acres to each Native American
(5) adult. However, the Native Americans were not granted outright title to their lands. The act defined each grant as a "trust patent," meaning that the Bureau of Indian Affairs (BIA), the governmental agency in charge of administering policy regarding
(10) Native Americans, would hold the allotted land in trust for 25 years, during which time the Native American owners could use, but not alienate (sell) the land. After the 25-year period, the Native American allottee would receive a "fee patent"
(15) awarding full legal ownership of the land.

Two main reasons were advanced for the restriction on the Native Americans' ability to sell their lands. First, it was claimed that free alienability would lead to immediate transfer of
(20) large amounts of former reservation land to non-Native Americans, consequently threatening the traditional way of life on those reservations. A second objection to free alienation was that Native Americans were unaccustomed to, and did not
(25) desire, a system of private landownership. Their custom, it was said, favored communal use of land.

However, both of these arguments bear only on the transfer of Native American lands to non-Native Americans; neither offers a reason for prohibiting
(30) Native Americans from transferring land among themselves. Selling land to each other would not threaten the Native American culture. Additionally, if communal land use remained preferable to Native Americans after allotment, free
(35) alienability would have allowed allottees to sell their lands back to the tribe.

When stated rationales for government policies prove empty, using an interest-group model often provides an explanation. While neither Native
(40) Americans nor the potential non-Native American purchasers benefited from the restraint on alienation contained in the Dawes Act, one clearly defined group did benefit: the BIA bureaucrats. It has been convincingly demonstrated that bureaucrats
(45) seek to maximize the size of their staffs and their budgets in order to compensate for the lack of other sources of fulfillment, such as power and prestige. Additionally, politicians tend to favor the growth of governmental bureaucracy because such
(50) growth provides increased opportunity for the exercise of political patronage. The restraint on alienation vastly increased the amount of work, and hence the budgets, necessary to implement the statute. Until allotment was ended in 1934,
(55) granting fee patents and leasing Native American lands were among the principal activities of the United States government. One hypothesis, then, for the temporary restriction on alienation in the Dawes Act is that it reflected a compromise
(60) between non-Native Americans favoring immediate alienability so they could purchase land and the BIA bureaucrats who administered the privatization system.

21. Which one of the following best summarizes the main idea of the passage?

(A) United States government policy toward Native Americans has tended to disregard their needs and consider instead the needs of non-Native American purchasers of land.

(B) In order to preserve the unique way of life on Native American reservations, use of Native American lands must be communal rather than individual.

(C) The Dawes Act's restriction on the right of Native Americans to sell their land may have been implemented primarily to serve the interests of politicians and bureaucrats.

(D) The clause restricting free alienability in the Dawes Act greatly expanded United States governmental activity in the area of land administration.

(E) Since passage of the Dawes Act in 1887, Native Americans have not been able to sell or transfer their former reservation land freely.

22. Which one of the following statements concerning the reason for the end of allotment, if true, would provide the most support for the author's view of politicians?

(A) Politicians realized that allotment was damaging the Native American way of life.

(B) Politicians decided that allotment would be more congruent with the Native American custom of communal land use.

(C) Politicians believed that allotment's continuation would not enhance their opportunities to exercise patronage.

(D) Politicians felt that the staff and budgets of the BIA had grown too large.

(E) Politicians were concerned that too much Native American land was falling into the hands of non-Native Americans.

GO ON TO THE NEXT PAGE.

23. Which one of the following best describes the organization of the passage?

(A) The passage of a law is analyzed in detail, the benefits and drawbacks of one of its clauses are studied, and a final assessment of the law is offered.
(B) The history of a law is narrated, the effects of one of its clauses on various populations are studied, and repeal of the law is advocated.
(C) A law is examined, the political and social backgrounds of one of its clauses are characterized, and the permanent effects of the law are studied.
(D) A law is described, the rationale put forward for one of its clauses is outlined and dismissed, and a different rationale for the clause is presented.
(E) The legal status of an ethnic group is examined with respect to issues of landownership and commercial autonomy, and the benefits to rival groups due to that status are explained.

24. The author's attitude toward the reasons advanced for the restriction on alienability in the Dawes Act at the time of its passage can best be described as

(A) completely credulous
(B) partially approving
(C) basically indecisive
(D) mildly questioning
(E) highly skeptical

25. It can be inferred from the passage that which one of the following was true of Native American life immediately before passage of the Dawes Act?

(A) Most Native Americans supported themselves through farming.
(B) Not many Native Americans personally owned the land on which they lived.
(C) The land on which most Native Americans lived had been bought from their tribes.
(D) Few Native Americans had much contact with their non-Native American neighbors.
(E) Few Native Americans were willing to sell their land to non-Native Americans.

26. According to the passage, the type of landownership initially obtainable by Native Americans under the Dawes Act differed from the type of ownership obtainable after a 25-year period in that only the latter allowed

(A) owners of land to farm it
(B) owners of land to sell it
(C) government some control over how owners disposed of land
(D) owners of land to build on it with relatively minor governmental restrictions
(E) government to charge owners a fee for developing their land

27. Which one of the following, if true, would most strengthen the author's argument regarding the true motivation for the passage of the Dawes Act?

(A) The legislators who voted in favor of the Dawes Act owned land adjacent to Native American reservations.
(B) The majority of Native Americans who were granted fee patents did not sell their land back to their tribes.
(C) Native Americans managed to preserve their traditional culture even when they were geographically dispersed.
(D) The legislators who voted in favor of the Dawes Act were heavily influenced by BIA bureaucrats.
(E) Non-Native Americans who purchased the majority of Native American lands consolidated them into larger farm holdings.

S T O P

IF YOU FINISH BEFORE TIME IS CALLED, YOU MAY CHECK YOUR WORK ON THIS SECTION ONLY.
DO NOT WORK ON ANY OTHER SECTION IN THE TEST.

SECTION IV

Time—35 minutes

25 Questions

<u>Directions:</u> The questions in this section are based on the reasoning contained in brief statements or passages. For some questions, more than one of the choices could conceivably answer the question. However, you are to choose the <u>best</u> answer; that is, the response that most accurately and completely answers the question. You should not make assumptions that are by commonsense standards implausible, superfluous, or incompatible with the passage. After you have chosen the best answer, blacken the corresponding space on your answer sheet.

1. In 1974 the speed limit on highways in the United States was reduced to 55 miles per hour in order to save fuel. In the first 12 months after the change, the rate of highway fatalities dropped 15 percent, the sharpest one-year drop in history. Over the next 10 years, the fatality rate declined by another 25 percent. It follows that the 1974 reduction in the speed limit saved many lives.

Which one of the following, if true, most strengthens the argument?

(A) The 1974 fuel shortage cut driving sharply for more than a year.

(B) There was no decline in the rate of highway fatalities during the twelfth year following the reduction in the speed limit.

(C) Since 1974 automobile manufacturers have been required by law to install lifesaving equipment, such as seat belts, in all new cars.

(D) The fatality rate in highway accidents involving motorists driving faster than 55 miles per hour is much higher than in highway accidents that do not involve motorists driving at such speeds.

(E) Motorists are more likely to avoid accidents by matching their speed to that of the surrounding highway traffic than by driving at faster or slower speeds.

2. Some legislators refuse to commit public funds for new scientific research if they cannot be assured that the research will contribute to the public welfare. Such a position ignores the lessons of experience. Many important contributions to the public welfare that resulted from scientific research were never predicted as potential outcomes of that research. Suppose that a scientist in the early twentieth century had applied for public funds to study molds: who would have predicted that such research would lead to the discovery of antibiotics—one of the greatest contributions ever made to the public welfare?

Which one of the following most accurately expresses the main point of the argument?

(A) The committal of public funds for new scientific research will ensure that the public welfare will be enhanced.

(B) If it were possible to predict the general outcome of a new scientific research effort, then legislators would not refuse to commit public funds for that effort.

(C) Scientific discoveries that have contributed to the public welfare would have occurred sooner if public funds had been committed to the research that generated those discoveries.

(D) In order to ensure that scientific research is directed toward contributing to the public welfare, legislators must commit public funds to new scientific research.

(E) Lack of guarantees that new scientific research will contribute to the public welfare is not sufficient reason for legislators to refuse to commit public funds to new scientific research.

GO ON TO THE NEXT PAGE.

3. When workers do not find their assignments challenging, they become bored and so achieve less than their abilities would allow. On the other hand, when workers find their assignments too difficult, they give up and so again achieve less than what they are capable of achieving. It is, therefore, clear that no worker's full potential will ever be realized.

Which one of the following is an error of reasoning contained in the argument?

(A) mistakenly equating what is actual and what is merely possible
(B) assuming without warrant that a situation allows only two possibilities
(C) relying on subjective rather than objective evidence
(D) confusing the coincidence of two events with a causal relation between the two
(E) depending on the ambiguous use of a key term

4. Our tomato soup provides good nutrition: for instance, a warm bowl of it contains more units of vitamin C than does a serving of apricots or fresh carrots!

The advertisement is misleading if which one of the following is true?

(A) Few people depend exclusively on apricots and carrots to supply vitamin C to their diets.
(B) A liquid can lose vitamins if it stands in contact with the air for a protracted period of time.
(C) Tomato soup contains important nutrients other than vitamin C.
(D) The amount of vitamin C provided by a serving of the advertised soup is less than the amount furnished by a serving of fresh strawberries.
(E) Apricots and fresh carrots are widely known to be nutritious, but their contribution consists primarily in providing a large amount of vitamin A, not a large amount of vitamin C.

Questions 5–6

The government provides insurance for individuals' bank deposits, but requires the banks to pay the premiums for this insurance. Since it is depositors who primarily benefit from the security this insurance provides, the government should take steps to ensure that depositors who want this security bear the cost of it and thus should make depositors pay the premiums for insuring their own accounts.

5. Which one of the following principles, if established, would do most to justify drawing the conclusion of the argument on the basis of the reasons offered in its support?

(A) The people who stand to benefit from an economic service should always be made to bear the costs of that service.
(B) Any rational system of insurance must base the size of premiums on the degree of risk involved.
(C) Government-backed security for investors, such as bank depositors, should be provided only when it does not reduce incentives for investors to make responsible investments.
(D) The choice of not accepting an offered service should always be available, even if there is no charge for the service.
(E) The government should avoid any actions that might alter the behavior of corporations and individuals in the market.

6. Which one of the following is assumed by the argument?

(A) Banks are not insured by the government against default on the loans the banks make.
(B) Private insurance companies do not have the resources to provide banks or individuals with deposit insurance.
(C) Banks do not always cover the cost of the deposit-insurance premiums by paying depositors lower interest rates on insured deposits than the banks would on uninsured deposits.
(D) The government limits the insurance protection it provides by insuring accounts up to a certain legally defined amount only.
(E) The government does not allow banks to offer some kinds of accounts in which deposits are not insured.

GO ON TO THE NEXT PAGE.

7. When individual students are all treated equally in that they have identical exposure to curriculum material, the rate, quality, and quantity of learning will vary from student to student. If all students are to master a given curriculum, some of them need different types of help than others, as any experienced teacher knows.

If the statements above are both true, which one of the following conclusions can be drawn on the basis of them?

(A) Unequal treatment, in a sense, of individual students is required in order to ensure equality with respect to the educational tasks they master.

(B) The rate and quality of learning, with learning understood as the acquiring of the ability to solve problems within a given curriculum area, depend on the quantity of teaching an individual student receives in any given curriculum.

(C) The more experienced the teacher is, the more the students will learn.

(D) All students should have identical exposure to learn the material being taught in any given curriculum.

(E) Teachers should help each of their students to learn as much as possible.

8. George: Some scientists say that global warming will occur because people are releasing large amounts of carbon dioxide into the atmosphere by burning trees and fossil fuels. We can see, though, that the predicted warming is occurring already. In the middle of last winter, we had a month of springlike weather in our area, and this fall, because of unusually mild temperatures, the leaves on our town's trees were three weeks late in turning color.

Which one of the following would it be most relevant to investigate in evaluating the conclusion of George's argument?

(A) whether carbon dioxide is the only cause of global warming

(B) when leaves on the trees in the town usually change color

(C) what proportion of global emissions of carbon dioxide is due to the burning of trees by humans

(D) whether air pollution is causing some trees in the area to lose their leaves

(E) whether unusually warm weather is occurring elsewhere on the globe more frequently than before

9. Student representative: Our university, in expelling a student who verbally harassed his roommate, has erred by penalizing the student for doing what he surely has a right to do: speak his mind!

Dean of students: But what you're saying is that our university should endorse verbal harassment. Yet surely if we did that, we would threaten the free flow of ideas that is the essence of university life.

Which one of the following is a questionable technique that the dean of students uses in attempting to refute the student representative?

(A) challenging the student representative's knowledge of the process by which the student was expelled

(B) invoking a fallacious distinction between speech and other sorts of behavior

(C) misdescribing the student representative's position, thereby making it easier to challenge

(D) questioning the motives of the student representative rather than offering reasons for the conclusion defended

(E) relying on a position of power to silence the opposing viewpoint with a threat

10. Famous personalities found guilty of many types of crimes in well-publicized trials are increasingly sentenced to the performance of community service, though unknown defendants convicted of similar crimes almost always serve prison sentences. However, the principle of equality before the law rules out using fame and publicity as relevant considerations in the sentencing of convicted criminals.

The statements above, if true, most strongly support which one of the following conclusions?

(A) The principle of equality before the law is rigorously applied in only a few types of criminal trials.

(B) The number of convicted celebrities sentenced to community service should equal the number of convicted unknown defendants sentenced to community service.

(C) The principle of equality before the law can properly be overridden by other principles in some cases.

(D) The sentencing of celebrities to community service instead of prison constitutes a violation of the principle of equality before the law in many cases.

(E) The principle of equality before the law does not allow for leniency in sentencing.

GO ON TO THE NEXT PAGE.

11. Scientific research at a certain university was supported in part by an annual grant from a major foundation. When the university's physics department embarked on weapons-related research, the foundation, which has a purely humanitarian mission, threatened to cancel its grant. The university then promised that none of the foundation's money would be used for the weapons research, whereupon the foundation withdrew its threat, concluding that the weapons research would not benefit from the foundation's grant.

Which one of the following describes a flaw in the reasoning underlying the foundation's conclusion?

(A) It overlooks the possibility that the availability of the foundation's money for humanitarian uses will allow the university to redirect other funds from humanitarian uses to weapons research.

(B) It overlooks the possibility that the physics department's weapons research is not the only one of the university's research activities with other than purely humanitarian purposes.

(C) It overlooks the possibility that the university made its promise specifically in order to induce the foundation to withdraw its threat.

(D) It confuses the intention of not using a sum of money for a particular purpose with the intention of not using that sum of money at all.

(E) It assumes that if the means to achieve an objective are humanitarian in character, then the objective is also humanitarian in character.

12. To suit the needs of corporate clients, advertising agencies have successfully modified a strategy originally developed for political campaigns. This strategy aims to provide clients with free publicity and air time by designing an advertising campaign that is controversial, thus drawing prime-time media coverage and evoking public comment by officials.

The statements above, if true, most seriously undermine which one of the following assertions?

(A) The usefulness of an advertising campaign is based solely on the degree to which the campaign's advertisements persuade their audiences.

(B) Only a small percentage of eligible voters admit to being influenced by advertising campaigns in deciding how to vote.

(C) Campaign managers have transformed political campaigns by making increasing use of strategies borrowed from corporate advertising campaigns.

(D) Corporations are typically more concerned with maintaining public recognition of the corporate name than with enhancing goodwill toward the corporation.

(E) Advertising agencies that specialize in campaigns for corporate clients are not usually chosen for political campaigns.

13. The National Association of Fire Fighters says that 45 percent of homes now have smoke detectors, whereas only 30 percent of homes had them 10 years ago. This makes early detection of house fires no more likely, however, because over half of the domestic smoke detectors are either without batteries or else inoperative for some other reason.

In order for the conclusion above to be properly drawn, which one of the following assumptions would have to be made?

(A) Fifteen percent of domestic smoke detectors were installed less than 10 years ago.

(B) The number of fires per year in homes with smoke detectors has increased.

(C) Not all of the smoke detectors in homes are battery operated.

(D) The proportion of domestic smoke detectors that are inoperative has increased in the past ten years.

(E) Unlike automatic water sprinklers, a properly functioning smoke detector cannot by itself increase fire safety in a home.

GO ON TO THE NEXT PAGE.

14. Advertisement: HomeGlo Paints, Inc., has won the prestigious Golden Paintbrush Award—given to the one paint manufacturer in the country that has increased the environmental safety of its product most over the past three years— for HomeGlo Exterior Enamel. The Golden Paintbrush is awarded only on the basis of thorough tests by independent testing laboratories. So when you choose HomeGlo Exterior Enamel, you will know that you have chosen the most environmentally safe brand of paint manufactured in this country today.

The flawed reasoning in the advertisement most closely parallels that in which one of the following?

(A) The ZXC audio system received the overall top ranking for looks, performance, durability, and value in *Listeners' Report* magazine's ratings of currently produced systems. Therefore, the ZXC must have better sound quality than any other currently produced sound system.

(B) Morning Sunshine breakfast cereal contains, ounce for ounce, more of the nutrients needed for a healthy diet than any other breakfast cereal on the market today. Thus, when you eat Morning Sunshine, you will know you are eating the most nutritious food now on the market.

(C) The number of consumer visits increased more at Countryside Market last year than at any other market in the region. Therefore, Countryside's profits must also have increased more last year than those of any other market in the region.

(D) Jerrold's teachers recognize him as the student who has shown more academic improvement than any other student in the junior class this year. Therefore, if Jerrold and his classmates are ranked according to their current academic performance, Jerrold must hold the highest ranking.

(E) Margaret Durring's short story "The Power Lunch" won three separate awards for best short fiction of the year. Therefore, any of Margaret Durring's earlier stories certainly has enough literary merit to be included in an anthology of the best recent short fiction.

15. The consistency of ice cream is adversely affected by even slight temperature changes in the freezer. To counteract this problem, manufacturers add stabilizers to ice cream. Unfortunately, stabilizers, though inexpensive, adversely affect flavor. Stabilizers are less needed if storage temperatures are very low. However, since energy costs are constantly going up, those costs constitute a strong incentive in favor of relatively high storage temperatures.

Which one of the following can be properly inferred from the passage?

(A) Even slight deviations from the proper consistency for ice cream sharply impair its flavor.

(B) Cost considerations favor sacrificing consistency over sacrificing flavor.

(C) It would not be cost-effective to develop a new device to maintain the constancy of freezer temperatures.

(D) Stabilizers function well only at very low freezer temperatures.

(E) Very low, stable freezer temperatures allow for the best possible consistency and flavor of ice cream.

16. Edwina: True appreciation of Mozart's music demands that you hear it exactly as he intended it to be heard; that is, exactly as he heard it. Since he heard it on eighteenth-century instruments, it follows that so should we.

Alberto: But what makes you think that Mozart ever heard his music played as he had intended it to be played? After all, Mozart was writing at a time when the performer was expected, as a matter of course, not just to interpret but to modify the written score.

Alberto adopts which one of the following strategies in criticizing Edwina's position?

(A) He appeals to an academic authority in order to challenge the factual basis of her conclusion.

(B) He attacks her judgment by suggesting that she does not recognize the importance of the performer's creativity to the audience's appreciation of a musical composition.

(C) He defends a competing view of musical authenticity.

(D) He attacks the logic of her argument by suggesting that the conclusion she draws does not follow from the premises she sets forth.

(E) He offers a reason to believe that one of the premises of her argument is false.

GO ON TO THE NEXT PAGE.

17. Since the introduction of the Impanian National Health scheme, Impanians (or their private insurance companies) have had to pay only for the more unusual and sophisticated medical procedures. When the scheme was introduced, it was hoped that private insurance to pay for these procedures would be available at modest cost, since the insurers would no longer be paying for the bulk of health care costs, as they had done previously. Paradoxically, however, the cost of private health insurance did not decrease but has instead increased dramatically in the years since the scheme's introduction.

Which one of the following, if true, does most to explain the apparently paradoxical outcome?

(A) The National Health scheme has greatly reduced the number of medical claims handled annually by Impania's private insurers, enabling these firms to reduce overhead costs substantially.

(B) Before the National Health scheme was introduced, more than 80 percent of all Impanian medical costs were associated with procedures that are now covered by the scheme.

(C) Impanians who previously were unable to afford regular medical treatment now use the National Health scheme, but the number of Impanians with private health insurance has not increased.

(D) Impanians now buy private medical insurance only at times when they expect that they will need care of kinds not available in the National Health scheme.

(E) The proportion of total expenditures within Impania that is spent on health care has declined since the introduction of the National Health scheme.

18. In clinical trials of new medicines, half of the subjects receive the drug being tested and half receive a physiologically inert substance—a placebo. Trials are designed with the intention that neither subjects nor experimenters will find out which subjects are actually being given the drug being tested. However, this intention is frequently frustrated because _____.

Which one of the following, if true, most appropriately completes the explanation?

(A) often the subjects who receive the drug being tested develop symptoms that the experimenters recognize as side effects of the physiologically active drug

(B) subjects who believe they are receiving the drug being tested often display improvements in their conditions regardless of whether what is administered to them is physiologically active or not

(C) in general, when the trial is intended to establish the experimental drug's safety rather than its effectiveness, all of the subjects are healthy volunteers

(D) when a trial runs a long time, few of the experimenters will work on it from inception to conclusion

(E) the people who are subjects for clinical trials must, by law, be volunteers and must be informed of the possibility that they will receive a placebo

19. It takes 365.25 days for the Earth to make one complete revolution around the Sun. Long-standing convention makes a year 365 days long, with an extra day added every fourth year, and the year is divided into 52 seven-day weeks. But since 52 times 7 is only 364, anniversaries do not fall on the same day of the week each year. Many scheduling problems could be avoided if the last day of each year and an additional day every fourth year belonged to no week, so that January 1 would be a Sunday every year.

The proposal above, once put into effect, would be most likely to result in continued scheduling conflicts for which one of the following groups?

(A) people who have birthdays or other anniversaries on December 30 or 31

(B) employed people whose strict religious observances require that they refrain from working every seventh day

(C) school systems that require students to attend classes a specific number of days each year

(D) employed people who have three-day breaks from work when holidays are celebrated on Mondays or Fridays

(E) people who have to plan events several years before those events occur

GO ON TO THE NEXT PAGE.

20. Graphologists claim that it is possible to detect permanent character traits by examining people's handwriting. For example, a strong cross on the "t" is supposed to denote enthusiasm. Obviously, however, with practice and perseverance people can alter their handwriting to include this feature. So it seems that graphologists must hold that permanent character traits can be changed.

The argument against graphology proceeds by

(A) citing apparently incontestable evidence that leads to absurd consequences when conjoined with the view in question
(B) demonstrating that an apparently controversial and interesting claim is really just a platitude
(C) arguing that a particular technique of analysis can never be effective when the people analyzed know that it is being used
(D) showing that proponents of the view have no theoretical justification for the view
(E) attacking a technique by arguing that what the technique is supposed to detect can be detected quite readily without it

Questions 21–22

Historian: There is no direct evidence that timber was traded between the ancient nations of Poran and Nayal, but the fact that a law setting tariffs on timber imports from Poran was enacted during the third Nayalese dynasty does suggest that during that period a timber trade was conducted.

Critic: Your reasoning is flawed. During its third dynasty, Nayal may well have imported timber from Poran, but certainly on today's statute books there remain many laws regulating activities that were once common but in which people no longer engage.

21. The critic's response to the historian's reasoning does which one of the following?

(A) It implies an analogy between the present and the past.
(B) It identifies a general principle that the historian's reasoning violates.
(C) It distinguishes between what has been established as a certainty and what has been established as a possibility.
(D) It establishes explicit criteria that must be used in evaluating indirect evidence.
(E) It points out the dissimilar roles that law plays in societies that are distinct from one another.

22. The critic's response to the historian is flawed because it

(A) produces evidence that is consistent with there not having been any timber trade between Poran and Nayal during the third Nayalese dynasty
(B) cites current laws without indicating whether the laws cited are relevant to the timber trade
(C) fails to recognize that the historian's conclusion was based on indirect evidence rather than direct evidence
(D) takes no account of the difference between a law's enactment at a particular time and a law's existence as part of a legal code at a particular time
(E) accepts without question the assumption about the purpose of laws that underlies the historian's argument

GO ON TO THE NEXT PAGE.

23. The workers at Bell Manufacturing will shortly go on strike unless the management increases their wages. As Bell's president is well aware, however, in order to increase the workers' wages, Bell would have to sell off some of its subsidiaries. So, some of Bell's subsidiaries will be sold.

The conclusion above is properly drawn if which one of the following is assumed?

(A) Bell Manufacturing will begin to suffer increased losses.

(B) Bell's management will refuse to increase its workers' wages.

(C) The workers at Bell Manufacturing will not be going on strike.

(D) Bell's president has the authority to offer the workers their desired wage increase.

(E) Bell's workers will not accept a package of improved benefits in place of their desired wage increase.

24. One sure way you can tell how quickly a new idea—for example, the idea of "privatization"—is taking hold among the population is to monitor how fast the word or words expressing that particular idea are passing into common usage. Professional opinions of whether or not words can indeed be said to have passed into common usage are available from dictionary editors, who are vitally concerned with this question.

The method described above for determining how quickly a new idea is taking hold relies on which one of the following assumptions?

(A) Dictionary editors are not professionally interested in words that are only rarely used.

(B) Dictionary editors have exact numerical criteria for telling when a word has passed into common usage.

(C) For a new idea to take hold, dictionary editors have to include the relevant word or words in their dictionaries.

(D) As a word passes into common usage, its meaning does not undergo any severe distortions in the process.

(E) Words denoting new ideas tend to be used before the ideas denoted are understood.

25. Because migrant workers are typically not hired by any one employer for longer than a single season, migrant workers can legally be paid less than the minimum hourly wage that the government requires employers to pay all their permanent employees. Yet most migrant workers work long hours each day for eleven or twelve months a year and thus are as much full-time workers as are people hired on a year-round basis. Therefore, the law should require that migrant workers be paid the same minimum hourly wage that other full-time workers must be paid.

The pattern of reasoning displayed above most closely parallels that displayed in which one of the following arguments?

(A) Because day-care facilities are now regulated at the local level, the quality of care available to children in two different cities can differ widely. Since such differences in treatment clearly are unfair, day care should be federally rather than locally regulated.

(B) Because many rural areas have few restrictions on development, housing estates in such areas have been built where no adequate supply of safe drinking water could be ensured. Thus, rural areas should adopt building codes more like those large cities have.

(C) Because some countries regulate gun sales more strictly than do other countries, some people can readily purchase a gun, whereas others cannot. Therefore, all countries should cooperate in developing a uniform international policy regarding gun sales.

(D) Because it is a democratic principle that laws should have the consent of those affected by them, liquor laws should be formulated not by politicians but by club and restaurant owners, since such laws directly affect the profitability of their businesses.

(E) Because food additives are not considered drugs, they have not had to meet the safety standards the government applies to drugs. But food additives can be as dangerous as drugs. Therefore, food additives should also be subject to safety regulations as stringent as those covering drugs.

S T O P

**IF YOU FINISH BEFORE TIME IS CALLED, YOU MAY CHECK YOUR WORK ON THIS SECTION ONLY.
DO NOT WORK ON ANY OTHER SECTION IN THE TEST.**

LSAT® Writing Sample Topic

The city of Stockton must choose an event to inaugurate its new auditorium, an open-air stage with seats for about 15,000 people and a surrounding lawn with room for 30,000 more. Write an argument in favor of hiring either of the following performers with these considerations in mind.

- The city hopes the inaugural performance will raise as much money as possible to pay off the auditorium's construction loans.
- The city wants to obtain considerable positive publicity for the new auditorium.

Astrani, one of the legends of popular music, is giving a farewell concert tour before retiring. He has proposed holding the final three concerts in Stockton; because of his elaborate sets and costumes, tickets would be sold only for the auditorium's seats and no lawn seating would be available. Astrani never allows souvenirs to be sold at his concerts, but the city will receive 20 percent of the proceeds from ticket sales. If the tour ends in Stockton, a well-known director will film the historic event and plans to release a full-length feature which will share the final shows with fans around the world.

A number of prominent bands have organized "Animal-Aid" to raise money for endangered species. The concert has already generated significant attention in the press and a number of important arenas competed for the privilege of hosting the event. Stockton's new auditorium is the organizer's first choice as the site for the all-day concert and the city would be allowed to design and sell souvenirs commemorating the event. While tickets would be available for both the seats and surrounding lawn, all of the proceeds from ticket sales would go to "Animal-Aid." The auditorium's security expert is concerned that the facility's novice staff may not yet have the experience to handle a large crowd during an all-day event.

Directions:

1. Use the Answer Key on the next page to check your answers.

2. Use the Scoring Worksheet below to compute your raw score.

3. Use the Score Conversion Chart to convert your raw score into the 120-180 scale.

Scoring Worksheet

1. Enter the number of questions you answered correctly in each section.

                        Number
                        Correct

    SECTION I . . . . . . _____
    SECTION II . . . . . _____
    SECTION III . . . . . _____
    SECTION IV . . . . . _____

2. Enter the sum here: _____
                        This is your Raw Score.

Conversion Chart

For Converting Raw Score to the 120-180 LSAT Scaled Score

Reported Score	Raw Score Lowest	Raw Score Highest
180	98	101
179	97	97
178	95	96
177	94	94
176	93	93
175	92	92
174	91	91
173	90	90
172	89	89
171	88	88
170	86	87
169	85	85
168	84	84
167	82	83
166	81	81
165	79	80
164	78	78
163	76	77
162	75	75
161	73	74
160	72	72
159	70	71
158	68	69
157	67	67
156	65	66
155	64	64
154	62	63
153	60	61
152	59	59
151	57	58
150	56	56
149	54	55
148	53	53
147	51	52
146	50	50
145	48	49
144	47	47
143	45	46
142	44	44
141	42	43
140	41	41
139	39	40
138	38	38
137	37	37
136	35	36
135	34	34
134	33	33
133	31	32
132	30	30
131	29	29
130	28	28
129	27	27
128	26	26
127	24	25
126	23	23
125	22	22
124	21	21
123	20	20
122	19	19
121	18	18
120	0	17

SECTION I

1.	C	8.	A	15.	A	22.	E
2.	C	9.	D	16.	B	23.	D
3.	E	10.	B	17.	B	24.	A
4.	E	11.	C	18.	C	25.	D
5.	B	12.	A	19.	C		
6.	E	13.	C	20.	B		
7.	C	14.	E	21.	B		

SECTION II

1.	C	8.	B	15.	E	22.	D
2.	A	9.	C	16.	A	23.	B
3.	C	10.	E	17.	E	24.	A
4.	C	11.	E	18.	B		
5.	E	12.	E	19.	E		
6.	C	13.	B	20.	D		
7.	D	14.	C	21.	B		

SECTION III

1.	E	8.	D	15.	B	22.	C
2.	D	9.	A	16.	D	23.	D
3.	C	10.	B	17.	C	24.	E
4.	B	11.	C	18.	E	25.	B
5.	D	12.	C	19.	A	26.	B
6.	A	13.	E	20.	D	27.	D
7.	A	14.	D	21.	C		

SECTION IV

1.	D	8.	E	15.	E	22.	D
2.	E	9.	C	16.	E	23.	C
3.	B	10.	D	17.	D	24.	D
4.	E	11.	A	18.	A	25.	E
5.	A	12.	A	19.	B		
6.	C	13.	D	20.	A		
7.	A	14.	D	21.	A		

The Official LSAT PrepTest

9

- **October 1993**
- **Form 4LSS23**

The sample test that follows consists of four sections corresponding to the four scored sections of the October 1993 LSAT.

SECTION I

Time—35 minutes

27 Questions

<u>Directions:</u> Each passage in this section is followed by a group of questions to be answered on the basis of what is <u>stated</u> or <u>implied</u> in the passage. For some of the questions, more than one of the choices could conceivably answer the question. However, you are to choose the <u>best</u> answer; that is, the response that most accurately and completely answers the question, and blacken the corresponding space on your answer sheet.

Many argue that recent developments in electronic technology such as computers and videotape have enabled artists to vary their forms of expression. For example, video art can now
(5) achieve images whose effect is produced by "digitalization": breaking up the picture using computerized information processing. Such new technologies create new ways of seeing and hearing by adding different dimensions to older forms,
(10) rather than replacing those forms. Consider *Locale*, a film about a modern dance company. The camera operator wore a Steadicam™, an uncomplicated device that allows a camera to be mounted on a person so that the camera remains steady no matter
(15) how the operator moves. The Steadicam™ captures the dance in ways impossible with traditional mounts. Such new equipment also allows for the preservation of previously unrecordable aspects of performances, thus enriching archives.
(20) By contrast, others claim that technology subverts the artistic enterprise: that artistic efforts achieved with machines preempt human creativity, rather than being inspired by it. The originality of musical performance, for example, might suffer, as
(25) musicians would be deprived of the opportunity to spontaneously change pieces of music before live audiences. Some even worry that technology will eliminate live performance altogether; performances will be recorded for home viewing, abolishing the
(30) relationship between performer and audience. But these negative views assume both that technology poses an unprecedented challenge to the arts and that we are not committed enough to the artistic enterprise to preserve the live performance,
(35) assumptions that seem unnecessarily cynical. In fact, technology has traditionally assisted our capacity for creative expression and can refine our notions of any given art form.
For example, the portable camera and the
(40) snapshot were developed at the same time as the rise of Impressionist painting in the nineteenth century. These photographic technologies encouraged a new appreciation for the chance view and unpredictable angle, thus preparing an
(45) audience for a new style of painting. In addition, Impressionist artists like Degas studied the elements of light and movement captured by instantaneous photography and used their new understanding of the way our perceptions distort
(50) reality to try to more accurately capture reality in

their work. Since photos can capture the "moments" of a movement, such as a hand partially raised in a gesture of greeting, Impressionist artists were inspired to paint such moments in order to more
(55) effectively convey the quality of spontaneous human action. Photography freed artists from the preconception that a subject should be painted in a static, artificial entirety, and inspired them to capture the random and fragmentary qualities of
(60) our world. Finally, since photography preempted painting as the means of obtaining portraits, painters had more freedom to vary their subject matter, thus giving rise to the abstract creations characteristic of modern art.

1. Which one of the following statements best expresses the main idea of the passage?

   (A) The progress of art relies primarily on technology.
   (B) Technological innovation can be beneficial to art.
   (C) There are risks associated with using technology to create art.
   (D) Technology will transform the way the public responds to art.
   (E) The relationship between art and technology has a lengthy history.

2. It can be inferred from the passage that the author shares which one of the following opinions with the opponents of the use of new technology in art?

   (A) The live performance is an important aspect of the artistic enterprise.
   (B) The public's commitment to the artistic enterprise is questionable.
   (C) Recent technological innovations present an entirely new sort of challenge to art.
   (D) Technological innovations of the past have been very useful to artists.
   (E) The performing arts are especially vulnerable to technological innovation.

GO ON TO THE NEXT PAGE.

3. Which one of the following, if true, would most undermine the position held by opponents of the use of new technology in art concerning the effect of technology on live performance?

(A) Surveys show that when recordings of performances are made available for home viewing, the public becomes far more knowledgeable about different performing artists.

(B) Surveys show that some people feel comfortable responding spontaneously to artistic performances when they are viewing recordings of those performances at home.

(C) After a live performance, sales of recordings for home viewing of the particular performing artist generally increase.

(D) The distribution of recordings of artists' performances has begun to attract many new audience members to their live performances.

(E) Musicians are less apt to make creative changes in musical pieces during recorded performances than during live performances.

4. The author uses the example of the Steadicam™ primarily in order to suggest that

(A) the filming of performances should not be limited by inadequate equipment

(B) new technologies do not need to be very complex in order to benefit art

(C) the interaction of a traditional art form with a new technology will change attitudes toward technology in general

(D) the replacement of a traditional technology with a new technology will transform definitions of a traditional art form

(E) new technology does not so much preempt as enhance a traditional art form

5. According to the passage, proponents of the use of new electronic technology in the arts claim that which one of the following is true?

(A) Most people who reject the use of electronic technology in art forget that machines require a person to operate them.

(B) Electronic technology allows for the expansion of archives because longer performances can be recorded.

(C) Electronic technology assists artists in finding new ways to present their material.

(D) Electronic technology makes the practice of any art form more efficient by speeding up the creative process.

(E) Modern dance is the art form that will probably benefit most from the use of electronic technology.

6. It can be inferred from the passage that the author would agree with which one of the following statements regarding changes in painting since the nineteenth century?

(A) The artistic experiments of the nineteenth century led painters to use a variety of methods in creating portraits, which they then applied to other subject matter.

(B) The nineteenth-century knowledge of light and movement provided by photography inspired the abstract works characteristic of modern art.

(C) Once painters no longer felt that they had to paint conventional portraits, they turned exclusively to abstract portraiture.

(D) Once painters were less limited to the Impressionist style, they were able to experiment with a variety of styles of abstract art.

(E) Once painters painted fewer conventional portraits, they had greater opportunity to move beyond the literal depiction of objects.

GO ON TO THE NEXT PAGE.

During the 1940s and 1950s the United States government developed a new policy toward Native Americans, often known as "readjustment." Because the increased awareness of civil rights in
(5) these decades helped reinforce the belief that life on reservations prevented Native Americans from exercising the rights guaranteed to citizens under the United States Constitution, the readjustment movement advocated the end of the federal
(10) government's involvement in Native American affairs and encouraged the assimilation of Native Americans as individuals into mainstream society. However, the same years also saw the emergence of a Native American leadership and efforts to develop
(15) tribal institutions and reaffirm tribal identity. The clash of these two trends may be traced in the attempts on the part of the Bureau of Indian Affairs (BIA) to convince the Oneida tribe of Wisconsin to accept readjustment.

(20) The culmination of BIA efforts to sway the Oneida occurred at a meeting that took place in the fall of 1956. The BIA suggested that it would be to the Oneida's benefit to own their own property and, like other homeowners, pay real estate taxes
(25) on it. The BIA also emphasized that, after readjustment, the government would not attempt to restrict Native Americans' ability to sell their individually owned lands. The Oneida were then offered a one-time lump-sum payment of $60,000 in
(30) lieu of the $0.52 annuity guaranteed in perpetuity to each member of the tribe under the Canandaigua Treaty.

The efforts of the BIA to "sell" readjustment to the tribe failed because the Oneida realized that
(35) they had heard similar offers before. The Oneida delegates reacted negatively to the BIA's first suggestion because taxation of Native American lands had been one past vehicle for dispossessing the Oneida: after the distribution of some tribal
(40) lands to individual Native Americans in the late nineteenth century, Native American lands became subject to taxation, resulting in new and impossible financial burdens, foreclosures, and subsequent tax sales of property. The Oneida delegates were
(45) equally suspicious of the BIA's emphasis on the rights of individual landowners, since in the late nineteenth century many individual Native Americans had been convinced by unscrupulous speculators to sell their lands. Finally, the offer of a
(50) lump-sum payment was unanimously opposed by the Oneida delegates, who saw that changing the terms of a treaty might jeopardize the many pending land claims based upon the treaty.

As a result of the 1956 meeting, the Oneida
(55) rejected readjustment. Instead, they determined to improve tribal life by lobbying for federal monies for postsecondary education, for the improvement of drainage on tribal lands, and for the building of a convalescent home for tribal members. Thus, by
(60) learning the lessons of history, the Oneida were able to survive as a tribe in their homeland.

7. Which one of the following would be most consistent with the policy of readjustment described in the passage?

(A) the establishment among Native Americans of a tribal system of elected government
(B) the creation of a national project to preserve Native American language and oral history
(C) the establishment of programs to encourage Native Americans to move from reservations to urban areas
(D) the development of a large-scale effort to restore Native American lands to their original tribes
(E) the reaffirmation of federal treaty obligations to Native American tribes

8. According to the passage, after the 1956 meeting the Oneida resolved to

(A) obtain improved social services and living conditions for members of the tribe
(B) pursue litigation designed to reclaim tribal lands
(C) secure recognition of their unique status as a self-governing Native American nation within the United States
(D) establish new kinds of tribal institutions
(E) cultivate a life-style similar to that of other United States citizens

9. Which one of the following best describes the function of the first paragraph in the context of the passage as a whole?

(A) It summarizes the basis of a conflict underlying negotiations described elsewhere in the passage.
(B) It presents two positions, one of which is defended by evidence provided in succeeding paragraphs.
(C) It compares competing interpretations of a historical conflict.
(D) It analyzes the causes of a specific historical event and predicts a future development.
(E) It outlines the history of a government agency.

GO ON TO THE NEXT PAGE.

10. The author refers to the increased awareness of civil rights during the 1940s and 1950s most probably in order to

(A) contrast the readjustment movement with other social phenomena
(B) account for the stance of the Native American leadership
(C) help explain the impetus for the readjustment movement
(D) explain the motives of BIA bureaucrats
(E) foster support for the policy of readjustment

11. The passage suggests that advocates of readjustment would most likely agree with which one of the following statements regarding the relationship between the federal government and Native Americans?

(A) The federal government should work with individual Native Americans to improve life on reservations.
(B) The federal government should be no more involved in the affairs of Native Americans than in the affairs of other citizens.
(C) The federal government should assume more responsibility for providing social services to Native Americans.
(D) The federal government should share its responsibility for maintaining Native American territories with tribal leaders.
(E) The federal government should observe all provisions of treaties made in the past with Native Americans.

12. The passage suggests that the Oneida delegates viewed the Canandaigua Treaty as

(A) a valuable safeguard of certain Oneida rights and privileges
(B) the source of many past problems for the Oneida tribe
(C) a model for the type of agreement they hoped to reach with the federal government
(D) an important step toward recognition of their status as an independent Native American nation
(E) an obsolete agreement without relevance for their current condition

13. Which one of the following situations most closely parallels that of the Oneida delegates in refusing to accept a lump-sum payment of $60,000 ?

(A) A university offers a student a four-year scholarship with the stipulation that the student not accept any outside employment; the student refuses the offer and attends a different school because the amount of the scholarship would not have covered living expenses.
(B) A company seeking to reduce its payroll obligations offers an employee a large bonus if he will accept early retirement; the employee refuses because he does not want to compromise an outstanding worker's compensation suit.
(C) Parents of a teenager offer to pay her at the end of the month for performing weekly chores rather than paying her on a weekly basis; the teenager refuses because she has a number of financial obligations that she must meet early in the month.
(D) A car dealer offers a customer a $500 cash payment for buying a new car; the customer refuses because she does not want to pay taxes on the amount, and requests instead that her monthly payments be reduced by a proportionate amount.
(E) A landlord offers a tenant several months rent-free in exchange for the tenant's agreeing not to demand that her apartment be painted every two years, as is required by the lease; the tenant refuses because she would have to spend her own time painting the apartment.

GO ON TO THE NEXT PAGE.

Direct observation of contemporary societies at the threshold of widespread literacy has not assisted our understanding of how such literacy altered ancient Greek society, in particular its political
(5) culture. The discovery of what Goody has called the "enabling effects" of literacy in contemporary societies tends to seduce the observer into confusing often rudimentary knowledge of how to read with popular access to important books and documents;
(10) this confusion is then projected onto ancient societies. "In ancient Greece," Goody writes, "alphabetic reading and writing was important for the development of political democracy."

An examination of the ancient Greek city
(15) Athens exemplifies how this sort of confusion is detrimental to understanding ancient politics. In Athens, the early development of a written law code was retrospectively mythologized as the critical factor in breaking the power monopoly of
(20) the old aristocracy: hence the Greek tradition of the "law-giver," which has captured the imaginations of scholars like Goody. But the application and efficacy of all law codes depend on their interpretation by magistrates and courts, and unless the right of
(25) interpretation is "democratized," the mere existence of written laws changes little.

In fact, never in antiquity did any but the elite consult documents and books. Even in Greek courts the juries heard only the relevant statutes
(30) read out during the proceedings, as they heard verbal testimony, and they then rendered their verdict on the spot, without the benefit of any discussion among themselves. True, in Athens the juries were representative of a broad spectrum of
(35) the population, and these juries, drawn from diverse social classes, both interpreted what they had heard and determined matters of fact. However, they were guided solely by the speeches prepared for the parties by professional pleaders
(40) and by the quotations of laws or decrees within the speeches, rather than by their own access to any kind of document or book.

Granted, people today also rely heavily on a truly knowledgeable minority for information and
(45) its interpretation, often transmitted orally. Yet this is still fundamentally different from an ancient society in which there was no "popular literature," i.e., no newspapers, magazines, or other media that dealt with sociopolitical issues. An ancient law code
(50) would have been analogous to the Latin Bible, a venerated document but a closed book. The resistance of the medieval Church to vernacular translations of the Bible, in the West at least, is therefore a pointer to the realities of ancient literacy.
(55) When fundamental documents are accessible for study only to an elite, the rest of the society is subject to the elite's interpretation of the rules of behavior, including right political behavior. Athens, insofar as it functioned as a democracy, did
(60) so not because of widespread literacy, but because the elite had chosen to accept democratic institutions.

14. Which one of the following statements best expresses the main idea of the passage?

(A) Democratic political institutions grow organically from the traditions and conventions of a society.

(B) Democratic political institutions are not necessarily the outcome of literacy in a society.

(C) Religious authority, like political authority, can determine who in a given society will have access to important books and documents.

(D) Those who are best educated are most often those who control the institutions of authority in a society.

(E) Those in authority have a vested interest in ensuring that those under their control remain illiterate.

15. It can be inferred from the passage that the author assumes which one of the following about societies in which the people possess a rudimentary reading ability?

(A) They are more politically advanced than societies without rudimentary reading ability.

(B) They are unlikely to exhibit the positive effects of literacy.

(C) They are rapidly evolving toward widespread literacy.

(D) Many of their people might not have access to important documents and books.

(E) Most of their people would not participate in political decision-making.

GO ON TO THE NEXT PAGE.

16. The author refers to the truly knowledgeable minority in contemporary societies in the context of the fourth paragraph in order to imply which one of the following?

   (A) Because they have a popular literature that closes the gap between the elite and the majority, contemporary societies rely far less on the knowledge of experts than did ancient societies.
   (B) Contemporary societies rely on the knowledge of experts, as did ancient societies, because contemporary popular literature so frequently conveys specious information.
   (C) Although contemporary societies rely heavily on the knowledge of experts, access to popular literature makes contemporary societies less dependent on experts for information about rules of behavior than were ancient societies.
   (D) While only some members of the elite can become experts, popular literature gives the majority in contemporary society an opportunity to become members of such an elite.
   (E) Access to popular literature distinguishes ancient from contemporary societies because it relies on a level of educational achievement attainable only by a contemporary elite.

17. According to the passage, each of the following statements concerning ancient Greek juries is true EXCEPT:

   (A) They were somewhat democratic insofar as they were composed largely of people from the lowest social classes.
   (B) They were exposed to the law only insofar as they heard relevant statutes read out during legal proceedings.
   (C) They ascertained the facts of a case and interpreted the laws.
   (D) They did not have direct access to important books and documents that were available to the elite.
   (E) They rendered verdicts without benefit of private discussion among themselves.

18. The author characterizes the Greek tradition of the "law-giver" (line 21) as an effect of mythologizing most probably in order to

   (A) illustrate the ancient Greek tendency to memorialize historical events by transforming them into myths
   (B) convey the historical importance of the development of the early Athenian written law code
   (C) convey the high regard in which the Athenians held their legal tradition
   (D) suggest that the development of a written law code was not primarily responsible for diminishing the power of the Athenian aristocracy
   (E) suggest that the Greek tradition of the "law-giver" should be understood in the larger context of Greek mythology

19. The author draws an analogy between the Latin Bible and an early law code (lines 49-51) in order to make which one of the following points?

   (A) Documents were considered authoritative in premodern society in proportion to their inaccessibility to the majority.
   (B) Documents that were perceived as highly influential in premodern societies were not necessarily accessible to the society's majority.
   (C) What is most revered in a nondemocratic society is what is most frequently misunderstood.
   (D) Political documents in premodern societies exerted a social influence similar to that exerted by religious documents.
   (E) Political documents in premodern societies were inaccessible to the majority of the population because of the language in which they were written.

20. The primary purpose of the passage is to

   (A) argue that a particular method of observing contemporary societies is inconsistent
   (B) point out the weaknesses in a particular approach to understanding ancient societies
   (C) present the disadvantages of a particular approach to understanding the relationship between ancient and contemporary societies
   (D) examine the importance of developing an appropriate method for understanding ancient societies
   (E) convey the difficulty of accurately understanding attitudes in ancient societies

GO ON TO THE NEXT PAGE.

The English who in the seventeenth and eighteenth centuries inhabited those colonies that would later become the United States shared a common political vocabulary with the English in
(5) England. Steeped as they were in the English political language, these colonials failed to observe that their experience in America had given the words a significance quite different from that accepted by the English with whom they debated:
(10) in fact, they claimed that they were more loyal to the English political tradition than were the English in England.

In many respects the political institutions of England were reproduced in these American
(15) colonies. By the middle of the eighteenth century, all of these colonies except four were headed by Royal Governors appointed by the King and perceived as bearing a relation to the people of the colony similar to that of the King to the English
(20) people. Moreover, each of these colonies enjoyed a representative assembly, which was consciously modeled, in powers and practices, after the English Parliament. In both England and these colonies, only property holders could vote.

(25) Nevertheless, though English and colonial institutions were structurally similar, attitudes toward those institutions differed. For example, English legal development from the early seventeenth century had been moving steadily
(30) toward the absolute power of Parliament. The most unmistakable sign of this tendency was the legal assertion that the King was subject to the law. Together with this resolute denial of the absolute right of kings went the assertion that Parliament
(35) was unlimited in its power: it could change even the Constitution by its ordinary acts of legislation. By the eighteenth century the English had accepted the idea that the parliamentary representatives of the people were omnipotent.

(40) The citizens of these colonies did not look upon the English Parliament with such fond eyes, nor did they concede that their own assemblies possessed such wide powers. There were good historical reasons for this. To the English the word
(45) "constitution" meant the whole body of law and legal custom formulated since the beginning of the kingdom, whereas to these colonials a constitution was a specific written document, enumerating specific powers. This distinction in meaning can be
(50) traced to the fact that the foundations of government in the various colonies were written charters granted by the Crown. These express authorizations to govern were tangible, definite things. Over the years these colonials had often repaired to the charters to
(55) justify themselves in the struggle against tyrannical governors or officials of the Crown. More than a century of government under written constitutions convinced these colonists of the necessity for and efficacy of protecting their liberties against
(60) governmental encroachment by explicitly defining all governmental powers in a document.

21. Which one of the following best expresses the main idea of the passage?

(A) The colonials and the English mistakenly thought that they shared a common political vocabulary.
(B) The colonials and the English shared a variety of institutions.
(C) The colonials and the English had conflicting interpretations of the language and institutional structures that they shared.
(D) Colonial attitudes toward English institutions grew increasingly hostile in the eighteenth century.
(E) Seventeenth-century English legal development accounted for colonial attitudes toward constitutions.

22. The passage supports all of the following statements about the political conditions present by the middle of the eighteenth century in the American colonies discussed in the passage EXCEPT:

(A) Colonials who did not own property could not vote.
(B) All of these colonies had representative assemblies modeled after the British Parliament.
(C) Some of these colonies had Royal Governors.
(D) Royal Governors could be removed from office by colonial assemblies.
(E) In these colonies, Royal Governors were regarded as serving a function like that of a king.

23. The passage implies which one of the following about English kings prior to the early seventeenth century?

(A) They were the source of all law.
(B) They frequently flouted laws made by Parliament.
(C) Their power relative to that of Parliament was considerably greater than it was in the eighteenth century.
(D) They were more often the sources of legal reform than they were in the eighteenth century.
(E) They had to combat those who believed that the power of Parliament was absolute.

GO ON TO THE NEXT PAGE.

24. The author mentions which one of the following as evidence for the eighteenth-century English attitude toward Parliament?

    (A) The English had become uncomfortable with institutions that could claim absolute authority.
    (B) The English realized that their interests were better guarded by Parliament than by the King.
    (C) The English allowed Parliament to make constitutional changes by legislative enactment.
    (D) The English felt that the King did not possess the knowledge that would enable him to rule responsibly.
    (E) The English had decided that it was time to reform their representative government.

25. The passage implies that the colonials discussed in the passage would have considered which one of the following to be a source of their debates with England?

    (A) their changed use of the English political vocabulary
    (B) English commitment to parliamentary representation
    (C) their uniquely English experience
    (D) their refusal to adopt any English political institutions
    (E) their greater loyalty to the English political traditions

26. According to the passage, the English attitude toward the English Constitution differed from the colonial attitude toward constitutions in that the English regarded their Constitution as

    (A) the legal foundation of the kingdom
    (B) a document containing a collection of customs
    (C) a cumulative corpus of legislation and legal traditions
    (D) a record alterable by royal authority
    (E) an unchangeable body of governmental powers

27. The primary purpose of the passage is to

    (A) expose the misunderstanding that has characterized descriptions of the relationship between seventeenth- and eighteenth-century England and certain of its American colonies
    (B) suggest a reason for England's treatment of certain of its American colonies in the seventeenth and eighteenth centuries
    (C) settle an ongoing debate about the relationship between England and certain of its American colonies in the seventeenth and eighteenth centuries
    (D) interpret the events leading up to the independence of certain of England's American colonies in the eighteenth century
    (E) explain an aspect of the relationship between England and certain of its American colonies in the seventeenth and eighteenth centuries

S T O P

IF YOU FINISH BEFORE TIME IS CALLED, YOU MAY CHECK YOUR WORK ON THIS SECTION ONLY.
DO NOT WORK ON ANY OTHER SECTION IN THE TEST.

SECTION II

Time—35 minutes

25 Questions

<u>Directions:</u>   The questions in this section are based on the reasoning contained in brief statements or passages. For some questions, more than one of the choices could conceivably answer the question. However, you are to choose the <u>best</u> answer; that is, the response that most accurately and completely answers the question. You should not make assumptions that are by commonsense standards implausible, superfluous, or incompatible with the passage. After you have chosen the best answer, blacken the corresponding space on your answer sheet.

1. Crimes in which handguns are used are more likely than other crimes to result in fatalities. However, the majority of crimes in which handguns are used do not result in fatalities. Therefore, there is no need to enact laws that address crimes involving handguns as distinct from other crimes.

    The pattern of flawed reasoning displayed in the argument above most closely resembles that in which one of the following?

    (A)   Overweight people are at higher risk of developing heart disease than other people. However, more than half of all overweight people never develop heart disease. Hence it is unnecessary for physicians to be more careful to emphasize the danger of heart disease to their overweight patients than to their other patients.

    (B)   Many people swim daily in order to stay physically fit. Yet people who swim daily increase their risk of developing ear infections. Hence people who want to remain in good health are better off not following fitness programs that include swimming daily.

    (C)   Most physicians recommend a balanced diet for those who want to remain in good health. Yet many people find that nontraditional dietary regimens such as extended fasting do their health no serious harm. Therefore, there is no need for everyone to avoid nontraditional dietary regimens.

    (D)   Foods rich in cholesterol and fat pose a serious health threat to most people. However, many people are reluctant to give up eating foods that they greatly enjoy. Therefore, people who refuse to give up rich foods need to spend more time exercising than do other people.

    (E)   Many serious health problems are the result of dietary disorders. Yet these disorders are often brought about by psychological factors. Hence people suffering from serious health problems should undergo psychological evaluation.

2. Tall children can generally reach high shelves easily. Short children can generally reach high shelves only with difficulty. It is known that short children are more likely than are tall children to become short adults. Therefore, if short children are taught to reach high shelves easily, the proportion of them who become short adults will decrease.

    A reasoning error in the argument is that the argument

    (A)   attributes a characteristic of an individual member of a group to the group as a whole
    (B)   presupposes that which is to be proved
    (C)   refutes a generalization by means of an exceptional case
    (D)   assumes a causal relationship where only a correlation has been indicated
    (E)   takes lack of evidence for the existence of a state of affairs as evidence that there can be no such state of affairs

GO ON TO THE NEXT PAGE.

3. Balance is particularly important when reporting the background of civil wars and conflicts. Facts must not be deliberately manipulated to show one party in a favorable light, and the views of each side should be fairly represented. This concept of balance, however, does not justify concealing or glossing over basic injustices in an effort to be even-handed. If all the media were to adopt such a perverse interpretation of balanced reporting, the public would be given a picture of a world where each party in every conflict had an equal measure of justice on its side, contrary to our experience of life and, indeed, our common sense.

Which one of the following best expresses the main point of the argument?

(A) Balanced reporting presents the public with a picture of the world in which all sides to a conflict have equal justification.

(B) Balanced reporting requires impartially revealing injustices where they occur no less than fairly presenting the views of each party in a conflict.

(C) Our experience of life shows that there are indeed cases in which conflicts arise because of an injustice, with one party clearly in the wrong.

(D) Common sense tells us that balance is especially needed when reporting the background of civil wars and conflicts.

(E) Balanced reporting is an ideal that cannot be realized, because judgments of balance are necessarily subjective.

4. Data from satellite photographs of the tropical rain forest in Melonia show that last year the deforestation rate of this environmentally sensitive zone was significantly lower than in previous years. The Melonian government, which spent millions of dollars last year to enforce laws against burning and cutting of the forest, is claiming that the satellite data indicate that its increased efforts to halt the destruction are proving effective.

Which one of the following, if true, most seriously undermines the government's claim?

(A) Landowner opposition to the government's antideforestation efforts grew more violent last year in response to the increased enforcement.

(B) Rainfall during the usually dry 6-month annual burning season was abnormally heavy last year.

(C) Government agents had to issue fines totaling over $9 million to 3,500 violators of burning-and-cutting regulations.

(D) The inaccessibility of much of the rain forest has made it impossible to confirm the satellite data by direct observation from the field.

(E) Much of the money that was designated last year for forest preservation has been spent on research and not on enforcement.

5. Advertisement: Northwoods Maple Syrup, made the old-fashioned way, is simply tops for taste. And here is the proof: in a recent market survey, 7 out of every 10 shoppers who expressed a preference said that Northwoods was the only maple syrup for them, no ifs, ands, or buts.

Of the following, which one is the strongest reason why the advertisement is potentially misleading?

(A) The proportion of shoppers expressing no preference might have been very small.

(B) Other brands of maple syrup might also be made the old-fashioned way.

(C) No market survey covers more than a sizable minority of the total population of consumers.

(D) The preference for the Northwoods brand might be based on such a factor as an exceptionally low price.

(E) Shoppers who buy syrup might buy only maple syrup.

6. In the summer of 1936 a polling service telephoned 10,000 United States voters and asked how they planned to vote in the coming presidential election. The survey sample included a variety of respondents —rural and urban, male and female, from every state. The poll predicted that Alfred Landon would soundly defeat Franklin Roosevelt. Nevertheless, Roosevelt won in a landslide.

Which one of the following, if true, best explains why the poll's prediction was inaccurate?

(A) The interviewers did not reveal their own political affiliation to the respondents.

(B) Only people who would be qualified to vote by election time were interviewed, so the survey sample was not representative of the overall United States population.

(C) The survey sample was representative only of people who could afford telephones at a time when phone ownership was less common than it is today.

(D) No effort was made to determine the respondents' political affiliations.

(E) Because the poll asked only for respondents' candidate preference, it collected no information concerning their reasons for favoring Landon or Roosevelt.

GO ON TO THE NEXT PAGE.

7. Waste management companies, which collect waste for disposal in landfills and incineration plants, report that disposable plastics make up an ever-increasing percentage of the waste they handle. It is clear that attempts to decrease the amount of plastic that people throw away in the garbage are failing.

Which one of the following, if true, most seriously weakens the argument?

(A) Because plastics create harmful pollutants when burned, an increasing percentage of the plastics handled by waste management companies are being disposed of in landfills.
(B) Although many plastics are recyclable, most of the plastics disposed of by waste management companies are not.
(C) People are more likely to save and reuse plastic containers than containers made of heavier materials like glass or metal.
(D) An increasing proportion of the paper, glass, and metal cans that waste management companies used to handle is now being recycled.
(E) While the percentage of products using plastic packaging is increasing, the total amount of plastic being manufactured has remained unchanged.

8. Most of the ultraviolet radiation reaching the Earth's atmosphere from the Sun is absorbed by the layer of stratospheric ozone and never reaches the Earth's surface. Between 1969 and 1986, the layer of stratospheric ozone over North America thinned, decreasing by about 3 percent. Yet, the average level of ultraviolet radiation measured at research stations across North America decreased over the same period.

Which one of the following, if true, best reconciles the apparently discrepant facts described above?

(A) Ultraviolet radiation increases the risk of skin cancer and cataracts; the incidence of skin cancer and cataracts increased substantially between 1969 and 1986.
(B) Between 1969 and 1986, the layer of stratospheric ozone over Brazil thinned, and the average level of ultraviolet radiation reaching the Earth's surface in Brazil increased.
(C) Manufactured chlorine chemicals thin the layer of stratospheric ozone.
(D) Ozone pollution, which absorbs ultraviolet radiation, increased dramatically between 1969 and 1986.
(E) Thinning of the layer of stratospheric ozone varies from one part of the world to another and from year to year.

Questions 9–10

The number of aircraft collisions on the ground is increasing because of the substantial increase in the number of flights operated by the airlines. Many of the fatalities that occur in such collisions are caused not by the collision itself, but by an inherent flaw in the cabin design of most aircraft, in which seats, by restricting access to emergency exits, impede escape. Therefore, to reduce the total number of fatalities that result annually from such collisions, the airlines should be required to remove all seats that restrict access to emergency exits.

9. Which one of the following, if true, provides the most support for the proposal?

(A) The number of deaths that occurred in theater fires because theater patrons could not escape was greatly reduced when theaters were required to have aisles leading to each exit.
(B) Removing the seats that block emergency exits on aircraft will require a costly refitting of aircraft cabins.
(C) In the event of fire, public buildings equipped with smoke detectors have fewer fatalities than do public buildings not so equipped.
(D) In the event of collision, passengers on planes with a smaller passenger capacity generally suffer more serious injury than do passengers on planes with a larger passenger capacity.
(E) The safety belts attached to aircraft seats function to protect passengers from the full force of impact in the event of a collision.

10. Which one of the following proposals, if implemented together with the proposal made in the passage, would improve the prospects for achieving the stated objective of reducing fatalities?

(A) The airlines should be required, when buying new planes, to buy only planes with unrestricted access to emergency exits.
(B) The airlines should not be permitted to increase further the number of flights in order to offset the decrease in the number of seats on each aircraft.
(C) Airport authorities should be required to streamline their passenger check-in procedures to accommodate the increased number of passengers served by the airlines.
(D) Airport authorities should be required to refine security precautions by making them less conspicuous without making them less effective.
(E) The airlines should not be allowed to increase the ticket price for each passenger to offset the decrease in the number of seats on each aircraft.

GO ON TO THE NEXT PAGE.

11. Recently discovered fossil evidence casts doubt on the evolutionary theory that dinosaurs are more closely related to reptiles than to other classes of animals. Fossils show that some dinosaurs had hollow bones—a feature found today only in warm-blooded creatures, such as birds, that have a high metabolic rate. Dinosaurs had well-developed senses of sight and hearing, which is not true of present-day cold-blooded creatures like reptiles. The highly arched mouth roof of some dinosaurs would have permitted them to breathe while eating, as fast-breathing animals, such as birds, need to do. Today, all fast-breathing animals are warm-blooded. Finally, fossils reveal that many dinosaurs had a pattern of growth typical of warm-blooded animals.

The argument in the passage proceeds by

(A) attempting to justify one position by demonstrating that an opposing position is based on erroneous information
(B) establishing a general principle that it then uses to draw a conclusion about a particular case
(C) dismissing a claim made about the present on the basis of historical evidence
(D) assuming that if all members of a category have a certain property then all things with that property belong to the category
(E) presenting evidence that a past phenomenon is more similar to one rather than the other of two present-day phenomena

12. Purebred dogs are prone to genetically determined abnormalities. Although such abnormalities often can be corrected by surgery, the cost can reach several thousand dollars. Since nonpurebred dogs rarely suffer from genetically determined abnormalities, potential dog owners who want to reduce the risk of incurring costly medical bills for their pets would be well advised to choose nonpurebred dogs.

Which one of the following, if true, most seriously weakens the argument?

(A) Most genetically determined abnormalities in dogs do not seriously affect a dog's general well-being.
(B) All dogs, whether purebred or nonpurebred, are subject to the same common nongenetically determined diseases.
(C) Purebred dogs tend to have shorter natural life spans than do nonpurebred dogs.
(D) The purchase price of nonpurebred dogs tends to be lower than the purchase price of purebred dogs.
(E) A dog that does not have genetically determined abnormalities may nevertheless have offspring with such abnormalities.

13. Criticism that the press panders to public sentiment neglects to consider that the press is a profit-making institution. Like other private enterprises, it has to make money to survive. If the press were not profit-making, who would support it? The only alternative is subsidy and, with it, outside control. It is easy to get subsidies for propaganda, but no one will subsidize honest journalism.

It can be properly inferred from the passage that if the press is

(A) not subsidized, it is in no danger of outside control
(B) not subsidized, it will not produce propaganda
(C) not to be subsidized, it cannot be a profit-making institution
(D) to produce honest journalism, it must be a profit-making institution
(E) to make a profit, it must produce honest journalism

GO ON TO THE NEXT PAGE.

Questions 14–15

Lucien: Public-housing advocates claim that the many homeless people in this city are proof that there is insufficient housing available to them and therefore that more low-income apartments are needed. But that conclusion is absurd. Many apartments in my own building remain unrented and my professional colleagues report similar vacancies where they live. Since apartments clearly are available, homelessness is not a housing problem. Homelessness can, therefore, only be caused by people's inability or unwillingness to work to pay the rent.

Maria: On the contrary, all recent studies show that a significant percentage of this city's homeless people hold regular jobs. These are people who lack neither will nor ability.

14. Lucien's argument against the public-housing advocates' position is most vulnerable to which one of the following criticisms?

   (A) It offers no justification for dismissing as absurd the housing advocates' claim that there are many homeless people in the city.
   (B) It treats information acquired through informal conversations as though it provided evidence as strong as information acquired on the basis of controlled scientific studies.
   (C) It responds to a claim in which "available" is used in the sense of "affordable" by using "available" in the sense of "not occupied."
   (D) It overlooks the possibility that not all apartment buildings have vacant apartments for rent.
   (E) It fails to address the issue, raised by the public-housing advocates' argument, of who would pay for the construction of more low-income housing.

15. Maria responds to Lucien's argument by

   (A) challenging the accuracy of the personal experiences he offers in support of his position
   (B) showing that a presupposition of his argument is false
   (C) presenting evidence that calls into question his motives for adopting the view he holds
   (D) demonstrating that the evidence he offers supports a conclusion other than the conclusion he draws from it
   (E) offering an alternative explanation for the facts he cites as evidence supporting his conclusion

16. Some people take their moral cues from governmental codes of law; for them, it is inconceivable that something that is legally permissible could be immoral.

   Those whose view is described above hold inconsistent beliefs if they also believe that

   (A) law does not cover all circumstances in which one person morally wrongs another
   (B) a legally impermissible action is never morally excusable
   (C) governmental officials sometimes behave illegally
   (D) the moral consensus of a society is expressed in its laws
   (E) some governmental regulations are so detailed that they are burdensome to the economy

17. Certain instruments used in veterinary surgery can be made either of stainless steel or of nylon. In a study of such instruments, 50 complete sterilizations of a set of nylon instruments required 3.4 times the amount of energy used to manufacture that set of instruments, whereas 50 complete sterilizations of a set of stainless steel instruments required 2.1 times the amount of energy required to manufacture that set of instruments.

   If the statements above are true, each of the following could be true EXCEPT:

   (A) The 50 complete sterilizations of the nylon instruments used more energy than did the 50 complete sterilizations of the stainless steel instruments.
   (B) More energy was required for each complete sterilization of the nylon instruments than was required to manufacture the nylon instruments.
   (C) More nylon instruments than stainless steel instruments were sterilized in the study.
   (D) More energy was used to produce the stainless steel instruments than was used to produce the nylon instruments.
   (E) The total cost of 50 complete sterilizations of the stainless steel instruments was greater than the cost of manufacturing the stainless steel instruments.

GO ON TO THE NEXT PAGE.

18. A local group had planned a parade for tomorrow, but city hall has not yet acted on its application for a permit. The group had applied for the permit well in advance, had made sure their application satisfied all the requirements, and was clearly entitled to a permit. Although the law prohibits parades without a permit, the group plans to proceed with its parade. The group's leader defended its decision by appealing to the principle that citizens need not refrain from actions that fail to comply with the law if they have made a good-faith effort to comply but are prevented from doing so by government inaction.

Which one of the following actions would be justified by the principle to which the leader of the group appealed in defending the decision to proceed?

(A) A chemical-processing company commissioned an environmental impact report on its plant. The report described foul odors emanating from the plant but found no hazardous wastes being produced. Consequently, the plant did not alter its processing practices.

(B) A city resident applied for rezoning of her property so that she could build a bowling alley in a residential community. She based her application on the need for recreational facilities in the community. Her application was turned down by the zoning board, so she decided to forgo construction.

(C) The law requires that no car be operated without a certain amount of insurance coverage. But since the authorities have been unable to design an effective procedure for prosecuting owners of cars that are driven without insurance, many car owners are allowing their insurance to lapse.

(D) A real-estate developer obtained a permit to demolish a historic apartment building that had not yet been declared a governmentally protected historic landmark. Despite the protests of citizens' groups, the developer then demolished the building.

(E) A physician who had been trained in one country applied for a license to practice medicine in another country. Although he knew he met all the qualifications for this license, he had not yet received it one year after he applied for it. He began to practice medicine without the license in the second country despite the law's requirement for a license.

Questions 19–20

A university should not be entitled to patent the inventions of its faculty members. Universities, as guarantors of intellectual freedom, should encourage the free flow of ideas and the general dissemination of knowledge. Yet a university that retains the right to patent the inventions of its faculty members has a motive to suppress information about a potentially valuable discovery until the patent for it has been secured. Clearly, suppressing information concerning such discoveries is incompatible with the university's obligation to promote the free flow of ideas.

19. Which one of the following is an assumption that the argument makes?

(A) Universities are the only institutions that have an obligation to guarantee intellectual freedom.

(B) Most inventions by university faculty members would be profitable if patented.

(C) Publication of reports on research is the only practical way to disseminate information concerning new discoveries.

(D) Universities that have a motive to suppress information concerning discoveries by their faculty members will occasionally act on that motive.

(E) If the inventions of a university faculty member are not patented by that university, then they will be patented by the faculty member instead.

20. The claim that a university should not be entitled to patent the inventions of its faculty members plays which one of the following roles in the argument?

(A) It is the conclusion of the argument.

(B) It is a principle from which the conclusion is derived.

(C) It is an explicit assumption.

(D) It is additional but nonessential information in support of one of the premises.

(E) It is a claim that must be demonstrated to be false in order to establish the conclusion.

GO ON TO THE NEXT PAGE.

21. English and the Austronesian language Mbarbaram both use the word "dog" for canines. These two languages are unrelated, and since speakers of the two languages only came in contact with one another long after the word "dog" was first used in this way in either language, neither language could have borrowed the word from the other. Thus this case shows that sometimes when languages share words that are similar in sound and meaning the similarity is due neither to language relatedness nor to borrowing.

The argument requires that which one of the following be assumed?

(A) English and Mbarbaram share no words other than "dog."

(B) Several languages besides English and Mbarbaram use "dog" as the word for canines.

(C) Usually when two languages share a word, those languages are related to each other.

(D) There is no third language from which both English and Mbarbaram borrowed the word "dog."

(E) If two unrelated languages share a word, speakers of those two languages must have come in contact with one another at some time.

22. Politician: From the time our party took office almost four years ago the number of people unemployed city-wide increased by less than 20 percent. The opposition party controlled city government during the four preceding years, and the number of unemployed city residents rose by over 20 percent. Thus, due to our leadership, fewer people now find themselves among the ranks of the unemployed, whatever the opposition may claim.

The reasoning in the politician's argument is most vulnerable to the criticism that

(A) the claims made by the opposition are simply dismissed without being specified

(B) no evidence has been offered to show that any decline in unemployment over the past four years was uniform throughout all areas of the city

(C) the issue of how much unemployment in the city is affected by seasonal fluctuations is ignored

(D) the evidence cited in support of the conclusion actually provides more support for the denial of the conclusion

(E) the possibility has not been addressed that any increase in the number of people employed is due to programs supported by the opposition party

23. A poor farmer was fond of telling his children: "In this world, you are either rich or poor, and you are either honest or dishonest. All poor farmers are honest. Therefore, all rich farmers are dishonest."

The farmer's conclusion is properly drawn if the argument assumes that

(A) every honest farmer is poor

(B) every honest person is a farmer

(C) everyone who is dishonest is a rich farmer

(D) everyone who is poor is honest

(E) every poor person is a farmer

GO ON TO THE NEXT PAGE.

24. Journalist: Can you give me a summary of the novel you are working on?

Novelist: Well, I assume that by "summary" you mean something brief and not a version of the novel itself. The reason I write novels is that what I want to communicate can be communicated only in the form of a novel. So I am afraid I cannot summarize my novel for you in a way that would tell you what I am trying to communicate with this novel.

Which one of the following exhibits a pattern of reasoning that is most parallel to that used by the novelist?

(A) Only if a drawing can be used as a guide by the builder can it be considered a blueprint. This drawing of the proposed building can be used as a guide by the builder, so it can be considered a blueprint.

(B) Only a statement that does not divulge company secrets can be used as a press release. This statement does not divulge company secrets, but it is uninformative and therefore cannot be used as a press release.

(C) Watching a travelog is not the same as traveling. But a travelog confers some of the benefits of travel without the hardships of travel. So many people just watch travelogs and do not undergo the hardships of travel.

(D) Only a three-dimensional representation of a landscape can convey the experience of being in that landscape. A photograph taken with a traditional camera is not three-dimensional. Therefore a photograph taken with a traditional camera can never convey the experience of being in a landscape.

(E) A banquet menu foretells the content of a meal, but some people collect menus in order to remind themselves of great meals they have eaten. Thus a banquet menu has a function not only before, but also after, a meal has been served.

25. Medical research findings are customarily not made public prior to their publication in a medical journal that has had them reviewed by a panel of experts in a process called peer review. It is claimed that this practice delays public access to potentially beneficial information that, in extreme instances, could save lives. Yet prepublication peer review is the only way to prevent erroneous and therefore potentially harmful information from reaching a public that is ill equipped to evaluate medical claims on its own. Therefore, waiting until a medical journal has published the research findings that have passed peer review is the price that must be paid to protect the public from making decisions based on possibly substandard research.

The argument assumes that

(A) unless medical research findings are brought to peer review by a medical journal, peer review will not occur

(B) anyone who does not serve on a medical review panel does not have the necessary knowledge and expertise to evaluate medical research findings

(C) the general public does not have access to the medical journals in which research findings are published

(D) all medical research findings are subjected to prepublication peer review

(E) peer review panels are sometimes subject to political and professional pressures that can make their judgments less than impartial

S T O P

IF YOU FINISH BEFORE TIME IS CALLED, YOU MAY CHECK YOUR WORK ON THIS SECTION ONLY.
DO NOT WORK ON ANY OTHER SECTION IN THE TEST.

SECTION III

Time—35 minutes

24 Questions

Directions: Each group of questions in this section is based on a set of conditions. In answering some of the questions, it may be useful to draw a rough diagram. Choose the response that most accurately and completely answers each question and blacken the corresponding space on your answer sheet.

Questions 1–7

A florist is making three corsages from four types of flowers: gardenias, orchids, roses, and violets. Each of the corsages will contain exactly three flowers. The nine flowers used in the corsages must include at least one flower from each of the four types, and at least twice as many roses as orchids must be used. The corsages must also meet the following specifications:

Corsage 1 must contain exactly two types of flowers.

Corsage 2 must contain at least one rose.

Corsage 3 must contain at least one gardenia but no. orchids.

1. Which one of the following is an acceptable selection of flowers for the three corsages?

	Corsage 1	Corsage 2	Corsage 3
(A)	2 gardenias 1 rose	1 orchid 1 rose 1 violet	1 gardenia 1 orchid 1 violet
(B)	2 orchids 1 rose	2 orchids 1 rose	2 gardenias 1 rose
(C)	2 orchids 1 rose	3 roses	1 gardenia 2 violets
(D)	1 gardenia 1 orchid 1 rose	1 gardenia 1 rose 1 violet	1 gardenia 1 rose 1 violet
(E)	1 orchid 2 roses	3 violets	3 gardenias

2. The maximum total number of roses that can be used in the three corsages is

(A) three
(B) four
(C) five
(D) six
(E) seven

3. If corsage 1 contains two orchids and one rose, what is the maximum total number of violets that the florist can use in making the three corsages?

(A) one
(B) two
(C) three
(D) four
(E) five

4. If corsage 2 is exactly the same as corsage 3, the nine flowers used in the corsages can include exactly

(A) two orchids
(B) three gardenias
(C) three roses
(D) five roses
(E) five violets

5. If two of the corsages contain at least one orchid each, then the flowers in corsage 2 must include at least

(A) one gardenia and one orchid
(B) one gardenia and one rose
(C) one orchid and one rose
(D) one orchid and one violet
(E) one rose and one violet

6. If the greatest possible number of violets is used in the three corsages, the florist must use

(A) exactly one rose and exactly one gardenia
(B) exactly one orchid and exactly four violets
(C) exactly two orchids
(D) exactly two roses
(E) exactly six violets

7. If corsage 1 contains at least one gardenia and at least one violet, and if corsage 3 contains three different types of flowers, which one of the following could be used to make corsage 2 ?

(A) one rose, one orchid, and one gardenia
(B) one rose and two orchids
(C) one rose and two violets
(D) two roses and one gardenia
(E) two roses and one violet

GO ON TO THE NEXT PAGE.

Questions 8–13

From a group of seven people—J, K, L, M, N, P, and Q—exactly four will be selected to attend a diplomat's retirement dinner. Selection must conform to the following conditions:

Either J or K must be selected, but J and K cannot both be selected.

Either N or P must be selected, but N and P cannot both be selected.

N cannot be selected unless L is selected.

Q cannot be selected unless K is selected.

8. Which one of the following could be the four people selected to attend the retirement dinner?

(A) J, K, M, P
(B) J, L, N, Q
(C) J, M, N, Q
(D) K, M, P, Q
(E) L, M, N, P

9. Among the people selected to attend the retirement dinner there must be

(A) K or Q or both
(B) L or M or both
(C) N or M or both
(D) N or Q or both
(E) P or Q or both

10. Which one of the following is a pair of people who CANNOT both be selected to attend the retirement dinner?

(A) J and N
(B) J and Q
(C) K and L
(D) K and N
(E) N and Q

11. If M is not selected to attend the retirement dinner, the four people selected to attend must include which one of the following pairs of people?

(A) J and Q
(B) K and L
(C) K and P
(D) L and P
(E) N and Q

12. If P is not selected to attend the retirement dinner, then exactly how many different groups of four are there each of which would be an acceptable selection?

(A) one
(B) two
(C) three
(D) four
(E) five

13. There is only one acceptable group of four that can be selected to attend the retirement dinner if which one of the following pairs of people is selected?

(A) J and L
(B) K and M
(C) L and N
(D) L and Q
(E) M and Q

GO ON TO THE NEXT PAGE.

Questions 14–18

Three boys—Karl, Luis, and Miguel—and three girls—Rita, Sarah, and Tura—are giving a dance recital. Three dances—1, 2, and 3—are to be performed. Each dance involves three pairs of children, a boy and a girl partnering each other in each pair, according to the following conditions:

Karl partners Sarah in either dance 1 or dance 2.

Whoever partners Rita in dance 2 must partner Sarah in dance 3.

No two children can partner each other in more than one dance.

14. If Sarah partners Luis in dance 3, which one of the following is a complete and accurate list of the girls any one of whom could partner Miguel in dance 1?

(A) Rita
(B) Sarah
(C) Tura
(D) Rita, Sarah
(E) Rita, Tura

15. If Miguel partners Rita in dance 2, which one of the following could be true?

(A) Karl partners Tura in dance 1.
(B) Luis partners Sarah in dance 2.
(C) Luis partners Sarah in dance 3.
(D) Miguel partners Sarah in dance 1.
(E) Miguel partners Tura in dance 3.

16. If Miguel partners Sarah in dance 1, which one of the following is a pair of children who must partner each other in dance 3?

(A) Karl and Rita
(B) Karl and Tura
(C) Luis and Rita
(D) Luis and Tura
(E) Miguel and Tura

17. If Luis partners Sarah in dance 2, which one of the following is a pair of children who must partner each other in dance 1?

(A) Karl and Rita
(B) Karl and Tura
(C) Luis and Rita
(D) Luis and Tura
(E) Miguel and Rita

18. If Miguel partners Rita in dance 1, which one of the following must be true?

(A) Karl partners Rita in dance 2.
(B) Karl partners Sarah in dance 3.
(C) Karl partners Tura in dance 1.
(D) Luis partners Rita in dance 2.
(E) Luis partners Tura in dance 3.

GO ON TO THE NEXT PAGE.

Questions 19–24

Six cities are located within the numbered areas as follows:

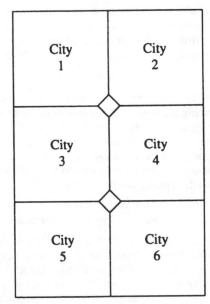

Within the six-city area there are exactly four hospitals, two jails, and two universities. These eight institutions are located as follows:

No institution is in more than one of the cities.

None of the cities contains more than one jail, and none contains more than one university.

None of the cities contains both a jail and a university.

Each jail is located in a city that contains at least one hospital.

The universities are located in two cities that do not share a common boundary.

City 3 contains a university, and city 6 contains a jail.

19. Which one of the following could be true?

   (A) City 5 contains a university.
   (B) City 6 contains a university.
   (C) City 2 contains a jail.
   (D) City 3 contains a jail.
   (E) City 3 contains a hospital.

20. Which one of the following could be true?

   (A) City 1 contains exactly one hospital.
   (B) City 1 contains exactly one university.
   (C) City 2 contains exactly one jail.
   (D) City 5 contains exactly one university.
   (E) City 6 contains exactly one university.

21. Which one of the following is a complete and accurate list of the cities any one of which could contain the jail that is not in city 6 ?

   (A) 1, 4
   (B) 2, 4
   (C) 4, 5
   (D) 1, 4, 5
   (E) 1, 2, 4, 5

22. If each of the six cities contains at least one of the eight institutions, then which one of the following must be true?

   (A) There is a jail in city 1.
   (B) There is a hospital in city 2.
   (C) There is a hospital in city 3.
   (D) There is a hospital in city 4.
   (E) There is a jail in city 4.

23. In which one of the following cities must there be fewer than three hospitals?

   (A) 1
   (B) 2
   (C) 4
   (D) 5
   (E) 6

24. If one of the cities contains exactly two hospitals and exactly one university, then which one of the following lists three cities that might, among them, contain no hospital?

   (A) 1, 3, 5
   (B) 1, 4, 5
   (C) 2, 3, 5
   (D) 2, 4, 6
   (E) 4, 5, 6

S T O P

IF YOU FINISH BEFORE TIME IS CALLED, YOU MAY CHECK YOUR WORK ON THIS SECTION ONLY.
DO NOT WORK ON ANY OTHER SECTION IN THE TEST.

SECTION IV
Time—35 minutes
25 Questions

Directions: The questions in this section are based on the reasoning contained in brief statements or passages. For some questions, more than one of the choices could conceivably answer the question. However, you are to choose the best answer; that is, the response that most accurately and completely answers the question. You should not make assumptions that are by commonsense standards implausible, superfluous, or incompatible with the passage. After you have chosen the best answer, blacken the corresponding space on your answer sheet.

1. People who accuse the postal service of incompetence and inefficiency while complaining of the proposed five-cent increase in postal rates do not know a bargain when they see one. Few experiences are more enjoyable than reading a personal letter from a friend. Viewed in this way, postal service is so underpriced that a five-cent increase is unworthy of serious debate.

   The reasoning in the argument is flawed because the argument

   (A) suggests that the postal service is both competent and efficient, but does not establish how competence and efficiency should be measured
   (B) claims that the proposed increase is insignificant but does not say at what level the increase would be worthy of serious debate
   (C) confuses the value of the object delivered with the value of delivering that object
   (D) appeals to an outside authority for support of a premise that should be established by argument
   (E) fails to establish whether or not the critics of the postal service are employees of the postal service

2. When a study of aspirin's ability to prevent heart attacks in humans yielded positive results, researchers immediately submitted those results to a medical journal, which published them six weeks later. Had the results been published sooner, many of the heart attacks that occurred during the delay could have been prevented.

   The conclusion drawn above would be most undermined if it were true that

   (A) the medical journal's staff worked overtime in order to publish the study's results as soon as possible
   (B) studies of aspirin's usefulness in reducing heart attacks in laboratory animals remain inconclusive
   (C) people who take aspirin regularly suffer a higher-than-average incidence of stomach ulcers
   (D) the medical journal's official policy is to publish articles only after an extensive review process
   (E) a person's risk of suffering a heart attack drops only after that person has taken aspirin regularly for two years

3. It might seem that an airline could increase profits by reducing airfares on all its flights in order to encourage discretionary travel and thus fill planes. Offers of across-the-board discount fares have, indeed, resulted in the sale of large numbers of reduced-price tickets. Nevertheless such offers have, in the past, actually cut the airline's profits.

   Which one of the following, if true, most helps to resolve the apparent discrepancy described above?

   (A) Fewer than 10 percent of all air travelers make no attempt to seek out discount fares.
   (B) Fares for trips between a large city and a small city are higher than those for trips between two large cities even when the distances involved are the same.
   (C) Across-the-board discounts in fares tend to decrease revenues on flights that are normally filled, but they fail to attract passengers to unpopular flights.
   (D) Only a small number of people who have never before traveled by air are persuaded to do so on the basis of across-the-board discount fares.
   (E) It is difficult to devise an advertising campaign that makes the public aware of across-the-board discount fares while fully explaining the restrictions applied to those discount fares.

4. Only if the electorate is moral and intelligent will a democracy function well.

   Which one of the following can be logically inferred from the claim above?

   (A) If the electorate is moral and intelligent, then a democracy will function well.
   (B) Either a democracy does not function well or else the electorate is not moral or not intelligent.
   (C) If the electorate is not moral or not intelligent, then a democracy will not function well.
   (D) If a democracy does not function well, then the electorate is not moral or not intelligent.
   (E) It cannot, at the same time, be true that the electorate is moral and intelligent and that a democracy will not function well.

GO ON TO THE NEXT PAGE.

5. Infants younger than six months who have normal hearing can readily distinguish between acoustically similar sounds that are used as part of any language —not only those used in the language spoken by the people who raise them. Young adults can readily distinguish between such sounds only in languages that they regularly use. It is known that the physiological capacity to hear begins to deteriorate after infancy. So the observed difference in the abilities of infants and young adults to distinguish between acoustically similar speech sounds must be the result of the physiological deterioration of hearing.

    The reasoning in the argument is flawed because the argument

    (A) sets an arbitrary cutoff point of six months for the age below which infants are able to distinguish acoustically similar speech sounds
    (B) does not explain the procedures used to measure the abilities of two very different populations
    (C) ignores the fact that certain types of speech sounds occur in almost all languages
    (D) assumes that what is true of a group of people taken collectively is also true of any individual within that group
    (E) takes a factor that might contribute to an explanation of the observed difference as a sufficient explanation for that difference

6. The economies of some industrialized countries face the prospect of large labor shortages in the decades ahead. Meanwhile, these countries will have a vast number of experienced and productive older workers who, as things stand, will be driven from the work force upon reaching the age of sixty-five by the widespread practice of requiring workers to retire at that age. Therefore, if the discriminatory practice of mandatory retirement at age sixty-five were eliminated, the labor shortages facing these economies would be averted.

    The argument assumes that

    (A) older workers have acquired skills that are extremely valuable and that their younger colleagues lack
    (B) workers in industrialized countries are often unprepared to face the economic consequences of enforced idleness
    (C) a large number of workers in some industrialized countries would continue working beyond the age of sixty-five if workers in those countries were allowed to do so
    (D) mandatory retirement at age sixty-five was first instituted when life expectancy was considerably lower than it is today
    (E) a substantial proportion of the population of officially retired workers is actually engaged in gainful employment

7. The incidence in Japan of most types of cancer is remarkably low compared to that in North America, especially considering that Japan has a modern life-style, industrial pollution included. The cancer rates, however, for Japanese people who immigrate to North America and adopt the diet of North Americans approximate the higher cancer rates prevalent in North America.

    If the statements above are true, they provide the most support for which one of the following?

    (A) The greater the level of industrial pollution in a country, the higher that country's cancer rate will tend to be.
    (B) The stress of life in North America is greater than that of life in Japan and predisposes to cancer.
    (C) The staple foods of the Japanese diet contain elements that cure cancer.
    (D) The relatively low rate of cancer among people in Japan does not result from a high frequency of a protective genetic trait among Japanese people.
    (E) The higher cancer rates of Japanese immigrants to North America are caused by fats in the North American diet.

8. A translation invariably reflects the writing style of the translator. Sometimes when a long document needs to be translated quickly, several translators are put to work on the job, each assigned to translate part of the document. In these cases, the result is usually a translation marked by different and often incompatible writing styles. Certain computer programs for language translation that work without the intervention of human translators can finish the job faster than human translators and produce a stylistically uniform translation with an 80 percent accuracy rate. Therefore, when a long document needs to be translated quickly, it is better to use a computer translation program than human translators.

    Which one of the following issues would be LEAST important to resolve in evaluating the argument?

    (A) whether the problem of stylistic variety in human translation could be solved by giving stylistic guidelines to human translators
    (B) whether numerical comparisons of the accuracy of translations can reasonably be made
    (C) whether computer translation programs, like human translators, each have their own distinct writing style
    (D) whether the computer translation contains errors of grammar and usage that drastically alter the meaning of the text
    (E) how the accuracy rate of computer translation programs compares with that of human translators in relation to the users' needs

GO ON TO THE NEXT PAGE.

Questions 9–10

Myrna: People should follow diets in which fat represents no more than 30 percent of total calories, not the 37 percent the average diet in this country contains.

Roland: If everyone in the country followed your recommendation during his or her entire life, just 0.2 percent would lengthen their lives at all, and then only by an average of 3 months. Modifying our diet is not worthwhile. A lifetime of sacrifice spent eating an unappealing low-fat diet is too high a price to pay for the chance of extending that sacrifice for 3 months.

Myrna: But for everyone who dies early from a high-fat diet, many more people suffer from serious chronic diseases because they followed such diets.

9. Myrna responds to Roland by

(A) disputing the correctness of the facts cited by Roland and offering facts that she considers correct

(B) showing that the factors considered by Roland are not the only ones relevant in evaluating her recommendation

(C) demonstrating that the statistics used by Roland to dispute her recommendation are inaccurate

(D) suggesting that Roland's evidence derives from unreliable sources

(E) pointing out that Roland's argument assumes the very proposition it sets out to prove

10. Roland's argument assumes that

(A) it is desirable to live in such a way as to lengthen life as much as possible

(B) a low-fat diet cannot readily be made appealing and satisfying to a person who follows it regularly

(C) diet is the only relevant factor to consider in computing influences on length of life

(D) the difference in tastiness between a diet in which fat represents 30 percent of total calories and one in which it represents 37 percent is not noticeable

(E) not everyone in the country eats the average diet

11. Some critics claim that it is unfair that so many great works of art are housed in huge metropolitan museums, since the populations served by these museums already have access to a wide variety of important artwork. But this criticism is in principle unwarranted because the limited number of masterpieces makes wider distribution of them impractical. Besides, if a masterpiece is to be fully appreciated, it must be seen alongside other works that provide a social and historical context for it.

Which one of the following, if established, could most logically serve as the principle appealed to in the argument countering the critics' claim?

(A) In providing facilities to the public, the goal should be to ensure that as many as possible of those people who could benefit from the facilities are able to do so.

(B) In providing facilities to the public, the goal should be to ensure that the greatest possible number of people gain the greatest benefit possible from them.

(C) It is unreasonable to enforce a redistribution of social goods that involves depriving some members of society of these goods in order to supply others.

(D) For it to be reasonable to criticize an arrangement as unfair, there must be a more equitable arrangement that is practically attainable.

(E) A work of art should be displayed in conditions resembling as closely as possible those in which the work was originally intended to be displayed.

12. Some accountants calculate with simple adding machines, and some use complex computers. One can perform more calculations in less time with a computer than with an adding machine. Therefore, assuming the costs of using the two types of machines are equal, an accountant who uses a computer generally can earn more per hour than an accountant who uses an adding machine.

Which one of the following is an assumption that would make the conclusion in the passage a logical one?

(A) More accountants use computers than use adding machines.

(B) The more hours an accountant spends on the job, the more money he or she will earn.

(C) The more calculations an accountant performs, the more money he or she will earn.

(D) An accountant who uses an adding machine can charge a higher hourly rate than one who uses a computer.

(E) In general, accountants vary in terms of the number of calculations they make and the amount of money they earn.

GO ON TO THE NEXT PAGE.

13. This summer, Jennifer, who has worked at KVZ Manufacturing for just over three years, plans to spend with her family the entire four weeks of paid vacation to which she is entitled this year. Anyone who has worked at KVZ Manufacturing for between one and four years is automatically entitled to exactly three weeks paid vacation each year but can apply up to half of any vacation time that remains unused at the end of one year to the next year's vacation.

If the statements above are all true, which one of the following must also be true on the basis of them?

(A) Jennifer did not use two weeks of the paid vacation time to which she was entitled last year.

(B) If Jennifer continues to work for KVZ Manufacturing, she will only be entitled to three weeks paid vacation next year.

(C) The majority of KVZ's employees use each year all of the paid vacation time to which they are entitled.

(D) Last year Jennifer took only one week of the paid vacation time to which she was entitled.

(E) KVZ Manufacturing sometimes allows extra vacation time to employees who need to spend more time with their families.

14. A careful review of hospital fatalities due to anesthesia during the last 20 years indicates that the most significant safety improvements resulted from better training of anesthetists. Equipment that monitors a patient's oxygen and carbon dioxide levels was not available in most operating rooms during the period under review. Therefore, the increased use of such monitoring equipment in operating rooms will not significantly cut fatalities due to anesthesia.

A flaw in the argument is that

(A) the evidence cited to show that one factor led to a certain result is not sufficient to show that a second factor will not also lead to that result

(B) the reasons given in support of the conclusion presuppose the truth of that conclusion

(C) the evidence cited to show that a certain factor was absent when a certain result occurred does not show that the absence of that factor caused that result

(D) the evidence cited in support of the conclusion is inconsistent with other information that is provided

(E) the reason indicated for the claim that one event caused a second more strongly supports the claim that both events were independent effects of a third event

15. New types of washing machines designed to consume less energy also extract less water from laundry during their final spin cycles than do washing machines that consume somewhat more energy. The wetter the laundry, the more energy required to dry it in an automatic dryer. Thus using these new types of washing machines could result in an overall increase in the energy needed to wash and dry a load of laundry.

In which one of the following is the pattern of reasoning most parallel to that in the argument above?

(A) The more skill required to operate a machine, the harder it is to find people able to do it, and thus the more those people must be paid. Therefore, if a factory installs machines that require highly skilled operators, it must be prepared to pay higher wages.

(B) There are two routes between Centerville and Mapletown, and the scenic route is the longer route. Therefore, a person who is not concerned with how long it will take to travel between Centerville and Mapletown will probably take the scenic route.

(C) The more people who work in the library's reading room, the noisier the room becomes; and the noisier the working environment, the less efficiently people work. Therefore, when many people are working in the reading room, those people are working less efficiently.

(D) Pine is a less expensive wood than cedar but is more susceptible to rot. Outdoor furniture made from wood susceptible to rot must be painted with more expensive paint. Therefore, building outdoor furniture from pine rather than cedar could increase the total cost of building and painting the furniture.

(E) The more weights added to an exercise machine, the greater the muscle strength needed to work out on the machine. Up to a point, using more muscle strength can make a person stronger. Thus an exercise machine with more weights can, but does not necessarily, make a person stronger.

GO ON TO THE NEXT PAGE.

Questions 16–17

G: The group of works exhibited in this year's Metropolitan Art Show reveals a bias in favor of photographers. Equal numbers of photographers, sculptors, and painters submitted works that met the traditional criteria for the show, yet more photographs were exhibited than either sculptures or paintings. As you know, each artist was allowed to submit work in one medium only.

H: How could there have been bias? All submitted works that met the traditional criteria—and only those works—were exhibited in the show.

16. If both G's assertions and H's assertion are true, which one of the following must also be true?

(A) More photographers than sculptors or painters submitted works to be considered for exhibition in the Metropolitan Art Show.

(B) All the works submitted for the Metropolitan Art Show met the traditional criteria for the show.

(C) The quality of photographs exhibited in the Metropolitan Art Show was inferior to the quality of the sculptures or paintings exhibited.

(D) Some of the photographs submitted for the Metropolitan Art Show did not meet the traditional criteria for the show.

(E) More works that met the traditional criteria for the Metropolitan Art Show were submitted by photographers than by sculptors or painters.

17. Which one of the following, if true, most strongly supports G's allegation of bias?

(A) If an artist has had one of his or her works exhibited in the Metropolitan Art Show, that artist has an advantage in getting commissions and selling works over artists who have never had a work exhibited in the show.

(B) The fee for entering photographs in the Metropolitan Art Show was $25 per work submitted, while the fee for each painting or sculpture submitted was $75.

(C) The committee that selected from the submitted works the ones to be exhibited in this year's Metropolitan Art Show had four members: one photographer, one sculptor, one painter, and one who works in all three media but is the least known of the four members.

(D) Reviews of this year's Metropolitan Art Show that appeared in major newspapers and magazines tended to give more coverage to the photographs in the show than to the sculptures and paintings that were exhibited.

(E) In previous years, it has often happened that more paintings or more sculptures were exhibited in the Metropolitan Art Show than photographs, even though the total number of works exhibited each year does not vary widely.

Questions 18–19

Marcus: For most ethical dilemmas the journalist is likely to face, traditional journalistic ethics is clear, adequate, and essentially correct. For example, when journalists have uncovered newsworthy information, they should go to press with it as soon as possible. No delay motivated by the journalists' personal or professional interests is permissible.

Anita: Well, Marcus, of course interesting and important information should be brought before the public —that is a journalist's job. But in the typical case, where a journalist has some information but is in a quandary about whether it is yet important or "newsworthy," this guidance is inadequate.

18. The point made by Anita's statements is most accurately expressed by which one of the following?

(A) Marcus' claim that traditional journalistic ethics is clear for most ethical dilemmas in journalism is incorrect.

(B) A typical case illustrates that Marcus is wrong in claiming that traditional journalistic ethics is essentially correct for most ethical dilemmas in journalism.

(C) The ethical principle that Marcus cites does not help the journalist in a typical kind of situation in which a decision needs to be made.

(D) There are common situations in which a journalist must make a decision and in which no principle of journalistic ethics can be of help.

(E) Traditional journalistic ethics amounts to no more than an unnecessarily convoluted description of the journalist's job.

19. In order to conclude properly from Anita's statements that Marcus' general claim about traditional journalistic ethics is incorrect, it would have to be assumed that

(A) whether a piece of information is or is not newsworthy can raise ethical dilemmas for journalists

(B) there are circumstances in which it would be ethically wrong for a journalist to go to press with legitimately acquired, newsworthy information

(C) the most serious professional dilemmas that a journalist is likely to face are not ethical dilemmas

(D) there are no ethical dilemmas that a journalist is likely to face that would not be conclusively resolved by an adequate system of journalistic ethics

(E) for a system of journalistic ethics to be adequate it must be able to provide guidance in every case in which a journalist must make a professional decision

GO ON TO THE NEXT PAGE.

Questions 20-21

Of every 100 burglar alarms police answer, 99 are false alarms. This situation causes an enormous and dangerous drain on increasingly scarce public resources. Each false alarm wastes an average of 45 minutes of police time. As a result police are consistently taken away from responding to other legitimate calls for service, and a disproportionate share of police service goes to alarm system users, who are mostly businesses and affluent homeowners. However, burglar alarm systems, unlike car alarm systems, are effective in deterring burglaries, so the only acceptable solution is to fine burglar alarm system owners the cost of 45 minutes of police time for each false alarm their systems generate.

20. The statement that burglar alarm systems, unlike car alarm systems, are effective in deterring burglaries plays which one of the following roles in the argument?

(A) It justifies placing more restrictions on owners of burglar alarms than on owners of car alarms.

(B) It provides background information needed to make plausible the claim that the number of burglar alarms police are called on to answer is great enough to be a drain on public resources.

(C) It provides a basis for excluding as unacceptable one obvious alternative to the proposal of fining owners of burglar alarm systems for false alarms.

(D) It gives a reason why police might be more inclined to respond to burglar alarms than to car alarms.

(E) It explains why a disproportionate number of the burglar alarms responded to by police come from alarm systems owned by businesses.

21. On the basis of the premises advanced, which one of the following principles, if established, would provide the most justification for the concluding recommendation?

(A) No segment of a community should be permitted to engage in a practice that has been shown to result in a disproportionate share of police service being devoted to that segment of the community.

(B) When public resources are in short supply, any individual who wants special services from public agencies such as police and fire departments should be required to pay for those services if he or she can afford to do so.

(C) Police departments are not justified in improving service to one segment of the community at the expense of other segments of the community unless doing so reduces the crime level throughout the entire area served.

(D) Anyone who directly benefits from a service provided by public employees should be required to reimburse the general public fund an amount equivalent to the average cost of providing that service.

(E) If receipt of a service results in the waste of scarce public resources and people with other legitimate needs are disadvantaged in consequence, the recipient of that service should compensate the public for the resources wasted.

GO ON TO THE NEXT PAGE.

22. When butterfat was considered nutritious and healthful, a law was enacted requiring that manufacturers use the term "imitation butter" to indicate butter whose butterfat content had been diminished through the addition of water. Today, it is known that the high cholesterol content of butterfat makes it harmful to human health. Since the public should be encouraged to eat foods with lower rather than higher butterfat content and since the term "imitation" with its connotations of falsity deters many people from purchasing products so designated, manufacturers who wish to give reduced-butterfat butter the more appealing name of "lite butter" should be allowed to do so.

Which one of the following, if true, most seriously undermines the argument?

(A) The manufacturers who prefer to use the word "lite" instead of "imitation" are motivated principally by the financial interest of their stockholders.

(B) The manufacturers who wish to call their product "lite butter" plan to change the composition of the product so that it contains more water than it now does.

(C) Some individuals who need to reduce their intake of cholesterol are not deterred from using the reduced-butterfat product by the negative connotations of the term "imitation."

(D) Cholesterol is only one of many factors that contribute to the types of health problems with which the consumption of excessive amounts of cholesterol is often associated.

(E) Most people deterred from eating "imitation butter" because of its name choose alternatives with a lower butterfat content than this product has.

23. Farm animals have certain behavioral tendencies that result from the evolutionary history of these species. By imposing on these animals a type of organization that conflicts with their behavioral tendencies, current farm-management practices cause the animals more pain and distress than do practices that more closely conform to the animals' behavioral tendencies. Because the animals tend to resist this type of organization, current practices can also be less efficient than those other farm-management practices.

If the statements above are true, which one of the following can be properly inferred from them?

(A) Some of the behavioral tendencies of farm animals can be altered by efficient farm-management practices.

(B) In order to implement efficient farm-management practices, it is necessary to be familiar with the evolutionary history of farm animals.

(C) In order to create farm-management practices that cause less pain and distress to farm animals, a significant loss of efficiency will be required.

(D) Farm-management practices that cause the least amount of pain and distress to farm animals are also the most efficient management practices.

(E) Some changes in farm-management practices that lessen the pain and distress experienced by farm animals can result in gains in efficiency.

GO ON TO THE NEXT PAGE.

24. It now seems clear that the significant role initially predicted for personal computers in the classroom has not become fact. One need only look to the dramatic decline in sales of computers for classroom use in the past year for proof that the fad has passed.

Which one of the following arguments contains flawed reasoning parallel to that in the argument above?

(A) Clearly, government legislation mandating the reduction of automobile emissions has been at least partially successful, as is demonstrated by the fact that the air of the 20 largest cities now contains smaller amounts of the major pollutants mentioned in the legislation than it did before the legislation was passed.

(B) Mechanical translation from one language into another, not merely in narrow contexts such as airline reservations but generally, is clearly an idea whose time has come. Since experts have been working on the problem for 40 years, it is now time for the accumulated expertise to achieve a breakthrough.

(C) Sales of computers for home use will never reach the levels optimistically projected by manufacturers. The reason is that home use was envisioned as encompassing tasks, such as menu planning and checkbook reconciliation, that most homemakers perform in much simpler ways than using a computer would require.

(D) It is apparent that consumers have tired of microwave ovens as quickly as they initially came to accept this recent invention. In contrast to several years of increasing sales following the introduction of microwave ovens, sales of microwave ovens flattened last year, indicating that consumers have found relatively little use for these devices.

(E) Creating incentives for a particular kind of investment inevitably engenders boom-and-bust cycles. The evidence is in the recent decline in the value of commercial real estate, which shows that, although the government can encourage people to put up buildings, it cannot guarantee that those buildings will be fully rented or sold.

25. Scientists attempting to replicate certain controversial results reported by a group of experienced researchers failed to get the same results as those reported. The conclusion drawn from this by the scientists who conducted the replication experiments was that the originally reported results had been due to faulty measurements.

The argument of the scientists who conducted the replication experiments assumes that

(A) the original experiments had not been described in sufficient detail to make an exact replication possible

(B) the fact that the originally reported results aroused controversy made it highly likely that they were in error

(C) the theoretical principles called into question by the originally reported results were themselves based on weak evidence

(D) the replication experiments were not so likely as the original experiments to be marred by faulty measurements

(E) the researchers who originally reported the controversial results had themselves observed those results only once

S T O P

IF YOU FINISH BEFORE TIME IS CALLED, YOU MAY CHECK YOUR WORK ON THIS SECTION ONLY.
DO NOT WORK ON ANY OTHER SECTION IN THE TEST.

LSAT® Writing Sample Topic

Directions: The scenario presented below describes two choices, either one of which can be supported on the basis of the information given. Your essay should consider both choices and argue for one over the other, based on the two specified criteria and the facts provided. There is no "right" or "wrong" choice: a reasonable argument can be made for either.

Valerie, a first-year graduate student in mathematics, needs a part-time job, and competition for jobs in the small town where her university is located is keen. With the following considerations in mind, write an argument in support of one of Valerie's two job offers over the other:

- Valerie wants the income from her job to minimize the money she must borrow for living expenses.
- Valerie wants the job to interfere with her graduate program as little as possible.

The university's Undergraduate Learning Center has offered Valerie a job tutoring groups of students taking introductory mathematics courses. Valerie has been assigned five 1:00 PM to 5:00 PM sessions, for which she will receive $160 per week. The ULC also provides free individual tutoring for students in advanced mathematics courses who request it. As a graduate student employee, Valerie would be eligible to serve as an individual tutor, in addition to her regular sessions, for which she would receive $15 per hour. The schedule of this job will require her to make changes in the courses she had planned to take this semester. She will also miss the afternoon office hours that most professors set aside to work individually with graduate students.

Milano's, a local restaurant, has offered Valerie a job as a food server. She will work Tuesday, Thursday, Friday, and Saturday nights each week, starting at 5:00 PM. The salary is $130 per week plus tips, which can range anywhere from $80 to $140 for four nights of work. Milano's is often crowded on Friday and Saturday nights but rarely during the week. A server at Milano's told Valerie that although the restaurant's kitchen closes at 11:00 PM, servers must stay until all customers have left, which can be midnight or later. Valerie's most demanding class meets at 8:00 AM Wednesdays and Fridays and cannot be rescheduled. Taking this job also means that she must give up the evening meetings of her study group.

Directions:

1. Use the Answer Key on the next page to check your answers.

2. Use the Scoring Worksheet below to compute your raw score.

3. Use the Score Conversion Chart to convert your raw score into the 120-180 scale.

Scoring Worksheet

1. Enter the number of questions you answered correctly in each section.

	Number Correct
SECTION I	_____
SECTION II	_____
SECTION III	_____
SECTION IV	_____

2. Enter the sum here: _____
   This is your Raw Score.

Conversion Chart

For Converting Raw Score to the 120-180 LSAT Scaled Score
LSAT Form 4LSS23

Reported Score	Raw Score Lowest	Raw Score Highest
180	98	101
179	97	97
178	96	96
177	95	95
176	94	94
175	93	93
174	92	92
173	90	91
172	89	89
171	88	88
170	86	87
169	85	85
168	83	84
167	82	82
166	80	81
165	78	79
164	77	77
163	75	76
162	73	74
161	71	72
160	70	70
159	68	69
158	66	67
157	64	65
156	63	63
155	61	62
154	59	60
153	58	58
152	56	57
151	54	55
150	53	53
149	51	52
148	49	50
147	48	48
146	46	47
145	45	45
144	43	44
143	42	42
142	40	41
141	39	39
140	37	38
139	36	36
138	35	35
137	33	34
136	32	32
135	31	31
134	29	30
133	28	28
132	27	27
131	26	26
130	25	25
129	24	24
128	23	23
127	22	22
126	21	21
125	20	20
124	19	19
123	18	18
122	17	17
121	—*	—*
120	0	16

*There is no raw score that will produce this scaled score for this form.

SECTION I

1.	B	8.	A	15.	D	22.	D
2.	A	9.	A	16.	C	23.	C
3.	D	10.	C	17.	A	24.	C
4.	E	11.	B	18.	D	25.	E
5.	C	12.	A	19.	B	26.	C
6.	E	13.	B	20.	B	27.	E
7.	C	14.	B	21.	C		

SECTION II

1.	A	8.	D	15.	B	22.	D
2.	D	9.	A	16.	A	23.	A
3.	B	10.	B	17.	B	24.	D
4.	B	11.	E	18.	E	25.	A
5.	D	12.	A	19.	D		
6.	C	13.	D	20.	A		
7.	D	14.	C	21.	D		

SECTION III

1.	C	8.	D	15.	B	22.	D
2.	D	9.	B	16.	B	23.	B
3.	B	10.	B	17.	C	24.	A
4.	A	11.	B	18.	D		
5.	C	12.	C	19.	E		
6.	D	13.	E	20.	A		
7.	A	14.	D	21.	D		

SECTION IV

1.	C	8.	C	15.	D	22.	E
2.	E	9.	B	16.	E	23.	E
3.	C	10.	B	17.	B	24.	D
4.	C	11.	D	18.	C	25.	D
5.	E	12.	C	19.	A		
6.	C	13.	A	20.	C		
7.	D	14.	A	21.	E		

The Official LSAT PrepTest

- February 1994
- Form 3LSS20

The sample test that follows consists of four sections corresponding to the four scored sections of the February 1994 LSAT.

SECTION I
Time—35 minutes
25 Questions

Directions: The questions in this section are based on the reasoning contained in brief statements or passages. For some questions, more than one of the choices could conceivably answer the question. However, you are to choose the best answer; that is, the response that most accurately and completely answers the question. You should not make assumptions that are by commonsense standards implausible, superfluous, or incompatible with the passage. After you have chosen the best answer, blacken the corresponding space on your answer sheet.

1. Educational television is a contradiction in terms. While a classroom encourages social interaction, television encourages solitude. School is centered on the development of language, but television depends upon constantly changing visual images. And in a classroom, fun is merely a means to an end, but on television it is the end in itself.

   Upon which one of the following assumptions does the author rely in the passage?

   (A) The classroom should not be a place where anyone has fun.
   (B) Only experiences that closely resemble what takes place in the school environment can be educational.
   (C) Television programs reinforce some of the values of the school environment.
   (D) Educational television programs are qualitatively better than most other television programs.
   (E) The potential of television as a powerful learning tool has not yet been realized.

2. Switching to "low-yield" cigarettes, those that yield less nicotine, tar, and carbon monoxide than regular cigarettes when tested on a standard machine, does not, in general, reduce the incidence of heart attack. This result is surprising, since nicotine and carbon monoxide have been implicated as contributing to heart disease.

   Which one of the following, if true, most helps to resolve the apparent discrepancy?

   (A) Smoking low-yield cigarettes has become fashionable, as relatively healthier styles of life have become more popular than those that have been identified as risky.
   (B) For those who are themselves smokers, inhaling the smoke of others is not generally a significant factor contributing to an increased risk of heart disease.
   (C) Nicotine does not contribute as much to heart disease as does carbon monoxide.
   (D) Carbon monoxide and cigarette tar are not addictive substances.
   (E) People who switch from high-yield to low-yield cigarettes often compensate by increasing the number and depth of puffs in order to maintain their accustomed nicotine levels.

Questions 3–4

Sally: I cannot study at a university where there is an alcohol problem, so unless something is done about the alcohol problem at this university, I'll have to transfer to a university where there are no fraternities.

Yolanda: I don't agree that fraternities are responsible for the alcohol problem at this university. Alcohol problems exist at all universities, including those where there are no fraternities. We all should become more aware of alcohol abuse. It's not simply a fraternity problem; it's a cultural problem.

3. Which one of the following is an assumption on which Sally's argument depends?

   (A) Most universities have fraternities.
   (B) Nothing will be done about the alcohol problem at Sally's university.
   (C) Alcohol problems are becoming more widespread at universities.
   (D) Some fraternity members who drink alcoholic beverages are too young to do so legally.
   (E) There could be universities that have no alcohol problems.

4. In the conversation, Yolanda does which one of the following?

   (A) She argues that if people become more aware of alcohol abuse, fewer people will themselves abuse alcohol.
   (B) She makes an overly broad generalization from one university to all universities.
   (C) She concludes that because alcohol problems are cultural problems, they cannot be fraternity problems.
   (D) She tries to undermine what she supposes to be Sally's position by pointing out that alcohol problems occur even at universities where there are no fraternities.
   (E) She suggests that even if alcohol problems existed only at universities with fraternities, she would still conclude that alcoholism is a cultural rather than a fraternity problem.

GO ON TO THE NEXT PAGE.

5. Some people have questioned why the Homeowners Association is supporting Cooper's candidacy for mayor. But if the Association wants a mayor who will attract more businesses to the town, Cooper is the only candidate it could support. So, since the Association is supporting Cooper, it must have a goal of attracting more businesses to the town.

The reasoning in the argument is in error because

(A) the reasons the Homeowners Association should want to attract more businesses to the town are not given

(B) the Homeowners Association could be supporting Cooper's candidacy for reasons unrelated to attracting businesses to the town

(C) other groups besides the Homeowners Association could be supporting Cooper's candidacy

(D) the Homeowners Association might discover that attracting more businesses to the town would not be in the best interest of its members

(E) Cooper might not have all of the skills that are needed by a mayor who wants to attract businesses to a town

6. Advertisement: Most power hedge trimmers on the market do an adequate job of trimming hedges, but many power hedge trimmers are dangerous to operate and can cause serious injury when used by untrained operators. Bolter Industries' hedge trimmer has been tested by National Laboratories, the most trusted name in safety testing. So you know, if you buy a Bolter's, you are buying a power hedge trimmer whose safety is assured.

The answer to which one of the following questions would be most useful in evaluating the truth of the conclusion drawn in the advertisement?

(A) Has National Laboratories performed safety tests on other machines made by Bolter Industries?

(B) How important to the average buyer of a power hedge trimmer is safety of operation?

(C) What were the results of National Laboratories' tests of Bolter Industries' hedge trimmer?

(D) Are there safer ways of trimming a hedge than using a power hedge trimmer?

(E) Does any other power hedge trimmer on the market do a better job of trimming hedges than does Bolter Industries' hedge trimmer?

7. Slash-and-burn agriculture involves burning several acres of forest, leaving vegetable ash that provides ample fertilizer for three or four years of bountiful crops. On the cleared land nutrients leach out of the soil, however, and the land becomes too poor to support agriculture. New land is then cleared by burning and the process starts again. Since most farming in the tropics uses this method, forests in this region will eventually be permanently eradicated.

The argument depends on the assumption that

(A) forests in the tropics do not regenerate well enough to restore themselves once they have been cleared by the slash-and-burn method

(B) some other methods of agriculture are not as destructive to the environment in tropical regions as the slash-and-burn method is

(C) forests in the tropics are naturally deficient in nutrients that are needed to support the growth of plants that are not native to those regions

(D) slash-and-burn agriculture is particularly suitable for farming in tropical areas

(E) slash-and-burn agriculture produces a more bountiful crop than do other agriculture methods for the first year

8. Of 2,500 people who survived a first heart attack, those who did not smoke had their first heart attack at a median age of 62. However, of those 2,500, people who smoked two packs of cigarettes a day had their first heart attack at a median age of 51. On the basis of this information, it can be concluded that nonsmokers tend to have a first heart attack eleven years later than do people who smoke two packs of cigarettes a day.

The conclusion is incorrectly drawn from the information given because this information does not include

(A) the relative severity of heart attacks suffered by smokers and nonsmokers

(B) the nature of the different medical treatments that smokers and nonsmokers received after they had survived their first heart attack

(C) how many of the 2,500 people studied suffered a second heart attack

(D) the earliest age at which a person who smoked two packs a day had his or her first heart attack

(E) data on people who did not survive a first heart attack

GO ON TO THE NEXT PAGE.

9. Paleontologists have discovered fossils of centipedes that are 414 million years old. These fossils are at least 20 million years older than the earliest land-dwelling animals previously identified. The paleontologists are confident that these centipedes lived on land, even though the fossilized centipedes were discovered in rock that also contained fossilized remains of animals known to be water-dwelling.

    The paleontologists' view would be LEAST supported by the truth of which one of the following?

    (A) The legs of the fossilized centipedes were particularly suited to being a means of locomotion on land.
    (B) All of the centipedes that had previously been discovered were land dwellers.
    (C) The rock in which the fossilized centipedes were found was formed from mud flats that were occasionally covered by river water.
    (D) Fossils of the earliest land-dwelling animals that had previously been identified were found in rock that did not contain fossilized remains of water-dwelling animals.
    (E) Fossils of spiders with respiratory systems adapted only to breathing air were found in the same rock as the centipede fossils.

10. Broadcaster: Our radio station has a responsibility to serve the public interest. Hence, when our critics contend that our recent exposé of events in the private lives of local celebrities was excessively intrusive, we can only reply that the overwhelming public interest in these matters makes it our responsibility to publicize them.

    Which one of the following is a flaw in the broadcaster's defense of the radio station's practice?

    (A) assuming without argument that there is a right to privacy
    (B) ignoring grounds for criticism of the exposé aside from intrusion into people's private lives
    (C) intentionally failing to specify what is meant by "excessively intrusive"
    (D) confusing legal responsibility with moral obligation
    (E) improperly exploiting an ambiguity in the phrase "public interest"

Questions 11–12

The fire that destroyed the Municipal Building started before dawn this morning, and the last fire fighters did not leave until late this afternoon. No one could have been anywhere in the vicinity of a fire like that one and fail to notice it. Thomas must have seen it, whatever he now says to the contrary. He admits that, as usual, he went from his apartment to the library this morning, and there is no way for him to get from his apartment to the library without going past the Municipal Building.

11. The main conclusion of the argument is that

    (A) Thomas was in the vicinity of the fire this morning
    (B) Thomas claimed not to have seen the fire
    (C) Thomas saw the fire this morning
    (D) Thomas went directly from his apartment to the library this morning
    (E) Thomas went by the Municipal Building this morning

12. The argument employs which one of the following reasoning techniques?

    (A) presenting several different pieces of evidence, each of which by itself would allow the conclusion to be properly drawn
    (B) establishing that one thing occurred by showing that another thing occurred and that this second thing was enough to ensure the occurrence of the first thing
    (C) justifying a claim that a view held by someone else is false by explaining why that view, despite its falsity, is a tempting one for that person to hold under the circumstances
    (D) relying on evidence that a certain kind of event has regularly occurred in the past as a basis for concluding that an event of that kind occurred in the present case
    (E) drawing a general conclusion about what is possible in a certain kind of situation on the basis of firsthand experience with one such situation

GO ON TO THE NEXT PAGE.

13. Editorial: In rejecting the plan proposed by parliament to reform the electoral process, the president clearly acted in the best interests of the nation. Anyone who thinks otherwise should remember that the president made this decision knowing it would be met with fierce opposition at home and widespread disapproval abroad. All citizens who place the nation's well-being above narrow partisan interests will applaud this courageous action.

The reasoning in the editorial is in error because

(A) it confuses a quality that is merely desirable in a political leader with a quality that is essential to effective political decision-making

(B) it fails to distinguish between evidence concerning the courage required to make a certain decision and evidence concerning the wisdom of making that decision

(C) it ignores the likelihood that many citizens have no narrow partisan interest in the proposed election reform plan

(D) it overlooks the possibility that there was strong opposition to the parliament's plan among members of the president's own party

(E) it depends on the unwarranted assumption that any plan proposed by a parliament will necessarily serve only narrow partisan interests

14. Once consumers recognize that a period of inflation has begun, there is generally an increase in consumer spending. This increase can be readily explained by consumers' desire not to postpone purchases that will surely increase in price. But during protracted periods of inflation, consumers eventually begin to put off making even routine purchases, despite the fact that consumers continue to expect prices to rise and despite the fact that salaries also rise during inflationary periods.

Which one of the following, if true, most helps to explain the apparent inconsistency in consumer behavior described above?

(A) During times of inflation consumers save more money than they do in noninflationary periods.

(B) There is usually a lag between the leading economic indicators' first signaling the onset of an inflationary period and consumers' recognition of its onset.

(C) No generalization that describes human behavior will be true of every type of human behavior.

(D) If significant numbers of consumers are unable to make purchases, prices will eventually fall but salaries will not be directly affected.

(E) Consumers' purchasing power decreases during periods of protracted inflation since salaries do not keep pace with prices.

Questions 15–16

A favored theory to explain the extinction of dinosaurs, together with many other species, has been the globally catastrophic collision of a large asteroid with the Earth. Supporting evidence is an extraterrestrial chemical element in a layer of dust found worldwide at a geological level laid down contemporaneously with the supposed event. A new competing theory contends that any asteroid impact was irrelevant, because it was massive volcanic activity that caused the extinctions by putting enough dust into the atmosphere to cool the planet. The Deccan region of India contains extensive volcanic flows that occurred within the same time period as the supposed asteroid impact and the extinctions.

15. The new theory assumes that

(A) the massive volcanic activity was not caused by the impact of an asteroid

(B) no individual dinosaurs survived the impact of the asteroid, if it occurred

(C) the extinctions took place over a longer time period than they would have if caused by the impact of an asteroid

(D) other volcanic eruptions were not occurring at the same time as those in the Deccan region

(E) it is not possible to determine which would have occurred first, the volcanic flows in the Deccan region or the supposed impact of an asteroid

16. Which one of the following, if true, most strongly indicates that the asteroid-impact theory is at least incomplete, if not false?

(A) Large concentrations of dinosaur nests with fossil eggs found in Alberta indicate that at least some species of dinosaurs congregated in large groups during some part of their lives.

(B) Dinosaur remains indicate that some species of dinosaur could have migrated in herds over wide ranges, so that they could have traveled to escape the local effects of certain catastrophes.

(C) Legends from many cultures, such as the Greek legend that Cadmus raised an army by sowing dragons' teeth in the ground, show that various ancient peoples worldwide were familiar with the fossils of dinosaurs.

(D) In the Gobi desert in China, where now only small animals can eke out an existence, fossil dinosaur skeletons 27 feet long were found in circumstances indicating that the climate there was as dry when the dinosaurs lived as it is now.

(E) The fossil record in Montana from below the layer of extraterrestrial dust shows a diminution over time in dinosaur species from 35 to 13, and dinosaur teeth found above the dust layer show a diminution in species from 13 to 5.

GO ON TO THE NEXT PAGE.

17. A contract, whether expressed or unexpressed, exists when two parties engage with each other for the reciprocal transfer of benefits. Thus, in accepting support from public funds, an artist creates at least an unexpressed contract between himself or herself and the public, and the public can rightly expect to benefit from the artist's work.

Which one of the following most accurately describes an error in reasoning in the passage?

(A) attempting to justify a rule of conduct on the grounds that it confers benefits on all of the parties involved

(B) concluding that a definition is fully applicable to a situation when it is known only that the situation conforms partially to that definition

(C) speaking only in abstract terms about matters that involve contingencies and that must be judged on a case-by-case basis

(D) confusing the type of mental or emotional activity in which an individual can engage with the mental or emotional states that can characterize groups of individuals

(E) treating an issue that requires resolution through political processes as if it were merely a matter of opinion

18. People cannot be morally responsible for things over which they have no control. Therefore, they should not be held morally responsible for any inevitable consequences of such things, either. Determining whether adults have any control over the treatment they are receiving can be difficult. Hence in some cases it can be difficult to know whether adults bear any moral responsibility for the way they are treated. Everyone, however, sometimes acts in ways that are an inevitable consequence of treatment received as an infant, and infants clearly cannot control, and so are not morally responsible for, the treatment they receive.

Anyone making the claims above would be logically committed to which one of the following further claims?

(A) An infant should never be held morally responsible for an action that infant has performed.

(B) There are certain commonly performed actions for which no one performing those actions should ever be held morally responsible.

(C) Adults who claim that they have no control over the treatment they are receiving should often be held at least partially responsible for being so treated.

(D) If a given action is within a certain person's control that person should be held morally responsible for the consequences of that action.

(E) No adult should be held morally responsible for every action he or she performs.

19. Fares on the city-run public buses in Greenville are subsidized by city tax revenues, but among the beneficiaries of the low fares are many people who commute from outside the city to jobs in Greenville. Some city councillors argue that city taxes should be used primarily to benefit the people who pay them, and therefore that bus fares should be raised enough to cover the cost of the service.

Each of the following, if true, would weaken the argument advanced by the city councillors EXCEPT:

(A) Many businesses whose presence in the city is beneficial to the city's taxpayers would relocate outside the city if public-transit fares were more expensive.

(B) By providing commuters with economic incentives to drive to work, higher transit fares would worsen air pollution in Greenville and increase the cost of maintaining the city's streets.

(C) Increasing transit fares would disadvantage those residents of the city whose low incomes make them exempt from city taxes, and all city councillors agree that these residents should be able to take advantage of city-run services.

(D) Voters in the city, many of whom benefit from the low transit fares, are strongly opposed to increasing local taxes.

(E) People who work in Greenville and earn wages above the nationally mandated minimum all pay the city wage tax of 5 percent.

GO ON TO THE NEXT PAGE.

20. Government official: Clearly, censorship exists if we, as citizens, are not allowed to communicate what we are ready to communicate at our own expense or if other citizens are not permitted access to our communications at their own expense. Public unwillingness to provide funds for certain kinds of scientific, scholarly, or artistic activities cannot, therefore, be described as censorship.

The flawed reasoning in the government official's argument is most parallel to that in which one of the following?

(A)   All actions that cause unnecessary harm to others are unjust; so if a just action causes harm to others, that action must be necessary.

(B)   Since there is more to good manners than simply using polite forms of address, it is not possible to say on first meeting a person whether or not that person has good manners.

(C)   Acrophobia, usually defined as a morbid fear of heights, can also mean a morbid fear of sharp objects. Since both fears have the same name, they undoubtedly have the same origin.

(D)   There is no doubt that a deed is heroic if the doer risks his or her own life to benefit another person. Thus an action is not heroic if the only thing it endangers is the reputation of the doer.

(E)   Perception of beauty in an object is determined by past and present influences on the mind of the beholder. Thus no object can be called beautiful, since not everyone will see beauty in it.

21. The Japanese *haiku* is defined as a poem of three lines with five syllables in the first line, seven syllables in the second line, and five syllables in the third line. English poets tend to ignore this fact. Disregarding syllable count, they generally call any three-line English poem with a "*haiku* feel" a *haiku*. This demonstrates that English poets have little respect for foreign traditions, even those from which some of their own poetry derives.

The reasoning is flawed because it

(A)   confuses matters of objective fact with matters of subjective feeling

(B)   draws a conclusion that is broader in scope than is warranted by the evidence advanced

(C)   relies on stereotypes instead of presenting evidence

(D)   overlooks the possibility that the case it cites is not unique

(E)   fails to acknowledge that ignoring something implies a negative judgment about that thing

GO ON TO THE NEXT PAGE.

Questions 22–23

No one knows what purposes, if any, dreams serve, although there are a number of hypotheses. According to one hypothesis, dreams are produced when the brain is erasing "parasitic connections" (meaningless, accidental associations between ideas), which accumulate during the day and which would otherwise clog up our memories. Interestingly, the only mammal that does not have rapid eye movement sleep, in which we humans typically have our most vivid dreams, is the spiny anteater, which has been seen as anomalous in that it has a very large brain relative to the animal's size. This fact provides some confirmation for the parasitic-connection hypothesis, since the hypothesis predicts that for an animal that did not dream to have an effective memory that animal would need extra memory space for the parasitic connections.

22. The parasitic-connection hypothesis, if true, most strongly supports which one of the following?

(A) The animals with the smallest brains spend the most time sleeping.

(B) Immediately after a person awakens from normal sleep, her or his memory contains virtually no accidental associations between ideas.

(C) When a mammal that would normally dream is prevented from dreaming, the functioning of its memory will be impaired.

(D) Insofar as a person's description of a dream involves meaningful associations between ideas, it is an inaccurate description.

(E) All animals other than the spiny anteater dream.

23. The reasoning in the argument most closely conforms to which one of the following principles?

(A) Facts about one species of animal can provide confirmation for hypotheses about all species that are similar in all relevant respects to the particular species in question.

(B) A hypothesis from which several predictions can be drawn as logical conclusions is confirmed only when the majority of these predictions turn out to be true.

(C) A hypothesis about the purpose of an action or object is confirmed when it is shown that the hypothesized purpose is achieved with the help of the action or object and could not be achieved without that action or object.

(D) A hypothesis is partially confirmed whenever a prediction derived from that hypothesis provides an explanation for an otherwise unexplained set of facts.

(E) When several competing hypotheses exist, one of them is confirmed only when it makes a correct prediction that its rivals fail to make.

GO ON TO THE NEXT PAGE.

24. The body of anyone infected by virus X will, after a week, produce antibodies to fight the virus; the antibodies will increase in number for the next year or so. There is now a test that reliably indicates how many antibodies are present in a person's body. If positive, this test can be used during the first year of infection to estimate to within a month how long that person has had the virus.

Which one of the following conclusions is best supported by the statements above?

(A) Antibodies increase in number only until they have defeated the virus.

(B) Without the test for antibodies, there is no way of establishing whether a person has virus X.

(C) Antibodies are produced only for viral infections that cannot be fought by any other body defenses.

(D) If a person remains infected by virus X indefinitely, there is no limit to the number of antibodies that can be present in the person's body.

(E) Anyone infected by virus X will for a time fail to exhibit infection if tested by the antibody test.

25. Large inequalities in wealth always threaten the viability of true democracy, since wealth is the basis of political power, and true democracy depends on the equal distribution of political power among all citizens.

The reasoning in which one of the following arguments most closely parallels the reasoning in the argument above?

(A) Consumer culture and an emphasis on technological innovation are a dangerous combination, since together they are uncontrollable and lead to irrational excess.

(B) If Sara went to the bookstore every time her pocket was full, Sara would never have enough money to cover her living expenses, since books are her love and they are getting very expensive.

(C) It is very difficult to write a successful science fiction novel that is set in the past, since historical fiction depends on historical accuracy, whereas science fiction does not.

(D) Honesty is important in maintaining friendships. But sometimes honesty can lead to arguments, so it is difficult to predict the effect a particular honest act will have on a friendship.

(E) Repeated encroachments on one's leisure time by a demanding job interfere with the requirements of good health. The reason is that good health depends on regular moderate exercise, but adequate leisure time is essential to regular exercise.

S T O P

IF YOU FINISH BEFORE TIME IS CALLED, YOU MAY CHECK YOUR WORK ON THIS SECTION ONLY.
DO NOT WORK ON ANY OTHER SECTION IN THE TEST.

SECTION II

Time—35 minutes

24 Questions

Directions: Each group of questions in this section is based on a set of conditions. In answering some of the questions, it may be useful to draw a rough diagram. Choose the response that most accurately and completely answers each question and blacken the corresponding space on your answer sheet.

Questions 1–5

On the basis of an examination, nine students—Fred, Glen, Hilary, Ida, Jan, Kathy, Laura, Mike, and Nick—are each placed in one of three classes. The three highest scorers are placed in the level 1 class; the three lowest scorers are placed in the level 3 class. The remaining three are placed in the level 2 class. Each class has exactly three students.

Ida scores higher than Glen.
Glen scores higher than both Jan and Kathy.
Jan scores higher than Mike.
Mike scores higher than Hilary.
Hilary scores higher than Nick.
Kathy scores higher than both Fred and Laura.

1. How many different combinations of students could form the level 1 class?

    (A) one
    (B) two
    (C) three
    (D) four
    (E) six

2. Which one of the following students could be in the level 2 class but cannot be in the level 3 class?

    (A) Fred
    (B) Glen
    (C) Jan
    (D) Kathy
    (E) Nick

3. Which one of the following students could be placed in any one of the three classes?

    (A) Fred
    (B) Jan
    (C) Kathy
    (D) Laura
    (E) Mike

4. The composition of each class can be completely determined if which one of the following pairs of students is known to be in the level 2 class?

    (A) Fred and Kathy
    (B) Fred and Mike
    (C) Hilary and Jan
    (D) Kathy and Laura
    (E) Laura and Mike

5. Which one of the following pairs of students cannot be in the same class as Fred?

    (A) Hilary and Nick
    (B) Jan and Laura
    (C) Kathy and Laura
    (D) Jan and Mike
    (E) Laura and Mike

GO ON TO THE NEXT PAGE.

Questions 6-12

Six reviewers—Frank, George, Hilda, Jackie, Karl, and Lena—will review four movies—*Mystery, Retreat, Seasonings,* and *Wolves*—according to the following conditions:

Each reviewer reviews exactly one movie, and each movie is reviewed by at least one of the six reviewers.
Hilda reviews the same movie as Frank.
Lena reviews the same movie as exactly one other reviewer.
George reviews *Mystery*.
Jackie reviews either *Mystery* or else *Wolves*.
Hilda does not review *Wolves*.

6. If Lena reviews *Seasonings*, which one of the following must be true?

    (A) Hilda reviews *Retreat*.
    (B) Jackie reviews *Seasonings*.
    (C) Karl reviews *Mystery*.
    (D) Karl reviews *Retreat*.
    (E) Karl reviews *Wolves*.

7. If Karl does not review *Seasonings*, which one of the following must be true?

    (A) Lena reviews *Mystery*.
    (B) Lena reviews *Retreat*.
    (C) Lena reviews *Seasonings*.
    (D) Frank and Hilda review *Retreat*.
    (E) Frank and Hilda review *Seasonings*.

8. Which one of the following is a complete and accurate list of the movies each of which could be the movie that Lena reviews?

    (A) *Mystery, Retreat*
    (B) *Retreat, Seasonings*
    (C) *Mystery, Seasonings, Wolves*
    (D) *Retreat, Seasonings, Wolves*
    (E) *Mystery, Retreat, Seasonings, Wolves*

9. Which one of the following can be true?

    (A) Frank and George review *Mystery*.
    (B) Frank and Lena review *Wolves*.
    (C) George and Jackie review *Mystery*.
    (D) Karl reviews *Wolves* and Lena reviews *Mystery*.
    (E) Lena reviews *Retreat* and Frank reviews *Seasonings*.

10. Lena can review any of the following EXCEPT

    (A) *Mystery* with George
    (B) *Mystery* with Karl
    (C) *Retreat* with Karl
    (D) *Seasonings* with Karl
    (E) *Wolves* with Jackie

11. If Karl reviews the same movie as exactly one other reviewer, which one of the following is a complete and accurate list of the movies any one of which could be the movie that these two reviewers review?

    (A) *Mystery, Retreat*
    (B) *Mystery, Seasonings*
    (C) *Retreat, Seasonings*
    (D) *Mystery, Seasonings, Wolves*
    (E) *Retreat, Seasonings, Wolves*

12. Which one of the following is an acceptable assignment of reviewers to movies?

	Mystery	*Retreat*	*Seasonings*	*Wolves*
(A)	George	Frank, Hilda	Jackie, Lena	Karl
(B)	George	Frank, Hilda	Karl, Lena	Jackie
(C)	George	Karl, Lena	Jackie	Frank, Hilda
(D)	George, Karl	Frank, Hilda	Lena	Jackie
(E)	Jackie	George, Lena	Frank, Hilda	Karl

GO ON TO THE NEXT PAGE.

Questions 13-18

In a game, "words" (real or nonsensical) consist of any combination of at least four letters of the English alphabet. Any "sentence" consists of exactly five words and satisfies the following conditions:

The five words are written from left to right on a single line in alphabetical order.

The sentence is started by any word, and each successive word is formed by applying exactly one of three operations to the word immediately to its left: delete one letter; add one letter; replace one letter with another letter.

At most three of the five words begin with the same letter as one another.

Except for the leftmost word, each word is formed by a different operation from that which formed the word immediately to its left.

13. Which one of the following could be a sentence in the word game?

(A) bzeak   bleak   leak   peak   pea
(B) crbek   creek   reek   seek   sxeek
(C) dteam   gleam   glean   lean   mean
(D) feed   freed   reed   seed   seeg
(E) food   fool   fools   fopls   opls

14. The last letter of the alphabet that the first word of a sentence in the word game can begin with is

(A) t
(B) w
(C) x
(D) y
(E) z

15. If the first word in a sentence is "blender" and the third word is "slender," then the second word can be

(A) bender
(B) gender
(C) lender
(D) sender
(E) tender

16. If the first word in a sentence consists of nine letters, then the minimum number of letters that the fourth word can contain is

(A) four
(B) five
(C) six
(D) seven
(E) eight

17. If "clean" is the first word in a sentence and "learn" is another word in the sentence, then which one of the following is a complete and accurate list of the positions each of which could be the position in which "learn" occurs in the sentence?

(A) second
(B) third
(C) fourth, fifth
(D) second, third, fourth
(E) third, fourth, fifth

18. If the first word in a sentence consists of four letters, then the maximum number of letters that the fifth word in this sentence could contain is

(A) four
(B) five
(C) six
(D) seven
(E) eight

GO ON TO THE NEXT PAGE.

Questions 19–24

A soloist will play six different guitar concertos, exactly one each Sunday for six consecutive weeks. Two concertos will be selected from among three concertos by Giuliani— H, J, and K; two from among four concertos by Rodrigo— M, N, O, and P; and two from among three concertos by Vivaldi—X, Y, and Z. The following conditions apply without exception:

If N is selected, then J is also selected.
If M is selected, then neither J nor O can be selected.
If X is selected, then neither Z nor P can be selected.
If both J and O are selected, then J is played at some time before O.
X cannot be played on the fifth Sunday unless one of Rodrigo's concertos is played on the first Sunday.

19. Which one of the following is an acceptable selection of concertos that the soloist could play on the first through the sixth Sunday?

	1	2	3	4	5	6
(A)	H	Z	M	N	Y	K
(B)	K	J	Y	O	Z	N
(C)	K	Y	P	J	Z	M
(D)	P	Y	J	H	X	O
(E)	X	N	K	O	J	Z

20. If the six concertos to be played are J, K, N, O, Y, and Z and if N is to be played on the first Sunday, then which one of the following concertos CANNOT be played on the second Sunday?

(A) J
(B) K
(C) O
(D) Y
(E) Z

21. If J, O, and Y are the first three concertos to be played, not necessarily in the order given, which one of the following is a concerto that CANNOT be played on the fifth Sunday?

(A) H
(B) K
(C) N
(D) P
(E) X

22. If O is selected for the first Sunday, which one of the following is a concerto that must also be selected?

(A) J
(B) K
(C) M
(D) N
(E) X

23. Which one of the following is a concerto that must be selected?

(A) J
(B) K
(C) O
(D) Y
(E) Z

24. Which one of the following is a concerto that CANNOT be selected together with N ?

(A) M
(B) O
(C) P
(D) X
(E) Z

S T O P

IF YOU FINISH BEFORE TIME IS CALLED, YOU MAY CHECK YOUR WORK ON THIS SECTION ONLY.
DO NOT WORK ON ANY OTHER SECTION IN THE TEST.

SECTION III

Time—35 minutes

27 Questions

<u>Directions:</u> Each passage in this section is followed by a group of questions to be answered on the basis of what is <u>stated</u> or <u>implied</u> in the passage. For some of the questions, more than one of the choices could conceivably answer the question. However, you are to choose the <u>best</u> answer; that is, the response that most accurately and completely answers the question, and blacken the corresponding space on your answer sheet.

Oil companies need offshore platforms primarily because the oil or natural gas the companies extract from the ocean floor has to be processed before pumps can be used to move the substances ashore.
(5) But because processing crude (unprocessed oil or gas) on a platform rather than at facilities onshore exposes workers to the risks of explosion and to an unpredictable environment, researchers are attempting to diminish the need for human labor
(10) on platforms and even to eliminate platforms altogether by redesigning two kinds of pumps to handle crude. These pumps could then be used to boost the natural pressure driving the flow of crude, which, by itself, is sufficient only to bring
(15) the crude to the platform, located just above the wellhead. Currently, pumps that could boost this natural pressure sufficiently to drive the crude through a pipeline to the shore do not work consistently because of the crude's content. Crude
(20) may consist of oil or natural gas in multiphase states—combinations of liquids, gases, and solids under pressure—that do not reach the wellhead in constant proportions. The flow of crude oil, for example, can change quickly from 60 percent liquid
(25) to 70 percent gas. This surge in gas content causes loss of "head," or pressure inside a pump, with the result that a pump can no longer impart enough energy to transport the crude mixture through the pipeline and to the shore.
(30) Of the two pumps being redesigned, the positive-displacement pump is promising because it is immune to sudden shifts in the proportion of liquid to gas in the crude mixture. But the pump's design, which consists of a single or twin screw
(35) pushing the fluid from one end of the pump to the other, brings crude into close contact with most parts of the pump, and thus requires that it be made of expensive, corrosion-resistant material. The alternative is the centrifugal pump, which has a
(40) rotating impeller that sucks fluid in at one end and forces fluid out at the other. Although this pump has a proven design and has worked for years with little maintenance in waste-disposal plants, researchers have discovered that because the swirl
(45) of its impeller separates gas out from the oil that normally accompanies it, significant reductions in head can occur as it operates.
Research in the development of these pumps is focused mainly on trying to reduce the cost of the
(50) positive-displacement pump and attempting to

make the centrifugal pump more tolerant of gas. Other researchers are looking at ways of adapting either kind of pump for use underwater, so that crude could be moved directly from the sea bottom
(55) to processing facilities onshore, eliminating platforms.

1. Which one of the following best expresses the main idea of the passage?

    (A) Oil companies are experimenting with technologies that may help diminish the danger to workers from offshore crude processing.
    (B) Oil companies are seeking methods of installing processing facilities underwater.
    (C) Researchers are developing several new pumps designed to enhance human labor efficiency in processing facilities.
    (D) Researchers are seeking to develop equipment that would preempt the need for processing facilities onshore.
    (E) Researchers are seeking ways to separate liquids from gases in crude in order to enable safer processing.

2. The passage supports which one of the following statements about the natural pressure driving the flow of crude?

    (A) It is higher than that created by the centrifugal pump.
    (B) It is constant, regardless of relative proportions of gas and liquid.
    (C) It is able to carry the crude only as far as the wellhead.
    (D) It is able to carry the crude to the platform.
    (E) It is able to carry the crude to the shore.

GO ON TO THE NEXT PAGE.

3. Which one of the following best describes the relationship of the second paragraph to the passage as a whole?

(A) It offers concrete detail designed to show that the argument made in the first paragraph is flawed.

(B) It provides detail that expands upon the information presented in the first paragraph.

(C) It enhances the author's discussion by objectively presenting in detail the pros and cons of a claim made in the first paragraph.

(D) It detracts from the author's discussion by presenting various problems that qualify the goals presented.

(E) It modifies an observation made in the first paragraph by detailing viewpoints against it.

4. Which one of the following phrases, if substituted for the word "head" in line 47, would LEAST change the meaning of the sentence?

(A) the flow of the crude inside the pump

(B) the volume of oil inside the pump

(C) the volume of gas inside the pump

(D) the speed of the impeller moving the crude

(E) the pressure inside of the pump

5. With which one of the following statements regarding offshore platforms would the author most likely agree?

(A) If a reduction of human labor on offshore platforms is achieved, there is no real need to eliminate platforms altogether.

(B) Reducing human labor on offshore platforms is desirable because researchers' knowledge about the transportation of crude is dangerously incomplete.

(C) The dangers involved in working on offshore platforms make their elimination a desirable goal.

(D) The positive-displacement pump is the better alternative for researchers, because it would allow them to eliminate platforms altogether.

(E) Though researchers have succeeded in reducing human labor on offshore platforms, they think that it would be inadvisable to eliminate platforms altogether, because these platforms have other uses.

6. Which one of the following can be inferred from the passage about pumps that are currently available to boost the natural pressure of crude?

(A) The efficiency of these pumps depends on there being no gas in the flow of crude.

(B) These pumps are more efficient when the crude is less subject to sudden increases in the proportion of gas to liquid.

(C) A sudden change from solid to liquid in the flow of crude increases the efficiency of these pumps.

(D) The proportion of liquid to gas in the flow of crude does not affect the efficiency of these pumps.

(E) A sudden change from liquid to gas in the flow of crude increases the risk of explosion due to rising pressure inside these pumps.

7. The passage implies that the positive-displacement pump differs from the centrifugal pump in that the positive-displacement pump

(A) is more promising, but it also is more expensive and demands more maintenance

(B) is especially well researched, since it has been used in other settings

(C) involves the use of a single or twin screw that sucks fluid in at one end of the pump

(D) is problematic because it causes rapid shifts from liquid to gas content in crude

(E) involves exposure of many parts of the pump to crude

8. The passage implies that the current state of technology necessitates that crude be moved to shore

(A) in a multiphase state

(B) in equal proportions of gas to liquid

(C) with small proportions of corrosive material

(D) after having been processed

(E) largely in the form of a liquid

GO ON TO THE NEXT PAGE.

To critics accustomed to the style of fifteenth-century narrative paintings by Italian artists from Tuscany, the Venetian examples of narrative paintings with religious subjects that
(5) Patricia Fortini Brown analyzes in a recent book will come as a great surprise. While the Tuscan paintings present large-scale figures, clear narratives, and simple settings, the Venetians filled their pictures with dozens of small figures and
(10) elaborate buildings, in addition to a wealth of carefully observed anecdotal detail often irrelevant to the paintings' principal subjects—the religious stories they narrate. Although it occasionally obscured these stories, this accumulation of
(15) circumstantial detail from Venetian life—the inclusion of prominent Venetian citizens, for example—was considered appropriate to the narration of historical subjects and underlined the authenticity of the historical events depicted.
(20) Indeed, Brown argues that the distinctive style of the Venetian paintings—what she calls the "eyewitness style"—was influenced by Venetian affinity for a strongly parochial type of historical writing, consisting almost exclusively of vernacular
(25) chronicles of local events embroidered with all kinds of inconsequential detail.

And yet, while Venetian attitudes toward history that are reflected in their art account in part for the difference in style between Venetian and Tuscan
(30) narrative paintings, Brown has overlooked some practical influences, such as climate. Tuscan churches are filled with frescoes that, in contrast to Venetian narrative paintings, consist mainly of large figures and easily recognized religious stories, as one would
(35) expect of paintings that are normally viewed from a distance and are designed primarily to remind the faithful of their religious tenets. In Venice, where the damp climate is unsuited to fresco, narrative frescoes in churches were almost nonexistent, with
(40) the result that Venetian artists and their public had no practical experience of the large-scale representation of familiar religious stories. Their model for painted stories was the cycle of secular historical paintings in the Venetian magistrate's
(45) palace, which were indeed the counterpart of written history and were made all the more authoritative by a proliferation of circumstantial detail.

Moreover, because painting frescoes requires an
(50) unusually sure hand, particularly in the representation of the human form, the development of drawing skill was central to artistic training in Tuscany, and by 1500 the public there tended to distinguish artists on the basis of how well they could draw
(55) human figures. In Venice, a city virtually without frescoes, this kind of skill was acquired and appreciated much later. Gentile Bellini, for example, although regarded as one of the supreme painters of the day, was feeble at drawing. On the
(60) other hand, the emphasis on architecture so evident

in the Venetian narrative paintings was something that local painters obviously prized, largely because painting architecture in perspective was seen as a particular test of the Venetian painter's skill.

9. Which one of the following best states the main idea of the passage?

(A) Tuscan painters' use of fresco explains the prominence of human figures in the narrative paintings that they produced during the fifteenth century.

(B) In addition to fifteenth-century Venetian attitudes toward history, other factors may help to explain the characteristic features of Venetian narrative paintings with religious subjects produced during that period.

(C) The inclusion of authentic detail from Venetian life distinguished fifteenth-century Venetian narrative paintings from those that were produced in Tuscany.

(D) Venetian painters were generally more skilled at painting buildings than Tuscan painters were at drawing human forms.

(E) The cycle of secular historical paintings in the Venetian magistrate's palace was the primary influence on fifteenth-century Venetian narrative paintings with religious subjects.

10. In the passage, the author is primarily concerned with

(A) pointing out the superiority of one painting style over another

(B) citing evidence that requires a reevaluation of a conventionally held view

(C) discussing factors that explain a difference in painting styles

(D) outlining the strengths and weaknesses of two opposing views regarding the evolution of a painting style

(E) arguing for the irrelevance of one theory and for its replacement by a more plausible alternative

GO ON TO THE NEXT PAGE.

11. As it is described in the passage, Brown's explanation of the use of the eyewitness style in Venetian narrative painting suggests that

(A) the painting of architecture in perspective requires greater drawing skill than does the representation of a human form in a fresco

(B) certain characteristics of a style of painting can reflect a style of historical writing that was common during the same period

(C) the eyewitness style in Venetian narrative paintings with religious subjects was largely the result of the influence of Tuscan artists who worked primarily in fresco

(D) the historical detail in Venetian narrative paintings with religious subjects can be traced primarily to the influence of the paintings in the Venetian magistrate's palace

(E) a style of painting can be dramatically transformed by a sudden influx of artists from another region

12. The author suggests that fifteenth-century Venetian narrative paintings with religious subjects were painted by artists who

(A) were able to draw human figures with more skill after they were apprenticed to painters in Tuscany

(B) assumed that their paintings would typically be viewed from a distance

(C) were a major influence on the artists who produced the cycle of historical paintings in the Venetian magistrate's palace

(D) were reluctant to paint frescoes primarily because they lacked the drawing skill that painting frescoes required

(E) were better at painting architecture in perspective than they were at drawing human figures

13. The author implies that Venetian narrative paintings with religious subjects included the representation of elaborate buildings in part because

(A) the ability to paint architecture in perspective was seen in Venice as proof of a painter's skill

(B) the subjects of such paintings were often religious stories

(C) large frescoes were especially conducive to representing architecture in perspective

(D) the architecture of Venice in the fifteenth century was more elaborate than was the architecture of Tuscany

(E) the paintings were imitations of a kind of historical writing that was popular in Tuscany

14. Which one of the following, if true, would most weaken the author's contention that fifteenth-century Venetian artists "had no practical experience of the large-scale representation of familiar religious stories" (lines 40–42)?

(A) The style of secular historical paintings in the palace of the Venetian magistrate was similar to that of Venetian narrative paintings with religious subjects.

(B) The style of the historical writing produced by fifteenth-century Venetian authors was similar in its inclusion of anecdotal details to secular paintings produced during that century in Tuscany.

(C) Many of the artists who produced Venetian narrative paintings with religious subjects served as apprentices in Tuscany, where they had become familiar with the technique of painting frescoes.

(D) Few of the frescoes painted in Tuscany during the fifteenth century had secular subjects, and those that did often betrayed the artist's inability to represent elaborate architecture in perspective.

(E) Few of the Venetian narrative paintings produced toward the end of the fifteenth century show evidence of the enhanced drawing skill that characterized the paintings produced in Venice a century later.

GO ON TO THE NEXT PAGE.

Currently, legal scholars agree that in some cases legal rules do not specify a definite outcome. These scholars believe that such indeterminacy results from the vagueness of language: the boundaries of
(5) the application of a term are often unclear. Nevertheless, they maintain that the system of legal rules by and large rests on clear core meanings that do determine definite outcomes for most cases. Contrary to this view, an earlier group of legal
(10) philosophers, called "realists," argued that indeterminacy pervades every part of the law.

The realists held that there is always a cluster of rules relevant to the decision in any litigated case. For example, deciding whether an aunt's promise to
(15) pay her niece a sum of money if she refrained from smoking is enforceable would involve a number of rules regarding such issues as offer, acceptance, and revocation. Linguistic vagueness in any one of these rules would affect the outcome of the case, making
(20) possible multiple points of indeterminacy, not just one or two, in any legal case.

For the realists, an even more damaging kind of indeterminacy stems from the fact that in a common-law system based on precedent, a judge's
(25) decision is held to be binding on judges in subsequent similar cases. Judicial decisions are expressed in written opinions, commonly held to consist of two parts: the holding (the decision for or against the plaintiff and the essential grounds or
(30) legal reasons for it, that is, what subsequent judges are bound by), and the dicta (everything in an opinion not essential to the decision, for example, comments about points of law not treated as the basis of the outcome). The realists argued that in
(35) practice the common-law system treats the "holding/dicta" distinction loosely. They pointed out that even when the judge writing an opinion characterizes part of it as "the holding," judges writing subsequent opinions, although unlikely to
(40) dispute the decision itself, are not bound by the original judge's perception of what was essential to the decision. Later judges have tremendous leeway in being able to redefine the holding and the dicta in a precedential case. This leeway enables judges to
(45) choose which rules of law formed the basis of the decision in the earlier case. When judging almost any case, then, a judge can find a relevant precedential case which, in subsequent opinions, has been read by one judge as stating one legal
(50) rule, and by another judge as stating another, possibly contradictory one. A judge thus faces an indeterminate legal situation in which he or she has to choose which rules are to govern the case at hand.

15. According to the passage, the realists argued that which one of the following is true of a common-law system?

(A) It gives rise to numerous situations in which the decisions of earlier judges are found to be in error by later judges.

(B) It possesses a clear set of legal rules in theory, but in practice most judges are unaware of the strict meaning of those rules.

(C) Its strength lies in the requirement that judges decide cases according to precedent rather than according to a set of abstract principles.

(D) It would be improved if judges refrained from willfully misinterpreting the written opinions of prior judges.

(E) It treats the difference between the holding and the dicta in a written opinion rather loosely in practice.

16. According to the passage, which one of the following best describes the relationship between a judicial holding and a judicial decision?

(A) The holding is not commonly considered binding on subsequent judges, but the decision is.

(B) The holding formally states the outcome of the case, while the decision explains it.

(C) The holding explains the decision but does not include it.

(D) The holding consists of the decision and the dicta.

(E) The holding sets forth and justifies a decision.

17. The information in the passage suggests that the realists would most likely have agreed with which one of the following statements about the reaction of judges to past interpretations of a precedential case, each of which states a different legal rule?

(A) The judges would most likely disagree with one or more of the interpretations and overturn the earlier judges' decisions.

(B) The judges might differ from each other concerning which of the interpretations would apply in a given case.

(C) The judges probably would consider themselves bound by all the legal rules stated in the interpretations.

(D) The judges would regard the lack of unanimity among interpretations as evidence that no precedents existed.

(E) The judges would point out in their holdings the inherent contradictions arising from the earlier judges' differing interpretations.

GO ON TO THE NEXT PAGE.

18. It can be inferred from the passage that most legal scholars today would agree with the realists that

   (A) linguistic vagueness can cause indeterminacy regarding the outcome of a litigated case
   (B) in any litigated case, several different and possibly contradictory legal rules are relevant to the decision of the case
   (C) the distinction between holding and dicta in a written opinion is usually difficult to determine in practice
   (D) the boundaries of applicability of terms may sometimes be difficult to determine, but the core meanings of the terms are well established
   (E) a common-law system gives judges tremendous leeway in interpreting precedents, and contradictory readings of precedential cases can usually be found

19. The passage suggests that the realists believed which one of the following to be true of the dicta in a judge's written opinion?

   (A) The judge writing the opinion is usually careful to specify those parts of the opinion he or she considers part of the dicta.
   (B) The appropriateness of the judge's decision would be disputed by subsequent judges on the basis of legal rules expressed in the dicta.
   (C) A consensus concerning what constitutes the dicta in a judge's opinion comes to be fixed over time as subsequent similar cases are decided.
   (D) Subsequent judges can consider parts of what the original judge saw as the dicta to be essential to the original opinion.
   (E) The judge's decision and the grounds for it are usually easily distinguishable from the dicta.

20. Which one of the following best describes the overall organization of the passage?

   (A) A traditional point of view is explained and problems arising from it are described.
   (B) Two conflicting systems of thought are compared point for point and then evaluated.
   (C) A legal concept is defined and arguments justifying that definition are refuted.
   (D) Two viewpoints on an issue are briefly described and one of those viewpoints is discussed at greater length.
   (E) A theoretical description of how a system develops is contrasted with the actual practices characterizing the system.

21. Which one of the following titles best reflects the content of the passage?

   (A) Legal Indeterminacy: The Debate Continues
   (B) Holding Versus Dicta: A Distinction Without a Difference
   (C) Linguistic Vagueness: Is It Circumscribed in Legal Terminology?
   (D) Legal Indeterminacy: The Realist's View of Its Scope
   (E) Legal Rules and the Precedential System: How Judges Interpret the Precedents

GO ON TO THE NEXT PAGE.

Years after the movement to obtain civil rights for black people in the United States made its most important gains, scholars are reaching for a theoretical perspective capable of clarifying its

(5) momentous developments. New theories of social movements are being discussed, not just among social psychologists, but also among political theorists.

Of the many competing formulations of the

(10) "classical" social psychological theory of social movement, three are prominent in the literature on the civil rights movement: "rising expectations," "relative deprivation," and "J-curve." Each conforms to a causal sequence characteristic of

(15) classical social movement theory, linking some unusual condition, or "system strain," to the generation of unrest. When these versions of the classical theory are applied to the civil rights movement, the source of strain is identified as a

(20) change in black socioeconomic status that occurred shortly before the widespread protest activity of the movement.

For example, the theory of rising expectations asserts that protest activity was a response to

(25) psychological tensions generated by gains experienced immediately prior to the civil rights movement. Advancement did not satisfy ambition, but created the desire for further advancement. Only slightly different is the theory of relative

(30) deprivation. Here the impetus to protest is identified as gains achieved during the premovement period, coupled with simultaneous failure to make any appreciable headway relative to the dominant group. The J-curve theory argues that the movement

(35) occurred because a prolonged period of rising expectations and gratification was followed by a sharp reversal.

Political theorists have been dismissive of these applications of classical theory to the civil rights

(40) movement. Their arguments rest on the conviction that, implicitly, the classical theory trivializes the political ends of movement participants, focusing rather on presumed psychological dysfunctions; reduction of complex social situations to simple

(45) paradigms of stimulus and response obviates the relevance of all but the shortest-term analysis. Furthermore, the theories lack predictive value: "strain" is always present to some degree, but social movement is not. How can we know which

(50) strain will provoke upheaval?

These very legitimate complaints having frequently been made, it remains to find a means of testing the strength of the theories. Problematically, while proponents of the various theories have

(55) contradictory interpretations of socioeconomic conditions leading to the civil rights movement, examination of various statistical records regarding the material status of black Americans yields ample evidence to support any of the three theories. The

(60) steady rise in median black family income supports

the rising expectations hypothesis; the stability of the economic position of black vis-à-vis white Americans lends credence to the relative deprivation interpretation; unemployment data are consistent

(65) with the J-curve theory. A better test is the comparison of each of these economic indicators with the frequency of movement-initiated events reported in the press; unsurprisingly, none correlates significantly with the pace of reports

(70) about movement activity.

22. It can be inferred from the passage that the classical theory of social movement would not be appropriately applied to an annual general election because such an election

(A) may focus on personalities rather than on political issues
(B) is not provoked primarily by an unusual condition
(C) may be decided according to the psychological needs of voters
(D) may not entail momentous developments
(E) actually entails two or more distinct social movements

23. According to the passage, the "rising expectations" and "relative deprivation" models differ in which one of the following ways?

(A) They predict different responses to the same socioeconomic conditions.
(B) They disagree about the relevance of psychological explanations for protest movements.
(C) They are meant to explain different kinds of social change.
(D) They describe the motivation of protesters in slightly different ways.
(E) They disagree about the relevance of socioeconomic status to system strain.

24. The author implies that political theorists attribute which one of the following assumptions to social psychologists who apply the classical theory of social movements to the civil rights movement?

(A) Participants in any given social movement have conflicting motivations.
(B) Social movements are ultimately beneficial to society.
(C) Only strain of a socioeconomic nature can provoke a social movement.
(D) The political ends of movement participants are best analyzed in terms of participants' psychological motivations.
(E) Psychological motivations of movement participants better illuminate the causes of social movements than do participants' political motivations.

GO ON TO THE NEXT PAGE.

25. Which one of the following statements is supported by the results of the "better test" discussed in the last paragraph of the passage?

    (A) The test confirms the three classical theories discussed in the passage.
    (B) The test provides no basis for deciding among the three classical theories discussed in the passage.
    (C) The test shows that it is impossible to apply any theory of social movements to the civil rights movement.
    (D) The test indicates that press coverage of the civil rights movement was biased.
    (E) The test verifies that the civil rights movement generated socioeconomic progress.

26. The validity of the "better test" (line 65) as proposed by the author might be undermined by the fact that

    (A) the press is selective about the movement activities it chooses to cover
    (B) not all economic indicators receive the same amount of press coverage
    (C) economic indicators often contradict one another
    (D) a movement-initiated event may not correlate significantly with any of the three economic indicators
    (E) the pace of movement-initiated events is difficult to anticipate

27. The main purpose of the passage is to

    (A) persuade historians of the indispensability of a theoretical framework for understanding recent history
    (B) present a new model of social movement
    (C) account for a shift in a theoretical debate
    (D) show the unity underlying the diverse classical models of social movement
    (E) discuss the reasoning behind and shortcomings of certain social psychological theories

S T O P

IF YOU FINISH BEFORE TIME IS CALLED, YOU MAY CHECK YOUR WORK ON THIS SECTION ONLY.
DO NOT WORK ON ANY OTHER SECTION IN THE TEST.

SECTION IV

Time—35 minutes

25 Questions

<u>Directions:</u> The questions in this section are based on the reasoning contained in brief statements or passages. For some questions, more than one of the choices could conceivably answer the question. However, you are to choose the <u>best</u> answer; that is, the response that most accurately and completely answers the question. You should not make assumptions that are by commonsense standards implausible, superfluous, or incompatible with the passage. After you have chosen the best answer, blacken the corresponding space on your answer sheet.

Questions 1–2

A physician who is too thorough in conducting a medical checkup is likely to subject the patient to the discomfort and expense of unnecessary tests. One who is not thorough enough is likely to miss some serious problem and therefore give the patient a false sense of security. It is difficult for physicians to judge exactly how thorough they should be. Therefore, it is generally unwise for patients to have medical checkups when they do not feel ill.

1. Which one of the following, if true, would most seriously weaken the argument in the passage?

    (A) Some serious diseases in their early stages have symptoms that physicians can readily detect, although patients are not aware of any problem.

    (B) Under the pressure of reduced reimbursements, physicians have been reducing the average amount of time they spend on each medical checkup.

    (C) Patients not medically trained are unable to judge for themselves what degree of thoroughness is appropriate for physicians in conducting medical checkups.

    (D) Many people are financially unable to afford regular medical checkups.

    (E) Some physicians sometimes exercise exactly the right degree of thoroughness in performing a medical checkup.

2. Which one of the following, if true, would provide the most support for the conclusion in the passage?

    (A) Not all medical tests entail significant discomfort.

    (B) Sometimes, unnecessary medical tests cause healthy people to become ill.

    (C) Some patients refuse to accept a physician's assurance that the patient is healthy.

    (D) The more complete the series of tests performed in a medical checkup, the more likely it is that a rare disease, if present, will be discovered.

    (E) Physicians can eliminate the need to order certain tests by carefully questioning patients and rejecting some possibilities on that basis.

3. People often pronounce a word differently when asked to read written material aloud than when speaking spontaneously. These differences may cause problems for those who develop computers that recognize speech. Usually the developers "train" the computers by using samples of written material read by the people who will be using the computer.

    The observations above provide most evidence for the conclusion that

    (A) it will be impossible to develop computers that decode spontaneous speech

    (B) when reading written material, people who have different accents pronounce the same word in the same way as one another

    (C) computers may be less reliable in decoding spontaneous speech than in decoding samples that have been read aloud

    (D) a "trained" computer never correctly decodes the spontaneous speech of a person whose voice sample was used to train it

    (E) computers are now able to interpret oral speech without error

4. One of the requirements for admission to the Lunnville Roller Skating Club is a high degree of skill in roller skating. The club president has expressed concern that the club may have discriminated against qualified women in its admissions this year. Yet half of the applicants admitted to the club this year were women. This proves that there was no discrimination against qualified women applicants in the club's admissions this year.

    Which one of the following is an assumption on which the conclusion of the argument depends?

    (A) Only a few applicants were found to be qualified and were admitted to the club this year.

    (B) No more than half of all the roller skaters in Lunnville are women.

    (C) No more than half of all the roller skaters in Lunnville are men.

    (D) This year no more than half of the applicants who met all the qualifications for admission to the club were women.

    (E) This year no more than half of the members of the club's committee that makes decisions about applicants' qualifications were men.

GO ON TO THE NEXT PAGE.

5. When girls are educated in single-sex secondary schools, they tend to do better academically than girls who attend mixed-sex schools. Since Alice achieved higher grades than any other woman in her first year at the university, she was probably educated at a single-sex school.

Which one of the following most closely parallels the flawed reasoning used in the argument above?

(A) When students have individual tutoring in math, they usually get good grades on their final exams. Celia had individual tutoring in math so she will probably get a good grade.

(B) When babies are taught to swim, they have more than the average number of ear infections as they grow up. Janice has more ear infections than any other person at the local swimming club, so she probably was taught to swim when she was a baby.

(C) When children study music at an early age, they later tend to appreciate a wide variety of music, so the talent of future musicians is best fostered at an early age.

(D) When children practice their piano scales for half an hour each day, they usually pass their piano exams. Sally practices scales for less than half an hour each day, so she will probably fail her piano exam.

(E) When children have parents who help them with their homework, they usually do well in school. Therefore, having help with homework is probably the cause of high academic achievement.

6. In the past century, North America has shifted its main energy source first from wood to coal, then from coal to oil and natural gas. With each transition, the newly dominant fuel has had less carbon and more hydrogen than its predecessor had. It is logical to conclude that in the future the main energy source will be pure hydrogen.

Which one of the following expresses a general principle that could underlie the argument?

(A) If a series of transitions from one state of a system to another state of that system is allowed to continue without interference, the initial state of the series will eventually recur.

(B) If each of two desirable attributes belongs to a useful substance, then the most useful form of that substance will have those two attributes in equal amounts.

(C) If the second stage of a process has been completed more quickly than the first stage, the third stage of that process will be completed more quickly than the second stage.

(D) If each step in a series of changes involves a decrease of one attribute of the thing undergoing the change and an increase of another, the series will terminate with the first attribute eliminated and only the second attribute present.

(E) If one substance is better for a certain purpose than another substance is, then the best substance for that purpose is one that includes among its attributes all of the attributes of the first substance and none of the attributes of the second substance.

GO ON TO THE NEXT PAGE.

Questions 7-8

X: Since many chemicals useful for agriculture and medicine derive from rare or endangered plant species, it is likely that many plant species that are now extinct could have provided us with substances that would have been a boon to humanity. Therefore, if we want to ensure that chemicals from plants are available for use in the future, we must make more serious efforts to preserve for all time our natural resources.

Y: But living things are not our "resources." Yours is a selfish approach to conservation. We should rather strive to preserve living species because they deserve to survive, not because of the good they can do us.

7. Which one of the following is an issue about which X and Y disagree?

    (A)   whether the benefits humans derive from exploiting nonhuman species provide a good reason for preserving nonhuman species
    (B)   whether the cost of preserving plant species outweighs the cost of artificially synthesizing chemicals that could otherwise be derived from those species
    (C)   whether it is prudent to conserve natural resources
    (D)   whether humans should make efforts to prevent the extinction of living species
    (E)   whether all nonhuman species are equally valuable as natural resources

8. X's argument relies on which one of the following assumptions?

    (A)   Medicine would now be more advanced than it is if there had been a serious conservation policy in the past.
    (B)   All living things exist to serve humankind.
    (C)   The use of rare and endangered plant species as a source for chemicals will not itself render those species extinct.
    (D)   The only way to persuade people to preserve natural resources is to convince them that it is in their interest to do so.
    (E)   Few, if any, plant species have been saved from extinction through human efforts.

9. There is relatively little room for growth in the overall carpet market, which is tied to the size of the population. Most who purchase carpet do so only once or twice, first in their twenties or thirties, and then perhaps again in their fifties or sixties. Thus as the population ages, companies producing carpet will be able to gain market share in the carpet market only through purchasing competitors, and not through more aggressive marketing.

    Which one of the following, if true, casts the most doubt on the conclusion above?

    (A)   Most of the major carpet producers market other floor coverings as well.
    (B)   Most established carpet producers market several different brand names and varieties, and there is no remaining niche in the market for new brands to fill.
    (C)   Two of the three mergers in the industry's last ten years led to a decline in profits and revenues for the newly merged companies.
    (D)   Price reductions, achieved by cost-cutting in production, by some of the dominant firms in the carpet market are causing other producers to leave the market altogether.
    (E)   The carpet market is unlike most markets in that consumers are becoming increasingly resistant to new patterns and styles.

10. Decision makers tend to have distinctive styles. One such style is for the decision maker to seek the widest possible input from advisers and to explore alternatives while making up his or her mind. In fact, decision makers of this sort will often argue vigorously for a particular idea, emphasizing its strong points and downplaying its weaknesses, not because they actually believe in the idea but because they want to see if their real reservations about it are idiosyncratic or are held independently by their advisers.

    Which one of the following is most strongly supported by the statements above?

    (A)   If certain decision makers' statements are quoted accurately and at length, the content of the quote could nonetheless be greatly at variance with the decision eventually made.
    (B)   Certain decision makers do not know which ideas they do not really believe in until after they have presented a variety of ideas to their advisers.
    (C)   If certain decision makers dismiss an idea out of hand, it must be because its weaknesses are more pronounced than any strong points it may have.
    (D)   Certain decision makers proceed in a way that makes it likely that they will frequently decide in favor of ideas in which they do not believe.
    (E)   If certain decision makers' advisers know the actual beliefs of those they advise, those advisers will give better advice than they would if they did not know those beliefs.

GO ON TO THE NEXT PAGE.

Questions 11–12

The foreign minister of Zeria announced today that her country was severing diplomatic relations with Nandalo because of Nandalo's flagrant violations of human rights. But Zeria continues to maintain diplomatic relations with many countries that the minister knows to have far worse human-rights records than Nandalo does. Therefore, despite the foreign minister's claim, this latest diplomatic move cannot be explained exclusively by Zeria's commitment to upholding human rights.

11. Which one of the following, if true, provides the most support for the argument in the passage?

(A) The country that currently buys most of Zeria's exports recently suggested that it might severely restrict its imports from Zeria unless Zeria broke off diplomatic relations with Nandalo.

(B) Two weeks after the Zerian minister's announcement, several other countries cited human-rights violations as a reason for severing diplomatic relations with Nandalo.

(C) More countries have expressed concern over reported human-rights violations in Nandalo than have expressed concern over human-rights violations in Zeria.

(D) Nandalo has considered accusing Zeria of violating the human rights of Nandalo citizens living in Zeria.

(E) The opposition party in Zeria has long advocated severing trade relations with countries that systematically violate human rights but has opposed severing diplomatic relations.

12. The argumentative structure of which one of the following most closely parallels that of the argument in the passage?

(A) Henry's parents insist that he eat breakfast before leaving for school because not doing so would be bad for his health. But his parents themselves almost never eat breakfast, so their insistence cannot be completely explained by their concern for his health.

(B) Professor Walsh says that only typed term papers will be accepted because most handwriting is difficult to read. But since she lectures from handwritten notes, her policy cannot be exclusively explained by any difficulty she has with handwritten material.

(C) James claims that he stole only because he was hungry. But although hunger could account for stealing if food could not be readily obtained in any other way, in this case food was otherwise readily available, and so James' theft cannot be completely explained by his hunger.

(D) Armand declined Helen's invitation to dinner on the grounds that socializing with coworkers is imprudent. But since Armand went to a movie with another coworker, Maria, that same evening, his expressed concern for prudence cannot fully explain his refusal.

(E) It is often asserted that there are fewer good teachers than there used to be because teachers' salaries have reached a new low. But teachers have always been poorly paid, so low salaries cannot fully explain this perceived decline in the effectiveness of teachers.

GO ON TO THE NEXT PAGE.

13. Few politicians will support legislation that conflicts with their own self-interest. A case in point is August Frenson, who throughout his eight terms in office consistently opposed measures limiting the advantage incumbents enjoy over their challengers. Therefore, if such measures are to be enacted, they must result from direct popular vote rather than from legislative action.

The case of August Frenson plays which one of the following roles in the argument?

(A) It provides evidence, the falsity of which would guarantee the falsity of the author's conclusion.
(B) It is cited as an example illustrating the generalization that is invoked.
(C) It gives essential background information concerning a measure being advocated.
(D) It demonstrates the extent to which incumbents have the advantage over challengers.
(E) It gives an example of the limits of direct popular vote.

14. In a learning experiment a researcher ran rats through a maze. Some of the rats were blind, others deaf, others lacked a sense of smell, and others had no sensory deficiencies; yet all the rats learned the task in much the same amount of time. Of the senses other than sight, hearing, and smell, only kinesthesia had not previously been shown to be irrelevant to maze-learning. The researcher concluded on the basis of these facts that kinesthesia, the sensation of bodily movement, is sufficient for maze-learning.

The researcher's reasoning is most vulnerable to which one of the following criticisms?

(A) The small differences in proficiency found by the researcher did not appear to fall into a systematic pattern by group.
(B) The possibility that the interaction of kinesthesia with at least one other sense is required for maze-learning cannot be ruled out on the basis of the data above.
(C) It can be determined from the data that rats who are deprived of one of their sources of sensory stimulation become more reliant on kinesthesia than they had been, but the data do not indicate how such a transference takes place.
(D) It can be determined from the data that rats can learn to run mazes by depending on kinesthesia alone, but the possibility that rats respond to nonkinesthetic stimulation is not ruled out.
(E) It can be determined from the data that maze-learning in rats depends on at least two sources of sensory stimulation, one of which is kinesthesia, but which of the remaining sources must also be employed is not determinable.

15. New legislation would require a seven-day waiting period in the sale of handguns to private individuals, in order that records of prisons could be checked and the sale of handguns to people likely to hurt other people thereby prevented. People opposed to this legislation claim that prison records are so full of errors that the proposed law would prevent as many law-abiding citizens as criminals from having access to handguns.

If the claim made by people opposed to the new legislation is true, which one of the following is a principle that, if established, would do the most to justify opposition to the new legislation on the basis of that claim?

(A) The rights of law-abiding citizens are more worthy of protection than are the rights of criminals.
(B) Nothing should be done to restrict potential criminals at the cost of placing restrictions on law-abiding citizens.
(C) Legislation should not be enacted if no benefit could accrue to society as a result of that legislation.
(D) No restrictions should be placed on the sale of merchandise unless sale of that merchandise could endanger innocent people.
(E) Even citizens who are neither fugitives nor felons should not be permitted to own a handgun unless they have received adequate training.

GO ON TO THE NEXT PAGE.

Questions 16–17

The Gulches is an area of volcanic rock that is gashed by many channels that lead downhill from the site of a prehistoric glacier to a river. The channels clearly were cut by running water. It was once accepted as fact that the cutting occurred gradually, as the glacier melted. But one geologist theorized that the channels were cut in a short time by an enormous flood. The channels do show physical evidence of having been formed quickly, but the flood theory was originally rejected because scientists knew of no natural process that could melt so much ice so quickly. Paradoxically, today the scientific community accepts the flood theory even though scientists still do not know of a process that can melt so much ice so quickly.

16. Which one of the following is supported by the information in the passage?

(A) Only running water can cause deep channels in volcanic rock.
(B) The river did not exist before the channels were cut.
(C) Geologists cannot determine the amount of heat required to melt a glacier quickly.
(D) The physical effects of water on rock vary with the speed with which those effects are produced.
(E) Geologists are compelled to reject physical evidence when it leads to an unexplainable conclusion.

17. Which one of the following, if true, most helps to resolve the apparent paradox in the passage?

(A) Ripples, which indicate that the channels were cut by water, have been discovered in the floors of the channels.
(B) The Gulches is known to be similar in certain respects to many other volcanic rock formations.
(C) More than one glacier was present in the area during prehistoric times.
(D) Volcanic rock is more easily cut by water than are other forms of rock.
(E) Scientists now believe that the prehistoric glacier dammed a source of water, created a huge lake in the process, and then retreated.

18. Advertisement: Attention pond owners! Ninety-eight percent of mosquito larvae in a pond die within minutes after the pond has been treated with BTI. Yet BTI is not toxic to fish, birds, animals, plants, or beneficial insects. So by using BTI regularly to destroy their larvae, you can greatly reduce populations of pesky mosquitoes that hatch in your pond, and you can do so without diminishing the populations of fish, frogs, or beneficial insects in and around the pond.

Which one of the following is an assumption on which the argument depends?

(A) The most effective way to control the numbers of mosquitoes in a given area is to destroy the mosquito larvae in that area.
(B) Populations of mosquitoes are not dependent on a single body of water within an area as a place for their larvae to hatch and develop.
(C) There are no insect pests besides mosquitoes that pond owners might want to eliminate from in and around their ponds.
(D) The effectiveness of BTI in destroying mosquito larvae in a pond does not require the pond owner's strict adherence to specific application procedures.
(E) The fish, frogs, and beneficial insects in and around a pond-owner's pond do not depend on mosquito larvae as an important source of food.

GO ON TO THE NEXT PAGE.

19. Many people change their wills on their own every few years, in response to significant changes in their personal or financial circumstances. This practice can create a problem for the executor when these people are careless and do not date their wills: the executor will then often know neither which one of several undated wills is the most recent, nor whether the will drawn up last has ever been found. Therefore, people should not only date their wills but also state in any new will which will it supersedes, for then there would not be a problem to begin with.

The reasoning in the argument is flawed because the argument

(A) treats a partial solution to the stated problem as though it were a complete solution
(B) fails to distinguish between prevention of a problem and successful containment of the adverse effects that the problem might cause
(C) proposes a solution to the stated problem that does not actually solve the problem but merely makes someone else responsible for solving the problem
(D) claims that a certain action would be a change for the better without explicitly considering what negative consequences the action might have
(E) proposes that a certain action be based on information that would be unavailable at the time proposed for that action

20. Some flowering plant species, entirely dependent on bees for pollination, lure their pollinators with abundant nectar and pollen, which are the only source of food for bees. Often the pollinating species is so highly adapted that it can feed from—and thus pollinate—only a single species of plant. Similarly, some plant species have evolved flowers that only a single species of bee can pollinate—an arrangement that places the plant species at great risk of extinction. If careless applications of pesticides destroy the pollinating bee species, the plant species itself can no longer reproduce.

The information above, if true, most strongly supports which one of the following?

(A) The earliest species of flowering plants appeared on Earth contemporaneously with the earliest bee species.
(B) If the sole pollinator of a certain plant species is in no danger of extinction, the plant species it pollinates is also unlikely to become extinct.
(C) Some bees are able to gather pollen and nectar from any species of plant.
(D) The blossoms of most species of flowering plants attract some species of bees and do not attract others.
(E) The total destruction of the habitat of some plant species could cause some bee species to become extinct.

21. The proper way to plan a scientific project is first to decide its goal and then to plan the best way to accomplish that goal. The United States space station project does not conform to this ideal. When the Cold War ended, the project lost its original purpose, so another purpose was quickly grafted onto the project, that of conducting limited-gravity experiments, even though such experiments can be done in an alternative way. It is, therefore, abundantly clear that the space station should not be built.

The reasoning in the argument is flawed because the argument

(A) attacks the proponents of a claim rather than arguing against the claim itself
(B) presupposes what it sets out to prove
(C) faults planners for not foreseeing a certain event, when in fact that event was not foreseeable
(D) contains statements that lead to a self-contradiction
(E) concludes that a shortcoming is fatal, having produced evidence only of the existence of that shortcoming

22. Only an expert in some branch of psychology could understand why Patrick is behaving irrationally. But no expert is certain of being able to solve someone else's problem. Patrick wants to devise a solution to his own behavioral problem.

Which one of the following conclusions can be validly drawn from the passage?

(A) Patrick does not understand why he is behaving in this way.
(B) Patrick is not an expert in psychology.
(C) Patrick is not certain of being able to devise a solution to his own behavioral problem.
(D) Unless Charles is an expert in some branch of psychology, Charles should not offer a solution to Patrick's behavioral problem.
(E) If Charles is certain of being able to solve Patrick's behavioral problem, then Charles does not understand why Patrick is behaving in this way.

GO ON TO THE NEXT PAGE.

23. Throughout European history famines have generally been followed by periods of rising wages, because when a labor force is diminished, workers are more valuable in accordance with the law of supply and demand. The Irish potato famine of the 1840s is an exception; it resulted in the death or emigration of half of Ireland's population, but there was no significant rise in the average wages in Ireland in the following decade.

Which one of the following, if true, would LEAST contribute to an explanation of the exception to the generalization?

(A) Improved medical care reduced the mortality rate among able-bodied adults in the decade following the famine to below prefamine levels.

(B) Eviction policies of the landowners in Ireland were designed to force emigration of the elderly and infirm, who could not work, and to retain a high percentage of able-bodied workers.

(C) Advances in technology increased the efficiency of industry and agriculture, and so allowed maintenance of economic output with less demand for labor.

(D) The birth rate increased during the decade following the famine, and this compensated for much of the loss of population that was due to the famine.

(E) England, which had political control of Ireland, legislated artificially low wages to provide English-owned industry and agriculture in Ireland with cheap labor.

24. When the rate of inflation exceeds the rate of return on the most profitable investment available, the difference between those two rates will be the percentage by which, at a minimum, the value of any investment will decline. If in such a circumstance the value of a particular investment declines by more than that percentage, it must be true that _____.

Which one of the following logically completes the argument?

(A) the rate of inflation has risen

(B) the investment in question is becoming less profitable

(C) the investment in question is less profitable than the most profitable investment available

(D) the rate of return on the most profitable investment available has declined

(E) there has been a change in which particular investment happens to be the most profitable available

25. Philosopher: The eighteenth-century thesis that motion is absolute asserts that the change in an object's position over time could be measured without reference to the position of any other object. A well-respected physicist, however, claims that this thesis is incoherent. Since a thesis that is incoherent cannot be accepted as a description of reality, motion cannot be absolute.

The argument uses which one of the following argumentative techniques?

(A) attempting to persuade by the mere use of technical terminology

(B) using experimental results to justify a change in definition

(C) relying on the authority of an expert to support a premise

(D) inferring from what has been observed to be the case under experimental conditions to what is in principle true

(E) generalizing from what is true in one region of space to what must be true in all regions of space

S T O P

IF YOU FINISH BEFORE TIME IS CALLED, YOU MAY CHECK YOUR WORK ON THIS SECTION ONLY.
DO NOT WORK ON ANY OTHER SECTION IN THE TEST.

LSAT® Writing Sample Topic

The program director of a television station must select the guest for the first edition of <u>Timewaves</u>, a new talk show. Write an argument in favor of selecting one of the guests over the other, with the following considerations in mind:

- <u>Timewaves</u> must have enough mass appeal to attract a significant viewing audience in a competitive time slot.
- <u>Timewaves</u> must continue the company's tradition of providing serious commentary on current topics.

Jeanne Josephs—a popular writer, is known for her sharp analysis of national issues. Her most recent article, published in a widely read news magazine, was entitled "Success: Who's Got It and Why." In the article, Josephs interviews celebrities in various fields, including sports, business, and the arts, about their views on success and how they achieved it. Josephs has not appeared on a television talk show in several years. Last year, however, she won a prestigious journalism award for "The Private Pain of Politics," a series of articles on the toll public office has taken on the family lives of prominent politicians. At that time reports about Josephs and her work appeared in many major newspapers.

Dr. Kingston Evans—a prominent psychologist, recently led an expert panel in a study of drug use in several affluent suburban communities. The panel's controversial final report, "Drugs in Suburbia," is to be published as a book soon after the first edition of <u>Timewaves</u> is shown. The report is said to expose establishment figures, including public officials, as narcotics suppliers to the suburban market. The study received some media attention after the panel's conclusion—that drugs are more prevalent though less visible in the suburbs than in the inner city—was inadvertently revealed. At the same time, there have been accusations that the study is an inaccurate, sensationalized account of a serious issue. Dr. Evans, however, is a distinguished professor with a well-respected body of academic research to his credit.

Directions:

1. Use the Answer Key on the next page to check your answers.

2. Use the Scoring Worksheet below to compute your raw score.

3. Use the Score Conversion Chart to convert your raw score into the 120-180 scale.

Scoring Worksheet

1. Enter the number of questions you answered correctly in each section.

$$\begin{array}{l} \textbf{Number} \\ \textbf{Correct} \end{array}$$

SECTION I . . . . . . _____
SECTION II . . . . . _____
SECTION III . . . . . _____
SECTION IV . . . . . _____

2. Enter the sum here: _____
This is your Raw Score.

Conversion Chart

For Converting Raw Score to the 120-180 LSAT Scaled Score
LSAT Form 3LSS20

Reported Score	Raw Score	
	Lowest	Highest
180	100	101
179	99	99
178	98	98
177	97	97
176	96	96
175	—*	—*
174	95	95
173	94	94
172	93	93
171	92	92
170	90	91
169	89	89
168	88	88
167	86	87
166	85	85
165	83	84
164	82	82
163	80	81
162	78	79
161	76	77
160	74	75
159	73	73
158	71	72
157	69	70
156	67	68
155	65	66
154	63	64
153	61	62
152	59	60
151	57	58
150	56	56
149	54	55
148	52	53
147	50	51
146	49	49
145	47	48
144	45	46
143	44	44
142	42	43
141	41	41
140	39	40
139	38	38
138	36	37
137	35	35
136	33	34
135	32	32
134	31	31
133	29	30
132	28	28
131	27	27
130	26	26
129	24	25
128	23	23
127	22	22
126	21	21
125	20	20
124	19	19
123	18	18
122	—*	—*
121	17	17
120	0	16

*There is no raw score that will produce this scaled score for this form.

SECTION I

1. B	8. E	15. A	22. C
2. E	9. D	16. E	23. D
3. E	10. E	17. B	24. E
4. D	11. C	18. E	25. E
5. B	12. B	19. D	
6. C	13. B	20. D	
7. A	14. E	21. B	

SECTION II

1. B	8. E	15. C	22. B
2. C	9. E	16. D	23. D
3. C	10. B	17. E	24. A
4. C	11. C	18. C	
5. E	12. B	19. B	
6. A	13. B	20. C	
7. E	14. D	21. E	

SECTION III

1. A	8. D	15. E	22. B
2. D	9. B	16. E	23. D
3. B	10. C	17. B	24. E
4. E	11. B	18. A	25. B
5. C	12. E	19. D	26. A
6. B	13. A	20. D	27. E
7. E	14. C	21. D	

SECTION IV

1. A	8. C	15. B	22. E
2. B	9. D	16. D	23. D
3. C	10. A	17. E	24. C
4. D	11. A	18. E	25. C
5. B	12. D	19. A	
6. D	13. B	20. E	
7. A	14. B	21. E	

The Official LSAT PrepTest

1

- June 1994
- Form 5LSS22

The sample test that follows consists of four sections corresponding to the four scored sections of the June 1994 LSAT.

SECTION I
Time—35 minutes
24 Questions

Directions: Each group of questions in this section is based on a set of conditions. In answering some of the questions, it may be useful to draw a rough diagram. Choose the response that most accurately and completely answers each question and blacken the corresponding space on your answer sheet.

Questions 1–6

Eight camp counselors—Fran, George, Henry, Joan, Kathy, Lewis, Nathan, and Olga—must each be assigned to supervise exactly one of three activities—swimming, tennis, and volleyball. The assignment of counselors must conform to the following conditions:

Each activity is supervised by at least two, but not more than three, of the eight counselors.

Henry supervises swimming.

Neither Kathy nor Olga supervises tennis.

Neither Kathy nor Nathan supervises the same activity as Joan.

If George supervises swimming, both Nathan and Olga supervise volleyball.

1. Which one of the following is an acceptable assignment of the counselors to the activities?

    (A) Swimming: Fran, George, Henry; Tennis: Joan, Lewis; Volleyball: Kathy, Nathan, Olga
    (B) Swimming: George, Henry, Olga; Tennis: Fran, Joan, Lewis; Volleyball: Kathy, Nathan
    (C) Swimming: Henry; Tennis: Fran, George, Joan, Lewis; Volleyball: Kathy, Nathan, Olga
    (D) Swimming: Henry, Joan, Kathy; Tennis: George, Nathan; Volleyball: Fran, Lewis, Olga
    (E) Swimming: Henry, Nathan; Tennis: Fran, Kathy, Lewis; Volleyball: George, Joan, Olga

2. Which one of the following is a pair of counselors who could be two of three counselors assigned to supervise swimming?

    (A) George and Nathan
    (B) George and Olga
    (C) Joan and Kathy
    (D) Joan and Nathan
    (E) Joan and Olga

3. Which one of the following is a pair of counselors who could together be assigned to supervise tennis?

    (A) Fran and Kathy
    (B) George and Nathan
    (C) Henry and Lewis
    (D) Joan and Nathan
    (E) Joan and Olga

4. If George and Kathy are two of three counselors assigned to supervise swimming, which one of the following could be true of the assignment?

    (A) Fran supervises swimming.
    (B) Henry supervises tennis.
    (C) Joan supervises volleyball.
    (D) Lewis supervises volleyball.
    (E) Nathan supervises tennis.

5. If Fran and Lewis are two of three counselors assigned to supervise swimming, which one of the following must be true of the assignment?

    (A) George supervises volleyball.
    (B) Henry supervises volleyball.
    (C) Joan supervises tennis.
    (D) Kathy supervises swimming.
    (E) Nathan supervises tennis.

6. If Joan is assigned to supervise the same activity as Olga, which one of the following CANNOT be true of the assignment?

    (A) Fran supervises swimming.
    (B) George supervises swimming.
    (C) Kathy supervises volleyball.
    (D) Lewis supervises volleyball.
    (E) Nathan supervises tennis.

GO ON TO THE NEXT PAGE.

Questions 7–11

A fire chief is determining the work schedules of five firefighters: Fuentes, Graber, Howell, Iman, and Jackson. The schedule must meet the following conditions:

Except for Saturday and Sunday, when none of them works, exactly one of the firefighters works each day.

None of the firefighters can work more than two days per week.

No firefighter works on two consecutive days.

Fuentes never works later in the week than Jackson.

If Howell works, then Graber must work on the following day.

7. Which one of the following CANNOT be a Monday-to-Friday work schedule?

  (A) Fuentes, Iman, Fuentes, Jackson, Iman
  (B) Fuentes, Jackson, Howell, Graber, Fuentes
  (C) Graber, Fuentes, Graber, Fuentes, Jackson
  (D) Graber, Howell, Graber, Fuentes, Jackson
  (E) Howell, Graber, Iman, Graber, Iman

8. If each firefighter is required to have at least two consecutive days off during the Monday-to-Friday workweek, which one of the following could be a possible work schedule?

  (A) Howell, Graber, Howell, Graber, Iman
  (B) Howell, Howell, Graber, Fuentes, Iman
  (C) Iman, Fuentes, Jackson, Iman, Iman
  (D) Fuentes, Howell, Graber, Fuentes, Jackson
  (E) Jackson, Howell, Graber, Iman, Fuentes

9. If both Fuentes and Jackson work during a week, which one of the following statements CANNOT be true?

  (A) Fuentes works on Monday and Wednesday.
  (B) Jackson works on Monday and Wednesday.
  (C) Fuentes works on Tuesday and Thursday.
  (D) Jackson works on Tuesday and Thursday.
  (E) Jackson works on Wednesday and Friday.

10. If Fuentes works two days during the week and Jackson works on Thursday, which one of the following statements could be true?

  (A) Fuentes works on Tuesday.
  (B) Graber works on Tuesday.
  (C) Howell works on Tuesday.
  (D) Graber works on Wednesday.
  (E) Howell works on Wednesday.

11. If Graber does not work during the week, which one of the following statements must be true?

  (A) Fuentes works exactly one day during the week.
  (B) Fuentes works exactly two days during the week.
  (C) Iman works exactly one day during the week.
  (D) Iman works exactly two days during the week.
  (E) Jackson works exactly one day during the week.

GO ON TO THE NEXT PAGE.

Questions 12–19

A housing committee will consist of exactly five representatives, one of whom will be its chairperson. The representatives will be selected from among a group of five tenants—F, G, J, K, and M—and a group of four homeowners—P, Q, R, and S. The following conditions must be met:

The committee must include at least two representatives from each group.
The chairperson must be a representative belonging to the group from which exactly two representatives are selected.
If F is selected, Q must be selected.
If G is selected, K must be selected.
If either J or M is selected, the other must also be selected.
M and P cannot both be selected.

12. Which one of the following is an acceptable selection of representatives for the committee?

(A) F, G, Q, R, S
(B) F, J, K, P, Q
(C) F, P, Q, R, S
(D) J, K, M, Q, S
(E) J, M, P, Q, S

13. Which one of the following lists three representatives who could be selected together for the committee?

(A) F, G, J
(B) F, G, M
(C) F, J, M
(D) G, J, K
(E) G, J, M

14. If M is the chairperson of the committee, which one of the following is among the people who must also be on the committee?

(A) F
(B) G
(C) K
(D) P
(E) R

15. If F is the chairperson of the committee, which one of the following is among the people who must also be on the committee?

(A) G
(B) K
(C) P
(D) R
(E) S

16. If F is selected, any one of the following people could be the chairperson of the committee EXCEPT:

(A) G
(B) K
(C) P
(D) Q
(E) S

17. If neither F nor K is selected for the committee, which one of the following can be true?

(A) G is selected.
(B) P is selected.
(C) J is the chairperson.
(D) Q is the chairperson.
(E) S is the chairperson.

18. If the chairperson of the committee is to be a homeowner, which one of the following must be true?

(A) If G is selected, Q is also selected.
(B) If G is selected, R is also selected.
(C) If J is selected, F is also selected.
(D) If J is selected, Q is also selected.
(E) If J is selected, R is also selected.

19. The committee must include at least one representative from which one of the following pairs?

(A) F, P
(B) G, J
(C) K, Q
(D) M, P
(E) R, S

GO ON TO THE NEXT PAGE.

Questions 20–24

Four apprentices—Louis, Madelyn, Nora, and Oliver—are initially assigned to projects Q, R, S, and T, respectively. During the year in which they are apprentices, two reassignments of apprentices to projects will be made, each time according to a different one of the following plans, which can be used in any order:

Plan 1. The apprentice assigned to project Q switches projects with the apprentice assigned to project S and the apprentice assigned to project R switches projects with the apprentice assigned to project T.

Plan 2. The apprentice assigned to project S switches projects with the apprentice assigned to project T.

Plan 3. Louis and Madelyn switch projects with each other.

20. Which one of the following must be true after the second reassignment of apprentices to projects during the year if that reassignment assigns Nora to project T ?

(A) Louis is assigned to project S.
(B) Madelyn is assigned to project R.
(C) Madelyn is assigned to project S.
(D) Oliver is assigned to project R.
(E) Oliver is assigned to project S.

21. Which one of the following could be true after only one reassignment during the year?

(A) Louis is assigned to project T.
(B) Nora is assigned to project R.
(C) Oliver is assigned to project Q.
(D) Louis and Nora each remain assigned to the same projects as before.
(E) Nora and Oliver each remain assigned to the same projects as before.

22. If at some time during the year, Louis is reassigned to project R, which one of the following could have been the assignment of apprentices to the projects immediately before the reassignment?

(A) Q: Louis; R: Madelyn; S: Oliver; T: Nora
(B) Q: Louis; R: Nora; S: Oliver; T: Madelyn
(C) Q: Nora; R: Madelyn; S: Louis; T: Oliver
(D) Q: Nora; R: Oliver; S: Louis; T: Madelyn
(E) Q: Oliver; R: Nora; S: Louis; T: Madelyn

23. Which one of the following is an acceptable assignment of apprentices to the projects after only one reassignment during the year?

(A) Q: Louis; R: Madelyn; S: Nora; T: Oliver
(B) Q: Madelyn; R: Louis; S: Nora; T: Oliver
(C) Q: Madelyn; R: Oliver; S: Nora; T: Louis
(D) Q: Nora; R: Louis; S: Oliver; T: Madelyn
(E) Q: Nora; R: Madelyn; S: Oliver; T: Louis

24. If the first reassignment is made according to plan 1, which one of the following must be true?

(A) Louis is assigned to project T as a result of the second reassignment.
(B) Madelyn is assigned to project Q as a result of the second reassignment.
(C) Madelyn is assigned to project T as a result of the second reassignment.
(D) Oliver is assigned to project S as a result of the second reassignment.
(E) Oliver is assigned to project T as a result of the second reassignment.

S T O P

IF YOU FINISH BEFORE TIME IS CALLED, YOU MAY CHECK YOUR WORK ON THIS SECTION ONLY.
DO NOT WORK ON ANY OTHER SECTION IN THE TEST.

SECTION II

Time—35 minutes

26 Questions

Directions: The questions in this section are based on the reasoning contained in brief statements or passages. For some questions, more than one of the choices could conceivably answer the question. However, you are to choose the best answer; that is, the response that most accurately and completely answers the question. You should not make assumptions that are by commonsense standards implausible, superfluous, or incompatible with the passage. After you have chosen the best answer, blacken the corresponding space on your answer sheet.

Questions 1–2

Sea turtles nest only at their own birthplaces. After hatching on the beach, the turtles enter the water to begin their far-ranging migration, only returning to their birthplaces to nest some 15 to 30 years later. It has been hypothesized that newborn sea turtles learn the smell of their birth environment, and it is this smell that stimulates the turtles to return to nest.

1. Which one of the following, if true, would cast the most serious doubt on the hypothesis in the passage?

   (A) Beaches on which sea turtles nest tend to be in secluded locations such as on islands.
   (B) Sea turtles exposed to a variety of environments under experimental conditions preferred the environment that contained sand from their own birthplaces.
   (C) Electronic tags attached to sea turtles did not alter their nesting patterns.
   (D) Unlike other types of turtles, sea turtles have a well-developed sense of smell.
   (E) Sea turtles that had their sense of smell destroyed by exposure to petroleum products returned to nest at their own birthplaces.

2. Which one of the following would be most important to know in evaluating the hypothesis in the passage?

   (A) how long the expected life span of sea turtles is
   (B) what the maximum migratory range of mature sea turtles is
   (C) whether many beaches on which sea turtles were hatched have since been destroyed by development
   (D) whether immediately before returning to nest, sea turtles are outside the area where the smell of their birthplace would be perceptible
   (E) whether both sexes of sea turtles are actively involved in the nesting process

3. For Juanita to get to the zoo she must take either the number 12 bus or else the subway. Everyone knows that the number 12 bus is not running this week; so although Juanita generally avoids using the subway, she must have used it today, since she was seen at the zoo this afternoon.

The method of the argument is to

   (A) assert that if something is true, it will be known to be true
   (B) demonstrate that certain possibilities are not exclusive
   (C) show that something is the case by ruling out the only alternative
   (D) explain why an apparent exception to a general rule is not a real exception
   (E) substitute a claim about what invariably occurs for a claim about what typically occurs

GO ON TO THE NEXT PAGE.

4. If the regulation of computer networks is to be modeled on past legislation, then its model must be either legislation regulating a telephone system or else legislation regulating a public broadcasting service. If the telephone model is used, computer networks will be held responsible only for ensuring that messages get transmitted. If the public broadcast model is used, computer networks will additionally be responsible for the content of those messages. Yet a computer network serves both these sorts of functions: it can serve as a private message service or as a publicly accessible information service. Thus neither of these models can be appropriate for computer networks.

The passage is structured to lead to which one of the following conclusions?

(A) Regulation of computer networks is required in order to ensure the privacy of the messages transmitted through such networks.

(B) The regulation of computer networks should not be modeled on any single piece of past legislation.

(C) Computer networks were developed by being modeled on both telephone systems and television networks.

(D) Legislators who do not have extensive experience with computers should not attempt to write legislation regulating computer networks.

(E) A computer network merely duplicates the functions of a telephone system and a television network.

5. The government has proposed a plan requiring young people to perform services to correct various current social ills, especially those in education and housing. Government service, however, should be compelled only in response to a direct threat to the nation's existence. For that reason, the proposed program should not be implemented.

Which one of the following is an assumption on which the argument depends?

(A) Government-required service by young people cannot correct all social ills.

(B) The nation's existence is directly threatened only in times of foreign attack.

(C) Crises in education and housing constitute a threat to the nation's existence.

(D) The nation's young people believe that current social ills pose no direct threat to the nation's existence.

(E) Some of the social ills that currently afflict the nation do not pose a direct threat to the nation's existence.

6. Cigarette smoking has been shown to be a health hazard; therefore, governments should ban all advertisements that promote smoking.

Which one of the following principles, if established, most strongly supports the argument?

(A) Advertisements should not be allowed to show people doing things that endanger their health.

(B) Advertisers should not make misleading claims about the healthfulness of their products.

(C) Advertisements should disclose the health hazards associated with the products they promote.

(D) All products should conform to strict government health and safety standards.

(E) Advertisements should promote only healthful products.

7. Every adult male woolly monkey is larger than even the largest female woolly monkey. In colonies of woolly monkeys, any adult male will dominate any female.

If the statements above are true, which one of the following must on the basis of them be true of woolly monkeys in colonies?

(A) Size is the primary determinant of relations of dominance among woolly monkeys.

(B) Some large adolescent male woolly monkeys dominate some smaller females of the species.

(C) If a male woolly monkey is larger than a female of the species, that male will dominate that female.

(D) If a female woolly monkey dominates a male of the species, the dominated male monkey is not an adult.

(E) An adult male woolly monkey can dominate a female of the species only if that female is also an adult.

GO ON TO THE NEXT PAGE.

8. S: Our nation is becoming too averse to risk.
        We boycott any food reported to contain
        a toxic chemical, even though the risk, as
        a mathematical ratio, might be minimal.
        With this mentality, Columbus would never
        have sailed west.

    T: A risk-taker in one context can be risk-averse in
        another: the same person can drive recklessly,
        but refuse to eat food not grown organically.

    T responds to S by showing that

    (A) a distinction should be made between
         avoidable and unavoidable risks
    (B) aversion to risk cannot be reliably assessed
         without reference to context
    (C) there is confusion about risk in the minds of
         many members of the public
    (D) mathematical odds concerning risk give an
         unwarranted impression of precision
    (E) risk cannot be defined in relation to perceived
         probable benefit

9. Any announcement authorized by the head of the
    department is important. However, announcements
    are sometimes issued, without authorization, by
    people other than the head of the department, so
    some announcements will inevitably turn out not to
    be important.

    The reasoning is flawed because the argument

    (A) does not specify exactly which communications
         are to be classified as announcements
    (B) overlooks the possibility that people other than
         the head of the department have the authority
         to authorize announcements
    (C) leaves open the possibility that the head of the
         department never, in fact, authorizes any
         announcements
    (D) assumes without warrant that just because
         satisfying a given condition is enough to
         ensure an announcement's importance,
         satisfying that condition is necessary for its
         importance
    (E) fails to distinguish between the importance of
         the position someone holds and the importance
         of what that person may actually be announcing
         on a particular occasion

Questions 10–11

   The labeling of otherwise high-calorie foods as
"sugar-free," based on the replacement of all sugar by
artificial sweeteners, should be prohibited by law. Such a
prohibition is indicated because many consumers who
need to lose weight will interpret the label "sugar-free" as
synonymous with "low in calories" and harm themselves
by building weight-loss diets around foods labeled
"sugar-free." Manufacturers of sugar-free foods are well
aware of this tendency on the part of consumers.

10. Which one of the following principles, if established,
     most helps to justify the conclusion in the passage?

     (A) Product labels that are literally incorrect
          should be prohibited by law, even if reliance
          on those labels is not likely to cause harm to
          consumers.
     (B) Product labels that are literally incorrect, but
          in such an obvious manner that no rational
          consumer would rely on them, should
          nevertheless be prohibited by law.
     (C) Product labels that are literally correct but
          cannot be interpreted by the average buyer
          of the product without expert help should be
          prohibited by law.
     (D) Product labels that are literally correct but will
          predictably be misinterpreted by some buyers
          of the product to their own harm should be
          prohibited by law.
     (E) Product labels that are literally correct, but
          only on one of two equally accurate
          interpretations, should be prohibited by law
          if buyers tend to interpret the label in the way
          that does not match the product's actual
          properties.

11. Which one of the following, if true, provides the
     strongest basis for challenging the conclusion in the
     passage?

     (A) Food manufacturers would respond to a ban
          on the label "sugar-free" by reducing the
          calories in sugar-free products by enough to
          be able to promote those products as diet
          foods.
     (B) Individuals who are diabetic need to be able to
          identify products that contain no sugar by
          reference to product labels that expressly state
          that the product contains no sugar.
     (C) Consumers are sometimes slow to notice changes
          in product labels unless those changes are
          themselves well advertised.
     (D) Consumers who have chosen a particular
          weight-loss diet tend to persist with this diet if
          they have been warned not to expect very
          quick results.
     (E) Exactly what appears on a product label is less
          important to consumer behavior than is the
          relative visual prominence of the different
          pieces of information that the label contains.

GO ON TO THE NEXT PAGE.

12. In the Centerville Botanical Gardens, all tulip trees are older than any maples. A majority, but not all, of the garden's sycamores are older than any of its maples. All the garden's maples are older than any of its dogwoods.

If the statements above are true, which one of the following must also be true of trees in the Centerville Botanical Gardens?

(A) Some dogwoods are as old as the youngest tulip trees.
(B) Some dogwoods are as old as the youngest sycamores.
(C) Some sycamores are not as old as the oldest dogwoods.
(D) Some tulip trees are not as old as the oldest sycamores.
(E) Some sycamores are not as old as the youngest tulip trees.

13. Emissions from automobiles that burn gasoline and automobiles that burn diesel fuel are threatening the quality of life on our planet, contaminating both urban air and global atmosphere. Therefore, the only effective way to reduce such emissions is to replace the conventional diesel fuel and gasoline used in automobiles with cleaner-burning fuels, such as methanol, that create fewer emissions.

Which one of the following is an assumption on which the argument depends?

(A) Reducing the use of automobiles would not be a more effective means to reduce automobile emissions than the use of methanol.
(B) There is no fuel other than methanol that is cleaner-burning than both diesel fuel and gasoline.
(C) If given a choice of automobile fuels, automobile owners would not select gasoline over methanol.
(D) Automobile emissions constitute the most serious threat to the global environment.
(E) At any given time there is a direct correlation between the level of urban air pollution and the level of contamination present in the global atmosphere.

14. Dr. Libokov: Certain islands near New Zealand are home to the tuatara, reptiles that are the sole surviving members of the sphenodontidans. Sphenodontidans were plentiful throughout the world during the age of the dinosaurs. But the survival of sphenodontidans near New Zealand, and their total disappearance elsewhere, is no mystery. New Zealand and nearby islands have no native land mammals. Land mammals, plentiful elsewhere, undoubtedly became major predators of sphenodontidans and their eggs, leading to their extinction.

Dr. Santos: In fact, the tuatara thrive only on a few islands near New Zealand. On all those where land mammals, such as rats, dogs, or cats, have been introduced in recent years, the tuatara are now extinct or nearly so.

Which one of the following most accurately characterizes Dr. Santos' response to the hypothesis advanced by Dr. Libokov?

(A) It identifies a flaw in Dr. Libokov's reasoning.
(B) It restates Dr. Libokov's major hypothesis and thus adds nothing to it.
(C) It contradicts one of Dr. Libokov's assertions.
(D) It offers a hypothesis that is incompatible with Dr. Libokov's position.
(E) It provides additional evidence in support of Dr. Libokov's hypothesis.

15. A standard problem for computer security is that passwords that have to be typed on a computer keyboard are comparatively easy for unauthorized users to steal or guess. A new system that relies on recognizing the voices of authorized users apparently avoids this problem. In a small initial trial, the system never incorrectly accepted someone seeking access to the computer's data. Clearly, if this result can be repeated in an operational setting, then there will be a way of giving access to those people who are entitled to access and to no one else.

The reasoning above is flawed because it

(A) makes a faulty comparison, in that a security system based on voice recognition would not be expected to suffer from the same problems as one that relied on passwords entered from a keyboard
(B) bases a general conclusion on a small amount of data
(C) fails to recognize that a security system based on voice recognition could easily have applications other than computer security
(D) ignores the possibility that the system sometimes denies access to people who are entitled to access
(E) states its conclusion in a heavily qualified way

GO ON TO THE NEXT PAGE.

16. Body temperature varies over a 24-hour period, with a low point roughly between 4 a.m. and 5 a.m. Speed of reaction varies in line with body temperature, such that whenever body temperature is low, speed of reaction is low. If low body temperature caused slow reaction, the speed of reaction should increase if we artificially raised body temperature during the period 4 a.m. to 5 a.m. But the speed of reaction does not increase.

Which one of the following conclusions can properly be drawn from the above statements?

(A) Low speeds of reaction cause low body temperature.

(B) Low speeds of reaction do not cause low body temperature.

(C) Low body temperatures do not cause low speeds of reaction.

(D) Low body temperatures cause low speeds of reaction.

(E) Artificially raising body temperature causes increased speed of reaction.

17. Of the two proposals for solving the traffic problems on Main Street, Chen's plan is better for the city as a whole, as is clear from the fact that the principal supporter of Ripley's plan is Smith Stores. Smith Stores, with its highly paid consultants, knows where its own interest lies and, moreover, has supported its own interests in the past, even to the detriment of the city as a whole.

The faulty reasoning in which one of the following is most parallel to that in the argument above?

(A) Surely Centreville should oppose adoption of the regional planning commission's new plan since it is not in Centreville's interest, even though it might be in the interest of some towns in the region.

(B) The school board should support the plan for the new high school since this plan was recommended by the well-qualified consultants whom the school board hired at great expense.

(C) Of the two budget proposals, the mayor's is clearly preferable to the city council's, since the mayor's budget addresses the needs of the city as a whole, whereas the city council is protecting special interests.

(D) Nomura is clearly a better candidate for college president than Miller, since Nomura has the support of the three deans who best understand the president's job and with whom the president will have to work most closely.

(E) The planned light-rail system will clearly serve suburban areas well, since its main opponent is the city government, which has always ignored the needs of the suburbs and sought only to protect the interests of the city.

GO ON TO THE NEXT PAGE.

Questions 18-19

The format of network television news programs generally allows advocates of a point of view only 30 seconds to convey their message. Consequently, regular watchers become accustomed to thinking of issues in terms only of slogans and catch phrases, and so the expectation of careful discussion of public issues gradually disappears from their awareness. The format of newspaper stories, on the other hand, leads readers to pursue details of stories headed by the most important facts and so has the opposite effect on regular readers—that of maintaining the expectation of careful discussion of public issues. Therefore, in contrast to regular newspaper reading, regular watching of network television news programs increases the tendency to think of public issues in oversimplified terms.

18. The argument assumes which one of the following?

(A) Viewers of network television news programs would be interested in seeing advocates of opposing views present their positions at length.

(B) Since it is not possible to present striking images that would symbolize events for viewers, and since images hold sway over words in television, television must oversimplify.

(C) It is not possible for television to present public issues in a way that allows for the nuanced presentation of diverse views and a good-faith interchange between advocates of opposing views.

(D) In network television news reports, it is not usual for a reporter to offer additional factual evidence and background information to develop a story in which opposing views are presented briefly by their advocates.

(E) Television news reporters introduce more of their own biases into news stories than do newspaper reporters.

19. Which one of the following, if true, most seriously weakens the argument?

(A) Regular watchers of network television news programs are much more likely than other people to be habitual readers of newspapers.

(B) Including any 30-second quotations from proponents of diverse views, the total amount of time devoted to a single topic on regular network television news programs averages less than one and a half minutes.

(C) The format of network television news programs does not include roundtable discussion of issues among informed proponents of diverse views.

(D) Television news reports tend to devote equal time to discussion of opposing views.

(E) People who watch the most television, measured in average number of hours of watching per week, tend not to be regular readers of newspapers.

Questions 20-21

A recent report on an environmental improvement program was criticized for focusing solely on pragmatic solutions to the large number of significant problems that plague the program instead of seriously trying to produce a coherent vision for the future of the program. In response the report's authors granted that the critics had raised a valid point but explained that, to do anything at all, the program needed continued government funding, and that to get such funding the program first needed to regain a reputation for competence.

20. The basic position taken by the report's authors on the criticism leveled against the report is that

(A) addressing the critics' concern now would be premature

(B) the critics' motives are self-serving

(C) the notion of a coherent vision would be inappropriate to a program of the sort at issue

(D) the authors of the report are more knowledgeable than its critics

(E) giving the report a single focus is less desirable than the critics claim

21. Which one of the following, if true, would best serve the critics of the report in their attempt to undermine the position taken by the report's authors?

(A) The government does not actually provide a full 100 percent of the program's funding.

(B) The program will continue to have numerous serious problems precisely because it lacks a coherent vision for its future.

(C) The program had a coherent vision at its inception, but that vision has proved impossible to sustain.

(D) The government has threatened to cut off funding for the program but has not acted yet on this threat.

(E) The program has acquired a worse reputation for incompetence than it deserves.

GO ON TO THE NEXT PAGE.

22. Oil company representative: We spent more money on cleaning the otters affected by our recent oil spill than has been spent on any previous marine mammal rescue project. This shows our concern for the environment.

Environmentalist: You have no such concern. Your real concern is evident in your admission to the press that news photographs of oil-covered otters would be particularly damaging to your public image, which plays an important role in your level of sales.

The environmentalist's conclusion would be properly drawn if it were true that the

(A) oil company cannot have more than one motive for cleaning the otters affected by the oil spill

(B) otter population in the area of the oil spill could not have survived without the cleaning project

(C) oil company has always shown a high regard for its profits in choosing its courses of action

(D) government would have spent the money to clean the otters if the oil company had not agreed to do it

(E) oil company's efforts toward cleaning the affected otters have been more successful than have such efforts in previous projects to clean up oil spills

23. A group of scientists studying calcium metabolism in laboratory rats discovered that removing the rats' parathyroid glands resulted in the rats' having substantially lower than normal levels of calcium in their blood. This discovery led the scientists to hypothesize that the function of the parathyroid gland is to regulate the level of calcium in the blood by raising that level when it falls below the normal range. In a further experiment, the scientists removed not only the parathyroid gland but also the adrenal gland from rats. They made the surprising discovery that the level of calcium in the rats' blood decreased much less sharply than when the parathyroid gland alone was removed.

Which one of the following, if true, explains the surprising discovery in a way most consistent with the scientists' hypothesis?

(A) The adrenal gland acts to lower the level of calcium in the blood.

(B) The adrenal gland and the parathyroid gland play the same role in regulating calcium blood levels.

(C) The absence of a parathyroid gland causes the adrenal gland to increase the level of calcium in the blood.

(D) If the adrenal gland, and no other gland, of a rat were removed, the rat's calcium level would remain stable.

(E) The only function of the parathyroid gland is to regulate the level of calcium in the blood.

24. Since Mayor Drabble always repays her political debts as soon as possible, she will almost certainly appoint Lee to be the new head of the arts commission. Lee has wanted that job for a long time, and Drabble owes Lee a lot for his support in the last election.

Which one of the following is an assumption on which the argument depends?

(A) Mayor Drabble has no political debt that is both of longer standing than the one she owes to Lee and could as suitably be repaid by an appointment to be the new head of the arts commission.

(B) There is no one to whom Mayor Drabble owes a greater political debt for support in the last election than the political debt she owes to Lee.

(C) Lee is the only person to whom Mayor Drabble owes a political debt who would be willing to accept an appointment from her as the new head of the arts commission.

(D) Whether Lee is qualified to head the arts commission is irrelevant to Mayor Drabble's decision.

(E) The only way that Mayor Drabble can adequately repay her political debt to Lee is by appointing him to head the arts commission.

GO ON TO THE NEXT PAGE.

25. The fact that tobacco smoke inhaled by smokers harms the smokers does not prove that the much smaller amount of tobacco smoke inhaled by nonsmokers who share living space with smokers harms the nonsmokers to some degree. Many substances, such as vitamin A, are toxic in large quantities but beneficial in small quantities.

In which one of the following is the pattern of reasoning most similar to that in the argument above?

(A) The fact that a large concentration of bleach will make fabric very white does not prove that a small concentration of bleach will make fabric somewhat white. The effect of a small concentration of bleach may be too slight to change the color of the fabric.

(B) Although a healthful diet should include a certain amount of fiber, it does not follow that a diet that includes large amounts of fiber is more healthful than one that includes smaller amounts of fiber. Too much fiber can interfere with proper digestion.

(C) The fact that large amounts of chemical fertilizers can kill plants does not prove that chemical fertilizers are generally harmful to plants. It proves only that the quantity of chemical fertilizer used should be adjusted according to the needs of the plants and the nutrients already in the soil.

(D) From the fact that five professional taste testers found a new cereal product tasty, it does not follow that everyone will like it. Many people find broccoli a tasty food, but other people have a strong dislike for the taste of broccoli.

(E) Although watching television for half of every day would be a waste of time, watching television briefly every day is not necessarily even a small waste of time. After all, it would be a waste to sleep half of every day, but some sleep every day is necessary.

26. Why should the government, rather than industry or universities, provide the money to put a network of supercomputers in place? Because there is a range of problems that can be attacked only with the massive data-managing capacity of a supercomputer network. No business or university has the resources to purchase by itself enough machines for a whole network, and no business or university wants to invest in a part of a network if no mechanism exists for coordinating establishment of the network as a whole.

Which one of the following indicates a weakness in the argument?

(A) It does not furnish a way in which the dilemma concerning the establishment of the network can be resolved.

(B) It does not establish the impossibility of creating a supercomputer network as an international network.

(C) It fails to address the question of who would maintain the network if the government, rather than industry or universities, provides the money for establishing it.

(D) It takes for granted and without justification that it would enhance national preeminence in science for the government to provide the network.

(E) It overlooks the possibility that businesses or universities, or both, could cooperate to build the network.

S T O P

IF YOU FINISH BEFORE TIME IS CALLED, YOU MAY CHECK YOUR WORK ON THIS SECTION ONLY.
DO NOT WORK ON ANY OTHER SECTION IN THE TEST.

SECTION III

Time—35 minutes

27 Questions

<u>Directions</u>: Each passage in this section is followed by a group of questions to be answered on the basis of what is <u>stated</u> or <u>implied</u> in the passage. For some of the questions, more than one of the choices could conceivably answer the question. However, you are to choose the <u>best</u> answer; that is, the response that most accurately and completely answers the question, and blacken the corresponding space on your answer sheet.

Nearly every writer on the philosophy of civil rights activist Martin Luther King, Jr., makes a connection between King and Henry David Thoreau, usually via Thoreau's famous essay,
(5) "Civil Disobedience" (1849). In his book *Stride Toward Freedom* (1958), King himself stated that Thoreau's essay was his first intellectual contact with the theory of passive resistance to governmental laws that are perceived as morally unjust. However,
(10) this emphasis on Thoreau's influence on King is unfortunate: first, King would not have agreed with many other aspects of Thoreau's philosophy, including Thoreau's ultimate acceptance of violence as a form of protest; second, an overemphasis on
(15) the influence of one essay has kept historians from noting other correspondences between King's philosophy and transcendentalism. "Civil Disobedience" was the only example of transcendentalist writing with which King was
(20) familiar, and in many other transcendentalist writings, including works by Ralph Waldo Emerson and Margaret Fuller, King would have found ideas more nearly akin to his own.

The kind of civil disobedience King had in
(25) mind was, in fact, quite different from Thoreau's view of civil disobedience. Thoreau, like most other transcendentalists, was primarily interested in reform of the individual, whereas King was primarily interested in reform of society. As a protest against
(30) the Mexican War, Thoreau refused to pay taxes, but he did not hope by his action to force a change in national policy. While he encouraged others to adopt similar protests, he did not attempt to mount any mass protest action against unjust laws. In
(35) contrast to Thoreau, King began to advocate the use of mass civil disobedience to effect revolutionary changes within the social system.

However, King's writings suggest that, without realizing it, he was an incipient transcendentalist.
(40) Most transcendentalists subscribed to the concept of "higher law" and included civil disobedience to unjust laws as part of their strategy. They often invoked the concept of higher law to justify their opposition to slavery and to advocate disobedience
(45) to the strengthened Fugitive Slave Law of 1850. In his second major book, King's discussion of just and unjust laws and the responsibility of the individual is very similar to the transcendentalists' discussion of higher law. In reference to how one
(50) can advocate breaking some laws and obeying

others, King notes that there are two types of laws, just and unjust; he describes a just law as a "code that squares with the moral law" and an unjust law as a "code that is out of harmony with the moral
(55) law." Thus, King's opposition to the injustice of legalized segregation in the twentieth century is philosophically akin to the transcendentalists' opposition to the Fugitive Slave Law in the nineteenth century.

1. Which one of the following best states the main idea of the passage?

(A) King's philosophy was more influenced by Thoreau's essay on civil disobedience than by any other writing of the transcendentalists.
(B) While historians may have overestimated Thoreau's influence on King, King was greatly influenced by a number of the transcendentalist philosophers.
(C) Thoreau's and King's views on civil disobedience differed in that King was more concerned with the social reform than with the economic reform of society.
(D) Although historians have overemphasized Thoreau's influence on King, there are parallels between King's philosophy and transcendentalism that have not been fully appreciated.
(E) King's ideas about law and civil disobedience were influenced by transcendentalism in general and Thoreau's essays in particular.

2. Which one of the following statements about "Civil Disobedience" would the author consider most accurate?

(A) It was not King's first contact with the concept of passive resistance to unjust laws.
(B) It was one of many examples of transcendentalist writing with which King was familiar.
(C) It provided King with a model for using passive resistance to effect social change.
(D) It contains a number of ideas with which other transcendentalists strongly disagreed.
(E) It influenced King's philosophy on passive resistance to unjust laws.

GO ON TO THE NEXT PAGE.

3. In the first paragraph, the author is primarily concerned with

(A) chronicling the development of King's philosophy on passive resistance to unjust law
(B) suggesting that a common emphasis on one influence on King's philosophy has been misleading
(C) providing new information about the influence of twentieth-century philosophers on King's work
(D) summarizing the work of historians on the most important influences on King's philosophy
(E) providing background information about nineteenth-century transcendentalist philosophers

4. According to the passage, which one of the following is true of Emerson and Fuller?

(A) Some of their ideas were less typical of transcendentalism than were some of Thoreau's ideas.
(B) They were more concerned with the reform of society than with the reform of the individual.
(C) They would have been more likely than Thoreau to agree with King on the necessity of mass protest in civil disobedience.
(D) Their ideas about civil disobedience and unjust laws are as well known as Thoreau's are.
(E) Some of their ideas were more similar to King's than were some of Thoreau's.

5. According to the passage, King differed from most transcendentalists in that he

(A) opposed violence as a form of civil protest
(B) opposed war as an instrument of foreign policy under any circumstances
(C) believed that just laws had an inherent moral value
(D) was more interested in reforming society than in reforming the individual
(E) protested social and legal injustice in United States society rather than United States foreign policy

6. The passage suggests which one of the following about Thoreau?

(A) He was the first to develop fully the theory of civil disobedience.
(B) His work has had a greater influence on contemporary thinkers than has the work of Emerson and Fuller.
(C) His philosophy does not contain all of the same elements as the philosophies of the other transcendentalists.
(D) He advocated using civil disobedience to force the federal government to change its policies on war.
(E) He is better known for his ideas on social and legal reform than for his ideas on individual reform.

7. The passage provides support for which one of the following statements about the quotations in lines 52-55 ?

(A) They are an example of a way in which King's ideas differed from Thoreau's but were similar to the ideas of other transcendentalists.
(B) They provide evidence that proves that King's philosophy was affected by transcendentalist thought.
(C) They suggest that King, like the transcendentalists, judged human laws by ethical standards.
(D) They suggest a theoretical basis for King's philosophy of government.
(E) They provide a paraphrase of Thoreau's position on just and unjust laws.

GO ON TO THE NEXT PAGE.

In *Democracy and its Critics*, Robert Dahl defends both democratic values and pluralist democracies, or polyarchies (a rough shorthand term for Western political systems). Dahl argues
(5) convincingly that the idea of democracy rests on political equality—the equal capacity of all citizens to determine or influence collective decisions. Of course, as Dahl recognizes, if hierarchical ordering is inevitable in any structure of government, and if
(10) no society can guarantee perfect equality in the resources that may give rise to political influence, the democratic principle of political equality is incapable of full realization. So actual systems can be deemed democratic only as approximations to
(15) the ideal. It is on these grounds that Dahl defends polyarchy.

As a representative system in which elected officials both determine government policy and are accountable to a broad-based electorate, polyarchy
(20) reinforces a diffusion of power away from any single center and toward a variety of individuals, groups, and organizations. It is this centrifugal characteristic, Dahl argues, that makes polyarchy the nearest possible approximation to the democratic
(25) ideal. Polyarchy achieves this diffusion of power through party competition and the operation of pressure groups. Competing for votes, parties seek to offer different sections of the electorate what they most want; they do not ask what the majority
(30) thinks of an issue, but what policy commitments will sway the electoral decisions of particular groups. Equally, groups that have strong feelings about an issue can organize in pressure groups to influence public policy.
(35) During the 1960s and 1970s, criticism of the theory of pluralist democracy was vigorous. Many critics pointed to a gap between the model and the reality of Western political systems. They argued that the distribution of power resources other than
(40) the vote was so uneven that the political order systematically gave added weight to those who were already richer or organizationally more powerful. So the power of some groups to exclude issues altogether from the political agenda effectively
(45) countered any diffusion of influence on decision-making.

Although such criticism became subdued during the 1980s, Dahl himself seems to support some of the earlier criticism. Although he regrets that some
(50) Western intellectuals demand more democracy from polyarchies than is possible, and is cautious about the possibility of further democratization, he nevertheless ends his book by asking what changes in structures and consciousness might make political
(55) life more democratic in present polyarchies. One answer, he suggests, is to look at the economic order of polyarchies from the point of view of the citizen as well as from that of producers and consumers. This would require a critical examination
(60) of both the distribution of those economic resources

that are at the same time political resources, and the relationship between political structures and economic enterprises.

8. The characterization of polyarchies as "centrifugal" (line 22) emphasizes the

   (A) way in which political power is decentralized in a polyarchy
   (B) central role of power resources in a polyarchy
   (C) kind of concentrated power that political parties generate in a polyarchy
   (D) dynamic balance that exists between economic enterprises and elected officials in a polyarchy
   (E) dynamic balance that exists between voters and elected officials in a polyarchy

9. In the third paragraph, the author of the passage refers to criticism of the theory of pluralist democracy primarily in order to

   (A) refute Dahl's statement that Western intellectuals expect more democracy from polyarchies than is possible
   (B) advocate the need for rethinking the basic principles on which the theory of democracy rests
   (C) suggest that the structure of government within pluralist democracies should be changed
   (D) point out a flaw in Dahl's argument that the principle of political equality cannot be fully realized
   (E) point out an objection to Dahl's defense of polyarchy

10. According to the passage, the aim of a political party in a polyarchy is to do which one of the following?

   (A) determine what the position of the majority of voters is on a particular issue
   (B) determine what position on an issue will earn the support of particular groups of voters
   (C) organize voters into pressure groups in order to influence public policy on a particular issue
   (D) ensure that elected officials accurately represent the position of the party on specific issues
   (E) ensure that elected officials accurately represent the position of the electorate on specific issues

GO ON TO THE NEXT PAGE.

11. It can be inferred from the passage that Dahl assumes which one of the following in his defense of polyarchies?

(A) Polyarchies are limited in the extent to which they can embody the idea of democracy.

(B) The structure of polyarchical governments is free of hierarchical ordering.

(C) The citizens of a polyarchy have equal access to the resources that provide political influence.

(D) Polyarchy is the best political system to foster the growth of political parties.

(E) Polyarchy is a form of government that is not influenced by the interests of economic enterprises.

12. Which one of the following is most closely analogous to pluralist democracies as they are described in relation to the democratic principle of political equality?

(A) an exact copy of an ancient artifact that is on display in a museum

(B) a performance of a musical score whose range of tonality cannot be completely captured by any actual instruments

(C) a lecture by a former astronaut to a class of young students who would like to be astronauts

(D) the commemoration of a historical event each year by a historian presenting a lecture on a topic related to the event

(E) the mold from which a number of identical castings of a sculpture are made

13. Which one of the following, if true, would most strengthen Dahl's defense of polyarchy?

(A) The political agenda in a polyarchy is strongly influenced by how power resources other than the vote are distributed.

(B) The outcome of elections is more often determined by the financial resources candidates are able to spend during campaigns than by their stands on political issues.

(C) Public policy in a polyarchy is primarily determined by decision-makers who are not accountable to elected officials.

(D) Political parties in a polyarchy help concentrate political power in the central government.

(E) Small and diverse pressure groups are able to exert as much influence on public policy in a polyarchy as are large and powerful groups.

14. The passage can best be described as

(A) an inquiry into how present-day polyarchies can be made more democratic

(B) a commentary on the means pressure groups employ to exert influence within polyarchies

(C) a description of the relationship between polyarchies and economic enterprises

(D) a discussion of the strengths and weaknesses of polyarchy as a form of democracy

(E) an overview of the similarities between political parties and pressure groups in a polyarchy

GO ON TO THE NEXT PAGE.

The old belief that climatic stability accounts for the high level of species diversity in the Amazon River basin of South America emerged, strangely enough, from observations of the deep sea. Sanders
(5) discovered high diversity among the mud-dwelling animals of the deep ocean. He argued that such diversity could be attributed to the absence of significant fluctuations in climate and physical conditions, without which the extinction of species
(10) should be rare. In the course of time new species would continue to evolve, and so the rate of speciation would be greater than the rate of extinction, resulting in the accumulation of great diversity. Sanders argued that the Amazon tropical
(15) rain forest is analogous to the deep sea: because the rain forest has a stable climate, extinction should be rare. Evidence that some species of rain-forest trees have persisted for some 30 million years in the Amazon basin, added to the absence of
(20) winter and glaciation, supports this view.

Recently, however, several observations have cast doubt on the validity of the stability hypothesis and suggest that the climate of the Amazon basin has fluctuated significantly in the past. Haffer
(25) noted that different species of birds inhabit different corners of the basin in spite of the fact that essentially unbroken green forest spreads from the western edge to the eastern edge of the region. This pattern presented a puzzle to biologists
(30) studying the distributions of plants and animals: why would different species inhabit different parts of the forest if the habitat in which they lived had a stable climate?

Haffer proposed a compelling explanation for
(35) the distribution of species. Observing that species found on high ground are different from those on low ground, and knowing that in the Amazon lowlands are drier than uplands, he proposed that during the ice ages the Amazon lowlands became a
(40) near-desert arid plain; meanwhile, the more elevated regions became islands of moisture and hence served as refuges for the fauna and flora of the rain forest. Populations that were once continuous diverged and became permanently
(45) separated. Haffer's hypothesis appears to explain the distribution of species as well as the unusual species diversity. The ice-age refuges would have protected existing species from extinction. But the periodic geographic isolation of related populations
(50) (there have been an estimated 13 ice ages to date) would have facilitated the development of new species as existing species on the lowlands adapted to changing climates.

Although no conclusive proof has yet been
(55) found to support Haffer's hypothesis, it has led other researchers to gauge the effects of climatic changes, such as storms and flooding, on species diversity in the Amazon basin. Their research suggests that climatic disturbances help account for
(60) the splendid diversity of the Amazon rain forest today.

15. As discussed in the first paragraph of the passage, Sanders' analogy between the deep sea and the Amazon basin involves which one of the following assumptions?

(A) Both the Amazon basin and the deep sea support an unusually high rate of speciation.
(B) Both the rain-forest trees in the Amazon basin and the mud-dwelling animals in the deep sea have survived for 30 million years.
(C) Both the deep sea and the Amazon basin have not experienced dramatic changes in climate or physical conditions.
(D) A dependable supply of water to the Amazon basin and the deep sea has moderated the rate of extinction in both habitats.
(E) The rate of speciation in the Amazon basin is equivalent to the rate of speciation in the deep sea.

16. The author of the passage would most likely agree with which one of the following statements about Haffer's hypothesis?

(A) It provides an intriguing and complete explanation for the high rate of species diversity in the Amazon basin.
(B) It is partially correct in that a number of climatic disturbances account for species diversity in the Amazon basin.
(C) It has not yet been verified, but it has had an influential effect on current research on species diversity in the Amazon basin.
(D) It is better than Sanders' theory in accounting for the low rate of species extinction in the Amazon basin.
(E) It provides a compelling explanation for the distribution of species in the Amazon basin but does not account for the high species diversity.

17. According to the passage, lowlands in the Amazon basin currently differ from uplands in which one of the following respects?

(A) Lowlands are desertlike, whereas uplands are lush.
(B) Lowlands are less vulnerable to glaciation during the ice ages than are uplands.
(C) Uplands support a greater diversity of species than do lowlands.
(D) Uplands are wetter than are lowlands.
(E) Uplands are more densely populated than are lowlands.

GO ON TO THE NEXT PAGE.

18. Which one of the following best describes the organization of the passage?

(A) A hypothesis is discussed, evidence that undercuts that hypothesis is presented, and a new hypothesis that may account for the evidence is described.

(B) A recently observed phenomenon is described, an explanation for that phenomenon is discussed, and the explanation is evaluated in light of previous research findings.

(C) Several hypotheses that may account for a puzzling phenomenon are described and discounted, and a more promising hypothesis is presented.

(D) A hypothesis and the assumptions on which it is based are described, and evidence is provided to suggest that the hypothesis is only partially correct.

(E) Two alternative explanations for a phenomenon are presented and compared, and experiments designed to test each theory are described.

19. The author of the passage mentions the number of ice ages in the third paragraph most probably in order to

(A) provide proof that cooler and drier temperatures are primarily responsible for the distribution of species in the Amazon

(B) explain how populations of species were protected from extinction in the Amazon basin

(C) explain how most existing species were able to survive periodic climatic disturbances in the Amazon basin

(D) suggest that certain kinds of climatic disturbances cause more species diversity than do other kinds of climatic disturbances

(E) suggest that geographic isolation may have occurred often enough to cause high species diversity in the Amazon basin

20. The passage suggests that which one of the following is true of Sanders' hypothesis?

(A) He underestimated the effects of winter and glaciation in the Amazon basin on the tropical rain forest.

(B) He failed to recognize the similarity in physical conditions of the Amazon lowlands and the Amazon uplands.

(C) He failed to take into account the relatively high rate of extinction during the ice ages in the Amazon basin.

(D) He overestimated the length of time that species have survived in the Amazon basin.

(E) He failed to account for the distribution of species in the Amazon basin.

21. Which one of the following is evidence that would contribute to the "proof" mentioned in line 54 ?

(A) Accurately dated sediment cores from a freshwater lake in the Amazon indicate that the lake's water level rose significantly during the last ice age.

(B) Data based on radiocarbon dating of fossils suggest that the Amazon uplands were too cold to support rain forests during the last ice age.

(C) Computer models of climate during global ice ages predict only insignificant reductions of monsoon rains in tropical areas such as the Amazon.

(D) Fossils preserved in the Amazon uplands during the last ice age are found together with minerals that are the products of an arid landscape.

(E) Fossilized pollen from the Amazon lowlands indicates that during the last ice age the Amazon lowlands supported vegetation that needs little water rather than the rain forests they support today.

GO ON TO THE NEXT PAGE.

Although surveys of medieval legislation, guild organization, and terminology used to designate different medical practitioners have demonstrated
(5) that numerous medical specialities were recognized in Europe during the Middle Ages, most historians continue to equate the term "woman medical practitioner," wherever they encounter it in medieval records, with "midwife." This common
(10) practice obscures the fact that, although women were not represented on all levels of medicine equally, they were represented in a variety of specialties throughout the broad medical community. A reliable study by Wickersheimer and Jacquart
(15) documents that, of 7,647 medical practitioners in France during the twelfth through fifteenth centuries, 121 were women; of these, only 44 were identified as midwives, while the rest practiced as physicians, surgeons, apothecaries, barbers, and other healers.

While preserving terminological distinctions
(20) somewhat increases the quality of the information extracted from medieval documents concerning women medical practitioners, scholars must also reopen the whole question of why documentary evidence for women medical practitioners
(25) comprises such a tiny fraction of the evidence historians of medieval medicine usually present. Is this due to the limitations of the historical record, as has been claimed, or does it also result from the methods historians use? Granted, apart from
(30) medical licenses, the principal sources of information regarding medical practitioners available to researchers are wills, property transfers, court records, and similar documents, all of which typically underrepresent women because of
(35) restrictive medieval legal traditions. Nonetheless, the parameters researchers choose when they define their investigations may contribute to the problem. Studies focusing on the upper echelons of "learned" medicine, for example, tend to exclude healers on
(40) the legal and social fringes of medical practice, where most women would have been found.

The advantages of broadening the scope of such studies is immediately apparent in Pelling and Webster's study of sixteenth-century London.
(45) Instead of focusing solely on officially recognized and licensed practitioners, the researchers defined a medical practitioner as "any individual whose occupation is basically concerned with the care of the sick." Using this definition, they found primary
(50) source information suggesting that there were 60 women medical practitioners in the city of London in 1560. Although this figure may be slightly exaggerated, the evidence contrasts strikingly with that of Gottfried, whose earlier survey identified
(55) only 28 women medical practitioners in all of England between 1330 and 1530.

Finally, such studies provide only statistical information about the variety and prevalence of women's medical practice in medieval Europe.
(60) Future studies might also make profitable use of analyses developed in other areas of women's history as a basis for exploring the social context of women's medical practice. Information about economic rivalry in medicine, women's literacy, and
(65) the control of medical knowledge could add much to our growing understanding of women medical practitioners' role in medieval society.

22. Which one of the following best expresses the main point of the passage?

(A) Recent studies demonstrate that women medical practitioners were more common in England than in the rest of Western Europe during the Middle Ages.

(B) The quantity and quality of the information historians uncover concerning women's medical practice in medieval Europe would be improved if they changed their methods of study.

(C) The sparse evidence for women medical practitioners in studies dealing with the Middle Ages is due primarily to the limitations of the historical record.

(D) Knowledge about the social issues that influenced the role women medical practitioners played in medieval society has been enhanced by several recent studies.

(E) Analyses developed in other areas of women's history could probably be used to provide more information about the social context of women's medical practice during the Middle Ages.

23. Which one of the following is most closely analogous to the error the author believes historians make when they equate the term "woman medical practitioner" with "midwife"?

(A) equating pear with apple
(B) equating science with biology
(C) equating supervisor with subordinate
(D) equating member with nonmember
(E) equating instructor with trainee

GO ON TO THE NEXT PAGE.

24. It can be inferred from the passage that the author would be most likely to agree with which one of the following assertions regarding Gottfried's study?

   (A)   Gottfried's study would have recorded a much larger number of women medical practitioners if the time frame covered by the study had included the late sixteenth century.
   (B)   The small number of women medical practitioners identified in Gottfried's study is due primarily to problems caused by inaccurate sources.
   (C)   The small number of women medical practitioners identified in Gottfried's study is due primarily to the loss of many medieval documents.
   (D)   The results of Gottfried's study need to be considered in light of the social changes occurring in Western Europe during the fourteenth and fifteenth centuries.
   (E)   In setting the parameters for his study, Gottfried appears to have defined the term "medical practitioner" very narrowly.

25. The passage suggests that a future study that would be more informative about medieval women medical practitioners might focus on which one of the following?

   (A)   the effect of social change on the political and economic structure of medieval society
   (B)   the effect of social constraints on medieval women's access to a medical education
   (C)   the types of medical specialties that developed during the Middle Ages
   (D)   the reasons why medieval historians tend to equate the term "woman medical practitioner" with midwife
   (E)   the historical developments responsible for the medieval legal tradition's restrictions on women

26. The author refers to the study by Wickersheimer and Jacquart in order to

   (A)   demonstrate that numerous medical specialties were recognized in Western Europe during the Middle Ages
   (B)   demonstrate that women are often underrepresented in studies of medieval medical practitioners
   (C)   prove that midwives were officially recognized as members of the medical community during the Middle Ages
   (D)   prove that midwives were only a part of a larger community of women medical practitioners during the Middle Ages
   (E)   prove that the existence of midwives can be documented in Western Europe as early as the twelfth century

27. In the passage, the author is primarily concerned with doing which one of the following?

   (A)   describing new methodological approaches
   (B)   revising the definitions of certain concepts
   (C)   comparing two different analyses
   (D)   arguing in favor of changes in method
   (E)   chronicling certain historical developments

S T O P

IF YOU FINISH BEFORE TIME IS CALLED, YOU MAY CHECK YOUR WORK ON THIS SECTION ONLY.
DO NOT WORK ON ANY OTHER SECTION IN THE TEST.

SECTION IV

Time—35 minutes

24 Questions

<u>Directions:</u> The questions in this section are based on the reasoning contained in brief statements or passages. For some questions, more than one of the choices could conceivably answer the question. However, you are to choose the <u>best</u> answer; that is, the response that most accurately and completely answers the question. You should not make assumptions that are by commonsense standards implausible, superfluous, or incompatible with the passage. After you have chosen the best answer, blacken the corresponding space on your answer sheet.

1. Megatrash Co., the country's largest waste-disposal company, has been sued by environmental groups who have accused the firm of negligent handling of hazardous waste. The fines and legal fees that have resulted from the legal attacks against Megatrash have cost the company substantial amounts of money. Surprisingly, as successful lawsuits against the company have increased in number, the company has grown stronger and more profitable.

   Which one of the following, if true, does the most to resolve the apparent paradox?

   (A) Although waste-disposal firms merely handle but do not generate toxic waste, these firms have been held legally responsible for environmental damage caused by this waste.
   (B) Megatrash has made substantial contributions to environmental causes, as have other large waste-disposal companies.
   (C) Some of the judgments against Megatrash have legally barred it from entering the more profitable areas of the waste-management business.
   (D) The example of Megatrash's legal entanglements has driven most of the company's competitors from the field and deterred potential rivals from entering it.
   (E) In cases in which Megatrash has been acquitted of charges of negligence, the company has paid more in legal fees than it would have been likely to pay in fines.

2. Lewis: Those who do not learn from past mistakes —their own and those of others—are condemned to repeat them. In order to benefit from the lessons of history, however, we first have to know history. That is why the acquisition of broad historical knowledge is so important.

   Morris: The trouble is that the past is infinitely various. From its inexhaustible storehouse of events it is possible to prove anything or its contrary.

   The issue that Morris raises in objecting to Lewis' view is whether

   (A) there are any uncontested historical facts
   (B) historical knowledge can be too narrow to be useful
   (C) history teaches any unequivocal lessons
   (D) there are conventional criteria for calling a past action a mistake
   (E) events in the present are influenced by past events

3. A group of scientists who have done research on the health effects of food irradiation has discovered no evidence challenging its safety. Supporters of food irradiation have cited this research as certain proof that food irradiation is a safe practice.

   A flaw in the reasoning of the supporters of food irradiation is that they

   (A) assume that the scientists doing the research set out to prove that food irradiation is an unsafe practice
   (B) are motivated by a biased interest in proving the practice to be safe
   (C) overlook the possibility that objections about safety are not the only possible objections to the practice
   (D) neglect to provide detailed information about the evidence used to support the conclusion
   (E) use the lack of evidence contradicting a claim as conclusive evidence for that claim

4. Cooking teacher: Lima beans generally need about an hour of boiling to reach the proper degree of doneness. The precise amount of time it takes depends on size: larger beans require a longer cooking time than smaller beans do. It is important that lima beans not be overcooked since overcooking robs beans of many of their nutrients. Undercooking should also be avoided, since undercooked beans cannot be completely digested.

   If the statements above are true, they most strongly support which one of the following?

   (A) Lima beans that are completely digestible have lost many of their nutrients in cooking.
   (B) The nutrients that are lost when lima beans are overcooked are the same as those that the body fails to assimilate when lima beans are not completely digested.
   (C) Large lima beans, even when fully cooked, are more difficult to digest than small lima beans.
   (D) Lima beans that are added to the pot together should be as close to the same size as possible if they are to yield their full nutritional value.
   (E) From the standpoint of good nutrition, it is better to overcook than to undercook lima beans.

GO ON TO THE NEXT PAGE.

Questions 5–6

Large quantities of lead dust can be released during renovations in houses with walls painted with lead-based paint. Because the dust puts occupants at high risk of lead poisoning, such renovations should be done only in unoccupied houses by contractors who are experienced in removing all traces of lead from houses and who have the equipment to protect themselves from lead dust. Even when warned, however, many people will not pay to have someone else do renovations they believe they could do less expensively themselves. Therefore, *Homeowners' Journal* should run an article giving information to homeowners on how to reduce the risk of lead poisoning associated with do-it-yourself renovation.

5. Which one of the following, if true, argues most strongly against the passage's recommendation about an article?

   (A) Most homeowners know whether or not the walls of their houses are painted with lead-based paint, even if the walls were painted by previous owners.

   (B) Most people who undertake do-it-yourself renovation projects do so for the satisfaction of doing the work themselves and so are unlikely to hire a professional to do that sort of work.

   (C) Whenever information on do-it-yourself home renovation is published, many people who would otherwise hire professionals decide to perform the renovations themselves, even when there are risks involved.

   (D) In many areas, it is difficult to find professional renovators who have the equipment and qualifications to perform safely renovations involving lead dust.

   (E) When professionally done home renovations are no more expensive than do-it-yourself renovations, most people choose to have their homes renovated by professionals.

6. Which one of the following principles most helps to justify the passage's recommendation about an article?

   (A) Potentially dangerous jobs should always be left to those who have the training and experience to perform them safely, even if additional expense results.

   (B) If people refuse to change their behavior even when warned that they are jeopardizing their health, information that enables them to minimize the risks of that behavior should be made available to them.

   (C) A journal for homeowners should provide its readers with information on do-it-yourself projects only if such projects do not entail substantial risks.

   (D) No one should be encouraged to perform a potentially dangerous procedure if doing so could place any other people at risk.

   (E) People who are willing to do work themselves and who are competent to do so should not be discouraged from doing that work.

GO ON TO THE NEXT PAGE.

7. The scientific theory of evolution has challenged the view of human origin as divine creation and sees us as simply descended from the same ancestors as the apes. While science and technology have provided brilliant insights into our world and eased our everyday life, they have simultaneously deprived us of a view in which our importance is assured. Thus, while science has given us many things, it has taken away much that is also greatly valued.

    Which one of the following is assumed in the passage?

    (A) Science and technology are of less value than religion.
    (B) People have resisted the advances of science and technology.
    (C) The assurance that people are important is highly valued.
    (D) The world was a better place before the advent of science and technology.
    (E) The need of people to feel important is now met by science and technology.

Questions 8–9

   That long-term cigarette smoking can lead to health problems including cancer and lung disease is a scientifically well-established fact. Contrary to what many people seem to believe, however, it is not necessary to deny this fact in order to reject the view that tobacco companies should be held either morally or legally responsible for the poor health of smokers. After all, excessive consumption of candy undeniably leads to such health problems as tooth decay, but no one seriously believes that candy eaters who get cavities should be able to sue candy manufacturers.

8. The main point of the argument is that

    (A) no one should feel it necessary to deny the scientifically well-established fact that long-term cigarette smoking can lead to health problems
    (B) people who get cavities should not be able to sue candy manufacturers
    (C) the fact that smokers' health problems can be caused by their smoking is not enough to justify holding tobacco companies either legally or morally responsible for those problems
    (D) excessive consumption of candy will lead to health problems just as surely as long-term cigarette smoking will
    (E) if candy manufacturers were held responsible for tooth decay among candy eaters then tobacco companies should also be held responsible for health problems suffered by smokers

9. The reasoning in the argument is most vulnerable to criticism on the grounds that it

    (A) fails to establish that the connection between tooth decay and candy eating is as scientifically well documented as that between smoking and the health problems suffered by smokers
    (B) depends on the obviously false assumption that everyone who gets cavities does so only as a result of eating too much candy
    (C) leaves undefined such critical qualifying terms as "excessive" and "long-term"
    (D) attributes certain beliefs to "many people" without identifying the people who allegedly hold those beliefs
    (E) fails to address the striking differences in the nature of the threat to health posed by tooth decay on the one hand and cancer and lung disease on the other

GO ON TO THE NEXT PAGE.

10. Lydia: Each year, thousands of seabirds are injured when they become entangled in equipment owned by fishing companies. Therefore, the fishing companies should assume responsibility for funding veterinary treatment for the injured birds.

Jonathan: Your feelings for the birds are admirable. Your proposal, however, should not be adopted because treatment of the most seriously injured birds would inhumanely prolong the lives of animals no longer able to live in the wild, as all wildlife should.

Jonathan uses which one of the following techniques in his response to Lydia?

(A) He directs a personal attack against her rather than addressing the argument she advances.

(B) He suggests that her proposal is based on self-interest rather than on real sympathy for the injured birds.

(C) He questions the appropriateness of interfering with wildlife in any way, even if the goal of the interference is to help.

(D) He attempts to discredit her proposal by discussing its implications for only those birds that it serves least well.

(E) He evades discussion of her proposal by raising the issue of whether her feelings about the birds are justified.

11. Logging industry official: Harvesting trees from old-growth forests for use in manufacture can reduce the amount of carbon dioxide in the atmosphere, since when large old trees die in the forest they decompose, releasing their stored carbon dioxide. Harvesting old-growth forests would, moreover, make room for rapidly growing young trees, which absorb more carbon dioxide from the atmosphere than do trees in old-growth forests.

Which one of the following, if true, most seriously weakens the official's argument?

(A) Many old-growth forests are the home of thousands of animal species that would be endangered if the forests were to be destroyed.

(B) Much of the organic matter from old-growth trees, unusable as lumber, is made into products that decompose rapidly.

(C) A young tree contains less than half the amount of carbon dioxide that is stored in an old tree of the same species.

(D) Much of the carbon dioxide present in forests is eventually released when wood and other organic debris found on the forest floor decomposes.

(E) It can take many years for the trees of a newly planted forest to reach the size of those found in existing old-growth forests.

12. A survey of a group of people between the ages of 75 and 80 found that those who regularly played the card game bridge tended to have better short-term memory than those who did not play bridge. It was originally concluded from this that playing bridge can help older people to retain and develop their memory. However, it may well be that bridge is simply a more enjoyable game for people who already have good short-term memory and who are thus more inclined to play.

In countering the original conclusion the reasoning above uses which one of the following techniques?

(A) challenging the representativeness of the sample surveyed

(B) conceding the suggested relationship between playing bridge and short-term memory, but questioning whether any conclusion about appropriate therapy can be drawn

(C) arguing that the original conclusion relied on an inaccurate understanding of the motives that the people surveyed have for playing bridge

(D) providing an alternative hypothesis to explain the data on which the original conclusion was based

(E) describing a flaw in the reasoning on which the original conclusion was based

13. There are tests to detect some of the rare genetic flaws that increase the likelihood of certain diseases. If these tests are performed, then a person with a rare genetic flaw that is detected can receive the appropriate preventive treatment. Since it costs the health-care system less to prevent a disease than to treat it after it has occurred, widespread genetic screening will reduce the overall cost of health care.

The argument assumes which one of the following?

(A) The cost of treating patients who would, in the absence of screening, develop diseases that are linked to rare genetic flaws would be more than the combined costs of widespread screening and preventive treatment.

(B) Most diseases linked to rare genetic flaws are preventable.

(C) The resources allocated by hospitals to the treatment of persons with diseases linked to genetic flaws will increase once screening is widely available.

(D) Even if the genetic tests are performed, many people whose rare genetic flaws are detected will develop diseases linked to the flaws as a consequence of not receiving the appropriate preventive treatment.

(E) If preventive treatment is given to patients with rare genetic flaws, additional funds will be available for treating the more common diseases.

GO ON TO THE NEXT PAGE.

14. In the 1960s paranoia was viewed by social scientists as ungrounded fear of powerlessness, and the theme of paranoia as it relates to feelings of powerlessness was dominant in films of that period. In the 1970s paranoia instead was viewed by social scientists as a response to real threats from society. Films of this period portray paranoia as a legitimate response to a world gone mad.

Which one of the following is a conclusion that the statements above, if true, most strongly support?

(A) Images of paranoia presented in films made in a period reflect trends in social science of that period.
(B) Responses to real threats can, and often do, degenerate into groundless fears.
(C) The world is becoming more and more threatening.
(D) Paranoia is a condition that keeps changing along with changes in society.
(E) The shift in perception by social scientists from the 1960s to the 1970s resulted from an inability to find a successful cure for paranoia.

15. A certain experimental fungicide causes no harm to garden plants, though only if it is diluted at least to ten parts water to one part fungicide. Moreover, this fungicide is known to be so effective against powdery mildew that it has the capacity to eliminate it completely from rose plants. Thus this fungicide, as long as it is sufficiently diluted, provides a means of eliminating powdery mildew from rose plants that involves no risk of harming the plants.

Which one of the following is an assumption on which the argument depends?

(A) There is not an alternative method, besides application of this fungicide, for eliminating powdery mildew from rose plants without harming the plants.
(B) When the fungicide is sufficiently diluted, it does not present any risk of harm to people, animals, or beneficial insects.
(C) Powdery mildew is the only fungal infection that affects rose plants.
(D) If a fungicide is to be effective against powdery mildew on rose plants, it must eliminate the powdery mildew completely.
(E) The effectiveness of the fungicide does not depend on its being more concentrated than one part in ten parts of water.

16. When glass products are made from recycled glass, the resulting products can be equal in quality to glass products made from quartz sand, the usual raw material. When plastics are recycled, however, the result is inevitably a plastic of a lower grade than the plastic from which it is derived. Moreover, no applications have been found for grades of plastic that are lower than the currently lowest commercial grade.

Which one of the following is a conclusion that can be properly drawn from the statements above?

(A) Products cannot presently be made out of plastic recycled entirely from the currently lowest commercial grade.
(B) It is impossible to make glass products from recycled glass that are equal in quality to the best glass products made from the usual raw material.
(C) Glass products made from recycled glass are less expensive than comparable products made from quartz sand.
(D) Unless recycled plastic bears some symbol revealing its origin, not even materials scientists can distinguish it from virgin plastic.
(E) The difference in quality between different grades of glass is not as great as that between different grades of plastic.

GO ON TO THE NEXT PAGE.

Questions 17–18

Teacher: Journalists who conceal the identity of the sources they quote stake their professional reputations on what may be called the logic of anecdotes. This is so because the statements reported by such journalists are dissociated from the precise circumstances in which they were made and thus will be accepted for publication only if the statements are high in plausibility or originality or interest to a given audience—precisely the properties of a good anecdote.

Student: But what you are saying, then, is that the journalist need not bother with sources in the first place. Surely, any reasonably resourceful journalist can invent plausible, original, or interesting stories faster than they can be obtained from unidentified sources.

17. The student's response contains which one of the following reasoning flaws?

(A) confusing a marginal journalistic practice with the primary work done by journalists

(B) ignoring the possibility that the teacher regards as a prerequisite for the publication of an unattributed statement that the statement have actually been made

(C) confusing the characteristics of reported statements with the characteristics of the situations in which the statements were made

(D) judging the merits of the teacher's position solely by the most extreme case to which the position applies

(E) falsely concluding that if three criteria, met jointly, assure an outcome, then each criterion, met individually, also assures that outcome

18. Which one of the following, if true, most strengthens the teacher's argument?

(A) A journalist undermines his or her own professional standing by submitting for publication statements that, not being attributed to a named source, are rejected for being implausible, unoriginal, or dull.

(B) Statements that are attributed to a fully identified source make up the majority of reported statements included by journalists in stories submitted for publication.

(C) Reported statements that are highly original will often seem implausible unless submitted by a journalist who is known for solid, reliable work.

(D) Reputable journalists sometimes do not conceal the identity of their sources from their publishers but insist that the identity of those sources be concealed from the public.

(E) Journalists who have special access to sources whose identity they must conceal are greatly valued by their publishers.

19. The proposal to extend clinical trials, which are routinely used as systematic tests of pharmaceutical innovations, to new surgical procedures should not be implemented. The point is that surgical procedures differ in one important respect from medicinal drugs: a correctly prescribed drug depends for its effectiveness only on the drug's composition, whereas the effectiveness of even the most appropriate surgical procedure is transparently related to the skills of the surgeon who uses it.

The reasoning in the argument is flawed because the argument

(A) does not consider that new surgical procedures might be found to be intrinsically more harmful than the best treatment previously available

(B) ignores the possibility that the challenged proposal is deliberately crude in a way designed to elicit criticism to be used in refining the proposal

(C) assumes that a surgeon's skills remain unchanged throughout the surgeon's professional life

(D) describes a dissimilarity without citing any scientific evidence for the existence of that dissimilarity

(E) rejects a proposal presumably advanced in good faith without acknowledging any such good faith

GO ON TO THE NEXT PAGE.

20. If the majority of the residents of the apartment complex complain that their apartments are infested with ants, then the management of the complex will have to engage the services of an exterminator. But the majority of the residents of the complex indicate that their apartments are virtually free of ants. Therefore, the management of the complex will not have to engage the services of an exterminator.

Which one of the following arguments contains a flawed pattern of reasoning parallel to that contained in the argument above?

(A) A theater will be constructed in the fall if funds collected are at least sufficient to cover its cost. To date, the funds collected exceed the theater's cost, so the theater will be constructed in the fall.

(B) The number of flights operated by the airlines cannot be reduced unless the airlines can collect higher airfares. But people will not pay higher airfares, so it is not the case that the number of flights will be reduced.

(C) In order for the company to start the proposed building project, both the town council and the mayor must approve. Since the mayor has already approved, the building project will be started soon.

(D) Most employees will attend the company picnic if the entertainment committee is successful in getting a certain band to play at the picnic. But that band will be out of the country on the day of the picnic, so it is not true that most employees will attend.

(E) Either the school's principal or two-thirds of the parent council must approve a change in the school dress code in order for the code to be changed. Since the principal will not approve a change in the dress code, the code will not be changed.

21. When the supply of a given resource dwindles, alternative technologies allowing the use of different resources develop, and demand for the resource that was in short supply naturally declines. Then the existing supplies of that resource satisfy whatever demand remains. Among the once-dwindling resources that are now in more than adequate supply are flint for arrowheads, trees usable for schooner masts, and good mules. Because new technologies constantly replace old ones, we can never run out of important natural resources.

Which one of the following, if true, most seriously undermines the conclusion?

(A) The masts and hulls of some sailing ships built today are still made of wood.

(B) There are considerably fewer mules today than there were 100 years ago.

(C) The cost of some new technologies is often so high that the companies developing them might actually lose money at first.

(D) Dwindling supplies of a natural resource often result in that resource's costing more to use.

(E) The biological requirements for substances like clean air and clean water are unaffected by technological change.

GO ON TO THE NEXT PAGE.

22. Paulsville and Longtown cannot both be included in the candidate's itinerary of campaign stops. The candidate will make a stop in Paulsville unless Salisbury is made part of the itinerary. Unfortunately, a stop in Salisbury is out of the question. Clearly, then, a stop in Longtown can be ruled out.

The reasoning in the argument above most closely parallels that in which one of the following arguments?

(A) The chef never has both fresh radishes and fresh green peppers available for the chef's salad at the same time. If she uses fresh radishes, she also uses spinach. But currently there is no spinach to be had. It can be inferred, then, that she will not be using fresh green peppers.

(B) Tom will definitely support Parker if Mendoza does not apply; and Tom will not support both Parker and Chung. Since, as it turns out, Mendoza will not apply, it follows that Chung will not get Tom's support.

(C) The program committee never selects two plays by Shaw for a single season. But when they select a play by Coward, they do not select any play by Shaw at all. For this season, the committee has just selected a play by Shaw, so they will not select any play by Coward.

(D) In agricultural pest control, either pesticides or the introduction of natural enemies of the pest, but not both, will work. Of course, neither will be needed if pest-resistant crops are planted. So if pesticides are in fact needed, it must be that there are no natural enemies of the pest.

(E) The city cannot afford to build both a new stadium and the new road that would be needed to get there. But neither of the two projects is worth doing without the other. Since the city will not undertake any but worthwhile projects, the new stadium will not be constructed at this time.

23. A study of adults who suffer from migraine headaches revealed that a significant proportion of the study participants suffer from a complex syndrome characterized by a set of three symptoms. Those who suffer from the syndrome experienced excessive anxiety during early childhood. As adolescents, these people began experiencing migraine headaches. As these people approached the age of 20, they also began to experience recurring bouts of depression. Since this pattern is invariant, always with excessive anxiety at its beginning, it follows that excessive anxiety in childhood is one of the causes of migraine headaches and depression in later life.

The reasoning in the argument is vulnerable to criticism on which one of the following grounds?

(A) It does not specify the proportion of those in the general population who suffer from the syndrome.

(B) It fails to rule out the possibility that all of the characteristic symptoms of the syndrome have a common cause.

(C) It makes a generalization that is inconsistent with the evidence.

(D) It fails to demonstrate that the people who participated in the study are representative of migraine sufferers.

(E) It does not establish why the study of migraine sufferers was restricted to adult participants.

24. Mainstream economic theory holds that manufacturers, in deciding what kinds of products to manufacture and what form those products should have, simply respond to the needs and desires of consumers. However, most major manufacturers manipulate and even create consumer demand, as anyone who watches television knows. Since even mainstream economic theorists watch television, their motive in advancing this theory must be something other than disinterested concern for scientific truth.

The claim that manufacturers manipulate and create consumer demand plays which one of the following roles in the argument?

(A) It is one of the claims on which the conclusion is based.

(B) It is the conclusion of the argument.

(C) It states the position argued against.

(D) It states a possible objection to the argument's conclusion.

(E) It provides supplementary background information.

S T O P

IF YOU FINISH BEFORE TIME IS CALLED, YOU MAY CHECK YOUR WORK ON THIS SECTION ONLY. DO NOT WORK ON ANY OTHER SECTION IN THE TEST.

LSAT® Writing Sample Topic

Directions: The scenario presented below describes two choices, either one of which can be supported on the basis of the information given. Your essay should consider both choices and argue for one over the other, based on the two specified criteria and the facts provided. There is no "right" or "wrong" choice: a reasonable argument can be made for either.

The publisher of *Willow Creek Dispatch*, the morning newspaper in the small town of Willow Creek, is hiring a new editor in chief. Write an argument favoring one candidate over the other based on the following considerations:

- The *Dispatch* wants to gain a reputation as a leader among small town newspapers.
- The *Dispatch* needs an editor in chief who understands the issues that are important to the residents of Willow Creek.

Amanda Fitzgerald is currently the editor of the local news section of a major city newspaper, where she worked as a reporter for over a decade before becoming an editor eight years ago. While a reporter, she won five national journalism awards for articles on public housing, community control of schools, and the demise of neighborhood businesses. Her colleagues describe her as "an advocate for excellence" as an editor. She grew up in Forest Knolls, a small town near Willow Creek; though she has not lived there for 23 years, she returns occasionally to visit her brother and his family.

Molly Chu was born and raised in a large city. She is the editor in chief of the *Lumberton Gazette*, the morning paper in Lumberton, a nearby town of comparable size to Willow Creek. She has worked at the *Gazette* for the past eleven years, becoming the editor in chief two years ago after a highly praised stint as the newspaper's only staff reporter. The Association of Small Town Newspapers awarded her third place in last year's editorial competition. In addition, parts of her article about health care in small towns were quoted in a story about health care that was the lead article in a national magazine.

Directions:

1. Use the Answer Key on the next page to check your answers.

2. Use the Scoring Worksheet below to compute your raw score.

3. Use the Score Conversion Chart to convert your raw score into the 120-180 scale.

Scoring Worksheet

1. Enter the number of questions you answered correctly in each section.

	Number Correct
SECTION I	_____
SECTION II	_____
SECTION III	_____
SECTION IV	_____

2. Enter the sum here: _____
   This is your Raw Score.

Conversion Chart

For Converting Raw Score to the 120-180 LSAT Scaled Score
LSAT Form 5LSS22

Reported Score	Raw Score Lowest	Raw Score Highest
180	99	101
179	—*	—*
178	98	98
177	97	97
176	96	96
175	95	95
174	94	94
173	93	93
172	92	92
171	91	91
170	90	90
169	89	89
168	88	88
167	86	87
166	85	85
165	84	84
164	82	83
163	81	81
162	79	80
161	77	78
160	76	76
159	74	75
158	72	73
157	71	71
156	69	70
155	67	68
154	65	66
153	63	64
152	61	62
151	59	60
150	58	58
149	56	57
148	54	55
147	52	53
146	50	51
145	48	49
144	46	47
143	44	45
142	43	43
141	41	42
140	39	40
139	37	38
138	36	36
137	34	35
136	32	33
135	30	31
134	29	29
133	27	28
132	26	26
131	24	25
130	23	23
129	22	22
128	20	21
127	19	19
126	18	18
125	17	17
124	16	16
123	15	15
122	14	14
121	13	13
120	0	12

*There is no raw score that will produce this scaled score for this form.

SECTION I

1.	A	8.	D	15.	B	22.	A
2.	E	9.	B	16.	A	23.	B
3.	B	10.	B	17.	C	24.	A
4.	D	11.	D	18.	A		
5.	C	12.	D	19.	C		
6.	B	13.	C	20.	E		
7.	B	14.	E	21.	E		

SECTION II

1.	E	8.	B	15.	D	22.	A
2.	D	9.	D	16.	C	23.	A
3.	C	10.	D	17.	E	24.	A
4.	B	11.	B	18.	D	25.	E
5.	E	12.	E	19.	A	26.	E
6.	E	13.	A	20.	A		
7.	D	14.	E	21.	B		

SECTION III

1.	D	8.	A	15.	C	22.	B
2.	E	9.	E	16.	C	23.	B
3.	B	10.	B	17.	D	24.	E
4.	E	11.	A	18.	A	25.	B
5.	D	12.	B	19.	E	26.	D
6.	C	13.	E	20.	E	27.	D
7.	C	14.	D	21.	E		

SECTION IV

1.	D	8.	C	15.	E	22.	B
2.	C	9.	E	16.	A	23.	B
3.	E	10.	D	17.	B	24.	A
4.	D	11.	B	18.	A		
5.	C	12.	D	19.	A		
6.	B	13.	A	20.	D		
7.	C	14.	A	21.	E		

The Official LSAT PrepTest

12

- October 1994
- Form 4LSS26

The sample test that follows consists of four sections corresponding to the four scored sections of the October 1994 LSAT.

SECTION I

Time—35 minutes

26 Questions

Directions: The questions in this section are based on the reasoning contained in brief statements or passages. For some questions, more than one of the choices could conceivably answer the question. However, you are to choose the best answer; that is, the response that most accurately and completely answers the question. You should not make assumptions that are by commonsense standards implausible, superfluous, or incompatible with the passage. After you have chosen the best answer, blacken the corresponding space on your answer sheet.

1. It is probably within the reach of human technology to make the climate of Mars inhabitable. It might be several centuries before people could live there, even with breathing apparatuses, but some of the world's great temples and cathedrals took centuries to build. Research efforts now are justified if there is even a chance of making another planet inhabitable. Besides, the intellectual exercise of understanding how the Martian atmosphere might be changed could help in understanding atmospheric changes inadvertently triggered by human activity on Earth.

The main point of the argument is that

(A) it is probably technologically possible for humankind to alter the climate of Mars
(B) it would take several centuries to make Mars even marginally inhabitable
(C) making Mars inhabitable is an effort comparable to building a great temple or cathedral
(D) research efforts aimed at discovering how to change the climate of Mars are justified
(E) efforts to change the climate of Mars could facilitate understanding of the Earth's climate

Questions 2–3

Adults have the right to vote; so should adolescents. Admittedly, adolescents and adults are not the same. But to the extent that adolescents and adults are different, adults cannot be expected to represent the interests of adolescents. If adults cannot represent the interests of adolescents, then only by giving adolescents the vote will these interests be represented.

2. The argument relies on which one of the following assumptions?

(A) The right to vote is a right that all human beings should have.
(B) Adolescents and adults differ in most respects that are important.
(C) Adolescents should have their interests represented.
(D) Anyone who has the right to vote has all the rights an adult has.
(E) Adolescents have never enjoyed the right to vote.

3. The statement that adolescents and adults are not the same plays which one of the following roles in the argument?

(A) It presents the conclusion of the argument.
(B) It makes a key word in the argument more precise.
(C) It illustrates a consequence of one of the claims that are used to support the conclusion.
(D) It distracts attention from the point at issue.
(E) It concedes a point that is then used to support the conclusion.

GO ON TO THE NEXT PAGE.

4. When deciding where to locate or relocate, businesses look for an educated work force, a high level of services, a low business-tax rate, and close proximity to markets and raw materials. However, although each of these considerations has approximately equal importance, the lack of proximity either to markets or to raw materials often causes municipalities to lose prospective businesses, whereas having a higher-than-average business-tax rate rarely has this effect.

Which one of the following, if true, most helps to resolve the apparent discrepancy in the statements above?

(A) Taxes paid by businesses constitute only a part of the tax revenue collected by most municipalities.

(B) In general, the higher the rate at which municipalities tax businesses, the more those municipalities spend on education and on providing services to businesses.

(C) Businesses sometimes leave a municipality after that municipality has raised its taxes on businesses.

(D) Members of the work force who are highly educated are more likely to be willing to relocate to secure work than are less highly educated workers.

(E) Businesses have sometimes tried to obtain tax reductions from municipalities by suggesting that without such a reduction the business might be forced to relocate elsewhere.

Questions 5–6

Oscar: I have been accused of plagiarizing the work of Ethel Myers in my recent article. But that accusation is unwarranted. Although I admit I used passages from Myers' book without attribution, Myers gave me permission in private correspondence to do so.

Millie: Myers cannot give you permission to plagiarize. Plagiarism is wrong, not only because it violates authors' rights to their own words, but also because it misleads readers: it is fundamentally a type of lie. A lie is no less a lie if another person agrees to the deception.

5. Which one of the following principles, if established, would justify Oscar's judgment?

(A) A writer has no right to quote passages from another published source if the author of that other source has not granted the writer permission to do so.

(B) The writer of an article must cite the source of all passages that were not written by that writer if those passages are more than a few sentences long.

(C) Plagiarism is never justified, but writers are justified in occasionally quoting without attribution the work of other writers if the work quoted has not been published.

(D) An author is entitled to quote freely without attribution the work of a writer if that writer relinquishes his or her exclusive right to the material.

(E) Authors are entitled to quote without attribution passages that they themselves have written and published in other books or articles.

6. Millie uses which one of the following argumentative strategies in contesting Oscar's position?

(A) analyzing plagiarism in a way that undermines Oscar's position

(B) invoking evidence to show that Oscar did quote Myers' work without attribution

(C) challenging Oscar's ability to prove that he had received Myers' permission to quote Myers' work without attribution

(D) citing a theory of rights that prohibits plagiarism and suggesting that Oscar is committed to that theory

(E) showing that Oscar's admission demonstrates his lack of credibility

GO ON TO THE NEXT PAGE.

7. Soil scientists studying the role of compost in horticulture have found that, while compost is useful for building soil structure, it does not supply large enough quantities of the nutrients essential for plant growth to make it a replacement for fertilizer. Many home gardeners, however, have found they can grow healthy and highly productive plants in soil that lacked essential nutrients by enriching the soil with nothing but compost.

Which one of the following, if true, most helps to explain the discrepant findings of the soil scientists and the home gardeners?

(A) The findings of soil scientists who are employed by fertilizer manufacturers do not differ widely from those of scientists employed by the government or by universities.

(B) Compost used in research projects is usually made from leaves and grass clippings only, whereas compost used in home gardens is generally made from a wide variety of ingredients.

(C) Most plants grown in home gardens and in scientists' test plots need a favorable soil structure, as well as essential nutrients, in order to thrive.

(D) The soil in test plots, before it is adjusted in the course of experiments, tends to contain about the same quantities of plant nutrients as does soil in home gardens to which no compost or fertilizer has been added.

(E) Some of the varieties of plants grown by home gardeners require greater quantities of nutrients in order to be healthy than do the varieties of plants generally grown by the soil scientists in test plots.

8. At Happywell, Inc., last year the average annual salary for dieticians was $50,000, while the average annual salary for physical therapists was $42,000. The average annual salary for all Happywell employees last year was $40,000.

If the information above is correct, which one of the following conclusions can properly be drawn on the basis of it?

(A) There were more physical therapists than dieticians at Happywell last year.

(B) There was no dietician at Happywell last year who earned less than the average for a physical therapist.

(C) At least one Happywell employee earned less than the average for a physical therapist last year.

(D) At least one physical therapist earned less than the lowest-paid Happywell dietician last year.

(E) At least one dietician earned more than the highest-paid Happywell physical therapist last year.

9. Since multinational grain companies operate so as to maximize profits, they cannot be relied on to initiate economic changes that would reform the world's food-distribution system. Although it is true that the actions of multinational companies sometimes do result in such economic change, this result is incidental, arising not from the desire for reform but from the desire to maximize profits. The maximization of profits normally depends on a stable economic environment, one that discourages change.

The main point of the argument is that

(A) the maximization of profits depends on a stable economic environment

(B) when economic change accompanies business activity, that change is initiated by concern for the profit motive

(C) multinational grain companies operate so as to maximize profits

(D) the world's current food-distribution system is not in need of reform

(E) multinational grain companies cannot be relied on to initiate reform of the world's food-distribution system

10. Stage performances are judged to be realistic to the degree that actors reproduce on stage the behaviors generally associated by audiences with the emotional states of the characters portrayed. Traditional actors imitate those behaviors, whereas Method actors, through recollection of personal experience, actually experience the same emotions that their characters are meant to be experiencing. Audiences will therefore judge the performances of Method actors to be more realistic than the performances of traditional actors.

Which one of the following is an assumption on which the argument depends?

(A) Performances based on an actor's own experience of emotional states are more likely to affect an audience's emotions than are performances based on imitations of the behaviors generally associated with those emotional states.

(B) The behavior that results when a Method actor feels a certain emotion will conform to the behavior that is generally associated by audiences with that emotion.

(C) Realism is an essential criterion for evaluating the performances of both traditional actors and Method actors.

(D) Traditional actors do not aim to produce performances that are realistic representations of a character's emotional states.

(E) In order to portray a character, a Method actor need not have had experiences identical to those of the character portrayed.

GO ON TO THE NEXT PAGE.

11. The demand for used cars has risen dramatically in Germany in recent years. Most of this demand is generated by former East Germans who cannot yet afford new cars and for whom cars were generally unavailable prior to unification. This demand has outstripped supply and thus has exerted an upward pressure on the prices of used cars. Consequently, an increasing number of former West Germans, in order to take advantage of the improved market, will be selling the cars they have owned for several years. Hence, the German new-car market will most likely improve soon as well.

Which one of the following, if true, would most help to support the conclusion about the German new-car market?

(A) The demand for old cars in former West Germany is greater than the demand for new cars in former East Germany.

(B) In most European countries, the sale of a used car is subject to less tax than is the sale of a new car.

(C) Most Germans own very few cars in the course of their lives.

(D) Most former West Germans purchase new cars once they sell their used cars.

(E) Many former East Germans prefer to buy cars imported from North America because they are generally larger than European cars.

12. In 1980 health officials began to publicize the adverse effects of prolonged exposure to the sun, and since then the number of people who sunbathe for extended periods of time has decreased considerably each year. Nevertheless, in 1982 there was a dramatic rise in newly reported cases of melanoma, a form of skin cancer found mostly in people who have had prolonged exposure to the sun.

Which one of the following, if true, helps to resolve the apparent discrepancy in the information above?

(A) Before 1980 a considerable number of the people who developed melanoma as a result of prolonged exposure to the sun were over forty years of age.

(B) Before 1980, when most people had not yet begun to avoid prolonged exposure to the sun, sunbathing was widely thought to be healthful.

(C) In 1982 scientists reported that the body's need for exposure to sunlight in order to produce vitamin D, which helps prevent the growth of skin cancers, is less than was previously thought.

(D) In 1982 medical researchers perfected a diagnostic technique that allowed them to detect the presence of melanoma much earlier than had previously been possible.

(E) Since 1980, those people who have continued to sunbathe for extended periods of time have used sunblocks that effectively screen out the ultraviolet rays that help cause melanoma.

13. The tiny country of Minlandia does not produce its own television programming. Instead, the citizens of Minlandia, who generally are fluent not only in their native Minlandian, but also in Boltese, watch Boltese-language television programs from neighboring Bolta. Surveys show that the Minlandians spend on average more hours per week reading for pleasure and fewer hours per week watching television than people anywhere else in the world. A prominent psychologist accounts for the survey results by explaining that people generally prefer to be entertained in their native language, even if they are perfectly fluent in other languages.

The explanation offered by the psychologist accounts for the Minlandians' behavior only if which one of the following is assumed?

(A) Some Minlandians derive no pleasure from watching television in a language other than their native Minlandian.

(B) The study of Boltese is required of Minlandian children as part of their schooling.

(C) The proportion of bilingual residents to total population is greater in Minlandia than anywhere else in the world.

(D) At least some of what the Minlandians read for pleasure is in the Minlandian language.

(E) When Minlandians watch Boltese television programs, they tend to ignore the fact that they are hearing a foreign language spoken.

14. Morris High School has introduced a policy designed to improve the working conditions of its new teachers. As a result of this policy, only one-quarter of all part-time teachers now quit during their first year. However, a third of all full-time teachers now quit during their first year. Thus, more full-time than part-time teachers at Morris now quit during their first year.

The argument's reasoning is questionable because the argument fails to rule out the possibility that

(A) before the new policy was instituted, more part-time than full-time teachers at Morris High School used to quit during their first year

(B) before the new policy was instituted, the same number of full-time teachers as part-time teachers at Morris High School used to quit during their first year

(C) Morris High School employs more new full-time teachers than new part-time teachers

(D) Morris High School employs more new part-time teachers than new full-time teachers

(E) Morris High School employs the same number of new part-time as new full-time teachers

GO ON TO THE NEXT PAGE.

Questions 15–16

Salmonella is a food-borne microorganism that can cause intestinal illness. The illness is sometimes fatal, especially if not identified quickly and treated. Conventional *Salmonella* tests on food samples are slow and can miss unusual strains of the microorganism. A new test identifies the presence or absence of *Salmonella* by the one piece of genetic material common to all strains. Clearly, public health officials would be well advised to replace the previous *Salmonella* tests with the new test.

15. Which one of the following, if true, most strengthens the argument?

   (A) The level of skill required for laboratory technicians to perform the new test is higher than that required to perform previous tests for *Salmonella*.

   (B) The new test returns results very soon after food samples are submitted for testing.

   (C) A proposed new treatment for *Salmonella* poisoning would take effect faster than the old treatment.

   (D) *Salmonella* poisoning is becoming less frequent in the general population.

   (E) Some remedies for *Salmonella* poisoning also cure intestinal disorders caused by other microorganisms.

16. Which one of the following, if true, most substantially weakens the argument?

   (A) The new test identifies genetic material from *Salmonella* organisms only and not from similar bacteria.

   (B) The new test detects the presence of *Salmonella* at levels that are too low to pose a health risk to people.

   (C) *Salmonella* is only one of a variety of food-borne microorganisms that can cause intestinal illness.

   (D) The new test has been made possible only recently by dramatic advances in biological science.

   (E) Symptoms of *Salmonella* poisoning are often mistaken for those of other common intestinal illnesses.

17. On average, city bus drivers who are using the new computerized fare-collection system have a much better on-time record than do drivers using the old fare-collection system. Millicent Smith has the best on-time record of any bus driver in the city. Therefore, she must be using the computerized fare-collection system.

Which one of the following contains flawed reasoning most similar to that contained in the argument above?

   (A) All the city's solid-waste collection vehicles acquired after 1988 have a larger capacity than any of those acquired before 1988. This vehicle has the largest capacity of any the city owns, so it must have been acquired after 1988.

   (B) The soccer players on the blue team are generally taller than the players on the gold team. Since Henri is a member of the blue team, he is undoubtedly taller than most of the members of the gold team.

   (C) This tomato is the largest of this year's crop. Since the tomatoes in the experimental plot are on average larger than those grown in the regular plots, this tomato must have been grown in the experimental plot.

   (D) Last week's snowstorm in Toronto was probably an average storm for the area. It was certainly heavier than any snowstorm known to have occurred in Miami, but any average snowstorm in Toronto leaves more snow than ever falls in Miami.

   (E) Lawn mowers powered by electricity generally require less maintenance than do lawn mowers powered by gasoline. This lawn mower is powered by gasoline, so it will probably require a lot of maintenance.

GO ON TO THE NEXT PAGE.

18. Frieda: Lightning causes fires and damages electronic equipment. Since lightning rods can prevent any major damage, every building should have one.

    Erik: Your recommendation is pointless. It is true that lightning occasionally causes fires, but faulty wiring and overloaded circuits cause far more fires and damage to equipment than lightning does.

    Erik's response fails to establish that Frieda's recommendation should not be acted on because his response

    (A) does not show that the benefits that would follow from Frieda's recommendation would be offset by any disadvantages
    (B) does not offer any additional way of lessening the risk associated with lightning
    (C) appeals to Frieda's emotions rather than to her reason
    (D) introduces an irrelevant comparison between overloaded circuits and faulty wiring
    (E) confuses the notion of preventing damage with that of causing inconvenience

19. The use of automobile safety seats by children aged 4 and under has nearly doubled in the past 8 years. It is clear that this increase has prevented child fatalities that otherwise would have occurred, because although the number of children aged 4 and under who were killed while riding in cars involved in accidents rose 10 percent over the past 8 years, the total number of serious automobile accidents rose by 20 percent during that period.

    Which one of the following, if true, most strengthens the argument?

    (A) Some of the automobile safety seats purchased for children under 4 continue to be used after the child reaches the age of 5.
    (B) The proportion of serious automobile accidents involving child passengers has remained constant over the past 8 years.
    (C) Children are taking more trips in cars today than they were 8 years ago, but the average total time they spend in cars has remained constant.
    (D) The sharpest increase in the use of automobile safety seats over the past 8 years has been for children over the age of 2.
    (E) The number of fatalities among adults involved in automobile accidents rose by 10 percent over the past 8 years.

Questions 20–21

The new perfume Aurora smells worse to Joan than any comparably priced perfume, and none of her friends likes the smell of Aurora as much as the smell of other perfumes. However, she and her friends must have a defect in their sense of smell, since Professor Jameson prefers the smell of Aurora to that of any other perfume and she is one of the world's foremost experts on the physiology of smell.

20. The reasoning is flawed because it

    (A) calls into question the truthfulness of the opponent rather than addressing the point at issue
    (B) ignores the well-known fact that someone can prefer one thing to another without liking either very much
    (C) fails to establish that there is widespread agreement among the experts in the field
    (D) makes an illegitimate appeal to the authority of an expert
    (E) misrepresents the position against which it is directed

21. From the information presented in support of the conclusion, it can be properly inferred that

    (A) none of Joan's friends is an expert on the physiology of smell
    (B) Joan prefers all other perfumes to Aurora
    (C) Professor Jameson is not one of Joan's friends
    (D) none of Joan's friends likes Aurora perfume
    (E) Joan and her friends all like the same kinds of perfumes

GO ON TO THE NEXT PAGE.

22. At the end of the year, Wilson's Department Store awards free merchandise to its top salespeople. When presented with the fact that the number of salespeople receiving these awards has declined markedly over the past fifteen years, the newly appointed president of the company responded, "In that case, since our award criterion at present is membership in the top third of our sales force, we can also say that the number of salespeople passed over for these awards has similarly declined."

Which one of the following is an assumption that would allow the company president's conclusion to be properly drawn?

(A) Policies at Wilson's with regard to hiring salespeople have not become more lax over the past fifteen years.

(B) The number of salespeople at Wilson's has increased over the past fifteen years.

(C) The criterion used by Wilson's for selecting its award recipients has remained the same for the past fifteen years.

(D) The average total sales figures for Wilson's salespeople have been declining for fifteen years.

(E) Wilson's calculates its salespeople's sales figures in the same way as it did fifteen years ago.

23. The capture of a wild animal is justified only as a last resort to save that animal's life. But many wild animals are captured not because their lives are in any danger but so that they can be bred in captivity. Hence, many animals that have been captured should not have been captured.

Which one of the following arguments is most similar in its pattern of reasoning to the argument above?

(A) Punishing a child is justified if it is the only way to reform poor behavior. But punishment is never the only way to reform poor behavior. Hence, punishing a child is never justified.

(B) Parents who never punish a child are not justified in complaining if the child regularly behaves in ways that disturb them. But many parents who prefer not to punish their children complain regularly about their children's behavior. Hence, many parents who complain about their children have no right to complain.

(C) Punishing a young child is justified only if it is done out of concern for the child's future welfare. But many young children are punished not in order to promote their welfare but to minimize sibling rivalry. Hence, many children who are punished should not have been punished.

(D) A teacher is entitled to punish a child only if the child's parents have explicitly given the teacher the permission to do so. But many parents never give their child's teacher the right to punish their child. Hence, many teachers should not punish their pupils.

(E) Society has no right to punish children for deeds that would be crimes if the children were adults. But society does have the right to protect itself from children who are known threats. Hence, confinement of such children does not constitute punishment.

GO ON TO THE NEXT PAGE.

24. Until recently it was thought that ink used before the sixteenth century did not contain titanium. However, a new type of analysis detected titanium in the ink of the famous Bible printed by Johannes Gutenberg and in that of another fifteenth-century Bible known as B-36, though not in the ink of any of numerous other fifteenth-century books analyzed. This finding is of great significance, since it not only strongly supports the hypothesis that B-36 was printed by Gutenberg but also shows that the presence of titanium in the ink of the purportedly fifteenth-century Vinland Map can no longer be regarded as a reason for doubting the map's authenticity.

The reasoning in the passage is vulnerable to criticism on the ground that

(A) the results of the analysis are interpreted as indicating that the use of titanium as an ingredient in fifteenth-century ink both was, and was not, extremely restricted

(B) if the technology that makes it possible to detect titanium in printing ink has only recently become available, it is unlikely that printers or artists in the fifteenth century would know whether their ink contained titanium or not

(C) it is unreasonable to suppose that determination of the date and location of a document's printing or drawing can be made solely on the basis of the presence or absence of a single element in the ink used in the document

(D) both the B-36 Bible and the Vinland Map are objects that can be appreciated on their own merits whether or not the precise date of their creation or the identity of the person who made them is known

(E) the discovery of titanium in the ink of the Vinland Map must have occurred before titanium was discovered in the ink of the Gutenberg Bible and the B-36 Bible

25. All actors are exuberant people and all exuberant people are extroverts, but nevertheless it is true that some shy people are actors.

If the statements above are true, each of the following must also be true EXCEPT:

(A) Some shy people are extroverts.
(B) Some shy extroverts are not actors.
(C) Some exuberant people who are actors are shy.
(D) All people who are not extroverts are not actors.
(E) Some extroverts are shy.

26. Science Academy study: It has been demonstrated that with natural methods, some well-managed farms are able to reduce the amounts of synthetic fertilizer and pesticide and also of antibiotics they use without necessarily decreasing yields; in some cases yields can be increased.

Critics: Not so. The farms the academy selected to study were the ones that seemed most likely to be successful in using natural methods. What about the farmers who have tried such methods and failed?

Which one of the following is the most adequate evaluation of the logical force of the critics' response?

(A) Success and failure in farming are rarely due only to luck, because farming is the management of chance occurrences.

(B) The critics show that the result of the study would have been different if twice as many farms had been studied.

(C) The critics assume without justification that the failures were not due to soil quality.

(D) The critics demonstrate that natural methods are not suitable for the majority of farmers.

(E) The issue is only to show that something is possible, so it is not relevant whether the instances studied were representative.

S T O P

IF YOU FINISH BEFORE TIME IS CALLED, YOU MAY CHECK YOUR WORK ON THIS SECTION ONLY.
DO NOT WORK ON ANY OTHER SECTION IN THE TEST.

SECTION II

Time—35 minutes

24 Questions

<u>Directions</u>: Each group of questions in this section is based on a set of conditions. In answering some of the questions, it may be useful to draw a rough diagram. Choose the response that most accurately and completely answers each question and blacken the corresponding space on your answer sheet.

Questions 1–6

A piano instructor will schedule exactly one lesson for each of six students—Grace, Henry, Janet, Steve, Tom, and Una—one lesson per day for six consecutive days. The schedule must conform to the following conditions:

Henry's lesson is later in the schedule than Janet's lesson.

Una's lesson is later in the schedule than Steve's lesson.

Steve's lesson is exactly three days after Grace's lesson.

Janet's lesson is on the first day or else the third day.

1. If Janet's lesson is scheduled for the first day, then the lesson for which one of the following students must be scheduled for the sixth day?

(A) Grace
(B) Henry
(C) Steve
(D) Tom
(E) Una

2. For which one of the following students is there an acceptable schedule in which the student's lesson is on the third day and another acceptable schedule in which the student's lesson is on the fifth day?

(A) Grace
(B) Henry
(C) Steve
(D) Tom
(E) Una

3. Which one of the following is a complete and accurate list of the students any one of whom could be the student whose lesson is scheduled for the second day?

(A) Grace
(B) Tom
(C) Grace, Tom
(D) Henry, Tom
(E) Grace, Henry, Tom

4. If Henry's lesson is scheduled for a day either immediately before or immediately after Tom's lesson, then Grace's lesson must be scheduled for the

(A) first day
(B) second day
(C) third day
(D) fourth day
(E) fifth day

5. If Janet's lesson is scheduled for the third day, which one of the following could be true?

(A) Grace's lesson is scheduled for a later day than Henry's lesson.
(B) Grace's lesson is scheduled for a later day than Una's lesson.
(C) Henry's lesson is scheduled for a later day than Una's lesson.
(D) Tom's lesson is scheduled for a later day than Henry's lesson.
(E) Tom's lesson is scheduled for a later day than Una's lesson.

6. Which one of the following is a complete and accurate list of days any one of which could be the day for which Tom's lesson is scheduled?

(A) first, second, third
(B) second, third, fourth
(C) second, fifth, sixth
(D) first, second, third, fourth
(E) second, third, fourth, sixth

GO ON TO THE NEXT PAGE.

Questions 7–11

Five children—F, G, H, J, and K—and four adults—Q, R, S, and T—are planning a canoeing trip. The canoeists will be divided into three groups—groups 1, 2, and 3—of three canoeists each, according to the following conditions:

There must be at least one adult in each group.
F must be in the same group as J.
G cannot be in the same group as T.
H cannot be in the same group as R.
Neither H nor T can be in group 2.

7. If F is in group 1, which one of the following could be true?

(A) G and K are in group 3.
(B) G and R are in group 3.
(C) J and S are in group 2.
(D) K and R are in group 1.
(E) Q and S are in group 2.

8. If F and S are in group 3, which one of the following must be true?

(A) G is in group 2.
(B) H is in group 3.
(C) K is in group 1.
(D) Q is in group 2.
(E) R is in group 1.

9. If G and K are in group 3, which one of the following must be true?

(A) H is in group 3.
(B) J is in group 1.
(C) R is in group 2.
(D) S is in group 3.
(E) T is in group 1.

10. If Q is in group 1 and S is in group 3, which one of the following CANNOT be true?

(A) G is in group 2.
(B) T is in group 1.
(C) There is exactly one child in group 1.
(D) There is exactly one child in group 2.
(E) There is exactly one child in group 3.

11. If G is the only child in group 1, which one of the following must be true?

(A) F is in group 3.
(B) K is in group 3.
(C) Q is in group 2.
(D) R is in group 1.
(E) S is in group 2.

GO ON TO THE NEXT PAGE.

Questions 12–17

Lara, Mendel, and Nastassia each buy at least one kind of food from a street vendor who sells only fruit cups, hot dogs, pretzels, and shish kebabs. They make their selections in accordance with the following restrictions:

None of the three buys more than one portion of each kind of food.

If any of the three buys a hot dog, that person does not also buy a shish kebab.

At least one of the three buys a hot dog, and at least one buys a pretzel.

Mendel buys a shish kebab.

Nastassia buys a fruit cup.

Neither Lara nor Nastassia buys a pretzel.

Mendel does not buy any kind of food that Nastassia buys.

12. Which one of the following statements must be true?

    (A) Lara buys a hot dog.
    (B) Lara buys a shish kebab.
    (C) Mendel buys a hot dog.
    (D) Mendel buys a pretzel.
    (E) Nastassia buys a hot dog.

13. If the vendor charges $1 for each portion of food, what is the minimum amount the three people could spend?

    (A) $3
    (B) $4
    (C) $5
    (D) $6
    (E) $7

14. If the vendor charges $1 for each portion of food, what is the greatest amount the three people could spend?

    (A) $5
    (B) $6
    (C) $7
    (D) $8
    (E) $9

15. If Lara and Mendel buy exactly two kinds of food each, which one of the following statements must be true?

    (A) Lara buys a fruit cup.
    (B) Lara buys a hot dog.
    (C) Mendel buys a fruit cup.
    (D) There is exactly one kind of food that Lara and Mendel both buy.
    (E) There is exactly one kind of food that Lara and Nastassia both buy.

16. If Lara buys a shish kebab, which one of the following statements must be true?

    (A) Lara buys a fruit cup.
    (B) Mendel buys a fruit cup.
    (C) Nastassia buys a hot dog.
    (D) Nastassia buys exactly one kind of food.
    (E) Exactly one person buys a fruit cup.

17. Assume that the condition is removed that prevents a customer who buys a hot dog from buying a shish kebab but all other conditions remain the same. If the vendor charges $1 for each portion of food, what is the maximum amount the three people could spend?

    (A) $5
    (B) $6
    (C) $7
    (D) $8
    (E) $9

GO ON TO THE NEXT PAGE.

Questions 18–24

A science student has exactly four flasks—1, 2, 3, and 4—originally containing a red, a blue, a green, and an orange chemical, respectively. An experiment consists of mixing exactly two of these chemicals together by completely emptying the contents of one of the flasks into another of the flasks. The following conditions apply:

The product of an experiment cannot be used in further experiments.

Mixing the contents of 1 and 2 produces a red chemical.

Mixing the contents of 2 and 3 produces an orange chemical.

Mixing the contents of 3 with the contents of either 1 or 4 produces a blue chemical.

Mixing the contents of 4 with the contents of either 1 or 2 produces a green chemical.

18. If the student performs exactly one experiment, which one of the following could be the colors of the chemicals in the resulting three nonempty flasks?

    (A) blue, blue, green
    (B) blue, orange, orange
    (C) blue, orange, red
    (D) green, green, red
    (E) green, orange, orange

19. If the student performs exactly two experiments, which one of the following could be the colors of the chemicals in the resulting two nonempty flasks?

    (A) blue, blue
    (B) blue, orange
    (C) blue, red
    (D) green, red
    (E) orange, orange

20. If the student performs exactly one experiment and none of the resulting three nonempty flasks contains a red chemical, which one of the following could be the colors of the chemicals in the three flasks?

    (A) blue, blue, green
    (B) blue, green, green
    (C) blue, green, orange
    (D) blue, orange, orange
    (E) green, green, orange

21. If the student performs exactly one experiment and exactly one of the resulting three nonempty flasks contains a blue chemical, which one of the following must be the colors of the chemicals in the other two flasks?

    (A) both green
    (B) both orange
    (C) both red
    (D) one green and one red
    (E) one orange and one red

22. If the student will perform exactly two experiments and after the first experiment exactly one of the resulting three nonempty flasks contains an orange chemical, then in the second experiment the student could mix together the contents of flasks

    (A) 1 and 2
    (B) 1 and 3
    (C) 1 and 4
    (D) 2 and 3
    (E) 3 and 4

23. If the student performs exactly one experiment and none of the resulting three nonempty flasks contains an orange chemical, then the student must have mixed the contents of

    (A) flask 1 with flask 2
    (B) flask 1 with flask 4
    (C) flask 2 with flask 4
    (D) flask 2 with one of the other flasks
    (E) flask 4 with one of the other flasks

24. If the student performs exactly two experiments and exactly one of the resulting two nonempty flasks contains an orange chemical, then it must be true that the contents of the other nonempty flask is

    (A) obtained by mixing flasks 1 and 2
    (B) obtained by mixing flasks 2 and 4
    (C) blue
    (D) green
    (E) red

S T O P

IF YOU FINISH BEFORE TIME IS CALLED, YOU MAY CHECK YOUR WORK ON THIS SECTION ONLY.
DO NOT WORK ON ANY OTHER SECTION IN THE TEST.

SECTION III
Time—35 minutes
27 Questions

Directions: Each passage in this section is followed by a group of questions to be answered on the basis of what is <u>stated</u> or <u>implied</u> in the passage. For some of the questions, more than one of the choices could conceivably answer the question. However, you are to choose the <u>best</u> answer; that is, the response that most accurately and completely answers the question, and blacken the corresponding space on your answer sheet.

Modern architecture has been criticized for emphasizing practical and technical issues at the expense of aesthetic concerns. The high-rise buildings constructed throughout the industrialized
(5) world in the 1960s and 1970s provide ample evidence that cost-efficiency and utility have become the overriding concerns of the modern architect. However, Otto Wagner's seminal text on modern architecture, first published in Germany in
(10) 1896, indicates that the failures of modern architecture cannot be blamed on the ideals of its founders.

Wagner's *Modern Architecture* called for a new style based on modern technologies and modes of
(15) construction. He insisted that there could be no return to traditional, preindustrial models; only by accepting wholeheartedly the political and technological revolutions of the nineteenth century could the architect establish the forms appropriate
(20) to a modern, urban society. "All modern creations," Wagner wrote, "must correspond to the new materials and demands of the present. . .must illustrate our own better, democratic, self-confident, ideal nature," and must incorporate the new
(25) "colossal technical and scientific achievements" of the age. This would indeed seem to be the basis of a purely materialist definition of architecture, a prototype for the simplistic form-follows-function dogma that opponents have identified as the
(30) intellectual basis of modern architecture.

But the picture was more complex, for Wagner was always careful to distinguish between art and engineering. Ultimately, he envisaged the architect developing the skills of the engineer without losing
(35) the powers of aesthetic judgment that Wagner felt were unique to the artist. "Since the engineer is seldom a born artist and the architect must learn as a rule to be an engineer, architects will in time succeed in extending their influence into the realm
(40) occupied by the engineers, so that legitimate aesthetic demands can be met in a satisfactory way." In this symbiotic relationship essential to Modernism, art was to exercise the controlling influence.
(45) No other prospect was imaginable for Wagner, who was firmly rooted as a designer and, indeed, as a teacher in the Classical tradition. The apparent inconsistency of a confessed Classicist advising against the mechanical imitation of historical
(50) models and arguing for new forms appropriate to

the modern age created exactly the tension that made Wagner's writings and buildings so interesting. While he justified, for example, the choice of a circular ground plan for churches in
(55) terms of optimal sight-lines and the technology of the gasometer, the true inspiration was derived from the centralized churches of the Italian Renaissance. He acknowledged as a rationalist that there was no way back to the social and
(60) technological conditions that had produced the work of Michelangelo or Fischer von Erlach, but he recognized his emotional attachment to the great works of the Italian Renaissance and Austrian Baroque.

1. Which one of the following best expresses the main idea of the passage?

(A) Modern architecture has been criticized for emphasizing practical and technical issues and for failing to focus on aesthetic concerns.

(B) Critics have failed to take into account the technological innovations and aesthetic features that architects have incorporated into modern buildings.

(C) Wagner's *Modern Architecture* provides architects with a chronicle of the origins of modern architecture.

(D) Wagner's *Modern Architecture* indicates that the founders of modern architecture did not believe that practical issues should supersede the aesthetic concerns of the past.

(E) Wagner's seminal text, *Modern Architecture*, provides the intellectual basis for the purely materialistic definition of modern architecture.

GO ON TO THE NEXT PAGE.

2. According to the passage, Wagner asserts which one of the following about the roles of architect and engineer?

   (A) The architect should make decisions about aesthetic issues and leave decisions about technical matters to the engineer.

   (B) The engineer has often developed the powers of aesthetic judgment previously thought to be unique to the architect.

   (C) The judgment of the engineer should be as important as the judgment of the architect when decisions are made about aesthetic issues.

   (D) The technical judgment of the engineer should prevail over the aesthetic judgment of the architect in the design of modern buildings.

   (E) The architect should acquire the knowledge of technical matters typically held by the engineer.

3. The passage suggests that Wagner would be LEAST likely to agree with which one of the following statements about classical architecture and the modern architect?

   (A) The modern architect should avoid the mechanical imitation of the models of the Italian Renaissance and Austrian Baroque.

   (B) The modern architect cannot design buildings appropriate to a modern, urban society and still retain emotional attachments to the forms of the Italian Renaissance and Austrian Baroque.

   (C) The modern architect should possess knowledge of engineering as well as of the architecture of the past.

   (D) The modern architect should not base designs on the technological conditions that underlay the designs of the models of the Italian Renaissance and Austrian Baroque.

   (E) The designs of modern architects should reflect political ideals different from those reflected in the designs of classical architecture.

4. The passage suggests which one of the following about the quotations from *Modern Architecture* cited in the second paragraph?

   (A) They represent the part of Wagner's work that has had the least influence on the architects who designed the high-rise buildings of the 1960s and 1970s.

   (B) They describe the part of Wagner's work that is most often evoked by proponents of Wagner's ideas on art and technology.

   (C) They do not adequately reflect the complexity of Wagner's ideas on the use of modern technology in architecture.

   (D) They reflect Wagner's active participation in the political revolutions of the nineteenth century.

   (E) They provide an overview of Wagner's ideas on the relationship between art and technology.

5. The author of the passage states which one of the following about the concerns of modern architecture?

   (A) Cost-efficiency, utility, and aesthetic demands are the primary concerns of the modern architect.

   (B) Practical issues supersede aesthetic concerns in the design of many modern buildings.

   (C) Cost-efficiency is more important to the modern architect than are other practical concerns.

   (D) The design of many new buildings suggests that modern architects are still inspired by architectural forms of the past.

   (E) Many modern architects use current technology to design modern buildings that are aesthetically pleasing.

6. The author mentions Wagner's choice of a "circular ground plan for churches" (line 54) most likely in order to

   (A) provide an example of the kinds of technological innovations Wagner introduced into modern architecture

   (B) provide an example of Wagner's dismissal of historical forms from the Italian Renaissance

   (C) provide an example of a modern building where technological issues were much less significant than aesthetic demands

   (D) provide evidence of Wagner's tendency to imitate Italian Renaissance and Austrian Baroque models

   (E) provide evidence of the tension between Wagner's commitment to modern technology and to the Classical tradition

7. The passage is primarily concerned with

   (A) summarizing the history of a debate
   (B) explaining a traditional argument
   (C) describing and evaluating a recent approach
   (D) justifying a recent criticism by presenting new evidence
   (E) supporting an assertion by discussing an important work

GO ON TO THE NEXT PAGE.

In order to explain the socioeconomic achievement, in the face of disadvantages due to racial discrimination, of Chinese and Japanese immigrants to the United States and their
(5) descendants, sociologists have typically applied either culturally based or structurally based theories—but never both together. To use an economic metaphor, culturally based explanations assert the importance of the supply side of the labor
(10) market, emphasizing the qualities immigrant groups bring with them for competition in the United States labor market. Such explanations reflect a human-capital perspective in which status attainment is seen as a result of individuals' ability
(15) to generate resources. Structurally based explanations, on the other hand, examine the market condition of the immigrants' host society, particularly its discriminatory practices and their impact on the status attainment process of
(20) immigrant groups. In the economic metaphor, structural explanations assert the importance of the demand side of the labor market.

In order to understand the socioeconomic mobility of Chinese and Japanese immigrants and
(25) their descendants, only an analysis of supply-side and demand-side factors together, in the context of historical events, will suffice. On the cultural or supply side, differences in immigration pattern and family formation resulted in different rates of
(30) socioeconomic achievement for Chinese and Japanese immigrants. For various reasons, Chinese immigrants remained sojourners and did not (except for urban merchants) establish families. They were also hampered by ethnic conflict in the
(35) labor market. Japanese immigrants, on the other hand, were less constrained, made the transition from sojourner to settler within the first two decades of immigration, and left low-wage labor to establish small businesses based on a household
(40) mode of production. Chinese sojourners without families were more vulnerable to demoralization, whereas Japanese immigrants faced societal hostility with the emotional resources provided by a stable family life. Once Chinese immigrants began
(45) to establish nuclear families and produce a second generation, instituting household production similar to that established by Japanese immigrants, their socioeconomic attainment soon paralleled that of Japanese immigrants and their descendants.
(50) On the structural or demand side, changes in institutional constraints, immigration laws, labor markets, and societal hostility were rooted in the dynamics of capitalist economic development. Early capitalist development generated a demand for
(55) low-wage labor that could not be fulfilled. Early Chinese and Japanese immigration was a response to this demand. In an advanced capitalist economy, the demand for immigrant labor is more differentiated: skilled professional and technical
(60) labor fills empty positions in the primary labor

market and, with the traditional unskilled low-wage labor, creates two immigrant streams. The high levels of education attained by the descendants of Chinese and Japanese immigrants and their
(65) concentration in strategic states such as California paved the way for the movement of the second generation into the expanding primary labor market in the advanced capitalist economy that existed after the Second World War.

8. Which one of the following best expresses the main idea of the passage?

(A) The socioeconomic achievement of Chinese and Japanese immigrants and their descendants is best explained by a historical examination of the economic structures prevalent in the United States when such immigrant groups arrived.

(B) The socioeconomic achievement of Chinese and Japanese immigrants and their descendants is best explained by an examination of their cultural backgrounds, in particular their level of educational attainment.

(C) The socioeconomic achievement of Chinese and Japanese immigrants and their descendants has taken place in the context of a culturally based emphasis on the economic welfare of the nuclear family.

(D) Only the market structure of the capitalist economy of the United States in which supply has historically been regulated by demand can account for the socioeconomic achievement of Chinese and Japanese immigrants and their descendants.

(E) Only an analysis that combines an examination of the culture of Chinese and Japanese immigrant groups and the socioeconomic structure of the host country can adequately explain the socioeconomic achievement of Chinese and Japanese immigrants and their descendants.

9. Which one of the following can best be described as a supply-side element in the labor market, as such elements are explained in the passage?

(A) concentration of small businesses in a given geographical area
(B) need for workers with varying degrees of skill
(C) high value placed by immigrants on work
(D) expansion of the primary labor market
(E) development of an advanced capitalist economy

GO ON TO THE NEXT PAGE.

10. Which one of the following best states the function of the author's mention of "two immigrant streams" (line 62)?

    (A) It demonstrates the effects of changes in human capital.

    (B) It illustrates the operation of the primary labor market.

    (C) It explains the nature of early Chinese and Japanese immigration.

    (D) It characterizes the result of changing demand-side factors.

    (E) It underscores an influence on the labor market.

11. It can be inferred that the author's analysis of the socioeconomic achievement of Chinese and Japanese immigrants and their descendants differs from that of most sociologists primarily in that most sociologists

    (A) address the effects of the interaction of causal factors

    (B) exclude the factor of a developing capitalist economy

    (C) do not apply an economic metaphor

    (D) emphasize the disadvantageous effects of racial discrimination

    (E) focus on a single type of theoretical explanation

12. It can be inferred that which one of the following was an element of the experience of both Chinese and Japanese immigrants in the United States?

    (A) initial status as sojourners

    (B) slow accumulation of capital

    (C) quick transition from laborer to manager

    (D) rapid establishment of nuclear families

    (E) rapid acquisition of technical skills

13. The author is primarily concerned with

    (A) advancing a synthesis of approaches to an issue

    (B) challenging a tentative answer to a question

    (C) evaluating the soundness of theories

    (D) resolving the differences between schools of thought

    (E) outlining the achievements of a group

GO ON TO THE NEXT PAGE.

Although the legal systems of England and the United States are superficially similar, they differ profoundly in their approaches to and uses of legal reasons: substantive reasons are more common

(5) than formal reasons in the United States, whereas in England the reverse is true. This distinction reflects a difference in the visions of law that prevail in the two countries. In England the law has traditionally been viewed as a system of rules; the

(10) United States favors a vision of law as an outward expression of the community's sense of right and justice.

Substantive reasons, as applied to law, are based on moral, economic, political, and other

(15) considerations. These reasons are found both "in the law" and "outside the law," so to speak. Substantive reasons inform the content of a large part of the law: constitutions, statutes, contracts, verdicts, and the like. Consider, for example, a

(20) statute providing that "no vehicles shall be taken into public parks." Suppose that no specific rationales or purposes were explicitly written into this statute, but that it was clear (from its legislative history) that the substantive purpose of the statute

(25) was to ensure quiet and safety in the park. Now suppose that a veterans' group mounts a World War II jeep (in running order but without a battery) as a war memorial on a concrete slab in the park, and charges are brought against its members. Most

(30) judges in the United States would find the defendants not guilty because what they did had no adverse effect on park quiet and safety.

Formal reasons are different in that they frequently prevent substantive reasons from coming

(35) into play, even when substantive reasons are explicitly incorporated into the law at hand. For example, when a document fails to comply with stipulated requirements, the court may render the document legally ineffective. A will requiring

(40) written witness may be declared null and void and, therefore, unenforceable for the formal reason that the requirement was not observed. Once the legal rule—that a will is invalid for lack of proper witnessing—has been clearly established, and the

(45) legality of the rule is not in question, application of that rule precludes from consideration substantive arguments in favor of the will's validity or enforcement.

Legal scholars in England and the United States

(50) have long bemused themselves with extreme examples of formal and substantive reasoning. On the one hand, formal reasoning in England has led to wooden interpretations of statutes and an unwillingness to develop the common law through

(55) judicial activism. On the other hand, freewheeling substantive reasoning in the United States has resulted in statutory interpretations so liberal that the texts of some statutes have been ignored altogether.

14. Which one of the following best describes the content of the passage as a whole?

(A) an analysis of similarities and differences between the legal systems of England and the United States

(B) a reevaluation of two legal systems with the use of examples

(C) a contrast between the types of reasons embodied in the United States and English legal systems

(D) an explanation of how two distinct visions of the law shaped the development of legal reasoning

(E) a presentation of two types of legal reasons that shows the characteristics they have in common

15. It can be inferred from the passage that English judges would be likely to find the veterans' group discussed in the second paragraph guilty of violating the statute because

(A) not to do so would encourage others to act as the group did

(B) not to do so would be to violate the substantive reasons underlying the law

(C) the veterans failed to comply with the substantive purpose of the statute

(D) the veterans failed to demonstrate that their activities had no adverse effect on the public

(E) the veterans failed to comply with the stipulated requirements of the statute

16. From the discussion of wills in the third paragraph it can be inferred that substantive arguments as to the validity of a will might be considered under which one of the following circumstances?

(A) The legal rule requiring that a will be witnessed in writing does not stipulate the format of the will.

(B) The legal rule requiring that a will be witnessed stipulates that the will must be witnessed in writing by two people.

(C) The legal ruling requiring that a will be witnessed in writing stipulates that the witnessing must be done in the presence of a judge.

(D) A judge rules that the law requires a will to be witnessed in writing regardless of extenuating circumstances.

(E) A judge rules that the law can be interpreted to allow for a verbal witness to a will in a case involving a medical emergency.

GO ON TO THE NEXT PAGE.

17. The author of the passage makes use of all of the following in presenting the discussion of the English and the United States legal systems EXCEPT

(A) comparison and contrast
(B) generalization
(C) explication of terms
(D) a chronology of historical developments
(E) a hypothetical case

18. Which one of the following best describes the function of the last paragraph of the passage?

(A) It presents the consequences of extreme interpretations of the two types of legal reasons discussed by the author.
(B) It shows how legal scholars can incorrectly use extreme examples to support their views.
(C) It corrects inaccuracies in legal scholars' views of the nature of the two types of legal systems.
(D) It suggests how characterizations of the two types of legal reasons can become convoluted and inaccurate.
(E) It presents scholars' characterizations of both legal systems that are only partially correct.

19. The author of the passage suggests that in English law a substantive interpretation of a legal rule might be warranted under which one of the following circumstances?

(A) Social conditions have changed to the extent that to continue to enforce the rule would be to decide contrary to present-day social norms.
(B) The composition of the legislature has changed to the extent that to enforce the rule would be contrary to the views of the majority in the present legislative assembly.
(C) The legality of the rule is in question and its enforcement is open to judicial interpretation.
(D) Individuals who have violated the legal rule argue that application of the rule would lead to unfair judicial interpretations.
(E) Superior court judges have consistently ruled in decisions regarding the interpretation of the legal rule.

20. According to the passage, which one of the following statements about substantive reasons is true?

(A) They may be written into laws, but they may also exert an external influence on the law.
(B) They must be explicitly written into the law in order to be relevant to the application of the law.
(C) They are legal in nature and determine particular applications of most laws.
(D) They often provide judges with specific rationales for disregarding the laws of the land.
(E) They are peripheral to the law, whereas formal reasons are central to the law.

GO ON TO THE NEXT PAGE.

How does the brain know when carbohydrates
have been or should be consumed? The answer to
this question is not known, but one element in the
explanation seems to be the neurotransmitter
(5) serotonin, one of a class of chemical mediators that
may be released from a presynaptic neuron and that
cause the transmission of a nerve impulse across a
synapse to an adjacent postsynaptic neuron. In
general, it has been found that drugs that selectively
(10) facilitate serotonin-mediated neurotransmission
tend to cause weight loss, whereas drugs that block
serotonin-mediated transmission often have the
opposite effect: they often induce carbohydrate
craving and consequent weight gain.
(15) Serotonin is a derivative of tryptophan, an amino
acid that is normally present at low levels in the
bloodstream. The rate of conversion is affected by
the proportion of carbohydrates in an individual's
diet: carbohydrates stimulate the secretion of
(20) insulin, which facilitates the uptake of most amino
acids into peripheral tissues, such as muscles. Blood
tryptophan levels, however, are unaffected by
insulin, so the proportion of tryptophan in the
blood relative to the other amino acids increases
(25) when carbohydrates are consumed. Since
tryptophan competes with other amino acids for
transport across the blood–brain barrier into the
brain, insulin secretion indirectly speeds
tryptophan's entry into the central nervous system
(30) where, in a special cluster of neurons, it is
converted into serotonin.
The level of serotonin in the brain in turn affects
the amount of carbohydrate an individual chooses
to eat. Rats that are allowed to choose among
(35) synthetic foods containing different proportions of
carbohydrate and protein will normally alternate
between foods containing mostly protein and those
containing mostly carbohydrate. However, if rats
are given drugs that enhance the effect of serotonin,
(40) the rats' carbohydrate intake is reduced. On the
other hand, when rats are given drugs that interrupt
serotonin-mediated neurotransmission, their brains
fail to respond when carbohydrates are eaten, so
the desire for them persists.
(45) In human beings a serotoninlike drug,
d-fenfluramine (which releases serotonin into brain
synapses and then prolongs its action by blocking its
reabsorption into the presynaptic neuron),
selectively suppresses carbohydrate snacking (and
(50) its associated weight gain) in people who crave
carbohydrates. In contrast, drugs that block
serotonin-mediated transmission or that interact
with neurotransmitters other than serotonin have
the opposite effect: they often induce carbohydrate
(55) craving and subsequent weight gain. People who
crave carbohydrates report feeling refreshed and
invigorated after eating a carbohydrate-rich meal
(which would be expected to increase brain
serotonin levels). In contrast, those who do not
(60) crave carbohydrates become sleepy following a

high-carbohydrate meal. These findings suggest that
serotonin has other effects that may be useful
indicators of serotonin levels in human beings.

21. Which one of the following best states the main idea
of the passage?

(A) The body's need for carbohydrates varies with
the level of serotonin in the blood.
(B) The body's use of carbohydrates can be
regulated by the administration of
serotoninlike drugs.
(C) The role of serotonin in regulating the
consumption of carbohydrates is similar in
rats and in humans.
(D) The body's desire for carbohydrates can be
influenced by serotonin or serotoninlike
drugs.
(E) Tryptophan initiates a chain of events that
regulates the body's use of carbohydrates.

22. The term "rate" (line 17) refers to the rate at which

(A) serotonin is produced from tryptophan
(B) carbohydrates are taken into the body
(C) carbohydrates stimulate the secretion of
insulin
(D) insulin facilitates the uptake of amino acids
into peripheral tissues
(E) tryptophan enters the bloodstream

23. It can be inferred that a person is likely to crave
carbohydrates when

(A) the amount of insulin produced is too high
(B) the amount of serotonin in the brain is too low
(C) more tryptophan than usual crosses the
blood–brain barrier
(D) neurotransmission by neurotransmitters other
than serotonin is interrupted
(E) amino acids other than tryptophan are taken
up by peripheral tissues

GO ON TO THE NEXT PAGE.

24. The information in the passage indicates that if human beings were given a drug that inhibits the action of serotonin, which one of the following might be expected to occur?

   (A) Subjects would probably show a preference for carbohydrate-rich snacks rather than protein-rich snacks.
   (B) Subjects would probably become sleepy after eating a carbohydrate-rich meal.
   (C) Subjects would be more likely to lose weight than before they took the drug.
   (D) Subjects' blood tryptophan levels would probably increase.
   (E) Subjects' desire for both carbohydrates and proteins would increase.

25. The primary purpose of the second paragraph in the passage is to

   (A) provide an overview of current research concerning the effect of serotonin on carbohydrate consumption
   (B) contrast the role of tryptophan in the body with that of serotonin
   (C) discuss the role of serotonin in the transmission of neural impulses
   (D) explain how the brain knows that carbohydrates should be consumed
   (E) establish a connection between carbohydrate intake and the production of serotonin

26. It can be inferred that after a person has taken *d*-fenfluramine, he or she will probably be

   (A) inclined to gain weight
   (B) sleepy much of the time
   (C) unlikely to crave carbohydrates
   (D) unable to sleep as much as usual
   (E) likely to secrete more insulin than usual

27. The author's primary purpose is to

   (A) defend a point of view
   (B) correct a misconception
   (C) assess conflicting evidence
   (D) suggest new directions for investigation
   (E) provide information that helps explain a phenomenon

S T O P

IF YOU FINISH BEFORE TIME IS CALLED, YOU MAY CHECK YOUR WORK ON THIS SECTION ONLY.
DO NOT WORK ON ANY OTHER SECTION IN THE TEST.

SECTION IV
Time—35 minutes
24 Questions

Directions: The questions in this section are based on the reasoning contained in brief statements or passages. For some questions, more than one of the choices could conceivably answer the question. However, you are to choose the best answer; that is, the response that most accurately and completely answers the question. You should not make assumptions that are by commonsense standards implausible, superfluous, or incompatible with the passage. After you have chosen the best answer, blacken the corresponding space on your answer sheet.

1. Most regular coffee is made from arabica coffee beans because the great majority of consumers prefer its generally richer flavor to that of coffee made from robusta beans. Coffee drinkers who switch to decaffeinated coffee, however, overwhelmingly prefer coffee made from robusta beans, which are unlike arabica beans in that their flavor is not as greatly affected by decaffeination. Depending on the type of bean involved, decaffeination reduces or removes various substances, most of which are flavor-neutral but one of which contributes to the richness of the coffee's flavor.

    The statements above provide the most support for which one of the following conclusions?

    (A) The annual world crop of arabica beans is not large enough to satisfy completely the world demand for regular coffee.
    (B) Arabica beans contain more caffeine per unit of weight than do robusta beans.
    (C) Coffee drinkers who drink decaffeinated coffee almost exclusively are the ones who prefer regular coffee made from robusta beans to regular coffee made from arabica beans.
    (D) Decaffeination of arabica beans extracts more of the substance that enhances a coffee's flavor than does decaffeination of robusta beans.
    (E) There are coffee drinkers who switch from drinking regular coffee made from arabica beans to drinking decaffeinated coffee made from arabica beans because coffee made from arabica beans is less costly.

2. For the past 13 years, high school guidance counselors nationwide have implemented an aggressive program to convince high school students to select careers requiring college degrees. The government reported that the percentage of last year's high school graduates who went on to college was 15 percent greater than the percentage of those who graduated 10 years ago and did so. The counselors concluded from this report that the program had been successful.

    The guidance counselors' reasoning depends on which one of the following assumptions about high school graduates?

    (A) The number of graduates who went on to college remained constant each year during the 10-year period.
    (B) Any college courses that the graduates take will improve their career prospects.
    (C) Some of the graduates who went on to college never received guidance from a high school counselor.
    (D) There has been a decrease in the number of graduates who go on to college without career plans.
    (E) Many of last year's graduates who went on to college did so in order to prepare for careers requiring college degrees.

GO ON TO THE NEXT PAGE.

3. Insectivorous plants, which unlike other plants have the ability to trap and digest insects, can thrive in soils that are too poor in minerals to support noninsectivorous plants. Yet the mineral requirements of insectivorous plants are not noticeably different from the mineral requirements of noninsectivorous plants.

The statements above, if true, most strongly support which one of the following hypotheses?

(A) The insects that insectivorous plants trap and digest are especially abundant where the soil is poor in minerals.

(B) Insectivorous plants thrive only in soils that are too poor in minerals to support noninsectivorous plants.

(C) The types of minerals required by noninsectivorous plants are more likely than are the types of minerals required by insectivorous plants to be found in soils poor in minerals.

(D) The number of different environments in which insectivorous plants thrive is greater than the number of different environments in which noninsectivorous plants thrive.

(E) Insectivorous plants can get some of the minerals they require from the insects they trap and digest.

4. The region's water authority is responding to the current drought by restricting residential water use. Yet reservoir levels are now at the same height they were during the drought ten years ago when no restrictions were put into effect and none proved necessary. Therefore, imposing restrictions now is clearly premature.

Which one of the following, if true, most seriously calls the conclusion above into question?

(A) There are now more water storage reservoirs in the region than there were ten years ago.

(B) The population of the region is approximately three times greater than it was ten years ago.

(C) The region currently has more sources outside the drought-stricken area from which to draw water than it did ten years ago.

(D) The water-consuming home appliances and fixtures sold today are designed to use water more efficiently than those sold ten years ago.

(E) The price of water for residential use is significantly higher in the region than it is in regions that are not drought-stricken.

5. Montgomery, a biologist who is also well read in archaeology, has recently written a book on the origin and purpose of ancient monumental architecture. This book has received much positive attention in the popular press but has been severely criticized by many professional archaeologists for being too extreme. Montgomery's views do not deserve a negative appraisal, however, since those views are no more extreme than the views of some professional archaeologists.

The argument is most vulnerable to which one of the following criticisms?

(A) It fails to establish that professional archaeologists' views that are at least as extreme as Montgomery's views do not deserve negative appraisal for that reason.

(B) It assumes without warrant that many professional archaeologists consider biologists unqualified to discuss ancient architecture.

(C) It overlooks the possibility that many professional archaeologists are unfamiliar with Montgomery's views.

(D) It provides no independent evidence to show that the majority of professional archaeologists do not support Montgomery's views.

(E) It attempts to support its position by calling into question the motives of anyone who supports an opposing position.

6. Chronic fatigue syndrome is characterized by prolonged fatigue, muscular pain, and neurological problems. It is not known whether these symptoms are all caused by a single virus or whether each symptom is the result of a separate viral infection. A newly synthesized drug has been tested on those who suffer from chronic fatigue syndrome. Although the specific antiviral effects of this drug are unknown, it has lessened the severity of all of the symptoms of chronic fatigue syndrome. Thus there is evidence that chronic fatigue syndrome is, in fact, caused by one virus.

The argument assumes which one of the following?

(A) All those who suffer from prolonged fatigue also suffer from neurological problems.

(B) It is more likely that the new drug counteracts one virus than that it counteracts several viruses.

(C) The symptoms of chronic fatigue syndrome are dissimilar to those of any other syndrome.

(D) Most syndromes that are characterized by related symptoms are each caused by a single viral infection.

(E) An antiviral medication that eliminates the most severe symptoms of chronic fatigue syndrome thereby cures chronic fatigue syndrome.

GO ON TO THE NEXT PAGE.

7. DataCom, a company that filed many patents last year, was financially more successful last year than were its competitors, none of which filed many patents. It is therefore likely that DataCom owed its greater financial success to the fact that it filed many patents last year.

The argument is most vulnerable to criticism on the grounds that it

(A) presupposes what it sets out to demonstrate about the relationship between the financial success of DataCom's competitors and the number of patents they filed

(B) confuses a company's financial success with its technological innovativeness

(C) fails to establish whether any one of DataCom's competitors was financially more successful last year than was any other

(D) gives no reason to exclude the possibility that other differences between DataCom and its competitors accounted for its comparative financial success

(E) applies a generalization to an exceptional case

8. A history book written hundreds of years ago contains several inconsistencies. Some scholars argue that because the book contains inconsistencies, the author must have been getting information from more than one source.

The conclusion cited does not follow unless

(A) authors generally try to reconcile discrepancies between sources

(B) the inconsistencies would be apparent to the average reader of the history book at the present time

(C) the history book's author used no source that contained inconsistencies repeated in the history book

(D) the author of the history book was aware of the kinds of inconsistencies that can arise when multiple sources are consulted

(E) the author of the history book was familiar with all of the available source material that was relevant to the history book

9. Some games, such as chess and soccer, are competitive and played according to rules, but others, such as children's games of make believe, are neither. Therefore, being competitive and involving rules are not essential to being a game.

Which one of the following is most similar in its logical features to the argument above?

(A) Both the gourmet and the glutton enjoy eating. However, one can be a glutton, but not a gourmet, without having an educated palate. Therefore, having an educated palate is essential to being a gourmet, but enjoying food is not.

(B) All North American bears eat meat. Some taxonomists, however, have theorized that the giant panda, which eats only bamboo shoots, is a kind of bear. Either these taxonomists are wrong or eating meat is not essential to being a bear.

(C) It is true that dogs occasionally eat vegetation, but if dogs were not carnivorous they would be shaped quite differently from the way they are. Therefore, being carnivorous is essential to being a dog.

(D) Most automobiles, and nearly all of those produced today, are gasoline-fueled and four-wheeled, but others, such as some experimental electric cars, are neither. Therefore, being gasoline-fueled and having four wheels are not essential to being an automobile.

(E) Montréal's most vaunted characteristics, such as its cosmopolitanism and its vitality, are all to be found in many other cities. Therefore, cosmopolitanism and vitality are not essential properties of Montréal.

GO ON TO THE NEXT PAGE.

Questions 10–11

Household indebtedness, which some theorists regard as causing recession, was high preceding the recent recession, but so was the value of assets owned by households. Admittedly, if most of the assets were owned by quite affluent households, and most of the debt was owed by low-income households, high household debt levels could have been the cause of the recession despite high asset values: low-income households might have decreased spending in order to pay off debts while the quite affluent ones might simply have failed to increase spending. But, in fact, quite affluent people must have owed most of the household debt, since money is not lent to those without assets. Therefore, the real cause must lie elsewhere.

10. The argument is structured to lead to which one of the following conclusions?

(A) High levels of household debt did not cause the recent recession.
(B) Low-income households succeeded in paying off their debts despite the recent recession.
(C) Affluent people probably increased their spending levels during the recent recession.
(D) High levels of household debt have little impact on the economy.
(E) When people borrowed money prior to the recent recession, they did not use it to purchase assets.

11. Which one of the following, if true, casts the most doubt on the argument?

(A) Prior to the recent recession, middle-income households owed enough debt that they had begun to decrease spending.
(B) The total value of the economy's household debt is exceeded by the total value of assets held by households.
(C) Low-income households somewhat decreased their spending during the recent recession.
(D) During a recession the affluent usually borrow money only in order to purchase assets.
(E) Household debt is the category of debt least likely to affect the economy.

12. Fossil-fuel emissions, considered a key factor in the phenomenon known as global warming, contain two gases, carbon dioxide and sulfur dioxide, that have opposite effects on atmospheric temperatures. Carbon dioxide traps heat, tending to warm the atmosphere, whereas sulfur dioxide turns into sulfate aerosols that reflect sunlight back toward space, thereby tending to cool the atmosphere. Given that the heat-trapping effect is stronger than the cooling effect, cutting fossil-fuel emissions might be expected to slow the rise in global temperatures. Yet, surprisingly, if fossil-fuel emissions were cut today, global warming would actually be enhanced for more than three decades before the temperature rise began to slow.

Which one of the following, if true, most helps to explain the claim made in the last sentence above?

(A) Carbon dioxide stays in the atmosphere for many decades, while the sulfate aerosols fall out within days.
(B) Sulfur pollution is not spread evenly around the globe but is concentrated in the Northern Hemisphere, where there is a relatively high concentration of industry.
(C) While it has long been understood that sulfur dioxide is a harmful pollutant, it has been understood only recently that carbon dioxide might also be a harmful pollutant.
(D) Carbon dioxide is produced not only by automobiles but also by power plants that burn fossil fuels.
(E) Because fossil-fuel emissions contain sulfur dioxide, they contribute not only to global warming but also to acid rain.

GO ON TO THE NEXT PAGE.

13. Police published a "wanted" poster for a criminal fugitive in a medical journal, because the fugitive was known to have a certain acute noninfectious skin problem that would eventually require a visit to a doctor. The poster asked for information about the whereabouts of the fugitive. A physician's responding to the poster's request for information would not violate medical ethics, since physicians are already subject to requirements to report gunshot wounds to police and certain infectious diseases to health authorities. These exceptions to confidentiality are clearly ethical.

Which one of the following principles, while remaining compatible with the requirements cited above, supports the view that a physician's responding to the request would violate medical ethics?

(A) Since a physician acts both as a professional person and as a citizen, it is not ethical for a physician to conceal information about patients from duly constituted law enforcement agencies that have proper jurisdiction.

(B) Since a patient comes to a physician with the expectation that the patient's visit and medical condition will remain confidential, it is not ethical for a physician to share this information with anyone except personnel within the physician's office.

(C) Since the primary concern of medicine is individual and public health, it is not ethical for a physician, except in the case of gunshot wounds, to reduce patients' willingness to come for treatment by a policy of disclosing their identities to law-enforcement agencies.

(D) Except as required by the medical treatment of the patient, physicians cannot ethically disclose to others information about a patient's identity or medical condition without the patient's consent.

(E) Except to other medical personnel working to preserve or restore the health of a patient or of other persons, physicians cannot ethically disclose information about the identity of patients or their medical condition.

14. Ingrid: Rock music has produced no songs as durable as the songs of the 1940s, which continue to be recorded by numerous performers.

Jerome: True, rock songs are usually recorded only once. If the original recording continues to be popular, however, that fact can indicate durability, and the best rock songs will prove to be durable.

Jerome responds to Ingrid's claim by

(A) intentionally misinterpreting the claim
(B) showing that the claim necessarily leads to a contradiction
(C) undermining the truth of the evidence that Ingrid presents
(D) suggesting an alternative standard for judging the point at issue
(E) claiming that Ingrid's knowledge of the period under discussion is incomplete

15. Health insurance insulates patients from the expense of medical care, giving doctors almost complete discretion in deciding the course of most medical treatments. Moreover, with doctors being paid for each procedure performed, they have an incentive to overtreat patients. It is thus clear that medical procedures administered by doctors are frequently prescribed only because these procedures lead to financial rewards.

The argument uses which one of the following questionable techniques?

(A) assigning responsibility for a certain result to someone whose involvement in the events leading to that result was purely coincidental
(B) inferring the performance of certain actions on no basis other than the existence of both incentive and opportunity for performing those actions
(C) presenting as capricious and idiosyncratic decisions that are based on the rigorous application of well-defined principles
(D) depicting choices as having been made arbitrarily by dismissing without argument reasons that have been given for these choices
(E) assuming that the irrelevance of a consideration for one participant in a decision makes that consideration irrelevant for each participant in the decision

GO ON TO THE NEXT PAGE.

16. Chlorofluorocarbons are the best possible solvents to have in car engines for cleaning the electronic sensors in modern automobile ignition systems. These solvents have contributed significantly to automakers' ability to meet legally mandated emission standards. Now automakers will have to phase out the use of chlorofluorocarbons at the same time that emission standards are becoming more stringent.

If under the circumstances described above cars continue to meet emission standards, which one of the following is the most strongly supported inference?

(A) As emission standards become more stringent, automakers will increasingly cooperate with each other in the area of emission control.

(B) Car engines will be radically redesigned so as to do away with the need for cleaning the electronic ignition sensors.

(C) There will be a marked shift toward smaller, lighter cars that will have less powerful engines but will use their fuel more efficiently.

(D) The solvents developed to replace chlorofluorocarbons in car engines will be only marginally less effective than the chlorofluorocarbons themselves.

(E) Something other than the cleansers for electronic ignition sensors will make a relatively greater contribution to meeting emission standards than at present.

Questions 17–18

Two alternative drugs are available to prevent blood clots from developing after a heart attack. According to two major studies, drug Y does this no more effectively than the more expensive drug Z, but drug Z is either no more or only slightly more effective than drug Y. Drug Z's manufacturer, which has engaged in questionable marketing practices such as offering stock options to doctors who participate in clinical trials of drug Z, does not contest the results of the studies but claims that they do not reveal drug Z's advantages. However, since drug Z does not clearly treat the problem more effectively than drug Y, there is no established medical reason for doctors to use drug Z rather than drug Y on their heart-attack victims.

17. A major flaw in the argument is that the argument

(A) does not consider drugs or treatments other than drug Y and drug Z that may be used to prevent blood clotting in heart-attack patients

(B) neglects to compare the marketing practices of drug Y's manufacturer with those of drug Z's manufacturer

(C) fails to recognize that there may be medical criteria relevant to the choice between the two drugs other than their effectiveness as a treatment

(D) assumes without proof that the two drugs are similar in their effectiveness as treatments because they are similar in their chemical composition

(E) confuses economic reasons for selecting a treatment with medical reasons

18. Which one of the following principles, if established, would most help to justify a doctor's decision to use drug Z rather than drug Y when treating a patient?

(A) Only patients to whom the cost of an expensive treatment will not be a financial hardship should receive that treatment rather than a less expensive alternative one.

(B) Doctors who are willing to assist in research on the relative effectiveness of drugs by participating in clinical trials deserve fair remuneration for that participation.

(C) The decision to use a particular drug when treating a patient should not be influenced by the marketing practices employed by the company manufacturing that drug.

(D) A drug company's criticism of studies of its product that do not report favorably on that product is unavoidably biased and therefore invalid.

(E) Where alternative treatments exist and there is a chance that one is more effective than the other, the possibly more effective one should be employed, regardless of cost.

GO ON TO THE NEXT PAGE.

19. Jane: According to an article in this newsmagazine, children's hand-eye coordination suffers when they spend a great amount of time watching television. Therefore, we must restrict the amount of time Jacqueline and Mildred are allowed to watch television.

    Alan: Rubbish! The article says that only children under three are affected in that way. Jacqueline is ten and Mildred is eight. Therefore, we need not restrict their television viewing.

    Alan's argument against Jane's conclusion makes which one of the following errors in reasoning?

    (A) It relies on the same source that Jane cited in support of her conclusion.
    (B) It confuses undermining an argument in support of a given conclusion with showing that the conclusion itself is false.
    (C) It does not address the main point of Jane's argument and focuses instead on a side issue.
    (D) It makes an irrelevant appeal to an authority.
    (E) It fails to distinguish the consequences of a certain practice from the causes of the practice.

20. A new gardening rake with an S-shaped handle reduces compression stress on the spine during the pull stroke to about one-fifth of what it is with a straight-handled rake. During the push stroke, however, compression stress is five times more with the new rake than with a straight-handled rake. Neither the push stroke nor the pull stroke with a straight-handled rake produces enough compression stress to cause injury, but compression stress during the push stroke with the new rake is above the danger level. Therefore, straight-handled rakes are better than the new rakes for minimizing risk of spinal injury.

    The conclusion above is properly drawn from the premises given if which one of the following is true?

    (A) Compression stress resulting from pushing is the only cause of injuries to the spine that occur as a result of raking.
    (B) Raking is a frequent cause of spinal injury among gardeners.
    (C) The redesign of a tool rarely results in a net gain of efficiency, since gains tend to be counterbalanced by losses.
    (D) A garden rake can never be used in such a way that all the strokes with that rake are push strokes.
    (E) It is not possible to design a garden rake with a handle that is other than straight or S-shaped.

21. Some people fear that global warming will cause the large ice formations in the polar seas to melt, thereby warming the waters of those seas and threatening the plankton that is crucial to the marine food chain. Some scientists contend that it is unlikely that the melting process has begun, since water temperatures in the polar seas are the same today as they were a century ago.

    Which one of the following, if true, most seriously undermines the scientists' contention?

    (A) Much of the marine plant life that flourishes in the polar seas will die in the event that the water temperatures rise above their present levels.
    (B) The overall effect of the melting process will be an increase in global sea levels.
    (C) The mean air temperature above both land and water in the polar regions has not varied significantly over the past 100 years.
    (D) The temperature of water that contains melting ice tends to remain constant until all of the ice in the ice-and-water mixture has melted.
    (E) The mean temperature of ocean waters near the equator has remained constant over the past 100 years.

22. A long-term health study that followed a group of people who were age 35 in 1950 found that those whose weight increased by approximately half a kilogram or one pound per year after the age of 35 tended, on the whole, to live longer than those who maintained the weight they had at age 35. This finding seems at variance with other studies that have associated weight gain with a host of health problems that tend to lower life expectancy.

    Which one of the following, if true, most helps to resolve the apparently conflicting findings?

    (A) As people age, muscle and bone tissue tends to make up a smaller and smaller proportion of total body weight.
    (B) Individuals who reduce their cholesterol levels by losing weight can thereby also reduce their risk of dying from heart attacks or strokes.
    (C) Smokers, who tend to be leaner than nonsmokers, tend to have shorter life spans than nonsmokers.
    (D) The normal deterioration of the human immune system with age can be slowed down by a reduction in the number of calories consumed.
    (E) Diets that tend to lead to weight gain often contain not only excess fat but also unhealthful concentrations of sugar and sodium.

GO ON TO THE NEXT PAGE.

23. Insurance industry statistics demonstrate that cars with alarms or other antitheft devices are more likely to be stolen or broken into than cars without such devices or alarms. Therefore antitheft devices do not protect cars against thieves.

The pattern of flawed reasoning in the argument above is most similar to that in which one of the following?

(A) Since surveys reveal that communities with flourishing public libraries have, on average, better-educated citizens, it follows that good schools are typically found in communities with public libraries.

(B) Most public libraries are obviously intended to serve the interests of the casual reader, because most public libraries contain large collections of fiction and relatively small reference collections.

(C) Studies reveal that people who are regular users of libraries purchase more books per year than do people who do not use libraries regularly. Hence using libraries regularly does not reduce the number of books that library patrons purchase.

(D) Since youngsters who read voraciously are more likely to have defective vision than youngsters who do not read very much, it follows that children who do not like to read usually have perfect vision.

(E) Societies that support free public libraries are more likely to support free public universities than are societies without free public libraries. Hence a society that wishes to establish a free public university should first establish a free public library.

24. The problem that environmental economics aims to remedy is the following: people making economic decisions cannot readily compare environmental factors, such as clean air and the survival of endangered species, with other costs and benefits. As environmental economists recognize, solving this problem requires assigning monetary values to environmental factors. But monetary values result from people comparing costs and benefits in order to arrive at economic decisions. Thus, environmental economics is stymied by what motivates it.

If the considerations advanced in its support are true, the passage's conclusion is supported

(A) strongly, on the assumption that monetary values for environmental factors cannot be assigned unless people make economic decisions about these factors

(B) strongly, unless economic decision-making has not yet had any effect on the things categorized as environmental factors

(C) at best weakly, because the passage fails to establish that economic decision-makers do not by and large take adequate account of environmental factors

(D) at best weakly, because the argument assumes that pollution and other effects on environmental factors rarely result from economic decision-making

(E) not at all, since the argument is circular, taking that conclusion as one of its premises

S T O P

**IF YOU FINISH BEFORE TIME IS CALLED, YOU MAY CHECK YOUR WORK ON THIS SECTION ONLY.
DO NOT WORK ON ANY OTHER SECTION IN THE TEST.**

LSAT® Writing Sample Topic

Directions: The scenario presented below describes two choices, either one of which can be supported on the basis of the information given. Your essay should consider both choices and argue for one over the other, based on the two specified criteria and the facts provided. There is no "right" or "wrong" choice: a reasonable argument can be made for either.

Newhall City's television station is choosing between two shows on steroid drug use. Write an argument supporting one show over the other based on the following considerations:
- The station wants to attract younger viewers to its informational programs.
- The station wants its educational programs to be recognized for their in-depth analysis.

"A Question of Health" is an investigation of teenage steroid use in Newhall City's four high schools narrated by Marlene Seligman, prizewinning health columnist for the local newspaper. Seligman interviews a number of local students as well as school administrators, coaches, and faculty about the effects of steroid use on the students' lives. She also visits local hospitals and counseling centers to interview doctors and psychologists, who outline the serious physical and psychological effects of using steroids. Included in the show are detailed descriptions of treatment options available in Newhall City and their costs, as well as advice for parents who suspect their children of using steroids.

"David's Game" follows the story of 16-year-old David Worsley, a high school track star from another city who was removed from the team and lost a college scholarship offer after using and selling steroids. A physician who worked with David is interviewed, but the show focuses primarily on David, his family, and his teammates, all of whom describe how David's increasing dependence on steroids gradually distorted both his appearance and his personality. Family and friends discuss their helplessness as they watched him become more aggressive and violent. David explains the pressures he felt to excel in sports, to the exclusion of all other interests, and he suggests ways in which the larger culture intensifies this pressure. David ends the show by directing a plea to other teenagers to avoid steroids.

Directions:

1. Use the Answer Key on the next page to check your answers.

2. Use the Scoring Worksheet below to compute your raw score.

3. Use the Score Conversion Chart to convert your raw score into the 120-180 scale.

Scoring Worksheet

1. Enter the number of questions you answered correctly in each section.

	Number Correct
SECTION I	_____
SECTION II	_____
SECTION III	_____
SECTION IV	_____

2. Enter the sum here: _____
   This is your Raw Score.

Conversion Chart

For Converting Raw Score to the 120-180 LSAT Scaled Score
LSAT Form 4LSS26

Reported Score	Raw Score Lowest	Raw Score Highest
180	100	101
179	99	99
178	98	98
177	—*	—*
176	97	97
175	96	96
174	—*	—*
173	95	95
172	94	94
171	93	93
170	92	92
169	90	91
168	89	89
167	88	88
166	86	87
165	84	85
164	83	83
163	81	82
162	79	80
161	77	78
160	75	76
159	73	74
158	72	72
157	70	71
156	68	69
155	66	67
154	64	65
153	62	63
152	60	61
151	58	59
150	56	57
149	54	55
148	52	53
147	51	51
146	49	50
145	47	48
144	45	46
143	44	44
142	42	43
141	41	41
140	39	40
139	37	38
138	36	36
137	34	35
136	33	33
135	32	32
134	30	31
133	29	29
132	28	28
131	27	27
130	26	26
129	25	25
128	24	24
127	23	23
126	22	22
125	21	21
124	20	20
123	—*	—*
122	19	19
121	18	18
120	0	17

*There is no raw score that will produce this scaled score for this form.

SECTION I

1.	D	8.	C	15.	B	22.	C
2.	C	9.	E	16.	B	23.	C
3.	E	10.	B	17.	C	24.	A
4.	B	11.	D	18.	A	25.	B
5.	D	12.	D	19.	B	26.	E
6.	A	13.	D	20.	D		
7.	B	14.	D	21.	C		

SECTION II

1.	E	8.	A	15.	A	22.	E
2.	B	9.	E	16.	C	23.	E
3.	C	10.	D	17.	C	24.	D
4.	B	11.	B	18.	D		
5.	C	12.	D	19.	C		
6.	D	13.	B	20.	B		
7.	E	14.	B	21.	A		

SECTION III

1.	D	8.	E	15.	E	22.	A
2.	E	9.	C	16.	E	23.	B
3.	B	10.	D	17.	D	24.	A
4.	C	11.	E	18.	A	25.	E
5.	B	12.	A	19.	C	26.	C
6.	E	13.	A	20.	A	27.	E
7.	E	14.	C	21.	D		

SECTION IV

1.	D	8.	C	15.	B	22.	C
2.	E	9.	D	16.	E	23.	C
3.	E	10.	A	17.	C	24.	A
4.	B	11.	A	18.	E		
5.	A	12.	A	19.	B		
6.	B	13.	C	20.	A		
7.	D	14.	D	21.	D		

The Official LSAT PrepTest

13

- December 1994
- Form 5LSS28

The sample test that follows consists of four sections corresponding to the four scored sections of the December 1994 LSAT.

SECTION I

Time—35 minutes

24 Questions

Directions: Each group of questions in this section is based on a set of conditions. In answering some of the questions, it may be useful to draw a rough diagram. Choose the response that most accurately and completely answers each question and blacken the corresponding space on your answer sheet.

Questions 1–6

Exactly eight consumers—F, G, H, J, K, L, M, and N—will be interviewed by market researchers. The eight will be divided into exactly two 4-person groups—group 1 and group 2—before interviews begin. Each person is assigned to exactly one of the two groups according to the following conditions:

F must be in the same group as J.
G must be in a different group from M.
If H is in group 1, then L must be in group 1.
If N is in group 2, then G must be in group 1.

1. Group 1 could consist of

    (A) F, G, H, and J
    (B) F, H, L, and M
    (C) F, J, K, and L
    (D) G, H, L, and N
    (E) G, K, M, and N

2. If K is in the same group as N, which one of the following must be true?

    (A) G is in group 1.
    (B) H is in group 2.
    (C) J is in group 1.
    (D) K is in group 2.
    (E) M is in group 1.

3. If F is in the same group as H, which one of the following must be true?

    (A) G is in group 2.
    (B) J is in group 1.
    (C) K is in group 1.
    (D) L is in group 2.
    (E) M is in group 2.

4. If L and M are in group 2, then a person who could be assigned either to group 1 or, alternatively, to group 2 is

    (A) F
    (B) G
    (C) H
    (D) J
    (E) K

5. Each of the following is a pair of people who could be in group 1 together EXCEPT

    (A) F and G
    (B) F and H
    (C) F and L
    (D) H and G
    (E) H and N

6. If L is in group 2, then each of the following is a pair of people who could be in group 1 together EXCEPT

    (A) F and M
    (B) G and N
    (C) J and N
    (D) K and M
    (E) M and N

GO ON TO THE NEXT PAGE.

Questions 7–11

Five people—Harry, Iris, Kate, Nancy, and Victor—are to be scheduled as contestants on a television show, one contestant per day, for five consecutive days from Monday through Friday. The following restrictions governing the scheduling of contestants must be observed:

Nancy is not scheduled for Monday.

If Harry is scheduled for Monday, Nancy is scheduled for Friday.

If Nancy is scheduled for Tuesday, Iris is scheduled for Monday.

Kate is scheduled for the next day after the day for which Victor is scheduled.

7. Victor can be scheduled for any day EXCEPT

(A) Monday
(B) Tuesday
(C) Wednesday
(D) Thursday
(E) Friday

8. If Iris is scheduled for the next day after Harry, which one of the following lists all those days any one of which could be the day for which Harry is scheduled?

(A) Monday, Tuesday
(B) Monday, Wednesday
(C) Monday, Thursday
(D) Monday, Tuesday, Wednesday
(E) Monday, Wednesday, Thursday

9. If Kate is scheduled for Wednesday, which one of the following could be true?

(A) Iris is scheduled for Friday.
(B) Nancy is scheduled for Tuesday.
(C) Nancy is scheduled for an earlier day than the day for which Harry is scheduled.
(D) Nancy is scheduled for an earlier day than the day for which Iris is scheduled.
(E) Nancy is scheduled for an earlier day than the day for which Kate is scheduled.

10. If Kate is scheduled for Friday, which one of the following must be true?

(A) Harry is scheduled for Tuesday.
(B) Harry is scheduled for Wednesday.
(C) Iris is scheduled for Monday.
(D) Iris is scheduled for Wednesday.
(E) Nancy is scheduled for Wednesday.

11. If Iris is scheduled for Wednesday, which one of the following must be true?

(A) Harry is scheduled for an earlier day than the day for which Nancy is scheduled.
(B) Harry is scheduled for an earlier day than the day for which Kate is scheduled.
(C) Kate is scheduled for an earlier day than the day for which Harry is scheduled.
(D) Nancy is scheduled for an earlier day than the day for which Kate is scheduled.
(E) Nancy is scheduled for an earlier day than the day for which Iris is scheduled.

GO ON TO THE NEXT PAGE.

Questions 12–17

An art teacher will schedule exactly six of eight lectures—fresco, history, lithography, naturalism, oils, pastels, sculpture, and watercolors—for three days—1, 2, and 3. There will be exactly two lectures each day—morning and afternoon. Scheduling is governed by the following conditions:

Day 2 is the only day for which oils can be scheduled.

Neither sculpture nor watercolors can be scheduled for the afternoon.

Neither oils nor pastels can be scheduled for the same day as lithography.

If pastels is scheduled for day 1 or day 2, then the lectures scheduled for the day immediately following pastels must be fresco and history, not necessarily in that order.

12. Which one of the following is an acceptable schedule of lectures for days 1, 2, and 3, respectively?

(A) Morning: lithography, history, sculpture
    Afternoon: pastels, fresco, naturalism
(B) Morning: naturalism, oils, fresco
    Afternoon: lithography, pastels, history
(C) Morning: oils, history, naturalism
    Afternoon: pastels, fresco, lithography
(D) Morning: sculpture, lithography, naturalism
    Afternoon: watercolors, fresco, pastels
(E) Morning: sculpture, pastels, fresco
    Afternoon: lithography, history, naturalism

13. If lithography and fresco are scheduled for the afternoons of day 2 and day 3, respectively, which one of the following is a lecture that could be scheduled for the afternoon of day 1 ?

(A) history
(B) oils
(C) pastels
(D) sculpture
(E) watercolors

14. If lithography and history are scheduled for the mornings of day 2 and day 3, respectively, which one of the following lectures could be scheduled for the morning of day 1 ?

(A) fresco
(B) naturalism
(C) oils
(D) pastels
(E) sculpture

15. If oils and lithography are scheduled for the mornings of day 2 and day 3, respectively, which one of the following CANNOT be scheduled for any day?

(A) fresco
(B) history
(C) naturalism
(D) pastels
(E) sculpture

16. If neither fresco nor naturalism is scheduled for any day, which one of the following must be scheduled for day 1 ?

(A) history
(B) lithography
(C) oils
(D) pastels
(E) sculpture

17. If the lectures scheduled for the mornings are fresco, history, and lithography, not necessarily in that order, which one of the following could be true?

(A) Lithography is scheduled for day 3.
(B) Naturalism is scheduled for day 2.
(C) Fresco is scheduled for the same day as naturalism.
(D) History is scheduled for the same day as naturalism.
(E) History is scheduled for the same day as oils.

GO ON TO THE NEXT PAGE.

Questions 18–24

The population of a small country is organized into five clans—N, O, P, S, and T. Each year exactly three of the five clans participate in the annual harvest ceremonies. The rules specifying the order of participation of the clans in the ceremonies are as follows:

Each clan must participate at least once in any two consecutive years.

No clan participates for three consecutive years.

Participation takes place in cycles, with each cycle ending when each of the five clans has participated three times. Only then does a new cycle begin.

No clan participates more than three times within any cycle.

18. If the clans participating in the first year of a given cycle are N, O, and P, which one of the following could be the clans participating in the second year of that cycle?

  (A) N, O, S
  (B) N, O, T
  (C) N, P, S
  (D) O, P, T
  (E) O, S, T

19. Which one of the following can be true about the clans' participation in the ceremonies?

  (A) N participates in the first, second, and third years.
  (B) N participates in the second, third, and fourth years.
  (C) Both O and S participate in the first and third years.
  (D) Both N and S participate in the first, third, and fifth years.
  (E) Both S and T participate in the second, third, and fifth years.

20. Any cycle for the clans' participation in the ceremonies must be completed at the end of exactly how many years?

  (A) five
  (B) six
  (C) seven
  (D) eight
  (E) nine

21. Which one of the following must be true about the three clans that participate in the ceremonies in the first year?

  (A) At most two of them participate together in the third year.
  (B) At least two of them participate together in the second year.
  (C) All three of them participate together in the fourth year.
  (D) All three of them participate together in the fifth year.
  (E) None of them participates in the third year.

22. If, in a particular cycle, N, O, and S participate in the ceremonies in the first year, which one of the following must be true?

  (A) N participates in the second and third years.
  (B) O participates in the third and fourth years.
  (C) N and O both participate in the third year.
  (D) P and T both participate in the fifth year.
  (E) S and T both participate in the fifth year.

23. If, in a particular cycle, N, O, and T participate in the first year and if O and P participate in the fourth year, any of the following could be a clan that participates in the third year EXCEPT

  (A) N
  (B) O
  (C) P
  (D) S
  (E) T

24. If, in a particular cycle, N, O, and S participate in the ceremonies in the first year and O, S, and T participate in the third year, then which one of the following could be the clans that participate in the fifth year?

  (A) N, O, P
  (B) N, O, S
  (C) N, P, S
  (D) O, P, S
  (E) P, S, T

S T O P

IF YOU FINISH BEFORE TIME IS CALLED, YOU MAY CHECK YOUR WORK ON THIS SECTION ONLY.
DO NOT WORK ON ANY OTHER SECTION IN THE TEST.

SECTION II

Time—35 minutes

26 Questions

Directions: The questions in this section are based on the reasoning contained in brief statements or passages. For some questions, more than one of the choices could conceivably answer the question. However, you are to choose the best answer; that is, the response that most accurately and completely answers the question. You should not make assumptions that are by commonsense standards implausible, superfluous, or incompatible with the passage. After you have chosen the best answer, blacken the corresponding space on your answer sheet.

1. Paperback books wear out more quickly than hardcover books do, but paperback books cost much less. Therefore, users of public libraries would be better served if public libraries bought only paperback books, since by so doing these libraries could increase the number of new book titles added to their collections without increasing their budgets.

   Which one of the following, if true, most seriously weakens the argument?

   (A) If a public library's overall budget is cut, the budget for new acquisitions is usually cut back more than is that for day-to-day operations.
   (B) Paperback books can very inexpensively have their covers reinforced in order to make them last longer.
   (C) Many paperback books are never published in hardcover.
   (D) Library users as a group depend on their public library for access to a wide variety of up-to-date reference books that are published in hardcover only.
   (E) People are more likely to buy for themselves a copy of a book they had previously borrowed from the public library if that book is available in paperback.

2. Garbage in this neighborhood probably will not be collected until Thursday this week. Garbage is usually collected here on Wednesdays, and the garbage collectors in this city are extremely reliable. However, Monday was a public holiday, and after a public holiday that falls on a Monday, garbage throughout the city is supposed to be collected one day later than usual.

   The argument proceeds by

   (A) treating several pieces of irrelevant evidence as though they provide support for the conclusion
   (B) indirectly establishing that one thing is likely to occur by directly ruling out all of the alternative possibilities
   (C) providing information that allows application of a general rule to a specific case
   (D) generalizing about all actions of a certain kind on the basis of a description of one such action
   (E) treating something that is probable as though it were inevitable

3. When compact discs first entered the market, they were priced significantly higher than vinyl records. Manufacturers attributed the difference in price to the difference in production costs, saying that compact disc production was expensive because the technology was new and unfamiliar. As the technology became more efficient, the price of the discs did indeed come down. But vinyl records, whose production technology has long been established, then went up in price to approach that of compact discs.

   Which one of the following most helps to explain why the price of vinyl records went up?

   (A) Consumers were so enthusiastic about the improved sound quality offered by compact disc technology that they were willing to pay a higher price to obtain it.
   (B) Some consumers who continued to buy vinyl records instead of compact discs did so because they were unwilling to pay a higher price for compact discs.
   (C) As consumers bought compact discs instead of vinyl records, the number of vinyl records produced decreased, making their production less cost-efficient.
   (D) Compact disc player technology continued to change and develop even after compact discs first entered the market.
   (E) When compact discs first entered the market, many consumers continued to buy vinyl records rather than buying the equipment necessary to play compact discs.

GO ON TO THE NEXT PAGE.

4. Conservationists have established land reserves to preserve the last remaining habitat for certain species whose survival depends on the existence of such habitat. A grove of trees in Mexico that provide habitat for North American monarch butterflies in winter is a typical example of such a land reserve. If global warming occurs as predicted, however, the temperature bands within which various types of vegetation can grow will shift into regions that are currently cooler.

If the statements above are true, they provide the most support for which one of the following?

(A) If global warming occurs as predicted, the conservation land reserves will cease to serve their purpose.
(B) Monarch butterflies will succeed in adapting to climatic change by shortening their migration.
(C) If global warming occurs, it will melt polar ice and so will cause the sea level to rise so high that many coastal plants and animals will become extinct.
(D) The natural world has adapted many times in the past to drastic global warming and cooling.
(E) If global warming occurs rapidly, species of plants and animals now protected in conservation land reserves will move to inhabit areas that are currently used for agriculture.

5. Financial success does not guarantee happiness. This claim is not mere proverbial wisdom but a fact verified by statistics. In a recently concluded survey, only one-third of the respondents who claimed to have achieved financial success reported that they were happy.

Which one of the following, if true, most strongly supports the conclusion drawn from the survey results?

(A) The respondents who reported financial success were, for the most part, financially successful.
(B) Financial success was once thought to be necessary for happiness but is no longer considered a prerequisite for happiness.
(C) Many of the respondents who claimed not to have achieved financial success reported that they were happy five years ago.
(D) Many of the respondents who failed to report financial success were in fact financially successful.
(E) Most of the respondents who reported they were unhappy were in fact happy.

6. The distance that animals travel each day and the size of the groups in which they live are highly correlated with their diets. And diet itself depends in large part on the sizes and shapes of animals' teeth and faces.

The statements above provide the most support for which one of the following?

(A) Animals that eat meat travel in relatively small groups and across relatively small ranges compared to animals that eat plants.
(B) Animals that have varied diets can be expected to be larger and more robust than animals that eat only one or two kinds of food.
(C) When individual herd animals lose their teeth through age or injury, those animals are likely to travel at the rear of their herd.
(D) Information about the size and shape of an animal's face is all that is needed to identify the species to which that animal belongs.
(E) Information about the size and shape of an extinct animal's teeth and face can establish whether that animal is likely to have been a herd animal.

7. It is not correct that the people of the United States, relative to comparable countries, are the most lightly taxed. True, the United States has the lowest tax, as percent of gross domestic product, of the Western industrialized countries, but tax rates alone do not tell the whole story. People in the United States pay out of pocket for many goods and services provided from tax revenues elsewhere. Consider universal health care, which is an entitlement supported by tax revenues in every other Western industrialized country. United States government health-care expenditures are equivalent to about 5 percent of the gross domestic product, but private health-care expenditures represent another 7 percent. This 7 percent, then, amounts to a tax.

The argument concerning whether the people of the United States are the most lightly taxed is most vulnerable to which one of the following criticisms?

(A) It bases a comparison on percentages rather than on absolute numbers.
(B) It unreasonably extends the application of a key term.
(C) It uses negatively charged language instead of attempting to give a reason.
(D) It generalizes from only a few instances.
(E) It sets up a dichotomy between alternatives that are not exclusive.

GO ON TO THE NEXT PAGE.

8. Various mid-fourteenth-century European writers show an interest in games, but no writer of this period mentions the playing of cards. Nor do any of the mid-fourteenth-century statutes that proscribe or limit the play of games mention cards, though they do mention dice, chess, and other games. It is therefore likely that, contrary to what is sometimes claimed, at that time playing cards was not yet common in Europe.

The pattern of reasoning in which one of the following is most similar to that in the argument above?

(A) Neither today's newspapers nor this evening's television news mentioned a huge fire that was rumored to have happened in the port last night. Therefore, there probably was no such fire.

(B) This evening's television news reported that the cruise ship was only damaged in the fire last night, whereas the newspaper reported that it was destroyed. The television news is based on more recent information, so probably the ship was not destroyed.

(C) Among the buildings that are near the port is the newspaper's printing plant. Early editions of this morning's paper were very late. Therefore, the fire at the port probably affected areas beyond the port itself.

(D) The newspaper does not explicitly say that the port reopened after the fire, but in its listing of newly arrived ships it mentions some arrival times after the fire. Therefore, the port was probably not closed for long.

(E) The newspaper is generally more reliable than the television news, and the newspaper reported that the damage from last night's fire in the port was not severe. Therefore, the damage probably was not severe.

9. In a mature tourist market such as Bellaria there are only two ways hotel owners can increase profits: by building more rooms or by improving what is already there. Rigid land-use laws in Bellaria rule out construction of new hotels or, indeed, any expansion of hotel capacity. It follows that hotel owners cannot increase their profits in Bellaria since Bellarian hotels _____.

Which one of the following logically completes the argument?

(A) are already operating at an occupancy rate approaching 100 percent year-round

(B) could not have been sited any more attractively than they are even in the absence of land-use laws

(C) have to contend with upward pressures on the cost of labor which stem from an incipient shortage of trained personnel

(D) already provide a level of luxury that is at the limits of what even wealthy patrons are prepared to pay for

(E) have shifted from serving mainly Bellarian tourists to serving foreign tourists traveling in organized tour groups

10. Every political philosopher of the early twentieth century who was either a socialist or a communist was influenced by Rosa Luxemburg. No one who was influenced by Rosa Luxemburg advocated a totalitarian state.

If the statements above are true, which one of the following must on the basis of them also be true?

(A) No early-twentieth-century socialist political philosopher advocated a totalitarian state.

(B) Every early-twentieth-century political philosopher who did not advocate a totalitarian state was influenced by Rosa Luxemburg.

(C) Rosa Luxemburg was the only person to influence every early-twentieth-century political philosopher who was either socialist or communist.

(D) Every early-twentieth-century political philosopher who was influenced by Rosa Luxemburg and was not a socialist was a communist.

(E) Every early-twentieth-century political philosopher who did not advocate a totalitarian state was either socialist or communist.

GO ON TO THE NEXT PAGE.

Questions 11–12

Harris: Currently, hybrid animals are not protected by international endangered-species regulations. But new techniques in genetic research suggest that the red wolf, long thought to be an independent species, is a hybrid of the coyote and the gray wolf. Hence, since the red wolf clearly deserves protection, these regulations should be changed to admit the protection of hybrids.

Vogel: Yet hybrids do not need protection. Since a breeding population that arises through hybridization descends from independent species, if any such population were to die out, it could easily be revived by interbreeding members of the species from which the hybrid is descended.

11. Which one of the following is a point at issue between Harris and Vogel?

(A) whether the red wolf descends from the gray wolf and the coyote

(B) whether there are some species that are currently considered endangered that are not in fact in any danger

(C) whether the packs of red wolves that currently exist are in danger of dying out

(D) whether there are some hybrids that ought to be protected by endangered-species regulations

(E) whether new techniques in genetic research should be used to determine which groups of animals constitute species and which constitute hybrids

12. Which one of the following is an assumption on which Vogel's argument relies?

(A) The techniques currently being used to determine whether a population of animals is a hybrid of other species have proven to be reliable.

(B) The international regulations that protect endangered species and subspecies are being enforced successfully.

(C) The gray wolf has been successfully bred in captivity.

(D) All hybrids are the descendants of species that are currently extant.

(E) The coyote and the red wolf are not related genetically.

13. From an analysis of broken pottery and statuary, archaeologists have estimated that an ancient settlement in southwestern Arabia was established around 1000 B.C. However, new evidence suggests that the settlement is considerably older: tests show that a piece of building timber recently uncovered at the site is substantially older than the pottery and statuary.

Which one of the following, if true, most seriously undermines the conclusion drawn from the new evidence?

(A) The building timber bore marks suggesting that it had been salvaged from an earlier settlement.

(B) The pieces of pottery and fragments of statues that were analyzed come from several parts of the site.

(C) The tests used to determine the age of the pottery and statuary had been devised more recently than those used to determine the age of the building timber.

(D) The site has yielded many more samples of pottery and statuary than of building timber.

(E) The type of pottery found at the site is similar to a type of pottery associated with civilizations that existed before 1000 B.C.

14. The book *To Save the Earth* is so persuasive that no one who reads it can fail to heed its environmentalist message. Members of the Earth Association have given away 2,000 copies in the last month. Thus the Earth Association can justly claim credit for at least 2,000 people in one month converted to the environmentalist cause.

Which one of the following is an assumption on which the argument depends?

(A) No other environmental organization gave away copies of *To Save the Earth* during the month in which the Earth Association gave away its 2,000 copies.

(B) The people to whom the Earth Association gave copies of *To Save the Earth* would not have been willing to pay to receive it from the Earth Association.

(C) The copies of *To Save the Earth* given away by members of the Earth Association were printed on recycled paper.

(D) None of those who received *To Save the Earth* from a member of the Earth Association were already committed to the environmentalist cause when they received this book.

(E) Every recipient of *To Save the Earth* will embrace the environmental program advocated by the Earth Association.

GO ON TO THE NEXT PAGE.

15. Smokers of pipes or cigars run a distinctly lower risk to their health than do cigarette smokers. However, whereas cigarette smokers who quit smoking altogether sharply reduce their risk of smoking-related health problems, those who give up cigarettes and take up pipes or cigars remain in as much danger as before.

Which one of the following, if true, offers the best prospects for an explanation of why the two changes in smoking habits do not both result in reduced health risks?

(A) Smokers of pipes or cigars who quit smoking thereby reduce their risk of smoking-related health problems.

(B) Cigarette smokers who quit smoking for a time and who then resume cigarette smoking do not necessarily reduce their risk of smoking-related health problems.

(C) The kinds of illnesses that smokers run an increased risk of contracting develop no earlier in cigarette smokers than they do in smokers of pipes or cigars.

(D) At any given period in their lives, virtually all smokers smoke either cigarettes exclusively or cigars exclusively or pipes exclusively, rather than alternating freely among various ways of smoking.

(E) People who switch from cigarette smoking to smoking pipes or cigars inhale smoke in a way that those who have never smoked cigarettes do not.

Questions 16–17

Production manager: The building materials that we produce meet industry safety codes but pose some safety risk. Since we have recently developed the technology to make a safer version of our product, we should stop producing our current product and sell only the safer version in order to protect public safety.

Sales manager: If we stop selling our current product, we will have no money to develop and promote the safer product. We need to continue to sell the less-safe product in order to be in a position to market the safer product successfully.

16. Which one of the following principles, if established, most helps to justify the production manager's conclusion?

(A) Companies should be required to develop safer products if such development can be funded from sales of existing products.

(B) That a product does not meet industry safety codes should be taken as sufficient indication that the product poses some safety risks.

(C) Companies should not sell a product that poses safety risks if they are technologically capable of producing a safer version of that product.

(D) Product safety codes should be reviewed whenever an industry replaces one version of a product with a technologically more advanced version of that product.

(E) In order to make building materials safer, companies should continually research new technologies whether or not they are required to do so in order to comply with safety codes.

17. The sales manager counters the production manager's argument by

(A) pointing out that one part of the production manager's proposal would have consequences that would prevent successful execution of another part

(B) challenging the production manager's authority to dictate company policy

(C) questioning the product manager's assumption that a product is necessarily safe just because it is safer than another product

(D) proposing a change in the standards by which product safety is judged

(E) presenting evidence to show that the production manager has overestimated the potential impact of the new technology

GO ON TO THE NEXT PAGE.

Questions 18–19

Each year, an official estimate of the stock of cod in the Grand Banks is announced. This estimate is obtained by averaging two separate estimates of how many cod are available, one based on the number of cod caught by research vessels during a once-yearly sampling of the area and the other on the average number of tons of cod caught by various commercial vessels per unit of fishing effort expended there in the past year—a unit of fishing effort being one kilometer of net set out in the water for one hour. In previous decades, the two estimates usually agreed closely. However, for the last decade the estimate based on commercial tonnage has been increasing markedly, by about the same amount as the sampling-based estimate has been decreasing.

18. If the statements in the passage are true, which one of the following is most strongly supported by them?

(A) Last year's official estimate was probably not much different from the official estimate ten years ago.

(B) The number of commercial vessels fishing for cod in the Grand Banks has increased substantially over the past decade.

(C) The sampling-based estimate is more accurate than the estimate based on commercial tonnage in that the data on which it relies is less likely to be inaccurate.

(D) The once-yearly sampling by research vessels should be used as the sole basis for arriving at the official estimate of the stock of cod.

(E) Twenty years ago, the overall stock of cod in the Grand Banks was officially estimated to be much larger than it is estimated to be today.

19. Which one of the following, if true, most helps to account for the growing discrepancy between the estimate based on commercial tonnage and the research-based estimate?

(A) Fishing vessels often exceed their fishing quotas for cod and therefore often underreport the number of tons of cod that they catch.

(B) More survey vessels are now involved in the yearly sampling effort than were involved 10 years ago.

(C) Improvements in technology over the last 10 years have allowed commercial fishing vessels to locate and catch large schools of cod more easily.

(D) Survey vessels count only those cod caught during a 30-day survey period, whereas commercial fishing vessels report all cod caught during the course of a year.

(E) Because of past overfishing of cod, fewer fishing vessels now catch the maximum tonnage of cod each vessel is allowed by law to catch.

20. Pretzels can cause cavities. Interestingly, the longer that a pretzel remains in contact with the teeth when it is being eaten, the greater the likelihood that a cavity will result. What is true of pretzels in this regard is also true of caramels. Therefore, since caramels dissolve more quickly in the mouth than pretzels do, eating a caramel is less likely to result in a cavity than eating a pretzel is.

The reasoning in the argument is vulnerable to criticism on the grounds that the argument

(A) treats a correlation that holds within individual categories as thereby holding across categories as well

(B) relies on the ambiguous use of a key term

(C) makes a general claim based on particular examples that do not adequately represent the respective classes that they are each intended to represent

(D) mistakes the cause of a particular phenomenon for the effect of that phenomenon

(E) is based on premises that cannot all be true

GO ON TO THE NEXT PAGE.

Questions 21–22

Mark: Plastic-foam cups, which contain environmentally harmful chlorofluorocarbons, should no longer be used; paper cups are preferable. Styrene, a carcinogenic by-product, is generated in foam production, and foam cups, once used, persist indefinitely in the environment.

Tina: You overlook the environmental effects of paper cups. A study done 5 years ago showed that making paper for their production burned more petroleum than was used for foam cups and used 12 times as much steam, 36 times as much electricity, and twice as much cooling water. Because paper cups weigh more, their transportation takes more energy. Paper mills produce water pollution, and when the cups decay they produce methane, a gas that contributes to harmful global warming. So they are a worse choice.

21. Which one of the following, if true, could Mark cite to counter evidence offered by Tina?

(A) The use of energy for chain saws that cut down trees and for trucks that haul logs is part of the environmental cost of manufacturing paper.

(B) Foam cups are somewhat more acceptable to consumers than paper cups because of their better insulating qualities.

(C) The production and transportation of petroleum occasions serious environmental pollution, but the energy that runs paper mills now comes from burning waste wood rather than petroleum.

(D) The amount of styrene escaping into the environment or remaining in foam cups after their manufacture is negligible.

(E) Acre for acre, tree farms for the production of wood for paper have fewer beneficial effects on the environment than do natural forests that remain uncut.

22. To decide the issue between Mark and Tina, it would first be most important to decide

(A) how soon each of the kinds of harm cited by Mark and Tina would be likely to be at its maximum level

(B) whether members of some societies use, on average, more disposable goods than do members of other societies

(C) whether it is necessary to seek a third alternative that has none of the negative consequences cited with respect to the two products

(D) how much of the chains of causation involved in the production, marketing, and disposal of the products should be considered in analyzing their environmental impact

(E) whether paper and foam cups, in their most popular sizes, hold the same quantities of liquid

23. When people experience throbbing in their teeth or gums, they have serious dental problems, and if a dental problem is serious, it will be a problem either of tooth decay or of gum disease. Therefore, since throbbing in the teeth or gums is a sign of serious dental problems, and neither Sabina's teeth nor her gums are throbbing, Sabina can be suffering from neither tooth decay nor gum disease.

Which one of the following contains an error of reasoning most similar to that made in the argument above?

(A) People who drink a lot of coffee are said to have jittery nerves. Therefore, medical students who drink a lot of coffee should not become neonatologists or surgeons since neither neonatology nor surgery should be practiced by people with jittery nerves.

(B) A legally practicing psychiatrist must have both a medical degree and psychiatric training. Thus, since Emmett has not undergone psychiatric training, if he is practicing as a psychiatrist, he is not doing so legally.

(C) Someone with severe nasal congestion has a sinus infection or else is suffering from an allergy. Therefore, if Barton does not have a sinus infection, Barton probably does not have severe nasal congestion.

(D) If a person is interested in either physics or chemistry, then that person would be wise to consider a career in medicine. Yolanda, however, is interested in neither physics nor chemistry, so it would not be wise for her to consider a career in medicine.

(E) Someone who is neither an ophthalmologist nor an optometrist lacks specialized training for diagnosing defects of the eye. Therefore, Kim must have been trained in ophthalmology or optometry, given that she accurately diagnosed John's eye defect.

GO ON TO THE NEXT PAGE.

24. A certain airport security scanner designed to detect explosives in luggage will alert the scanner's operator whenever the piece of luggage passing under the scanner contains an explosive. The scanner will erroneously alert the operator for only one percent of the pieces of luggage that contain no explosives. Thus in ninety-nine out of a hundred alerts explosives will actually be present.

The reasoning in the argument is flawed because the argument

(A) ignores the possibility of the scanner's failing to signal an alert when the luggage does contain an explosive

(B) draws a general conclusion about reliability on the basis of a sample that is likely to be biased

(C) ignores the possibility of human error on the part of the scanner's operator once the scanner has alerted him or her

(D) fails to acknowledge the possibility that the scanner will not be equally sensitive to all kinds of explosives

(E) substitutes one group for a different group in the statement of a percentage

25. Unless negotiations begin soon, the cease-fire will be violated by one of the two sides to the dispute. Negotiations will be held only if other countries have pressured the two sides to negotiate; an agreement will emerge only if other countries continue such pressure throughout the negotiations. But no negotiations will be held until international troops enforcing the cease-fire have demonstrated their ability to counter any aggression from either side, thus suppressing a major incentive for the two sides to resume fighting.

If the statements above are true, and if negotiations between the two sides do begin soon, at the time those negotiations begin each of the following must also be true EXCEPT:

(A) The cease-fire has not been violated by either of the two sides.

(B) International troops enforcing the cease-fire have demonstrated that they can counter aggression from either of the two sides.

(C) A major incentive for the two sides to resume hostilities has been suppressed.

(D) Other countries have exerted pressure on the two sides to the dispute.

(E) The negotiations' reaching an agreement depends in part on the actions of other countries.

26. If Blankenship Enterprises has to switch suppliers in the middle of a large production run, the company will not show a profit for the year. Therefore, if Blankenship Enterprises in fact turns out to show no profit for the year, it will also turn out to be true that the company had to switch suppliers during a large production run.

The reasoning in the argument is most vulnerable to criticism on which one of the following grounds?

(A) The argument is a circular argument made up of an opening claim followed by a conclusion that merely paraphrases that claim.

(B) The argument fails to establish that a condition under which a phenomenon is said to occur is the only condition under which that phenomenon occurs.

(C) The argument involves an equivocation, in that the word "profit" is allowed to shift its meaning during the course of the argument.

(D) The argument erroneously uses an exceptional, isolated case to support a universal conclusion.

(E) The argument explains one event as being caused by another event, even though both events must actually have been caused by some third, unidentified event.

S T O P

IF YOU FINISH BEFORE TIME IS CALLED, YOU MAY CHECK YOUR WORK ON THIS SECTION ONLY.
DO NOT WORK ON ANY OTHER SECTION IN THE TEST.

SECTION III
Time—35 minutes
27 Questions

<u>Directions:</u> Each passage in this section is followed by a group of questions to be answered on the basis of what is <u>stated</u> or <u>implied</u> in the passage. For some of the questions, more than one of the choices could conceivably answer the question. However, you are to choose the <u>best</u> answer; that is, the response that most accurately and completely answers the question, and blacken the corresponding space on your answer sheet.

A major tenet of the neurosciences has been that all neurons (nerve cells) in the brains of vertebrate animals are formed early in development. An adult vertebrate, it was believed, must make do with a
(5) fixed number of neurons: those lost through disease or injury are not replaced, and adult learning takes place not through generation of new cells but through modification of connections among existing ones.
(10) However, new evidence for neurogenesis (the birth of new neurons) has come from the study of canary song. Young canaries and other songbirds learn to sing much as humans learn to speak, by imitating models provided by their elders. Several
(15) weeks after birth, a young bird produces its first rudimentary attempts at singing; over the next few months the song becomes more structured and stable, reaching a fully developed state by the time the bird approaches its first breeding season. But
(20) this repertoire of song is not permanently learned. After each breeding season, during late summer and fall, the bird loses mastery of its developed "vocabulary," and its song becomes as unstable as that of a juvenile bird. During the following winter
(25) and spring, however, the canary acquires new songs, and by the next breeding season it has developed an entirely new repertoire.
Recent neurological research into this learning and relearning process has shown that the two most
(30) important regions of the canary's brain related to the learning of songs actually vary in size at different times of the year. In the spring, when the bird's song is highly developed and uniform, the regions are roughly twice as large as they are in the
(35) fall. Further experiments tracing individual nerve cells within these regions have shown that the number of neurons drops by about 38 percent after the breeding season, but by the following breeding season, new ones have been generated to replace
(40) them. A possible explanation for this continual replacement of nerve cells may have to do with the canary's relatively long life span and the requirements of flight. Its brain would have to be substantially larger and heavier than might be
(45) feasible for flying if it had to carry all the brain cells needed to process and retain all the information gathered over a lifetime. Although the idea of neurogenesis in the adult mammalian brain is still not generally accepted,
(50) these findings might help uncover a mechanism that

would enable the human brain to repair itself through neurogenesis. Whether such replacement of neurons would disrupt complex learning processes or long-term memory is not known, but
(55) songbird research challenges scientists to identify the genes or hormones that orchestrate neurogenesis in the young human brain and to learn how to activate them in the adult brain.

1. Which one of the following best expresses the main idea of the passage?

   (A) New evidence of neurogenesis in canaries challenges an established neurological theory concerning brain cells in vertebrates and suggests the possibility that human brains may repair themselves.
   (B) The brains of canaries differ from the brains of other vertebrate animals in that the brains of adult canaries are able to generate neurons.
   (C) Recent studies of neurogenesis in canaries, building on established theories of vertebrate neurology, provide important clues as to why researchers are not likely to discover neurogenesis in adult humans.
   (D) Recent research into neurogenesis in canaries refutes a long-held belief about the limited supply of brain cells and provides new information about neurogenesis in the adult human brain.
   (E) New information about neurogenesis in canaries challenges older hypotheses and clarifies the importance of the yearly cycle in learning processes and neurological replacement among vertebrates.

GO ON TO THE NEXT PAGE.

2. According to the passage, which one of the following is true of the typical adult canary during the late summer and fall?

(A) The canary's song repertoire takes on a fully structured and stable quality.

(B) A process of neurogenesis replaces the song-learning neurons that were lost during the preceding months.

(C) The canary begins to learn an entirely new repertoire of songs based on the models of other canaries.

(D) The regions in the canary's brain that are central to the learning of song decrease in size.

(E) The canary performs slightly modified versions of the songs it learned during the preceding breeding season.

3. Information in the passage suggests that the author would most likely regard which one of the following as LEAST important in future research on neurogenesis in humans?

(A) research on possible similarities between the neurological structures of humans and canaries

(B) studies that compare the ratio of brain weight to body weight in canaries to that in humans

(C) neurological research on the genes or hormones that activate neurogenesis in the brain of human infants

(D) studies about the ways in which long-term memory functions in the human brain

(E) research concerning the processes by which humans learn complicated tasks

4. Which one of the following, if true, would most seriously undermine the explanation proposed by the author in the third paragraph?

(A) A number of songbird species related to the canary have a shorter life span than the canary and do not experience neurogenesis.

(B) The brain size of several types of airborne birds with life spans similar to those of canaries has been shown to vary according to a two-year cycle of neurogenesis.

(C) Several species of airborne birds similar to canaries in size are known to have brains that are substantially heavier than the canary's brain.

(D) Individual canaries that have larger-than-average repertoires of songs tend to have better developed muscles for flying.

(E) Individual canaries with smaller and lighter brains than the average tend to retain a smaller-than-average repertoire of songs.

5. The use of the word "vocabulary" (line 23) serves primarily to

(A) demonstrate the presence of a rudimentary grammatical structure in canary song

(B) point out a similarity between the patterned groupings of sounds in a canary's song and the syllabic structures of words

(C) stress the stability and uniformity of the canary's song throughout its lifetime

(D) suggest a similarity between the possession of a repertoire of words among humans and a repertoire of songs among canaries

(E) imply that the complexity of the canary's song repertoire is equal to that of human language

6. According to the passage, which one of the following factors may help account for the occurrence of neurogenesis in canaries?

(A) the life span of the average canary

(B) the process by which canaries learn songs

(C) the frequency of canary breeding seasons

(D) the number of regions in the canary brain related to song learning

(E) the amount of time an average canary needs to learn a repertoire of songs

7. Which one of the following best describes the organization of the third paragraph?

(A) A theory is presented, analyzed, and modified, and a justification for the modification is offered.

(B) Research results are advanced and reconciled with results from other studies, and a shared principle is described.

(C) Research results are presented, further details are provided, and a hypothesis is offered to explain the results.

(D) Research findings are described, their implications are explained, and an application to a related field is proposed.

(E) Research results are reported, their significance is clarified, and they are reconciled with previously established neurological tenets.

8. It can be inferred from the passage that the author would most likely describe the current understanding of neurogenesis as

(A) exhaustive
(B) progressive
(C) incomplete
(D) antiquated
(E) incorrect

GO ON TO THE NEXT PAGE.

For too many years scholars of African American history focused on the harm done by slaveholders and by the institution of slavery, rather than on what Africans in the United States were
(5) able to accomplish despite the effects of that institution. In *Myne Owne Ground*, T. H. Breen and Stephen Innes contribute significantly to a recent, welcome shift from a white-centered to a black-centered inquiry into the role of African Americans
(10) in the American colonial period. Breen and Innes focus not on slaves, but on a small group of freed indentured servants in Northampton County (in the Chesapeake Bay region of Virginia) who, according to the authors, maintained their freedom, secured
(15) property, and interacted with persons of different races and economic standing from 1620 through the 1670s. African Americans living on the Chesapeake were to some extent disadvantaged, say Breen and Innes, but this did not preclude the attainment of
(20) status roughly equal to that of certain white planters of the area. Continuously acting within black social networks, and forming economic relationships with white planters, local Native Americans, indentured servants, and white settlers outside the gentry class,
(25) the free African Americans of Northampton County held their own in the rough-hewn world of Chesapeake Bay.

The authors emphasize that in this early period, when the percentage of African Americans in any
(30) given Chesapeake county was still no more than 10 percent of the population, very little was predetermined so far as racial status or race relations were concerned. By schooling themselves in the local legal process and by working
(35) prodigiously on the land, African Americans acquired property, established families, and warded off contentious white neighbors. Breen and Innes do acknowledge that political power on the Chesapeake was asymmetrically distributed among
(40) black and white residents. However, they underemphasize much evidence that customary law, only gradually embodied in statutory law, was closing in on free African Americans well before the 1670s: during the 1660s, when the proportion
(45) of African Americans in Virginia increased dramatically, Virginia tightened a law regulating interracial relations (1662) and enacted a statute prohibiting baptism from altering slave status (1667). Anthony Johnson, a leader in the
(50) community of free African Americans in the Chesapeake Bay region, sold the land he had cultivated for more than twenty years and moved north with his family around 1665, an action that the authors attribute to a search for "fresh, more
(55) productive land." But the answer to why the Johnsons left that area where they had labored so long may lie in their realization that their white neighbors were already beginning the transition from a largely white indentured labor force to
(60) reliance on a largely black slave labor force, and that the institution of slavery was threatening their descendants' chances for freedom and success in Virginia.

9. The author of the passage objects to many scholarly studies of African American history for which one of the following reasons?

(A) Their emphases have been on statutory law rather than on customary law.
(B) They have ignored specific historical situations and personages in favor of broad interpretations.
(C) They have focused on the least eventful periods in African American history.
(D) They have underemphasized the economic system that was the basis of the institution of slavery.
(E) They have failed to focus to a sufficient extent on the achievements of African Americans.

10. Which one of the following can be inferred from the passage concerning the relationship between the African American population and the law in the Chesapeake Bay region of Virginia between 1650 and 1670 ?

(A) The laws affecting black citizens were embodied in statutes much more gradually than were laws affecting white citizens.
(B) As the percentage of black citizens in the population grew, the legal restrictions placed on them also increased.
(C) Because of discriminatory laws, black farmers suffered more economic setbacks than did white farmers.
(D) Because of legal constraints on hiring indentured servants, black farmers faced a chronic labor shortage on their farms.
(E) The adherence to customary law was more rigid in regions with relatively large numbers of free black citizens.

GO ON TO THE NEXT PAGE.

11. The author of the passage most probably refers to Anthony Johnson and his family in order to

   (A) provide a specific example of the potential shortcomings of Breen and Innes's interpretation of historical events

   (B) provide a specific example of relevant data overlooked by Breen and Innes in their discussion of historical events

   (C) provide a specific example of data that Breen and Innes might profitably have used in proving their thesis

   (D) argue that the standard interpretation of historical events is superior to Breen and Innes's revisionist interpretation

   (E) argue that a new historiographical method is needed to provide a full and coherent reading of historical events

12. The attitude of the author of the passage toward Breen and Innes's study can best be described as one of

   (A) condescending dismissal
   (B) wholehearted acceptance
   (C) contentious challenge
   (D) qualified approval
   (E) sincere puzzlement

13. The primary purpose of the passage is to

   (A) summarize previous interpretations
   (B) advocate a new approach
   (C) propose and then illustrate a thesis
   (D) present and evaluate an interpretation
   (E) describe a historical event

GO ON TO THE NEXT PAGE.

Late-nineteenth-century books about the French artist Watteau (1684–1721) betray a curious blind spot: more than any single artist before or since, Watteau provided his age with an influential image
(5) of itself, and nineteenth-century writers accepted this image as genuine. This was largely due to the enterprise of Watteau's friends who, soon after his death, organized the printing of engraved reproductions of the great bulk of his work—both
(10) his paintings and his drawings—so that Watteau's total artistic output became and continued to be more accessible than that of any other artist until the twentieth-century advent of art monographs illustrated with photographs. These engravings
(15) presented aristocratic (and would-be aristocratic) eighteenth-century French society with an image of itself that was highly acceptable and widely imitated by other artists, however little relationship that image bore to reality. By 1884, the bicentenary of
(20) Watteau's birth, it was standard practice for biographers to refer to him as "the personification of the witty and amiable eighteenth century."

In fact, Watteau saw little enough of that "witty and amiable" century for which so much nostalgia
(25) was generally felt between about 1870 and 1920, a period during which enthusiasm for the artist reached its peak. The eighteenth century's first decades, the period of his artistic activity, were fairly calamitous ones. During his short life, France
(30) was almost continually at war: his native region was overrun with foreign troops, and Paris was threatened by siege and by a rampaging army rabble. The dreadful winter of 1709, the year of Watteau's first Paris successes, was marked by
(35) military defeat and a disastrous famine.

Most of Watteau's nineteenth-century admirers simply ignored the grim background of the works they found so lyrical and charming. Those who took the inconvenient historical facts into consideration
(40) did so only in order to refute the widely held deterministic view that the content and style of an artist's work were absolutely dictated by heredity and environment. (For Watteau admirers, such determinism was unthinkable: the artist was born
(45) in a Flemish town only six years after it first became part of France, yet Watteau was quintessentially French. As one patriotic French biographer put it, "In Dresden, Potsdam, and Berlin I have never come across a Watteau without feeling refreshed by
(50) a breath of native air.") Even such writers, however, persisted in according Watteau's canvases a privileged status as representative "personifications" of the eighteenth century. The discrepancy between historical fact and artistic
(55) vision, useful in refuting the extreme deterministic position, merely forced these writers to seek a new formula that allowed them to preserve the desired identity between image and reality, this time a rather suspiciously psychic one: Watteau did not
(60) record the society he knew, but rather "foresaw" a society that developed shortly after his death.

14. Which one of the following best describes the overall organization of the passage?

(A) A particular phenomenon is discussed, the reasons that it is atypical are put forward, and these reasons are evaluated and refined.

(B) An assumption is made, results deriving from it are compared with what is known to be true, and the assumption is finally rejected as counterfactual.

(C) A point of view is described, one hypothesis accounting for it is introduced and rejected, and a better hypothesis is offered for consideration.

(D) A general characterization is offered, examples supporting it are introduced, and its special applicability to a particular group is asserted.

(E) A particular viewpoint is explained, its shortcomings are discussed, and its persistence in the face of these is noted.

15. The passage suggests that late-nineteenth-century biographers of Watteau considered the eighteenth century to be "witty and amiable" in large part because of

(A) what they saw as Watteau's typical eighteenth-century talent for transcending reality through art

(B) their opposition to the determinism that dominated late-nineteenth-century French thought

(C) a lack of access to historical source material concerning the early eighteenth century in France

(D) the nature of the image conveyed by the works of Watteau and his many imitators

(E) their political bias in favor of aristocratic regimes and societies

GO ON TO THE NEXT PAGE.

16. According to the passage, explanations of artistic production based on determinism were unthinkable to Watteau admirers for which one of the following reasons?

(A) If such explanations were widely accepted, too many people who would otherwise have admired Watteau would cease to appreciate Watteau's works.

(B) If such explanations were adopted, they would make it difficult for Watteau admirers to explain why Watteau's works were purchased and admired by foreigners.

(C) If such explanations were correct, many artists who, like Watteau, considered themselves French would have to be excluded from histories of French art.

(D) If such simple explanations were offered, other more complex arguments concerning what made Watteau's works especially charming would go unexplored.

(E) If such explanations were true, Watteau's works would reflect a "Flemish" sensibility rather than the especially "French" one these admirers saw in them.

17. The phrase "curious blind spot" (lines 2–3) can best be interpreted as referring to which one of the following?

(A) some biographers' persistent inability to appreciate what the author considers a particularly admirable quality

(B) certain writers' surprising lack of awareness of what the author considers an obvious discrepancy

(C) some writers' willful refusal to evaluate properly what the author considers a valuable source of information about the past

(D) an inexplicable tendency on the part of some writers to undervalue an artist whom the author considers extremely influential

(E) a marked bias in favor of a certain painter and a concomitant prejudice against contemporaries the author considers equally talented

18. It can be inferred from the passage that the author's view of Watteau's works differs most significantly from that of most late-nineteenth-century Watteau admirers in which one of the following ways?

(A) Unlike most late-nineteenth-century Watteau admirers, the author appreciates the importance of Watteau's artistic accomplishment.

(B) The author finds Watteau's works to be much less lyrical and charming than did most late-nineteenth-century admirers of the works.

(C) In contrast to most late-nineteenth-century Watteau admirers, the author finds it misleading to see Watteau's works as accurately reflecting social reality.

(D) The author is much more willing to entertain deterministic explanations of the origins of Watteau's works than were most late-nineteenth-century Watteau admirers.

(E) Unlike most late-nineteenth-century admirers of Watteau, the author considers it impossible for any work of art to personify or represent a particular historical period.

19. The author asserts that during the period of Watteau's artistic activity French society was experiencing which one of the following?

(A) widespread social upheaval caused by war

(B) a pervasive sense of nostalgia for an idealized past

(C) increased domination of public affairs by a powerful aristocracy

(D) rapid adoption by the middle classes of aristocratic manners and life-styles

(E) a need to reconcile the French self-image with French social realities

20. The information given in the passage suggests that which one of the following principles accurately characterizes the relationship between an artist's work and the impact it is likely to have on a society?

(A) An artist's recognition by a society is most directly determined by the degree to which his or her works are perceived as lyrical and charming.

(B) An artist will have the greatest influence on a society that values art particularly highly.

(C) The works of an artist who captures the true and essential nature of a given society will probably have a great impact on that society.

(D) The degree of influence an artist's vision will have on a society is conditional on the visibility of the artist's work.

(E) An artist who is much imitated by contemporaries will usually fail to have an impact on a society unless the imitators are talented.

GO ON TO THE NEXT PAGE.

Faced with the problems of insufficient evidence, of conflicting evidence, and of evidence relayed through the flawed perceptual, retentive, and narrative abilities of witnesses, a jury is forced to
(5) draw inferences in its attempt to ascertain the truth. By applying the same cognitive tools they have developed and used over a lifetime, jurors engage in the inferential exercise that lawyers call fact-finding. In certain decision-making contexts that are
(10) relevant to the trial of lawsuits, however, these normally reliable cognitive tools may cause jurors to commit inferential errors that distort rather than reveal the truth.

Although juries can make a variety of inferential
(15) errors, most of these mistakes in judgment involve the drawing of an unwarranted conclusion from the evidence, that is, deciding that the evidence proves something that, in reality, it does not prove. For example, evidence that the defendant in a criminal
(20) prosecution has a prior conviction may encourage jurors to presume the defendant's guilt, because of their preconception that a person previously convicted of a crime must be inclined toward repeated criminal behavior. That commonly held
(25) belief is at least a partial distortion of reality; not all former convicts engage in repeated criminal behavior. Also, a jury may give more probative weight than objective analysis would allow to vivid photographic evidence depicting a shooting victim's
(30) wounds, or may underestimate the weight of defense testimony that is not delivered in a sufficiently forceful or persuasive manner. Finally, complex or voluminous evidence might be so confusing to a jury that its members would draw
(35) totally unwarranted conclusions or even ignore the evidence entirely.

Recent empirical research in cognitive psychology suggests that people tend to commit inferential errors like these under certain
(40) predictable circumstances. By examining the available information, the situation, and the type of decision being made, cognitive psychologists can describe the kinds of inferential errors a person or group is likely to make. These patterns of human
(45) decision-making may provide the courts with a guide to evaluating the effect of evidence on the reliability of the jury's inferential processes in certain situations.

The notion that juries can commit inferential
(50) errors that jeopardize the accuracy of the fact-finding process is not unknown to the courts. In fact, one of a presiding judge's duties is to minimize jury inferential error through explanation and clarification. Nonetheless, most judges now employ
(55) only a limited and primitive concept of jury inferential error: limited because it fails to recognize the potential for error outside certain traditional situations, primitive because it ignores the research and conclusions of psychologists in
(60) favor of notions about human cognition held by lawyers.

21. Which one of the following best expresses the main idea of the passage?

(A) When making decisions in certain predictable situations, juries may commit inferential errors that obscure rather than reveal the truth.
(B) The views of human cognition taken by cognitive psychologists on the one hand and by the legal profession on the other are demonstrably dissimilar.
(C) When confronting powerful preconceptions, particularly shocking evidence, or complex situations, jurors make errors in judgment.
(D) The problem of inferential error by juries is typical of the difficulties with cognitive processes that people face in their everyday lives.
(E) Juries would probably make more reliable decisions if cognitive psychologists, rather than judges, instructed them about the problems inherent in drawing unwarranted conclusions.

22. Of the following hypothetical reforms in trial procedure, which one would the author be most likely to support as the best way to address the problem of jury inferential error?

(A) a move away from jury trials
(B) the institution of minimum formal educational requirements for jurors
(C) the development of strict guidelines for defense testimony
(D) specific training for judges in the area of jury instruction
(E) restrictions on lawyers' use of psychological research

23. In the second paragraph, the author's primary purpose is to

(A) refute the idea that the fact-finding process is a complicated exercise
(B) emphasize how carefully evidence must be presented in order to avoid jury inferential error
(C) explain how commonly held beliefs affect the jury's ability to ascertain the truth
(D) provide examples of situations that may precipitate jury errors
(E) recommend a method for minimizing mistakes by juries

GO ON TO THE NEXT PAGE.

24. Which one of the following best describes the author's attitude toward the majority of judges today?

   (A) apprehensive about whether they are consistent in their instruction of juries
   (B) doubtful of their ability to draw consistently correct conclusions based on the evidence
   (C) critical of their failure to take into account potentially helpful research
   (D) pessimistic about their willingness to make significant changes in trial procedure
   (E) concerned about their allowing the presentation of complex and voluminous evidence in the courtroom

25. Which one of the following statements, if true, would most seriously undermine the author's suggestion about the use of current psychological research in the courtroom?

   (A) All guidelines about human behavior must take account of variations in the patterns of human decision-making.
   (B) Current models of how humans make decisions apply reliably to individuals but do not hold for decisions made by groups.
   (C) The current conception of jury inferential error employed by judges has been in use for nearly a century.
   (D) Inferential errors can be more easily predicted in controlled situations such as the trial of lawsuits than in other kinds of decision-making processes.
   (E) In certain predictable circumstances, juries are less susceptible to inferential errors than they are in other circumstances.

26. It can be inferred from the passage that the author would be most likely to agree with which one of the following generalizations about lawyers?

   (A) They have a less sophisticated understanding of human cognition than do psychologists.
   (B) They often present complex or voluminous information merely in order to confuse a jury.
   (C) They are no better at making logical inferences from the testimony at a trial than are most judges.
   (D) They have worked to help judges minimize jury inferential error.
   (E) They are unrealistic about the ability of jurors to ascertain the truth.

27. The author would be most likely to agree with which one of the following generalizations about a jury's decision-making process?

   (A) The more evidence that a jury has, the more likely it is that the jury will reach a reliable verdict.
   (B) Juries usually overestimate the value of visual evidence such as photographs.
   (C) Jurors have preconceptions about the behavior of defendants that prevent them from making an objective analysis of the evidence in a criminal trial.
   (D) Most of the jurors who make inferential errors during a trial do so because they are unaccustomed to having to make difficult decisions based on inferences.
   (E) The manner in which evidence is presented to a jury may influence the jury either to overestimate or to underestimate the value of that evidence.

S T O P

IF YOU FINISH BEFORE TIME IS CALLED, YOU MAY CHECK YOUR WORK ON THIS SECTION ONLY.
DO NOT WORK ON ANY OTHER SECTION IN THE TEST.

SECTION IV

Time—35 minutes

24 Questions

Directions: The questions in this section are based on the reasoning contained in brief statements or passages. For some questions, more than one of the choices could conceivably answer the question. However, you are to choose the best answer; that is, the response that most accurately and completely answers the question. You should not make assumptions that are by commonsense standards implausible, superfluous, or incompatible with the passage. After you have chosen the best answer, blacken the corresponding space on your answer sheet.

1. James: In my own house, I do what I want. In banning smoking on passenger airlines during domestic flights, the government has ignored the airlines' right to set smoking policies on their own property.

   Eileen: Your house is for your own use. Because a passenger airline offers a service to the public, the passengers' health must come first.

   The basic step in Eileen's method of attacking James' argument is to

   (A) draw a distinction
   (B) offer a definition
   (C) establish an analogy
   (D) derive a contradiction from it
   (E) question its motivation

2. The company that produces XYZ, a computer spreadsheet program, estimates that millions of illegally reproduced copies of XYZ are being used. If legally purchased, this number of copies would have generated millions of dollars in sales for the company, yet despite a company-wide effort to boost sales, the company has not taken available legal measures to prosecute those who have copied the program illegally.

   Which one of the following, if true, most helps to explain why the company has not taken available legal measures?

   (A) XYZ is very difficult to copy illegally, because a sophisticated anticopying mechanism in the program must first be disabled.
   (B) The legal measures that the company that produces XYZ could take against those who have copied its product became available several years before XYZ came on the market.
   (C) Many people who purchase a software program like XYZ are willing to purchase that program only after they have already used it.
   (D) The number of illegally reproduced copies of XYZ currently in use exceeds the number of legally reproduced copies currently in use.
   (E) The company that produces ABC, the spreadsheet program that is XYZ's main rival in the marketplace, is well known for taking legal action against people who have copied ABC illegally.

Questions 3–4

Kim: Some people claim that the battery-powered electric car represents a potential solution to the problem of air pollution. But they forget that it takes electricity to recharge batteries and that most of our electricity is generated by burning polluting fossil fuels. Increasing the number of electric cars on the road would require building more generating facilities since current facilities are operating at maximum capacity. So even if all of the gasoline-powered cars on the roads today were replaced by electric cars, it would at best be an exchange of one source of fossil-fuel pollution for another.

3. The main point made in Kim's argument is that

   (A) replacing gasoline-powered cars with battery-powered electric cars will require building more generating facilities
   (B) a significant reduction in air pollution cannot be achieved unless people drive less
   (C) all forms of automobile transportation are equally harmful to the environment in terms of the air pollution they produce
   (D) battery-powered electric cars are not a viable solution to the air-pollution problem
   (E) gasoline-powered cars will probably remain a common means of transportation for the foreseeable future

4. Which one of the following is an assumption on which Kim's argument depends?

   (A) Replacing gasoline-powered cars with battery-powered electric cars will not lead to a net increase in the total number of cars on the road.
   (B) Gasoline-powered cars are currently not the most significant source of fossil-fuel pollution.
   (C) Replacing gasoline-powered cars with battery-powered electric cars is justified only if electric cars produce less air pollution.
   (D) While it is being operated, a battery-powered electric car does not cause any significant air pollution.
   (E) At least some of the generating facilities built to meet the demand for electricity for battery-powered electric cars would be of a type that burns fossil fuel.

GO ON TO THE NEXT PAGE.

5. Planetary bodies differ from one another in their composition, but most of those in the Solar System have solid surfaces. Unless the core of such a planetary body generates enough heat to cause volcanic action, the surface of the body will not be renewed for millions of years. Any planetary body with a solid surface whose surface is not renewed for millions of years becomes heavily pockmarked by meteorite craters, just like the Earth's Moon. Some old planetary bodies in the Solar System, such as Europa, a very cold moon belonging to Jupiter, have solid icy surfaces with very few meteorite craters.

If the claims above are true, which one of the following must, on the basis of them, be true?

(A) The Earth's Moon does not have an icy surface.

(B) If a planetary body does not have a heavily pockmarked surface, its core does not generate enough heat to cause volcanic action.

(C) Some planetary bodies whose cores generate enough heat to cause volcanic action do not have solid icy surfaces.

(D) Some of Jupiter's moons are heavily pockmarked by meteorite craters.

(E) Some very cold planetary bodies have cores that generate enough heat to cause volcanic action.

6. Patient: Pharmacists maintain that doctors should not be permitted to sell the medicine that they prescribe because doctors would then be tempted to prescribe unnecessary medicines in order to earn extra income. But pharmacists have a financial interest in having a monopoly on the sale of prescription medicines, so their objection to the sale of medicines by doctors cannot be taken seriously.

The patient's argument proceeds by

(A) pointing out an unstated assumption on which the pharmacists' argument relies and then refuting it

(B) attempting to discredit a position by questioning the motives of the proponents of that position

(C) undermining the pharmacists' conclusion by demonstrating that one of the statements used to support the conclusion is false

(D) rejecting a questionable position on the grounds that the general public does not support that position

(E) asserting that pharmacists lack the appropriate knowledge to have informed opinions on the subject under discussion

7. Murray: You claim Senator Brandon has accepted gifts from lobbyists. You are wrong to make this criticism. That it is motivated by personal dislike is shown by the fact that you deliberately avoid criticizing other politicians who have done what you accuse Senator Brandon of doing.

Jane: You are right that I dislike Senator Brandon, but just because I have not criticized the same failing in others doesn't mean you can excuse the senator's offense.

If Murray and Jane are both sincere in what they say, then it can properly be concluded that they agree that

(A) Senator Brandon has accepted gifts from lobbyists

(B) it is wrong for politicians to accept gifts from lobbyists

(C) Jane's criticism of Senator Brandon is motivated only by personal dislike

(D) Senator Brandon should be criticized for accepting gifts from lobbyists

(E) one or more politicians have accepted gifts from lobbyists

GO ON TO THE NEXT PAGE.

Questions 8–9

Oscar: Emerging information technologies will soon make speed of information processing the single most important factor in the creation of individual, corporate, and national wealth. Consequently, the division of the world into northern countries—in general rich—and southern countries—in general poor—will soon be obsolete. Instead, there simply will be fast countries and slow countries, and thus a country's economic well-being will not be a function of its geographical position but just a matter of its relative success in incorporating those new technologies.

Sylvia: But the poor countries of the south lack the economic resources to acquire those technologies and will therefore remain poor. The technologies will thus only widen the existing economic gap between north and south.

8.   Sylvia's reasoning depends on the assumption that

(A)   the prosperity of the rich countries of the north depends, at least in part, on the natural resources of the poor countries of the south

(B)   the emergence of new information technologies will not result in a significant net increase in the total amount of global wealth

(C)   there are technologies other than information technologies whose development could help narrow the existing economic gap between north and south

(D)   at least some of the rich countries of the north will be effective in incorporating new information technologies into their economies

(E)   the speed at which information processing takes place will continue to increase indefinitely

9.   The reasoning that Oscar uses in supporting his prediction is vulnerable to criticism on the ground that it

(A)   overlooks the possibility that the ability of countries to acquire new technologies at some time in the future will depend on factors other than those countries' present economic status

(B)   fails to establish that the division of the world into rich countries and poor countries is the single most important problem that will confront the world economy in the future

(C)   ignores the possibility that, in determining a country's future wealth, the country's incorporation of information-processing technologies might be outweighed by a combination of other factors

(D)   provides no reason to believe that faster information processing will have only beneficial effects on countries that successfully incorporate new information technologies into their economies

(E)   makes no distinction between those of the world's rich countries that are the wealthiest and those that are less wealthy

10.   At the beginning of each month, companies report to the federal government their net loss or gain in jobs over the past month. These reports are then consolidated by the government and reported as the total gain or loss for the past month. Despite accurate reporting by companies and correct tallying by the government, the number of jobs lost was significantly underestimated in the recent recession.

Which one of the following, if true, contributes most to a resolution of the apparent discrepancy described?

(A)   More jobs are lost in a recession than in a period of growth.

(B)   The expenses of collecting and reporting employment data have steadily increased.

(C)   Many people who lose their jobs start up their own businesses.

(D)   In the recent recession a large number of failing companies abruptly ceased all operations.

(E)   The recent recession contributed to the growing preponderance of service jobs over manufacturing jobs.

GO ON TO THE NEXT PAGE.

Questions 11–12

Beverage company representative: The plastic rings that hold six-packs of beverage cans together pose a threat to wild animals, which often become entangled in the discarded rings and suffocate as a result. Following our lead, all beverage companies will soon use only those rings consisting of a new plastic that disintegrates after only three days' exposure to sunlight. Once we all complete the switchover from the old to the new plastic rings, therefore, the threat of suffocation that plastic rings pose to wild animals will be eliminated.

11. The argument depends on which one of the following assumptions?

   (A) None of the new plastic rings can disintegrate after only two days' exposure to sunlight.
   (B) The switchover to the new plastic rings can be completed without causing significant financial hardship to the beverage companies.
   (C) Wild animals will not become entangled in the new plastic rings before the rings have had sufficient exposure to sunlight to disintegrate.
   (D) Use of the old plastic rings poses no substantial threat to wild animals other than that of suffocation.
   (E) Any wild animal that becomes entangled in the old plastic rings will suffocate as a result.

12. Which one of the following, if true, most seriously weakens the representative's argument?

   (A) The switchover to the new plastic rings will take at least two more years to complete.
   (B) After the beverage companies have switched over to the new plastic rings, a substantial number of the old plastic rings will persist in most aquatic and woodland environments.
   (C) The new plastic rings are slightly less expensive than the old rings.
   (D) The new plastic rings rarely disintegrate during shipping of beverage six-packs because most trucks that transport canned beverages protect their cargo from sunlight.
   (E) The new plastic rings disintegrate into substances that are harmful to aquatic animals when ingested in substantial quantities by them.

13. Alcohol consumption has been clearly linked to high blood pressure, which increases the likelihood of developing heart disease. Yet in a study of the effects of alcohol consumption, the incidence of heart disease was lower among participants who drank moderate quantities of alcohol every day than it was among participants identified as nondrinkers.

Which one of the following, if true, most helps to resolve the apparent discrepancy in the information above?

   (A) Because many people who do not drink alcohol are conscious of their health habits, they are likely to engage in regular exercise and to eat nutritionally well-balanced meals.
   (B) Many of the participants identified as nondrinkers were people who had been heavy drinkers but had stopped drinking alcohol prior to participating in the study.
   (C) Some of the participants who drank moderate quantities of alcohol every day said that they occasionally drank large quantities of alcohol.
   (D) Some of the participants who drank moderate quantities of alcohol every day had high blood pressure.
   (E) The two groups of participants were similar to each other with respect to the participants' age, sex, geographical origin, and economic background.

14. Some of the world's most beautiful cats are Persian cats. However, it must be acknowledged that all Persian cats are pompous, and pompous cats are invariably irritating.

If the statements above are true, each of the following must also be true on the basis of them EXCEPT:

   (A) Some of the world's most beautiful cats are irritating.
   (B) Some irritating cats are among the world's most beautiful cats.
   (C) Any cat that is not irritating is not a Persian cat.
   (D) Some pompous cats are among the world's most beautiful cats.
   (E) Some irritating and beautiful cats are not Persian cats.

GO ON TO THE NEXT PAGE.

15. At Flordyce University any student who wants to participate in a certain archaeological dig is eligible to do so but only if the student has taken at least one archaeology course and has shown an interest in the field. Many students who have shown an interest in archaeology never take even one archaeology course. Therefore, many students who want to participate in the dig will be ineligible to do so.

The flawed reasoning of which one of the following arguments is most similar to that of the argument above?

(A) Theoretically, any jar is worth saving regardless of its size, but only if it has a lid. Therefore, since some jars are sure not to have lids, there are certain sizes of jar that are actually not worth saving.

(B) For a horse that is well schooled to be ideal for beginning riders that horse must also be surefooted and gentle. Many horses that are surefooted are not gentle. Therefore many well-schooled horses are not ideal for beginning riders.

(C) If an author's first novel has a romantic setting and a suspenseful plot, it will become a best-seller. Since many authors' first novels have neither, not many first novels become best-sellers.

(D) Any automobile that is more than a few years old is eventually sure to need repairs if it is not regularly maintained. Many automobiles are more than a few years old, but still do not need repairs. Therefore, many automobiles are regularly maintained.

(E) An expensive new building will prove to be a good investment only if it is aesthetically pleasing or provides lots of office space. However, since many expensive new buildings are not aesthetically pleasing, few expensive new buildings will prove to be good investments.

16. From the observation that each member of a group could possess a characteristic, it is fallacious to conclude immediately that it is possible for all the group's members to possess the characteristic. An example in which the fallacy is obvious: arguing that because each of the players entering a tennis tournament has a possibility of winning it, there is therefore a possibility that all will win the tournament.

Which one of the following commits the fallacy described above?

(A) You can fool some of the people all of the time and all of the people some of the time, but you cannot fool all of the people all of the time.

(B) Each of the candidates for mayor appears at first glance to possess the necessary qualifications. It would therefore be a mistake to rule out any of them without more careful examination.

(C) Each of the many nominees could be appointed to any one of the three openings on the committee. Therefore it is possible for all of the nominees to be appointed to the openings on the committee.

(D) If a fair coin is tossed five times, then on each toss the chance of heads being the result is half. Therefore the chance of heads being the result on all five tosses is also half.

(E) It is estimated that ten million planets capable of supporting life exist in our galaxy. Thus to rule out the possibility of life on worlds other than Earth, ten million planetary explorations would be needed.

GO ON TO THE NEXT PAGE.

17. Recent research shows that hesitation, shifting posture, and failure to maintain eye contact are not reliable indicators in discriminating between those who are lying and those who are telling the truth. The research indicates that behavior that cannot be controlled is a much better clue, at least when the lie is important to the liar. Such behavior includes the dilation of eye pupils, which indicates emotional arousal, and small movements of facial muscles, which indicate distress, fear, or anger.

Which one of the following provides the strongest reason for exercising caution when relying on the "better" clues mentioned above in order to discover whether someone is lying?

(A) A person who is lying might be aware that he or she is being closely observed for indications of lying.

(B) Someone who is telling the truth might nevertheless have a past history of lying.

(C) A practiced liar might have achieved great control over body posture and eye contact.

(D) A person telling the truth might be affected emotionally by being suspected of lying or by some other aspect of the situation.

(E) Someone who is lying might exhibit hesitation and shifting posture as well as dilated pupils.

Questions 18–19

Orthodox medicine is ineffective at both ends of the spectrum of ailments. At the more trivial end, orthodox medicine is largely ineffective in treating aches, pains, and allergies, and, at the other extreme, it has yet to produce a cure for serious, life-threatening diseases such as advanced cancer and lupus. People turn to alternative medicine when orthodox medicine fails to help them and when it produces side effects that are unacceptable to them. One of the reasons alternative medicine is free of such side effects is that it does not have any effects at all.

18. If the statements above are true, which one of the following can be properly inferred from them?

(A) Practitioners of alternative medicine are acting in bad faith.

(B) There are some medical conditions for which no orthodox or alternative treatment is effective.

(C) There are some trivial illnesses that can be treated effectively by the methods of alternative medicine.

(D) There are no effective medical treatments that are free from unacceptable side effects.

(E) Orthodox medicine will eventually produce a solution for the diseases that are currently incurable.

19. The charge made above against alternative medicine is most seriously weakened if it is true that

(A) predictions based on orthodox medicine have sometimes failed, as when a patient has recovered despite the judgment of doctors that an illness is fatal

(B) alternative medicine relies on concepts of the body and of the nature of healing that differ from those on which orthodox medicine is based

(C) alternative medicine provides hope to those for whom orthodox medicine offers no cure

(D) a patient's belief in the medical treatment the patient is receiving can release the body's own chemical painkillers, diminish allergic reactions, and promote healing

(E) many treatments used for a time by orthodox medicine have later been found to be totally ineffective

GO ON TO THE NEXT PAGE.

20. Humans began to spread across North America around 12,000 years ago, as the climate became warmer. During the same period the large mammals that were once abundant in North America, such as the mastodon, the woolly mammoth, and the saber-toothed tiger, became extinct. Thus, contrary to the myth that humans formerly lived in harmony with the rest of nature, it is clear that even 12,000 years ago human activity was causing the extinction of animal species.

The argument is most vulnerable to the criticism that

(A) it adopts without question a view of the world in which humans are seen as not included in nature
(B) in calling the idea that humans once lived in harmony with nature a myth the argument presupposes what it attempts to prove
(C) for early inhabitants of North America the destruction of mastodons, woolly mammoths, and saber-toothed tigers might have had very different significance than the extinction of mammal species does for modern humans
(D) there might have been many other species of animals, besides mastodons, woolly mammoths, and saber-toothed tigers, that became extinct as the result of the spread of humans across North America
(E) the evidence it cites is consistent with the alternative hypothesis that the large mammals' extinction was a direct result of the same change in climate that allowed humans to spread across North America

21. The town of Greenfield recently instituted a substantial supplementary tax on all households, whereby each household is taxed in proportion to the volume of the trash that it puts out for trash collectors to pick up, as measured by the number of standard-sized garbage bags put out. In order to reduce the volume of the trash on which their tax bill is based, Greenfield households can deliver their recyclable trash to a conveniently located local commercial recycling center, where such trash is accepted free of charge.

The supplementary tax provides some financial incentive to Greenfield households to do each of the following EXCEPT

(A) sort out recyclable trash thoroughly from their other trash
(B) dump nonrecyclable trash illegally at parks and roadsides
(C) compress and nest items of nonrecyclable trash before putting them out for pickup
(D) deliver recyclable materials to the recycling center instead of passing them on to neighbors who want to reuse them
(E) buy products without packaging or with recyclable rather than nonrecyclable packaging

22. In a survey of consumers in an Eastern European nation, respondents were asked two questions about each of 400 famous Western brands: whether or not they recognized the brand name and whether or not they thought the products bearing that name were of high quality. The results of the survey were a rating and corresponding rank order for each brand based on recognition, and a second rating-plus-ranking based on approval. The brands ranked in the top 27 for recognition were those actually available in that nation. The approval rankings of these 27 brands often differed sharply from their recognition rankings. By contrast, most of the other brands had ratings, and thus rankings, that were essentially the same for recognition as for approval.

Which one of the following, if each is a principle about consumer surveys, is violated by the survey described?

(A) Never ask all respondents a question if it cannot reasonably be answered by respondents who make a particular response to another question in the same survey.
(B) Never ask a question that is likely to generate a large variety of responses that are difficult to group into a manageable number of categories.
(C) Never ask all respondents a question that respondents cannot answer without giving up their anonymity.
(D) It is better to ask the same question about ten different products than to ask ten different questions about a single product.
(E) It is best to ask questions that a respondent can answer without fear of having gotten the answer wrong.

GO ON TO THE NEXT PAGE.

23. A certain species of bird has two basic varieties, crested and noncrested. The birds, which generally live in flocks that contain only crested or only noncrested birds, tend to select mates of the same variety as themselves. However, if a bird that is raised in a flock in which all other members are crested is later moved to a mixed flock, then that bird—whether crested or noncrested—is likely to select a crested mate. This fact indicates that the birds' preference for crested or noncrested mates is learned rather than genetically determined.

Which one of the following, if true, provides the most support for the argument?

(A) Birds of other species also tend to show preferences for mates that have one or another specific physical feature.

(B) In general there are few behavioral differences between the crested and noncrested birds of the species.

(C) Both the crested and noncrested birds of the species tend to select mates that are similar to themselves in size and age.

(D) If a crested bird of the species is raised in captivity apart from other birds and is later moved to a mixed flock, that bird is likely to select a crested mate.

(E) If a bird of the species is raised in a flock that contains both crested and noncrested birds, that bird shows no preference for one variety or the other in its selection of a mate.

24. Plant species differ in that renewed growth in spring can be triggered by day length or by temperature or else by a combination of both. Day length is the same, year after year, for any given date. Therefore, any plant species that starts to grow again on widely different dates in different years resumes growth at least in part in response to temperature.

Which one of the following arguments is most similar in its pattern of reasoning to the argument above?

(A) In Xandia, medical assistant trainees must either complete a formal training course or work for one year under the close supervision of a physician. Since few physicians are willing to act as supervisors, it must be true that most medical assistant trainees in Xandia take the training course.

(B) In the Crawford area, easterly winds mean rain will come and westerly winds mean dry weather will come; winds from other directions do not occur. Therefore, since it is currently raining in Crawford, there must be an easterly wind blowing there now.

(C) Some landfills charge garbage companies by volume only, some charge by weight only, and all others use a formula sensitive to both volume and weight. So if at a particular landfill the charges for two particular loads of equal volume dumped on the same day are different, weight must determine, or help determine, charges at that landfill.

(D) Depending on volume of business, either one or two or three store detectives are needed for adequate protection against shoplifting. Therefore, if on any particular day store management has decided that three detectives will be needed, it must be because business that day is expected to be heavy.

(E) A call is more likely to be heard if it is loud rather than soft, if it is high-pitched rather than low-pitched, and especially if it is both loud and high-pitched. Therefore, anyone whose call goes unheard in spite of being at maximum loudness should try to raise the pitch of the call.

S T O P

IF YOU FINISH BEFORE TIME IS CALLED, YOU MAY CHECK YOUR WORK ON THIS SECTION ONLY.
DO NOT WORK ON ANY OTHER SECTION IN THE TEST.

LSAT® Writing Sample Topic

Sea Coast University is hiring new faculty for its science program and has narrowed its selection to Louise Park or the team of Joe Echevarria and Jeanne Myrdal. Assuming the cost of hiring Park alone or the team is comparable, write an argument supporting one choice over the other based on the following considerations:

- Sea Coast University wants to develop a science program that will attract more undergraduate science majors.
- Sea Coast University wants to increase private and public support for its scientific research.

Louise Park, an internationally recognized scientist, plans to retire in three to five years. The recipient of numerous prizes for several key discoveries, Dr. Park has published extensively in scientific journals. While many of her graduate students have become influential scientists, undergraduates often find her inaccessible. Dr. Park is eager to leave her current university for Sea Coast's warmer climate, and she will bring a large, well-equipped laboratory if she comes to Sea Coast. This year, as usual, Dr. Park has secured grants from public and private sources to support her research.

Joe Echevarria and Jeanne Myrdal number among the most promising young scientists in the country. They have begun to publish in respected journals and have received research grants from major foundations. Last year, their team-teaching approach won them a national teaching award. They recently published an article detailing their ground-breaking research on commercial uses of biotechnology; this research has attracted the attention of major corporations, several of whom are eager to fund their future work.

Directions:

1. Use the Answer Key on the next page to check your answers.

2. Use the Scoring Worksheet below to compute your raw score.

3. Use the Score Conversion Chart to convert your raw score into the 120-180 scale.

Scoring Worksheet

1. Enter the number of questions you answered correctly in each section.

	Number Correct
SECTION I	_____
SECTION II	_____
SECTION III	_____
SECTION IV	_____

2. Enter the sum here: _____
   This is your Raw Score.

Conversion Chart

For Converting Raw Score to the 120-180 LSAT Scaled Score
LSAT Form 5LSS28

Reported Score	Raw Score Lowest	Raw Score Highest
180	98	101
179	97	97
178	96	96
177	95	95
176	94	94
175	93	93
174	91	92
173	90	90
172	89	89
171	88	88
170	87	87
169	86	86
168	84	85
167	83	83
166	81	82
165	80	80
164	78	79
163	77	77
162	75	76
161	74	74
160	72	73
159	71	71
158	69	70
157	67	68
156	66	66
155	64	65
154	62	63
153	60	61
152	59	59
151	57	58
150	55	56
149	53	54
148	52	52
147	50	51
146	48	49
145	47	47
144	45	46
143	43	44
142	42	42
141	40	41
140	39	39
139	37	38
138	35	36
137	34	34
136	32	33
135	31	31
134	30	30
133	28	29
132	27	27
131	26	26
130	24	25
129	23	23
128	22	22
127	21	21
126	20	20
125	18	19
124	17	17
123	16	16
122	15	15
121	14	14
120	0	13

SECTION I

1.	D	8.	E	15.	D	22.	D
2.	B	9.	C	16.	B	23.	C
3.	C	10.	C	17.	E	24.	E
4.	E	11.	C	18.	E		
5.	B	12.	B	19.	C		
6.	D	13.	A	20.	A		
7.	E	14.	E	21.	A		

SECTION II

1.	D	8.	A	15.	E	22.	D
2.	C	9.	D	16.	C	23.	D
3.	C	10.	A	17.	A	24.	E
4.	A	11.	D	18.	A	25.	A
5.	A	12.	D	19.	C	26.	B
6.	E	13.	A	20.	A		
7.	B	14.	D	21.	C		

SECTION III

1.	A	8.	C	15.	D	22.	D
2.	D	9.	E	16.	E	23.	D
3.	B	10.	B	17.	B	24.	C
4.	C	11.	A	18.	C	25.	B
5.	D	12.	D	19.	A	26.	A
6.	A	13.	D	20.	D	27.	E
7.	C	14.	E	21.	A		

SECTION IV

1.	A	8.	D	15.	B	22.	A
2.	C	9.	C	16.	C	23.	E
3.	D	10.	D	17.	D	24.	C
4.	E	11.	C	18.	B		
5.	E	12.	B	19.	D		
6.	B	13.	B	20.	E		
7.	E	14.	E	21.	D		

The Official LSAT PrepTest

14

- February 1995
- Form 3LSS19

The sample test that follows consists of four sections corresponding to the four scored sections of the February 1995 LSAT.

$$\boxed{1}$$

SECTION I

Time—35 minutes

24 Questions

<u>Directions:</u> Each group of questions in this section is based on a set of conditions. In answering some of the questions, it may be useful to draw a rough diagram. Choose the response that most accurately and completely answers each question and blacken the corresponding space on your answer sheet.

<u>Questions 1–6</u>

A newly formed company has five employees—F, G, H, K, and L. Each employee holds exactly one of the following positions: president, manager, or technician. Only the president is not supervised. Other employees are each supervised by exactly one employee, who is either the president or a manager. Each supervised employee holds a different position than his or her supervisor. The following conditions apply:

    There is exactly one president.

    At least one of the employees whom the president supervises is a manager.

    Each manager supervises at least one employee.

    F does not supervise any employee.

    G supervises exactly two employees.

1. Which one of the following is an acceptable assignment of employees to the positions?

	President	Manager	Technician
(A)	G	H, K, L	F
(B)	G	H	F, K, L
(C)	H	F, G	K, L
(D)	H, K	G	F, L
(E)	K	F, G, H, L	—

2. Which one of the following must be true?

    (A) There are at most three technicians.
    (B) There is exactly one technician.
    (C) There are at least two managers.
    (D) There are exactly two managers.
    (E) There are exactly two employees who supervise no one.

3. Which one of the following is a pair of employees who could serve as managers together?

    (A) F, H
    (B) F, L
    (C) G, K
    (D) G, L
    (E) K, L

4. Which one of the following could be true?

    (A) There is exactly one technician.
    (B) There are exactly two managers.
    (C) There are exactly two employees who are not supervised.
    (D) There are more managers than technicians.
    (E) The president supervises all of the other employees.

5. If F is supervised by the president, which one of the following must be true?

    (A) G is the president.
    (B) H is the president.
    (C) L is a technician.
    (D) There is exactly one manager.
    (E) There are exactly two technicians.

6. If K supervises exactly two employees, which one of the following must be true?

    (A) F is supervised by K.
    (B) G is a manager.
    (C) L is supervised.
    (D) There are exactly two managers.
    (E) There are exactly two technicians.

GO ON TO THE NEXT PAGE.

Questions 7–12

Ron washed a total of seven objects after eating his lunch. Two of the objects were pieces of china: a mug and a plate. Two were pieces of glassware: a water glass and a juice glass. Three were utensils: a fork, a knife, and a spoon. Ron washed the two pieces of china consecutively, the two glasses consecutively, and the three utensils consecutively. He washed the objects as follows:

Ron washed each of the objects exactly once.
Ron washed the glassware after either the china or the utensils but not after both.
He washed the knife before the spoon, and he washed the mug before the plate.
He did not wash any two objects at the same time.

7. Which one of the following statements CANNOT be true?

(A) Ron washed the fork first.
(B) Ron washed the fork second.
(C) Ron washed the mug first.
(D) Ron washed the plate second.
(E) Ron washed the plate third.

8. Which one of the following statements can be true?

(A) Ron washed the knife second.
(B) Ron washed the knife seventh.
(C) Ron washed the mug second.
(D) Ron washed the mug third.
(E) Ron washed the mug fourth.

9. Which one of the following CANNOT be an accurate list of the objects Ron washed second, third, and fourth, respectively?

(A) fork, spoon, water glass
(B) knife, fork, juice glass
(C) knife, spoon, juice glass
(D) knife, spoon, water glass
(E) plate, water glass, juice glass

10. It is NOT possible that Ron washed the knife

(A) first
(B) second
(C) third
(D) fifth
(E) sixth

11. If Ron washed the spoon immediately before the fork, then which one of the following statements can be true?

(A) He washed the knife second.
(B) He washed the knife third.
(C) He washed the plate third.
(D) He washed the plate sixth.
(E) He washed the plate seventh.

12. If Ron washed a glass and the knife consecutively, but not necessarily in that order, then which one of the following statements must be false?

(A) He washed the fork before the plate.
(B) He washed the fork before the spoon.
(C) He washed the juice glass before the knife.
(D) He washed the plate before the water glass.
(E) He washed the spoon before the fork.

GO ON TO THE NEXT PAGE.

Questions 13–18

A breeder has ten birds:

Kind	Male	Female
Goldfinches	H	J, K
Lovebirds	M	N
Parakeets	Q, R, S	T, W

The breeder exhibits pairs of birds consisting of one male and one female of the same kind. At most two pairs can be exhibited at a time; the remaining birds must be distributed between two cages. The breeder is constrained by the following conditions:

Neither cage can contain more than four birds.

Any two birds that are both of the same sex and of the same kind as each other cannot be caged together.

Whenever either J or W is exhibited, S cannot be exhibited.

13. Which one of the following is a possible assignment of the birds?

	First Cage	Second Cage	Exhibition
(A)	H, M, N	J, K, S	Q, R, T, W
(B)	K, M, Q	N, R, W	H, J, S, T
(C)	K, Q, S	R, T, W	H, J, M, N
(D)	H, J, M, R	K, N, S, W	Q, T
(E)	H, J, M, R, W	K, N, S	Q, T, W

14. Which one of the following lists two pairs of birds that the breeder can exhibit at the same time?

(A) H and J; M and N
(B) H and J; S and T
(C) H and K; M and N
(D) H and K; R and W
(E) M and N; S and W

15. If Q and R are among the birds that are assigned to the cages, then it must be true that

(A) H is exhibited
(B) K is exhibited
(C) N is exhibited
(D) J is assigned to one of the cages
(E) T is assigned to one of the cages

16. If Q and T are among the birds assigned to the cages, which one of the following is a pair of birds that must be exhibited?

(A) H and J
(B) H and K
(C) M and N
(D) R and W
(E) S and W

17. Which one of the following CANNOT be true?

(A) One pair of parakeets are the only birds exhibited together.
(B) One pair of goldfinches and one pair of lovebirds are exhibited together.
(C) One pair of goldfinches and one pair of parakeets are exhibited together.
(D) One pair of lovebirds and one pair of parakeets are exhibited together.
(E) Two pairs of parakeets are exhibited together.

18. If S is one of the birds exhibited, it must be true that

(A) H is exhibited
(B) M is exhibited
(C) K is assigned to a cage
(D) N is assigned to a cage
(E) R is assigned to a cage

GO ON TO THE NEXT PAGE.

Questions 19–24

During each of the fall, winter, spring, and summer seasons of one year, Nikki and Otto each participate in exactly one of the following five sports: hockey, kayaking, mountaineering, running, and volleyball.

Each child participates in exactly four different sports during the year.

In the fall, each child participates in mountaineering, running, or volleyball.

In the winter, each child participates in hockey or volleyball.

In the spring, each child participates in kayaking, mountaineering, running, or volleyball.

In the summer, each child participates in kayaking, mountaineering, or volleyball.

Nikki and Otto do not participate in the same sport during the same season.

Otto's summer sport is volleyball.

19. Which one of the following statements must be true?

    (A) Nikki's fall sport is running.
    (B) Nikki's winter sport is volleyball.
    (C) Nikki's spring sport is mountaineering.
    (D) Otto's fall sport is mountaineering.
    (E) Otto's spring sport is kayaking.

20. It CANNOT be true that both Nikki and Otto participate during the year in which one of the following sports?

    (A) hockey
    (B) kayaking
    (C) mountaineering
    (D) running
    (E) volleyball

21. If Nikki's fall sport is running, then which one of the following statements must be true?

    (A) Nikki's spring sport is kayaking.
    (B) Nikki's summer sport is mountaineering.
    (C) Otto's fall sport is mountaineering.
    (D) Otto's spring sport is kayaking.
    (E) Otto's spring sport is running.

22. Which one of the following statements could be true?

    (A) Nikki's fall sport is neither mountaineering nor running.
    (B) Nikki's spring sport is neither mountaineering nor running.
    (C) Nikki's summer sport is neither kayaking nor mountaineering.
    (D) Otto's fall sport is neither mountaineering nor running.
    (E) Otto's spring sport is neither kayaking, nor mountaineering, nor running.

23. If Otto does not run during the year, then which one of the following statements must be false?

    (A) Nikki's fall sport is running.
    (B) Nikki's spring sport is running.
    (C) Nikki's summer sport is kayaking.
    (D) Otto's fall sport is mountaineering.
    (E) Otto's spring sport is kayaking.

24. Which one of the following statements could be true?

    (A) Nikki's fall sport is mountaineering and Otto's spring sport is running.
    (B) Nikki's spring sport is running and her summer sport is mountaineering.
    (C) Nikki's spring sport is mountaineering and Otto's fall sport is mountaineering.
    (D) Nikki's spring sport is running and Otto's fall sport is mountaineering.
    (E) Nikki's summer sport is mountaineering and Otto's spring sport is mountaineering.

S T O P

**IF YOU FINISH BEFORE TIME IS CALLED, YOU MAY CHECK YOUR WORK ON THIS SECTION ONLY.
DO NOT WORK ON ANY OTHER SECTION IN THE TEST.**

SECTION II

Time—35 minutes

25 Questions

<u>Directions:</u> The questions in this section are based on the reasoning contained in brief statements or passages. For some questions, more than one of the choices could conceivably answer the question. However, you are to choose the <u>best</u> answer; that is, the response that most accurately and completely answers the question. You should not make assumptions that are by commonsense standards implausible, superfluous, or incompatible with the passage. After you have chosen the best answer, blacken the corresponding space on your answer sheet.

1. Rainfall in the drought-plagued metropolitan area was heavier than usual for the month of June. Nevertheless, by the first of July the city's water shortage was more severe than ever, and officials proposed drastic restrictions on the use of water.

Which one of the following, if true, helps to explain why the city's water shortage was not alleviated by the first of July?

(A) Moderate restrictions on the industrial use of water had gone into effect in the metropolitan area several months earlier.

(B) Because of the heavier rainfall, people watered their lawns much less in June than they usually do in the metropolitan area during that month.

(C) People in the metropolitan area who had voluntarily reduced their use of water in earlier months when officials voiced alarm used greater than normal amounts of water when rainfall seemed plentiful in June.

(D) During the drought most residents of the metropolitan area had been informed about water conservation methods that would help them to reduce their water consumption significantly with a minimal reduction in their standard of living.

(E) The per capita rate of the use of water in the metropolitan area was slightly lower in June than in each of the three previous months and significantly lower than in June of the previous year.

2. Manager: I have circulated a posting for the position of Social Scientific Researcher. Applicants must have either an earned doctorate and a track record of published research, or else five years' work experience. The relevant fields for these requirements are sociology, psychology, and education.

Which one of the applicants, as described below, does NOT meet the manager's requirements?

(A) Joanne Bernstein has worked for the department of education as coordinator of research for the past eleven years. She also served for six years as director of the Save the Children Fund, for which she was awarded an honorary doctorate from the liberal arts college where she earned her bachelor's degree.

(B) Alvin Johnson is a doctoral candidate at a local university and is currently working on a dissertation. Prior to undertaking doctoral studies, he worked as a psychology researcher for seven years.

(C) Edward St. John has worked as a business consultant for the past ten years, during which time he has published six novels. He holds an earned doctorate from one of the nation's foremost business schools.

(D) Michael Roberts has published two highly regarded books on the problems of urban public schools and has a master's degree in special education. He taught special education classes for two years and then for four years served as a research associate with the Mayor's Task Force on Education.

(E) Alicia Arias holds an earned doctorate in sociology from a prestigious university and has published one book and fifteen research articles in sociology.

GO ON TO THE NEXT PAGE.

3. Deer mice normally do not travel far from their nests, and deer mice that are moved more than half a kilometer from their nests generally never find their way back. Yet in one case, when researchers camped near a deer mouse nest and observed a young deer mouse for several weeks before moving it to an area over two kilometers away, the deer mouse found its way back to its nest near their camp in less than two days.

Which one of the following, if true, most helps to explain how the deer mouse might have found its way back to its nest?

(A) The area to which the deer mouse was moved was dryer and more rocky than the area in which its nest was located.

(B) The researchers released the deer mouse in a flat area across which their campfire smoke drifted.

(C) There were very few deer mice in the area to which the deer mouse was moved.

(D) The researchers had moved the deer mouse in a small dark box, keeping the mouse calm before it was released.

(E) Animals that prey on deer mice were common in the area to which the deer mouse was moved.

4. The government's proposed 8 percent cut in all subsidies to arts groups will be difficult for those groups to absorb. As can be seen, however, from their response to last year's cut, it will not put them out of existence. Last year there was also an 8 percent cut, and though private fund-raising was very difficult for the arts groups in the current recessionary economy, they did survive.

The reasoning in the argument is flawed because the argument

(A) relies without warrant on the probability that the economy will improve

(B) does not raise the issue of whether there should be any government subsidies to arts groups at all

(C) equates the mere survival of the arts groups with their flourishing

(D) does not take into account that the dollar amount of the proposed cut is lower than the dollar amount of last year's cut

(E) overlooks the possibility that the cumulative effect of the cuts will be more than the arts groups can withstand

5. The average literate person today spends significantly less time reading than the average literate person did 50 years ago, yet many more books are sold per year now than were sold 50 years ago.

Each of the following, if true, helps resolve the apparent discrepancy above EXCEPT:

(A) The population of literate people is significantly larger today than it was 50 years ago.

(B) People who read books 50 years ago were more likely to read books borrowed from libraries than are people who read books today.

(C) The average scholar or other person who uses books professionally today owns and consults many more different books than did the average scholar or similar professional 50 years ago.

(D) People of 50 years ago were more likely than people are today to display large collections of books as a sign of education and good taste.

(E) Books sold now tend to be shorter and easier to read than were books sold 50 years ago.

6. Some scientists believe that the relationship between mice and humans has, over time, diminished the ability of mice to survive in nature, so that now they must depend upon human civilization for their continued existence. This opinion, however, ignores significant facts. Despite numerous predators and humanity's enmity, mice have distributed themselves more widely across the planet than any other mammal except humans. Mice reproduce rapidly and, more important to their survival, they have the ability to adapt to an extraordinary range of habitats. Should the environment ever become too extreme to support human life, naturalists predict that mice would be able to adapt and survive.

Which one of the following, if true, would most support the naturalists' prediction?

(A) The size of the mouse population is limited by the availability of food.

(B) Under optimum conditions, mice reproduce every four weeks, with five to seven pups per litter.

(C) Fossil remains prove that mice inhabited North America prior to the arrival of humans.

(D) Mice have colonized an island near Antarctica which is too bleak and harsh to support human life.

(E) A significant percentage of the world's mouse population lives in urban areas.

GO ON TO THE NEXT PAGE.

7. All zebras have stripes, and the most widespread subspecies has the best-defined stripes. The stripes must therefore be of importance to the species. Since among these grassland grazers the stripes can hardly function as camouflage, they must serve as some sort of signal for other zebras.

Which one of the following, if true, most strongly supports the conclusion regarding a signaling function?

(A) The subspecies of zebras with the best-defined stripes is also characterized by exceptional size and vigor.

(B) In certain tall grasses zebras can be harder to spot than grazing animals with a coat of uniform color.

(C) A visual signal transmitted among the members of a species can consist of a temporary change of color perceptible to other members of the species.

(D) Zebras react much faster to moving shapes that have stripes than they do to moving shapes that are otherwise identical but lack stripes.

(E) Zebras have a richer repertoire of vocal signals than do similar species such as horses.

8. Some years ago, an editorial defended United States government restrictions on academic freedom, arguing that scientists who receive public funding cannot rightly "detach themselves from the government's policies on national security." Yet the same editorial criticized the Soviet government for not allowing scientists to "detach themselves from politics." If there is a significant difference between the principles involved in each case, the editorial should have explained what that difference is.

The author of the passage criticizes the editorial by

(A) disputing certain factual claims made in the editorial

(B) pointing out an apparent inconsistency in the editorial

(C) describing an alleged exception to a general claim made in the editorial

(D) refuting an assumption on which the argument of the editorial appears to have been based

(E) drawing a conclusion from the editorial different from the conclusion drawn by the writer of the editorial

9. Ph.D. programs are valuable only if they inculcate good scholarship and expedite the student's full participation in the field. Hence, doctoral dissertations should not be required in the humanities. Undertaking a quality book-length dissertation demands an accumulation of knowledge virtually impossible for those relatively new to their disciplines. The student consequently either seeks to compensate for poor quality with quantity or ends up spending years producing a work of quality. Either way, the dissertation is counterproductive and frustrates the appropriate goals of the doctoral program.

The claim that doctoral dissertations should not be required in the humanities plays which one of the following roles in the argument?

(A) It provides essential support for the conclusion.

(B) It is an example illustrative of a general principle concerning the goals of Ph.D. programs.

(C) It is what the argument is attempting to establish.

(D) It provides evidence for the assumption that requirements for degrees in the humanities differ from requirements for degrees in other disciplines.

(E) It confirms the observation that the requirement for a dissertation can frustrate the goals of a doctoral program.

GO ON TO THE NEXT PAGE.

10. The government of Penglai, an isolated island, proposed eliminating outdoor advertising except for small signs of standard shape that identify places of business. Some island merchants protested that the law would reduce the overall volume of business in Penglai, pointing to a report done by the government indicating that in every industry the Penglai businesses that used outdoor advertising had a larger market share than those that did not.

Which one of the following describes an error of reasoning in the merchants' argument?

(A) presupposing that there are no good reasons for restricting the use of outdoor advertising in Penglai

(B) assuming without giving justification that the outdoor advertising increased market share by some means other than by diverting trade from competing businesses

(C) ignoring the question of whether the government's survey of the island could be objective

(D) failing to establish whether the market-share advantage enjoyed by businesses employing outdoor advertising was precisely proportionate to the amount of advertising

(E) disregarding the possibility that the government's proposed restrictions are unconstitutional

11. Unless they are used as strictly temporary measures, rent-control ordinances (municipal regulations placing limits on rent increases) have several negative effects for renters. One of these is that the controls will bring about a shortage of rental units. This disadvantage for renters occurs over the long run, but the advantage—smaller rent increases—occurs immediately. In many municipalities, specifically in all those where tenants of rent-control units have a secure hold on political power and can get rent-control ordinances enacted or repealed, it is invariably the desire for short-term gain that guides those tenants in the exercise of that power.

If the statements above are true, which one of the following can be properly inferred from them?

(A) It is impossible for landlords to raise rents when rent controls are in effect.

(B) In many municipalities rent-control ordinances are repealed as soon as shortages of rental units arise.

(C) The only negative effect of rent control for renters is that it brings about a shortage of rental units.

(D) In many municipalities there is now, or eventually will be, a shortage of rental units.

(E) In the long term, a shortage of rental units will raise rents substantially.

Questions 12–13

In many languages other than English there is a word for "mother's brother" which is different from the word for "father's brother," whereas English uses the word "uncle" for both. Thus, speakers of these languages evidence a more finely discriminated kinship system than English speakers do. The number of basic words for colors also varies widely from language to language. Therefore, speakers of languages that have fewer basic words for colors than English has must be perceptually unable to distinguish as many colors as speakers of English can distinguish.

12. Which one of the following, if true, undermines the conclusion concerning words for colors?

(A) Speakers of English are able to distinguish between lighter and darker shades of the color they call "blue," for which Russian has two different basic words.

(B) Almost every language distinguishes red from the other colors.

(C) Khmer uses a basic word corresponding to English "blue" for most leaves, but uses its basic word corresponding to English "green" for unripe bananas.

(D) The word "orange" in English has the same origin as the equivalent word in Spanish.

(E) Most languages do not have a basic word that distinguishes gray from other colors, although gray is commonly found in nature.

13. The conclusion concerning words for colors would be properly drawn if which one of the following were assumed?

(A) Most languages have distinct words for "sister" and "brother."

(B) Each language has a different basic word for each sensory quality that its speakers can perceptually distinguish.

(C) Every language makes some category distinctions that no other language makes.

(D) In any language short, frequently used words express categories that are important for its speakers to distinguish perceptually from each other.

(E) Speakers of languages with relatively few basic words for colors live in geographical regions where flora and fauna do not vary greatly in color.

GO ON TO THE NEXT PAGE.

Questions 14–15

Zachary: One would have to be blind to the reality of moral obligation to deny that people who believe a course of action to be morally obligatory for them have both the right and the duty to pursue that action, and that no one else has any right to stop them from doing so.

Cynthia: But imagine an artist who feels morally obliged to do whatever she can to prevent works of art from being destroyed confronting a morally committed antipornography demonstrator engaged in destroying artworks he deems pornographic. According to your principle that artist has, simultaneously, both the right and the duty to stop the destruction and no right whatsoever to stop it.

14. Cynthia's response to Zachary's claim is structured to demonstrate that

(A) the concept of moral obligation is incoherent
(B) the ideas of right and duty should not be taken seriously since doing so leads to morally undesirable consequences
(C) Zachary's principle is untenable on its own terms
(D) because the term "moral obligation" is understood differently by different people, it is impossible to find a principle concerning moral rights and duties that applies to everyone
(E) Zachary's principle is based on an understanding of moral obligation that is too narrow to encompass the kind of moral obligation artists feel toward works of art

15. Which one of the following, if substituted for the scenario invoked by Cynthia, would preserve the force of her argument?

(A) a medical researcher who feels a moral obligation not to claim sole credit for work that was performed in part by someone else confronting another researcher who feels no such moral obligation
(B) a manufacturer who feels a moral obligation to recall potentially dangerous products confronting a consumer advocate who feels morally obliged to expose product defects
(C) an investment banker who believes that governments are morally obliged to regulate major industries confronting an investment banker who holds that governments have a moral obligation not to interfere with market forces
(D) an architect who feels a moral obligation to design only energy-efficient buildings confronting, as a potential client, a corporation that believes its primary moral obligation is to maximize shareholder profits
(E) a health inspector who feels morally obliged to enforce restrictions on the number of cats a householder may keep confronting a householder who, feeling morally obliged to keep every stray that comes along, has over twice that number of cats

16. A county airport, designed to serve the needs of private aircraft owners, planned to cover its operating expenses in part by charging user fees to private aircraft using the airport. The airport was unable to pay its operating expenses because the revenue from user fees was lower than expected.

If the statements above are true, which one of the following must also be true?

(A) Most of the county's citizens live a convenient distance from one or another airport now offering commercial airline services.
(B) Private aircraft owners were unwilling to pay the user fees charged at the airport.
(C) The airport's construction was financed exclusively by private funds.
(D) The airport's operating expenses were greater than the revenue raised from sources other than the airport user fees for private planes.
(E) The number of owners of private aircraft who use the county's airport facilities will not change appreciably in the future.

GO ON TO THE NEXT PAGE.

Questions 17–18

Consumer activist: By allowing major airlines to abandon, as they promptly did, all but their most profitable routes, the government's decision to cease regulation of the airline industry has worked to the disadvantage of everyone who lacks access to a large metropolitan airport.

Industry representative: On the contrary, where major airlines moved out, regional airlines have moved in and, as a consequence, there are more flights into and out of most small airports now than before the change in regulatory policy.

17. The industry representative's argument will not provide an effective answer to the consumer activist's claim unless which one of the following is true?

(A) No small airport has fewer flights now than it did before the change in policy regarding regulation of the airline industry.

(B) When permitted to do so by changes in regulatory policy, each major airline abandoned all but large metropolitan airports.

(C) Policies that result in an increase in the number of flights to which consumers have easy access do not generally work to the disadvantage of consumers.

(D) Regional airlines charge less to fly a given route now than the major airlines charged when they flew the same route.

(E) Any policy that leads to an increase in the number of competitors in a given field works to the long-term advantage of consumers.

18. Which one of the following is an assumption on which the consumer activist's argument depends?

(A) Before the recent change in regulatory policy, there was no advantage in having easy access to a large metropolitan airport.

(B) When any sizable group of consumers is seriously disadvantaged by a change in government policy, that change should be reversed.

(C) Government regulation of industry almost always works to the advantage of consumers.

(D) At the time of the regulatory change, the major airlines were maintaining their less profitable routes at least in part because of government requirements.

(E) Regional airlines lack the resources to provide consumers with service of the same quality as that provided by the major airlines.

19. A report on the likely effects of current levels of air pollution on forest growth in North America concluded that, since nitrogen is a necessary nutrient for optimal plant growth, the nitrogen deposited on forest soil as a result of air pollution probably benefits eastern forests. However, European soil scientists have found that in forests saturated with sulfate and nitrate, trees begin to die when the nitrogen deposited exceeds the amount of nitrogen absorbed by the forest system. Since this finding is likely to apply to forests everywhere, large areas of eastern forests of North America are, undoubtedly, already being affected adversely.

Which one of the following most accurately expresses the main point of the passage?

(A) The implication of the report cited is that the amount of nitrogen reaching eastern forests by way of polluted air is approximately what those forests need for optimal growth.

(B) If large areas of eastern forests were increasingly saturated with sulfate and nitrate, the capacity of those forest systems for absorbing nitrogen would also increase.

(C) The type of analysis used by European soil scientists does not necessarily apply to eastern forests of North America.

(D) The eastern forests are the only forests of North America currently affected by polluted air.

(E) Contrary to the report cited, the nitrogen pollution now in the air is more likely to cause trees to die in eastern forests than to benefit them.

GO ON TO THE NEXT PAGE.

20. Railroad spokesperson: Of course it is a difficult task to maintain quality of service at the same time that the amount of subsidy the taxpayers give the railroad network is reduced. Over recent years, however, the number of passengers has increased in spite of subsidy reductions. This fact leads to the conclusion that our quality of service has been satisfactory.

The spokesperson's argument is based on which one of the following assumptions?

(A) Taxpayers do not wish to have their taxes raised to subsidize the railroads.

(B) Some people refuse to travel by train if they are dissatisfied with the quality of service.

(C) The quality of service on the trains must have improved in spite of subsidy reductions.

(D) It is impossible to reduce subsidies to the railroad network without some effect on the quality of service.

(E) The increase in the number of passengers will increase revenue sufficiently to offset the subsidy reductions.

21. In response to high mortality in area hospitals, surgery was restricted to emergency procedures during a five-week period. Mortality in these hospitals was found to have fallen by nearly one-third during the period. The number of deaths rose again when elective surgery (surgery that can be postponed) was resumed. It can be concluded that, before the five-week period, the risks of elective surgery had been incurred unnecessarily often in the area.

Which one of the following, if true, most seriously undermines the conclusion above?

(A) The conditions for which elective surgery was performed would in the long run have been life-threatening, and surgery for them would have become riskier with time.

(B) The physicians planning elective surgery performed before the five-week period had fully informed the patients who would undergo it of the possible risks of the procedures.

(C) Before the suspension of elective surgery, surgical operations were performed in area hospitals at a higher rate, per thousand residents of the area, than was usual elsewhere.

(D) Elective surgery is, in general, less risky than is emergency surgery because the conditions requiring or indicating surgery are often less severe.

(E) Even if a surgical procedure is successful, the patient can die of a hospital-contracted infection with a bacterium that is resistant to antibiotic treatment.

22. Gallery owner: Because this painting appears in no catalog of van Gogh's work, we cannot guarantee that he painted it. But consider: the subject is one he painted often, and experts agree that in his later paintings van Gogh invariably used just such broad brushstrokes and distinctive combinations of colors as we find here. Internal evidence, therefore, makes it virtually certain that this is a previously uncataloged, late van Gogh, and as such, a bargain at its price.

The reasoning used by the gallery owner is flawed because it

(A) ignores the fact that there can be general agreement that something is the case without its being the case

(B) neglects to cite expert authority to substantiate the claim about the subject matter of the painting

(C) assumes without sufficient warrant that the only reason anyone would want to acquire a painting is to make a profit

(D) provides no evidence that the painting is more likely to be an uncataloged van Gogh than to be a painting by someone else who painted that particular subject in van Gogh's style

(E) attempts to establish a particular conclusion because doing so is in the reasoner's self-interest rather than because of any genuine concern for the truth of the matter

23. Government-subsidized insurance available to homeowners makes it feasible for anyone to build a house on a section of coastline regularly struck by hurricanes. Each major storm causes billions of dollars worth of damage in such coastal areas, after which owners who have insurance are able to collect an amount of money sufficient to recoup a high percentage of their losses.

The passage provides the most support for an argument against a government bill proposing

(A) that power companies be required to bury power lines in areas of the coastline regularly struck by hurricanes

(B) an increase in funding of weather service programs that provide a hurricane watch and warning system for coastal areas

(C) renewal of federal funding for emergency life-support programs in hurricane-stricken areas

(D) establishment of an agency committed to managing coastal lands in ecologically responsible ways

(E) establishment of a contingency fund protecting owners of uninsured houses in the coastal areas from catastrophic losses due to the hurricane damage

GO ON TO THE NEXT PAGE.

24. Between 1951 and 1963, it was illegal in the country of Geronia to manufacture, sell, or transport any alcoholic beverages. Despite this prohibition, however, the death rate from diseases related to excessive alcohol consumption was higher during the first five years of the period than it was during the five years prior to 1951. Therefore, the attempt to prevent alcohol use merely made people want and use alcohol more than they would have if it had not been forbidden.

Each of the following, if true, weakens the argument EXCEPT:

(A) Death from an alcohol-related disease generally does not occur until five to ten years after the onset of excessive alcohol consumption.

(B) The diseases that can be caused by excessive alcohol consumption can also be caused by other kinds of behavior that increased between 1951 and 1963.

(C) The death rate resulting from alcohol-related diseases increased just as sharply during the ten years before and the ten years after the prohibition of alcohol as it did during the years of prohibition.

(D) Many who died of alcohol-related diseases between 1951 and 1963 consumed illegally imported alcoholic beverages produced by the same methods as those used within Geronia.

(E) Between 1951 and 1963, among the people with preexisting alcohol-related diseases, the percentage who obtained lifesaving medical attention declined because of a social stigma attached to excessive alcohol consumption.

25. A letter submitted to the editor of a national newsmagazine was written and signed by a Dr. Shirley Martin who, in the text of the letter, mentions being a professor at a major North American medical school. Knowing that fewer than 5 percent of the professors at such schools are women, the editor reasons that the chances are better than 19 to 1 that the letter was written by a man.

Which one of the following involves flawed reasoning most like that used by the editor?

(A) Since 19 out of 20 home computers are purchased primarily for use with computer games, and the first computer sold today was purchased solely for word processing, the next 19 computers sold will almost certainly be used primarily for computer games.

(B) Fewer than 1 in 20 of the manuscripts submitted to Argon Publishing Co. are accepted for publication. Since only 15 manuscripts were submitted last week, there is almost no chance that any of them will be accepted for publication.

(C) Fewer than 5 percent of last year's graduating class took Latin in secondary school. Howard took Latin in secondary school, so if he had graduated last year, it is likely that one of the other Latin scholars would not have graduated.

(D) More than 95 percent of the planes built by UBC last year met government standards for large airliners. Since small planes account for just under 5 percent of UBC's output last year, it is almost certain that all their large planes met government standards.

(E) Since more than 19 out of every 20 animals in the wildlife preserve are mammals and fewer than 1 out of 20 are birds, there is a greater than 95 percent chance that the animal Emily saw flying between two trees in the wildlife refuge yesterday morning was a mammal.

S T O P

IF YOU FINISH BEFORE TIME IS CALLED, YOU MAY CHECK YOUR WORK ON THIS SECTION ONLY. DO NOT WORK ON ANY OTHER SECTION IN THE TEST.

SECTION III

Time—35 minutes

27 Questions

Directions: Each passage in this section is followed by a group of questions to be answered on the basis of what is <u>stated</u> or <u>implied</u> in the passage. For some of the questions, more than one of the choices could conceivably answer the question. However, you are to choose the <u>best</u> answer; that is, the response that most accurately and completely answers the question, and blacken the corresponding space on your answer sheet.

It is a fundamental tenet of geophysics that the Earth's magnetic field can exist in either of two polarity states: a "normal" state, in which north-seeking compass needles point to the

(5) geographic north, and a "reverse" state, in which they point to the geographic south. Geological evidence shows that periodically the field's polarity reverses, and that these reversals have been taking place at an increasing rate. Evidence also indicates

(10) that the field does not reverse instantaneously from one polarity state to another; rather, the process involves a transition period that typically spans a few thousand years.

Though this much is known, the underlying

(15) causes of the reversal phenomenon are not well understood. It is generally accepted that the magnetic field itself is generated by the motion of free electrons in the outer core, a slowly churning mass of molten metal sandwiched between the

(20) Earth's mantle (the region of the Earth's interior lying below the crust) and its solid inner core. In some way that is not completely understood, gravity and the Earth's rotation, acting on temperature and density differences within the

(25) outer core fluid, provide the driving forces behind the generation of the field. The reversal phenomenon may be triggered when something disturbs the heat circulation pattern of the outer core fluid, and with it the magnetic field.

(30) Several explanations for this phenomenon have been proposed. One proposal, the "heat-transfer hypothesis," is that the triggering process is intimately related to the way the outer core vents its heat into the mantle. For example, such heat

(35) transfer could create hotter (rising) or cooler (descending) blobs of material from the inner and outer boundaries of the fluid core, thereby perturbing the main heat-circulation pattern. A more controversial alternative proposal is the

(40) "asteroid-impact hypothesis." In this scenario an extended period of cold and darkness results from the impact of an asteroid large enough to send a great cloud of dust into the atmosphere. Following this climatic change, ocean temperatures drop and

(45) the polar ice caps grow, redistributing the Earth's seawater. This redistribution increases the rotational acceleration of the mantle, causing friction and turbulence near the outer core-mantle boundary and initiating a reversal of the magnetic field.

(50) How well do these hypotheses account for such

observations as the long-term increase in the frequency of reversal? In support of the asteroid-impact model, it has been argued that the gradual cooling of the average ocean temperature

(55) would enable progressively smaller asteroid impacts (which are known to occur more frequently than larger impacts) to cool the Earth's climate sufficiently to induce ice-cap growth and reversals. But theories that depend on extraterrestrial

(60) intervention seem less convincing than theories like the first, which account for the phenomenon solely by means of the thermodynamic state of the outer core and its effect on the mantle.

1. Which one of the following statements regarding the Earth's outer core is best supported by information presented in the passage?

(A) Heat circulation in the outer core controls the growth and diminution of the polar ice caps.
(B) Impact of asteroids on the Earth's surface alters the way in which the outer core vents its heat into the mantle.
(C) Motion of electrons within the metallic fluid in the outer core produces the Earth's magnetic field.
(D) Friction and turbulence near the boundary between the outer core and the mantle are typically caused by asteroid impacts.
(E) Cessation of heat circulation within the outer core brings on multiple reversals in the Earth's magnetic field.

GO ON TO THE NEXT PAGE.

2. The author's objection to the second hypothesis discussed in the passage is most applicable to which one of the following explanations concerning the extinction of the dinosaurs?

(A) The extinction of the dinosaurs was the result of gradual changes in the composition of the Earth's atmosphere that occurred over millions of years.

(B) The dinosaurs became extinct when their food supply was disrupted following the emergence of mammals.

(C) The dinosaurs succumbed to the new, colder environment brought about by a buildup of volcanic ash in the atmosphere.

(D) After massively overpopulating the planet, dinosaurs disappeared due to widespread starvation and the rapid spread of disease.

(E) After radical climatic changes resulted from the impact of a comet, dinosaurs disappeared from the Earth.

3. The author mentions the creation of blobs of different temperatures in the Earth's outer core (lines 34-38) primarily in order to

(A) present a way in which the venting of heat from the outer core might disturb the heat-circulation pattern within the outer core

(B) provide proof for the proposal that ventilation of heat from the outer core into the mantle triggers polarity reversal

(C) give an example of the way in which heat circulates between the Earth's outer core and the Earth's exterior

(D) describe how the outer core maintains its temperature by venting its excess heat into the Earth's mantle

(E) argue in favor of the theory that heat circulation in the Earth's interior produces the magnetic field

4. Which one of the following statements regarding the polarity of the Earth's magnetic field is best supported by information in the passage?

(A) Most, but not all, geophysicists agree that the Earth's magnetic field may exist in two distinct polarity states.

(B) Changes in the polarity of the Earth's magnetic field have occurred more often in the recent past than in the distant past.

(C) Heat transfer would cause reversals of the polarity of the Earth's magnetic field to occur more quickly than would asteroid impact.

(D) Geophysicists' understanding of the reversal of the Earth's magnetic field has increased significantly since the introduction of the heat-transfer hypothesis.

(E) Friction near the boundary of the inner and outer cores brings on reversal of the polarity of the geomagnetic field.

5. Which one of the following can be inferred regarding the two proposals discussed in the passage?

(A) Since their introduction they have sharply divided the scientific community.

(B) Both were formulated in order to explain changes in the frequency of polarity reversal.

(C) Although no firm conclusions regarding them have yet been reached, both have been extensively investigated.

(D) They are not the only proposals scientists have put forward to explain the phenomenon of polarity reversal.

(E) Both were introduced some time ago and have since fallen into disfavor among geophysicists.

6. The author mentions each of the following as possible contributing causes to reversals of the Earth's magnetic field EXCEPT

(A) changes in the way heat circulates within the outer core fluid

(B) extended periods of colder temperatures on the Earth's surface

(C) the creation of circulating blobs of outer core material of different temperatures

(D) changes in circulation patterns in the Earth's oceans

(E) clouding of the Earth's atmosphere by a large amount of dust

GO ON TO THE NEXT PAGE.

Innovations in language are never completely new. When the words used for familiar things change, or words for new things enter the language, they are usually borrowed or adapted from stock.
(5) Assuming new roles, they drag their old meanings along behind them like flickering shadows. This seems especially true of the language of the contemporary school of literary criticism that now prefers to describe its work simply and rather
(10) presumptuously as "theory" but is still popularly referred to as poststructuralism or deconstruction.

The first neologisms adopted by this movement were *signifier* and *signified*, employed to distinguish words from their referents, and to illustrate the
(15) arbitrariness of the terms we choose. The use of these particular terms (rather than, respectively, *word* and *thing*) underlined the seriousness of the naming process and its claim on our attention. Since in English "to signify" can also mean "to
(20) portend," these terms also suggest that words predict coming events.

With the use of the term *deconstruction* we move into another and more complex realm of meaning. The most common use of the terms *construction*
(25) and *deconstruction* is in the building trades, and their borrowing by literary theorists for a new type of criticism cannot help but have certain overtones to the outsider. First, the usage suggests that the creation and critical interpretation of literature are
(30) not organic but mechanical processes; that the author of any piece of writing is not an inspired, intuitive artist, but merely a laborer who cobbles existing materials (words) into more or less conventional structures. The term *deconstruction*
(35) implies that the text has been put together like a building or a piece of machinery, and that it is in need of being taken apart, not so much in order to repair it as to demonstrate underlying inadequacies, false assumptions, and inherent contradictions.
(40) This process can supposedly be repeated many times and by many literary hard hats; it is expected that each deconstruction will reveal additional flaws and expose the illusions or bad faith of the builder. The fact that deconstructionists prefer to
(45) describe their activities as *deconstruction* rather than *criticism* is also revealing. *Criticism* and *critic* derive from the Greek *kritikos*, "skillful in judging, decisive." *Deconstruction*, on the other hand, has no overtones of skill or wisdom; it merely suggests
(50) demolition of an existing building. In popular usage *criticism* suggests censure but not change. If we find fault with a building, we may condemn it, but we do not carry out the demolition ourselves. The deconstructionist, by implication, is both judge and
(55) executioner who leaves a text totally dismantled, if not reduced to a pile of rubble.

7. Which one of the following best expresses the main idea of the passage?

(A) Implicit in the terminology of the school of criticism known as *deconstruction* are meanings that reveal the true nature of the deconstructionist's endeavor.
(B) The appearance of the terms *signifier* and *signified* in the field of literary theory anticipated the appearance of an even more radical idea known as *deconstruction*.
(C) Innovations in language and the relations between old and new meanings of terms are a special concern of the new school of criticism known as *deconstruction*.
(D) Deconstructionists maintain that it is insufficient merely to judge a work; the critic must actively dismantle it.
(E) Progress in the field of literary theory is best achieved by looking for new terms like *signifier* and *deconstruction* that might suggest new critical approaches to a work.

8. Which one of the following is a claim that the author of the passage makes about deconstructionists?

(A) Deconstructionists would not have been able to formulate their views adequately without the terms *signifier* and *signified*.
(B) Deconstructionists had no particular purpose in mind in choosing to use neologisms.
(C) Deconstructionists do not recognize that their own theory contains inherent contradictions.
(D) Deconstructionists find little interest in the relationship between words and their referents.
(E) Deconstructionists use the terms *signifier* and *signified* to stress the importance of the process of naming.

GO ON TO THE NEXT PAGE.

9. Which one of the following generalizations about inventions is most analogous to the author's point about innovation in language?

   (A) A new invention usually consists of components that are specifically manufactured for the new invention.
   (B) A new invention is usually behind the times, never making as much use of all the available modern technology as it could.
   (C) A new invention usually consists of components that are already available but are made to function in new ways.
   (D) A new invention is most useful when it is created with attention to the historical tradition established by implements previously used to do the same job.
   (E) A new invention is rarely used to its full potential because it is surrounded by out-of-date technology that hinders its application.

10. The author of the passage uses the word "*criticism*" in lines 46-56 primarily in order to

    (A) give an example
    (B) introduce a contrast
    (C) undermine an argument
    (D) codify a system
    (E) dismiss an objection

11. Which one of the following best describes the function of the second paragraph within the passage as a whole?

    (A) It introduces a hypothesis that the author later expands upon.
    (B) It qualifies a claim made earlier by the author.
    (C) It develops an initial example of the author's general thesis.
    (D) It predicts a development.
    (E) It presents a contrasting view.

12. The passage suggests that the author most probably holds the view that an important characteristic of literary criticism is that it

    (A) demonstrate false assumptions and inherent contradictions
    (B) employ skill and insight
    (C) be carried out by one critic rather than many
    (D) reveal how a text is put together like a building
    (E) point out the superiority of conventional text structures

13. The passage suggests that which one of the following most accurately describes the author's view of deconstructionist thought?

    (A) The author is guardedly optimistic about the ability of deconstruction to reveal the intentions and biases of a writer.
    (B) The author endorses the utility of deconstruction for revealing the role of older meanings of words.
    (C) The author is enthusiastic about the significant neologisms that deconstruction has introduced into literary criticism.
    (D) The author regards deconstruction's tendency to focus only on the problems and faults of literary texts as too mechanical.
    (E) The author condemns deconstruction's attempts to define literary criticism as a creative act.

GO ON TO THE NEXT PAGE.

(The following passage was written in 1986.)

The legislature of a country recently considered a bill designed to reduce the uncertainty inherent in the ownership of art by specifying certain conditions that must be met before an allegedly stolen work of art can be reclaimed by a plaintiff. The bill places the burden of proof in reclamation litigation entirely on the plaintiff, who must demonstrate that the holder of an item knew at the time of purchase that it had been stolen. Additionally, the bill creates a uniform national statute of limitations for reclamation of stolen cultural property.

Testifying in support of the bill, James D. Burke, a citizen of the country and one of its leading art museum directors, specifically praised the inclusion of a statute of limitations; otherwise, he said, other countries could seek to reclaim valuable art objects, no matter how long they have been held by the current owner or how legitimately they were acquired. Any country could enact a patrimony law stating that anything ever made within the boundaries of that country is its cultural property. Burke expressed the fear that widespread reclamation litigation would lead to ruinous legal defense costs for museums.

However, because such reclamation suits have not yet been a problem, there is little basis for Burke's concern. In fact, the proposed legislation would establish too many unjustifiable barriers to the location and recovery of stolen objects. The main barrier is that the bill considers the announcement of an art transaction in a museum publication to be adequate evidence of an attempt to notify a possible owner. There are far too many such publications for the victim of a theft to survey, and with only this form of disclosure, a stolen object could easily remain unlocated even if assiduously searched for. Another stipulation requires that a purchaser show the object to a scholar for verification that it is not stolen, but it is a rare academic who is aware of any but the most publicized art thefts. Moreover, the time limit specified by the statute of limitations is very short, and the requirement that the plaintiff demonstrate that the holder had knowledge of the theft is unrealistic. Typically, stolen art changes hands several times before rising to the level in the marketplace where a curator or collector would see it. At that point, the object bears no trace of the initial transaction between the thief and the first purchaser, perhaps the only one in the chain who knowingly acquired a stolen work of art.

Thus, the need for new legislation to protect holders of art is not obvious. Rather, what is necessary is legislation remedying the difficulties that legitimate owners of works of art, and countries from which such works have been stolen, have in locating and reclaiming these stolen works.

14. Which one of the following most accurately summarizes the main point of the passage?

(A) Various legal disputes have recently arisen that demonstrate the need for legislation clarifying the legal position of museums in suits involving the repossession of cultural property.

(B) A bill intended to prevent other governments from recovering cultural property was recently introduced into the legislature of a country at the behest of its museum directors.

(C) A bill intended to protect good-faith purchasers of works of art from reclamation litigation is unnecessary and fails to address the needs of legitimate owners attempting to recover stolen art works.

(D) Clashes between museum professionals and members of the academic community regarding governmental legislation of the arts can best be resolved by negotiation and arbitration, not by litigation.

(E) The desire of some governments to use legislation and litigation to recover cultural property stolen from their countries has led to abuses in international patrimony legislation.

15. The uncertainty mentioned in line 2 of the passage refers to the

(A) doubt that owners of works of art often harbor over whether individuals have a moral right to possess great art

(B) concern that owners of works of art often have that their possession of such objects may be legally challenged at any time

(C) questions that owners of works of art often have concerning the correct identification of the age and origin of their objects

(D) disputes that often arise between cultural institutions vying for the opportunity to purchase a work of art

(E) apprehension that owners of works of art often feel concerning the possibility that their objects may be damaged or stolen from them

GO ON TO THE NEXT PAGE.

16. Which one of the following is an example of the kind of action that Burke feared would pose a serious threat to museums in his country?

(A) the passage of a law by another country forbidding the future export of any archaeological objects uncovered at sites within its territory

(B) an international accord establishing strict criteria for determining whether a work of art can be considered stolen and specifying the circumstances under which it must be returned to its country of origin

(C) the passage of a law by another country declaring that all objects created by its aboriginal people are the sole property of that country

(D) an increase in the acquisition of culturally significant works of art by private collectors, who are more capable than museums of bearing the cost of litigation but who rarely display their collections to the public

(E) the recommendation of a United Nations committee studying the problem of art theft that all international sales of cultural property be coordinated by a central regulatory body

17. According to the passage, Burke envisaged the most formidable potential adversaries of his country's museums in reclamation litigation to be

(A) commercial dealers in art
(B) law enforcement officials in his own country
(C) governments of other countries
(D) private collectors of art
(E) museums in other countries

18. The author suggests that in the country mentioned in line 1, litigation involving the reclamation of stolen works of art has been

(A) less common than Burke fears it will become without passage of a national statute of limitations for reclamation of stolen cultural property

(B) increasing as a result of the passage of legislation that aids legitimate owners of art in their attempts to recover stolen works

(C) a serious threat to museums and cultural institutions that have unwittingly added stolen artifacts to their collections

(D) a signal of the legitimate frustrations of victims of art theft

(E) increasing as a result of an increase in the amount of art theft

19. Which one of the following best describes the author's attitude toward the proposed bill?

(A) impassioned support
(B) measured advocacy
(C) fearful apprehension
(D) reasoned opposition
(E) reluctant approval

20. Which one of the following best exemplifies the sort of legislation considered necessary by the author of the passage?

(A) a law requiring museums to notify foreign governments and cultural institutions of all the catalogs and scholarly journals that they publish

(B) a law providing for the creation of a national warehouse for storage of works of art that are the subject of litigation

(C) a law instituting a national fund for assisting museums to bear the expenses of defending themselves against reclamation suits

(D) a law declaring invalid all sales of cultural property during the last ten years by museums of one country to museums of another

(E) a law requiring that a central archive be established for collecting and distributing information concerning all reported thefts of cultural property

GO ON TO THE NEXT PAGE.

Until recently, few historians were interested in analyzing the similarities and differences between serfdom in Russia and slavery in the United States. Even Alexis de Tocqueville, who recognized the
(5) significant comparability of the two nations, never compared their systems of servitude, despite his interest in United States slavery. Moreover, the almost simultaneous abolition of Russian serfdom and United States slavery in the 1860s—a riveting
(10) coincidence that should have drawn more modern scholars to a comparative study of the two systems of servitude—has failed to arouse the interest of scholars. Though some historians may have been put off by the forbidding political differences
(15) between nineteenth-century Russia and the United States—one an imperial monarchy, the other a federal democracy—a recent study by Peter Kolchin identifies differences that are illuminating, especially with regard to the different kinds of
(20) rebellion exhibited by slaves and serfs.

Kolchin points out that nobles owning serfs in Russia constituted only a tiny proportion of the population, while in the southern United States, about a quarter of all White people were members
(25) of slave-owning families. And although in the southern United States only 2 percent of slaves worked on plantations where more than a hundred slaves worked, in Russia almost 80 percent of the serfs worked for nobles who owned more than a
(30) hundred serfs. In Russia most serfs rarely saw their owners, who tended to rely on intermediaries to manage their estates, while most southern planters lived on their land and interacted with slaves on a regular basis.

(35) These differences in demographics partly explain differences in the kinds of resistance that slaves and serfs practiced in their respective countries. Both serfs and slaves engaged in a wide variety of rebellious activity, from silent sabotage, much of
(40) which has escaped the historical record, to organized armed rebellions, which were more common in Russia. The practice of absentee ownership, combined with the large numbers in which serfs were owned, probably contributed
(45) significantly to the four great rebellions that swept across Russia at roughly fifty-year intervals in the seventeenth and eighteenth centuries. The last of these, occurring between 1773 and 1774, enlisted more than a million serfs in a futile attempt to
(50) overthrow the Russian nobility. Russian serfs also participated in smaller acts of collective defiance called the *volnenie*, which typically started with a group of serfs who complained of grievances by petition and went out on strike. Confrontations
(55) between slaves and plantation authorities were also common, but they tended to be much less collective in nature than those that occurred in Russia, probably in part because the number of workers on each estate was smaller in the United States than
(60) was the case in Russia.

21. Which one of the following best states the main idea of the passage?

(A) Differences in the demographics of United States slavery and Russian serfdom can help explain the different kinds of resistance practiced by slaves and serfs in their respective countries.

(B) Historians have yet to undertake an adequate comparison and contrast of Russian serfdom and United States slavery.

(C) Revolts by Russian serfs were commonly characterized by collective action.

(D) A recent study has questioned the value of comparing United States slavery to Russian serfdom, especially in light of the significant demographic and cultural differences between the two countries.

(E) De Tocqueville failed to recognize the fundamental differences between Russian serfdom and United States slavery which more recent historians have identified.

22. According to the author, de Tocqueville was similar to many modern historians in his

(A) interest in the demographic differences between Russia and the United States during the nineteenth century

(B) failure to undertake a comparison of Russian serfdom and United States slavery

(C) inability to explain why United States slavery and Russian serfdom were abolished during the same decade

(D) overestimation of the significance of the political differences between Russia and the United States

(E) recognition of the essential comparability of Russia and the United States

GO ON TO THE NEXT PAGE.

23. Which one of the following assertions, if true, would provide the most support for Kolchin's principal conclusion regarding the relationship of demographics to rebellion among Russian serfs and United States slaves?

(A) Collective defiance by serfs during the nineteenth century was confined almost exclusively to their participation in the *volnenie*.

(B) The rebellious activity of United States slaves was more likely to escape the historical record than was the rebellious activity of Russian serfs.

(C) Organized rebellions by slaves in the Western Hemisphere during the nineteenth century were most common in colonies with large estates that normally employed more than a hundred slaves.

(D) In the southern United States during the nineteenth century, those estates that were managed by intermediaries rather than by the owner generally relied upon the labor of at least a hundred slaves.

(E) The intermediaries who managed estates in Russia during the nineteenth century were in general much more competent as managers than the owners of the estates that they managed.

24. The fact that United States slavery and Russian serfdom were abolished during the same decade is cited by the author in the first paragraph primarily in order to

(A) emphasize that rebellions in both countries eventually led to the demise of the two institutions

(B) cite a coincidence that de Tocqueville should have been able to foresee

(C) suggest one reason why more historians should have been drawn to a comparative study of the two institutions

(D) cite a coincidence that Kolchin's study has failed to explain adequately

(E) emphasize the underlying similarities between the two institutions

25. The author cites which one of the following as a factor that might have discouraged historians from undertaking a comparative study of Russian serfdom and United States slavery?

(A) major differences in the political systems of the two countries

(B) major differences in the demographics of the two countries

(C) the failure of de Tocqueville to address the subject

(D) differences in the size of the estates on which slaves and serfs labored

(E) the comprehensiveness of Kolchin's own work

26. According to the passage, Kolchin's study asserts that which one of the following was true of Russian nobles during the nineteenth century?

(A) They agreed to the abolition of serfdom in the 1860s largely as a result of their having been influenced by the abolition of slavery in the United States.

(B) They became more directly involved in the management of their estates as a result of the rebellions that occurred in the previous century.

(C) They commonly agreed to at least some of the demands that arose out of the *volnenie*.

(D) They had relatively little direct contact with the serfs who worked on their estates.

(E) They hastened the abolition of serfdom by failing to devise an effective response to the collective nature of the serfs' rebellious activity.

27. The passage suggests that which one of the following was true of southern planters in the United States?

(A) They were as prepared for collective protest as were their Russian counterparts.

(B) Few of them owned plantations on which fewer than a hundred slaves worked.

(C) They managed their estates more efficiently than did their Russian counterparts.

(D) Few of them relied on intermediaries to manage their estates.

(E) The size of their estates was larger on average than the size of Russian estates.

S T O P

IF YOU FINISH BEFORE TIME IS CALLED, YOU MAY CHECK YOUR WORK ON THIS SECTION ONLY.
DO NOT WORK ON ANY OTHER SECTION IN THE TEST.

SECTION IV
Time—35 minutes
25 Questions

<u>Directions:</u> The questions in this section are based on the reasoning contained in brief statements or passages. For some questions, more than one of the choices could conceivably answer the question. However, you are to choose the <u>best</u> answer; that is, the response that most accurately and completely answers the question. You should not make assumptions that are by commonsense standards implausible, superfluous, or incompatible with the passage. After you have chosen the best answer, blacken the corresponding space on your answer sheet.

1. In a yearlong study, half of the participants were given a simple kit to use at home for measuring the cholesterol level of their blood. They reduced their cholesterol levels on average 15 percent more than did participants without the kit. Participants were selected at random from among people with dangerously high cholesterol levels.

    Which one of the following, if true, most helps to explain the study's finding?

    (A) The lower a blood-cholesterol level is, the less accurate are measurements made by the kit.
    (B) Participants with the kit were more likely to avoid foods that lower cholesterol level.
    (C) Participants with the kit used it more frequently during the first two months of the study.
    (D) All the participants in the study showed some lowering of cholesterol levels, the most striking decreases having been achieved in the first three months.
    (E) Participants using the kit reported that each reading reinforced their efforts to reduce their cholesterol levels.

2. You should not praise an act of apparent generosity unless you believe it is actually performed out of selfless motives, and you should not condemn an act of apparent selfishness unless you believe it is actually performed out of self-centered motives.

    Which one of the following judgments conforms to the principle stated above?

    (A) Caroline rightly blamed her coworker Monica for failing to assist her in doing a time-consuming project, even though she knew that Monica had offered to help in the project earlier but that her offer had been vetoed by their supervisor.
    (B) It was correct for Sarah not to praise Michael for being charitable when he told her that he donates a tenth of his income to charity, since she guessed that he only told that fact in order to impress her.
    (C) Enrique justifiably excused his friend William for failing to write or phone after William moved out of town because he realized that William never makes an effort to keep in contact with any of his friends.
    (D) Daniel was right not to praise Margaret for offering to share her house with a visiting French family, since he believed that she made the offer only because she hoped it would be reciprocated by an invitation to use the family's apartment in Paris.
    (E) Albert correctly criticized Louise for adopting an abandoned dog because he believed that, although she felt sorry for the dog, she did not have sufficient time or space to care for it adequately.

GO ON TO THE NEXT PAGE.

3. The government recently released a study of drinking water, in which it was reported that consumers who bought bottled water were in many cases getting water that was less safe than what they could obtain much more cheaply from the public water supply. In spite of the enormous publicity that the study received, sales of bottled water have continued to rise.

Which one of the following, if true, is most helpful in resolving the apparent paradox?

(A) Bottled water might contain levels of potentially harmful contaminants that are not allowed in drinking water.

(B) Most consumers who habitually drink the bottled water discussed in the study cannot differentiate between the taste of their usual brand of bottled water and that of water from public sources.

(C) Increased consumption of the five best-selling brands of bottled water, which the report said were safer than both public water and most other brands of bottled water, accounted for the increase in sales.

(D) The rate of increase in the sales of bottled water has slowed since the publication of the government study.

(E) Government health warnings concerning food have become so frequent that consumers have begun to doubt the safety of many everyday foods.

4. Many economically useful raw materials are nonrenewable and in limited supply on Earth. Therefore, unless those materials can be obtained somewhere other than Earth, people will eventually be unable to accomplish what they now accomplish using those materials.

Which one of the following, if true, most seriously weakens the argument?

(A) Some economically useful resources are renewable.

(B) It is extremely difficult to get raw materials from outer space.

(C) Functionally equivalent renewable substitutes could be found for nonrenewable resources that are in limited supply.

(D) What is accomplished now using nonrenewable resources is sometimes not worth accomplishing.

(E) It will be a few hundred years before the Earth is depleted of certain nonrenewable resources that are in limited supply.

5. Only some strains of the tobacco plant are naturally resistant to tobacco mosaic virus, never becoming diseased even when infected. When resistant strains were experimentally infected with the virus, levels of naturally occurring salicylic acid in these plants increased fivefold; no such increase occurred in the nonresistant plants. In a second experiment, 50 nonresistant tobacco plants were exposed to tobacco mosaic virus, and 25 of them were injected with salicylic acid. None of these 25 plants showed signs of infection; however, the other 25 plants succumbed to the disease.

Which one of the following conclusions is most strongly supported by the results of the experiments?

(A) Tobacco plants that have become diseased by infection with tobacco mosaic virus can be cured by injecting them with salicylic acid.

(B) Producing salicylic acid is at least part of the mechanism by which some tobacco plants naturally resist the disease caused by tobacco mosaic virus.

(C) Salicylic acid is not produced in strains of tobacco plants that are not resistant to tobacco mosaic virus.

(D) It is possible to test an uninfected tobacco plant for resistance to tobacco mosaic virus by measuring the level of salicylic acid it contains.

(E) The production of salicylic acid in certain strains of tobacco plants can be increased and thus the strains made resistant to tobacco mosaic virus.

GO ON TO THE NEXT PAGE.

Questions 6–7

The number of hospital emergency room visits by heroin users grew by more than 25 percent during the 1980s. Clearly, then, the use of heroin rose in that decade.

6. Which one of the following, if true, would account for the statistic above without supporting the author's conclusion?

(A) Widespread use of automatic weapons in the drug trade during the 1980s raised the incidence of physical injury to heroin users.

(B) The introduction of a smokable type of heroin during the 1980s removed the need for heroin to be injected intravenously and thus reduced the users' risk of infection.

(C) Many hospital emergency rooms were barely able to accommodate the dramatic increase in the number of medical emergencies related to drug abuse during the 1980s.

(D) Heroin use increased much more than is reflected in the rate of heroin-linked hospital emergency room visits.

(E) Viral and bacterial infections, malnourishment, and overdoses account for most hospital emergency room visits linked to heroin.

7. The author's conclusion is properly drawn if which one of the following is assumed?

(A) Those who seek medical care because of heroin use usually do so in the later stages of addiction.

(B) Many heroin users visit hospital emergency rooms repeatedly.

(C) The number of visits to hospital emergency rooms by heroin users is proportional to the incidence of heroin usage.

(D) The methods of using heroin have changed since 1980, and the new methods are less hazardous.

(E) Users of heroin identify themselves as such when they come to hospital emergency rooms.

8. The years 1917, 1937, 1956, 1968, 1979, and 1990 are all notable for the occurrence of both popular uprisings and near-maximum sunspot activity. During heavy sunspot activity, there is a sharp rise in positively charged ions in the air people breathe, and positively charged ions are known to make people anxious and irritable. Therefore, it is likely that sunspot activity has actually been a factor in triggering popular uprisings.

Which one of the following exhibits a pattern of reasoning most similar to that in the passage?

(A) The ancient Greeks sometimes attempted to predict the outcome of future events by watching the flight patterns of birds. Since the events themselves often matched the predictions, the birds were probably responding to some factor that also influenced the events.

(B) Martha, Sidney, and Hilary are the city's three most powerful politicians, and all three graduated from Ridgeview High School. Although Ridgeview never had a reputation for excellence, it must have been a good school to have produced three such successful graduates.

(C) Unusually cold weather last December coincided with a rise in fuel prices. When it is cold, people use more fuel to keep warm; and when more fuel is used, prices rise. Therefore if prices are high next winter, it will be the result of cold weather.

(D) The thirty healthiest people in a long-term medical study turned out to be the same thirty whose regular diets included the most vegetables. Since specific substances in vegetables are known to help the body fight disease, vegetables should be part of everyone's diet.

(E) Acme's most productive managers are consistently those who occupy the corner offices, which have more windows than other offices at Acme. Since people are more alert when they are exposed to abundant natural light, the greater productivity of these managers is probably at least in part a result of their working in the corner offices.

GO ON TO THE NEXT PAGE.

9. Since anyone who supports the new tax plan has no chance of being elected, and anyone who truly understands economics would not support the tax plan, only someone who truly understands economics would have any chance of being elected.

The reasoning in the argument is flawed because the argument ignores the possibility that some people who

(A) truly understand economics do not support the tax plan

(B) truly understand economics have no chance of being elected

(C) do not support the tax plan have no chance of being elected

(D) do not support the tax plan do not truly understand economics

(E) have no chance of being elected do not truly understand economics

10. Interviewer: You have shown that biofeedback, dietary changes, and adoption of proper sleep habits all succeed in curing insomnia. You go so far as to claim that, with rigorous adherence to the proper treatment, any case of insomnia is curable. Yet in fact some patients suffering from insomnia do not respond to treatment.

Therapist: If patients do not respond to treatment, this just shows that they are not rigorous in adhering to their treatment.

The therapist's reply to the interviewer is most vulnerable to which one of the following criticisms?

(A) It precludes the possibility of disconfirming evidence.

(B) It depends on the ambiguous use of the term "treatment."

(C) It fails to acknowledge that there may be different causes for different cases of insomnia.

(D) It does not provide statistical evidence to back up its claim.

(E) It overlooks the possibility that some cases of insomnia might improve without any treatment.

Questions 11–12

Conservative: Socialists begin their arguments with an analysis of history, from which they claim to derive certain trends leading inevitably to a socialist future. But in the day-to-day progress of history there are never such discernible trends. Only in retrospect does inevitability appear, for history occurs through accident, contingency, and individual struggle.

Socialist: If we thought the outcome of history were inevitable, we would not work so hard to transform the institutions of capitalist society. But to transform them we must first understand them, and we can only understand them by an analysis of their history. This is why historical analysis is important in socialist argument.

11. In the dispute the issue between the socialist and the conservative can most accurately be described as whether

(A) a socialist society is the inevitable consequence of historical trends that can be identified by an analysis of history

(B) the institutions of capitalist society stand in need of transformation

(C) socialists' arguments for the inevitability of socialism are justified

(D) it is possible for people by their own efforts to affect the course of history

(E) socialists analyze history in order to support the view that socialism is inevitable

12. The socialist's statements imply a conflict with the conservative's view of history if the conservative also holds that

(A) it would have been impossible for anyone to predict a significant period beforehand that the institutions of capitalist society would take the form that they actually took

(B) the apparent inevitability of historical change is deceptive; all historical events could have occurred otherwise than they actually did

(C) in the past, radical changes in social structures have mostly resulted in a deterioration of social conditions

(D) since socialism cannot arise by accident or contingency, it can only arise as a result of individual struggle

(E) because historical changes are mostly accidental, it is impossible for people to direct their efforts sensibly toward achieving large-scale changes in social conditions

GO ON TO THE NEXT PAGE.

13. "Addiction" has been defined as "dependence on and abuse of a psychoactive substance." Dependence and abuse do not always go hand in hand, however. For example, cancer patients can become dependent on morphine to relieve their pain, but this is not abusing the drug. Correspondingly, a person can abuse a drug without being dependent on it. Therefore, the definition of "addiction" is incorrect.

The relevance of the example of cancer patients to the argument depends on the assumption that

(A) cancer patients never abuse morphine
(B) cancer patients often become dependent on morphine
(C) cancer patients who are dependent on morphine are addicted to it
(D) cancer patients who abuse a drug are dependent on it
(E) cancer patients cannot depend on morphine without abusing it

14. The commissioner has announced that Judge Khalid, who was on the seven-member panel appointed to resolve the Amlec labor dispute, will have sole responsibility for resolving the Simdon labor dispute. Since in its decision the Amlec panel showed itself both reasonable and fair, the two sides in the Simdon dispute are undoubtedly justified in the confidence they have expressed in the reasonableness and fairness of the arbitrator assigned to their case.

Which one of the following contains flawed reasoning most parallel to that contained in the passage?

(A) Representing the school board, Marcia Barthes presented to the school's principal a list of recently elected school board members. Since only an elected member of the school board can act as its representative, Ms. Barthes's name undoubtedly appears on that list.
(B) Alan Caldalf, who likes being around young children, has decided to become a pediatrician. Since the one characteristic common to all good pediatricians is that they like young children, Mr. Caldalf will undoubtedly be a very good pediatrician.
(C) Jorge Diaz is a teacher at a music school nationally known for the excellence of its conducting faculty. Since Mr. Diaz has recently been commended for the excellence of his teaching, he is undoubtedly a member of the school's conducting faculty.
(D) Ula Borg, who has sold real estate for Arcande Realty for many years, undoubtedly sold fewer houses last year than she had the year before since the number of houses sold last year by Arcande Realty is far lower than the number sold the previous year.
(E) The members of the local historical society unanimously support designating the First National Bank building a historical landmark. Since Evelyn George is a member of that society, she undoubtedly favors according landmark status to the city hall as well.

15. Magazine article: The Environmental Commissioner's new proposals are called "Fresh Thinking on the Environment," and a nationwide debate on them has been announced. Well, "fresh thinking" from such an unlikely source as the commissioner does deserve closer inspection. Unfortunately we discovered that these proposals are virtually identical to those issued three months ago by Tsarque Inc. under the heading "New Environmentalism" (Tsarque Inc.'s chief is a close friend of the commissioner). Since Tsarque Inc.'s polluting has marked it as an environmental nightmare, in our opinion the "nationwide debate" can end here.

A flaw in the magazine article's reasoning is that it

(A) assumes without any justification that since two texts are similar one of them must be influenced by the other
(B) gives a distorted version of the commissioner's proposals and then attacks this distorted version
(C) dismisses the proposals because of their source rather than because of their substance
(D) uses emotive language in labeling the proposals
(E) appeals to the authority of Tsarque Inc.'s chief without giving evidence that this person's opinion should carry special weight

16. It is not reasonable to search out "organic" foods—those grown without the application of synthetic chemicals—as the only natural foods. A plant will take up the molecules it needs from the soil and turn them into the same natural compounds, whether or not those molecules come from chemicals applied to the soil. All compounds made by plants are part of nature, so all are equally natural.

The argument proceeds by

(A) redefining a term in a way that is favorable to the argument
(B) giving a reason why a recommended course of action would be beneficial
(C) appealing to the authority of scientific methods
(D) showing that a necessary condition for correctly applying the term "organic" is not satisfied
(E) reinterpreting evidence presented as supporting the position being rejected

GO ON TO THE NEXT PAGE.

17. On completing both the course in experimental design and the developmental psychology course, Angela will have earned a degree in psychology. Since experimental design, which must be completed before taking developmental psychology, will not be offered until next term, it will be at least two terms before Angela gets her psychology degree.

If the statements above are all true, which one of the following must also be true?

(A) The developmental psychology course Angela needs to take requires two terms to complete.
(B) The course in experimental design is an easier course than the course in developmental psychology.
(C) There are no prerequisites for the course in experimental design.
(D) Anyone who earns a degree in psychology from the university Angela attends will have completed the course in experimental design.
(E) Once Angela completes the developmental psychology course, she will have earned a degree in psychology.

18. According to a government official involved in overseeing airplane safety during the last year, over 75 percent of the voice-recorder tapes taken from small airplanes involved in relatively minor accidents record the whistling of the pilot during the fifteen minutes immediately preceding the accident. Even such minor accidents pose some safety risk. Therefore, if passengers hear the pilot start to whistle they should take safety precautions, whether instructed by the pilot to do so or not.

The argument is most vulnerable to criticism on the grounds that it

(A) accepts the reliability of the cited statistics on the authority of an unidentified government official
(B) ignores the fact that in nearly one-quarter of these accidents following the recommendation would not have improved passengers' safety
(C) does not indicate the criteria by which an accident is classified as "relatively minor"
(D) provides no information about the percentage of all small airplane flights during which the pilot whistles at some time during that flight
(E) fails to specify the percentage of all small airplane flights that involve relatively minor accidents

19. When permits for the discharge of chemicals into a waterway are issued, they are issued in terms of the number of pounds of each chemical that can be discharged into the waterway per day. These figures, calculated separately for each chemical for which a permit is issued, are based on an estimate of the effect of the dilution of the chemical by the amount of water flowing through the waterway. The waterway is therefore protected against being adversely affected by chemicals discharged under the permits.

The argument depends on the assumption that

(A) relatively harmless chemicals do not interact with each other in the water to form harmful compounds
(B) there is a swift flow of water in the waterway that ensures rapid dispersion of chemicals discharged
(C) there are no chemicals for which discharge into waterways is entirely prohibited
(D) those who receive the permits do not always discharge the entire quantity of chemicals that the permits allow
(E) the danger of chemical pollution of waterways is to be evaluated in terms of human health only and not in terms of the health of both human beings and wildlife

GO ON TO THE NEXT PAGE.

Questions 20–21

Monroe, despite his generally poor appetite, thoroughly enjoyed the three meals he ate at the Tip-Top Restaurant, but, unfortunately, after each meal he became ill. The first time he ate an extra-large sausage pizza with a side order of hot peppers; the second time he took full advantage of the all-you-can-eat fried shrimp and hot peppers special; and the third time he had two of Tip-Top's giant meatball sandwiches with hot peppers. Since the only food all three meals had in common was the hot peppers, Monroe concludes that it is solely due to Tip-Top's hot peppers that he became ill.

20. Monroe's reasoning is most vulnerable to which one of the following criticisms?

(A) He draws his conclusion on the basis of too few meals that were consumed at Tip-Top and that included hot peppers.

(B) He posits a causal relationship without ascertaining that the presumed cause preceded the presumed effect.

(C) He allows his desire to continue dining at Tip-Top to bias his conclusion.

(D) He fails to establish that everyone who ate Tip-Top's hot peppers became ill.

(E) He overlooks the fact that at all three meals he consumed what was, for him, an unusually large quantity of food.

21. If both Monroe's conclusion and the evidence on which he bases it are correct, they would provide the strongest support for which one of the following?

(A) Monroe can eat any of Tip-Top's daily all-you-can-eat specials without becoming ill as long as the special does not include the hot peppers.

(B) If, at his third meal at Tip-Top, Monroe had chosen to eat the baked chicken with hot peppers, he would have become ill after that meal.

(C) If the next time Monroe eats one of Tip-Top's extra-large sausage pizzas he does not have a side order of hot peppers, he will not become ill after his meal.

(D) Before eating Tip-Top's fried shrimp with hot peppers special, Monroe had eaten fried shrimp without suffering any ill effects.

(E) The only place Monroe has eaten hot peppers has been at Tip-Top.

22. "This company will not be training any more pilots in the foreseeable future, since we have 400 trained pilots on our waiting list who are seeking employment. The other five major companies each have roughly the same number of trained pilots on their waiting lists, and since the projected requirement of each company is for not many more than 100 additional pilots, there will be no shortage of personnel despite the current upswing in the aviation industry."

Which one of the following, if true, casts the most doubt on the accuracy of the above conclusion?

(A) Most of the trained pilots who are on a waiting list for a job are on the waiting lists of all the major companies.

(B) In the long run, pilot training will become necessary to compensate for ordinary attrition.

(C) If no new pilots are trained, there will be an age imbalance in the pilot work force.

(D) The quoted personnel projections take account of the current upswing in the aviation industry.

(E) Some of the other major companies are still training pilots but with no presumption of subsequent employment.

23. A car's antitheft alarm that sounds in the middle of the night in a crowded city neighborhood may stop an attempted car theft. On the other hand, the alarm might signal only a fault in the device, or a response to some harmless contact, such as a tree branch brushing the car. But whatever the cause, the sleep of many people in the neighborhood is disturbed. Out of consideration for others, people who have these antitheft alarms on their cars should deactivate them when they park in crowded city neighborhoods at night.

Which one of the following, if assumed by the author of the passage, would allow her properly to draw her conclusion that the owners of alarm-equipped cars should deactivate the alarms when parking in crowded city neighborhoods at night?

(A) The inconvenience of false alarms is a small price to pay for the security of a neighborhood.

(B) In most cases when a car alarm sounds at night, it is a false alarm.

(C) Allowing the residents of a crowded city neighborhood to sleep undisturbed is more important than preventing car theft.

(D) People who equip their cars with antitheft alarms are generally inconsiderate of others.

(E) The sounding of car antitheft alarms during the daytime does not disturb the residents of crowded city neighborhoods.

GO ON TO THE NEXT PAGE.

Questions 24–25

In Peru, ancient disturbances in the dark surface material of a desert show up as light-colored lines that are the width of a footpath and stretch for long distances. One group of lines branching out like rays from a single point crosses over curved lines that form a very large bird figure. Interpreting the lines in the desert as landing strips for spaceship-traveling aliens, an investigator argues that they could hardly have been Inca roads, asking, "What use to the Inca would have been closely spaced roads that ran parallel? That intersected in a sunburst pattern? That came abruptly to an end in the middle of an uninhabited plain?"

24. The argumentative strategy of the investigator quoted is to

(A) reject out of hand direct counterevidence to the investigator's own interpretation

(B) introduce evidence newly discovered by the investigator which discredits the alternative interpretation

(C) support one interpretation by calling into question the plausibility of the alternative interpretation

(D) challenge the investigative methods used by those who developed the alternative interpretation

(E) show that the two competing interpretations can be reconciled with one another

25. For someone who interprets the lines as referring to astronomical phenomena, which one of the following, if true, most effectively counters an objection that the crossing of the straight-line pattern over the bird figure shows that the two kinds of line pattern served unrelated purposes?

(A) In areas that were inhabited by ancient native North American peoples, arrangements of stones have been found that mark places where sunlight falls precisely on the spring solstice, an astronomically determined date.

(B) The straight lines are consistent with sight lines to points on the horizon where particular astronomical events could have been observed at certain plausible dates, and the figure could represent a constellation.

(C) The straight-line pattern is part of a large connected complex of patterns of straight-line rays connecting certain points with one another.

(D) Native Central American cultures, such as that of the Maya, left behind elaborate astronomical calendars that were engraved on rocks.

(E) There is evidence that the bird figure was made well before the straight-line pattern.

S T O P

IF YOU FINISH BEFORE TIME IS CALLED, YOU MAY CHECK YOUR WORK ON THIS SECTION ONLY.
DO NOT WORK ON ANY OTHER SECTION IN THE TEST.

LSAT® Writing Sample Topic

The economically depressed town of Sterling Falls has received a grant allowing it to provide a low-interest loan to fund one of the following development proposals. Assuming costs are roughly the same, write an argument supporting one proposal over the other based on the following criteria:

- The town wants to find a way to offset the unemployment caused by the recent closing of a nearby manufacturing plant.
- The town wants to preserve the integrity of its wildlife refuge area, which attracts thousands of migratory birds.

Lakeview Hotels proposes building a three-story hotel on the edge of the wildlife refuge. This wood and glass structure would be designed to fit into the natural environment with many of the 100 rooms having a view of the refuge's major lake. The hotel would also have a family restaurant and gift shop featuring work by area artisans. Lakeview wants to pave a one-lane road through parts of the refuge and provide several vans to take guests on guided tours. Lakeview promises to dedicate a substantial percentage of the hotel's profits toward maintenance of the refuge, whose upkeep costs have been rising steadily in recent years. Scientists familiar with the area have expressed concern that the traffic might cause many of the migratory birds to take refuge elsewhere.

Porterfield Associates, a family-owned development company prominent in the Sterling Falls area, proposes renovating the historical Sterling Hotel on the town's main street. A once-elegant structure, the building is currently a boardinghouse in need of repair. The renovated structure would have 30 rooms and a small gourmet restaurant. In support of this proposal, Bruce Alexander, a local philanthropist friendly with the Porterfield family, has offered to establish an educational center at the refuge. While the center would open with a staff of only twenty, Alexander believes that interest, along with external funding, would grow. Alexander will not fund the center if Lakeview's proposal is approved.

Directions:

1. Use the Answer Key on the next page to check your answers.

2. Use the Scoring Worksheet below to compute your raw score.

3. Use the Score Conversion Chart to convert your raw score into the 120-180 scale.

Scoring Worksheet

1. Enter the number of questions you answered correctly in each section.

	Number Correct
SECTION I	_____
SECTION II	_____
SECTION III	_____
SECTION IV	_____

2. Enter the sum here: _____
   This is your Raw Score.

Conversion Chart

For Converting Raw Score to the 120-180 LSAT Scaled Score
LSAT Form 3LSS19

Reported Score	Raw Score Lowest	Raw Score Highest
180	100	101
179	99	99
178	98	98
177	97	97
176	_*	_*
175	96	96
174	95	95
173	94	94
172	93	93
171	92	92
170	91	91
169	90	90
168	88	89
167	87	87
166	85	86
165	84	84
164	82	83
163	81	81
162	79	80
161	77	78
160	75	76
159	74	74
158	72	73
157	70	71
156	68	69
155	66	67
154	65	65
153	63	64
152	61	62
151	59	60
150	57	58
149	56	56
148	54	55
147	52	53
146	50	51
145	48	49
144	47	47
143	45	46
142	43	44
141	41	42
140	40	40
139	38	39
138	36	37
137	35	35
136	33	34
135	31	32
134	30	30
133	29	29
132	27	28
131	26	26
130	25	25
129	24	24
128	23	23
127	22	22
126	21	21
125	20	20
124	19	19
123	18	18
122	_*	_*
121	17	17
120	0	16

*There is no raw score that will produce this scaled score for this form.

SECTION I

1.	B	8.	A	15.	D	22.	B
2.	A	9.	B	16.	D	23.	B
3.	E	10.	C	17.	B	24.	C
4.	B	11.	E	18.	E		
5.	D	12.	A	19.	B		
6.	C	13.	D	20.	A		
7.	E	14.	D	21.	C		

SECTION II

1.	C	8.	B	15.	E	22.	D
2.	C	9.	C	16.	D	23.	E
3.	B	10.	B	17.	C	24.	D
4.	E	11.	D	18.	D	25.	E
5.	D	12.	A	19.	E		
6.	D	13.	B	20.	B		
7.	D	14.	C	21.	A		

SECTION III

1.	C	8.	E	15.	B	22.	B
2.	E	9.	C	16.	C	23.	C
3.	A	10.	B	17.	C	24.	C
4.	B	11.	C	18.	A	25.	A
5.	D	12.	B	19.	D	26.	D
6.	D	13.	D	20.	E	27.	D
7.	A	14.	C	21.	A		

SECTION IV

1.	E	8.	E	15.	C	22.	A
2.	D	9.	D	16.	A	23.	C
3.	C	10.	A	17.	E	24.	C
4.	C	11.	E	18.	D	25.	B
5.	B	12.	E	19.	A		
6.	A	13.	C	20.	E		
7.	C	14.	D	21.	B		

The Official LSAT PrepTest

15

- June 1995
- Form 6LSS27

The sample test that follows consists of four sections corresponding to the four scored sections of the June 1995 LSAT.

$$\boxed{1}$$

SECTION I

Time—35 minutes

27 Questions

Directions: Each passage in this section is followed by a group of questions to be answered on the basis of what is stated or implied in the passage. For some of the questions, more than one of the choices could conceivably answer the question. However, you are to choose the best answer; that is, the response that most accurately and completely answers the question, and blacken the corresponding space on your answer sheet.

Until the 1980s, most scientists believed that noncatastrophic geological processes caused the extinction of dinosaurs that occurred approximately 66 million years ago, at the end of the Cretaceous
(5) period. Geologists argued that a dramatic drop in sea level coincided with the extinction of the dinosaurs and could have caused the climatic changes that resulted in this extinction as well as the extinction of many ocean species.
(10) This view was seriously challenged in the 1980s by the discovery of large amounts of iridium in a layer of clay deposited at the end of the Cretaceous period. Because iridium is extremely rare in rocks on the Earth's surface but common in meteorites,
(15) researchers theorized that it was the impact of a large meteorite that dramatically changed the Earth's climate and thus triggered the extinction of the dinosaurs.
Currently available evidence, however, offers
(20) more support for a new theory, the volcanic-eruption theory. A vast eruption of lava in India coincided with the extinctions that occurred at the end of the Cretaceous period, and the release of carbon dioxide from this episode of volcanism could
(25) have caused the climatic change responsible for the demise of the dinosaurs. Such outpourings of lava are caused by instability in the lowest layer of the Earth's mantle, located just above the Earth's core. As the rock that constitutes this layer is heated by
(30) the Earth's core, it becomes less dense and portions of it eventually escape upward as blobs of molten rock, called "diapirs," that can, under certain circumstances, erupt violently through the Earth's crust.
(35) Moreover, the volcanic-eruption theory, like the impact theory, accounts for the presence of iridium in sedimentary deposits; it also explains matters that the meteorite-impact theory does not. Although iridium is extremely rare on the Earth's
(40) surface, the lower regions of the Earth's mantle have roughly the same composition as meteorites and contain large amounts of iridium, which in the case of a diapir eruption would probably be emitted as iridium hexafluoride, a gas that would disperse
(45) more uniformly in the atmosphere than the iridium-containing matter thrown out from a meteorite impact. In addition, the volcanic-eruption theory may explain why the end of the Cretaceous period was marked by a gradual change in sea level.
(50) Fossil records indicate that for several hundred thousand years prior to the relatively sudden disappearance of the dinosaurs, the level of the sea gradually fell, causing many marine organisms to die out. This change in sea level might well have
(55) been the result of a distortion in the Earth's surface that resulted from the movement of diapirs upward toward the Earth's crust, and the more cataclysmic extinction of the dinosaurs could have resulted from the explosive volcanism that occurred as material
(60) from the diapirs erupted onto the Earth's surface.

1. The passage suggests that during the 1980s researchers found meteorite impact a convincing explanation for the extinction of dinosaurs, in part because

    (A) earlier theories had failed to account for the gradual extinction of many ocean species at the end of the Cretaceous period
    (B) geologists had, up until that time, underestimated the amount of carbon dioxide that would be released during an episode of explosive volcanism
    (C) a meteorite could have served as a source of the iridium found in a layer of clay deposited at the end of the Cretaceous period
    (D) no theory relying on purely geological processes had, up until that time, explained the cause of the precipitous drop in sea level that occurred at the end of the Cretaceous period
    (E) the impact of a large meteorite could have resulted in the release of enough carbon dioxide to cause global climatic change

2. According to the passage, the lower regions of the Earth's mantle are characterized by

    (A) a composition similar to that of meteorites
    (B) the absence of elements found in rocks on the Earth's crust
    (C) a greater stability than that of the upper regions
    (D) the presence of large amounts of carbon dioxide
    (E) a uniformly lower density than that of the upper regions

GO ON TO THE NEXT PAGE.

3. It can be inferred from the passage that which one of the following was true of the lava that erupted in India at the end of the Cretaceous period?

(A) It contained less carbon dioxide than did the meteorites that were striking the Earth's surface during that period.

(B) It was more dense than the molten rock located just above the Earth's core.

(C) It released enough iridium hexafluoride into the atmosphere to change the Earth's climate dramatically.

(D) It was richer in iridium than rocks usually found on the Earth's surface.

(E) It was richer in iridium than were the meteorites that were striking the Earth's surface during that period.

4. In the passage, the author is primarily concerned with doing which one of the following?

(A) describing three theories and explaining why the latest of these appears to be the best of the three

(B) attacking the assumptions inherent in theories that until the 1980s had been largely accepted by geologists

(C) outlining the inadequacies of three different explanations of the same phenomenon

(D) providing concrete examples in support of the more general assertion that theories must often be revised in light of new evidence

(E) citing evidence that appears to confirm the skepticism of geologists regarding a view held prior to the 1980s

5. The author implies that if the theory described in the third paragraph is true, which one of the following would have been true of iridium in the atmosphere at the end of the Cretaceous period?

(A) Its level of concentration in the Earth's atmosphere would have been high due to a slow but steady increase in the atmospheric iridium that began in the early Cretaceous period.

(B) Its concentration in the Earth's atmosphere would have increased due to the dramatic decrease in sea level that occurred during the Cretaceous period.

(C) It would have been directly responsible for the extinction of many ocean species.

(D) It would have been more uniformly dispersed than iridium whose source had been the impact of a meteorite on the Earth's surface.

(E) It would have been more uniformly dispersed than iridium released into the atmosphere as a result of normal geological processes that occur on Earth.

6. The passage supports which one of the following claims about the volcanic-eruption theory?

(A) It does not rely on assumptions concerning the temperature of molten rock at the lowest part of the Earth's mantle.

(B) It may explain what caused the gradual fall in sea level that occurred for hundreds of thousands of years prior to the more sudden disappearance of the dinosaurs.

(C) It bases its explanation on the occurrence of periods of increased volcanic activity similar to those shown to have caused earlier mass extinctions.

(D) It may explain the relative scarcity of iridium in rocks on the Earth's surface, compared to its abundance in meteorites.

(E) It accounts for the relatively uneven distribution of iridium in the layer of clay deposited at the end of the Cretaceous period.

7. Which one of the following, if true, would cast the most doubt on the theory described in the last paragraph of the passage?

(A) Fragments of meteorites that have struck the Earth are examined and found to have only minuscule amounts of iridium hexafluoride trapped inside of them.

(B) Most diapir eruptions in the geological history of the Earth have been similar in size to the one that occurred in India at the end of the Cretaceous period and have not been succeeded by periods of climatic change.

(C) There have been several periods in the geological history of the Earth, before and after the Cretaceous period, during which large numbers of marine species have perished.

(D) The frequency with which meteorites struck the Earth was higher at the end of the Cretaceous period than at the beginning of the period.

(E) Marine species tend to be much more vulnerable to extinction when exposed to a dramatic and relatively sudden change in sea level than when they are exposed to a gradual change in sea level similar to the one that preceded the extinction of the dinosaurs.

GO ON TO THE NEXT PAGE.

It has become something of a truism in folklore studies that until recently the lore was more often studied than the folk. That is, folklorists concentrated on the folklore—the songs, tales, and
(5) proverbs themselves—and ignored the people who transmitted that lore as part of their oral culture. However, since the early 1970s, folklore studies have begun to regard folk performers as people of creativity who are as worthy of attention as are
(10) artists who transmit their ideas in writing. This shift of emphasis has also encouraged a growing interest in women folk performers.

Until recently, folklorists tended to collect folklore from women on only a few topics such as
(15) health and games. In other areas, as Weigle and Farrer have noted, if folklorists "had a choice between a story as told by a man or as told by a woman, the man's version was chosen." It is still too early to tell how profoundly this situation has
(20) changed, but one can point to several recent studies in which women performers play central roles. Perhaps more telling is the focus of the most recently published major folklore textbook, *The Dynamics of Folklore*. Whereas earlier textbooks
(25) gave little attention to women and their folklore, this book devotes many pages to women folk performers.

Recognition of women as important bearers of folklore is not entirely a recent phenomenon. As
(30) early as 1903, a few outstanding women folk performers were the focus of scholarly attention. But the scholarship devoted to these women tended to focus primarily on presenting the performer's repertoire. Recent works about women folk artists,
(35) however, have been more biographically oriented. Juha Pentikäinen's study of Marina Tokalo, a Finnish healer and narrator of folktales, is especially extensive and probing. Though interested in the problems of repertoire analysis, Pentikäinen
(40) gives considerable attention to the details of Tokalo's life and cultural background, so that a full picture of a woman and her folklore emerges. Another notable work is Roger Abraham's book, which presents a very clear picture of the
(45) significance of traditional singing in the life of noted ballad singer Almeda Riddle. Unfortunately, unlike Pentikäinen's study, Abraham's study contains little repertoire analysis.

These recent books reflect the current interest of
(50) folklorists in viewing folklore in context and thus answering questions about what folklore means to the people who use it. One unexpected result of this line of study has been the discovery that women may use the same folklore that men use, but for very
(55) different purposes. This realization has potential importance for future folklore studies in calling greater attention to the type of study required if a folklorist wants truly to understand the role folklore plays in a particular culture.

8. Which one of the following best describes the main point of the passage?

(A) It is only since the early 1970s that folklore studies have begun to recognize women as important bearers of folklore.

(B) A careful analysis of the repertoires of women folk performers has led to a new discovery with important implications for future folklore studies.

(C) Recent studies of women folk performers have focused primarily on the problems of repertoire analysis to the exclusion of a discussion of the culture within which the folklore was developed.

(D) The emphasis in folklore studies has shifted from a focus on the life and the cultural background of the folk performers themselves to a broader understanding of the role folklore plays in a culture.

(E) A change in the focus of folklore studies has led to increased interest in women folk performers and to a new understanding of the importance of the context in which folklore is produced.

9. The author of the passage refers to *The Dynamics of Folklore* primarily in order to

(A) support the idea that it is too soon to tell whether or not folklorists are giving greater attention to women's folklore

(B) refute Weigle and Farrer's contention that folklorists prefer to collect folklore from men rather than from women

(C) support the assertion that scholarship devoted to women folk performers tends to focus primarily on repertoire

(D) present an example of the new emphasis in folklore studies on the performer rather than on the folklore

(E) suggest that there are some signs that women folk performers are gaining increased critical attention in the field of folklore

GO ON TO THE NEXT PAGE.

10. The focus of which one of the following books would most clearly reflect the current interest of the folklorists mentioned in the last paragraph?

(A) an anthology of tales and songs collected exclusively from women in different cultures

(B) a compilation of tales and songs from both men and women covering a great variety of traditional and nontraditional topics

(C) a study of the purpose and meaning of a tale or song for the men and women in a particular culture

(D) an analysis of one particular tale or song that documents changes in the text of the folklore over a period of time

(E) a comparison of the creative process of performers who transmit folklore with that of artists who transmit their ideas in writing

11. According to the passage, which one of the following changes has occurred in the field of folklore since the early 1970s?

(A) increased recognition of the similar ways in which men and women use folklore

(B) increased recognition of folk performers as creative individuals

(C) increased emphasis on the need for repertoire analysis

(D) less emphasis on the relationship between cultural influences and folklore

(E) less emphasis on the individual performers and more emphasis on the meaning of folklore to a culture

12. It can be inferred from the passage that early folklorists assumed that which one of the following was true?

(A) The people who transmitted the folklore did not play a creative role in the development of that folklore.

(B) The people who transmitted the folklore were not consciously aware of the way in which they creatively shaped that folklore.

(C) The text of a song or tale did not change as the folklore was transmitted from one generation to another.

(D) Women were not involved in transmitting folklore except for songs or tales dealing with a few traditional topics.

(E) The meaning of a piece of folklore could differ depending on whether the tale or song was transmitted by a man or by a woman.

13. Based on the information in the passage, which one of the following is most closely analogous to the type of folklore studies produced before the early 1970s?

(A) An anthropologist studies the implements currently used by an isolated culture, but does not investigate how the people of that culture designed and used those implements.

(B) A manufacturer hires a consultant to determine how existing equipment in a plant might be modified to improve efficiency, but does not ask employees for their suggestions on how to improve efficiency.

(C) A historian studies different types of documents dealing with a particular historical event, but decides not to review newspaper accounts written by journalists who lived through that event.

(D) An archaeologist studies the artifacts of an ancient culture to reconstruct the life-style of that culture, but does not actually visit the site where those artifacts were unearthed.

(E) An architect designs a private home for a client, but ignores many of the client's suggestions concerning minor details about the final design of the home.

14. The author of the passage uses the term "context" (line 50) to refer to

(A) a holistic assessment of a piece of folklore rather than a critical analysis of its parts

(B) a study that examines a piece of folklore in light of earlier interpretations provided by other folklorists

(C) the parts of a piece of folklore that can shed light on the meaning of the entire piece

(D) the environment and circumstances in which a particular piece of folklore is used

(E) the location in which the story line of a piece of folklore is set

15. The author's attitude toward Roger Abraham's book can best be described as one of

(A) wholehearted approval
(B) qualified admiration
(C) uneasy ambivalence
(D) extreme skepticism
(E) trenchant criticism

GO ON TO THE NEXT PAGE.

J. G. A. Pocock's numerous investigations have all revolved around the fruitful assumption that a work of political thought can only be understood in light of the linguistic constraints to which its author
(5) was subject, for these prescribed both the choice of subject matter and the author's conceptualization of this subject matter. Only the occasional epic theorist, like Machiavelli or Hobbes, succeeded in breaking out of these bonds by redefining old terms
(10) and inventing new ones. The task of the modern commentator is to identify the "language" or "vocabulary" with and within which the author operated. While historians of literature have always been aware that writers work within particular
(15) traditions, the application of this notion to the history of political ideas forms a sharp contrast to the assumptions of the 1950s, when it was naïvely thought that the close reading of a text by an analytic philosopher was sufficient to establish its
(20) meaning, even if the philosopher had no knowledge of the period of the text's composition.

The language Pocock has most closely investigated is that of "civic humanism." For much of his career he has argued that eighteenth-century
(25) English political thought should be interpreted as a conflict between rival versions of the "virtue" central to civic humanism. On the one hand, he argues, this virtue is described by representatives of the Tory opposition using a vocabulary of public
(30) spirit and self-sufficiency. For these writers the societal ideal is the small, independent landowner in the countryside. On the other hand, Whig writers describe such virtue using a vocabulary of commerce and economic progress; for them the
(35) ideal is the merchant.

In making such linguistic discriminations Pocock has disassociated himself from historians like Namier, who deride all eighteenth-century English political language as "cant." But while Pocock's
(40) ideas have proved fertile when applied to England, they are more controversial when applied to the late-eighteenth-century United States. Pocock's assertion that Jefferson's attacks on the commercial policies of the Federalists simply echo the language
(45) of the Tory opposition in England is at odds with the fact that Jefferson rejected the elitist implications of that group's notion of virtue and asserted the right of all to participate in commercial society. Indeed, after promptings by Quentin
(50) Skinner, Pocock has admitted that a counterlanguage—one of rights and liberties—was probably as important in the political discourse of the late-eighteenth-century United States as the language of civic humanism. Fortunately, it is not
(55) necessary to rank the relative importance of all the different vocabularies in which eighteenth-century political argument was conducted. It is sufficient to recognize that any interesting text is probably a mixture of several of these vocabularies, and to
(60) applaud the historian who, though guilty of some exaggeration, has done the most to make us aware of their importance.

16. The main idea of the passage is that

(A) civic humanism, in any of its manifestations, cannot entirely explain eighteenth-century political discourse
(B) eighteenth-century political texts are less likely to reflect a single vocabulary than to combine several vocabularies
(C) Pocock's linguistic approach, though not applicable to all eighteenth-century political texts, provides a useful model for historians of political theory
(D) Pocock has more successfully accounted for the nature of political thought in eighteenth-century England than in the eighteenth-century United States
(E) Pocock's notion of the importance of language in political texts is a logical extension of the insights of historians of literature

17. According to the passage, Pocock most clearly associates the use of a vocabulary of economic progress with

(A) Jefferson
(B) Federalists
(C) English Whigs
(D) English Tories
(E) rural English landowners

18. The author's attitude toward Pocock is best revealed by which of the following pairs of words?

(A) "fruitful" (line 2) and "cant" (line 39)
(B) "sharp" (line 16) and "elitist" (line 46)
(C) "naïvely" (line 17) and "controversial" (line 41)
(D) "fertile" (line 40) and "applaud" (line 60)
(E) "simply" (line 44) and "importance" (line 55)

19. The passage suggests that one of the "assumptions of the 1950s" (line 17) regarding the meaning of a political text was that this meaning

(A) could be established using an approach similar to that used by literary historians
(B) could be definitively established without reference to the text's historical background
(C) could be closely read in several different ways depending on one's philosophic approach
(D) was constrained by certain linguistic preconceptions held by the text's author
(E) could be expressed most clearly by an analytic philosopher who had studied its historical context

GO ON TO THE NEXT PAGE.

20. The author of the passage would most likely agree that which one of the following is a weakness found in Pocock's work?

   (A) the use of the term "language" to describe the expressive features of several diverse kinds of discourse
   (B) the overemphatic denigration of the role of the analytic philosopher in establishing the meaning of a political, or indeed any, text
   (C) the emphasis on the overriding importance of civic humanism in eighteenth-century English political thought
   (D) the insistence on a single linguistic dichotomy to account for political thought in eighteenth-century England and the United States
   (E) the assignment of certain vocabularies to particular parties in eighteenth-century England without taking note of how these vocabularies overlapped

21. Which one of the following best describes the organization of the passage?

   (A) A description of a thesis is offered, specific cases are considered, and an evaluation is given.
   (B) A thesis is brought forward, the thesis is qualified, and evidence that calls the qualification into question is stated.
   (C) A hypothesis is described, examples that suggest it is incorrect are summarized, and supporting examples are offered.
   (D) A series of evaluations are given, concrete reasons are put forward, and a future direction for research is suggested.
   (E) Comparisons and contrasts are made, some categories of evaluation are suggested, and a framework for applying these categories is implied.

GO ON TO THE NEXT PAGE.

In 1964 the United States federal government began attempts to eliminate racial discrimination in employment and wages: the United States Congress enacted Title VII of the Civil Rights Act,
(5) prohibiting employers from making employment decisions on the basis of race. In 1965 President Johnson issued Executive Order 11,246, which prohibited discrimination by United States government contractors and emphasized direct
(10) monitoring of minority representation in contractors' work forces.

Nonetheless, proponents of the "continuous change" hypothesis believe that United States federal law had a marginal impact on the economic
(15) progress made by black people in the United States between 1940 and 1975. Instead they emphasize slowly evolving historical forces, such as long-term trends in education that improved segregated schools for black students during the 1940s and
(20) were operative during and after the 1960s. They argue that as the quality of black schools improved relative to that of white schools, the earning potential of those attending black schools increased relative to the earning potential of those attending
(25) white schools.

However, there is no direct evidence linking increased quality of underfunded segregated black schools to these improvements in earning potential. In fact, even the evidence on relative schooling
(30) quality is ambiguous. Although in the mid-1940s term length at black schools was approaching that in white schools, the rapid growth in another important measure of school quality, school expenditures, may be explained by increases in
(35) teachers' salaries, and, historically, such increases have not necessarily increased school quality. Finally, black individuals in all age groups, even those who had been educated at segregated schools before the 1940s, experienced post-1960 increases
(40) in their earning potential. If improvements in the quality of schooling were an important determinant of increased returns, only those workers who could have benefited from enhanced school quality should have received higher returns. The relative
(45) improvement in the earning potential of educated black people of all age groups in the United States is more consistent with a decline in employment discrimination.

An additional problem for continuity theorists is
(50) how to explain the rapid acceleration of black economic progress in the United States after 1964. Education alone cannot account for the rate of change. Rather, the coincidence of increased United States government antidiscrimination
(55) pressure in the mid-1960s with the acceleration in the rate of black economic progress beginning in 1965 argues against the continuity theorists' view. True, correlating federal intervention and the acceleration of black economic progress might be
(60) incorrect. One could argue that changing attitudes about employment discrimination sparked both the adoption of new federal policies and the rapid

acceleration in black economic progress. Indeed, the shift in national attitude that made possible the
(65) enactment of Title VII was in part produced by the persistence of racial discrimination in the southern United States. However, the fact that the law had its greatest effect in the South, in spite of the vigorous resistance of many Southern leaders,
(70) suggests its importance for black economic progress.

22. According to the passage, Title VII of the 1964 Civil Rights Act differs from Executive Order 11,246 in that Title VII

(A) monitors employers to ensure minority representation
(B) assesses the work forces of government contractors
(C) eliminates discriminatory disparities in wages
(D) focuses on determining minority representation in government
(E) governs hiring practices in a wider variety of workplaces

23. Which one of the following statements about schooling in the United States during the mid-1940s can be inferred from the passage?

(A) School expenditures decreased for white schools.
(B) The teachers in white schools had more time to cover material during a school year than did teachers in black schools.
(C) The basic curriculum of white schools was similar to the curriculum at black schools.
(D) White schools did not change substantially in quality.
(E) Although the salaries of teachers in black schools increased, they did not keep pace with the salaries of teachers in white schools.

GO ON TO THE NEXT PAGE.

24. The primary purpose of the passage is to

   (A) explain why an argument about black economic progress is incomplete
   (B) describe the impact of education on black economic progress
   (C) refute an argument about the factors influencing black economic progress
   (D) describe black economic progress before and after the 1960s
   (E) clarify the current view about the factors influencing black economic progress

25. Which one of the following best states the position of proponents of the "continuous change" hypothesis regarding the relationship between law and racial discrimination?

   (A) Individuals cannot be forced by legal means to behave in nondiscriminatory ways.
   (B) Discriminatory practices in education have been effectively altered by legal means.
   (C) Legislation alone has had little effect on racially discriminatory behavior.
   (D) Legislation is necessary, but not sufficient, to achieve changes in racial attitudes.
   (E) Legislation can only exacerbate conflicts about racially discriminatory behavior.

26. The author concedes that "correlating federal intervention and the acceleration of black economic progress might be incorrect" (lines 58–60) primarily in order to

   (A) strengthen the overall argument by anticipating an objection
   (B) introduce another factor that may have influenced black economic progress
   (C) concede a point to the continuity theorists
   (D) change the overall argument in light of the views of the continuity theorists
   (E) introduce a discussion about the impact of federal intervention on discrimination

27. The "continuous change" hypothesis, as it is presented in the passage, can best be applied to which one of the following situations?

   (A) Homes are found for many low-income families because the government funds a project to build subsidized housing in an economically depressed area.
   (B) A depressed economy does not cause the closing of small businesses in a local community because the government provides special grants to aid these businesses.
   (C) Unemployed people are able to obtain jobs because private contractors receive tax incentives for constructing office buildings in an area with a high unemployment rate.
   (D) A housing shortage is remedied because the changing state of the economy permits private investors to finance construction in a depressed area.
   (E) A community's sanitation needs are met because neighborhood organizations lobby aggressively for government assistance.

S T O P

IF YOU FINISH BEFORE TIME IS CALLED, YOU MAY CHECK YOUR WORK ON THIS SECTION ONLY. DO NOT WORK ON ANY OTHER SECTION IN THE TEST.

SECTION II

Time—35 minutes

24 Questions

<u>Directions:</u> The questions in this section are based on the reasoning contained in brief statements or passages. For some questions, more than one of the choices could conceivably answer the question. However, you are to choose the <u>best</u> answer; that is, the response that most accurately and completely answers the question. You should not make assumptions that are by commonsense standards implausible, superfluous, or incompatible with the passage. After you have chosen the best answer, blacken the corresponding space on your answer sheet.

1. Walter: Although cigarette smoking is legal, it should be banned on all airline flights. Cigarette smoking in the confines of an aircraft exposes nonsmokers to harmful secondhand smoke that they cannot avoid.

   Which one of the following principles, if established, would justify the proposal put forth by Walter?

   (A) People should be prohibited from engaging in an otherwise legal activity in those situations in which that activity would unavoidably expose others to harm.

   (B) An activity should be banned only if most situations in which a person engages in that activity would inevitably expose others to harm.

   (C) A legal activity that has the potential for causing harm to others in certain situations should be modified in those situations to render it harmless.

   (D) People who regularly engage in an activity that has the potential for harming others when that activity takes place in certain situations should be excluded from those situations.

   (E) If an activity is legal in some situations in which a person's engaging in that activity could harm others, then that activity should be legal in all situations.

2. Physicist: The claim that low-temperature nuclear fusion can be achieved entirely by chemical means is based on chemical experiments in which the measurements and calculations are inaccurate.

   Chemist: But your challenge is ineffectual, since you are simply jealous at the thought that chemists might have solved a problem that physicists have been unable to solve.

   Which one of the following is the strongest criticism of the chemist's response to the physicist's challenge?

   (A) It restates a claim in different words instead of offering evidence for this claim.

   (B) It fails to establish that perfect accuracy of measurements and calculations is possible.

   (C) It confuses two different meanings of the word "solve."

   (D) It is directed against the proponent of a claim rather than against the claim itself.

   (E) It rests on a contradiction.

3. A certain strain of bacteria was found in the stomachs of ulcer patients. A medical researcher with no history of ulcers inadvertently ingested some of the bacteria and within weeks developed an ulcer. Therefore, it is highly likely that the bacteria strain induces ulcers.

   Which one of the following, if true, most supports the argument above?

   (A) People who have the bacteria strain in their stomachs have been found to have no greater incidence of kidney disease than do people who lack the bacteria strain.

   (B) The researcher did not develop any other serious health problems within a year after ingesting the bacteria strain.

   (C) There is no evidence that the bacteria strain induces ulcers in laboratory animals.

   (D) The researcher is a recognized expert in the treatment of diseases of the stomach.

   (E) A study of 2,000 people who do not have ulcers found that none of these people had the bacteria strain in their stomachs.

GO ON TO THE NEXT PAGE.

4. A recent study monitored the blood pressure of people petting domestic animals in the laboratory. The blood pressure of some of these people lowered while petting the animals. Therefore, for any one of the people so affected, owning a pet would result in that person having a lower average blood pressure.

The flawed pattern of reasoning in the argument above is most similar to that in which one of the following?

(A) Because a single dose of a drug acts as a remedy for a particular ailment, a healthy person can ward off that ailment by taking single doses regularly.

(B) Because buying an automobile is very expensive, people should hold on to an automobile, once bought, for as long as it can be maintained in running condition.

(C) Since pruning houseplants is enjoyable for some people, those people should get rid of houseplants that do not require frequent pruning.

(D) Since riding in a boat for a few minutes is relaxing for some people, those people would be more relaxed generally if those people owned boats.

(E) Since giving a fence one coat of white paint makes the fence white, giving it two coats of white paint would make it even whiter.

5. Of the five bill collectors at Apex Collection Agency, Mr. Young has the highest rate of unsuccessful collections. Yet Mr. Young is the best bill collector on the agency's staff.

Which one of the following, if true, most helps to resolve the apparent discrepancy?

(A) Mr. Young is assigned the majority of the most difficult cases at the agency.

(B) The other four bill collectors at the agency all consider Mr. Young to be a very capable bill collector.

(C) Mr. Young's rate of collections per year has remained fairly steady in the last few years.

(D) Before joining the agency, Mr. Young was affiliated with the credit department of a large department store.

(E) None of the bill collectors at the agency has been on the agency's staff longer than Mr. Young has.

6. A primate jawbone found in Namibia in southern Africa has been identified by anthropologists as that of an ape that lived between 10 million and 15 million years ago. Researchers generally agree that such ancient primates lived only in dense forests. Consequently, the dry, treeless expanses now dominating the landscape in and around Namibia must have replaced an earlier, heavily forested terrain.

The argument assumes which one of the following?

(A) Modern apes also tend to live only in heavily forested terrain.

(B) The ape whose jawbone was found lived in or near the area that is now Namibia.

(C) There were no apes living in the area that is now Namibia prior to 15 million years ago.

(D) The ape whose jawbone was found was adapted to a diet that was significantly different from that of any modern ape.

(E) The ancient primates were numerous enough to have caused severe damage to the ecology of the forests in which they lived.

GO ON TO THE NEXT PAGE.

7. Workers may complain about many things at work, but stress is not high on the list. In fact, in a recent survey a majority placed boredom at the top of their list of complaints. The assumption that job-related stress is the most serious problem for workers in the corporate world is thus simply not warranted.

Which one of the following, if true, most seriously weakens the argument?

(A) Those workers who are responsible for the planning and supervision of long-term projects are less likely to complain of either boredom or stress.

(B) Workers who complain of boredom exhibit more stress-related symptoms than do those who claim their work is interesting.

(C) Workers responding to opinion surveys tend to emphasize those experiences that have happened most recently.

(D) Workers who feel that their salaries are commensurate with the amount of work they do are less likely to complain of boredom.

(E) Workers are less likely to complain about work if they feel that their jobs are secure.

8. Would it be right for the government to abandon efforts to determine at what levels to allow toxic substances in our food supply? Only if it can reasonably be argued that the only acceptable level of toxic substances in food is zero. However, virtually all foods contain perfectly natural substances that are toxic but cause no harm because they do not occur in food in toxic concentrations. Furthermore, we can never be certain of having reduced the concentration of any substance to zero; all we can ever know is that it has been reduced to below the threshold of detection of current analytical methods.

The main conclusion of the argument is that

(A) the government should continue trying to determine acceptable levels for toxic substances in our food supply

(B) the only acceptable level of toxic substances in food is zero

(C) naturally occurring toxic substances in food present little danger because they rarely occur in toxic concentrations

(D) the government will never be able to determine with certainty that a food contains no toxic substances

(E) the government needs to refine its methods of detecting toxic substances in our food supply

9. Over the past twenty-five years the introduction of labor-saving technologies has greatly reduced the average amount of time a worker needs to produce a given output, potentially both reducing the number of hours each worker works each week and increasing workers' leisure time correspondingly. The average amount of leisure time per worker, however, has increased at only half the rate at which the average hourly output per worker has grown.

If the statements above are true, which one of the following is most strongly supported by them?

(A) Workers, on average, spend more money on leisure activities today than they did twenty-five years ago.

(B) Labor-saving technologies have created fewer jobs than they have eliminated.

(C) The percentage of the population that is in the work force has grown over the past twenty-five years.

(D) The average hourly output per worker has not risen as much as had been anticipated when modern labor-saving technologies were first introduced.

(E) Twenty-five years ago the average weekly output per worker was less than it is today.

GO ON TO THE NEXT PAGE.

10. Ten thousand years ago many communities in western Asia stopped procuring food by hunting and gathering and began instead to cultivate food. Archaeological evidence reveals that, compared to their hunter-gatherer forebears, the early agricultural peoples ate a poorly balanced diet and had diet-related health problems, yet these peoples never returned to hunting and gathering.

Which one of the following, if true, most helps to explain why the agricultural peoples of western Asia never returned to hunting and gathering?

(A) The plants and animals that the agricultural peoples began to cultivate continued to exist in the wild.

(B) Both hunter-gatherers and agriculturalists sometimes depended on stored and preserved foods instead of fresh foods.

(C) An increase in population density at the time required a higher food production rate than hunting and gathering could provide.

(D) Thousands of years ago similar shifts from hunting and gathering to agriculture occurred in many other parts of the world.

(E) The physical labor involved in agriculture burns more calories than does that needed for hunting and gathering.

11. Should a journalist's story begin with the set phrase "in a surprise development," as routinely happens? Well, not if the surprise was merely the journalist's, since journalists should not intrude themselves into their stories, and not if the surprise was someone else's, because if some person's surprise was worth mentioning at all, it should have been specifically attributed. The one possibility remaining is that lots of people were surprised; in that case, however, there is no point in belaboring the obvious.

Which one of the following most accurately states the conclusion of the argument above?

(A) Journalists should reserve use of the phrase "in a surprise development" for major developments that are truly unexpected.

(B) The phrase "in a surprise development" is appropriately used only where someone's being surprised is itself interesting.

(C) The phrase "in a surprise development" is used in three distinct sorts of circumstances.

(D) Journalists should make the point that a development comes as a surprise when summing up, not when introducing, a story.

(E) Introducing stories with the phrase "in a surprise development" is not good journalistic practice.

12. Individual pyrrole molecules readily join together into larger molecules called polypyrroles. If polypyrroles form from pyrrole in the presence of zeolites, they do so by attaching to the zeolite either in lumps on the outer surface of the zeolite or in delicate chains within the zeolite's inner channels. When zeolite changes color from yellow to black, it means that on or in that zeolite polypyrroles have formed from pyrrole. Yellow zeolite free of any pyrrole was submerged in dissolved pyrrole. The zeolite turned black even though no polypyrroles formed on its outer surface.

If the statements above are true, which one of the following must on the basis of them be true?

(A) Polypyrroles had already formed on or in the zeolite before it was submerged.

(B) Lumps of polypyrrole attached to the zeolite were responsible for its color change.

(C) At least some of the pyrrole in which the zeolite was submerged formed polypyrrole chains.

(D) None of the pyrrole in which the zeolite was submerged attached itself to the zeolite.

(E) Little, if any, of the pyrrole in which the zeolite was submerged reached the zeolite's inner channels.

GO ON TO THE NEXT PAGE.

Questions 13–14

Pedigreed dogs, including those officially classified as working dogs, must conform to standards set by organizations that issue pedigrees. Those standards generally specify the physical appearance necessary for a dog to be recognized as belonging to a breed but stipulate nothing about other genetic traits, such as those that enable breeds originally developed as working dogs to perform the work for which they were developed. Since dog breeders try to maintain only those traits specified by pedigree organizations, and traits that breeders do not try to maintain risk being lost, certain traits like herding ability risk being lost among pedigreed dogs. Therefore, pedigree organizations should set standards requiring working ability in pedigreed dogs classified as working dogs.

13. Which one of the following principles, if valid, justifies the argument's conclusion that pedigree organizations should set standards for working ability in dogs?

   (A) Organizations that set standards for products or activities should not set standards calling for a particular characteristic if such standards increase the risk of some other characteristic being lost.

   (B) Any standard currently in effect for a product or an activity should be rigorously enforced regardless of when the standard was first set.

   (C) Organizations that set standards for products or activities should be responsible for seeing to it that those products or activities conform to all the specifications called for by those standards.

   (D) Any standard that is set for a product or an activity should reflect the uses to which that product or activity will eventually be put.

   (E) Organizations that set standards for products or activities should attempt to ensure that those products or activities can serve the purposes for which they were originally developed.

14. The phrase "certain traits like herding ability risk being lost among pedigreed dogs" serves which one of the following functions in the argument?

   (A) It is a claim on which the argument depends but for which no support is given.

   (B) It is a subsidiary conclusion used in support of the main conclusion.

   (C) It acknowledges a possible objection to the proposal put forth in the argument.

   (D) It summarizes the position that the argument as a whole is directed toward discrediting.

   (E) It provides evidence necessary to support a claim stated earlier in the argument.

15. In rheumatoid arthritis, the body's immune system misfunctions by attacking healthy cells in the joints, causing the release of a hormone that in turn causes pain and swelling. This hormone is normally activated only in reaction to injury or infection. A new arthritis medication will contain a protein that inhibits the functioning of the hormone that causes pain and swelling in the joints.

The statements above, if true, most strongly support which one of the following conclusions?

   (A) Unlike aspirin and other medications that reduce pain and swelling and that are currently available, the new medication would repair existing cell damage that had been caused by rheumatoid arthritis.

   (B) The benefits to rheumatoid arthritis sufferers of the new medication would outweigh the medication's possible harmful side effects.

   (C) A patient treated with the new medication for rheumatoid arthritis could sustain a joint injury without becoming aware of it.

   (D) The new medication could be adapted for use against a variety of immune system disorders, such as diabetes and lupus.

   (E) Joint diseases other than rheumatoid arthritis would not be affected by the new medication.

16. In their native habitat, amaryllis plants go dormant when the soil in which they are growing dries out during the dry season. Therefore, if amaryllis plants kept as houseplants are to thrive, water should be withheld from them during part of the year so that the plants go dormant.

Which one of the following is an assumption on which the argument depends?

   (A) Most kinds of plants go dormant at some time or other during the year.

   (B) Amaryllis are more difficult to keep as houseplants than other kinds of plants are.

   (C) Water should be withheld from amaryllis plants kept as houseplants during the exact time of year that corresponds to the dry season in their native habitat.

   (D) Any amaryllis plant that fails to thrive is likely to have been dormant for too short a time.

   (E) Going dormant benefits amaryllis plants in their native habitat in some way other than simply preventing death during overly dry periods.

GO ON TO THE NEXT PAGE.

17. Most people believe that yawning is most powerfully triggered by seeing someone else yawn. This belief about yawning is widespread not only today, but also has been commonplace in many parts of the world in the past, if we are to believe historians of popular culture. Thus, seeing someone else yawn must be the most irresistible cause of yawning.

The argument is most vulnerable to which one of the following criticisms?

(A) It attempts to support its conclusion solely by restating that conclusion in other words.

(B) It cites the evidence of historians of popular culture in direct support of a claim that lies outside their area of expertise.

(C) It makes a sweeping generalization about yawning based on evidence drawn from a limited number of atypical cases.

(D) It supports its conclusion by appealing solely to opinion in a matter that is largely factual.

(E) It takes for granted that yawns have no cause other than the one it cites.

18. Everyone who is a gourmet cook enjoys a wide variety of foods and spices. Since no one who enjoys a wide variety of foods and spices prefers bland foods to all other foods, it follows that anyone who prefers bland foods to all other foods is not a gourmet cook.

The pattern of reasoning displayed in the argument above is most similar to that displayed in which one of the following?

(A) All of the paintings in the Huang Collection will be put up for auction next week. Since the paintings to be auctioned next week are by a wide variety of artists, it follows that the paintings in the Huang Collection are by a wide variety of artists.

(B) All of the paintings in the Huang Collection are abstract. Since no abstract painting will be included in next week's art auction, nothing to be included in next week's art auction is a painting in the Huang Collection.

(C) All of the paintings in the Huang Collection are superb works of art. Since none of the paintings in the Huang Collection is by Roué, it stands to reason that no painting by Roué is a superb work of art.

(D) Every postimpressionist painting from the Huang Collection will be auctioned off next week. No pop art paintings from the Huang Collection will be auctioned off next week. Hence none of the pop art paintings to be auctioned off next week will be from the Huang Collection.

(E) Every painting from the Huang Collection that is to be auctioned off next week is a major work of art. No price can adequately reflect the true value of a major work of art. Hence the prices that will be paid at next week's auction will not adequately reflect the true value of the paintings sold.

19. Without information that could only have come from someone present at the secret meeting between the finance minister and the leader of the opposition party, the newspaper story that forced the finance minister to resign could not have been written. No one witnessed the meeting, however, except the minister's aide. It is clear, therefore, that the finance minister was ultimately brought down, not by any of his powerful political enemies, but by his own trusted aide.

The argument commits which one of the following errors of reasoning?

(A) drawing a conclusion on the basis of evidence that provides equally strong support for a competing conclusion

(B) assuming without warrant that if one thing cannot occur without another thing's already having occurred, then the earlier thing cannot occur without bringing about the later thing

(C) confusing evidence that a given outcome on one occasion was brought about in a certain way with evidence that the same outcome on a different occasion was brought about in that way

(D) basing its conclusion on evidence that is almost entirely irrelevant to the point at issue

(E) treating evidence that a given action contributed to bringing about a certain effect as though that evidence established that the given action by itself was sufficient to bring about that effect

GO ON TO THE NEXT PAGE.

20. S. R. Evans: A few critics have dismissed my poems as not being poems and have dismissed me as not being a poet. But one principle of criticism has it that only true poets can recognize poetic creativity or function as critics of poetry—and that the only true poets are those whose work conveys genuine poetic creativity. But I have read the work of these critics; none of it demonstrated poetic creativity. These critics' judgments should be rejected, since these critics are not true poets.

The argument above is vulnerable to criticism on the grounds that it

(A)   presupposes what it sets out to conclude, since the principle requires that only true poets can determine whether the critics' work demonstrates poetic creativity
(B)   uses the distinction between poets and critics as though everyone fell into one category or the other
(C)   gives no justification for the implicit claim that the standing of a poet can be judged independently of his or her poetry
(D)   makes an unjustifiable distinction, since it is possible that some critics are also poets
(E)   inevitably leads to the conclusion that poets can never learn to improve their poetry, since no poet is in a position to criticize his or her own work

21. Claim: Country X's government lowered tariff barriers because doing so served the interests of powerful foreign companies.

Principle: In order for a change to be explained by the advantage some person or group gained from it, it must be shown how the interests of the person or group played a role in bringing about the change.

Which one of the following, if true, can most logically serve as a premise for an argument that uses the principle to counter the claim?

(A)   Foreign companies did benefit when Country X lowered tariff barriers, but consumers in Country X benefited just as much.
(B)   In the period since tariff barriers were lowered, price competition among importers has severely limited importers' profits from selling foreign companies' products in Country X.
(C)   It was impossible to predict how Country X's economic reforms, which included lowering tariff barriers, would affect the economy in the short term.
(D)   Many of the foreign companies that benefited from Country X's lowering tariff barriers compete fiercely among themselves both in Country X and in other markets.
(E)   Although foreign companies benefited when Country X lowered tariff barriers, there is no other evidence that these foreign companies induced the change.

22. A scientist made three observations: (1) in the world's temperate zones, food is more plentiful in the ocean than it is in fresh water; (2) migratory fish in temperate zones generally mature in the ocean and spawn in fresh water; and (3) migratory fish need much nourishment as they mature but little or none during the part of their lives when they spawn. On the basis of those observations, the scientist formulated the hypothesis that food availability is a determining factor in the migration of migratory fish. Subsequently the scientist learned that in the tropics migratory fish generally mature in fresh water and spawn in the ocean.

Which one of the following would it be most helpful to know in order to judge whether what the scientist subsequently learned calls into question the hypothesis?

(A)   whether in the world's temperate zones, the temperatures of bodies of fresh water tend to be lower than those of the regions of the oceans into which they flow
(B)   whether the types of foods that migratory fish eat while they inhabit the ocean are similar to those that they eat while they inhabit bodies of fresh water
(C)   whether any species of fish with populations in temperate zones also have populations that live in the tropics
(D)   whether there are more species of migratory fish in the tropics than there are in temperate zones
(E)   whether in the tropics food is less plentiful in the ocean than in fresh water

GO ON TO THE NEXT PAGE.

23. No computer will ever be able to do everything that some human minds can do, for there are some problems that cannot be solved by following any set of mechanically applicable rules. Yet computers can only solve problems by following some set of mechanically applicable rules.

Which one of the following is an assumption on which the argument depends?

(A) At least one problem solvable by following some set of mechanically applicable rules is not solvable by any human mind.

(B) At least one problem not solvable by following any set of mechanically applicable rules is solvable by at least one human mind.

(C) At least one problem solvable by following some set of mechanically applicable rules is solvable by every human mind.

(D) Every problem that is solvable by following more than one set of mechanically applicable rules is solvable by almost every human mind.

(E) Every problem that is solvable by following at least one set of mechanically applicable rules is solvable by at least one human mind.

24. People were asked in a survey how old they felt. They replied, almost unanimously despite a great diversity of ages, with a number that was 75 percent of their real age. There is, however, a problem in understanding this sort of response. For example, suppose it meant that a 48-year-old man was claiming to feel as he felt at 36. But at age 36 he would have said he felt like a man of 27, and at 27 he would have said he felt just over 20, and so on into childhood. And surely, that 48-year-old man did not mean to suggest that he felt like a child!

Which one of the following techniques of reasoning is employed in the argument?

(A) projecting from responses collected at one time from many individuals of widely different ages to hypothetical earlier responses of a single individual at some of those ages

(B) reinterpreting what certain people actually said in the light of what would, in the circumstances, have been the most reasonable thing for them to say

(C) qualifying an overly sweeping generalization in light of a single, well chosen counterexample

(D) deriving a contradiction from a pair of statements in order to prove that at least one of those statements is false

(E) analyzing an unexpected unanimity among respondents as evidence, not of a great uniformity of opinion among those respondents, but of their successful manipulation by their questioners

S T O P

IF YOU FINISH BEFORE TIME IS CALLED, YOU MAY CHECK YOUR WORK ON THIS SECTION ONLY.
DO NOT WORK ON ANY OTHER SECTION IN THE TEST.

SECTION III

Time—35 minutes

26 Questions

<u>Directions:</u> The questions in this section are based on the reasoning contained in brief statements or passages. For some questions, more than one of the choices could conceivably answer the question. However, you are to choose the <u>best</u> answer; that is, the response that most accurately and completely answers the question. You should not make assumptions that are by commonsense standards implausible, superfluous, or incompatible with the passage. After you have chosen the best answer, blacken the corresponding space on your answer sheet.

<u>Questions 1–2</u>

Those who support the continued reading and performance of Shakespeare's plays maintain that in England appreciation for his work has always extended beyond educated elites and that ever since Shakespeare's own time his plays have always been known and loved by comparatively uneducated people. Skepticism about this claim is borne out by examining early eighteenth-century editions of the plays. These books, with their fine paper and good bindings, must have been far beyond the reach of people of ordinary means.

1. The main point of the argument is to

    (A) suggest that knowledge of Shakespeare's plays is a suitable criterion for distinguishing the educated elite from other members of English society

    (B) provide evidence that at some time in the past appreciation for Shakespeare's plays was confined to educated elites

    (C) prove that early eighteenth-century appreciation for Shakespeare's works rested on aspects of the works that are less appreciated today

    (D) demonstrate that since Shakespeare's time the people who have known and loved his work have all been members of educated elites

    (E) confirm the skepticism of the educated elite concerning the worth of Shakespeare's plays

2. Which one of the following describes a reasoning error in the argument?

    (A) The argument uses the popularity of Shakespeare's plays as a measure of their literary quality.

    (B) The argument bases an aesthetic conclusion about Shakespeare's plays on purely economic evidence.

    (C) The argument anachronistically uses the standards of the twentieth century to judge events that occurred in the early eighteenth century.

    (D) The argument judges the literary quality of a book's text on the basis of the quality of the volume in which the text is printed.

    (E) The argument does not allow for the possibility that people might know Shakespeare's plays without having read them.

3. Organization president: The stationery and envelopes used in all of the mailings from our national headquarters are made from recycled paper, and we never put anything but letters in the envelopes. When the envelopes have windows, these windows are also made from recycled material. Therefore the envelopes, and thus these mailings, are completely recyclable.

Which one of the following is an assumption on which the organization president's argument depends?

    (A) All the paper used by the organization for purposes other than mailings is recycled.

    (B) The mailings from the organization's national headquarters always use envelopes that have windows.

    (C) The envelope windows made from recycled material are recyclable.

    (D) The envelopes and stationery used in the organization's mailings are always recycled.

    (E) The organization sends mailings only from its national headquarters.

GO ON TO THE NEXT PAGE.

Questions 4–5

The frequently expressed view that written constitutions are inherently more liberal than unwritten ones is false. No written constitution is more than a paper with words on it until those words are both interpreted and applied. Properly understood, then, a constitution is the sum of those procedures through which the power of the state is legitimately exercised and limited. Therefore, even a written constitution becomes a liberal constitution only when it is interpreted and applied in a liberal way.

4. The main point of the argument above is that

   (A)   written constitutions are no more inherently liberal than are unwritten constitutions
   (B)   the idea of a written constitution, properly understood, is inherently self-contradictory
   (C)   unwritten constitutions are less subject to misinterpretation than are constitutions that have been written down
   (D)   liberal constitutions are extremely difficult to preserve
   (E)   there are criteria for evaluating the interpretation and application of a constitution

5. If the statements in the argument are all true, which one of the following must also be true on the basis of them?

   (A)   A careful analysis of the written text of a constitution can show that the constitution is not a liberal one.
   (B)   It is impossible to determine that a written constitution is liberal merely through careful analysis of the written text.
   (C)   There are no advantages to having a written rather than an unwritten constitution.
   (D)   Constitutions that are not written are more likely to be liberal than are constitutions that are written.
   (E)   A constitution is a liberal constitution if it is possible to interpret it in a liberal way.

6. As far as we know, Earth is the only planet on which life has evolved, and all known life forms are carbon-based. Therefore, although there might exist noncarbon-based life on planets very unlike Earth, our scientific estimates of the probability of extraterrestrial life should be generated from estimates of the number of planets like Earth and the likelihood of carbon-based life on those planets.

Which one of the following general principles most strongly supports the recommendation?

   (A)   There is no good reason to think that unobserved phenomena closely resemble those that have been observed.
   (B)   A scientific theory that explains a broad range of phenomena is preferable to a competing theory that explains only some of those phenomena.
   (C)   It is preferable for scientists to restrict their studies to phenomena that are observable and forego making estimates about unobservable things.
   (D)   A scientific theory that explains observed phenomena on the basis of a few principles that are independent of each other is preferable to a theory that explains those same phenomena on the basis of many independent principles.
   (E)   Estimations of probability that are more closely tied to what is known are preferable to those that are less closely tied to what is known.

7. Politician: Unless our nation redistributes wealth, we will be unable to alleviate economic injustice and our current system will lead inevitably to intolerable economic inequities. If the inequities become intolerable, those who suffer from the injustice will resort to violence to coerce social reform. It is our nation's responsibility to do whatever is necessary to alleviate conditions that would otherwise give rise to violent attempts at social reform.

The statements above logically commit the politician to which one of the following conclusions?

   (A)   The need for political reform never justifies a resort to violent remedies.
   (B)   It is our nation's responsibility to redistribute wealth.
   (C)   Politicians must base decisions on political expediency rather than on abstract moral principles.
   (D)   Economic injustice need not be remedied unless it leads to intolerable social conditions.
   (E)   All that is required to create conditions of economic justice is the redistribution of wealth.

GO ON TO THE NEXT PAGE.

8. Delta green ground beetles sometimes remain motionless for hours at a stretch, although they are more active in wet years than in dry years. In 1989 an observer spotted ten delta green ground beetles in nine hours; in 1985 the same observer at the same location had counted 38 in about two hours. This difference probably does not reflect a drop in the population of these rare beetles over this period, however, because 1985 was a wet year and 1989 was relatively dry.

    Which one of the following, if true, most strongly supports the conclusion drawn above?

    (A) Because of their excellent camouflage, delta green ground beetles are almost impossible to see if they are not moving.
    (B) The only habitat of delta green ground beetles is around pools formed by the collection of winter rains in low-lying areas.
    (C) Delta green ground beetles move about very little to get food; most of their moving from one place to another is related to their reproductive behavior.
    (D) Delta green ground beetles are so rare that, although the first specimen was found in 1878, a second was not found until 1974.
    (E) No predator relies on the delta green ground beetle for a major portion of its food supply.

9. Chronic fatigue syndrome, a condition that afflicts thousands of people, is invariably associated with lower-than-normal concentrations of magnesium in the blood. Further, malabsorption of magnesium from the digestive tract to the blood is also often associated with some types of fatigue. These facts in themselves demonstrate that treatments that raise the concentration of magnesium in the blood would provide an effective cure for the fatigue involved in the syndrome.

    The argument is most vulnerable to which one of the following criticisms?

    (A) It fails to establish that lower-than-normal concentrations of magnesium in the blood are invariably due to malabsorption of magnesium.
    (B) It offers no evidence that fatigue itself does not induce lowered concentrations of magnesium in the blood.
    (C) It ignores the possibility that, even in people who are not afflicted with chronic fatigue syndrome, concentration of magnesium in the blood fluctuates.
    (D) It neglects to state the exact concentration of magnesium in the blood which is considered the normal concentration.
    (E) It does not specify what methods would be most effective in raising the concentration of magnesium in the blood.

Questions 10–11

Consumer advocate: The toy-labeling law should require manufacturers to provide explicit safety labels on toys to indicate what hazards the toys pose. The only labels currently required by law are labels indicating the age range for which a toy is intended. For instance, a "three and up" label is required on toys that pose a choking hazard for children under three years of age. Although the current toy-labeling law has indeed reduced the incidence of injuries to children from toys, parents could prevent such injuries almost entirely if toy labels provided explicit safety information.

10. Which one of the following, if true, most strengthens the consumer advocate's argument?

    (A) Certain types of toys have never been associated with injury to children.
    (B) Most parents believe that the current labels are recommendations regarding level of cognitive skill.
    (C) The majority of children injured by toys are under three years of age.
    (D) Many parents do not pay attention to manufacturers' labels when they select toys for their children.
    (E) Choking is the most serious hazard presented to children by toys.

11. The statement that the law should require explicit safety labels on toys serves which one of the following functions in the consumer advocate's argument?

    (A) It is a general principle supporting the conclusion of the argument.
    (B) It is a proposed compromise between two conflicting goals.
    (C) It is the conclusion of the argument.
    (D) It is evidence that must be refuted in order to establish the conclusion of the argument.
    (E) It is a particular instance of the general position under discussion.

GO ON TO THE NEXT PAGE.

12. Proponents of organic farming claim that using chemical fertilizers and pesticides in farming is harmful to local wildlife. To produce the same amount of food, however, more land must be under cultivation when organic farming techniques are used than when chemicals are used. Therefore, organic farming leaves less land available as habitat for local wildlife.

Which one of the following is an assumption on which the author's argument depends?

(A) Chemical fertilizers and pesticides pose no health threat to wildlife.
(B) Wildlife living near farms where chemicals are used will not ingest any food or water containing those chemicals.
(C) The only disadvantage to using chemicals in farming is their potential effect on wildlife.
(D) The same crops are grown on organic farms as on farms where chemicals are used.
(E) Land cultivated by organic farming methods no longer constitutes a habitat for wildlife.

13. Reptiles are air-breathing vertebrates with completely ossified skeletons; so alligators must be air-breathing vertebrates with completely ossified skeletons.

In terms of its logical features, the argument above most resembles which one of the following?

(A) Green plants take in carbon dioxide and release oxygen back into the air; so it follows that grass takes in carbon dioxide and releases oxygen into the air.
(B) Some red butterflies are poisonous to birds that prey on them; so this particular red butterfly is poisonous to birds that prey on it.
(C) Knowledge about the empirical world can be gained from books; so Virginia Woolf's book *A Room of One's Own* must provide knowledge about the empirical world.
(D) Dierdre has seen every film directed by Rainer Werner Fassbinder; so Dierdre must have seen *Ali: Fear Eats the Soul*, a film directed by Fassbinder.
(E) Skiers run a high risk of bone fracture; so it is likely that Lindsey, who has been an avid skier for many years, has suffered a broken bone at some point.

14. Although inflated government spending for weapons research encourages waste at weapons research laboratories, weapons production plants must be viewed as equally wasteful of taxpayer dollars. After all, by the government's own admission, the weapons plant it plans to reopen will violate at least 69 environmental, health, and safety laws. The government has decided to reopen the plant and exempt it from compliance, even though the weapons to be produced there could be produced at the same cost at a safer facility.

The reasoning in the argument is most vulnerable to criticism on which one of the following grounds?

(A) It offers no evidence that the "safer" alternative production site actually complies with any of the laws mentioned.
(B) It concedes a point regarding weapons research laboratories that undermines its conclusion about weapons production plants.
(C) It relies on evidence that does not directly address the issue of wasteful spending.
(D) It confuses necessary expenditures for research with wasteful spending on weapons.
(E) It fails to establish that research laboratories and weapons production plants are similar enough to be meaningfully compared.

GO ON TO THE NEXT PAGE.

Questions 15–16

Dr. Godfrey: Now that high school students are allowed to work more than 15 hours per week at part-time jobs, those who actually do so show less interest in school and get lower grades than those who do not work as many hours at part-time jobs. Obviously, working long hours at part-time jobs during the school year contributes to the academic problems that many of our high school students experience.

Dr. Nash: That's not so. Many of our high school students set out to earn as much money as they can simply to compensate for their lack of academic success.

15.   Dr. Nash responds to Dr. Godfrey's argument by doing which one of the following?

(A)   attempting to downplay the seriousness of the problems facing academically troubled high school students

(B)   offering an alternative interpretation of the evidence cited by Dr. Godfrey

(C)   questioning the accuracy of the evidence on which Dr. Godfrey bases his conclusion

(D)   proposing that the schools are not at fault for the academic problems facing many high school students

(E)   raising the possibility that there is no relationship between academic problems among high school students and part-time employment

16.   The answer to which one of the following would be the most helpful in determining whether the conclusion that Dr. Godfrey draws could be logically defended against Dr. Nash's counterargument?

(A)   whether people who have had academic problems in high school are ultimately less successful in their careers than people who have not had such problems

(B)   whether students are allowed to spend more than 15 hours per week at school-sponsored nonacademic extracurricular activities such as team sports or clubs

(C)   whether the students who work more than 15 hours per week and have academic problems had such problems before they began to work that many hours

(D)   whether employers and high school students typically obey all the laws that regulate the conditions under which young people may legally be employed

(E)   whether high school students who have after-school jobs continue to work at those jobs after graduating from high school

17.   X: Medical research on animals should not be reduced in response to a concern for animals, because results of such research serve to avert human suffering. In such research a trade-off between human and animal welfare is always inevitable, but we should give greater weight to human welfare.

Y: With technology that is currently available, much of the research presently performed on animals could instead be done with computer modeling or human subjects without causing any suffering.

The relationship of Y's response to X's argument is that Y's response

(A)   contradicts a premise on which X's argument relies

(B)   disagrees with X about the weight to be given to animal suffering as opposed to human suffering

(C)   presents a logical consequence of the premises of X's argument

(D)   strengthens X's argument by presenting evidence not mentioned by X

(E)   supplies a premise to X's argument that was not explicitly stated

18.   In experiments in which certain kinds of bacteria were placed in a generous supply of nutrients, the populations of bacteria grew rapidly, and genetic mutations occurred at random in the populations. These experiments show that all genetic mutation is random.

Which one of the following, if true, enables the conclusion to be properly drawn?

(A)   Either all genetic mutations are random or none are random.

(B)   The bacteria tested in the experiments were of extremely common forms.

(C)   If all genetic mutations in bacteria are random, then all genetic mutations in every other life form are random also.

(D)   The kind of environment in which genetic mutation takes place has no effect on the way genetic mutation occurs.

(E)   The nutrients used were the same as those that nourish the bacteria in nature.

GO ON TO THE NEXT PAGE.

19. Thomas: The club president had no right to disallow Jeffrey's vote. Club rules say that only members in good standing may vote. You've admitted that club rules also say that all members whose dues are fully paid are members in good standing. And since, as the records indicate, Jeffrey has always paid his dues on time, clearly the president acted in violation of club rules.

Althea: By that reasoning my two-year-old niece can legally vote in next month's national election since she is a citizen of this country, and only citizens can legally vote in national elections.

The reasoning in Thomas' argument is flawed because his argument

(A) fails to take into account the distinction between something not being prohibited and its being authorized

(B) offers evidence that casts doubt on the character of the club president and thereby ignores the question of voting eligibility

(C) wrongly assumes that if a statement is not actually denied by someone, that statement must be regarded as true

(D) does not specify the issue with respect to which the disputed vote was cast

(E) overlooks the possibility that Althea is not an authority on the club's rules

20. Calories consumed in excess of those with which the body needs to be provided to maintain its weight are normally stored as fat and the body gains weight. Alcoholic beverages are laden with calories. However, those people who regularly drink two or three alcoholic beverages a day and thereby exceed the caloric intake necessary to maintain their weight do not in general gain weight.

Which one of the following, if true, most helps to resolve the apparent discrepancy?

(A) Some people who regularly drink two or three alcoholic beverages a day avoid exceeding the caloric intake necessary to maintain their weight by decreasing caloric intake from other sources.

(B) Excess calories consumed by people who regularly drink two or three alcoholic beverages a day tend to be dissipated as heat.

(C) Some people who do not drink alcoholic beverages but who eat high-calorie foods do not gain weight.

(D) Many people who regularly drink more than three alcoholic beverages a day do not gain weight.

(E) Some people who take in fewer calories than are normally necessary to maintain their weight do not lose weight.

21. When a person with temporal lobe epilepsy is having an epileptic seizure, part of the brain's temporal lobe produces abnormal electrical impulses, which can often, but not always, be detected through a test called an electroencephalogram (EEG). Therefore, although a positive EEG reading—that is, evidence of abnormal electrical impulses—during an apparent seizure is a reasonably reliable indicator of temporal lobe epilepsy, _____.

Of the following, which one logically completes the conclusion above?

(A) a positive reading is just as reliable an indicator of the absence of temporal lobe epilepsy

(B) a positive reading can also indicate the presence of other forms of epilepsy

(C) a positive reading is more frequently an erroneous reading than is a negative one

(D) a negative reading does not mean that temporal lobe epilepsy can be ruled out

(E) a negative reading is just as reliable an indicator of the presence of temporal lobe epilepsy

GO ON TO THE NEXT PAGE.

22. In Sheldon most bicyclists aged 18 and over have lights on their bicycles, whereas most bicyclists under the age of 18 do not. It follows that in Sheldon most bicyclists who have lights on their bicycles are at least 18 years old.

Which one of the following exhibits a pattern of flawed reasoning most similar to that in the argument above?

(A) Most of the people in Sheldon buy gasoline on Mondays only. But almost everyone in Sheldon buys groceries on Tuesdays only. It follows that fewer than half of the people in Sheldon buy gasoline on the same day on which they buy groceries.

(B) The Sheldon Library lent more books during the week after it began lending videos than it had in the entire preceding month. It follows that the availability of videos was responsible for the increase in the number of books lent.

(C) Most of the residents of Sheldon who voted in the last election are on the Conservative party's mailing list, whereas most of Sheldon's residents who did not vote are not on the list. It follows that most of the residents of Sheldon on the Conservative party's mailing list voted in the last election.

(D) In the county where Sheldon is located, every town that has two or more fire trucks has a town pool, whereas most towns that have fewer than two fire trucks do not have a town pool. It follows that Sheldon, which has a town pool, must have at least two fire trucks.

(E) In Sheldon everyone over the age of 60 who knits also sews, but not everyone over the age of 60 who sews also knits. It follows that among people over the age of 60 in Sheldon there are more who sew than there are who knit.

23. Asbestos, an almost indestructible mineral once installed as building insulation, poses no health risk unless the asbestos is disturbed and asbestos fibers are released into the environment. Since removing asbestos from buildings disturbs it, thereby releasing asbestos fibers, the government should not require removal of all asbestos insulation.

Which one of the following, if true, most strengthens the argument?

(A) Asbestos poses far less risk to health than does smoking, drug and alcohol abuse, improper diet, or lack of exercise.

(B) Asbestos can pose a health threat to workers who remove it without wearing required protective gear.

(C) Some kinds of asbestos, when disturbed, pose greater health risks than do other kinds.

(D) Asbestos is inevitably disturbed by building renovations or building demolition.

(E) Much of the time, removed asbestos is buried in landfills and forgotten, with no guarantee that it will not be disturbed again.

GO ON TO THE NEXT PAGE.

Questions 24–25

When volcanic lava solidifies, it becomes uniformly magnetized in the direction in which the Earth's magnetic field points. There are significant differences in the direction of magnetization among solidified lava flows from different volcanoes that erupted at different times over the past several million years. Therefore, it must be that the direction of the Earth's magnetic field has changed over time. Since lava flows differing by thousands of years in age often have very similar directions of magnetization, the change in the direction of the Earth's magnetic field must take place very gradually over hundreds of thousands of years.

24. The argument that the direction of the Earth's magnetic field has changed over time requires the assumption that

(A) only lava can be used to measure the direction of the Earth's magnetic field as it existed in the distant past

(B) a single volcano can produce lava of differing consistencies during different eruptions

(C) not all solidified lava has changed the direction of its magnetization unpredictably

(D) there are fewer volcanic eruptions now than there were millions of years ago

(E) as lava flows down the side of a volcano, it picks up magnetized rocks

25. Which one of the following, if true, most seriously undermines the conclusion that the change in the direction of the Earth's magnetic field happened very slowly?

(A) The changes in the direction of the Earth's magnetic field are determined by the chaotic movement of iron-containing liquids in the Earth's outer core.

(B) There has not been a change in the direction of the Earth's magnetic field since scientists have begun measuring the direction of magnetization of lava flows.

(C) The direction of the Earth's magnetic field has undergone a complete reversal several times over the past few million years.

(D) A lava flow has been found in which the direction of magnetization in the center of the flow differs significantly from that on the surface, even though the flow took only two weeks to solidify completely.

(E) Since the rate at which molten lava solidifies depends on the temperature and altitude of the environment, some lava flows from volcanoes in certain areas will take years to solidify completely.

26. When the manufacturers in a given country are slower to adopt new technologies than their foreign competitors are, their production costs will fall more slowly than their foreign competitors' costs will. But if manufacturers' production costs fall less rapidly than their foreign competitors' costs do, those manufacturers will be unable to lower their prices as rapidly as their foreign competitors can; and when a country's manufacturers cannot lower their prices as rapidly as their foreign competitors can, that country gets squeezed out of the global market.

If the statements above are true, which one of the following must also be true on the basis of them?

(A) If the manufacturers in one country raise their prices, it is because they have squeezed their foreign competitors out of the global market.

(B) If manufacturers in one country have been squeezed out of the global market, this shows that their foreign competitors have adopted new technologies more rapidly than they have.

(C) If a country's foreign competitors can lower their production costs more rapidly than the country's own manufacturers can, then their foreign competitors must have adopted new manufacturing techniques.

(D) If a country's manufacturers adopt new technologies at the same rate as their foreign competitors, neither group will be able to squeeze the other out of the global market.

(E) If a country's manufacturers can lower their prices as rapidly as their foreign competitors can, this shows that they adopt new technology at least as fast as their foreign competitors do.

S T O P

IF YOU FINISH BEFORE TIME IS CALLED, YOU MAY CHECK YOUR WORK ON THIS SECTION ONLY.
DO NOT WORK ON ANY OTHER SECTION IN THE TEST.

SECTION IV
Time—35 minutes
24 Questions

Directions: Each group of questions in this section is based on a set of conditions. In answering some of the questions, it may be useful to draw a rough diagram. Choose the response that most accurately and completely answers each question and blacken the corresponding space on your answer sheet.

Questions 1–6

A professor will listen to exactly one speech from each of six students—H, J, K, R, S, and T. The six speeches will be delivered one at a time, consecutively, according to the following conditions:

The speeches delivered by H, J, and K, no matter what their order relative to each other, cannot form a sequence of three consecutive speeches.

The speeches delivered by R, S, and T, no matter what their order relative to each other, cannot form a sequence of three consecutive speeches.

H's speech must be earlier than S's speech.

J's speech can be neither first nor sixth.

T's speech can be neither immediately before nor immediately after J's speech.

1. Which one of the following could be the order, from first to last, in which the students deliver their speeches?

    (A) H, J, R, S, T, K
    (B) H, R, T, K, S, J
    (C) K, J, T, H, S, R
    (D) R, J, K, T, H, S
    (E) T, R, J, S, K, H

2. If T delivers the third speech, which one of the following must be true?

    (A) H delivers the first speech.
    (B) J delivers the fifth speech.
    (C) K delivers the fourth speech.
    (D) R delivers the sixth speech.
    (E) S delivers the fourth speech.

3. If S delivers the third speech and T delivers the fourth speech, then which one of the following must be true?

    (A) H delivers the second speech.
    (B) J delivers the fifth speech.
    (C) K delivers the fifth speech.
    (D) K delivers the first speech.
    (E) R delivers the first speech.

4. If K delivers the first speech and H delivers the fifth speech, which one of the following must be true?

    (A) R delivers the third speech.
    (B) T delivers the fourth speech.
    (C) J's speech is immediately before H's speech.
    (D) K's speech is immediately before T's speech.
    (E) R's speech is immediately before J's speech.

5. If R's speech is immediately after S's speech and immediately before K's speech, then which one of the following could be true?

    (A) H's speech is immediately before S's speech.
    (B) H's speech is immediately before T's speech.
    (C) K's speech is immediately before J's speech.
    (D) K's speech is immediately before T's speech.
    (E) T's speech is immediately before S's speech.

6. If K delivers the third speech, any of the following could be the student who makes the fourth speech EXCEPT

    (A) H
    (B) J
    (C) R
    (D) S
    (E) T

GO ON TO THE NEXT PAGE.

Questions 7–13

The country of Zendu contains exactly four areas for radar detection: R, S, T, and U. Each detection area is circular and falls completely within Zendu. Part of R intersects T; part of S also intersects T; R does not intersect S. Area U is completely within R and also completely within T. At noon exactly four planes—J, K, L, M—are over Zendu, in a manner consistent with the following statements:

Each plane is in at least one of the four areas.
J is in area S.
K is not in any detection area that J is in.
L is not in any detection area that M is in.
M is in exactly one of the areas.

7. Which one of the following could be a complete listing of the planes located in the four areas at noon, with each plane listed in every area in which it is located?

(A) R: J, L;   S: J, M;   T: L;   U: L
(B) R: J, L;   S: K;   T: M;   U: none
(C) R: K;   S: J;   T: L;   U: M
(D) R: K, M;   S: J, L;   T: J;   U: none
(E) R: M;   S: J, K;   T: J, L;   U: none

8. If at noon K is within exactly two of the four areas, then which one of the following CANNOT be true at that time?

(A) J is within area T.
(B) K is within area R.
(C) K is within area T.
(D) L is within area R.
(E) L is within area T.

9. Which one of the following is a complete and accurate list of those planes any one of which could be within area T at noon?

(A) M
(B) J, L
(C) J, L, M
(D) K, L, M
(E) J, K, L, M

10. Which one of the following statements CANNOT be true at noon about the planes?

(A) K is within area T.
(B) K is within area U.
(C) L is within area R.
(D) M is within area R.
(E) M is within area U.

11. It CANNOT be true that at noon there is at least one plane that is within both area

(A) R and area T
(B) R and area U
(C) S and area T
(D) S and area U
(E) T and area U

12. If at noon M is within area T, then which one of the following statements CANNOT be true at that time?

(A) J is within area T.
(B) L is within area R.
(C) L is within area S.
(D) K is within exactly two areas.
(E) L is within exactly two areas.

13. If at noon plane L is within exactly three of the areas, which one of the following could be true at that time?

(A) J is within exactly two of the areas.
(B) J is within exactly three of the areas.
(C) K is within area S.
(D) M is within area R.
(E) M is within area T.

GO ON TO THE NEXT PAGE.

Questions 14–19

Four people—Fritz, Gina, Helen, and Jerry—have formed a car pool to commute to work together six days a week from Monday through Saturday. Each day exactly one of the people drives. The schedule of the car pool's drivers for any given week must meet the following conditions:

Each person drives on at least one day.
No person drives on two consecutive days.
Fritz does not drive on Monday.
Jerry drives on Wednesday or Saturday or both, and he may also drive on other days.
If Gina drives on Monday, then Jerry does not drive on Saturday.

14. Which one of the following could be the schedule of drivers for one week, for the days Monday through Saturday, respectively?

   (A) Gina, Fritz, Jerry, Helen, Gina, Gina
   (B) Gina, Fritz, Jerry, Helen, Fritz, Jerry
   (C) Helen, Fritz, Gina, Jerry, Helen, Fritz
   (D) Helen, Gina, Jerry, Fritz, Helen, Fritz
   (E) Helen, Gina, Jerry, Helen, Jerry, Gina

15. Which one of the following could be true of one week's schedule of drivers?

   (A) Fritz drives on both Wednesday and Saturday.
   (B) Gina drives on both Monday and Wednesday.
   (C) Jerry drives on both Tuesday and Friday.
   (D) Gina drives on Monday and Jerry drives on Thursday.
   (E) Jerry drives on Wednesday and Gina drives on Saturday.

16. If during one week Jerry drives on Wednesday and Saturday only, which one of the following must be true of that week?

   (A) Fritz drives on Tuesday.
   (B) Gina drives on Friday.
   (C) Helen drives on Monday.
   (D) Fritz drives on exactly two days.
   (E) Helen drives on exactly two days.

17. If during one week Gina drives on Monday and Saturday only, which one of the following must be true of that week?

   (A) One other person besides Gina drives on exactly two days.
   (B) The person who drives on Wednesday does not drive on Friday.
   (C) Helen drives on a day immediately before a day on which Fritz drives.
   (D) Either Fritz or Helen drives on Friday.
   (E) Either Helen or Jerry drives on Tuesday.

18. Which one of the following CANNOT be true of one week's schedule of drivers?

   (A) Fritz drives on Tuesday and Gina drives on Friday.
   (B) Gina drives on Monday and Jerry drives on Tuesday.
   (C) Gina drives on Monday and Jerry drives on Friday.
   (D) Helen drives on Monday and Jerry drives on Tuesday.
   (E) Helen drives on Tuesday and Jerry drives on Friday.

19. If during one week Fritz drives exactly twice but he drives on neither Tuesday nor Wednesday, which one of the following could be true of that week?

   (A) One person drives exactly three times during the week.
   (B) Three people drive exactly one time each during the week.
   (C) Jerry drives on no day that is immediately before a day on which Fritz drives.
   (D) Gina drives on Wednesday.
   (E) Jerry drives on Friday.

GO ON TO THE NEXT PAGE.

Questions 20–24

Five experienced plumbers—Frank, Gene, Jill, Kathy, and Mark—and four inexperienced plumbers—Roberta, Sally, Tim, and Vernon—must decide which of them will be assigned to four work teams of exactly two plumbers each. Assignments must meet the following restrictions:

Each plumber is assigned to at most one team.

At least one plumber on each team must be experienced.

Neither Mark nor Roberta nor Vernon can be assigned to a team with Frank.

If Tim is assigned to a team, either Gene or Kathy must be assigned to that team.

Jill cannot be assigned to a team with Roberta.

20. Which one of the following is an inexperienced plumber who can be assigned to a team with Frank?

   (A) Kathy
   (B) Roberta
   (C) Sally
   (D) Tim
   (E) Vernon

21. Which one of the following is a pair of plumbers who can be assigned together to a team?

   (A) Frank and Roberta
   (B) Frank and Vernon
   (C) Jill and Mark
   (D) Roberta and Tim
   (E) Sally and Vernon

22. If Tim is assigned to a team, and if Sally is assigned to a team with a plumber who could have been assigned to a team with Tim, then the only plumber with whom Frank could be assigned to a team is

   (A) Gene
   (B) Jill
   (C) Mark
   (D) Roberta
   (E) Vernon

23. If Gene is not assigned to a team, then Jill must be assigned to a team with

   (A) Vernon
   (B) Tim
   (C) Mark
   (D) Kathy
   (E) Frank

24. If all of the inexperienced plumbers are assigned to teams, and neither Roberta nor Tim nor Vernon is assigned to a team with Gene, then Sally must be assigned to a team with either

   (A) Frank or else Gene
   (B) Frank or else Mark
   (C) Gene or else Mark
   (D) Jill or else Kathy
   (E) Jill or else Mark

S T O P

IF YOU FINISH BEFORE TIME IS CALLED, YOU MAY CHECK YOUR WORK ON THIS SECTION ONLY.
DO NOT WORK ON ANY OTHER SECTION IN THE TEST.

LSAT® Writing Sample Topic

Coach Mineko Sato is choosing members of her team to form a squad that will compete in this year's Big Basin International Games. Each squad member will compete in one event, and the overall prize goes to the squad whose members win the most events. With four of the five squad members chosen, Coach Sato is selecting a skier to compete in the 10K cross-country event. Write an argument supporting one of two candidates over the other based on the following criteria:

- To win the overall prize, Coach Sato needs a skier who is likely to win the 10K event.
- Coach Sato wants a skier who will provide leadership and inspire the squad to work well together.

One of cross-country skiing's all-time greats, Andrea Anderson, has won the 10K event at the Big Basin games for four straight years, twice setting a new world record. Shortly after last year's games, Anderson suffered a serious knee injury that has hampered her performance for most of this season, although a team physician has predicted that her knee will be fully healed in time for the Big Basin games three months from now. Anderson is both outgoing and outspoken. Her vivid sense of humor and high energy have made her popular with teammates, yet several times in the last year she received bad press for publicly criticizing a teammate.

Undefeated so far this season, Bettina Schmidt is viewed by many as cross-country skiing's next great champion. Schmidt's recent achievements include her first-ever defeat of Anderson, a goal that had eluded her for several years. She performs best on hilly, winding courses like the one at Big Basin. She recently missed several team meetings, claiming that her time was better spent working out, and she rarely joins in the team's social activities. Her teammates, nonetheless, admire her skill and drive, and she is known for her encouragement during competition, especially when someone on the team suffers a difficulty or setback.

Directions:

1. Use the Answer Key on the next page to check your answers.

2. Use the Scoring Worksheet below to compute your raw score.

3. Use the Score Conversion Chart to convert your raw score into the 120-180 scale.

Scoring Worksheet

1. Enter the number of questions you answered correctly in each section.

	Number Correct
SECTION I	_____
SECTION II	_____
SECTION III	_____
SECTION IV	_____

2. Enter the sum here: _____
   This is your Raw Score.

Conversion Chart

For Converting Raw Score to the 120-180 LSAT Scaled Score
LSAT Form 6LSS27

Reported Score	Raw Score Lowest	Raw Score Highest
180	100	101
179	99	99
178	–*	–*
177	98	98
176	97	97
175	–*	–*
174	96	96
173	95	95
172	94	94
171	93	93
170	92	92
169	91	91
168	89	90
167	88	88
166	87	87
165	85	86
164	84	84
163	82	83
162	80	81
161	78	79
160	77	77
159	75	76
158	73	74
157	71	72
156	69	70
155	67	68
154	65	66
153	63	64
152	61	62
151	59	60
150	57	58
149	55	56
148	54	54
147	52	53
146	50	51
145	48	49
144	46	47
143	44	45
142	43	43
141	41	42
140	39	40
139	38	38
138	36	37
137	35	35
136	33	34
135	32	32
134	30	31
133	29	29
132	28	28
131	26	27
130	25	25
129	24	24
128	23	23
127	22	22
126	21	21
125	20	20
124	19	19
123	–*	–*
122	18	18
121	17	17
120	0	16

*There is no raw score that will produce this scaled score for this form.

SECTION I

1.	C	8.	E	15.	B	22.	E
2.	A	9.	E	16.	C	23.	B
3.	D	10.	C	17.	C	24.	C
4.	A	11.	B	18.	D	25.	C
5.	D	12.	A	19.	B	26.	A
6.	B	13.	A	20.	D	27.	D
7.	B	14.	D	21.	A		

SECTION II

1.	A	8.	A	15.	C	22.	E
2.	D	9.	E	16.	E	23.	B
3.	E	10.	C	17.	D	24.	A
4.	D	11.	E	18.	B		
5.	A	12.	C	19.	A		
6.	B	13.	E	20.	A		
7.	B	14.	B	21.	E		

SECTION III

1.	B	8.	A	15.	B	22.	C
2.	E	9.	B	16.	C	23.	E
3.	C	10.	B	17.	A	24.	C
4.	A	11.	C	18.	A	25.	D
5.	B	12.	E	19.	A	26.	E
6.	E	13.	A	20.	B		
7.	B	14.	C	21.	D		

SECTION IV

1.	D	8.	A	15.	E	22.	B
2.	B	9.	E	16.	C	23.	A
3.	C	10.	E	17.	A	24.	A
4.	A	11.	D	18.	B		
5.	D	12.	E	19.	E		
6.	A	13.	A	20.	C		
7.	D	14.	D	21.	C		

The Official LSAT PrepTest

16

- September 1995
- Form 4LSS25

The sample test that follows consists of four sections corresponding to the four scored sections of the September 1995 LSAT.

1

SECTION I
Time—35 minutes
24 Questions

Directions: Each group of questions in this section is based on a set of conditions. In answering some of the questions, it may be useful to draw a rough diagram. Choose the response that most accurately and completely answers each question and blacken the corresponding space on your answer sheet.

Questions 1–6

Eight new students—R, S, T, V, W, X, Y, Z—are being divided among exactly three classes—class 1, class 2, and class 3. Classes 1 and 2 will gain three new students each; class 3 will gain two new students. The following restrictions apply:

  R must be added to class 1.
  S must be added to class 3.
  Neither S nor W can be added to the same class as Y.
  V cannot be added to the same class as Z.
  If T is added to class 1, Z must also be added to class 1.

1. Which one of the following is an acceptable assignment of students to the three classes?

	1	2	3
(A)	R, T, Y	V, W, X	S, Z
(B)	R, T, Z	S, V, Y	W, X
(C)	R, W, X	V, Y, Z	S, T
(D)	R, X, Z	T, V, Y	S, W
(E)	R, X, Z	V, W, Y	S, T

2. Which one of the following is a complete and accurate list of classes any one of which could be the class to which V is added?

(A) class 1
(B) class 3
(C) class 1, class 3
(D) class 2, class 3
(E) class 1, class 2, class 3

3. If X is added to class 1, which one of the following is a student who must be added to class 2 ?

(A) T
(B) V
(C) W
(D) Y
(E) Z

4. If X is added to class 3, each of the following is a pair of students who can be added to class 1 EXCEPT

(A) Y and Z
(B) W and Z
(C) V and Y
(D) V and W
(E) T and Z

5. If T is added to class 3, which one of the following is a student who must be added to class 2 ?

(A) V
(B) W
(C) X
(D) Y
(E) Z

6. Which one of the following must be true?

(A) If T and X are added to class 2, V is added to class 3.
(B) If V and W are added to class 1, T is added to class 3.
(C) If V and W are added to class 1, Z is added to class 3.
(D) If V and X are added to class 1, W is added to class 3.
(E) If Y and Z are added to class 2, X is added to class 2.

GO ON TO THE NEXT PAGE.

Questions 7–12

Four lions—F, G, H, J—and two tigers—K and M—will be assigned to exactly six stalls, one animal per stall. The stalls are arranged as follows:

First Row: 1   2   3

Second Row: 4   5   6

The only stalls that face each other are stalls 1 and 4, stalls 2 and 5, and stalls 3 and 6. The following conditions apply:

The tigers' stalls cannot face each other.
A lion must be assigned to stall 1.
H must be assigned to stall 6.
J must be assigned to a stall numbered one higher than K's stall.
K cannot be assigned to the stall that faces H's stall.

7. Which one of the following must be true?

   (A)   F is assigned to an even-numbered stall.
   (B)   F is assigned to stall 1.
   (C)   J is assigned to stall 2 or else stall 3.
   (D)   J is assigned to stall 3 or else stall 4.
   (E)   K is assigned to stall 2 or else stall 4.

8. Which one of the following could be true?

   (A)   F's stall is numbered one higher than J's stall.
   (B)   H's stall faces M's stall.
   (C)   J is assigned to stall 4.
   (D)   K's stall faces J's stall.
   (E)   K's stall is in a different row than J's stall.

9. Which one of the following must be true?

   (A)   A tiger is assigned to stall 2.
   (B)   A tiger is assigned to stall 5.
   (C)   K's stall is in a different row from M's stall.
   (D)   Each tiger is assigned to an even-numbered stall.
   (E)   Each lion is assigned to a stall that faces a tiger's stall.

10. If K's stall is in the same row as H's stall, which one of the following must be true?

    (A)   F's stall is in the same row as J's stall.
    (B)   F is assigned to a lower-numbered stall than G.
    (C)   G is assigned to a lower-numbered stall than M.
    (D)   G's stall faces H's stall.
    (E)   M's stall is in the same row as G's stall.

11. If J is assigned to stall 3, which one of the following could be true?

    (A)   F is assigned to stall 2.
    (B)   F is assigned to stall 4.
    (C)   G is assigned to stall 1.
    (D)   G is assigned to stall 4.
    (E)   M is assigned to stall 5.

12. Which one of the following must be true?

    (A)   A tiger is assigned to stall 2.
    (B)   A tiger is assigned to stall 4.
    (C)   A tiger is assigned to stall 5.
    (D)   A lion is assigned to stall 3.
    (E)   A lion is assigned to stall 4.

GO ON TO THE NEXT PAGE.

Questions 13–18

On an undeveloped street, a developer will simultaneously build four houses on one side, numbered consecutively 1, 3, 5, and 7, and four houses on the opposite side, numbered consecutively 2, 4, 6, and 8. Houses 2, 4, 6, and 8 will face houses 1, 3, 5, and 7, respectively. Each house will be exactly one of three styles—ranch, split-level, or Tudor—according to the following conditions:

    Adjacent houses are of different styles.
    No split-level house faces another split-level house.
    Every ranch house has at least one Tudor house adjacent to it.
    House 3 is a ranch house.
    House 6 is a split-level house.

13. Any of the following could be a Tudor house EXCEPT house

    (A) 1
    (B) 2
    (C) 4
    (D) 7
    (E) 8

14. If there is one ranch house directly opposite another ranch house, which one of the following could be true?

    (A) House 8 is a ranch house.
    (B) House 7 is a split-level house.
    (C) House 4 is a Tudor house.
    (D) House 2 is a split-level house.
    (E) House 1 is a ranch house.

15. If house 4 is a Tudor house, then it could be true that house

    (A) 1 is a Tudor house
    (B) 2 is a Tudor house
    (C) 5 is a ranch house
    (D) 7 is a Tudor house
    (E) 8 is a ranch house

16. On the street, there could be exactly

    (A) one ranch house
    (B) one Tudor house
    (C) two Tudor houses
    (D) four ranch houses
    (E) five ranch houses

17. If no house faces a house of the same style, then it must be true that house

    (A) 1 is a split-level house
    (B) 1 is a Tudor house
    (C) 2 is a ranch house
    (D) 2 is a split-level house
    (E) 4 is a Tudor house

18. If the condition requiring house 6 to be a split-level house is suspended but all other original conditions remain the same, then any of the following could be an accurate list of the styles of houses 2, 4, 6, and 8, respectively, EXCEPT:

    (A) ranch, split-level, ranch, Tudor
    (B) split-level, ranch, Tudor, split-level
    (C) split-level, Tudor, ranch, split-level
    (D) Tudor, ranch, Tudor, split-level
    (E) Tudor, split-level, ranch, Tudor

GO ON TO THE NEXT PAGE.

1   1   1

Questions 19–24

Within a tennis league each of five teams occupies one of five positions, numbered 1 through 5 in order of rank, with number 1 as the highest position. The teams are initially in the order R, J, S, M, L, with R in position 1. Teams change positions only when a lower-positioned team defeats a higher-positioned team. The rules are as follows:

    Matches are played alternately in odd-position rounds and in even-position rounds.

    In an odd-position round, teams in positions 3 and 5 play against teams positioned immediately above them.

    In an even-position round, teams in positions 2 and 4 play against teams positioned immediately above them.

    When a lower-positioned team defeats a higher-positioned team, the two teams switch positions after the round is completed.

19. Which one of the following could be the order of teams, from position 1 through position 5 respectively, after exactly one round of even-position matches if no odd-position round has yet been played?

    (A)   J, R, M, L, S
    (B)   J, R, S, L, M
    (C)   R, J, M, L, S
    (D)   R, J, M, S, L
    (E)   R, S, J, L, M

20. If exactly two rounds of matches have been played, beginning with an odd-position round, and if the lower-positioned teams have won every match in those two rounds, then each of the following must be true EXCEPT:

    (A)   L is one position higher than J.
    (B)   R is one position higher than L.
    (C)   S is one position higher than R.
    (D)   J is in position 4.
    (E)   M is in position 3.

21. Which one of the following could be true after exactly two rounds of matches have been played?

    (A)   J has won two matches.
    (B)   L has lost two matches.
    (C)   R has won two matches.
    (D)   L's only match was played against J.
    (E)   M played against S in two matches.

22. If after exactly three rounds of matches M is in position 4, and J and L have won all of their matches, then which one of the following can be true?

    (A)   J is in position 2.
    (B)   J is in position 3.
    (C)   L is in position 2.
    (D)   R is in position 1.
    (E)   S is in position 3.

23. If after exactly three rounds M has won three matches and the rankings of the other four teams relative to each other remain the same, then which one of the following must be in position 3 ?

    (A)   J
    (B)   L
    (C)   M
    (D)   R
    (E)   S

24. If after exactly three rounds the teams, in order from first to fifth position, are R, J, L, S, and M, then which one of the following could be the order, from first to fifth position, of the teams after the second round?

    (A)   J, R, M, S, L
    (B)   J, L, S, M, R
    (C)   R, J, S, L, M
    (D)   R, L, M, S, J
    (E)   R, M, L, S, J

S T O P

IF YOU FINISH BEFORE TIME IS CALLED, YOU MAY CHECK YOUR WORK ON THIS SECTION ONLY.
DO NOT WORK ON ANY OTHER SECTION IN THE TEST.

SECTION II
Time—35 minutes
24 Questions

Directions: The questions in this section are based on the reasoning contained in brief statements or passages. For some questions, more than one of the choices could conceivably answer the question. However, you are to choose the best answer; that is, the response that most accurately and completely answers the question. You should not make assumptions that are by commonsense standards implausible, superfluous, or incompatible with the passage. After you have chosen the best answer, blacken the corresponding space on your answer sheet.

1. The city's center for disease control reports that the rabies epidemic is more serious now than it was two years ago: two years ago less than 25 percent of the local raccoon population was infected, whereas today the infection has spread to more than 50 percent of the raccoon population. However, the newspaper reports that whereas two years ago 32 cases of rabid raccoons were confirmed during a 12-month period, in the past 12 months only 18 cases of rabid raccoons were confirmed.

Which one of the following, if true, most helps to resolve the apparent discrepancy between the two reports?

(A) The number of cases of rabies in wild animals other than raccoons has increased in the past 12 months.
(B) A significant proportion of the raccoon population succumbed to rabies in the year before last.
(C) The symptoms of distemper, another disease to which raccoons are susceptible, are virtually identical to those of rabies.
(D) Since the outbreak of the epidemic, raccoons, which are normally nocturnal, have increasingly been seen during daylight hours.
(E) The number of confirmed cases of rabid raccoons in neighboring cities has also decreased over the past year.

2. Recently, reviewers of patent applications decided against granting a patent to a university for a genetically engineered mouse developed for laboratory use in studying cancer. The reviewers argued that the mouse was a new variety of animal and that rules governing the granting of patents specifically disallow patents for new animal varieties.

Which one of the following, if true, most weakens the patent reviewers' argument?

(A) The restrictions the patent reviewers cited pertain only to domesticated farm animals.
(B) The university's application for a patent for the genetically engineered mouse was the first such patent application made by the university.
(C) The patent reviewers had reached the same decision on all previous patent requests for new animal varieties.
(D) The patent reviewers had in the past approved patents for genetically engineered plant varieties.
(E) The patent reviewers had previously decided against granting patents for new animal varieties that were developed through conventional breeding programs rather than through genetic engineering.

GO ON TO THE NEXT PAGE.

Questions 3–4

Although water in deep aquifers does not contain disease-causing bacteria, when public water supplies are drawn from deep aquifers, chlorine is often added to the water as a disinfectant because contamination can occur as a result of flaws in pipes or storage tanks. Of 50 municipalities that all pumped water from the same deep aquifer, 30 chlorinated their water and 20 did not. The water in all of the municipalities met the regional government's standards for cleanliness, yet the water supplied by the 20 municipalities that did not chlorinate had less bacterial contamination than the water supplied by the municipalities that added chlorine.

3. Which one of the following can properly be concluded from the information given above?

(A) A municipality's initial decision whether or not to use chlorine is based on the amount of bacterial contamination in the water source.

(B) Water in deep aquifers does not contain any bacteria of any kind.

(C) Where accessible, deep aquifers are the best choice as a source for a municipal water supply.

(D) The regional government's standards allow some bacteria in municipal water supplies.

(E) Chlorine is the least effective disinfecting agent.

4. Which one of the following, if true, most helps explain the difference in bacterial contamination in the two groups of municipalities?

(A) Chlorine is considered by some experts to be dangerous to human health, even in the small concentrations used in municipal water supplies.

(B) When municipalities decide not to chlorinate their water supplies, it is usually because their citizens have voiced objections to the taste and smell of chlorine.

(C) The municipalities that did not add chlorine to their water supplies also did not add any of the other available water disinfectants, which are more expensive than chlorine.

(D) Other agents commonly added to public water supplies, such as fluoride and sodium hydroxide, were not used by any of the 50 municipalities.

(E) Municipalities that do not chlorinate their water supplies are subject to stricter regulation by the regional government in regard to pipes and water tanks than are municipalities that use chlorine.

5. The population of songbirds throughout England has decreased in recent years. Many people explain this decrease as the result of an increase during the same period in the population of magpies, which eat the eggs and chicks of songbirds.

Which one of the following, if true, argues most strongly against the explanation reported in the passage?

(A) Official records of the population of birds in England have been kept for only the past 30 years.

(B) The number of eggs laid yearly by a female songbird varies widely according to the songbird's species.

(C) Although the overall population of magpies has increased, in most areas of England in which the songbird population has decreased, the number of magpies has remained stable.

(D) The population of magpies has increased because farmers no longer shoot or trap magpies to any great extent, though farmers still consider magpies to be pests.

(E) Although magpies eat the eggs and chicks of songbirds, magpies' diets consist of a wide variety of other foods as well.

6. The introduction of symbols for numbers is an event lost in prehistory, but the earliest known number symbols, in the form of simple grooves and scratches on bones and stones, date back 20,000 years or more. Nevertheless, since it was not until 5,500 years ago that systematic methods for writing numerals were invented, it was only then that any sort of computation became possible.

Which one of the following is an assumption on which the argument relies?

(A) Grooves and scratches found on bones and stones were all made by people, and none resulted from natural processes.

(B) Some kinds of surfaces upon which numeric symbols could have been made in the period before 5,500 years ago were not used for that purpose.

(C) Grooves and scratches inscribed on bones and stones do not date back to the time of the earliest people.

(D) Computation of any sort required a systematic method for writing numerals.

(E) Systematic methods for writing numerals were invented only because the need for computation arose.

GO ON TO THE NEXT PAGE.

7. Politician: Now that we are finally cleaning up the industrial pollution in the bay, we must start making the bay more accessible to the public for recreational purposes.

   Reporter: But if we increase public access to the bay, it will soon become polluted again.

   Politician: Not true. The public did not have access to the bay, and it got polluted. Therefore, if and when the public is given access to the bay, it will not get polluted.

   Which one of the following most closely parallels the flawed pattern of reasoning in the politician's reply to the reporter?

   (A) If there had been a full moon last night, the tide would be higher than usual today. Since the tide is no higher than usual, there must not have been a full moon last night.

   (B) The detective said that whoever stole the money would be spending it conspicuously by now. Jones is spending money conspicuously, so he must be the thief.

   (C) When prisoners convicted of especially violent crimes were kept in solitary confinement, violence in the prisons increased. Therefore, violence in the prisons will not increase if such prisoners are allowed to mix with fellow prisoners.

   (D) To get a driver's license, one must pass a written test. Smith passed the written test, so she must have gotten a driver's license.

   (E) In order to like abstract art, you have to understand it. Therefore, in order to understand abstract art, you have to like it.

8. Because learned patterns of behavior, such as the association of a green light with "go" or the expectation that switches will flip up for "on," become deeply ingrained, designers should make allowances for that fact, in order not to produce machines that are inefficient or dangerous.

   In which one of the following situations is the principle expressed most clearly violated?

   (A) Manufacturers have refused to change the standard order of letters on the typewriter keyboard even though some people who have never learned to type find this arrangement of letters bewildering.

   (B) Government regulations require that crucial instruments in airplane cockpits be placed in exactly the same array in all commercial aircraft.

   (C) Automobile manufacturers generally design for all of their automobiles a square or oblong ignition key and a round or oval luggage compartment key.

   (D) The only traffic signs that are triangular in shape are "yield" signs.

   (E) On some tape recorders the "start" button is red and the "stop" button is yellow.

9. From 1973 to 1989 total energy use in this country increased less than 10 percent. However, the use of electrical energy in this country during this same period grew by more than 50 percent, as did the gross national product—the total value of all goods and services produced in the nation.

   If the statements above are true, then which one of the following must also be true?

   (A) Most of the energy used in this country in 1989 was electrical energy.

   (B) From 1973 to 1989 there was a decline in the use of energy other than electrical energy in this country.

   (C) From 1973 to 1989 there was an increase in the proportion of energy use in this country that consisted of electrical energy use.

   (D) In 1989 electrical energy constituted a larger proportion of the energy used to produce the gross national product than did any other form of energy.

   (E) In 1973 the electrical energy that was produced constituted a smaller proportion of the gross national product than did all other forms of energy combined.

10. A fundamental illusion in robotics is the belief that improvements in robots will liberate humanity from "hazardous and demeaning work." Engineers are designing only those types of robots that can be properly maintained with the least expensive, least skilled human labor possible. Therefore, robots will not eliminate demeaning work—only substitute one type of demeaning work for another.

    The reasoning in the argument is most vulnerable to the criticism that it

    (A) ignores the consideration that in a competitive business environment some jobs might be eliminated if robots are not used in the manufacturing process

    (B) assumes what it sets out to prove, that robots create demeaning work

    (C) does not specify whether or not the engineers who design robots consider their work demeaning

    (D) attempts to support its conclusion by an appeal to the emotion of fear, which is often experienced by people faced with the prospect of losing their jobs to robots

    (E) fails to address the possibility that the amount of demeaning work eliminated by robots might be significantly greater than the amount they create

GO ON TO THE NEXT PAGE.

11. If the needle on an industrial sewing machine becomes badly worn, the article being sewn can be ruined. In traditional apparel factories, the people who operate the sewing machines monitor the needles and replace those that begin to wear out. Industrial sewing operations are becoming increasingly automated, however, and it would be inefficient for a factory to hire people for the sole purpose of monitoring needles. Therefore a sophisticated new acoustic device that detects wear in sewing machine needles is expected to become standard equipment in the automated apparel factories of the future.

Which one of the following is most strongly supported by the information above?

(A) In automated apparel factories, items will be ruined by faulty needles less frequently than happens in traditional apparel factories.

(B) In the automated apparel factories of the future, each employee will perform only one type of task.

(C) Traditional apparel factories do not use any automated equipment.

(D) The needles of industrial sewing machines wear out at unpredictable rates.

(E) As sewing machine needles become worn, the noise they make becomes increasingly loud.

Questions 12–13

Alexander: The chemical waste dump outside our town should be cleaned up immediately. Admittedly, it will be very costly to convert that site into woodland, but we have a pressing obligation to redress the harm we have done to local forests and wildlife.

Teresa: But our town's first priority is the health of its people. So even if putting the dump there was environmentally disastrous, we should not spend our resources on correcting it unless it presents a significant health hazard to people. If it does, then we only need to remove that hazard.

12. Teresa's statement most closely conforms to which one of the following principles?

(A) Environmental destruction should be redressed only if it is in the economic interest of the community to do so.

(B) Resources should be allocated only to satisfy goals that have the highest priority.

(C) No expense should be spared in protecting the community's health.

(D) Environmental hazards that pose slight health risks to people should be rectified if the technology is available to do so.

(E) It is the community as a whole that should evaluate the importance of eliminating various perceived threats to public health.

13. Which one of the following is the point at issue between Alexander and Teresa?

(A) whether the maintenance of a chemical waste dump inflicts significant damage on forests and wildlife

(B) whether it is extremely costly to clean up a chemical waste dump in order to replace it by a woodland

(C) whether the public should be consulted in determining the public health risk posed by a chemical waste dump

(D) whether the town has an obligation to redress damage to local forests and wildlife if that damage poses no significant health hazard to people

(E) whether destroying forests and wildlife in order to establish a chemical waste dump amounts to an environmental disaster

GO ON TO THE NEXT PAGE.

14. In 1980, Country A had a per capita gross domestic product (GDP) that was $5,000 higher than that of the European Economic Community. By 1990, the difference, when adjusted for inflation, had increased to $6,000. Since a rising per capita GDP indicates a rising average standard of living, the average standard of living in Country A must have risen between 1980 and 1990.

Which one of the following is an assumption on which the argument depends?

(A) Between 1980 and 1990, Country A and the European Economic Community experienced the same percentage increase in population.
(B) Between 1980 and 1990, the average standard of living in the European Economic Community fell.
(C) Some member countries of the European Economic Community had, during the 1980s, a higher average standard of living than Country A.
(D) The per capita GDP of the European Economic Community was not lower by more than $1,000 in 1990 than it had been in 1980.
(E) In 1990, no member country of the European Economic Community had a per capita GDP higher than that of Country A.

15. Municipal officials originally estimated that it would be six months before municipal road crews could complete repaving a stretch of road. The officials presumed that private contractors could not finish any sooner. However, when the job was assigned to a private contractor, it was completed in just 28 days.

Which one of the following, if true, does most to resolve the discrepancy between the time estimated for completion of the repaving job, and the actual time taken by the private contractor?

(A) Road repaving work can only be done in the summer months of June, July, and August.
(B) The labor union contract for road crews employed by both municipal agencies and private contractors stipulates that employees can work only eight hours a day, five days a week, before being paid overtime.
(C) Many road-crew workers for private contractors have previously worked for municipal road crews, and vice versa.
(D) Private contractors typically assign 25 workers to each road-repaving job site, whereas the number assigned to municipal road crews is usually 30.
(E) Municipal agencies must conduct a lengthy bidding process to procure supplies after repaving work is ordered and before they can actually start work, whereas private contractors can obtain supplies readily as needed.

16. Researchers in South Australia estimate changes in shark populations inhabiting local waters by monitoring what is termed the "catch per unit effort" (CPUE). The CPUE for any species of shark is the number of those sharks that commercial shark-fishing boats catch per hour for each kilometer of gill net set out in the water. Since 1973 the CPUE for a particular species of shark has remained fairly constant. Therefore, the population of that species in the waters around South Australia must be at approximately its 1973 level.

Which one of the following, if true, most seriously weakens the argument?

(A) The waters around South Australia are the only area in the world where that particular species of shark is found.
(B) The sharks that are the most profitable to catch are those that tend to remain in the same area of ocean year after year and not migrate far from where they were born.
(C) A significant threat to shark populations, in addition to commercial shark fishing, is "incidental mortality" that results from catching sharks in nets intended for other fish.
(D) Most of the quotas designed to protect shark populations limit the tonnage of sharks that can be taken and not the number of individual sharks.
(E) Since 1980 commercial shark-fishing boats have used sophisticated electronic equipment that enables them to locate sharks with greater accuracy.

GO ON TO THE NEXT PAGE.

Questions 17–18

Winston: The Public Transportation Authority (PTA) cannot fulfill its mandate to operate without a budget deficit unless it eliminates service during late-night periods of low ridership. Since the fares collected during these periods are less than the cost of providing the service, these cuts would reduce the deficit and should be made. Transit law prohibits unauthorized fare increases, and fare-increase authorization would take two years.

Ping: Such service cuts might cost the PTA more in lost fares than they would save in costs, for the PTA would lose those riders who leave home during the day but must return late at night. Thus the PTA would lose two fares, while realizing cost savings for only one leg of such trips.

17. The relationship of Ping's response to Winston's argument is that Ping's response

(A) carefully redefines a term used in Winston's argument

(B) questions Winston's proposal by raising considerations not addressed by Winston

(C) supplies a premise that could have been used as part of the support for Winston's argument

(D) introduces detailed statistical evidence that is more persuasive than that offered by Winston

(E) proposes a solution to the PTA's dilemma by contradicting Winston's conclusion

18. Which one of the following, if true, most strongly supports Ping's conclusion?

(A) Over 23 percent of the round trips made by PTA riders are either initiated or else completed during late-night periods.

(B) Reliable survey results show that over 43 percent of the PTA's riders oppose any cut in PTA services.

(C) The last time the PTA petitioned for a 15 percent fare increase, the petition was denied.

(D) The PTA's budget deficit is 40 percent larger this year than it was last year.

(E) The PTA's bus drivers recently won a new contract that guarantees them a significant cash bonus each time they work the late-night shifts.

19. The Volunteers for Literacy Program would benefit if Dolores takes Victor's place as director, since Dolores is far more skillful than Victor is at securing the kind of financial support the program needs and Dolores does not have Victor's propensity for alienating the program's most dedicated volunteers.

The pattern of reasoning in the argument above is most closely paralleled in which one of the following?

(A) It would be more convenient for Dominique to take a bus to school than to take the subway, since the bus stops closer to her house than does the subway and, unlike the subway, the bus goes directly to the school.

(B) Joshua's interest would be better served by taking the bus to get to his parent's house rather than by taking an airplane, since his primary concern is to travel as cheaply as possible and taking the bus is less expensive than going by airplane.

(C) Belinda will get to the concert more quickly by subway than by taxi, since the concert takes place on a Friday evening and on Friday evenings traffic near the concert hall is exceptionally heavy.

(D) Anita would benefit financially by taking the train to work rather than driving her car, since when she drives she has to pay parking fees and the daily fee for parking a car is higher than a round-trip train ticket.

(E) It would be to Fred's advantage to exchange his bus tickets for train tickets, since he needs to arrive at his meeting before any of the other participants and if he goes by bus at least one of the other participants will arrive first.

GO ON TO THE NEXT PAGE.

20. Students from outside the province of Markland, who in any given academic year pay twice as much tuition each as do students from Markland, had traditionally accounted for at least two-thirds of the enrollment at Central Markland College. Over the past 10 years academic standards at the college have risen, and the proportion of students who are not Marklanders has dropped to around 40 percent.

Which one of the following can be properly inferred from the statements above?

(A) If it had not been for the high tuition paid by students from outside Markland, the college could not have improved its academic standards over the past 10 years.

(B) If academic standards had not risen over the past 10 years, students who are not Marklanders would still account for at least two-thirds of the college's enrollment.

(C) Over the past 10 years, the number of students from Markland increased and the number of students from outside Markland decreased.

(D) Over the past 10 years, academic standards at Central Markland College have risen by more than academic standards at any other college in Markland.

(E) If the college's per capita revenue from tuition has remained the same, tuition fees have increased over the past 10 years.

21. Several years ago, as a measure to reduce the population of gypsy moths, which depend on oak leaves for food, entomologists introduced into many oak forests a species of fungus that is poisonous to gypsy moth caterpillars. Since then, the population of both caterpillars and adult moths has significantly declined in those areas. Entomologists have concluded that the decline is attributable to the presence of the poisonous fungus.

Which one of the following, if true, most strongly supports the conclusion drawn by the entomologists?

(A) A strain of gypsy moth whose caterpillars are unaffected by the fungus has increased its share of the total gypsy moth population.

(B) The fungus that was introduced to control the gypsy moth population is poisonous to few insect species other than the gypsy moth.

(C) An increase in numbers of both gypsy moth caterpillars and gypsy moth adults followed a drop in the number of some of the species that prey on the moths.

(D) In the past several years, air pollution and acid rain have been responsible for a substantial decline in oak tree populations.

(E) The current decline in the gypsy moth population in forests where the fungus was introduced is no greater than a decline that occurred concurrently in other forests.

22. Director of personnel: Ms. Tours has formally requested a salary adjustment on the grounds that she was denied merit raises to which she was entitled. Since such grounds provide a possible basis for adjustments, an official response is required. Ms. Tours presents compelling evidence that her job performance has been both excellent in itself and markedly superior to that of others in her department who were awarded merit raises. Her complaint that she was treated unfairly thus appears justified. Nevertheless, her request should be denied. To raise Ms. Tours's salary because of her complaint would jeopardize the integrity of the firm's merit-based reward system by sending the message that employees can get their salaries raised if they just complain enough.

The personnel director's reasoning is most vulnerable to criticism on the grounds that it

(A) fails to consider the possibility that Ms. Tours's complaint could be handled on an unofficial basis

(B) attempts to undermine the persuasiveness of Ms. Tours's evidence by characterizing it as "mere complaining"

(C) sidesteps the issue of whether superior job performance is a suitable basis for awarding salary increases

(D) ignores the possibility that some of the people who did receive merit increases were not entitled to them

(E) overlooks the implications for the integrity of the firm's merit-based reward system of denying Ms. Tours's request

GO ON TO THE NEXT PAGE.

23. **S:** People who are old enough to fight for their country are old enough to vote for the people who make decisions about war and peace. This government clearly regards 17 year olds as old enough to fight, so it should acknowledge their right to vote.

    T: Your argument is a good one only to the extent that fighting and voting are the same kind of activity. Fighting well requires strength, muscular coordination, and in a modern army, instant and automatic response to orders. Performed responsibly, voting, unlike fighting, is essentially a deliberative activity requiring reasoning power and knowledge of both history and human nature.

T responds to S's argument by

(A) citing evidence overlooked by S that would have supported S's conclusion

(B) calling into question S's understanding of the concept of rights

(C) showing that S has ignored the distinction between having a right to do something and having an obligation to do that thing

(D) challenging the truth of a claim on which S's conclusion is based

(E) arguing for a conclusion opposite to the one drawn by S

24. The role of the Uplandian supreme court is to protect all human rights against abuses of government power. Since the constitution of Uplandia is not explicit about all human rights, the supreme court must sometimes resort to principles outside the explicit provisions of the constitution in justifying its decisions. However, human rights will be subject to the whim of whoever holds judicial power unless the supreme court is bound to adhere to a single objective standard, namely, the constitution. Therefore, nothing but the explicit provisions of the constitution can be used to justify the court's decisions. Since these conclusions are inconsistent with each other, it cannot be true that the role of the Uplandian supreme court is to protect all human rights against abuses of government power.

The reasoning that leads to the conclusion that the first sentence in the passage is false is flawed because the argument

(A) ignores data that offer reasonable support for a general claim and focuses on a single example that argues against that claim

(B) seeks to defend a view on the grounds that the view is widely held and that decisions based on that view are often accepted as correct

(C) rejects a claim as false on the grounds that those who make that claim could profit if that claim is accepted by others

(D) makes an unwarranted assumption that what is true of each member of a group taken separately is also true of the group as a whole

(E) concludes that a particular premise is false when it is equally possible for that premise to be true and some other premise false

S T O P

IF YOU FINISH BEFORE TIME IS CALLED, YOU MAY CHECK YOUR WORK ON THIS SECTION ONLY.
DO NOT WORK ON ANY OTHER SECTION IN THE TEST.

SECTION III
Time—35 minutes

26 Questions

<u>Directions:</u> The questions in this section are based on the reasoning contained in brief statements or passages. For some questions, more than one of the choices could conceivably answer the question. However, you are to choose the <u>best</u> answer; that is, the response that most accurately and completely answers the question. You should not make assumptions that are by commonsense standards implausible, superfluous, or incompatible with the passage. After you have chosen the best answer, blacken the corresponding space on your answer sheet.

1. The painted spider spins webs that are much stickier than the webs spun by the other species of spiders that share the same habitat. Stickier webs are more efficient at trapping insects that fly into them. Spiders prey on insects by trapping them in their webs; therefore, it can be concluded that the painted spider is a more successful predator than its competitors.

    Which one of the following, if true, most seriously weakens the argument?

    (A) Not all of the species of insects living in the painted spider's habitat are flying insects.
    (B) Butterflies and moths, which can shed scales, are especially unlikely to be trapped by spider webs that are not very sticky.
    (C) Although the painted spider's venom does not kill insects quickly, it paralyzes them almost instantaneously.
    (D) Stickier webs reflect more light, and so are more visible to insects, than are less-sticky webs.
    (E) The webs spun by the painted spider are no larger than the webs spun by the other species of spiders in the same habitat.

2. Despite the best efforts of astronomers, no one has yet succeeded in exchanging messages with intelligent life on other planets or in other solar systems. In fact, no one has even managed to prove that any kind of extraterrestrial life exists. Thus, there is clearly no intelligent life anywhere but on Earth.

    The argument's reasoning is flawed because the argument

    (A) fails to consider that there might be extraterrestrial forms of intelligence that are not living beings
    (B) confuses an absence of evidence for a hypothesis with the existence of evidence against the hypothesis
    (C) interprets a disagreement over a scientific theory as a disproof of that theory
    (D) makes an inference that relies on the vagueness of the term "life"
    (E) relies on a weak analogy rather than on evidence to draw a conclusion

GO ON TO THE NEXT PAGE.

Questions 3–4

Bart: A mathematical problem that defied solution for hundreds of years has finally yielded to a supercomputer. The process by which the supercomputer derived the result is so complex, however, that no one can fully comprehend it. Consequently, the result is unacceptable.

Anne: In scientific research, if the results of a test can be replicated in other tests, the results are acceptable even though the way they were derived might not be fully understood. Therefore, if a mathematical result derived by a supercomputer can be reproduced by other supercomputers following the same procedure, it is acceptable.

3. Bart's argument requires which one of the following assumptions?

(A)   The mathematical result in question is unacceptable because it was derived with the use of a supercomputer.
(B)   For the mathematical result in question to be acceptable, there must be someone who can fully comprehend the process by which it was derived.
(C)   To be acceptable, the mathematical result in question must be reproduced on another supercomputer.
(D)   Making the mathematical result in question less complex would guarantee its acceptability.
(E)   The supercomputer cannot derive an acceptable solution to the mathematical problem in question.

4. The exchange between Bart and Anne most strongly supports the view that they disagree as to

(A)   whether a scientific result that has not been replicated can properly be accepted
(B)   whether the result that a supercomputer derives for a mathematical problem must be replicated on another supercomputer before it can be accepted
(C)   the criterion to be used for accepting a mathematical result derived by a supercomputer
(D)   the level of complexity of the process to which Bart refers in his statements
(E)   the relative complexity of mathematical problems as compared to scientific problems

5. It is commonly held among marketing experts that in a nonexpanding market a company's best strategy is to go after a bigger share of the market and that the best way to do this is to run comparative advertisements that emphasize weaknesses in the products of rivals. In the stagnant market for food oil, soybean-oil and palm-oil producers did wage a two-year battle with comparative advertisements about the deleterious effect on health of each other's products. These campaigns, however, had little effect on respective market shares; rather, they stopped many people from buying any edible oils at all.

The statements above most strongly support the conclusion that comparative advertisements

(A)   increase a company's market share in all cases in which that company's products are clearly superior to the products of rivals
(B)   should not be used in a market that is expanding or likely to expand
(C)   should under no circumstances be used as a retaliatory measure
(D)   carry the risk of causing a contraction of the market at which they are aimed
(E)   yield no long-term gains unless consumers can easily verify the claims made

6. Recent unexpectedly heavy rainfalls in the metropolitan area have filled the reservoirs and streams; water rationing, therefore, will not be necessary this summer.

Which one of the following, if true, most undermines the author's prediction?

(A)   Water rationing was imposed in the city in three of the last five years.
(B)   A small part of the city's water supply is obtained from deep underground water systems that are not reached by rainwater.
(C)   The water company's capacity to pump water to customers has not kept up with the increased demand created by population growth in the metropolitan area.
(D)   The long-range weather forecast predicts lower-than-average temperatures for this summer.
(E)   In most years the city receives less total precipitation in the summer than it receives in any other season.

GO ON TO THE NEXT PAGE.

7. John: In 80 percent of car accidents, the driver at fault was within five miles of home, so people evidently drive less safely near home than they do on long trips.

 Judy: But people do 80 percent of their driving within five miles of home.

How is Judy's response related to John's argument?

(A) It shows that the evidence that John presents, by itself, is not enough to prove his claim.
(B) It restates the evidence that John presents in different terms.
(C) It gives additional evidence that is needed by John to support his conclusion.
(D) It calls into question John's assumption that whenever people drive more than five miles from home they are going on a long trip.
(E) It suggests that John's conclusion is merely a restatement of his argument's premise.

8. Reasonable people adapt themselves to the world; unreasonable people persist in trying to adapt the world to themselves. Therefore, all progress depends on unreasonable people.

If all of the statements in the passage above are true, which one of the following statements must also be true?

(A) Reasonable people and unreasonable people are incompatible.
(B) If there are only reasonable people, there cannot be progress.
(C) If there are unreasonable people, there will be progress.
(D) Some unreasonable people are unable to bring about progress.
(E) Unreasonable people are more persistent than reasonable people.

9. Theater critic: The theater is in a dismal state. Audiences are sparse and revenue is down. Without the audience and the revenue, the talented and creative people who are the lifeblood of the theater are abandoning it. No wonder standards are deteriorating.

 Producer: It's not true that the theater is in decline. Don't you realize that your comments constitute a self-fulfilling prophecy? By publishing these opinions, you yourself are discouraging new audiences from emerging and new talent from joining the theater.

Which one of the following is a questionable technique employed by the producer in responding to the critic?

(A) focusing on the effects of the critic's evaluation rather than on its content
(B) accusing the critic of relying solely on opinion unsupported by factual evidence
(C) challenging the motives behind the critic's remarks rather than the remarks themselves
(D) relying on emphasis rather than on argument
(E) invoking authority in order to intimidate the critic

10. Michelangelo's sixteenth-century Sistine Chapel paintings are currently being restored. A goal of the restorers is to uncover Michelangelo's original work, and so additions made to Michelangelo's paintings by later artists are being removed. However, the restorers have decided to make one exception: to leave intact additions that were painted by da Volterra.

Which one of the following, if true, most helps to reconcile the restorers' decision with the goal stated in the passage?

(A) The restorers believe that da Volterra stripped away all previous layers of paint before he painted his own additions to the Sistine Chapel.
(B) Because da Volterra used a type of pigment that is especially sensitive to light, the additions to the Sistine Chapel that da Volterra painted have relatively muted colors.
(C) Da Volterra's additions were painted in a style that was similar to the style used by Michelangelo.
(D) Michelangelo is famous primarily for his sculptures and only secondarily for his paintings, whereas da Volterra is known exclusively for his paintings.
(E) Da Volterra's work is considered by certain art historians to be just as valuable as the work of some of the other artists who painted additions to Michelangelo's work.

11. A controversial program rewards prison inmates who behave particularly well in prison by giving them the chance to receive free cosmetic plastic surgery performed by medical students. The program is obviously morally questionable, both in its assumptions about what inmates might want and in its use of the prison population to train future surgeons. Putting these moral issues aside, however, the surgery clearly has a powerful rehabilitative effect, as is shown by the fact that, among recipients of the surgery, the proportion who are convicted of new crimes committed after release is only half that for the prison population as a whole.

A flaw in the reasoning of the passage is that it

(A) allows moral issues to be a consideration in presenting evidence about matters of fact
(B) dismisses moral considerations on the grounds that only matters of fact are relevant
(C) labels the program as "controversial" instead of discussing the issues that give rise to controversy
(D) asserts that the rehabilitation of criminals is not a moral issue
(E) relies on evidence drawn from a sample that there is reason to believe is unrepresentative

GO ON TO THE NEXT PAGE.

12. The retina scanner, a machine that scans the web of tiny blood vessels in the retina, stores information about the pattern formed by the blood vessels. This information allows it to recognize any pattern it has previously scanned. No two eyes have identical patterns of blood vessels in the retina. A retina scanner can therefore be used successfully to determine for any person whether it has ever scanned a retina of that person before.

The reasoning in the argument depends upon assuming that

(A) diseases of the human eye do not alter the pattern of blood vessels in the retina in ways that would make the pattern unrecognizable to the retina scanner

(B) no person has a different pattern of blood vessels in the retina of the left eye than in the retina of the right eye

(C) there are enough retina scanners to store information about every person's retinas

(D) the number of blood vessels in the human retina is invariant, although the patterns they form differ from person to person

(E) there is no person whose retinas have been scanned by two or more different retina scanners

13. There are just two ways a moon could have been formed from the planet around which it travels: either part of the planet's outer shell spun off into orbit around the planet or else a large object, such as a comet or meteoroid, struck the planet so violently that it dislodged a mass of material from inside the planet. Earth's moon consists primarily of materials different from those of the Earth's outer shell.

If the statements above are true, which one of the following, if also true, would most help to justify drawing the conclusion that Earth's moon was not formed from a piece of the Earth?

(A) The moons of some planets in Earth's solar system were not formed primarily from the planets' outer shells.

(B) Earth's moon consists primarily of elements that differ from those inside the Earth.

(C) Earth's gravity cannot have trapped a meteoroid and pulled it into its orbit as the Moon.

(D) The craters on the surface of Earth's moon show that it has been struck by many thousands of large meteoroids.

(E) Comets and large meteoroids normally move at very high speeds.

14. Caffeine can kill or inhibit the growth of the larvae of several species of insects. One recent experiment showed that tobacco hornworm larvae die when they ingest a preparation that consists, in part, of finely powdered tea leaves, which contain caffeine. This result is evidence for the hypothesis that the presence of non-negligible quantities of caffeine in various parts of many diverse species of plants is not accidental but evolved as a defense for those plants.

The argument assumes that

(A) caffeine-producing plants are an important raw material in the manufacture of commercial insecticides

(B) caffeine is stored in leaves and other parts of caffeine-producing plants in concentrations roughly equal to the caffeine concentration of the preparation fed to the tobacco hornworm larvae

(C) caffeine-producing plants grow wherever insect larvae pose a major threat to indigenous plants or once posed a major threat to the ancestors of those plants

(D) the tobacco plant is among the plant species that produce caffeine for their own defense

(E) caffeine-producing plants or their ancestors have at some time been subject to being fed upon by creatures sensitive to caffeine

15. The only plants in the garden were tulips, but they were tall tulips. So the only plants in the garden were tall plants.

Which one of the following exhibits faulty reasoning most similar to the faulty reasoning in the argument above?

(A) The only dogs in the show were poodles, and they were all black poodles. So all the dogs in the show were black.

(B) All the buildings on the block were tall. The only buildings on the block were office buildings and residential towers. So all the office buildings on the block were tall buildings.

(C) All the primates in the zoo were gorillas. The only gorillas in the zoo were small gorillas. Thus the only primates in the zoo were small primates.

(D) The only fruit in the kitchen was pears, but the pears were not ripe. Thus none of the fruit in the kitchen was ripe.

(E) All the grand pianos here are large. All the grand pianos here are heavy. Thus everything large is heavy.

GO ON TO THE NEXT PAGE.

16. Scientific research will be properly channeled whenever those who decide which research to fund give due weight to the scientific merits of all proposed research. But when government agencies control these funding decisions, political considerations play a major role in determining which research will be funded, and whenever political considerations play such a role, the inevitable result is that scientific research is not properly channeled.

Which one of the following can be properly inferred from the statements above?

(A) There is no proper role for political considerations to play in determining who will decide which scientific research to fund.
(B) It is inevitable that considerations of scientific merit will be neglected in decisions regarding the funding of scientific research.
(C) Giving political considerations a major role in determining which scientific research to fund is incompatible with giving proper weight to the scientific merits of proposed research.
(D) When scientific research is not properly channeled, governments tend to step in and take control of the process of choosing which research to fund.
(E) If a government does not control investment in basic scientific research, political consideration will inevitably be neglected in deciding which research to fund.

17. A new silencing device for domestic appliances operates by producing sound waves that cancel out the sound waves produced by the appliance. The device, unlike conventional silencers, actively eliminates the noise the appliance makes, and for that reason vacuum cleaners designed to incorporate the new device will operate with much lower electricity consumption than conventional vacuum cleaners.

Which one of the following, if true, most helps to explain why the new silencing device will make lower electricity consumption possible?

(A) Designers of vacuum cleaner motors typically have to compromise the motors' efficiency in order to reduce noise production.
(B) The device runs on electricity drawn from the appliance's main power supply.
(C) Conventional vacuum cleaners often use spinning brushes to loosen dirt in addition to using suction to remove dirt.
(D) Governmental standards for such domestic appliances as vacuum cleaners allow higher electricity consumption when vacuum cleaners are quieter.
(E) The need to incorporate silencers in conventional vacuum cleaners makes them heavier and less mobile than they might otherwise be.

18. Because dinosaurs were reptiles, scientists once assumed that, like all reptiles alive today, dinosaurs were cold-blooded. The recent discovery of dinosaur fossils in the northern arctic, however, has led a number of researchers to conclude that at least some dinosaurs might have been warm-blooded. These researchers point out that only warm-blooded animals could have withstood the frigid temperatures that are characteristic of arctic winters, whereas cold-blooded animals would have frozen to death in the extreme cold.

Which one of the following, if true, weakens the researchers' argument?

(A) Today's reptiles are generally confined to regions of temperate or even tropical climates.
(B) The fossils show the arctic dinosaurs to have been substantially smaller than other known species of dinosaurs.
(C) The arctic dinosaur fossils were found alongside fossils of plants known for their ability to withstand extremely cold temperatures.
(D) The number of fossils found together indicates herds of dinosaurs so large that they would need to migrate to find a continual food supply.
(E) Experts on prehistoric climatic conditions believe that winter temperatures in the prehistoric northern arctic were not significantly different from what they are today.

GO ON TO THE NEXT PAGE.

Questions 19–20

Maria: Calling any state totalitarian is misleading: it implies total state control of all aspects of life. The real world contains no political entity exercising literally total control over even one such aspect. This is because any system of control is inefficient, and, therefore, its degree of control is partial.

James: A one-party state that has tried to exercise control over most aspects of a society and that has, broadly speaking, managed to do so is totalitarian. Such a system's practical inefficiencies do not limit the aptness of the term, which does not describe a state's actual degree of control as much as it describes the nature of a state's ambitions.

19. Which one of the following most accurately expresses Maria's main conclusion?

(A) No state can be called totalitarian without inviting a mistaken belief.
(B) To be totalitarian, a state must totally control society.
(C) The degree of control exercised by a state is necessarily partial.
(D) No existing state currently has even one aspect of society under total control.
(E) Systems of control are inevitably inefficient.

20. James responds to Maria's argument by

(A) pointing out a logical inconsistency between two statements she makes in support of her argument
(B) offering an alternative explanation for political conditions she mentions
(C) rejecting some of the evidence she presents without challenging what she infers from it
(D) disputing the conditions under which a key term of her argument can be appropriately applied
(E) demonstrating that her own premises lead to a conclusion different from hers

21. The similarity between ichthyosaurs and fish is an example of convergence, a process by which different classes of organisms adapt to the same environment by independently developing one or more similar external body features. Ichthyosaurs were marine reptiles and thus do not belong to the same class of organisms as fish. However, ichthyosaurs adapted to their marine environment by converging on external body features similar to those of fish. Most strikingly, ichthyosaurs, like fish, had fins.

If the statements above are true, which one of the following is an inference that can be properly drawn on the basis of them?

(A) The members of a single class of organisms that inhabit the same environment must be identical in all their external body features.
(B) The members of a single class of organisms must exhibit one or more similar external body features that differentiate that class from all other classes of organisms.
(C) It is only as a result of adaptation to similar environments that one class of organisms develops external body features similar to those of another class of organisms.
(D) An organism does not necessarily belong to a class simply because the organism has one or more external body features similar to those of members of that class.
(E) Whenever two classes of organisms share the same environment, members of one class will differ from members of the other class in several external body features.

GO ON TO THE NEXT PAGE.

22. Further evidence bearing on Jamison's activities must have come to light. On the basis of previously available evidence alone, it would have been impossible to prove that Jamison was a party to the fraud, and Jamison's active involvement in the fraud has now been definitively established.

The pattern of reasoning exhibited in the argument above most closely parallels that exhibited in which one of the following?

(A) Smith must not have purchased his house within the last year. He is listed as the owner of that house on the old list of property owners, and anyone on the old list could not have purchased his or her property within the last year.

(B) Turner must not have taken her usual train to Nantes today. Had she done so, she could not have been in Nantes until this afternoon, but she was seen having coffee in Nantes at 11 o'clock this morning.

(C) Norris must have lied when she said that she had not authorized the investigation. There is no doubt that she did authorize it, and authorizing an investigation is not something anyone is likely to have forgotten.

(D) Waugh must have known that last night's class was canceled. Waugh was in the library yesterday, and it would have been impossible for anyone in the library not to have seen the cancellation notices.

(E) LaForte must have deeply resented being passed over for promotion. He maintains otherwise, but only someone who felt badly treated would have made the kind of remark LaForte made at yesterday's meeting.

23. Reporting on a civil war, a journalist encountered evidence that refugees were starving because the government would not permit food shipments to a rebel-held area. Government censors deleted all mention of the government's role in the starvation from the journalist's report, which had not implicated either nature or the rebels in the starvation. The journalist concluded that it was ethically permissible to file the censored report, because the journalist's news agency would precede it with the notice "Cleared by government censors."

Which one of the following ethical criteria, if valid, would serve to support the journalist's conclusion while placing the least constraint on the flow of reported information?

(A) It is ethical in general to report known facts but unethical to do so while omitting other known facts if the omitted facts would substantially alter an impression of a person or institution that would be congruent with the reported facts.

(B) In a situation of conflict, it is ethical to report known facts and unethical to fail to report known facts that would tend to exonerate one party to the conflict.

(C) In a situation of censorship, it is unethical to make any report if the government represented by the censor deletes from the report material unfavorable to that government.

(D) It is ethical in general to report known facts but unethical to make a report in a situation of censorship if relevant facts have been deleted by the censor, unless the recipient of the report is warned that censorship existed.

(E) Although it is ethical in general to report known facts, it is unethical to make a report from which a censor has deleted relevant facts, unless the recipient of the report is warned that there was censorship and the reported facts do not by themselves give a misleading impression.

GO ON TO THE NEXT PAGE.

24. A birth is more likely to be difficult when the mother is over the age of 40 than when she is younger. Regardless of the mother's age, a person whose birth was difficult is more likely to be ambidextrous than is a person whose birth was not difficult. Since other causes of ambidexterity are not related to the mother's age, there must be more ambidextrous people who were born to women over 40 than there are ambidextrous people who were born to younger women.

The argument is most vulnerable to which one of the following criticisms?

(A) It assumes what it sets out to establish.
(B) It overlooks the possibility that fewer children are born to women over 40 than to women under 40.
(C) It fails to specify what percentage of people in the population as a whole are ambidextrous.
(D) It does not state how old a child must be before its handedness can be determined.
(E) It neglects to explain how difficulties during birth can result in a child's ambidexterity.

Questions 25–26

The government has no right to tax earnings from labor. Taxation of this kind requires the laborer to devote a certain percentage of hours worked to earning money for the government. Thus, such taxation forces the laborer to work, in part, for another's purpose. Since involuntary servitude can be defined as forced work for another's purpose, just as involuntary servitude is pernicious, so is taxing earnings from labor.

25. The argument uses which one of the following argumentative techniques?

(A) deriving a general principle about the rights of individuals from a judgment concerning the obligations of governments
(B) inferring what will be the case merely from a description of what once was the case
(C) inferring that since two institutions are similar in one respect, they are similar in another respect
(D) citing the authority of an economic theory in order to justify a moral principle
(E) presupposing the inevitability of a hierarchical class system in order to oppose a given economic practice

26. Which one of the following is an error of reasoning committed by the argument?

(A) It ignores a difference in how the idea of forced work for another's purpose applies to the two cases.
(B) It does not take into account the fact that labor is taxed at different rates depending on income.
(C) It mistakenly assumes that all work is taxed.
(D) It ignores the fact that the government also taxes income from investment.
(E) It treats definitions as if they were matters of subjective opinion rather than objective facts about language.

S T O P

IF YOU FINISH BEFORE TIME IS CALLED, YOU MAY CHECK YOUR WORK ON THIS SECTION ONLY.
DO NOT WORK ON ANY OTHER SECTION IN THE TEST.

SECTION IV

Time—35 minutes

27 Questions

Three kinds of study have been performed on Byron. There is the biographical study—the very valuable examination of Byron's psychology and the events in his life; Escarpit's 1958 work is an example
(5) of this kind of study, and biographers to this day continue to speculate about Byron's life. Equally valuable is the study of Byron as a figure important in the history of ideas; Russell and Praz have written studies of this kind. Finally, there are
(10) studies that primarily consider Byron's poetry. Such literary studies are valuable, however, only when they avoid concentrating solely on analyzing the verbal shadings of Byron's poetry to the exclusion of any discussion of biographical considerations. A
(15) study with such a concentration would be of questionable value because Byron's poetry, for the most part, is simply not a poetry of subtle verbal meanings. Rather, on the whole, Byron's poems record the emotional pressure of certain moments
(20) in his life. I believe we cannot often read a poem of Byron's, as we often can one of Shakespeare's, without wondering what events or circumstances in his life prompted him to write it.

No doubt the fact that most of Byron's poems
(25) cannot be convincingly read as subtle verbal creations indicates that Byron is not a "great" poet. It must be admitted too that Byron's literary craftsmanship is irregular and often his temperament disrupts even his lax literary method
(30) (although the result, an absence of method, has a significant purpose: it functions as a rebuke to a cosmos that Byron feels he cannot understand). If Byron is not a "great" poet, his poetry is nonetheless of extraordinary interest to us because
(35) of the pleasure it gives us. Our main pleasure in reading Byron's poetry is the contact with a singular personality. Reading his work gives us illumination—self-understanding—after we have seen our weaknesses and aspirations mirrored in
(40) the personality we usually find in the poems. Anyone who thinks that this kind of illumination is not a genuine reason for reading a poet should think carefully about why we read Donne's sonnets.

It is Byron and Byron's idea of himself that hold
(45) his work together (and that enthralled early-nineteenth-century Europe). Different characters speak in his poems, but finally it is usually he himself who is speaking: a far cry from the impersonal poet Keats. Byron's poetry alludes to
(50) Greek and Roman myth in the context of

contemporary affairs, but his work remains generally of a piece because of his close presence in the poetry. In sum, the poetry is a shrewd personal performance, and to shut out Byron the man is to
(55) fabricate a work of pseudocriticism.

1. Which one of the following titles best expresses the main idea of the passage?

(A) An Absence of Method: Why Byron Is Not a "Great" Poet
(B) Byron: The Recurring Presence in Byron's Poetry
(C) Personality and Poetry: The Biographical Dimension of Nineteenth-Century Poetry
(D) Byron's Poetry: Its Influence on the Imagination of Early-Nineteenth-Century Europe
(E) Verbal Shadings: The Fatal Flaw of Twentieth-Century Literary Criticism

2. The author's mention of Russell and Praz serves primarily to

(A) differentiate them from one another
(B) contrast their conclusions about Byron with those of Escarpit
(C) point out the writers whose studies suggest a new direction for Byron scholarship
(D) provide examples of writers who have written one kind of study of Byron
(E) give credit to the writers who have composed the best studies of Byron

GO ON TO THE NEXT PAGE.

3. Which one of the following would the author most likely consider to be a valuable study of Byron?

(A) a study that compared Byron's poetic style with Keats' poetic style

(B) a study that argued that Byron's thought ought not to be analyzed in terms of its importance in the history of ideas

(C) a study that sought to identify the emotions felt by Byron at a particular time in his life

(D) a study in which a literary critic argues that the language of Byron's poetry was more subtle than that of Keats' poetry

(E) a study in which a literary critic drew on experiences from his or her own life

4. Which one of the following statements best describes the organization of the first paragraph of the passage?

(A) A generalization is made and then gradually refuted.

(B) A number of theories are discussed and then the author chooses the most convincing one.

(C) Several categories are mentioned and then one category is discussed in some detail.

(D) A historical trend is delineated and then a prediction about the future of the trend is offered.

(E) A classification is made and then a rival classification is substituted in its place.

5. The author mentions that "Byron's literary craftsmanship is irregular" (lines 27–28) most probably in order to

(A) contrast Byron's poetic skill with that of Shakespeare

(B) dismiss craftsmanship as a standard by which to judge poets

(C) offer another reason why Byron is not a "great" poet

(D) point out a negative consequence of Byron's belief that the cosmos is incomprehensible

(E) indicate the most-often-cited explanation of why Byron's poetry lacks subtle verbal nuances

6. According to the author, Shakespeare's poems differ from Byron's in that Shakespeare's poems

(A) have elicited a wider variety of responses from both literary critics and biographers

(B) are on the whole less susceptible to being read as subtle verbal creations

(C) do not grow out of, or are not motivated by, actual events or circumstances in the poet's life

(D) provide the attentive reader with a greater degree of illumination concerning his or her own weaknesses and aspirations

(E) can often be read without the reader's being curious about what biographical factors motivated the poet to write them

7. The author indicates which one of the following about biographers' speculation concerning Byron's life?

(A) Such speculation began in earnest with Escarpit's study.

(B) Such speculation continues today.

(C) Such speculation is less important than consideration of Byron's poetry.

(D) Such speculation has not given us a satisfactory sense of Byron's life.

(E) Such speculation has been carried out despite the objections of literary critics.

8. The passage supplies specific information that provides a definitive answer to which one of the following questions?

(A) What does the author consider to be the primary enjoyment derived from reading Byron?

(B) Who among literary critics has primarily studied Byron's poems?

(C) Which moments in Byron's life exerted the greatest pressure on his poetry?

(D) Has Byron ever been considered to be a "great" poet?

(E) Did Byron exert an influence on Europeans in the latter part of the nineteenth century?

GO ON TO THE NEXT PAGE.

The United States Supreme Court has not always resolved legal issues of concern to Native Americans in a manner that has pleased the Indian nations. Many of the Court's decisions have been
(5) products of political compromise that looked more to the temper of the times than to enduring principles of law. But accommodation is part of the judicial system in the United States, and judicial decisions must be assessed with this fact in mind.

(10) Despite the "accommodating" nature of the judicial system, it is worth noting that the power of the Supreme Court has been exercised in a manner that has usually been beneficial to Native Americans, at least on minor issues, and has not
(15) been wholly detrimental on the larger, more important issues. Certainly there have been decisions that cast doubt on the validity of this assertion. Some critics point to the patronizing tone of many Court opinions and the apparent rejection
(20) of Native American values as important points to consider when reviewing a case. However, the validity of the assertion can be illustrated by reference to two important contributions that have resulted from the exercise of judicial power.

(25) First, the Court has created rules of judicial construction that, in general, favor the rights of Native American litigants. The Court's attitude has been conditioned by recognition of the distinct disadvantages Native Americans faced when
(30) dealing with settlers in the past. Treaties were inevitably written in English for the benefit of their authors, whereas tribal leaders were accustomed to making treaties without any written account, on the strength of mutual promises sealed by religious
(35) commitment and individual integrity. The written treaties were often broken, and Native Americans were confronted with fraud and political and military aggression. The Court recognizes that past unfairness to Native Americans cannot be
(40) sanctioned by the force of law. Therefore, ambiguities in treaties are to be interpreted in favor of the Native American claimants, treaties are to be interpreted as the Native Americans would have understood them, and, under the reserved rights
(45) doctrine, treaties reserve to Native Americans all rights that have not been specifically granted away in other treaties.

A second achievement of the judicial system is the protection that has been provided against
(50) encroachment by the states into tribal affairs. Federal judges are not inclined to view favorably efforts to extend states' powers and jurisdictions because of the direct threat that such expansion poses to the exercise of federal powers. In the
(55) absence of a federal statute directly and clearly allocating a function to the states, federal judges are inclined to reserve for the federal government—and the tribal governments under its charge—all those powers and rights they can be said to have
(60) possessed historically.

9. According to the passage, one reason why the United States Supreme Court "has not always resolved legal issues of concern to Native Americans in a manner that has pleased the Indian nations" (lines 1–4) is that

(A) Native Americans have been prevented from presenting their concerns persuasively
(B) the Court has failed to recognize that the Indian nations' concerns are different from those of other groups or from those of the federal government
(C) the Court has been reluctant to curtail the powers of the federal government
(D) Native Americans faced distinct disadvantages in dealing with settlers in the past
(E) the Court has made political compromises in deciding some cases

10. It can be inferred that the objections raised by the critics mentioned in line 18 would be most clearly answered by a United States Supreme Court decision that

(A) demonstrated respect for Native Americans and the principles and qualities they consider important
(B) protected the rights of the states in conflicts with the federal government
(C) demonstrated recognition of the unfair treatment Native Americans received in the past
(D) reflected consideration of the hardships suffered by Native Americans because of unfair treaties
(E) prevented repetition of inequities experienced by Native Americans in the past

GO ON TO THE NEXT PAGE.

11. It can be inferred that the author calls the judicial system of the United States "accommodating" (line 10) primarily in order to

(A) suggest that the decisions of the United States Supreme Court have been less favorable to Native Americans than most people believe
(B) suggest that the United States Supreme Court should be more supportive of the goals of Native Americans
(C) suggest a reason why the decisions of the United States Supreme Court have not always favored Native Americans
(D) indicate that the United States Supreme Court has made creditable efforts to recognize the values of Native Americans
(E) indicate that the United States Supreme Court attempts to be fair to all parties to a case

12. The author's attitude toward the United States Supreme Court's resolution of legal issues of concern to Native Americans can best be described as one of

(A) wholehearted endorsement
(B) restrained appreciation
(C) detached objectivity
(D) cautious opposition
(E) suppressed exasperation

13. It can be inferred that the author believes that the extension of the states' powers and jurisdictions with respect to Native American affairs would be

(A) possible only with the consent of the Indian nations
(B) favorably viewed by the United States Supreme Court
(C) in the best interests of both state and federal governments
(D) detrimental to the interests of Native Americans
(E) discouraged by most federal judges in spite of legal precedents supporting the extension

14. The author's primary purpose is to

(A) contrast opposing views
(B) reevaluate traditional beliefs
(C) reconcile divergent opinions
(D) assess the claims made by disputants
(E) provide evidence to support a contention

15. It can be inferred that the author believes the United States Supreme Court's treatment of Native Americans to have been

(A) irreproachable on legal grounds
(B) reasonably supportive in most situations
(C) guided by enduring principles of law
(D) misguided but generally harmless
(E) harmful only in a few minor cases

GO ON TO THE NEXT PAGE.

When catastrophe strikes, analysts typically blame some combination of powerful mechanisms. An earthquake is traced to an immense instability along a fault line; a stock market crash is blamed on
(5) the destabilizing effect of computer trading. These explanations may well be correct. But systems as large and complicated as the Earth's crust or the stock market can break down not only under the force of a mighty blow but also at the drop of a pin.
(10) In a large interactive system, a minor event can start a chain reaction that leads to a catastrophe.

Traditionally, investigators have analyzed large interactive systems in the same way they analyze small orderly systems, mainly because the methods
(15) developed for small systems have proved so successful. They believed they could predict the behavior of a large interactive system by studying its elements separately and by analyzing its component mechanisms individually. For lack of a better
(20) theory, they assumed that in large interactive systems the response to a disturbance is proportional to that disturbance.

During the past few decades, however, it has become increasingly apparent that many large
(25) complicated systems do not yield to traditional analysis. Consequently, theorists have proposed a "theory of self-organized criticality": many large interactive systems evolve naturally to a critical state in which a minor event starts a chain reaction
(30) that can affect any number of elements in the system. Although such systems produce more minor events than catastrophes, the mechanism that leads to minor events is the same one that leads to major events.
(35) A deceptively simple system serves as a paradigm for self-organized criticality: a pile of sand. As sand is poured one grain at a time onto a flat disk, the grains at first stay close to the position where they land. Soon they rest on top of one
(40) another, creating a pile that has a gentle slope. Now and then, when the slope becomes too steep, the grains slide down, causing a small avalanche. The system reaches its critical state when the amount of sand added is balanced, on average, by the amount
(45) falling off the edge of the disk.

Now when a grain of sand is added, it can start an avalanche of any size, including a "catastrophic" event. Most of the time the grain will fall so that no avalanche occurs. By studying a specific area of the
(50) pile, one can even predict whether avalanches will occur there in the near future. To such a local observer, however, large avalanches would remain unpredictable because they are a consequence of the total history of the entire pile. No matter what
(55) the local dynamics are, catastrophic avalanches would persist at a relative frequency that cannot be altered. Criticality is a global property of the sandpile.

16. The passage provides support for all of the following generalizations about large interactive systems EXCEPT:

(A) They can evolve to a critical state.
(B) They do not always yield to traditional analysis.
(C) They make it impossible for observers to make any predictions about them.
(D) They are subject to the effects of chain reactions.
(E) They are subject to more minor events than major events.

17. According to the passage, the criticality of a sandpile is determined by the

(A) size of the grains of sand added to the sandpile
(B) number of grains of sand the sandpile contains
(C) rate at which sand is added to the sandpile
(D) shape of the surface on which the sandpile rests
(E) balance between the amount of sand added to and the amount lost from the sandpile

GO ON TO THE NEXT PAGE.

18. It can be inferred from the passage that the theory employed by the investigators mentioned in the second paragraph would lead one to predict that which one of the following would result from the addition of a grain of sand to a sandpile?

(A) The grain of sand would never cause anything more than a minor disturbance.
(B) The grain of sand would usually cause a minor disturbance, but would occasionally cause a small avalanche.
(C) The grain of sand would usually cause either a minor disturbance or a small avalanche, but would occasionally cause a catastrophic event.
(D) The grain of sand would usually cause a catastrophic event, but would occasionally cause only a small avalanche or an even more minor disturbance.
(E) The grain of sand would invariably cause a catastrophic event.

19. Which one of the following best describes the organization of the passage?

(A) A traditional procedure is described and its application to common situations is endorsed; its shortcomings in certain rare but critical circumstances are then revealed.
(B) A common misconception is elaborated and its consequences are described; a detailed example of one of these consequences is then given.
(C) A general principle is stated and supported by several examples; an exception to the rule is then considered and its importance evaluated.
(D) A number of seemingly unrelated events are categorized; the underlying processes that connect them are then detailed.
(E) A traditional method of analysis is discussed and the reasons for its adoption are explained; an alternative is then described and clarified by means of an example.

20. Which one of the following is most analogous to the method of analysis employed by the investigators mentioned in the second paragraph?

(A) A pollster gathers a sample of voter preferences and on the basis of this information makes a prediction about the outcome of an election.
(B) A historian examines the surviving documents detailing the history of a movement and from these documents reconstructs a chronology of the events that initiated the movement.
(C) A meteorologist measures the rainfall over a certain period of the year and from this data calculates the total annual rainfall for the region.
(D) A biologist observes the behavior of one species of insect and from these observations generalizes about the behavior of insects as a class.
(E) An engineer analyzes the stability of each structural element of a bridge and from these analyses draws a conclusion about the structural soundness of the bridge.

21. In the passage, the author is primarily concerned with

(A) arguing against the abandonment of a traditional approach
(B) describing the evolution of a radical theory
(C) reconciling conflicting points of view
(D) illustrating the superiority of a new theoretical approach
(E) advocating the reconsideration of an unfashionable explanation

GO ON TO THE NEXT PAGE.

Historians have long accepted the notion that women of English descent who lived in the English colonies of North America during the seventeenth and eighteenth centuries were better off than either
(5) the contemporary women in England or the colonists' own nineteenth-century daughters and granddaughters. The "golden age" theory originated in the 1920s with the work of Elizabeth Dexter, who argued that there were relatively few
(10) women among the colonists, and that all hands—male and female—were needed to sustain the growing settlements. Rigid sex-role distinctions could not exist under such circumstances; female colonists could accordingly engage in whatever
(15) occupations they wished, encountering few legal or social constraints if they sought employment outside the home. The surplus of male colonists also gave women crucial bargaining power in the marriage market, since women's contributions were vital to
(20) the survival of colonial households.

Dexter's portrait of female colonists living under conditions of rough equality with their male counterparts was eventually incorporated into studies of nineteenth-century middle-class women.
(25) The contrast between the self-sufficient colonial woman and the oppressed nineteenth-century woman, confined to her home by stultifying ideologies of domesticity and by the fact that industrialization eliminated employment
(30) opportunities for middle-class women, gained an extraordinarily tenacious hold on historians. Even scholars who have questioned the "golden age" view of colonial women's status have continued to accept the paradigm of a nineteenth-century
(35) decline from a more desirable past. For example, Joan Hoff-Wilson asserted that there was no "golden age" and yet emphasized that the nineteenth century brought "increased loss of function and authentic status for" middle-class
(40) women.

Recent publications about colonial women have exposed the concept of a decline in status as simplistic and unsophisticated, a theory that based its assessment of colonial women's status solely on
(45) one factor (their economic function in society) and assumed all too readily that a relatively simple social system automatically brought higher standing to colonial women. The new scholarship presents a far more complicated picture, one in which
(50) definitions of gender roles, the colonial economy, demographic patterns, religion, the law, and household organization all contributed to defining the circumstances of colonial women's lives. Indeed, the primary concern of modern scholarship is not to
(55) generalize about women's status but to identify the specific changes and continuities in women's lives during the colonial period. For example, whereas earlier historians suggested that there was little change for colonial women before 1800, the new
(60) scholarship suggests that a three-part chronological division more accurately reflects colonial women's experiences. First was the initial period of English colonization (from the 1620s to about 1660); then a period during which patterns of family and
(65) community were challenged and reshaped (roughly from 1660 to 1750); and finally the era of revolution (approximately 1750 to 1815), which brought other changes to women's lives.

22. Which one of the following best expresses the main idea of the passage?

(A) An earlier theory about the status of middle-class women in the nineteenth century has been supported by recent scholarship.
(B) Recent studies of middle-class nineteenth-century women have altered an earlier theory about the status of colonial women.
(C) Recent scholarship has exposed an earlier theory about the status of colonial women as too narrowly based and oversimplified.
(D) An earlier theory about colonial women has greatly influenced recent studies on middle-class women in the nineteenth century.
(E) An earlier study of middle-class women was based on insufficient research on the status of women in the nineteenth century.

23. The author discusses Hoff-Wilson primarily in order to

(A) describe how Dexter's theory was refuted by historians of nineteenth-century North America
(B) describe how the theory of middle-class women's nineteenth-century decline in status was developed
(C) describe an important influence on recent scholarship about the colonial period
(D) demonstrate the persistent influence of the "golden age" theory
(E) provide an example of current research on the colonial period

24. It can be inferred from the passage that the author would be most likely to describe the views of the scholars mentioned in line 32 as

(A) unassailable
(B) innovative
(C) paradoxical
(D) overly sophisticated
(E) without merit

GO ON TO THE NEXT PAGE.

25. It can be inferred from the passage that, in proposing the "three-part chronological division" (lines 60–61), scholars recognized which one of the following?

(A) The circumstances of colonial women's lives were defined by a broad variety of social and economic factors.

(B) Women's lives in the English colonies of North America were similar to women's lives in seventeenth- and eighteenth-century England.

(C) Colonial women's status was adversely affected when patterns of family and community were established in the late seventeenth century.

(D) Colonial women's status should be assessed primarily on the basis of their economic function in society.

(E) Colonial women's status was low when the colonies were settled but changed significantly during the era of revolution.

26. According to the author, the publications about colonial women mentioned in the third paragraph had which one of the following effects?

(A) They undermined Dexter's argument on the status of women colonists during the colonial period.

(B) They revealed the tenacity of the "golden age" theory in American history.

(C) They provided support for historians, such as Hoff-Wilson, who study the nineteenth century.

(D) They established that women's status did not change significantly from the colonial period to the nineteenth century.

(E) They provided support for earlier theories about women colonists in the English colonies of North America.

27. Practitioners of the new scholarship discussed in the last paragraph would be most likely to agree with which one of the following statements about Dexter's argument?

(A) It makes the assumption that women's status is determined primarily by their political power in society.

(B) It makes the assumption that a less complex social system necessarily confers higher status on women.

(C) It is based on inadequate research on women's economic role in the colonies.

(D) It places too much emphasis on the way definitions of gender roles affected women colonists in the colonial period.

(E) It accurately describes the way women's status declined in the nineteenth century.

S T O P

IF YOU FINISH BEFORE TIME IS CALLED, YOU MAY CHECK YOUR WORK ON THIS SECTION ONLY.
DO NOT WORK ON ANY OTHER SECTION IN THE TEST.

LSAT® Writing Sample Topic

Zelmar Corporation, an advertising company, must move its offices from their current downtown location. The company is considering an alternate building downtown and a suburban location. Write an argument favoring one of these choices over the other based on the following considerations:

- Zelmar wants as many employees as possible to remain with the company.
- Due to recent financial setbacks, Zelmar wants to make the coming year as profitable as possible.

The downtown location is in a somewhat smaller building a few blocks away from Zelmar's current offices and within the general area where a large proportion of the company's clients have offices. Rental costs would be slightly lower than those of its current location. Near a subway stop and close to numerous shops and restaurants, the building is located one block from a day care center that promises discounts to Zelmar employees, many of whom have preschool children. Because of space restrictions, about half of Zelmar's employees would have to give up their offices and work in a large open area subdivided by portable walls.

The suburban location is twenty miles from downtown, and the commute for many employees would at least double. While there is ample free parking, the subway line does not extend to this location; there is a bus stop directly outside the building. Zelmar would pay far less in rent than it currently does, and most employees could have their own offices. Located in an office park complex, this building has excellent facilities for large meetings and ample space for Zelmar to expand its business. A large cafeteria in the building offers food from 7 A.M. until 6 P.M. at a cost considerably below that of commercial restaurants. Employees from other offices have proposed a day care center to serve the entire complex.

Directions:

1. Use the Answer Key on the next page to check your answers.

2. Use the Scoring Worksheet below to compute your raw score.

3. Use the Score Conversion Chart to convert your raw score into the 120-180 scale.

Scoring Worksheet

1. Enter the number of questions you answered correctly in each section.

Number Correct

SECTION I . . . . . . _____
SECTION II . . . . . _____
SECTION III . . . . . _____
SECTION IV . . . . . _____

2. Enter the sum here: _____
This is your Raw Score.

Conversion Chart

For Converting Raw Score to the 120-180 LSAT Scaled Score
LSAT Form 4LSS25

Reported Score	Raw Score Lowest	Raw Score Highest
180	98	101
179	97	97
178	96	96
177	95	95
176	94	94
175	93	93
174	92	92
173	90	91
172	89	89
171	88	88
170	87	87
169	86	86
168	84	85
167	83	83
166	82	82
165	80	81
164	79	79
163	77	78
162	76	76
161	74	75
160	73	73
159	71	72
158	69	70
157	68	68
156	66	67
155	65	65
154	63	64
153	61	62
152	60	60
151	58	59
150	56	57
149	55	55
148	53	54
147	51	52
146	50	50
145	48	49
144	46	47
143	45	45
142	43	44
141	42	42
140	40	41
139	39	39
138	37	38
137	36	36
136	34	35
135	33	33
134	31	32
133	30	30
132	29	29
131	27	28
130	26	26
129	25	25
128	24	24
127	23	23
126	22	22
125	21	21
124	20	20
123	18	19
122	17	17
121	_*	_*
120	0	16

*There is no raw score that will produce this scaled score for this form.

SECTION I

#	Ans	#	Ans	#	Ans	#	Ans
1.	D	8.	B	15.	A	22.	C
2.	E	9.	C	16.	A	23.	C
3.	A	10.	E	17.	E	24.	C
4.	E	11.	C	18.	A		
5.	C	12.	B	19.	D		
6.	D	13.	D	20.	E		
7.	E	14.	B	21.	A		

SECTION II

#	Ans	#	Ans	#	Ans	#	Ans
1.	B	8.	E	15.	E	22.	E
2.	A	9.	C	16.	E	23.	D
3.	D	10.	C	17.	B	24.	E
4.	E	11.	D	18.	A		
5.	C	12.	B	19.	A		
6.	D	13.	D	20.	E		
7.	C	14.	D	21.	A		

SECTION III

#	Ans	#	Ans	#	Ans	#	Ans
1.	D	8.	B	15.	C	22.	B
2.	B	9.	A	16.	C	23.	D
3.	B	10.	A	17.	A	24.	B
4.	C	11.	E	18.	D	25.	C
5.	D	12.	A	19.	A	26.	A
6.	C	13.	B	20.	D		
7.	A	14.	E	21.	D		

SECTION IV

#	Ans	#	Ans	#	Ans	#	Ans
1.	B	8.	A	15.	B	22.	C
2.	D	9.	E	16.	C	23.	D
3.	C	10.	A	17.	E	24.	C
4.	C	11.	C	18.	A	25.	C
5.	C	12.	B	19.	E	26.	A
6.	E	13.	D	20.	E	27.	B
7.	B	14.	E	21.	D		

The Official LSAT PrepTest

18

- December 1992
- Form 3LSS17

The sample test that follows consists of four sections corresponding to the four scored sections of the December 1992 LSAT.

SECTION I

Time—35 minutes

24 Questions

<u>Directions:</u> Each group of questions in this section is based on a set of conditions. In answering some of the questions, it may be useful to draw a rough diagram. Choose the response that most accurately and completely answers each question and blacken the corresponding space on your answer sheet.

Questions 1–6

Each of five students—Hubert, Lori, Paul, Regina, and Sharon—will visit exactly one of three cities—Montreal, Toronto, or Vancouver—for the month of March, according to the following conditions:

Sharon visits a different city than Paul.

Hubert visits the same city as Regina.

Lori visits Montreal or else Toronto.

If Paul visits Vancouver, Hubert visits Vancouver with him.

Each student visits one of the cities with at least one of the other four students.

1. Which one of the following could be true for March?

(A) Hubert, Lori, and Paul visit Toronto, and Regina and Sharon visit Vancouver.
(B) Hubert, Lori, Paul, and Regina visit Montreal, and Sharon visits Vancouver.
(C) Hubert, Paul, and Regina visit Toronto, and Lori and Sharon visit Montreal.
(D) Hubert, Regina, and Sharon visit Montreal, and Lori and Paul visit Vancouver.
(E) Lori, Paul, and Sharon visit Montreal, and Hubert and Regina visit Toronto.

2. If Hubert and Sharon visit a city together, which one of the following could be true in March?

(A) Hubert visits the same city as Paul.
(B) Lori visits the same city as Regina.
(C) Paul visits the same city as Regina.
(D) Paul visits Toronto.
(E) Paul visits Vancouver.

3. If Sharon visits Vancouver, which one of the following must be true for March?

(A) Hubert visits Montreal.
(B) Lori visits Montreal.
(C) Paul visits Toronto.
(D) Lori visits the same city as Paul.
(E) Lori visits the same city as Regina.

4. Which one of the following could be false in March?

(A) Sharon must visit Montreal if Paul visits Vancouver.
(B) Regina must visit Vancouver if Paul visits Vancouver.
(C) Regina visits a city with exactly two of the other four students.
(D) Lori visits a city with exactly one of the other four students.
(E) Lori visits a city with Paul or else with Sharon.

5. If Regina visits Toronto, which one of the following could be true in March?

(A) Lori visits Toronto.
(B) Lori visits Vancouver.
(C) Paul visits Toronto.
(D) Paul visits Vancouver.
(E) Sharon visits Vancouver.

6. Which one of the following must be true for March?

(A) If any of the students visits Montreal, Lori visits Montreal.
(B) If any of the students visits Montreal, exactly two of them do.
(C) If any of the students visits Toronto, exactly three of them do.
(D) If any of the students visits Vancouver, Paul visits Vancouver.
(E) If any of the students visits Vancouver, exactly three of them do.

GO ON TO THE NEXT PAGE.

Questions 7–13

A college offers one course in each of three subjects—mathematics, nutrition, and oceanography—in the fall and again in the spring. Students' book orders for these course offerings are kept in six folders, numbered 1 through 6, from which labels identifying the folders' contents are missing. The following is known:

Each folder contains only the orders for one of the six course offerings.

Folder 1 contains orders for the same subject as folder 2 does.

The orders in folder 3 are for a different subject than are the orders in folder 4.

The fall mathematics orders are in folder 1 or else folder 4.

The spring oceanography orders are in folder 1 or else folder 4.

The spring nutrition orders are not in folder 5.

7. Which one of the following could be the list of the contents of the folders, in order from folder 1 to folder 6 ?

(A) fall mathematics, spring mathematics, fall oceanography, fall nutrition, spring nutrition, spring oceanography

(B) fall oceanography, spring nutrition, fall nutrition, fall mathematics, spring mathematics, spring oceanography

(C) spring mathematics, fall mathematics, spring nutrition, fall oceanography, fall nutrition, spring oceanography

(D) spring oceanography, fall oceanography, fall nutrition, fall mathematics, spring mathematics, spring nutrition

(E) spring oceanography, fall oceanography, spring mathematics, fall mathematics, fall nutrition, spring nutrition

8. Which one of the following statements must be false?

(A) The spring mathematics orders are in folder 3.

(B) The fall nutrition orders are in folder 3.

(C) The spring oceanography orders are in folder 1.

(D) The spring nutrition orders are in folder 6.

(E) The fall oceanography orders are in folder 5.

9. If the fall oceanography orders are in folder 2, then which one of the following statements could be true?

(A) The spring mathematics orders are in folder 4.

(B) The spring mathematics orders are in folder 6.

(C) The fall nutrition orders are in folder 1.

(D) The spring nutrition orders are in neither folder 3 nor folder 6.

(E) Neither the spring nor the fall nutrition orders are in folder 3.

10. Which one of the following statements could be true?

(A) The spring mathematics orders are in folder 1.

(B) The fall oceanography orders are in folder 1.

(C) The fall nutrition orders are in folder 4, and the fall oceanography orders are in folder 6.

(D) The fall oceanography orders are in folder 2, and the spring oceanography orders are in folder 1.

(E) The spring oceanography orders are in folder 1, and neither the spring nor the fall nutrition orders are in folder 3.

11. If the fall oceanography orders are in folder 2, then for exactly how many of the remaining five folders can it be deduced which course offering's orders are in that folder?

(A) one
(B) two
(C) three
(D) four
(E) five

12. Which one of the following lists a pair of folders that must together contain orders for two different subjects?

(A) 3 and 5
(B) 4 and 5
(C) 3 and 6
(D) 4 and 6
(E) 5 and 6

13. Which one of the following could be true?

(A) The fall mathematics and spring oceanography orders are in folders with consecutive numbers.

(B) Folder 5 contains the orders for a spring course in a subject other than mathematics.

(C) Folder 6 contains the orders for a subject other than nutrition.

(D) The mathematics orders are in folders 1 and 4.

(E) The orders for the fall courses are in folders 1, 3, and 6.

GO ON TO THE NEXT PAGE.

Questions 14–19

Greenburg has exactly five subway lines: L1, L2, L3, L4, and L5. Along each of the lines, trains run in both directions, stopping at every station.

L1 runs in a loop connecting exactly seven stations, their order being Rincon-Tonka-French-Semplain-Urstine-Quetzal-Park-Rincon in one direction of travel, and the reverse in the other direction.

L2 connects Tonka with Semplain, and with no other station.

L3 connects Rincon with Urstine, and with no other station.

L4 runs from Quetzal through exactly one other station, Greene, to Rincon.

L5 connects Quetzal with Tonka, and with no other station.

14. How many different stations are there that a traveler starting at Rincon could reach by using the subway lines without making any intermediate stops?

    (A) two
    (B) three
    (C) four
    (D) five
    (E) six

15. In order to go from Greene to Semplain taking the fewest possible subway lines and making the fewest possible stops, a traveler must make a stop at

    (A) French
    (B) Park
    (C) Quetzal
    (D) Rincon
    (E) Tonka

16. If L3 is not running and a traveler goes by subway from Urstine to Rincon making the fewest possible stops, which one of the following lists all of the intermediate stations in sequence along one of the routes that the traveler could take?

    (A) Quetzal, Tonka
    (B) Semplain, French
    (C) Semplain, Park
    (D) Quetzal, Park, Greene
    (E) Semplain, French, Tonka

17. In order to go by subway from French to Greene, the minimum number of intermediate stops a traveler must make is

    (A) zero
    (B) one
    (C) two
    (D) three
    (E) four

18. If the tracks that directly connect Urstine and Quetzal are blocked in both directions, a traveler going from Semplain to Park and making the fewest possible intermediate stops must pass through

    (A) French or Tonka
    (B) Greene or Urstine
    (C) Quetzal or Tonka
    (D) Quetzal or Urstine or both
    (E) Rincon or Tonka or both

19. If a sixth subway line is to be constructed so that all of the stations would have two or more lines reaching them, the stations connected by the new subway line must include at least

    (A) French, Greene, and Park
    (B) French, Greene, and Quetzal
    (C) French, Greene, and Rincon
    (D) Park, Tonka, and Urstine
    (E) Park, Semplain, and Tonka

GO ON TO THE NEXT PAGE.

Questions 20–24

Prior to this year's annual promotion review, the staff of a law firm consisted of partners Harrison and Rafael, associate Olivos, and assistants Ganz, Johnson, Lowry, Stefano, Turner, and Wilford. During each annual review, each assistant and associate is considered for promotion to the next higher rank, and at least one person is promoted from each of the two lower ranks. An assistant is promoted to associate when a majority of higher-ranking staff votes for promotion. An associate is promoted to partner when a majority of partners vote for promotion. Everyone eligible votes on every promotion. No one joins or leaves the firm.

Olivos never votes for promoting Ganz, Johnson, or Turner.
Rafael never votes for promoting Lowry or Stefano.
Harrison never votes for promoting Johnson or Wilford.

20. Which one of the following could be the distribution of staff resulting from this year's review?

	Partner	Associate	Assistant
(A)	Harrison, Olivos, Rafael	Ganz, Johnson, Lowry	Stefano, Turner, Wilford
(B)	Harrison, Rafael	Lowry, Olivos, Stefano	Ganz, Johnson, Turner, Wilford
(C)	Harrison, Olivos, Rafael, Stefano	Ganz, Lowry, Turner, Wilford	Johnson
(D)	Harrison, Olivos, Rafael		Ganz, Johnson, Lowry, Stefano, Turner, Wilford
(E)	Harrison, Olivos, Rafael	Ganz, Lowry, Stefano, Turner	Johnson, Wilford

21. If Rafael votes for promoting only Ganz, Olivos, and Wilford, and if Harrison votes for promoting only Lowry, Olivos, and Stefano, then which one of the following could be the complete roster of associates resulting from this year's review?

(A) Ganz, Lowry, Wilford
(B) Johnson, Lowry, Stefano
(C) Lowry, Stefano, Turner
(D) Lowry, Stefano, Wilford
(E) Olivos, Turner, Wilford

22. If Johnson is to be promoted to associate during next year's review, which one of the following is the smallest number of assistants who must be promoted during this year's review?

(A) one
(B) two
(C) three
(D) four
(E) five

23. Which one of the following must be true after next year's review?

(A) Lowry is an assistant.
(B) Wilford is a partner.
(C) There are no assistants.
(D) There are at least two assistants.
(E) There are no more than four assistants.

24. What is the smallest possible number of associates in the firm immediately after next year's review?

(A) none
(B) one
(C) two
(D) three
(E) four

STOP

IF YOU FINISH BEFORE TIME IS CALLED, YOU MAY CHECK YOUR WORK ON THIS SECTION ONLY.
DO NOT WORK ON ANY OTHER SECTION IN THE TEST.

SECTION II

Time—35 minutes

24 Questions

<u>Directions:</u> The questions in this section are based on the reasoning contained in brief statements or passages. For some questions, more than one of the choices could conceivably answer the question. However, you are to choose the <u>best</u> answer; that is, the response that most accurately and completely answers the question. You should not make assumptions that are by commonsense standards implausible, superfluous, or incompatible with the passage. After you have chosen the best answer, blacken the corresponding space on your answer sheet.

1.   Parent 1:   Ten years ago, children in communities like ours did not date until they were thirteen to fifteen years old. Now our nine to eleven year olds are dating. Obviously, children in communities like ours are becoming romantically interested in members of the opposite sex at an earlier age today than they did ten years ago.

Parent 2:   I disagree. Our nine to eleven year olds do not want to date, but they feel intense peer pressure to act grown up by dating.

Parent 2, in responding to Parent 1, does which one of the following?

(A)   draws a conclusion about a new phenomenon by comparing it to a phenomenon that is known and understood

(B)   refutes a generalization about nine- to eleven-year-old children by means of an exceptional case overlooked by Parent 1

(C)   assumes that nine- to eleven-year-old children are as interested in dating as thirteen- to fifteen-year-old children

(D)   provides an alternative explanation for the changes in children's dating described by Parent 1

(E)   criticizes Parent 1 as a proponent of a claim rather than criticizing the claim itself

2.   All cattle ranchers dislike long winters.

All ski resort owners like long winters because long winters mean increased profits.

Some lawyers are cattle ranchers.

Which one of the following statements, if true and added to those above, most supports the conclusion that no ski resort owners are lawyers?

(A)   Some cattle ranchers are lawyers.

(B)   Some people who dislike long winters are not cattle ranchers.

(C)   All lawyers are cattle ranchers.

(D)   All people who dislike long winters are cattle ranchers.

(E)   All people with increasing profits own ski resorts.

3.   Citizen of Mooresville: Mooresville's current city council is having a ruinous effect on municipal finances. Since a majority of the incumbents are running for reelection, I am going to campaign against all these incumbents in the upcoming city council election. The only incumbent I will support and vote for is the one who represents my own neighborhood, because she has the experience necessary to ensure that our neighborhood's interests are served. If everyone in Mooresville would follow my example, we could substantially change the council's membership.

Assuming that each citizen of Mooresville is allowed to vote only for a city council representative from his or her own neighborhood, for the council's membership to be changed substantially, it must be true that

(A)   at least some other voters in Mooresville do not make the same exception for their own incumbent in the upcoming election

(B)   most of the eligible voters in Mooresville vote in the upcoming election

(C)   few of the incumbents on the Mooresville city council have run for reelection in previous elections

(D)   all of the seats on the Mooresville city council are filled by incumbents whose terms are expiring

(E)   none of the challengers in the upcoming election for seats on Mooresville's city council are better able to serve the interests of their neighborhoods than were the incumbents

GO ON TO THE NEXT PAGE.

4. Marianna: The problem of drunk driving has been somewhat ameliorated by public education and stricter laws. Additional measures are nevertheless needed. People still drive after drinking, and when they do the probability is greatly increased that they will cause an accident involving death or serious injury.

David: I think you exaggerate the dangers of driving while drunk. Actually, a driver who is in an automobile accident is slightly less likely to be seriously injured if drunk than if sober.

In responding to Marianna's argument, David makes which one of the following errors of reasoning?

(A) He contradicts himself.
(B) He assumes what he is seeking to establish.
(C) He contradicts Marianna's conclusion without giving any evidence for his point of view.
(D) He argues against a point that is not one that Marianna was making.
(E) He directs his criticism against the person making the argument rather than directing it against the argument itself.

5. From a magazine article: Self-confidence is a dangerous virtue: it often degenerates into the vice of arrogance. The danger of arrogance is evident to all who care to look. How much more humane the twentieth century would have been without the arrogant self-confidence of a Hitler or a Stalin!

The author attempts to persuade by doing all of the following EXCEPT

(A) using extreme cases to evoke an emotional response
(B) introducing value-laden terms, such as "vice"
(C) illustrating the danger of arrogance
(D) appealing to authority to substantiate an assertion
(E) implying that Hitler's arrogance arose from self-confidence

6. A study was designed to establish what effect, if any, the long-term operation of offshore oil rigs had on animal life on the bottom of the sea. The study compared the sea-bottom communities near rigs with those located in control sites several miles from any rig and found no significant differences. The researchers concluded that oil rigs had no adverse effect on sea-bottom animals.

Which one of the following, if true, most seriously weakens the researchers' conclusion?

(A) Commercially important fish depend on sea-bottom animals for much of their food, so a drop in catches of those fish would be evidence of damage to sea-bottom communities.
(B) The discharge of oil from offshore oil rigs typically occurs at the surface of the water, and currents often carry the oil considerable distances before it settles on the ocean floor.
(C) Contamination of the ocean floor from sewage and industrial effluent does not result in the destruction of all sea-bottom animals but instead reduces species diversity as well as density of animal life.
(D) Only part of any oil discharged into the ocean reaches the ocean floor: some oil evaporates, and some remains in the water as suspended drops.
(E) Where the ocean floor consists of soft sediment, contaminating oil persists much longer than where the ocean floor is rocky.

GO ON TO THE NEXT PAGE.

7. Scientists are sometimes said to assume that something is not the case until there is proof that it is the case. Now suppose the question arises whether a given food additive is safe. At that point, it would be neither known to be safe nor known not to be safe. By the characterization above, scientists would assume the additive not to be safe because it has not been proven safe. But they would also assume it to be safe because it has not been proven otherwise. But no scientist could assume without contradiction that a given substance is both safe and not safe; so this characterization of scientists is clearly wrong.

Which one of the following describes the technique of reasoning used above?

(A) A general statement is argued to be false by showing that it has deliberately been formulated to mislead.

(B) A statement is argued to be false by showing that taking it to be true leads to implausible consequences.

(C) A statement is shown to be false by showing that it directly contradicts a second statement that is taken to be true.

(D) A general statement is shown to be uninformative by showing that there are as many specific instances in which it is false as there are instances in which it is true.

(E) A statement is shown to be uninformative by showing that it supports no independently testable inferences.

8. During the 1980s the homicide rate in Britain rose by 50 percent. The weapon used usually was a knife. Potentially lethal knives are sold openly and legally in many shops. Most homicide deaths occur as a result of unpremeditated assaults within the family. Even if these are increasing, they would probably not result in deaths if it were not for the prevalence of such knives. Thus the blame lies with the permissiveness of the government that allows such lethal weapons to be sold.

Which one of the following is the strongest criticism of the argument above?

(A) There are other means besides knives, such as guns or poison, that can be used to accomplish homicide by a person who intends to cause the death of another.

(B) It is impossible to know how many unpremeditated assaults occur within the family, since many are not reported to the authorities.

(C) Knives are used in other homicides besides those that result from unpremeditated assaults within the family.

(D) The argument assumes without justification that the knives used to commit homicide are generally purchased as part of a deliberate plan to commit murder or to inflict grievous harm on a family member.

(E) If the potentially lethal knives referred to are ordinary household knives, such knives were common before the rise in the homicide rate; but if they are weaponry, such knives are not generally available in households.

9. Nutritionist: Vitamins synthesized by chemists are exactly the same as vitamins that occur naturally in foods. Therefore, it is a waste of money to pay extra for brands of vitamin pills that are advertised as made of higher-quality ingredients or more natural ingredients than other brands are.

The nutritionist's advice is based on which one of the following assumptions?

(A) It is a waste of money for people to supplement their diets with vitamin pills.

(B) Brands of vitamin pills made of natural ingredients always cost more money than brands that contain synthesized vitamins.

(C) All brands of vitamin pills contain some synthesized vitamins.

(D) Some producers of vitamin pills are guilty of false advertising.

(E) There is no nonvitamin ingredient in vitamin pills whose quality makes one brand worth more money than another brand.

GO ON TO THE NEXT PAGE.

10. Most people are indignant at the suggestion that they are not reliable authorities about their real wants. Such self-knowledge, however, is not the easiest kind of knowledge to acquire. Indeed, acquiring it often requires hard and even potentially risky work. To avoid such effort, people unconsciously convince themselves that they want what society says they should want.

The main point of the argument is that

(A) acquiring self-knowledge can be risky
(B) knowledge of what one really wants is not as desirable as it is usually thought to be
(C) people cannot really want what they should want
(D) people usually avoid making difficult decisions
(E) people are not necessarily reliable authorities about what they really want

11. Since 1945 pesticide use in the United States has increased tenfold despite an overall stability in number of acres planted. During the same period, crop loss from insects has approximately doubled, from about seven to thirteen percent.

Which one of the following, if true, contributes most to explaining the paradoxical findings above?

(A) Extension agents employed by state governments to advise farmers have recently advocated using smaller amounts of pesticide, though in past years they promoted heavy pesticide use.
(B) While pesticide-resistant strains of insects were developing, crop rotation, which for insects disrupts a stable food supply, was gradually abandoned because farmers' eligibility to receive government crop subsidies depended on continuing to plant the same crop.
(C) Since 1970 the pesticides most lethal to people have generally been replaced by less-lethal chemicals that are equally effective against insects and have a less-damaging effect on the fish in streams fed by water that runs off from treated agricultural fields.
(D) Because farmers' decisions about how much land to plant are governed by their expectations about crop prices at harvest time, the amount of pesticide they apply also depends in part on expected crop prices.
(E) Although some pesticides can be removed from foodstuffs through washing, others are taken up into the edible portion of plants, and consumers have begun to boycott foods containing pesticides that cannot be washed off.

12. In discussing the pros and cons of monetary union among several European nations, some politicians have claimed that living standards in the countries concerned would first have to converge if monetary union is not to lead to economic chaos. This claim is plainly false, as is demonstrated by the fact that living standards diverge widely between regions within countries that nevertheless have stable economies.

In attempting to refute the politicians' claim, the author does which one of the following?

(A) argues that those making the claim are mistaken about a temporal relationship that has been observed
(B) presents an earlier instance of the action being considered in which the predicted consequences did not occur
(C) argues that the feared consequence would occur regardless of what course of action was followed
(D) gives an example of a state of affairs, assumed to be relevantly similar, in which the allegedly incompatible elements coexist
(E) points out that if an implicit recommendation is followed, the claim can be neither shown to be true nor shown to be false

GO ON TO THE NEXT PAGE.

13. Because some student demonstrations protesting his scheduled appearance have resulted in violence, the president of the Imperialist Society has been prevented from speaking about politics on campus by the dean of student affairs. Yet to deny anyone the unrestricted freedom to speak is to threaten everyone's right to free expression. Hence, the dean's decision has threatened everyone's right to free expression.

The pattern of reasoning displayed above is most closely paralleled in which one of the following?

(A) Dr. Pacheco saved a child's life by performing emergency surgery. But surgery rarely involves any risk to the surgeon. Therefore, if an act is not heroic unless it requires the actor to take some risk, Dr. Pacheco's surgery was not heroic.

(B) Because anyone who performs an act of heroism acts altruistically rather than selfishly, a society that rewards heroism encourages altruism rather than pure self-interest.

(C) In order to rescue a drowning child, Isabel jumped into a freezing river. Such acts of heroism performed to save the life of one enrich the lives of all. Hence, Isabel's action enriched the lives of all.

(D) Fire fighters are often expected to perform heroically under harsh conditions. But no one is ever required to act heroically. Hence, fire fighters are often expected to perform actions they are not required to perform.

(E) Acts of extreme generosity are usually above and beyond the call of duty. Therefore, most acts of extreme generosity are heroic, since all actions that are above and beyond the call of duty are heroic.

14. Professor: Members of most species are able to communicate with other members of the same species, but it is not true that all communication can be called "language." The human communication system unquestionably qualifies as language. In fact, using language is a trait without which we would not be human.

Student: I understand that communication by itself is not language, but how do you know that the highly evolved communication systems of songbirds, dolphins, honeybees, and apes, for example, are not languages?

The student has interpreted the professor's remarks to mean that

(A) different species can have similar defining traits
(B) every human trait except using language is shared by at least one other species
(C) not all languages are used to communicate
(D) using language is a trait humans do not share with any other species
(E) humans cannot communicate with members of other species

Questions 15–16

Environmentalist: An increased number of oil spills and the consequent damage to the environment indicate the need for stricter safety standards for the oil industry. Since the industry refuses to take action, it is the national government that must regulate industry safety standards. In particular, the government has to at least require oil companies to put double hulls on their tankers and to assume financial responsibility for accidents.

Industry representative: The industry alone should be responsible for devising safety standards because of its expertise in handling oil and its understanding of the cost entailed. Implementing the double-hull proposal is not currently feasible because it creates new safety issues. Furthermore, the cost would be burdensome to the industry and consumers.

15. Which one of the following is an assumption on which the argument of the environmentalist depends?

(A) The only effective sources of increased stringency in safety standards for oil tankers are action by the industry itself or national government regulation.

(B) The requirement of two hulls on oil tankers, although initially costly, will save money over time by reducing cleanup costs.

(C) The oil industry's aging fleet of tankers must either be repaired or else replaced.

(D) Government safety regulations are developed in a process of negotiation with industry leaders and independent experts.

(E) Environmental concerns outweigh all financial considerations when developing safety standards.

16. Which one of the following, if true, most strongly supports the industry representative's position against the environmentalist's position?

(A) Recently a double-hulled tanker loaded with oil was punctured when it ran aground, but no oil was released.

(B) Proposed government regulation would mandate the creation of regional response teams within the Coast Guard to respond to oil spills and coordinate cleanup activities.

(C) Proposed legislation requires that new tankers have double hulls but that existing tankers either be refitted with double hulls in the next 20 years or else be retired.

(D) Fumes can become trapped between the two hull layers of double-hulled tankers, and the risk of explosions that could rupture the tanker's hull is thereby increased.

(E) From now on, the oil industry will be required by recent legislation to finance a newly established oil-spill cleanup fund.

GO ON TO THE NEXT PAGE.

17. Biographer: Arnold's belief that every offer of
assistance on the part of his colleagues was a
disguised attempt to make him look inadequate and that no expression of congratula-
tions on his promotion should be taken at face
value may seem irrational. In fact, this belief
was a consequence of his early experiences with
an admired older sister who always made fun
of his ambitions and achievements. In light of
this explanation, therefore, Arnold's stubborn
belief that his colleagues were duplicitous
emerges as clearly justified.

The flawed reasoning in the biographer's argument is
most similar to that in which one of the following?

(A) The fact that top executives generally have
much larger vocabularies than do their subor-
dinates explains why Sheldon's belief, instilled
in him during his childhood, that developing
a large vocabulary is the way to get to the top
in the world of business is completely justified.

(B) Emily suspected that apples are unhealthy ever
since she almost choked to death while eating
an apple when she was a child. Now, evidence
that apples treated with certain pesticides can
be health hazards shows that Emily's long-
held belief is fully justified.

(C) As a child, Joan was severely punished
whenever she played with her father's prize
Siamese cat. Therefore, since this information
makes her present belief that cats are not
good pets completely understandable, that
belief is justified.

(D) Studies show that when usually well-behaved
children become irritable, they often exhibit
symptoms of viral infections the next day.
The suspicion, still held by many adults, that
misbehavior must always be paid for is thus
both explained and justified.

(E) Sumayia's father and mother were both concert pianists, and as a child, Sumayia knew
several other people trying to make careers as
musicians. Thus Sumayia's opinion that her
friend Anthony lacks the drive to be a successful pianist is undoubtedly justified.

18. The television documentary went beyond the
save-the-wildlife pieties of some of those remote from
East Africa and showed that in a country pressed for
food, the elephant is a pest, and an intelligent pest at
that. There appears to be no way to protect East
African farms from the voracious foraging of
night-raiding elephant herds. Clearly this example
illustrates that _____.

Which one of the following most logically completes
the paragraph?

(A) the preservation of wildlife may endanger
human welfare

(B) it is time to remove elephants from the list of
endangered species

(C) television documentaries are incapable of
doing more than reiterating accepted pieties

(D) farmers and agricultural agents should work
closely with wildlife conservationists before
taking measures to control elephants

(E) it is unfair that people in any country should
have to endure food shortages

GO ON TO THE NEXT PAGE.

Questions 19–20

Oxygen-18 is a heavier-than-normal isotope of oxygen. In a rain cloud, water molecules containing oxygen-18 are rarer than water molecules containing normal oxygen. But in rainfall, a higher proportion of all water molecules containing oxygen-18 than of all water molecules containing ordinary oxygen descends to earth. Consequently, scientists were surprised when measurements along the entire route of rain clouds' passage from above the Atlantic Ocean, the site of their original formation, across the Amazon forests, where it rains almost daily, showed that the oxygen-18 content of each of the clouds remained fairly constant.

19. Which one of the following statements, if true, best helps to resolve the conflict between scientists' expectations, based on the known behavior of oxygen-18, and the result of their measurements of the rain clouds' oxygen-18 content?

   (A) Rain clouds above tropical forests are poorer in oxygen-18 than rain clouds above unforested regions.
   (B) Like the oceans, tropical rain forests can create or replenish rain clouds in the atmosphere above them.
   (C) The amount of rainfall over the Amazon rain forests is exactly the same as the amount of rain originally collected in the clouds formed above the Atlantic Ocean.
   (D) The amount of rain recycled back into the atmosphere from the leaves of forest vegetation is exactly the same as the amount of rain in river runoffs that is not recycled into the atmosphere.
   (E) Oxygen-18 is not a good indicator of the effect of tropical rain forests on the atmosphere above them.

20. Which one of the following inferences about an individual rain cloud is supported by the passage?

   (A) Once it is formed over the Atlantic, the rain cloud contains more ordinary oxygen than oxygen-18.
   (B) Once it has passed over the Amazon, the rain cloud contains a greater-than-normal percentage of oxygen-18.
   (C) The cloud's rainfall contains more oxygen-18 than ordinary oxygen.
   (D) During a rainfall, the cloud must surrender the same percentage of its ordinary oxygen as of its oxygen-18.
   (E) During a rainfall, the cloud must surrender more of its oxygen-18 than it retains.

21. It is very difficult to prove today that a painting done two or three hundred years ago, especially one without a signature or with a questionably authentic signature, is indubitably the work of this or that particular artist. This fact gives the traditional attribution of a disputed painting special weight, since that attribution carries the presumption of historical continuity. Consequently, an art historian arguing for a deattribution will generally convince other art historians only if he or she can persuasively argue for a specific reattribution.

Which one of the following, if true, most strongly supports the position that the traditional attribution of a disputed painting should not have special weight?

   (A) Art dealers have always been led by economic self-interest to attribute any unsigned paintings of merit to recognized masters rather than to obscure artists.
   (B) When a painting is originally created, there are invariably at least some eyewitnesses who see the artist at work, and thus questions of correct attribution cannot arise at that time.
   (C) There are not always clearly discernible differences between the occasional inferior work produced by a master and the very best work produced by a lesser talent.
   (D) Attribution can shape perception inasmuch as certain features that would count as marks of greatness in a master's work would be counted as signs of inferior artistry if a work were attributed to a minor artist.
   (E) Even though some masters had specialists assist them with certain detail work, such as depicting lace, the resulting works are properly attributed to the masters alone.

GO ON TO THE NEXT PAGE.

22. Much of the best scientific research of today shows that many of the results of earlier scientific work that was regarded in its time as good are in fact mistaken. Yet despite the fact that scientists are above all concerned to discover the truth, it is valuable for today's scientists to study firsthand accounts of earlier scientific work.

Which one of the following, if true, would best reconcile the two statements above?

(A) Many firsthand accounts of earlier, flawed scientific work are not generally known to be mistaken.
(B) Lessons in scientific methodology can be learned by seeing how earlier scientific work was carried out, sometimes especially when the results of that work are known to be incorrect.
(C) Scientists can make valuable contributions to the scientific work of their time even if the results of their work will later be shown to be mistaken.
(D) There are many scientists today who are not thoroughly familiar with earlier scientific research.
(E) Some of the better scientific research of today does not directly address earlier scientific work.

23. Teachers are effective only when they help their students become independent learners. Yet not until teachers have the power to make decisions in their own classrooms can they enable their students to make their own decisions. Students' capability to make their own decisions is essential to their becoming independent learners. Therefore, if teachers are to be effective, they must have the power to make decisions in their own classrooms.

According to the argument, each of the following could be true of teachers who have enabled their students to make their own decisions EXCEPT:

(A) Their students have not become independent learners.
(B) They are not effective teachers.
(C) They are effective teachers.
(D) They have the power to make decisions in their own classrooms.
(E) They do not have the power to make decisions in their own classrooms.

24. Dr. Ruiz: Dr. Smith has expressed outspoken antismoking views in public. Even though Dr. Smith is otherwise qualified, clearly she cannot be included on a panel that examines the danger of secondhand cigarette smoke. As an organizer of the panel, I want to ensure that the panel examines the issue in an unbiased manner before coming to any conclusion.

Which one of the following, if true, provides the strongest basis for countering Dr. Ruiz' argument that Dr. Smith should not be included on the panel?

(A) A panel composed of qualified people with strong but conflicting views on a particular topic is more likely to reach an unbiased conclusion than a panel composed of people who have kept their views, if any, private.
(B) People who hold strong views on a particular topic tend to accept new evidence on that topic only if it supports their views.
(C) A panel that includes one qualified person with publicly known strong views on a particular topic is more likely to have lively discussions than a panel that includes only people with no well-defined views on that topic.
(D) People who have expressed strong views in public on a particular topic are better at raising funds to support their case than are people who have never expressed strong views in public.
(E) People who have well-defined strong views on a particular topic prior to joining a panel are often able to impose their views on panel members who are not committed at the outset to any conclusion.

S T O P

IF YOU FINISH BEFORE TIME IS CALLED, YOU MAY CHECK YOUR WORK ON THIS SECTION ONLY.
DO NOT WORK ON ANY OTHER SECTION IN THE TEST.

SECTION III

Time—35 minutes

28 Questions

<u>Directions:</u> Each passage in this section is followed by a group of questions to be answered on the basis of what is <u>stated</u> or <u>implied</u> in the passage. For some of the questions, more than one of the choices could conceivably answer the question. However, you are to choose the <u>best</u> answer; that is, the response that most accurately and completely answers the question, and blacken the corresponding space on your answer sheet.

The law-and-literature movement claims to have introduced a valuable pedagogical innovation into legal study: instructing students in techniques of literary analysis for the purpose of interpreting laws
(5) and in the reciprocal use of legal analysis for the purpose of interpreting literary texts. The results, according to advocates, are not only conceptual breakthroughs in both law and literature but also more sensitive and humane lawyers. Whatever the
(10) truth of this last claim, there can be no doubt that the movement is a success: law-and-literature is an accepted subject in law journals and in leading law schools. Indeed, one indication of the movement's strength is the fact that its most distinguished critic,
(15) Richard A. Posner, paradoxically ends up expressing qualified support for the movement in a recent study in which he systematically refutes the writings of its leading legal scholars and cooperating literary critics.
(20) Critiquing the movement's assumption that lawyers can offer special insights into literature that deals with legal matters, Posner points out that writers of literature use the law loosely to convey a particular idea, or as a metaphor for the workings
(25) of the society envisioned in their fiction. Legal questions per se, about which a lawyer might instruct readers, are seldom at issue in literature. This is why practitioners of law-and-literature end up discussing the law itself far less than one might
(30) suppose. Movement leader James White, for example, in his discussion of arguments in the *Iliad,* barely touches on law, and then so generally as to render himself vulnerable to Posner's devastating remark that "any argument can be analogized to a
(35) legal dispute."
Similarly, the notion that literary criticism can be helpful in interpreting law is problematic. Posner argues that literary criticism in general aims at exploring richness and variety of meaning in texts,
(40) whereas legal interpretation aims at discovering a single meaning. A literary approach can thus only confuse the task of interpreting the law, especially if one adopts current fashions like deconstruction, which holds that all texts are inherently
(45) uninterpretable.
Nevertheless, Posner writes that law-and-literature is a field with "promise." Why? Perhaps, recognizing the success of a movement that, in the past, has singled him out for abuse, he
(50) is attempting to appease his detractors, paying

obeisance to the movement's institutional success by declaring that it "deserves a place in legal research" while leaving it to others to draw the conclusion from his cogent analysis that it is an
(55) entirely factitious undertaking, deserving of no intellectual respect whatsoever. As a result, his work stands both as a rebuttal of law-and-literature and as a tribute to the power it has come to exercise in academic circles.

1. The primary purpose of the passage is to

   (A) assess the law-and-literature movement by examining the position of one of its most prominent critics
   (B) assert that a mutually beneficial relationship exists between the study of law and the study of literature
   (C) provide examples of the law-and-literature movement in practice by discussing the work of its proponents
   (D) dismiss a prominent critic's recent study of the law-and-literature movement
   (E) describe the role played by literary scholars in providing a broader context for legal issues

2. Posner's stated position with regard to the law-and-literature movement is most analogous to which one of the following?

   (A) a musician who is trained in the classics but frequently plays modern music while performing on stage
   (B) a partisan who transfers allegiance to a new political party that demonstrates more promise but has fewer documented accomplishments
   (C) a sports fan who wholeheartedly supports the team most likely to win rather than his or her personal favorite
   (D) an ideologue who remains committed to his or her own view of a subject in spite of compelling evidence to the contrary
   (E) a salesperson who describes the faults in a fashionable product while conceding that it may have some value

GO ON TO THE NEXT PAGE.

3. The passage suggests that Posner regards legal practitioners as using an approach to interpreting law that

    (A) eschews discovery of multiple meanings
    (B) employs techniques like deconstruction
    (C) interprets laws in light of varying community standards
    (D) is informed by the positions of literary critics
    (E) de-emphasizes the social relevance of the legal tradition

4. The passage suggests that Posner might find legal training useful in the interpretation of a literary text in which

    (A) a legal dispute symbolizes the relationship between two characters
    (B) an oppressive law is used to symbolize an oppressive culture
    (C) one of the key issues involves the answer to a legal question
    (D) a legal controversy is used to represent a moral conflict
    (E) the working of the legal system suggests something about the political character of a society

5. The author uses the word "success" in line 11 to refer to the law-and-literature movement's

    (A) positive effect on the sensitivity of lawyers
    (B) widespread acceptance by law schools and law journals
    (C) ability to offer fresh insights into literary texts
    (D) ability to encourage innovative approaches in two disciplines
    (E) response to recent criticism in law journals

6. According to the passage, Posner argues that legal analysis is not generally useful in interpreting literature because

    (A) use of the law in literature is generally of a quite different nature than use of the law in legal practice
    (B) law is rarely used to convey important ideas in literature
    (C) lawyers do not have enough literary training to analyze literature competently
    (D) legal interpretations of literature tend to focus on legal issues to the exclusion of other important elements
    (E) legal interpretations are only relevant to contemporary literature

7. According to Posner, the primary difficulty in using literary criticism to interpret law is that

    (A) the goals of the two disciplines are incompatible
    (B) there are few advocates for the law-and-literature movement in the literary profession
    (C) the task of interpreting law is too complex for the techniques of literary criticism
    (D) the interpretation of law relies heavily on legal precedent
    (E) legal scholars are reluctant to adopt the practice in the classroom

GO ON TO THE NEXT PAGE.

A recent generation of historians of science, far from portraying accepted scientific views as objectively accurate reflections of a natural world, explain the acceptance of such views in terms of the
(5) ideological biases of certain influential scientists or the institutional and rhetorical power such scientists wield. As an example of ideological bias, it has been argued that Pasteur rejected the theory of spontaneous generation not because of
(10) experimental evidence but because he rejected the materialist ideology implicit in that doctrine. These historians seem to find allies in certain philosophers of science who argue that scientific views are not imposed by reality but are free inventions of
(15) creative minds, and that scientific claims are never more than brave conjectures, always subject to inevitable future falsification. While these philosophers of science themselves would not be likely to have much truck with the recent historians,
(20) it is an easy step from their views to the extremism of the historians.

While this rejection of the traditional belief that scientific views are objective reflections of the world may be fashionable, it is deeply implausible. We
(25) now know, for example, that water is made of hydrogen and oxygen and that parents each contribute one-half of their children's complement of genes. I do not believe any serious-minded and informed person can claim that these statements are
(30) not factual descriptions of the world or that they will inevitably be falsified.

However, science's accumulation of lasting truths about the world is not by any means a straightforward matter. We certainly need to
(35) get beyond the naïve view that the truth will automatically reveal itself to any scientist who looks in the right direction; most often, in fact, a whole series of prior discoveries is needed to tease reality's truths from experiment and observation.
(40) And the philosophers of science mentioned above are quite right to argue that new scientific ideas often correct old ones by indicating errors and imprecisions (as, say, Newton's ideas did to Kepler's). Nor would I deny that there are
(45) interesting questions to be answered about the social processes in which scientific activity is embedded. The persuasive processes by which particular scientific groups establish their experimental results as authoritative are themselves
(50) social activities and can be rewardingly studied as such. Indeed, much of the new work in the history of science has been extremely revealing about the institutional interactions and rhetorical devices that help determine whose results achieve prominence.
(55) But one can accept all this without accepting the thesis that natural reality never plays any part at all in determining what scientists believe. What the new historians ought to be showing us is how those doctrines that do in fact fit reality work their way
(60) through the complex social processes of scientific activity to eventually receive general scientific acceptance.

8. It can be inferred from the passage that the author would be most likely to agree with which one of the following characterizations of scientific truth?

(A) It is often implausible.
(B) It is subject to inevitable falsification.
(C) It is rarely obvious and transparent.
(D) It is rarely discovered by creative processes.
(E) It is less often established by experimentation than by the rhetorical power of scientists.

9. According to the passage, Kepler's ideas provide an example of scientific ideas that were

(A) corrected by subsequent inquiries
(B) dependent on a series of prior observations
(C) originally thought to be imprecise and then later confirmed
(D) established primarily by the force of an individual's rhetorical power
(E) specifically taken up for the purpose of falsification by later scientists

10. In the third paragraph of the passage, the author is primarily concerned with

(A) presenting conflicting explanations for a phenomenon
(B) suggesting a field for possible future research
(C) qualifying a previously expressed point of view
(D) providing an answer to a theoretical question
(E) attacking the assumptions that underlie a set of beliefs

11. The use of the words "any serious-minded and informed person" (lines 28-29) serves which one of the following functions in the context of the passage?

(A) to satirize chronologically earlier notions about the composition of water
(B) to reinforce a previously stated opinion about certain philosophers of science
(C) to suggest the author's reservations about the "traditional belief" mentioned in line 22
(D) to anticipate objections from someone who would argue for an objectively accurate description of the world
(E) to discredit someone who would argue that certain scientific assertions do not factually describe reality

GO ON TO THE NEXT PAGE.

12. It can be inferred from the passage that the author would most likely agree with which one of the following statements about the relationship between the views of "certain philosophers of science" (lines 12-13) and those of the recent historians?

(A) These two views are difficult to differentiate.
(B) These two views share some similarities.
(C) The views of the philosophers ought to be seen as the source of the historians' views.
(D) Both views emphasize the rhetorical power of scientists.
(E) The historians explicitly acknowledge that their views are indebted to those of the philosophers.

13. Which one of the following best characterizes the author's assessment of the opinions of the new historians of science, as these opinions are presented in the passage?

(A) They lack any credibility.
(B) They themselves can be rewardingly studied as social phenomena.
(C) They are least convincing when they concern the actions of scientific groups.
(D) Although they are gross overstatements, they lead to some valuable insights.
(E) Although they are now popular, they are likely to be refuted soon.

14. In concluding the passage, the author does which one of the following?

(A) offers a prescription
(B) presents a paradox
(C) makes a prediction
(D) concedes an argument
(E) anticipates objections

15. The author's attitude toward the "thesis" mentioned in line 56 is revealed in which one of the following pairs of words?

(A) "biases" (line 5) and "rhetorical" (line 6)
(B) "wield" (line 7) and "falsification" (line 17)
(C) "conjectures" (line 16) and "truck with" (line 19)
(D) "extremism" (line 20) and "implausible" (line 24)
(E) "naïve" (line 35) and "errors" (line 42)

GO ON TO THE NEXT PAGE.

Until recently, it was thought that the Cherokee, a Native American tribe, were compelled to assimilate Euro-American culture during the 1820s. During that decade, it was supposed, White (5) missionaries arrived and, together with their part-Cherokee intermediaries, imposed the benefits of "civilization" on Cherokee tribes while the United States government actively promoted acculturalization by encouraging the Cherokee to (10) switch from hunting to settled agriculture. This view was based on the assumption that the end of a Native American group's economic and political autonomy would automatically mean the end of its cultural autonomy as well.

(15) William G. McLoughlin has recently argued that not only did Cherokee culture flourish during and after the 1820s, but the Cherokee themselves actively and continually reshaped their culture. Missionaries did have a decisive impact during (20) these years, he argues, but that impact was far from what it was intended to be. The missionaries' tendency to cater to the interests of an acculturating part-Cherokee elite (who comprised the bulk of their converts) at the expense of the more (25) traditionalist full-Cherokee majority created great intratribal tensions. As the elite initiated reforms designed to legitimize their own and the Cherokee Nation's place in the new republic of the United States, antimission Cherokee reacted by fostering (30) revivals of traditional religious beliefs and practices. However, these revivals did not, according to McLoughlin, undermine the elitist reforms, but supplemented them with popular, traditionalist counterparts.

(35) Traditionalist Cherokee did not reject the elitist reforms outright, McLoughlin argues, simply because they recognized that there was more than one way to use the skills the missionaries could provide them. As he quotes one group as saying, (40) "We want our children to learn English so that the White man cannot cheat us." Many traditionalist Cherokee welcomed the missionaries for another reason: they perceived that it would be useful to have White allies. In the end, McLoughlin asserts, (45) most members of the Cherokee council, including traditionalists, supported a move which preserved many of the reforms of the part-Cherokee elite but limited the activities and influence of the missionaries and other White settlers. According to (50) McLoughlin, the identity and culture that resulted were distinctively Cherokee, yet reflected the larger political and social setting in which they flourished.

Because his work concentrates on the nineteenth century, McLoughlin unfortunately overlooks (55) earlier sources of influence, such as eighteenth-century White resident traders and neighbors, thus obscuring the relative impact of the missionaries of the 1820s in contributing to both acculturalization and resistance to it among the (60) Cherokee. However, McLoughlin is undoubtedly

correct in recognizing that culture is an ongoing process rather than a static entity, and he has made a significant contribution to our understanding of how Cherokee culture changed while retaining its (65) essential identity after confronting the missionaries.

16. Which one of the following best states the main idea of the passage?

(A) McLoughlin's studies of the impact of missionaries on Cherokee culture during the 1820s are fundamentally flawed, since McLoughlin ignores the greater impact of White resident traders in the eighteenth century.

(B) Though his work is limited in perspective, McLoughlin is substantially correct that changes in Cherokee culture in the 1820s were mediated by the Cherokee themselves rather than simply imposed by the missionaries.

(C) Although McLoughlin is correct in asserting that cultural changes among the Cherokee were autonomous and so not a result of the presence of missionaries, he overemphasizes the role of intratribal conflicts.

(D) McLoughlin has shown that Cherokee culture not only flourished during and after the 1820s, but that changes in Cherokee culture during this time developed naturally from elements already present in Cherokee culture.

(E) Although McLoughlin overlooks a number of relevant factors in Cherokee cultural change in the 1820s, he convincingly demonstrates that these changes were fostered primarily by missionaries.

GO ON TO THE NEXT PAGE.

17. Which one of the following statements regarding the Cherokee council in the 1820s can be inferred from the passage?

(A) Members of the Cherokee council were elected democratically by the entire Cherokee Nation.

(B) In order for a policy to come into effect for the Cherokee Nation, it had to have been approved by a unanimous vote of the Cherokee council.

(C) Despite the fact that the Cherokee were dominated politically and economically by the United States in the 1820s, the Cherokee council was able to override policies set by the United States government.

(D) Though it did not have complete autonomy in governing the Cherokee Nation, it was able to set some policies affecting the activities of White people living in tribal areas.

(E) The proportions of traditionalist and acculturating Cherokee in the Cherokee council were determined by the proportions of traditionalist and acculturating Cherokee in the Cherokee population.

18. Which one of the following statements regarding the attitudes of traditionalist Cherokee toward the reforms that were instituted in the 1820s can be inferred from the passage?

(A) They supported the reforms merely as a way of placating the increasingly vocal acculturating elite.

(B) They thought that the reforms would lead to the destruction of traditional Cherokee culture but felt powerless to stop the reforms.

(C) They supported the reforms only because they thought that they were inevitable and it was better that the reforms appear to have been initiated by the Cherokee themselves.

(D) They believed that the reforms were a natural extension of already existing Cherokee traditions.

(E) They viewed the reforms as a means of preserving the Cherokee Nation and protecting it against exploitation.

19. According to the passage, McLoughlin cites which one of the following as a contributing factor in the revival of traditional religious beliefs among the Cherokee in the 1820s?

(A) Missionaries were gaining converts at an increasing rate as the 1820s progressed.

(B) The traditionalist Cherokee majority thought that most of the reforms initiated by the missionaries' converts would corrupt Cherokee culture.

(C) Missionaries unintentionally created conflict among the Cherokee by favoring the interests of the acculturating elite at the expense of the more traditionalist majority.

(D) Traditionalist Cherokee recognized that only some of the reforms instituted by a small Cherokee elite would be beneficial to all Cherokee.

(E) A small group of Cherokee converted by missionaries attempted to institute reforms designed to acquire political supremacy for themselves in the Cherokee council.

20. Which one of the following, if true, would most seriously undermine McLoughlin's account of the course of reform among the Cherokee during the 1820s?

(A) Traditionalist Cherokee gained control over the majority of seats on the Cherokee council during the 1820s.

(B) The United States government took an active interest in political and cultural developments within Native American tribes.

(C) The missionaries living among the Cherokee in the 1820s were strongly in favor of the cultural reforms initiated by the acculturating elite.

(D) Revivals of traditional Cherokee religious beliefs and practices began late in the eighteenth century, before the missionaries arrived.

(E) The acculturating Cherokee elite of the 1820s did not view the reforms they initiated as beneficial to all Cherokee.

21. It can be inferred from the author's discussion of McLoughlin's views that the author thinks that Cherokee acculturalization in the 1820s

(A) was reversed in the decades following the 1820s

(B) may have been part of an already-existing process of acculturalization

(C) could have been the result of earlier contacts with missionaries

(D) would not have occurred without the encouragement of the United States government

(E) was primarily a result of the influence of White traders living near the Cherokee

GO ON TO THE NEXT PAGE.

In the history of nineteenth-century landscape painting in the United States, the Luminists are distinguished by their focus on atmosphere and light. The accepted view of Luminist paintings is
(5) that they are basically spiritual and imply a tranquil mysticism that contrasts with earlier American artists' concept of nature as dynamic and energetic. According to this view, the Luminist atmosphere, characterized by "pure and constant light," guides
(10) the onlooker toward a lucid transcendentalism, an idealized vision of the world.

What this view fails to do is to identify the true significance of this transcendental atmosphere in Luminist paintings. The prosaic factors that are
(15) revealed by a closer examination of these works suggest that the glowing appearance of nature in Luminism is actually a sign of nature's domestication, its adaptation to human use. The idealized Luminist atmosphere thus seems to
(20) convey, not an intensification of human responses to nature, but rather a muting of those emotions, like awe and fear, which untamed nature elicits.

One critic, in describing the spiritual quality of harbor scenes by Fitz Hugh Lane, an important
(25) Luminist, carefully notes that "at the peak of Luminist development in the 1850s and 1860s, spiritualism in America was extremely widespread." It is also true, however, that the 1850s and 1860s were a time of trade expansion. From 1848 until his
(30) death in 1865, Lane lived in a house with a view of the harbor of Gloucester, Massachusetts, and he made short trips to Maine, New York, Baltimore, and probably Puerto Rico. In all of these places he painted the harbors with their ships—the
(35) instruments of expanding trade.

Lane usually depicts places like New York Harbor, with ships at anchor, but even when he depicts more remote, less commercially active harbors, nature appears pastoral and domesticated
(40) rather than primitive or unexplored. The ships, rather than the surrounding landscapes—including the sea—are generally the active element in his pictures. For Lane the sea is, in effect, a canal or a trade route for commercial activity, not a free,
(45) powerful element, as it is in the early pictures of his predecessor, Cole. For Lane nature is subdued, even when storms are approaching; thus, the sea is always a viable highway for the transport of goods. In sum, I consider Lane's sea simply an environment
(50) for human activity—nature no longer inviolate. The luminescence that Lane paints symbolizes nature's humbled state, for the light itself is as docile as the Luminist sea, and its tranquillity in a sense signifies no more than good conditions on the
(55) highway to progress. Progress, probably even more than transcendence, is the secret message of Luminism. In a sense, Luminist pictures are an ideological justification of the atmosphere necessary for business, if also an exaggerated,
(60) idealistic rendering of that atmosphere.

22. The passage is primarily concerned with discussing

(A) the importance of religion to the art of a particular period
(B) the way one artist's work illustrates a tradition of painting
(C) the significance of the sea in one artist's work
(D) differences in the treatment of nature as a more active or a less active force
(E) variations in the artistic treatment of light among nineteenth-century landscape painters

23. The author argues that nature is portrayed in Lane's pictures as

(A) wild and unexplored
(B) idealized and distant
(C) continually changing
(D) difficult to understand
(E) subordinate to human concerns

24. The passage contains information to suggest that the author would most probably agree with which one of the following statements?

(A) The prevailing religious principles of a given time can be reflected in the art of that time.
(B) In order to interest viewers, works of art must depict familiar subjects in detail.
(C) Because commerce is unusual as a subject in art, the painter of commercial activity must travel and observe it widely.
(D) Knowing about the environment in which an artist lived can aid in an understanding of a work by that artist.
(E) The most popular works of art at a given time are devoted to furthering economic or social progress.

GO ON TO THE NEXT PAGE.

25. According to the author, a supporter of the view of Luminism described in the first paragraph would most likely

   (A) be unimpressed by the paintings' glowing light
   (B) consider Luminist scenes to be undomesticated and wild
   (C) interpret the Luminist depiction of nature incorrectly
   (D) see Luminist paintings as practical rather than mystical
   (E) focus on the paintings' subject matter instead of on atmosphere and light

26. According to the author, the sea is significant in Lane's paintings because of its association with

   (A) exploration
   (B) commerce
   (C) canals
   (D) idealism
   (E) mysticism

27. The author's primary purpose is to

   (A) refute a new theory
   (B) replace an inadequate analysis
   (C) summarize current critics' attitudes
   (D) support another critic's evaluation
   (E) describe the history of a misinterpretation

28. The author quotes a critic writing about Lane (lines 25-27) most probably in order to

   (A) suggest that Luminism was the dominant mode of painting in the 1850s and 1860s
   (B) support the idea that Lane was interested in spiritualism
   (C) provide an example of the primary cultural factors that influenced the Luminists
   (D) explain why the development of Luminism coincided with that of spiritualism
   (E) illustrate a common misconception concerning an important characteristic of Lane's paintings

S T O P

IF YOU FINISH BEFORE TIME IS CALLED, YOU MAY CHECK YOUR WORK ON THIS SECTION ONLY.
DO NOT WORK ON ANY OTHER SECTION IN THE TEST.

SECTION IV

Time—35 minutes

25 Questions

Directions: The questions in this section are based on the reasoning contained in brief statements or passages. For some questions, more than one of the choices could conceivably answer the question. However, you are to choose the best answer; that is, the response that most accurately and completely answers the question. You should not make assumptions that are by commonsense standards implausible, superfluous, or incompatible with the passage. After you have chosen the best answer, blacken the corresponding space on your answer sheet.

1. Biotechnology companies say that voluntary guidelines for their industry are sufficient to ensure that no harm will result when a genetically altered organism is released into the environment. It is foolish, however, to rely on assurances from producers of genetically altered organisms that their products will not be harmful. Therefore, a biotechnology company should be required to apply to an independent regulatory board composed of scientists outside the biotechnology industry for the right to sell newly created organisms.

   Which one of the following principles, if accepted, most strongly justifies drawing the conclusion above?

   (A) Voluntary guidelines are sufficient to regulate activities that pose little danger to the environment.
   (B) People who engage in an activity and have a financial stake in that activity should not be the sole regulators of that activity.
   (C) Methods that result in harm to the environment must sometimes be used in order to avoid even greater harm.
   (D) A company is obligated to ensure the effectiveness of its products but not their environmental safety.
   (E) Issues of environmental protection are so important that they should not be left to scientific experts.

2. Zoo director: The city is in a financial crisis and must reduce its spending. Nevertheless, at least one reduction measure in next year's budget, cutting City Zoo's funding in half, is false economy. The zoo's current budget equals less than 1 percent of the city's deficit, so withdrawing support from the zoo does little to help the city's financial situation. Furthermore, the zoo, which must close if its budget is cut, attracts tourists and tax dollars to the city. Finally, the zoo adds immeasurably to the city's cultural climate and thus makes the city an attractive place for business to locate.

   Which one of the following is the main conclusion of the zoo director's argument?

   (A) Reducing spending is the only means the city has of responding to the current financial crisis.
   (B) It would be false economy for the city to cut the zoo's budget in half.
   (C) City Zoo's budget is only a very small portion of the city's entire budget.
   (D) The zoo will be forced to close if its budget is cut.
   (E) The city's educational and cultural climate will be irreparably damaged if the zoo is forced to close.

GO ON TO THE NEXT PAGE.

3. A cat will not be affectionate toward people unless it is handled when it is a kitten. Since the cat that Paula plans to give to her friend was handled when it was a kitten, that cat will be affectionate toward people.

The flawed reasoning in the argument above most closely parallels that in which one of the following?

(A) Tulip bulbs will not produce flowers unless they are chilled for two months. Since the tulip bulbs in the clay pot were not chilled for two months, these bulbs will not produce flowers.

(B) Beets do not grow well unless the soil in which they are grown contains trace amounts of boron. Since the beets in this plot are growing well, the soil in the plot must contain trace amounts of boron.

(C) Fruit trees will not produce much fruit unless they are pruned properly. That the fruit trees at the local orchard produce a large amount of fruit proves that they have been pruned properly.

(D) Cranberries will not thrive unless they are grown in bogs. Since the cranberries in this area are not grown in bogs, these cranberries will not thrive.

(E) Grass seeds will not germinate well unless they are pressed firmly into the ground. The grass seeds sown in this yard were pressed firmly into the ground, so they will germinate well.

4. Until recently, anthropologists generally agreed that higher primates originated about 30 million years ago in the Al Fayyum region of Egypt. However, a 40-million-year-old fossilized fragment of a lower jawbone discovered in Burma (now called Myanmar) in 1978 was used to support the theory that the earliest higher primates originated in Burma. However, the claim is premature, for _____.

Which one of the following, if true, is the most logical completion of the paragraph above?

(A) there are no more primate species in Burma than there are in Egypt

(B) several anthropologists, using different dating methods, independently confirmed the estimated age of the jawbone fragment

(C) higher primates cannot be identified solely by their lower jawbones

(D) several prominent anthropologists do not believe that higher primates could have originated in either Egypt or Burma

(E) other archaeological expeditions in Burma have unearthed higher-primate fossilized bone fragments that are clearly older than 40 million years

5. The ends of modern centuries have been greeted with both apocalyptic anxieties and utopian fantasies. It is not surprising that both reactions have consistently proven to be misplaced. After all, the precise time when a century happens to end cannot have any special significance, since the Gregorian calendar, though widely used, is only one among many that people have devised.

Which one of the following, if true, could be substituted for the reason cited above while still preserving the force of the argument?

(A) It is logically impossible for both reactions to be correct at the same time.

(B) What is a utopian fantasy to one group of people may well be, for another group of people, a realization of their worst fears.

(C) The number system based on the number ten, in the absence of which one hundred years would not have the appearance of being a significant period of time, is by no means the only one that people have created.

(D) The firm expectation that something extraordinary is about to happen can make people behave in a manner that makes it less likely that something extraordinary will happen.

(E) Since a century far exceeds the normal human life span, people do not live long enough to learn from mistakes that they themselves made one hundred years before.

6. People who listen to certain recordings of music are in danger of being unduly influenced by spoken messages that have been recorded backwards on the records or tapes.

A consequence of the view above is that

(A) the spoken messages must be louder than the music on the recordings

(B) backwards messages can be added to a recording while still preserving all of the musical qualities of the recorded performance

(C) the recordings on which such messages appear are chosen for this purpose either because they are especially popular or because they induce a trancelike state

(D) if such messages must be comprehended to exert influence, then people must be able to comprehend spoken messages recorded backwards

(E) when people listen to recorded music, they pay full attention to the music as it plays

GO ON TO THE NEXT PAGE.

7. Advertisement: Over 80 percent of the people who test-drive a Zenith car end up buying one. So be warned: you should not test-drive a Zenith unless you are prepared to buy one, because if you so much as drive a Zenith around the block, there is a better than 80 percent chance you will choose to buy it.

If the advertisement is interpreted as implying that the quality of the car is unusually impressive, which one of the following, if true, most clearly casts doubt on that implication?

(A) Test-drives of Zenith cars are, according to Zenith sales personnel, generally more extensive than a drive around the block and encounter varied driving conditions.
(B) Usually dealers have enough Zenith models in stock that prospective purchasers are able to test-drive the exact model that they are considering for purchase.
(C) Those who take test-drives in cars are, in overwhelming proportions, people who have already decided to buy the model driven unless some fault should become evident.
(D) Almost 90 percent of the people who purchase a car do not do so on the day they take a first test-drive but do so after another test-drive.
(E) In some Zenith cars, a minor part has broken within the first year, and Zenith dealers have issued notices to owners that the dealers will replace the part with a redesigned one at no cost to owners.

8. In Malsenia sales of classical records are soaring. The buyers responsible for this boom are quite new to classical music and were drawn to it either by classical scores from television commercials or by theme tunes introducing major sports events on television. Audiences at classical concerts, however, are continually shrinking in Malsenia. It can be concluded from this that the new Malsenian converts to classical music, having initially experienced this music as recorded music, are most comfortable with classical music as recorded music and really have no desire to hear live performances.

The argument assumes which one of the following?

(A) To sell well in Malsenia, a classical record must include at least one piece familiar from television.
(B) At least some of the new Malsenian buyers of classical records have available to them the option of attending classical concerts.
(C) The number of classical concerts performed in Malsenia has not decreased in response to smaller audiences.
(D) The classical records available in Malsenia are, for the most part, not recordings of actual public concerts.
(E) Classical concerts in Malsenia are not limited to music that is readily available on recordings.

9. Brain scans of people exposed to certain neurotoxins reveal brain damage identical to that found in people suffering from Parkinson's disease. This fact shows not only that these neurotoxins cause this type of brain damage, but also that the brain damage itself causes Parkinson's disease. Thus brain scans can be used to determine who is likely to develop Parkinson's disease.

The argument contains which one of the following reasoning errors?

(A) It fails to establish that other methods that can be used to diagnose Parkinson's disease are less accurate than brain scans.
(B) It overestimates the importance of early diagnosis in determining appropriate treatments for people suffering from Parkinson's disease.
(C) It mistakes a correlation between the type of brain damage described and Parkinson's disease for a causal relation between the two.
(D) It assumes that people would want to know as early as possible whether they were likely to develop Parkinson's disease.
(E) It neglects to specify how the information provided by brain scans could be used either in treating Parkinson's disease or in monitoring the progression of the disease.

10. Almost all of the books published in the past 150 years were printed on acidic paper. Unfortunately, every kind of acidic paper gradually destroys itself due to its very acidity. This process of deterioration can be slowed if the books are stored in a cool, dry environment. Techniques, which are now being developed, to deacidify books will probably be applied only to books with historical significance.

If all of the statements in the passage above are true, which one of the following must also be true?

(A) If a book was published in the past 150 years and is historically insignificant, it will probably deteriorate completely.
(B) Almost all of the books published in the past 150 years will gradually destroy themselves.
(C) Almost all of the books that gradually deteriorate are made of acidic paper.
(D) If a book is of historical significance and was printed before 150 years ago, it will be deacidified.
(E) Books published on acidic paper in 1900 should now all be at about the same state of deterioration.

GO ON TO THE NEXT PAGE.

11. Civil libertarian: The categorical prohibition of any nonviolent means of expression inevitably poisons a society's intellectual atmosphere. Therefore, those advocating censorship of all potentially offensive art are pursuing a course that is harmful to society.

Censorship advocate: You're wrong, because many people are in agreement about what constitutes potentially offensive art.

The censorship advocate's rebuttal is flawed because it

(A) attempts to extract a general rule from a specific case

(B) extracts an erroneous principle from a commonly held belief

(C) attacks the civil libertarian's character instead of the argument

(D) relies on an irrelevant reason for rejecting the civil libertarian's argument

(E) uses hyperbolic, inflammatory language that obscures the issue at hand

12. Although most species of nondomestic mammals in Australia are marsupials, over 100 species— including seals, bats, and mice—are not marsupials but placentals. It is clear, however, that these placentals are not native to this island continent: all nonhuman placentals except the dingo, a dog introduced by the first humans that settled Australia, are animals whose ancestors could swim long distances, fly, or float on driftwood.

The conclusion above is properly drawn if which one of the following is assumed?

(A) Some marsupials now found in Australia might not be native to that continent, but rather might have been introduced to Australia by some other means.

(B) Humans who settled Australia probably introduced many of the placental mammal species now present on that continent.

(C) The only Australian placentals that could be native to Australia would be animals whose ancestors could not have reached Australia from elsewhere.

(D) No marsupials now found in Australia can swim long distances, fly, or float on driftwood.

(E) Seals, bats, and mice are typically found only in areas where there are no native marsupials.

13. I. Room air conditioners produced by Japanese manufacturers tend to be more reliable than those produced by United States manufacturers.

II. The average lifetime of room air conditioners produced by United States manufacturers is about fifteen years, the same as that of room air conditioners produced by Japanese manufacturers.

Which one of the following, if true, would best reconcile the two statements above?

(A) Reliability is a measure of how long a product functions without needing repair.

(B) Production facilities of firms designated as United States manufacturers are not all located in the United States.

(C) Damage to room air conditioners during shipping and installation does not occur with great frequency in the United States or in Japan.

(D) Room air conditioners have been manufactured for a longer time in the United States than in Japan.

(E) Japanese manufacturers often use more reliable components in their room air conditioners than do United States manufacturers.

14. In 1980 there was growing concern that the protective ozone layer over the Antarctic might be decreasing and thereby allowing so much harmful ultraviolet radiation to reach the Earth that polar marine life would be damaged. Some government officials dismissed these concerns, since statistics indicated that global atmospheric ozone levels remained constant.

The relevance of the evidence cited by the government officials in support of their position would be most seriously undermined if it were true that

(A) most species of plant and animal life flourish in warm climates rather than in the polar regions

(B) decreases in the amount of atmospheric ozone over the Antarctic ice cap tend to be seasonal rather than constant

(C) decreases in the amount of atmospheric ozone were of little concern before 1980

(D) quantities of atmospheric ozone shifted away from the polar caps, correspondingly increasing ozone levels in other regions

(E) even where the amount of atmospheric ozone is normal, some ultraviolet light reaches the Earth's surface

GO ON TO THE NEXT PAGE.

15. Goodbody, Inc., is in the process of finding tenants for its newly completed Parrot Quay commercial development, which will make available hundreds of thousands of square feet of new office space on what was formerly derelict property outside the financial center of the city. Surprisingly enough, the coming recession, though it will hurt most of the city's businesses, should help Goodbody to find tenants.

Which one of the following, if true, does most to help resolve the apparent paradox?

(A) Businesses forced to economize by the recession will want to take advantage of the lower rents available outside the financial center.

(B) Public transportation links the financial center with the area around Parrot Quay.

(C) The area in which the Parrot Quay development is located became derelict after the heavy industry that used to be there closed down in a previous recession.

(D) Many of Goodbody's other properties are in the financial center and will become vacant if the recession is severe enough to force Goodbody's tenants out of business.

(E) The recession is likely to have the most severe effect not on service industries, which require a lot of office space, but on manufacturers.

Questions 16-17

Dr. Kim: Electronic fetal monitors, now routinely used in hospital delivery rooms to check fetal heartbeat, are more intrusive than ordinary stethoscopes and do no more to improve the chances that a healthy baby will be born. Therefore, the additional cost of electronic monitoring is unjustified and such monitoring should be discontinued.

Dr. Anders: I disagree. Although you and I know that both methods are capable of providing the same information, electronic monitoring has been well worth the cost. Doctors now know the warning signs they need to listen for with stethoscopes, but only because of what was learned from using electronic monitors.

16. Which one of the following principles, if accepted, would provide the most support for Dr. Kim's contention that the use of electronic fetal monitors should be discontinued?

(A) Hospitals should discontinue the routine use of a monitoring method whenever an alternative method that provides more information becomes available.

(B) Monitoring procedures should be routinely used in delivery rooms only if they provide information of a kind that is potentially useful in ensuring that a healthy baby will be born.

(C) When two methods available to hospitals provide the same kind of information, the more intrusive method should not be used.

(D) When the use of a medical device has enabled doctors to learn something that improves the chances that babies will be born healthy, that device is well worth its cost.

(E) Routinely used medical procedures should be reevaluated periodically to be sure that these procedures provide reliable information.

17. As a reply to Dr. Kim's argument, Dr. Anders' response is inadequate because it

(A) misses the point at issue
(B) assumes what it sets out to prove
(C) confuses high cost with high quality
(D) overestimates the importance of technology to modern medicine
(E) overlooks the fact that a procedure can be extensively used without being the best procedure available

GO ON TO THE NEXT PAGE.

18. Professor Hartley's new book on moral philosophy contains numerous passages that can be found verbatim in an earlier published work by Hartley's colleague, Professor Lawrence. Therefore, in view of the fact that these passages were unattributed in Hartley's book, Hartley has been dishonest in not acknowledging the intellectual debt owed to Lawrence.

Which one of the following is an assumption on which the argument is based?

(A) Hartley could not have written the new book without the passages in question.

(B) While writing the new book, Hartley had access to the manuscript of Lawrence's book.

(C) A book on moral philosophy should contain only material representing the author's own convictions.

(D) Lawrence did not get the ideas in the passages in question or did not get their formulations originally from Hartley.

(E) Hartley considered the passages in question to be the best possible expressions of the ideas they contain.

19. People who receive unsolicited advice from someone whose advantage would be served if that advice is taken should regard the proffered advice with skepticism unless there is good reason to think that their interests substantially coincide with those of the advice giver in the circumstance in question.

This principle, if accepted, would justify which one of the following judgments?

(A) After learning by chance that Harriet is looking for a secure investment for her retirement savings, Floyd writes to her recommending the R&M Company as an especially secure investment. But since Floyd is the sole owner of R&M, Harriet should reject his advice out of hand and invest her savings elsewhere.

(B) While shopping for a refrigerator, Ramón is approached by a salesperson who, on the basis of her personal experience, warns him against the least expensive model. However, the salesperson's commission increases with the price of the refrigerator sold, so Ramón should not reject the least expensive model on the salesperson's advice alone.

(C) Mario wants to bring pastry to Yvette's party, and when he consults her Yvette suggests that he bring his favorite chocolate fudge brownies from the local bakery. However, since Yvette also prefers those brownies to any other pastry, Mario would be wise to check with others before following her recommendation.

(D) Sara overhears Ron talking about a course he will be teaching and interrupts to recommend a textbook for his course. However, even though Sara and Ron each wrote a chapter of this textbook, since the book's editor is a personal friend of Sara's, Ron should investigate further before deciding whether it is the best textbook for his course.

(E) Mei is buying fish for soup. Joel, who owns the fish market where Mei is a regular and valued customer, suggests a much less expensive fish than the fish Mei herself prefers. Since if Mei follows Joel's advice, Joel will make less profit on the sale than he would have otherwise, Mei should follow his recommendation.

GO ON TO THE NEXT PAGE.

20. Last year the county park system failed to generate enough revenue to cover its costs. Any business should be closed if it is unprofitable, but county parks are not businesses. Therefore, the fact that county parks are unprofitable does not by itself justify closing them.

The pattern of reasoning in the argument above is most closely paralleled in which one of the following?

(A) A prime-time television series should be canceled if it fails to attract a large audience, but the small audience attracted by the documentary series is not sufficient reason to cancel it, since it does not air during prime time.

(B) Although companies that manufacture and market automobiles in the United States must meet stringent air-quality standards, the OKESA company should be exempt from these standards since it manufactures bicycles in addition to automobiles.

(C) Although the province did not specifically intend to prohibit betting on horse races when it passed a law prohibiting gambling, such betting should be regarded as being prohibited because it is a form of gambling.

(D) Even though cockatiels are not, strictly speaking, members of the parrot family, they should be fed the same diet as most parrots since the cockatiel's dietary needs are so similar to those of parrots.

(E) Since minors are not subject to the same criminal laws as are adults, they should not be subject to the same sorts of punishments as those that apply to adults.

21. Jane: Professor Harper's ideas for modifying the design of guitars are of no value because there is no general agreement among musicians as to what a guitar should sound like and, consequently, no widely accepted basis for evaluating the merits of a guitar's sound.

Mark: What's more, Harper's ideas have had enough time to be adopted if they really resulted in superior sound. It took only ten years for the Torres design for guitars to be almost universally adopted because of the improvement it makes in tonal quality.

Which one of the following most accurately describes the relationship between Jane's argument and Mark's argument?

(A) Mark's argument shows how a weakness in Jane's argument can be overcome.

(B) Mark's argument has a premise in common with Jane's argument.

(C) Mark and Jane use similar techniques to argue for different conclusions.

(D) Mark's argument restates Jane's argument in other terms.

(E) Mark's argument and Jane's argument are based on conflicting suppositions.

Questions 22–23

Doctors in Britain have long suspected that patients who wear tinted eyeglasses are abnormally prone to depression and hypochondria. Psychological tests given there to hospital patients admitted for physical complaints like heart pain and digestive distress confirmed such a relationship. Perhaps people whose relationship to the world is psychologically painful choose such glasses to reduce visual stimulation, which is perceived as irritating. At any rate, it can be concluded that when such glasses are worn, it is because the wearer has a tendency to be depressed or hypochondriacal.

22. The argument assumes which one of the following?

(A) Depression is not caused in some cases by an organic condition of the body.

(B) Wearers do not think of the tinted glasses as a means of distancing themselves from other people.

(C) Depression can have many causes, including actual conditions about which it is reasonable for anyone to be depressed.

(D) For hypochondriacs wearing tinted glasses, the glasses serve as a visual signal to others that the wearer's health is delicate.

(E) The tinting does not dim light to the eye enough to depress the wearer's mood substantially.

23. Each of the following, if true, weakens the argument EXCEPT:

(A) Some people wear tinted glasses not because they choose to do so but because a medical condition of their eyes forces them to do so.

(B) Even a depressed or hypochondriacal person can have valid medical complaints, so a doctor should perform all the usual objective tests in diagnosing such persons.

(C) The confirmatory tests were not done for places such as western North America where the usual quality of light differs from that prevailing in Britain.

(D) Fashions with respect to wearing tinted glasses differ in different parts of the world.

(E) At the hospitals where the tests were given, patients who were admitted for conditions less ambiguous than heart pain or digestive distress did not show the relationship between tinted glasses and depression or hypochondria.

GO ON TO THE NEXT PAGE.

24. The only fossilized bones of large prey found in and around settlements of early humans bear teeth marks of nonhuman predators on areas of the skeleton that had the most meat, and cut marks made by humans on the areas that had the least meat. The predators that hunted large prey invariably ate the meatiest parts of the carcasses, leaving uneaten remains behind.

If the information above is true, it provides the most support for which one of the following?

(A) Early humans were predators of small prey, not of large prey.

(B) Early humans ate fruits and edible roots as well as meat.

(C) Early humans would have been more effective hunters of large prey if they had hunted in large groups rather than individually.

(D) Early humans were not hunters of large prey but scavenged the uneaten remains of prey killed by other predators.

(E) Early humans were nomadic, and their settlements followed the migratory patterns of predators of large prey.

25. George: A well-known educator claims that children who are read to when they are very young are more likely to enjoy reading when they grow up than are children who were not read to. But this claim is clearly false. My cousin Emory was regularly read to as a child and as an adult he seldom reads for pleasure, whereas no one read to me and reading is now my favorite form of relaxation.

Ursula : You and Emory prove nothing in this case. Your experience is enough to refute the claim that all avid adult readers were read to as children, but what the educator said about reading to children is not that sort of claim.

Which one of the following describes a flaw in George's reasoning?

(A) He treats his own experience and the experiences of other members of his own family as though they have more weight as evidence than do the experiences of other people.

(B) He does not distinguish between the quality and the quantity of the books that adults read to Emory when Emory was a child.

(C) He overlooks the well-known fact that not all reading is equally relaxing.

(D) He fails to establish that the claim made by this particular educator accurately reflects the position held by the majority of educators.

(E) He attempts to refute a general claim by reference to nonconforming cases, although the claim is consistent with the occurrence of such cases.

S T O P

IF YOU FINISH BEFORE TIME IS CALLED, YOU MAY CHECK YOUR WORK ON THIS SECTION ONLY.
DO NOT WORK ON ANY OTHER SECTION IN THE TEST.

LSAT® Writing Sample Topic

Increased traffic has made it almost impossible to drive on Main Street in the historic town of Winfield. The town council has been presented with two proposals for remedying the problem, write an essay supporting one proposal over the other with the following in mind:

- The council wants to facilitate the flow of traffic on Main Street.
- The council wants to preserve and improve the town's attractiveness as a historic site.

The first plan would prohibit parking on Main Street and construct a four-story concrete garage on what is now an empty lot at one end of Main Street. The garage could be built in less than a year, and buses would shuttle people up and down Main Street. The garage would be significantly taller than any building in town. If parking fees were set at the level currently charged on Main Street, the garage would pay for itself in five years; thereafter income could be used to renovate several historic buildings that have fallen into disrepair and to maintain the historic district along Main Street.

Proponents of the second plan point out that much of the traffic on Main Street is merely passing through Winfield on its way to various surrounding towns. They propose building a bypass around the town and continuing to allow parking on Main Street. The county government, eager to speed traffic between the surrounding towns, will provide funds for the project, but three years would be required to build the four-lane highway and the only available route separates Winfield from a local battlefield that is an important element in the town's history. However, the highway will provide access to the original, but later abandoned, site of the town of Winfield. If the highway is built, a nearby museum plans a historically accurate restoration of the settlement.

Directions:

1. Use the Answer Key on the next page to check your answers.

2. Use the Scoring Worksheet below to compute your raw score.

3. Use the Score Conversion Chart to convert your raw score into the 120-180 scale.

Scoring Worksheet

1. Enter the number of questions you answered correctly in each section.

                        Number
                        Correct

    SECTION I . . . . . . _____
    SECTION II . . . . . _____
    SECTION III . . . . . _____
    SECTION IV . . . . . _____

2. Enter the sum here: _____
                        This is your Raw Score.

Conversion Chart

For Converting Raw Score to the 120-180 LSAT Scaled Score
LSAT Form 3LSS17

Reported Score	Raw Score Lowest	Raw Score Highest
180	99	101
179	97	98
178	96	96
177	95	95
176	94	94
175	93	93
174	92	92
173	91	91
172	90	90
171	89	89
170	88	88
169	86	87
168	85	85
167	83	84
166	82	82
165	80	81
164	79	79
163	77	78
162	75	76
161	73	74
160	72	72
159	70	71
158	68	69
157	66	67
156	64	65
155	63	63
154	61	62
153	59	60
152	57	58
151	55	56
150	53	54
149	52	52
148	50	51
147	48	49
146	46	47
145	45	45
144	43	44
143	41	42
142	40	40
141	38	39
140	36	37
139	35	35
138	33	34
137	32	32
136	31	31
135	29	30
134	28	28
133	27	27
132	26	26
131	25	25
130	24	24
129	23	23
128	22	22
127	21	21
126	20	20
125	19	19
124	—*	—*
123	18	18
122	17	17
121	—*	—*
120	0	16

*There is no raw score that will produce this scaled score for this form.

SECTION I

1.	C	8.	A	15.	C	22.	B
2.	D	9.	B	16.	A	23.	E
3.	D	10.	D	17.	C	24.	B
4.	A	11.	B	18.	E		
5.	C	12.	E	19.	A		
6.	E	13.	C	20.	E		
7.	D	14.	C	21.	D		

SECTION II

1.	D	8.	E	15.	A	22.	B
2.	C	9.	E	16.	D	23.	E
3.	A	10.	E	17.	C	24.	A
4.	D	11.	B	18.	A		
5.	D	12.	D	19.	B		
6.	B	13.	C	20.	A		
7.	B	14.	D	21.	A		

SECTION III

1.	A	8.	C	15.	D	22.	B
2.	E	9.	A	16.	B	23.	E
3.	A	10.	C	17.	D	24.	D
4.	C	11.	E	18.	E	25.	C
5.	B	12.	B	19.	C	26.	B
6.	A	13.	D	20.	D	27.	B
7.	A	14.	A	21.	B	28.	E

SECTION IV

1.	B	8.	B	15.	A	22.	E
2.	B	9.	C	16.	C	23.	B
3.	E	10.	A	17.	A	24.	D
4.	C	11.	D	18.	D	25.	E
5.	C	12.	C	19.	B		
6.	D	13.	A	20.	A		
7.	C	14.	D	21.	E		

LSAT® PREP TOOLS

The Official LSAT SuperPrep II™

SuperPrep II contains everything you need to prepare for the LSAT—a guide to all three LSAT question types, three actual LSATs, explanations for all questions in the three practice tests, answer keys, writing samples, and score-conversion tables, plus invaluable test-taking instructions to help with pacing and timing. SuperPrep has long been our most comprehensive LSAT preparation book, and SuperPrep II is even better. The practice tests in SuperPrep II are PrepTest 62 (December 2010 LSAT), PrepTest 63 (June 2011 LSAT), and one test that has never before been disclosed.

With this book you can

- Practice on genuine LSAT questions
- Review explanations for right and wrong answers
- Target specific categories for intensive review
- Simulate actual LSAT conditions

LSAC sets the standard for LSAT prep—and SuperPrep II raises the bar!

Available at your favorite bookseller.

LSAC.org

General Directions for the LSAT Answer Sheet

The actual testing time for this portion of the test will be 2 hours 55 minutes. There are five sections, each with a time limit of 35 minutes. The supervisor will tell you when to begin and end each section. If you finish a section before time is called, you may check your work on that section **only**; do not turn to any other section of the test book and do not work on any other section either in the test book or on the answer sheet.

There are several different types of questions on the test, and each question type has its own directions. **Be sure you understand the directions for each question type before attempting to answer any questions in that section.**

Not everyone will finish all the questions in the time allowed. Do not hurry, but work steadily and as quickly as you can without sacrificing accuracy. You are advised to use your time effectively. If a question seems too difficult, go on to the next one and return to the difficult question after completing the section. **MARK THE BEST ANSWER YOU CAN FOR EVERY QUESTION. NO DEDUCTIONS WILL BE MADE FOR WRONG ANSWERS. YOUR SCORE WILL BE BASED ONLY ON THE NUMBER OF QUESTIONS YOU ANSWER CORRECTLY.**

ALL YOUR ANSWERS MUST BE MARKED ON THE ANSWER SHEET. Answer spaces for each question are lettered to correspond with the letters of the potential answers to each question in the test book. After you have decided which of the answers is correct, blacken the corresponding space on the answer sheet. **BE SURE THAT EACH MARK IS BLACK AND COMPLETELY FILLS THE ANSWER SPACE.** Give only one answer to each question. If you change an answer, be sure that all previous marks are **erased completely.** Since the answer sheet is machine scored, incomplete erasures may be interpreted as intended answers. **ANSWERS RECORDED IN THE TEST BOOK WILL NOT BE SCORED.**

There may be more question numbers on this answer sheet than there are questions in a section. Do not be concerned, but be certain that the section and number of the question you are answering matches the answer sheet section and question number. Additional answer spaces in any answer sheet section should be left blank. Begin your next section in the number one answer space for that section.

LSAC takes various steps to ensure that answer sheets are returned from test centers in a timely manner for processing. In the unlikely event that an answer sheet is not received, LSAC will permit the examinee either to retest at no additional fee or to receive a refund of his or her LSAT fee. **THESE REMEDIES ARE THE ONLY REMEDIES AVAILABLE IN THE UNLIKELY EVENT THAT AN ANSWER SHEET IS NOT RECEIVED BY LSAC.**

Score Cancellation

Complete this section only if you are absolutely certain you want to cancel your score. **A CANCELLATION REQUEST CANNOT BE RESCINDED. IF YOU ARE AT ALL UNCERTAIN, YOU SHOULD NOT COMPLETE THIS SECTION.**

To cancel your score from this administration, you **must:**

A. fill in both ovals here ...... ○ ○

AND

B. read the following statement. Then sign your name and enter the date.
   YOUR SIGNATURE ALONE IS NOT SUFFICIENT FOR SCORE CANCELLATION. BOTH OVALS ABOVE MUST BE FILLED IN FOR SCANNING EQUIPMENT TO RECOGNIZE YOUR REQUEST FOR SCORE CANCELLATION.

I certify that I wish to cancel my test score from this administration. I understand that my request is irreversible and that my score will not be sent to me or to the law schools to which I apply.

_____
Sign your name in full

_____
Date

FOR LSAC USE ONLY   ●

HOW DID YOU PREPARE FOR THE LSAT?
(Select all that apply.)

Responses to this item are voluntary and will be used for statistical research purposes only.

○ By studying the free sample questions available on LSAC's website.
○ By taking the free sample LSAT available on LSAC's website.
○ By working through official LSAT *PrepTests*, *ItemWise*, and/or other LSAC test prep products.
○ By using LSAT prep books or software **not** published by LSAC.
○ By attending a commercial test preparation or coaching course.
○ By attending a test preparation or coaching course offered through an undergraduate institution.
○ Self study.
○ Other preparation.
○ No preparation.

CERTIFYING STATEMENT

Please write the following statement. Sign and date.

I certify that I am the examinee whose name appears on this answer sheet and that I am here to take the LSAT for the sole purpose of being considered for admission to law school. I further certify that I will neither assist nor receive assistance from any other candidate, and I agree not to copy, retain, or transmit examination questions in any form or discuss them with any other person.

_____
_____
_____
_____
_____
_____
_____
_____
_____

SIGNATURE: _____   TODAY'S DATE: ___/___/___
                                                            MONTH DAY YEAR

SCANTRON® EliteView™ EM-295665-1:654321

INSTRUCTIONS FOR COMPLETING THE BIOGRAPHICAL AREA ARE ON THE BACK COVER OF YOUR TEST BOOKLET.
USE ONLY A NO. 2 OR HB PENCIL TO COMPLETE THIS ANSWER SHEET. DO NOT USE INK.

A

1 LAST NAME | **FIRST NAME** | **MI**

2 LAST 4 DIGITS OF SOCIAL SECURITY/ SOCIAL INSURANCE NO.

L

3 LSAC ACCOUNT NUMBER

4 CENTER NUMBER

5 DATE OF BIRTH

MONTH	DAY	YEAR
Jan		
Feb		
Mar		
Apr		
May		
June		
July		
Aug		
Sept		
Oct		
Nov		
Dec		

6 TEST FORM CODE

7 RACIAL/ETHNIC DESCRIPTION
Mark one or more
- 1 Amer. Indian/Alaska Native
- 2 Asian
- 3 Black/African American
- 4 Canadian Aboriginal
- 5 Caucasian/White
- 6 Hispanic/Latino
- 7 Native Hawaiian/ Other Pacific Islander
- 8 Puerto Rican
- 9 TSI/Aboriginal Australian

8 SEX
- Male
- Female

9 DOMINANT LANGUAGE
- English
- Other

10 ENGLISH FLUENCY
- Yes
- No

11 TEST DATE
MONTH / DAY / YEAR

12 TEST FORM

Law School Admission Test

Mark one and only one answer to each question. Be sure to fill in completely the space for your intended answer choice. If you erase, do so completely. Make no stray marks.

13 TEST BOOK SERIAL NO.

SECTION 1

1 A B C D E
2 A B C D E
3 A B C D E
4 A B C D E
5 A B C D E
6 A B C D E
7 A B C D E
8 A B C D E
9 A B C D E
10 A B C D E
11 A B C D E
12 A B C D E
13 A B C D E
14 A B C D E
15 A B C D E
16 A B C D E
17 A B C D E
18 A B C D E
19 A B C D E
20 A B C D E
21 A B C D E
22 A B C D E
23 A B C D E
24 A B C D E
25 A B C D E
26 A B C D E
27 A B C D E
28 A B C D E
29 A B C D E
30 A B C D E

SECTION 2
1 A B C D E
2 A B C D E
3 A B C D E
4 A B C D E
5 A B C D E
6 A B C D E
7 A B C D E
8 A B C D E
9 A B C D E
10 A B C D E
11 A B C D E
12 A B C D E
13 A B C D E
14 A B C D E
15 A B C D E
16 A B C D E
17 A B C D E
18 A B C D E
19 A B C D E
20 A B C D E
21 A B C D E
22 A B C D E
23 A B C D E
24 A B C D E
25 A B C D E
26 A B C D E
27 A B C D E
28 A B C D E
29 A B C D E
30 A B C D E

SECTION 3
1 A B C D E
2 A B C D E
3 A B C D E
4 A B C D E
5 A B C D E
6 A B C D E
7 A B C D E
8 A B C D E
9 A B C D E
10 A B C D E
11 A B C D E
12 A B C D E
13 A B C D E
14 A B C D E
15 A B C D E
16 A B C D E
17 A B C D E
18 A B C D E
19 A B C D E
20 A B C D E
21 A B C D E
22 A B C D E
23 A B C D E
24 A B C D E
25 A B C D E
26 A B C D E
27 A B C D E
28 A B C D E
29 A B C D E
30 A B C D E

SECTION 4
1 A B C D E
2 A B C D E
3 A B C D E
4 A B C D E
5 A B C D E
6 A B C D E
7 A B C D E
8 A B C D E
9 A B C D E
10 A B C D E
11 A B C D E
12 A B C D E
13 A B C D E
14 A B C D E
15 A B C D E
16 A B C D E
17 A B C D E
18 A B C D E
19 A B C D E
20 A B C D E
21 A B C D E
22 A B C D E
23 A B C D E
24 A B C D E
25 A B C D E
26 A B C D E
27 A B C D E
28 A B C D E
29 A B C D E
30 A B C D E

SECTION 5
1 A B C D E
2 A B C D E
3 A B C D E
4 A B C D E
5 A B C D E
6 A B C D E
7 A B C D E
8 A B C D E
9 A B C D E
10 A B C D E
11 A B C D E
12 A B C D E
13 A B C D E
14 A B C D E
15 A B C D E
16 A B C D E
17 A B C D E
18 A B C D E
19 A B C D E
20 A B C D E
21 A B C D E
22 A B C D E
23 A B C D E
24 A B C D E
25 A B C D E
26 A B C D E
27 A B C D E
28 A B C D E
29 A B C D E
30 A B C D E

14 PLEASE PRINT INFORMATION

LAST NAME

FIRST NAME

DATE OF BIRTH

B

INSTRUCTIONS FOR COMPLETING THE BIOGRAPHICAL AREA ARE ON THE BACK COVER OF YOUR TEST BOOKLET.
USE ONLY A NO. 2 OR HB PENCIL TO COMPLETE THIS ANSWER SHEET. DO NOT USE INK.

A

1 LAST NAME | FIRST NAME | MI

2 LAST 4 DIGITS OF SOCIAL SECURITY/ SOCIAL INSURANCE NO.

3 LSAC ACCOUNT NUMBER

4 CENTER NUMBER

5 DATE OF BIRTH
MONTH | DAY | YEAR
Jan
Feb
Mar
Apr
May
June
July
Aug
Sept
Oct
Nov
Dec

6 TEST FORM CODE

7 RACIAL/ETHNIC DESCRIPTION
Mark one or more
1 Amer. Indian/Alaska Nati
2 Asian
3 Black/African American
4 Canadian Aboriginal
5 Caucasian/White
6 Hispanic/Latino
7 Native Hawaiian/ Other Pacific Islander
8 Puerto Rican
9 TSI/Aboriginal Australia

8 SEX
Male
Female

9 DOMINANT LANGUAGE
English
Other

10 ENGLISH FLUENCY
Yes
No

11 TEST DATE
MONTH   DAY   YEAR

12 TEST FORM

Law School Admission Test

Mark one and only one answer to each question. Be sure to fill in completely the space for your intended answer choice. If you erase, do so completely. Make no stray marks.

13 TEST BOOK SERIAL NO.

SECTION 1 | **SECTION 2** | **SECTION 3** | **SECTION 4** | **SECTION 5**

1 A B C D E (rows 1–30 for each of the five sections)

14 PLEASE PRINT INFORMATION

LAST NAME

FIRST NAME

DATE OF BIRTH

B

SCANTRON® EliteView™ EM-295665-1:654321

INSTRUCTIONS FOR COMPLETING THE BIOGRAPHICAL AREA ARE ON THE BACK COVER OF YOUR TEST BOOKLET.
USE ONLY A NO. 2 OR HB PENCIL TO COMPLETE THIS ANSWER SHEET. DO NOT USE INK.

A

1 LAST NAME | FIRST NAME | MI

2 LAST 4 DIGITS OF SOCIAL SECURITY/ SOCIAL INSURANCE NO.

L

3 LSAC ACCOUNT NUMBER

4 CENTER NUMBER

5 DATE OF BIRTH
MONTH | DAY | YEAR
○ Jan
○ Feb
○ Mar
○ Apr
○ May
○ June
○ July
○ Aug
○ Sept
○ Oct
○ Nov
○ Dec

6 TEST FORM CODE

7 RACIAL/ETHNIC DESCRIPTION
Mark one or more
○ 1 Amer. Indian/Alaska Native
○ 2 Asian
○ 3 Black/African American
○ 4 Canadian Aboriginal
○ 5 Caucasian/White
○ 6 Hispanic/Latino
○ 7 Native Hawaiian/ Other Pacific Islander
○ 8 Puerto Rican
○ 9 TSI/Aboriginal Australian

8 SEX
○ Male
○ Female

9 DOMINANT LANGUAGE
○ English
○ Other

10 ENGLISH FLUENCY
○ Yes
○ No

11 TEST DATE
MONTH / DAY / YEAR

12 TEST FORM

Law School Admission Test

Mark one and only one answer to each question. Be sure to fill in completely the space for your intended answer choice. If you erase, do so completely. Make no stray marks.

SECTION 1 | **SECTION 2** | **SECTION 3** | **SECTION 4** | **SECTION 5**

(Each section numbered 1–30 with answer bubbles Ⓐ Ⓑ Ⓒ Ⓓ Ⓔ)

13 TEST BOOK SERIAL NO.

14 PLEASE PRINT INFORMATION

LAST NAME

FIRST NAME

DATE OF BIRTH

(B)

SCANTRON EliteView™ EM-295665-1:654321

INSTRUCTIONS FOR COMPLETING THE BIOGRAPHICAL AREA ARE ON THE BACK COVER OF YOUR TEST BOOKLET.
USE ONLY A NO. 2 OR HB PENCIL TO COMPLETE THIS ANSWER SHEET. DO NOT USE INK.

A

1 LAST NAME / FIRST NAME / MI

2 LAST 4 DIGITS OF SOCIAL SECURITY/ SOCIAL INSURANCE NO.

3 LSAC ACCOUNT NUMBER

4 CENTER NUMBER

5 DATE OF BIRTH

MONTH	DAY	YEAR
Jan		
Feb		
Mar		
Apr		
May		
June		
July		
Aug		
Sept		
Oct		
Nov		
Dec		

6 TEST FORM CODE

7 RACIAL/ETHNIC DESCRIPTION
Mark one or more
- 1 Amer. Indian/Alaska Nati
- 2 Asian
- 3 Black/African American
- 4 Canadian Aboriginal
- 5 Caucasian/White
- 6 Hispanic/Latino
- 7 Native Hawaiian/ Other Pacific Islander
- 8 Puerto Rican
- 9 TSI/Aboriginal Australia

8 SEX
- Male
- Female

9 DOMINANT LANGUAGE
- English
- Other

10 ENGLISH FLUENCY
- Yes
- No

11 TEST DATE
MONTH DAY YEAR

12 TEST FORM

Law School Admission Test

Mark one and only one answer to each question. Be sure to fill in completely the space for your intended answer choice. If you erase, do so completely. Make no stray marks.

13 TEST BOOK SERIAL NO.

SECTION 1	SECTION 2	SECTION 3	SECTION 4	SECTION 5
1–30 A B C D E	1–30 A B C D E	1–30 A B C D E	1–30 A B C D E	1–30 A B C D E

14 PLEASE PRINT INFORMATION

LAST NAME

FIRST NAME

DATE OF BIRTH

B

INSTRUCTIONS FOR COMPLETING THE BIOGRAPHICAL AREA ARE ON THE BACK COVER OF YOUR TEST BOOKLET.
USE ONLY A NO. 2 OR HB PENCIL TO COMPLETE THIS ANSWER SHEET. DO NOT USE INK.

A

1 LAST NAME / FIRST NAME / MI

2 LAST 4 DIGITS OF SOCIAL SECURITY/ SOCIAL INSURANCE NO.

L

3 LSAC ACCOUNT NUMBER

4 CENTER NUMBER

5 DATE OF BIRTH

MONTH	DAY	YEAR
◯ Jan		
◯ Feb		
◯ Mar		
◯ Apr		
◯ May		
◯ June		
◯ July		
◯ Aug		
◯ Sept		
◯ Oct		
◯ Nov		
◯ Dec		

6 TEST FORM CODE

7 RACIAL/ETHNIC DESCRIPTION
Mark one or more
- ◯ 1 Amer. Indian/Alaska Native
- ◯ 2 Asian
- ◯ 3 Black/African American
- ◯ 4 Canadian Aboriginal
- ◯ 5 Caucasian/White
- ◯ 6 Hispanic/Latino
- ◯ 7 Native Hawaiian/ Other Pacific Islander
- ◯ 8 Puerto Rican
- ◯ 9 TSI/Aboriginal Australian

8 SEX
- ◯ Male
- ◯ Female

9 DOMINANT LANGUAGE
- ◯ English
- ◯ Other

10 ENGLISH FLUENCY
- ◯ Yes
- ◯ No

11 TEST DATE
____ / ____ / ____
MONTH   DAY   YEAR

12 TEST FORM

Law School Admission Test

Mark one and only one answer to each question. Be sure to fill in completely the space for your intended answer choice. If you erase, do so completely. Make no stray marks.

13 TEST BOOK SERIAL NO.

SECTION 1	SECTION 2	SECTION 3	SECTION 4	SECTION 5
1 Ⓐ Ⓑ Ⓒ Ⓓ Ⓔ	1 Ⓐ Ⓑ Ⓒ Ⓓ Ⓔ	1 Ⓐ Ⓑ Ⓒ Ⓓ Ⓔ	1 Ⓐ Ⓑ Ⓒ Ⓓ Ⓔ	1 Ⓐ Ⓑ Ⓒ Ⓓ Ⓔ
2 Ⓐ Ⓑ Ⓒ Ⓓ Ⓔ	2 Ⓐ Ⓑ Ⓒ Ⓓ Ⓔ	2 Ⓐ Ⓑ Ⓒ Ⓓ Ⓔ	2 Ⓐ Ⓑ Ⓒ Ⓓ Ⓔ	2 Ⓐ Ⓑ Ⓒ Ⓓ Ⓔ
3 Ⓐ Ⓑ Ⓒ Ⓓ Ⓔ	3 Ⓐ Ⓑ Ⓒ Ⓓ Ⓔ	3 Ⓐ Ⓑ Ⓒ Ⓓ Ⓔ	3 Ⓐ Ⓑ Ⓒ Ⓓ Ⓔ	3 Ⓐ Ⓑ Ⓒ Ⓓ Ⓔ
4 Ⓐ Ⓑ Ⓒ Ⓓ Ⓔ	4 Ⓐ Ⓑ Ⓒ Ⓓ Ⓔ	4 Ⓐ Ⓑ Ⓒ Ⓓ Ⓔ	4 Ⓐ Ⓑ Ⓒ Ⓓ Ⓔ	4 Ⓐ Ⓑ Ⓒ Ⓓ Ⓔ
5 Ⓐ Ⓑ Ⓒ Ⓓ Ⓔ	5 Ⓐ Ⓑ Ⓒ Ⓓ Ⓔ	5 Ⓐ Ⓑ Ⓒ Ⓓ Ⓔ	5 Ⓐ Ⓑ Ⓒ Ⓓ Ⓔ	5 Ⓐ Ⓑ Ⓒ Ⓓ Ⓔ
6 Ⓐ Ⓑ Ⓒ Ⓓ Ⓔ	6 Ⓐ Ⓑ Ⓒ Ⓓ Ⓔ	6 Ⓐ Ⓑ Ⓒ Ⓓ Ⓔ	6 Ⓐ Ⓑ Ⓒ Ⓓ Ⓔ	6 Ⓐ Ⓑ Ⓒ Ⓓ Ⓔ
7 Ⓐ Ⓑ Ⓒ Ⓓ Ⓔ	7 Ⓐ Ⓑ Ⓒ Ⓓ Ⓔ	7 Ⓐ Ⓑ Ⓒ Ⓓ Ⓔ	7 Ⓐ Ⓑ Ⓒ Ⓓ Ⓔ	7 Ⓐ Ⓑ Ⓒ Ⓓ Ⓔ
8 Ⓐ Ⓑ Ⓒ Ⓓ Ⓔ	8 Ⓐ Ⓑ Ⓒ Ⓓ Ⓔ	8 Ⓐ Ⓑ Ⓒ Ⓓ Ⓔ	8 Ⓐ Ⓑ Ⓒ Ⓓ Ⓔ	8 Ⓐ Ⓑ Ⓒ Ⓓ Ⓔ
9 Ⓐ Ⓑ Ⓒ Ⓓ Ⓔ	9 Ⓐ Ⓑ Ⓒ Ⓓ Ⓔ	9 Ⓐ Ⓑ Ⓒ Ⓓ Ⓔ	9 Ⓐ Ⓑ Ⓒ Ⓓ Ⓔ	9 Ⓐ Ⓑ Ⓒ Ⓓ Ⓔ
10 Ⓐ Ⓑ Ⓒ Ⓓ Ⓔ	10 Ⓐ Ⓑ Ⓒ Ⓓ Ⓔ	10 Ⓐ Ⓑ Ⓒ Ⓓ Ⓔ	10 Ⓐ Ⓑ Ⓒ Ⓓ Ⓔ	10 Ⓐ Ⓑ Ⓒ Ⓓ Ⓔ
11 Ⓐ Ⓑ Ⓒ Ⓓ Ⓔ	11 Ⓐ Ⓑ Ⓒ Ⓓ Ⓔ	11 Ⓐ Ⓑ Ⓒ Ⓓ Ⓔ	11 Ⓐ Ⓑ Ⓒ Ⓓ Ⓔ	11 Ⓐ Ⓑ Ⓒ Ⓓ Ⓔ
12 Ⓐ Ⓑ Ⓒ Ⓓ Ⓔ	12 Ⓐ Ⓑ Ⓒ Ⓓ Ⓔ	12 Ⓐ Ⓑ Ⓒ Ⓓ Ⓔ	12 Ⓐ Ⓑ Ⓒ Ⓓ Ⓔ	12 Ⓐ Ⓑ Ⓒ Ⓓ Ⓔ
13 Ⓐ Ⓑ Ⓒ Ⓓ Ⓔ	13 Ⓐ Ⓑ Ⓒ Ⓓ Ⓔ	13 Ⓐ Ⓑ Ⓒ Ⓓ Ⓔ	13 Ⓐ Ⓑ Ⓒ Ⓓ Ⓔ	13 Ⓐ Ⓑ Ⓒ Ⓓ Ⓔ
14 Ⓐ Ⓑ Ⓒ Ⓓ Ⓔ	14 Ⓐ Ⓑ Ⓒ Ⓓ Ⓔ	14 Ⓐ Ⓑ Ⓒ Ⓓ Ⓔ	14 Ⓐ Ⓑ Ⓒ Ⓓ Ⓔ	14 Ⓐ Ⓑ Ⓒ Ⓓ Ⓔ
15 Ⓐ Ⓑ Ⓒ Ⓓ Ⓔ	15 Ⓐ Ⓑ Ⓒ Ⓓ Ⓔ	15 Ⓐ Ⓑ Ⓒ Ⓓ Ⓔ	15 Ⓐ Ⓑ Ⓒ Ⓓ Ⓔ	15 Ⓐ Ⓑ Ⓒ Ⓓ Ⓔ
16 Ⓐ Ⓑ Ⓒ Ⓓ Ⓔ	16 Ⓐ Ⓑ Ⓒ Ⓓ Ⓔ	16 Ⓐ Ⓑ Ⓒ Ⓓ Ⓔ	16 Ⓐ Ⓑ Ⓒ Ⓓ Ⓔ	16 Ⓐ Ⓑ Ⓒ Ⓓ Ⓔ
17 Ⓐ Ⓑ Ⓒ Ⓓ Ⓔ	17 Ⓐ Ⓑ Ⓒ Ⓓ Ⓔ	17 Ⓐ Ⓑ Ⓒ Ⓓ Ⓔ	17 Ⓐ Ⓑ Ⓒ Ⓓ Ⓔ	17 Ⓐ Ⓑ Ⓒ Ⓓ Ⓔ
18 Ⓐ Ⓑ Ⓒ Ⓓ Ⓔ	18 Ⓐ Ⓑ Ⓒ Ⓓ Ⓔ	18 Ⓐ Ⓑ Ⓒ Ⓓ Ⓔ	18 Ⓐ Ⓑ Ⓒ Ⓓ Ⓔ	18 Ⓐ Ⓑ Ⓒ Ⓓ Ⓔ
19 Ⓐ Ⓑ Ⓒ Ⓓ Ⓔ	19 Ⓐ Ⓑ Ⓒ Ⓓ Ⓔ	19 Ⓐ Ⓑ Ⓒ Ⓓ Ⓔ	19 Ⓐ Ⓑ Ⓒ Ⓓ Ⓔ	19 Ⓐ Ⓑ Ⓒ Ⓓ Ⓔ
20 Ⓐ Ⓑ Ⓒ Ⓓ Ⓔ	20 Ⓐ Ⓑ Ⓒ Ⓓ Ⓔ	20 Ⓐ Ⓑ Ⓒ Ⓓ Ⓔ	20 Ⓐ Ⓑ Ⓒ Ⓓ Ⓔ	20 Ⓐ Ⓑ Ⓒ Ⓓ Ⓔ
21 Ⓐ Ⓑ Ⓒ Ⓓ Ⓔ	21 Ⓐ Ⓑ Ⓒ Ⓓ Ⓔ	21 Ⓐ Ⓑ Ⓒ Ⓓ Ⓔ	21 Ⓐ Ⓑ Ⓒ Ⓓ Ⓔ	21 Ⓐ Ⓑ Ⓒ Ⓓ Ⓔ
22 Ⓐ Ⓑ Ⓒ Ⓓ Ⓔ	22 Ⓐ Ⓑ Ⓒ Ⓓ Ⓔ	22 Ⓐ Ⓑ Ⓒ Ⓓ Ⓔ	22 Ⓐ Ⓑ Ⓒ Ⓓ Ⓔ	22 Ⓐ Ⓑ Ⓒ Ⓓ Ⓔ
23 Ⓐ Ⓑ Ⓒ Ⓓ Ⓔ	23 Ⓐ Ⓑ Ⓒ Ⓓ Ⓔ	23 Ⓐ Ⓑ Ⓒ Ⓓ Ⓔ	23 Ⓐ Ⓑ Ⓒ Ⓓ Ⓔ	23 Ⓐ Ⓑ Ⓒ Ⓓ Ⓔ
24 Ⓐ Ⓑ Ⓒ Ⓓ Ⓔ	24 Ⓐ Ⓑ Ⓒ Ⓓ Ⓔ	24 Ⓐ Ⓑ Ⓒ Ⓓ Ⓔ	24 Ⓐ Ⓑ Ⓒ Ⓓ Ⓔ	24 Ⓐ Ⓑ Ⓒ Ⓓ Ⓔ
25 Ⓐ Ⓑ Ⓒ Ⓓ Ⓔ	25 Ⓐ Ⓑ Ⓒ Ⓓ Ⓔ	25 Ⓐ Ⓑ Ⓒ Ⓓ Ⓔ	25 Ⓐ Ⓑ Ⓒ Ⓓ Ⓔ	25 Ⓐ Ⓑ Ⓒ Ⓓ Ⓔ
26 Ⓐ Ⓑ Ⓒ Ⓓ Ⓔ	26 Ⓐ Ⓑ Ⓒ Ⓓ Ⓔ	26 Ⓐ Ⓑ Ⓒ Ⓓ Ⓔ	26 Ⓐ Ⓑ Ⓒ Ⓓ Ⓔ	26 Ⓐ Ⓑ Ⓒ Ⓓ Ⓔ
27 Ⓐ Ⓑ Ⓒ Ⓓ Ⓔ	27 Ⓐ Ⓑ Ⓒ Ⓓ Ⓔ	27 Ⓐ Ⓑ Ⓒ Ⓓ Ⓔ	27 Ⓐ Ⓑ Ⓒ Ⓓ Ⓔ	27 Ⓐ Ⓑ Ⓒ Ⓓ Ⓔ
28 Ⓐ Ⓑ Ⓒ Ⓓ Ⓔ	28 Ⓐ Ⓑ Ⓒ Ⓓ Ⓔ	28 Ⓐ Ⓑ Ⓒ Ⓓ Ⓔ	28 Ⓐ Ⓑ Ⓒ Ⓓ Ⓔ	28 Ⓐ Ⓑ Ⓒ Ⓓ Ⓔ
29 Ⓐ Ⓑ Ⓒ Ⓓ Ⓔ	29 Ⓐ Ⓑ Ⓒ Ⓓ Ⓔ	29 Ⓐ Ⓑ Ⓒ Ⓓ Ⓔ	29 Ⓐ Ⓑ Ⓒ Ⓓ Ⓔ	29 Ⓐ Ⓑ Ⓒ Ⓓ Ⓔ
30 Ⓐ Ⓑ Ⓒ Ⓓ Ⓔ	30 Ⓐ Ⓑ Ⓒ Ⓓ Ⓔ	30 Ⓐ Ⓑ Ⓒ Ⓓ Ⓔ	30 Ⓐ Ⓑ Ⓒ Ⓓ Ⓔ	30 Ⓐ Ⓑ Ⓒ Ⓓ Ⓔ

14 PLEASE PRINT INFORMATION

LAST NAME
_____

FIRST NAME
_____

DATE OF BIRTH
_____

●Ⓑ

SCANTRON® EliteView™ EM-295665-1:654321

A

INSTRUCTIONS FOR COMPLETING THE BIOGRAPHICAL AREA ARE ON THE BACK COVER OF YOUR TEST BOOKLET.
USE ONLY A NO. 2 OR HB PENCIL TO COMPLETE THIS ANSWER SHEET. DO NOT USE INK.

1 LAST NAME | FIRST NAME | MI

2 LAST 4 DIGITS OF SOCIAL SECURITY/ SOCIAL INSURANCE NO.

L

3 LSAC ACCOUNT NUMBER

4 CENTER NUMBER

5 DATE OF BIRTH

MONTH	DAY	YEAR
Jan		
Feb		
Mar		
Apr		
May		
June		
July		
Aug		
Sept		
Oct		
Nov		
Dec		

6 TEST FORM CODE

7 RACIAL/ETHNIC DESCRIPTION
Mark one or more
- 1 Amer. Indian/Alaska Nat
- 2 Asian
- 3 Black/African America
- 4 Canadian Aboriginal
- 5 Caucasian/White
- 6 Hispanic/Latino
- 7 Native Hawaiian/ Other Pacific Islander
- 8 Puerto Rican
- 9 TSI/Aboriginal Australi

8 SEX
- Male
- Female

9 DOMINANT LANGUAGE
- English
- Other

10 ENGLISH FLUENCY
- Yes
- No

11 TEST DATE
MONTH / DAY / YEAR

12 TEST FORM

Law School Admission Test

Mark one and only one answer to each question. Be sure to fill in completely the space for your intended answer choice. If you erase, do so completely. Make no stray marks.

13 TEST BOOK SERIAL NO.

SECTION 1

1 A B C D E
2 A B C D E
3 A B C D E
4 A B C D E
5 A B C D E
6 A B C D E
7 A B C D E
8 A B C D E
9 A B C D E
10 A B C D E
11 A B C D E
12 A B C D E
13 A B C D E
14 A B C D E
15 A B C D E
16 A B C D E
17 A B C D E
18 A B C D E
19 A B C D E
20 A B C D E
21 A B C D E
22 A B C D E
23 A B C D E
24 A B C D E
25 A B C D E
26 A B C D E
27 A B C D E
28 A B C D E
29 A B C D E
30 A B C D E

SECTION 2

1 A B C D E
2 A B C D E
3 A B C D E
4 A B C D E
5 A B C D E
6 A B C D E
7 A B C D E
8 A B C D E
9 A B C D E
10 A B C D E
11 A B C D E
12 A B C D E
13 A B C D E
14 A B C D E
15 A B C D E
16 A B C D E
17 A B C D E
18 A B C D E
19 A B C D E
20 A B C D E
21 A B C D E
22 A B C D E
23 A B C D E
24 A B C D E
25 A B C D E
26 A B C D E
27 A B C D E
28 A B C D E
29 A B C D E
30 A B C D E

SECTION 3

1 A B C D E
2 A B C D E
3 A B C D E
4 A B C D E
5 A B C D E
6 A B C D E
7 A B C D E
8 A B C D E
9 A B C D E
10 A B C D E
11 A B C D E
12 A B C D E
13 A B C D E
14 A B C D E
15 A B C D E
16 A B C D E
17 A B C D E
18 A B C D E
19 A B C D E
20 A B C D E
21 A B C D E
22 A B C D E
23 A B C D E
24 A B C D E
25 A B C D E
26 A B C D E
27 A B C D E
28 A B C D E
29 A B C D E
30 A B C D E

SECTION 4

1 A B C D E
2 A B C D E
3 A B C D E
4 A B C D E
5 A B C D E
6 A B C D E
7 A B C D E
8 A B C D E
9 A B C D E
10 A B C D E
11 A B C D E
12 A B C D E
13 A B C D E
14 A B C D E
15 A B C D E
16 A B C D E
17 A B C D E
18 A B C D E
19 A B C D E
20 A B C D E
21 A B C D E
22 A B C D E
23 A B C D E
24 A B C D E
25 A B C D E
26 A B C D E
27 A B C D E
28 A B C D E
29 A B C D E
30 A B C D E

SECTION 5

1 A B C D E
2 A B C D E
3 A B C D E
4 A B C D E
5 A B C D E
6 A B C D E
7 A B C D E
8 A B C D E
9 A B C D E
10 A B C D E
11 A B C D E
12 A B C D E
13 A B C D E
14 A B C D E
15 A B C D E
16 A B C D E
17 A B C D E
18 A B C D E
19 A B C D E
20 A B C D E
21 A B C D E
22 A B C D E
23 A B C D E
24 A B C D E
25 A B C D E
26 A B C D E
27 A B C D E
28 A B C D E
29 A B C D E
30 A B C D E

14 PLEASE PRINT INFORMATION

LAST NAME

FIRST NAME

DATE OF BIRTH

SCANTRON® EliteView™ EM-295665-1:654321

INSTRUCTIONS FOR COMPLETING THE BIOGRAPHICAL AREA ARE ON THE BACK COVER OF YOUR TEST BOOKLET.
USE ONLY A NO. 2 OR HB PENCIL TO COMPLETE THIS ANSWER SHEET. DO NOT USE INK.

A

1 LAST NAME | FIRST NAME | MI

(Bubble grid A–Z for Last Name, First Name, and MI columns)

2 LAST 4 DIGITS OF SOCIAL SECURITY/ SOCIAL INSURANCE NO.
L
(Bubble grid 0–9)

3 LSAC ACCOUNT NUMBER
(Bubble grid 0–9)

4 CENTER NUMBER
(Bubble grid 0–9)

5 DATE OF BIRTH
MONTH | DAY | YEAR
○ Jan
○ Feb
○ Mar
○ Apr
○ May
○ June
○ July
○ Aug
○ Sept
○ Oct
○ Nov
○ Dec
(Bubble grid 0–9 for DAY and YEAR)

6 TEST FORM CODE
(Bubble grid 0–9)

7 RACIAL/ETHNIC DESCRIPTION
Mark one or more
○ 1 Amer. Indian/Alaska Native
○ 2 Asian
○ 3 Black/African American
○ 4 Canadian Aboriginal
○ 5 Caucasian/White
○ 6 Hispanic/Latino
○ 7 Native Hawaiian/ Other Pacific Islander
○ 8 Puerto Rican
○ 9 TSI/Aboriginal Australian

8 SEX
○ Male
○ Female

9 DOMINANT LANGUAGE
○ English
○ Other

10 ENGLISH FLUENCY
○ Yes
○ No

11 TEST DATE
/ /
MONTH DAY YEAR

12 TEST FORM

Law School Admission Test

Mark one and only one answer to each question. Be sure to fill in completely the space for your intended answer choice. If you erase, do so completely. Make no stray marks.

13 TEST BOOK SERIAL NO.
(Bubble grid A–T and 0–9)

SECTION 1	SECTION 2	SECTION 3	SECTION 4	SECTION 5
1 Ⓐ Ⓑ Ⓒ Ⓓ Ⓔ	1 Ⓐ Ⓑ Ⓒ Ⓓ Ⓔ	1 Ⓐ Ⓑ Ⓒ Ⓓ Ⓔ	1 Ⓐ Ⓑ Ⓒ Ⓓ Ⓔ	1 Ⓐ Ⓑ Ⓒ Ⓓ Ⓔ
2 Ⓐ Ⓑ Ⓒ Ⓓ Ⓔ	2 Ⓐ Ⓑ Ⓒ Ⓓ Ⓔ	2 Ⓐ Ⓑ Ⓒ Ⓓ Ⓔ	2 Ⓐ Ⓑ Ⓒ Ⓓ Ⓔ	2 Ⓐ Ⓑ Ⓒ Ⓓ Ⓔ
3 Ⓐ Ⓑ Ⓒ Ⓓ Ⓔ	3 Ⓐ Ⓑ Ⓒ Ⓓ Ⓔ	3 Ⓐ Ⓑ Ⓒ Ⓓ Ⓔ	3 Ⓐ Ⓑ Ⓒ Ⓓ Ⓔ	3 Ⓐ Ⓑ Ⓒ Ⓓ Ⓔ
4 Ⓐ Ⓑ Ⓒ Ⓓ Ⓔ	4 Ⓐ Ⓑ Ⓒ Ⓓ Ⓔ	4 Ⓐ Ⓑ Ⓒ Ⓓ Ⓔ	4 Ⓐ Ⓑ Ⓒ Ⓓ Ⓔ	4 Ⓐ Ⓑ Ⓒ Ⓓ Ⓔ
5 Ⓐ Ⓑ Ⓒ Ⓓ Ⓔ	5 Ⓐ Ⓑ Ⓒ Ⓓ Ⓔ	5 Ⓐ Ⓑ Ⓒ Ⓓ Ⓔ	5 Ⓐ Ⓑ Ⓒ Ⓓ Ⓔ	5 Ⓐ Ⓑ Ⓒ Ⓓ Ⓔ
6 Ⓐ Ⓑ Ⓒ Ⓓ Ⓔ	6 Ⓐ Ⓑ Ⓒ Ⓓ Ⓔ	6 Ⓐ Ⓑ Ⓒ Ⓓ Ⓔ	6 Ⓐ Ⓑ Ⓒ Ⓓ Ⓔ	6 Ⓐ Ⓑ Ⓒ Ⓓ Ⓔ
7 Ⓐ Ⓑ Ⓒ Ⓓ Ⓔ	7 Ⓐ Ⓑ Ⓒ Ⓓ Ⓔ	7 Ⓐ Ⓑ Ⓒ Ⓓ Ⓔ	7 Ⓐ Ⓑ Ⓒ Ⓓ Ⓔ	7 Ⓐ Ⓑ Ⓒ Ⓓ Ⓔ
8 Ⓐ Ⓑ Ⓒ Ⓓ Ⓔ	8 Ⓐ Ⓑ Ⓒ Ⓓ Ⓔ	8 Ⓐ Ⓑ Ⓒ Ⓓ Ⓔ	8 Ⓐ Ⓑ Ⓒ Ⓓ Ⓔ	8 Ⓐ Ⓑ Ⓒ Ⓓ Ⓔ
9 Ⓐ Ⓑ Ⓒ Ⓓ Ⓔ	9 Ⓐ Ⓑ Ⓒ Ⓓ Ⓔ	9 Ⓐ Ⓑ Ⓒ Ⓓ Ⓔ	9 Ⓐ Ⓑ Ⓒ Ⓓ Ⓔ	9 Ⓐ Ⓑ Ⓒ Ⓓ Ⓔ
10 Ⓐ Ⓑ Ⓒ Ⓓ Ⓔ	10 Ⓐ Ⓑ Ⓒ Ⓓ Ⓔ	10 Ⓐ Ⓑ Ⓒ Ⓓ Ⓔ	10 Ⓐ Ⓑ Ⓒ Ⓓ Ⓔ	10 Ⓐ Ⓑ Ⓒ Ⓓ Ⓔ
11 Ⓐ Ⓑ Ⓒ Ⓓ Ⓔ	11 Ⓐ Ⓑ Ⓒ Ⓓ Ⓔ	11 Ⓐ Ⓑ Ⓒ Ⓓ Ⓔ	11 Ⓐ Ⓑ Ⓒ Ⓓ Ⓔ	11 Ⓐ Ⓑ Ⓒ Ⓓ Ⓔ
12 Ⓐ Ⓑ Ⓒ Ⓓ Ⓔ	12 Ⓐ Ⓑ Ⓒ Ⓓ Ⓔ	12 Ⓐ Ⓑ Ⓒ Ⓓ Ⓔ	12 Ⓐ Ⓑ Ⓒ Ⓓ Ⓔ	12 Ⓐ Ⓑ Ⓒ Ⓓ Ⓔ
13 Ⓐ Ⓑ Ⓒ Ⓓ Ⓔ	13 Ⓐ Ⓑ Ⓒ Ⓓ Ⓔ	13 Ⓐ Ⓑ Ⓒ Ⓓ Ⓔ	13 Ⓐ Ⓑ Ⓒ Ⓓ Ⓔ	13 Ⓐ Ⓑ Ⓒ Ⓓ Ⓔ
14 Ⓐ Ⓑ Ⓒ Ⓓ Ⓔ	14 Ⓐ Ⓑ Ⓒ Ⓓ Ⓔ	14 Ⓐ Ⓑ Ⓒ Ⓓ Ⓔ	14 Ⓐ Ⓑ Ⓒ Ⓓ Ⓔ	14 Ⓐ Ⓑ Ⓒ Ⓓ Ⓔ
15 Ⓐ Ⓑ Ⓒ Ⓓ Ⓔ	15 Ⓐ Ⓑ Ⓒ Ⓓ Ⓔ	15 Ⓐ Ⓑ Ⓒ Ⓓ Ⓔ	15 Ⓐ Ⓑ Ⓒ Ⓓ Ⓔ	15 Ⓐ Ⓑ Ⓒ Ⓓ Ⓔ
16 Ⓐ Ⓑ Ⓒ Ⓓ Ⓔ	16 Ⓐ Ⓑ Ⓒ Ⓓ Ⓔ	16 Ⓐ Ⓑ Ⓒ Ⓓ Ⓔ	16 Ⓐ Ⓑ Ⓒ Ⓓ Ⓔ	16 Ⓐ Ⓑ Ⓒ Ⓓ Ⓔ
17 Ⓐ Ⓑ Ⓒ Ⓓ Ⓔ	17 Ⓐ Ⓑ Ⓒ Ⓓ Ⓔ	17 Ⓐ Ⓑ Ⓒ Ⓓ Ⓔ	17 Ⓐ Ⓑ Ⓒ Ⓓ Ⓔ	17 Ⓐ Ⓑ Ⓒ Ⓓ Ⓔ
18 Ⓐ Ⓑ Ⓒ Ⓓ Ⓔ	18 Ⓐ Ⓑ Ⓒ Ⓓ Ⓔ	18 Ⓐ Ⓑ Ⓒ Ⓓ Ⓔ	18 Ⓐ Ⓑ Ⓒ Ⓓ Ⓔ	18 Ⓐ Ⓑ Ⓒ Ⓓ Ⓔ
19 Ⓐ Ⓑ Ⓒ Ⓓ Ⓔ	19 Ⓐ Ⓑ Ⓒ Ⓓ Ⓔ	19 Ⓐ Ⓑ Ⓒ Ⓓ Ⓔ	19 Ⓐ Ⓑ Ⓒ Ⓓ Ⓔ	19 Ⓐ Ⓑ Ⓒ Ⓓ Ⓔ
20 Ⓐ Ⓑ Ⓒ Ⓓ Ⓔ	20 Ⓐ Ⓑ Ⓒ Ⓓ Ⓔ	20 Ⓐ Ⓑ Ⓒ Ⓓ Ⓔ	20 Ⓐ Ⓑ Ⓒ Ⓓ Ⓔ	20 Ⓐ Ⓑ Ⓒ Ⓓ Ⓔ
21 Ⓐ Ⓑ Ⓒ Ⓓ Ⓔ	21 Ⓐ Ⓑ Ⓒ Ⓓ Ⓔ	21 Ⓐ Ⓑ Ⓒ Ⓓ Ⓔ	21 Ⓐ Ⓑ Ⓒ Ⓓ Ⓔ	21 Ⓐ Ⓑ Ⓒ Ⓓ Ⓔ
22 Ⓐ Ⓑ Ⓒ Ⓓ Ⓔ	22 Ⓐ Ⓑ Ⓒ Ⓓ Ⓔ	22 Ⓐ Ⓑ Ⓒ Ⓓ Ⓔ	22 Ⓐ Ⓑ Ⓒ Ⓓ Ⓔ	22 Ⓐ Ⓑ Ⓒ Ⓓ Ⓔ
23 Ⓐ Ⓑ Ⓒ Ⓓ Ⓔ	23 Ⓐ Ⓑ Ⓒ Ⓓ Ⓔ	23 Ⓐ Ⓑ Ⓒ Ⓓ Ⓔ	23 Ⓐ Ⓑ Ⓒ Ⓓ Ⓔ	23 Ⓐ Ⓑ Ⓒ Ⓓ Ⓔ
24 Ⓐ Ⓑ Ⓒ Ⓓ Ⓔ	24 Ⓐ Ⓑ Ⓒ Ⓓ Ⓔ	24 Ⓐ Ⓑ Ⓒ Ⓓ Ⓔ	24 Ⓐ Ⓑ Ⓒ Ⓓ Ⓔ	24 Ⓐ Ⓑ Ⓒ Ⓓ Ⓔ
25 Ⓐ Ⓑ Ⓒ Ⓓ Ⓔ	25 Ⓐ Ⓑ Ⓒ Ⓓ Ⓔ	25 Ⓐ Ⓑ Ⓒ Ⓓ Ⓔ	25 Ⓐ Ⓑ Ⓒ Ⓓ Ⓔ	25 Ⓐ Ⓑ Ⓒ Ⓓ Ⓔ
26 Ⓐ Ⓑ Ⓒ Ⓓ Ⓔ	26 Ⓐ Ⓑ Ⓒ Ⓓ Ⓔ	26 Ⓐ Ⓑ Ⓒ Ⓓ Ⓔ	26 Ⓐ Ⓑ Ⓒ Ⓓ Ⓔ	26 Ⓐ Ⓑ Ⓒ Ⓓ Ⓔ
27 Ⓐ Ⓑ Ⓒ Ⓓ Ⓔ	27 Ⓐ Ⓑ Ⓒ Ⓓ Ⓔ	27 Ⓐ Ⓑ Ⓒ Ⓓ Ⓔ	27 Ⓐ Ⓑ Ⓒ Ⓓ Ⓔ	27 Ⓐ Ⓑ Ⓒ Ⓓ Ⓔ
28 Ⓐ Ⓑ Ⓒ Ⓓ Ⓔ	28 Ⓐ Ⓑ Ⓒ Ⓓ Ⓔ	28 Ⓐ Ⓑ Ⓒ Ⓓ Ⓔ	28 Ⓐ Ⓑ Ⓒ Ⓓ Ⓔ	28 Ⓐ Ⓑ Ⓒ Ⓓ Ⓔ
29 Ⓐ Ⓑ Ⓒ Ⓓ Ⓔ	29 Ⓐ Ⓑ Ⓒ Ⓓ Ⓔ	29 Ⓐ Ⓑ Ⓒ Ⓓ Ⓔ	29 Ⓐ Ⓑ Ⓒ Ⓓ Ⓔ	29 Ⓐ Ⓑ Ⓒ Ⓓ Ⓔ
30 Ⓐ Ⓑ Ⓒ Ⓓ Ⓔ	30 Ⓐ Ⓑ Ⓒ Ⓓ Ⓔ	30 Ⓐ Ⓑ Ⓒ Ⓓ Ⓔ	30 Ⓐ Ⓑ Ⓒ Ⓓ Ⓔ	30 Ⓐ Ⓑ Ⓒ Ⓓ Ⓔ

14 PLEASE PRINT INFORMATION

LAST NAME

FIRST NAME

DATE OF BIRTH

● Ⓑ

SCANTRON® EliteView™ EM-295665-1:654321

A

INSTRUCTIONS FOR COMPLETING THE BIOGRAPHICAL AREA ARE ON THE BACK COVER OF YOUR TEST BOOKLET.
USE ONLY A NO. 2 OR HB PENCIL TO COMPLETE THIS ANSWER SHEET. DO NOT USE INK.

1 LAST NAME | FIRST NAME | MI

(Bubble grid A–Z for each letter position)

2 LAST 4 DIGITS OF SOCIAL SECURITY/ SOCIAL INSURANCE NO.
L
(Bubbles 0–9)

3 LSAC ACCOUNT NUMBER
(Bubbles 0–9)

4 CENTER NUMBER
(Bubbles 0–9)

5 DATE OF BIRTH

MONTH	DAY	YEAR
Jan		
Feb		
Mar		
Apr		
May		
June		
July		
Aug		
Sept		
Oct		
Nov		
Dec		

6 TEST FORM CODE
(Bubbles 0–9)

7 RACIAL/ETHNIC DESCRIPTION
Mark one or more
- 1 Amer. Indian/Alaska Nat
- 2 Asian
- 3 Black/African American
- 4 Canadian Aboriginal
- 5 Caucasian/White
- 6 Hispanic/Latino
- 7 Native Hawaiian/ Other Pacific Islander
- 8 Puerto Rican
- 9 TSI/Aboriginal Australia

8 SEX
- Male
- Female

9 DOMINANT LANGUAGE
- English
- Other

10 ENGLISH FLUENCY
- Yes
- No

11 TEST DATE
MONTH / DAY / YEAR

12 TEST FORM

Law School Admission Test

Mark one and only one answer to each question. Be sure to fill in completely the space for your intended answer choice. If you erase, do so completely. Make no stray marks.

SECTION 1 (Questions 1–30, choices A B C D E)
SECTION 2 (Questions 1–30, choices A B C D E)
SECTION 3 (Questions 1–30, choices A B C D E)
SECTION 4 (Questions 1–30, choices A B C D E)
SECTION 5 (Questions 1–30, choices A B C D E)

13 TEST BOOK SERIAL NO.
(Bubble grid A–T and 0–9)

14 PLEASE PRINT INFORMATION

LAST NAME

FIRST NAME

DATE OF BIRTH

B

INSTRUCTIONS FOR COMPLETING THE BIOGRAPHICAL AREA ARE ON THE BACK COVER OF YOUR TEST BOOKLET.
USE ONLY A NO. 2 OR HB PENCIL TO COMPLETE THIS ANSWER SHEET. DO NOT USE INK.

A

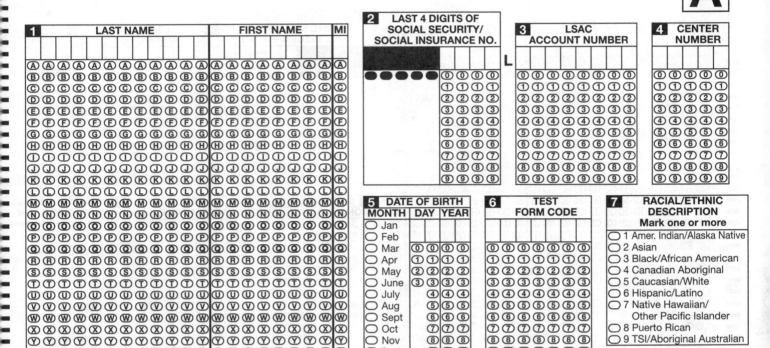

Law School Admission Test

Mark one and only one answer to each question. Be sure to fill in completely the space for your intended answer choice. If you erase, do so completely. Make no stray marks.

INSTRUCTIONS FOR COMPLETING THE BIOGRAPHICAL AREA ARE ON THE BACK COVER OF YOUR TEST BOOKLET.
USE ONLY A NO. 2 OR HB PENCIL TO COMPLETE THIS ANSWER SHEET. DO NOT USE INK.

A

1 LAST NAME | FIRST NAME | MI

2 LAST 4 DIGITS OF SOCIAL SECURITY/ SOCIAL INSURANCE NO.

L

3 LSAC ACCOUNT NUMBER

4 CENTER NUMBER

5 DATE OF BIRTH

MONTH	DAY	YEAR
Jan		
Feb		
Mar		
Apr		
May		
June		
July		
Aug		
Sept		
Oct		
Nov		
Dec		

6 TEST FORM CODE

7 RACIAL/ETHNIC DESCRIPTION
Mark one or more
- 1 Amer. Indian/Alaska Nati
- 2 Asian
- 3 Black/African American
- 4 Canadian Aboriginal
- 5 Caucasian/White
- 6 Hispanic/Latino
- 7 Native Hawaiian/ Other Pacific Islander
- 8 Puerto Rican
- 9 TSI/Aboriginal Australia

8 SEX
- Male
- Female

9 DOMINANT LANGUAGE
- English
- Other

10 ENGLISH FLUENCY
- Yes
- No

11 TEST DATE
MONTH / DAY / YEAR

12 TEST FORM

Law School Admission Test

Mark one and only one answer to each question. Be sure to fill in completely the space for your intended answer choice. If you erase, do so completely. Make no stray marks.

13 TEST BOOK SERIAL NO.

SECTION 1 — questions 1–30, choices (A) (B) (C) (D) (E)

SECTION 2 — questions 1–30, choices (A) (B) (C) (D) (E)

SECTION 3 — questions 1–30, choices (A) (B) (C) (D) (E)

SECTION 4 — questions 1–30, choices (A) (B) (C) (D) (E)

SECTION 5 — questions 1–30, choices (A) (B) (C) (D) (E)

14 PLEASE PRINT INFORMATION

LAST NAME

FIRST NAME

DATE OF BIRTH

(B)

A

INSTRUCTIONS FOR COMPLETING THE BIOGRAPHICAL AREA ARE ON THE BACK COVER OF YOUR TEST BOOKLET.
USE ONLY A NO. 2 OR HB PENCIL TO COMPLETE THIS ANSWER SHEET. DO NOT USE INK.

1 LAST NAME | FIRST NAME | MI

2 LAST 4 DIGITS OF SOCIAL SECURITY/ SOCIAL INSURANCE NO.

3 LSAC ACCOUNT NUMBER

4 CENTER NUMBER

5 DATE OF BIRTH
MONTH | DAY | YEAR
○ Jan
○ Feb
○ Mar
○ Apr
○ May
○ June
○ July
○ Aug
○ Sept
○ Oct
○ Nov
○ Dec

6 TEST FORM CODE

7 RACIAL/ETHNIC DESCRIPTION
Mark one or more
○ 1 Amer. Indian/Alaska Native
○ 2 Asian
○ 3 Black/African American
○ 4 Canadian Aboriginal
○ 5 Caucasian/White
○ 6 Hispanic/Latino
○ 7 Native Hawaiian/ Other Pacific Islander
○ 8 Puerto Rican
○ 9 TSI/Aboriginal Australian

8 SEX
○ Male
○ Female

9 DOMINANT LANGUAGE
○ English
○ Other

10 ENGLISH FLUENCY
○ Yes
○ No

11 TEST DATE
MONTH DAY YEAR

12 TEST FORM

Law School Admission Test

Mark one and only one answer to each question. Be sure to fill in completely the space for your intended answer choice. If you erase, do so completely. Make no stray marks.

13 TEST BOOK SERIAL NO.

SECTION 1	SECTION 2	SECTION 3	SECTION 4	SECTION 5
1 Ⓐ Ⓑ Ⓒ Ⓓ Ⓔ	1 Ⓐ Ⓑ Ⓒ Ⓓ Ⓔ	1 Ⓐ Ⓑ Ⓒ Ⓓ Ⓔ	1 Ⓐ Ⓑ Ⓒ Ⓓ Ⓔ	1 Ⓐ Ⓑ Ⓒ Ⓓ Ⓔ
2 Ⓐ Ⓑ Ⓒ Ⓓ Ⓔ	2 Ⓐ Ⓑ Ⓒ Ⓓ Ⓔ	2 Ⓐ Ⓑ Ⓒ Ⓓ Ⓔ	2 Ⓐ Ⓑ Ⓒ Ⓓ Ⓔ	2 Ⓐ Ⓑ Ⓒ Ⓓ Ⓔ
3 Ⓐ Ⓑ Ⓒ Ⓓ Ⓔ	3 Ⓐ Ⓑ Ⓒ Ⓓ Ⓔ	3 Ⓐ Ⓑ Ⓒ Ⓓ Ⓔ	3 Ⓐ Ⓑ Ⓒ Ⓓ Ⓔ	3 Ⓐ Ⓑ Ⓒ Ⓓ Ⓔ
4 Ⓐ Ⓑ Ⓒ Ⓓ Ⓔ	4 Ⓐ Ⓑ Ⓒ Ⓓ Ⓔ	4 Ⓐ Ⓑ Ⓒ Ⓓ Ⓔ	4 Ⓐ Ⓑ Ⓒ Ⓓ Ⓔ	4 Ⓐ Ⓑ Ⓒ Ⓓ Ⓔ
5 Ⓐ Ⓑ Ⓒ Ⓓ Ⓔ	5 Ⓐ Ⓑ Ⓒ Ⓓ Ⓔ	5 Ⓐ Ⓑ Ⓒ Ⓓ Ⓔ	5 Ⓐ Ⓑ Ⓒ Ⓓ Ⓔ	5 Ⓐ Ⓑ Ⓒ Ⓓ Ⓔ
6 Ⓐ Ⓑ Ⓒ Ⓓ Ⓔ	6 Ⓐ Ⓑ Ⓒ Ⓓ Ⓔ	6 Ⓐ Ⓑ Ⓒ Ⓓ Ⓔ	6 Ⓐ Ⓑ Ⓒ Ⓓ Ⓔ	6 Ⓐ Ⓑ Ⓒ Ⓓ Ⓔ
7 Ⓐ Ⓑ Ⓒ Ⓓ Ⓔ	7 Ⓐ Ⓑ Ⓒ Ⓓ Ⓔ	7 Ⓐ Ⓑ Ⓒ Ⓓ Ⓔ	7 Ⓐ Ⓑ Ⓒ Ⓓ Ⓔ	7 Ⓐ Ⓑ Ⓒ Ⓓ Ⓔ
8 Ⓐ Ⓑ Ⓒ Ⓓ Ⓔ	8 Ⓐ Ⓑ Ⓒ Ⓓ Ⓔ	8 Ⓐ Ⓑ Ⓒ Ⓓ Ⓔ	8 Ⓐ Ⓑ Ⓒ Ⓓ Ⓔ	8 Ⓐ Ⓑ Ⓒ Ⓓ Ⓔ
9 Ⓐ Ⓑ Ⓒ Ⓓ Ⓔ	9 Ⓐ Ⓑ Ⓒ Ⓓ Ⓔ	9 Ⓐ Ⓑ Ⓒ Ⓓ Ⓔ	9 Ⓐ Ⓑ Ⓒ Ⓓ Ⓔ	9 Ⓐ Ⓑ Ⓒ Ⓓ Ⓔ
10 Ⓐ Ⓑ Ⓒ Ⓓ Ⓔ	10 Ⓐ Ⓑ Ⓒ Ⓓ Ⓔ	10 Ⓐ Ⓑ Ⓒ Ⓓ Ⓔ	10 Ⓐ Ⓑ Ⓒ Ⓓ Ⓔ	10 Ⓐ Ⓑ Ⓒ Ⓓ Ⓔ
11 Ⓐ Ⓑ Ⓒ Ⓓ Ⓔ	11 Ⓐ Ⓑ Ⓒ Ⓓ Ⓔ	11 Ⓐ Ⓑ Ⓒ Ⓓ Ⓔ	11 Ⓐ Ⓑ Ⓒ Ⓓ Ⓔ	11 Ⓐ Ⓑ Ⓒ Ⓓ Ⓔ
12 Ⓐ Ⓑ Ⓒ Ⓓ Ⓔ	12 Ⓐ Ⓑ Ⓒ Ⓓ Ⓔ	12 Ⓐ Ⓑ Ⓒ Ⓓ Ⓔ	12 Ⓐ Ⓑ Ⓒ Ⓓ Ⓔ	12 Ⓐ Ⓑ Ⓒ Ⓓ Ⓔ
13 Ⓐ Ⓑ Ⓒ Ⓓ Ⓔ	13 Ⓐ Ⓑ Ⓒ Ⓓ Ⓔ	13 Ⓐ Ⓑ Ⓒ Ⓓ Ⓔ	13 Ⓐ Ⓑ Ⓒ Ⓓ Ⓔ	13 Ⓐ Ⓑ Ⓒ Ⓓ Ⓔ
14 Ⓐ Ⓑ Ⓒ Ⓓ Ⓔ	14 Ⓐ Ⓑ Ⓒ Ⓓ Ⓔ	14 Ⓐ Ⓑ Ⓒ Ⓓ Ⓔ	14 Ⓐ Ⓑ Ⓒ Ⓓ Ⓔ	14 Ⓐ Ⓑ Ⓒ Ⓓ Ⓔ
15 Ⓐ Ⓑ Ⓒ Ⓓ Ⓔ	15 Ⓐ Ⓑ Ⓒ Ⓓ Ⓔ	15 Ⓐ Ⓑ Ⓒ Ⓓ Ⓔ	15 Ⓐ Ⓑ Ⓒ Ⓓ Ⓔ	15 Ⓐ Ⓑ Ⓒ Ⓓ Ⓔ
16 Ⓐ Ⓑ Ⓒ Ⓓ Ⓔ	16 Ⓐ Ⓑ Ⓒ Ⓓ Ⓔ	16 Ⓐ Ⓑ Ⓒ Ⓓ Ⓔ	16 Ⓐ Ⓑ Ⓒ Ⓓ Ⓔ	16 Ⓐ Ⓑ Ⓒ Ⓓ Ⓔ
17 Ⓐ Ⓑ Ⓒ Ⓓ Ⓔ	17 Ⓐ Ⓑ Ⓒ Ⓓ Ⓔ	17 Ⓐ Ⓑ Ⓒ Ⓓ Ⓔ	17 Ⓐ Ⓑ Ⓒ Ⓓ Ⓔ	17 Ⓐ Ⓑ Ⓒ Ⓓ Ⓔ
18 Ⓐ Ⓑ Ⓒ Ⓓ Ⓔ	18 Ⓐ Ⓑ Ⓒ Ⓓ Ⓔ	18 Ⓐ Ⓑ Ⓒ Ⓓ Ⓔ	18 Ⓐ Ⓑ Ⓒ Ⓓ Ⓔ	18 Ⓐ Ⓑ Ⓒ Ⓓ Ⓔ
19 Ⓐ Ⓑ Ⓒ Ⓓ Ⓔ	19 Ⓐ Ⓑ Ⓒ Ⓓ Ⓔ	19 Ⓐ Ⓑ Ⓒ Ⓓ Ⓔ	19 Ⓐ Ⓑ Ⓒ Ⓓ Ⓔ	19 Ⓐ Ⓑ Ⓒ Ⓓ Ⓔ
20 Ⓐ Ⓑ Ⓒ Ⓓ Ⓔ	20 Ⓐ Ⓑ Ⓒ Ⓓ Ⓔ	20 Ⓐ Ⓑ Ⓒ Ⓓ Ⓔ	20 Ⓐ Ⓑ Ⓒ Ⓓ Ⓔ	20 Ⓐ Ⓑ Ⓒ Ⓓ Ⓔ
21 Ⓐ Ⓑ Ⓒ Ⓓ Ⓔ	21 Ⓐ Ⓑ Ⓒ Ⓓ Ⓔ	21 Ⓐ Ⓑ Ⓒ Ⓓ Ⓔ	21 Ⓐ Ⓑ Ⓒ Ⓓ Ⓔ	21 Ⓐ Ⓑ Ⓒ Ⓓ Ⓔ
22 Ⓐ Ⓑ Ⓒ Ⓓ Ⓔ	22 Ⓐ Ⓑ Ⓒ Ⓓ Ⓔ	22 Ⓐ Ⓑ Ⓒ Ⓓ Ⓔ	22 Ⓐ Ⓑ Ⓒ Ⓓ Ⓔ	22 Ⓐ Ⓑ Ⓒ Ⓓ Ⓔ
23 Ⓐ Ⓑ Ⓒ Ⓓ Ⓔ	23 Ⓐ Ⓑ Ⓒ Ⓓ Ⓔ	23 Ⓐ Ⓑ Ⓒ Ⓓ Ⓔ	23 Ⓐ Ⓑ Ⓒ Ⓓ Ⓔ	23 Ⓐ Ⓑ Ⓒ Ⓓ Ⓔ
24 Ⓐ Ⓑ Ⓒ Ⓓ Ⓔ	24 Ⓐ Ⓑ Ⓒ Ⓓ Ⓔ	24 Ⓐ Ⓑ Ⓒ Ⓓ Ⓔ	24 Ⓐ Ⓑ Ⓒ Ⓓ Ⓔ	24 Ⓐ Ⓑ Ⓒ Ⓓ Ⓔ
25 Ⓐ Ⓑ Ⓒ Ⓓ Ⓔ	25 Ⓐ Ⓑ Ⓒ Ⓓ Ⓔ	25 Ⓐ Ⓑ Ⓒ Ⓓ Ⓔ	25 Ⓐ Ⓑ Ⓒ Ⓓ Ⓔ	25 Ⓐ Ⓑ Ⓒ Ⓓ Ⓔ
26 Ⓐ Ⓑ Ⓒ Ⓓ Ⓔ	26 Ⓐ Ⓑ Ⓒ Ⓓ Ⓔ	26 Ⓐ Ⓑ Ⓒ Ⓓ Ⓔ	26 Ⓐ Ⓑ Ⓒ Ⓓ Ⓔ	26 Ⓐ Ⓑ Ⓒ Ⓓ Ⓔ
27 Ⓐ Ⓑ Ⓒ Ⓓ Ⓔ	27 Ⓐ Ⓑ Ⓒ Ⓓ Ⓔ	27 Ⓐ Ⓑ Ⓒ Ⓓ Ⓔ	27 Ⓐ Ⓑ Ⓒ Ⓓ Ⓔ	27 Ⓐ Ⓑ Ⓒ Ⓓ Ⓔ
28 Ⓐ Ⓑ Ⓒ Ⓓ Ⓔ	28 Ⓐ Ⓑ Ⓒ Ⓓ Ⓔ	28 Ⓐ Ⓑ Ⓒ Ⓓ Ⓔ	28 Ⓐ Ⓑ Ⓒ Ⓓ Ⓔ	28 Ⓐ Ⓑ Ⓒ Ⓓ Ⓔ
29 Ⓐ Ⓑ Ⓒ Ⓓ Ⓔ	29 Ⓐ Ⓑ Ⓒ Ⓓ Ⓔ	29 Ⓐ Ⓑ Ⓒ Ⓓ Ⓔ	29 Ⓐ Ⓑ Ⓒ Ⓓ Ⓔ	29 Ⓐ Ⓑ Ⓒ Ⓓ Ⓔ
30 Ⓐ Ⓑ Ⓒ Ⓓ Ⓔ	30 Ⓐ Ⓑ Ⓒ Ⓓ Ⓔ	30 Ⓐ Ⓑ Ⓒ Ⓓ Ⓔ	30 Ⓐ Ⓑ Ⓒ Ⓓ Ⓔ	30 Ⓐ Ⓑ Ⓒ Ⓓ Ⓔ

14 PLEASE PRINT INFORMATION

LAST NAME

FIRST NAME

DATE OF BIRTH

● Ⓑ

INSTRUCTIONS FOR COMPLETING THE BIOGRAPHICAL AREA ARE ON THE BACK COVER OF YOUR TEST BOOKLET.
USE ONLY A NO. 2 OR HB PENCIL TO COMPLETE THIS ANSWER SHEET. DO NOT USE INK.

A

1 LAST NAME / FIRST NAME / MI

2 LAST 4 DIGITS OF SOCIAL SECURITY/ SOCIAL INSURANCE NO.

L

3 LSAC ACCOUNT NUMBER

4 CENTER NUMBER

5 DATE OF BIRTH
MONTH | DAY | YEAR
Jan, Feb, Mar, Apr, May, June, July, Aug, Sept, Oct, Nov, Dec

6 TEST FORM CODE

7 RACIAL/ETHNIC DESCRIPTION
Mark one or more
1 Amer. Indian/Alaska Nat.
2 Asian
3 Black/African American
4 Canadian Aboriginal
5 Caucasian/White
6 Hispanic/Latino
7 Native Hawaiian/ Other Pacific Islander
8 Puerto Rican
9 TSI/Aboriginal Australian

8 SEX
Male
Female

9 DOMINANT LANGUAGE
English
Other

10 ENGLISH FLUENCY
Yes
No

11 TEST DATE
MONTH / DAY / YEAR

12 TEST FORM

Law School Admission Test

Mark one and only one answer to each question. Be sure to fill in completely the space for your intended answer choice. If you erase, do so completely. Make no stray marks.

SECTION 1 | SECTION 2 | SECTION 3 | SECTION 4 | SECTION 5
(1–30, each with A B C D E)

13 TEST BOOK SERIAL NO.

14 PLEASE PRINT INFORMATION
LAST NAME
FIRST NAME
DATE OF BIRTH

SCANTRON EliteView™ EM-295665-1:654321

INSTRUCTIONS FOR COMPLETING THE BIOGRAPHICAL AREA ARE ON THE BACK COVER OF YOUR TEST BOOKLET.

USE ONLY A NO. 2 OR HB PENCIL TO COMPLETE THIS ANSWER SHEET. DO NOT USE INK.

A

1 LAST NAME | FIRST NAME | MI

(A) through (Z) bubbles for each letter position

2 LAST 4 DIGITS OF SOCIAL SECURITY/ SOCIAL INSURANCE NO.

0 1 2 3 4 5 6 7 8 9

3 LSAC ACCOUNT NUMBER

L

0 1 2 3 4 5 6 7 8 9

4 CENTER NUMBER

0 1 2 3 4 5 6 7 8 9

5 DATE OF BIRTH

MONTH	DAY	YEAR
Jan		
Feb		
Mar	0 0	0 0
Apr	1 1	1 1
May	2 2	2 2
June	3 3	3 3
July	4	4 4
Aug	5	5 5
Sept	6	6 6
Oct	7	7 7
Nov	8	8 8
Dec	9	9 9

6 TEST FORM CODE

0 1 2 3 4 5 6 7 8 9

7 RACIAL/ETHNIC DESCRIPTION

Mark one or more

- 1 Amer. Indian/Alaska Native
- 2 Asian
- 3 Black/African American
- 4 Canadian Aboriginal
- 5 Caucasian/White
- 6 Hispanic/Latino
- 7 Native Hawaiian/ Other Pacific Islander
- 8 Puerto Rican
- 9 TSI/Aboriginal Australian

8 SEX
- Male
- Female

9 DOMINANT LANGUAGE
- English
- Other

10 ENGLISH FLUENCY
- Yes
- No

11 TEST DATE

___ / ___ / ___

MONTH DAY YEAR

12 TEST FORM

Law School Admission Test

Mark one and only one answer to each question. Be sure to fill in completely the space for your intended answer choice. If you erase, do so completely. Make no stray marks.

SECTION 1	SECTION 2	SECTION 3	SECTION 4	SECTION 5
1 A B C D E	1 A B C D E	1 A B C D E	1 A B C D E	1 A B C D E
2 A B C D E	2 A B C D E	2 A B C D E	2 A B C D E	2 A B C D E
3 A B C D E	3 A B C D E	3 A B C D E	3 A B C D E	3 A B C D E
4 A B C D E	4 A B C D E	4 A B C D E	4 A B C D E	4 A B C D E
5 A B C D E	5 A B C D E	5 A B C D E	5 A B C D E	5 A B C D E
6 A B C D E	6 A B C D E	6 A B C D E	6 A B C D E	6 A B C D E
7 A B C D E	7 A B C D E	7 A B C D E	7 A B C D E	7 A B C D E
8 A B C D E	8 A B C D E	8 A B C D E	8 A B C D E	8 A B C D E
9 A B C D E	9 A B C D E	9 A B C D E	9 A B C D E	9 A B C D E
10 A B C D E	10 A B C D E	10 A B C D E	10 A B C D E	10 A B C D E
11 A B C D E	11 A B C D E	11 A B C D E	11 A B C D E	11 A B C D E
12 A B C D E	12 A B C D E	12 A B C D E	12 A B C D E	12 A B C D E
13 A B C D E	13 A B C D E	13 A B C D E	13 A B C D E	13 A B C D E
14 A B C D E	14 A B C D E	14 A B C D E	14 A B C D E	14 A B C D E
15 A B C D E	15 A B C D E	15 A B C D E	15 A B C D E	15 A B C D E
16 A B C D E	16 A B C D E	16 A B C D E	16 A B C D E	16 A B C D E
17 A B C D E	17 A B C D E	17 A B C D E	17 A B C D E	17 A B C D E
18 A B C D E	18 A B C D E	18 A B C D E	18 A B C D E	18 A B C D E
19 A B C D E	19 A B C D E	19 A B C D E	19 A B C D E	19 A B C D E
20 A B C D E	20 A B C D E	20 A B C D E	20 A B C D E	20 A B C D E
21 A B C D E	21 A B C D E	21 A B C D E	21 A B C D E	21 A B C D E
22 A B C D E	22 A B C D E	22 A B C D E	22 A B C D E	22 A B C D E
23 A B C D E	23 A B C D E	23 A B C D E	23 A B C D E	23 A B C D E
24 A B C D E	24 A B C D E	24 A B C D E	24 A B C D E	24 A B C D E
25 A B C D E	25 A B C D E	25 A B C D E	25 A B C D E	25 A B C D E
26 A B C D E	26 A B C D E	26 A B C D E	26 A B C D E	26 A B C D E
27 A B C D E	27 A B C D E	27 A B C D E	27 A B C D E	27 A B C D E
28 A B C D E	28 A B C D E	28 A B C D E	28 A B C D E	28 A B C D E
29 A B C D E	29 A B C D E	29 A B C D E	29 A B C D E	29 A B C D E
30 A B C D E	30 A B C D E	30 A B C D E	30 A B C D E	30 A B C D E

13 TEST BOOK SERIAL NO.

A–T letter bubbles (two columns); 0–9 digit bubbles (six columns)

14 PLEASE PRINT INFORMATION

LAST NAME

FIRST NAME

DATE OF BIRTH

B

INSTRUCTIONS FOR COMPLETING THE BIOGRAPHICAL AREA ARE ON THE BACK COVER OF YOUR TEST BOOKLET.
USE ONLY A NO. 2 OR HB PENCIL TO COMPLETE THIS ANSWER SHEET. DO NOT USE INK.

A

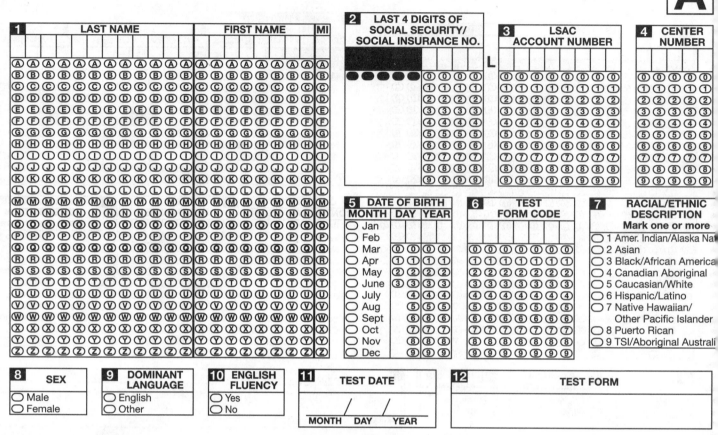

8 SEX
○ Male
○ Female

9 DOMINANT LANGUAGE
○ English
○ Other

10 ENGLISH FLUENCY
○ Yes
○ No

11 TEST DATE
/ /
MONTH DAY YEAR

12 TEST FORM

Law School Admission Test

Mark one and only one answer to each question. Be sure to fill in completely the space for your intended answer choice. If you erase, do so completely. Make no stray marks.

13 TEST BOOK SERIAL NO.

14 PLEASE PRINT INFORMATION

LAST NAME

FIRST NAME

DATE OF BIRTH

SECTION 1	SECTION 2	SECTION 3	SECTION 4	SECTION 5
1 Ⓐ Ⓑ Ⓒ Ⓓ Ⓔ	1 Ⓐ Ⓑ Ⓒ Ⓓ Ⓔ	1 Ⓐ Ⓑ Ⓒ Ⓓ Ⓔ	1 Ⓐ Ⓑ Ⓒ Ⓓ Ⓔ	1 Ⓐ Ⓑ Ⓒ Ⓓ Ⓔ
2 Ⓐ Ⓑ Ⓒ Ⓓ Ⓔ	2 Ⓐ Ⓑ Ⓒ Ⓓ Ⓔ	2 Ⓐ Ⓑ Ⓒ Ⓓ Ⓔ	2 Ⓐ Ⓑ Ⓒ Ⓓ Ⓔ	2 Ⓐ Ⓑ Ⓒ Ⓓ Ⓔ
3 Ⓐ Ⓑ Ⓒ Ⓓ Ⓔ	3 Ⓐ Ⓑ Ⓒ Ⓓ Ⓔ	3 Ⓐ Ⓑ Ⓒ Ⓓ Ⓔ	3 Ⓐ Ⓑ Ⓒ Ⓓ Ⓔ	3 Ⓐ Ⓑ Ⓒ Ⓓ Ⓔ
4 Ⓐ Ⓑ Ⓒ Ⓓ Ⓔ	4 Ⓐ Ⓑ Ⓒ Ⓓ Ⓔ	4 Ⓐ Ⓑ Ⓒ Ⓓ Ⓔ	4 Ⓐ Ⓑ Ⓒ Ⓓ Ⓔ	4 Ⓐ Ⓑ Ⓒ Ⓓ Ⓔ
5 Ⓐ Ⓑ Ⓒ Ⓓ Ⓔ	5 Ⓐ Ⓑ Ⓒ Ⓓ Ⓔ	5 Ⓐ Ⓑ Ⓒ Ⓓ Ⓔ	5 Ⓐ Ⓑ Ⓒ Ⓓ Ⓔ	5 Ⓐ Ⓑ Ⓒ Ⓓ Ⓔ
6 Ⓐ Ⓑ Ⓒ Ⓓ Ⓔ	6 Ⓐ Ⓑ Ⓒ Ⓓ Ⓔ	6 Ⓐ Ⓑ Ⓒ Ⓓ Ⓔ	6 Ⓐ Ⓑ Ⓒ Ⓓ Ⓔ	6 Ⓐ Ⓑ Ⓒ Ⓓ Ⓔ
7 Ⓐ Ⓑ Ⓒ Ⓓ Ⓔ	7 Ⓐ Ⓑ Ⓒ Ⓓ Ⓔ	7 Ⓐ Ⓑ Ⓒ Ⓓ Ⓔ	7 Ⓐ Ⓑ Ⓒ Ⓓ Ⓔ	7 Ⓐ Ⓑ Ⓒ Ⓓ Ⓔ
8 Ⓐ Ⓑ Ⓒ Ⓓ Ⓔ	8 Ⓐ Ⓑ Ⓒ Ⓓ Ⓔ	8 Ⓐ Ⓑ Ⓒ Ⓓ Ⓔ	8 Ⓐ Ⓑ Ⓒ Ⓓ Ⓔ	8 Ⓐ Ⓑ Ⓒ Ⓓ Ⓔ
9 Ⓐ Ⓑ Ⓒ Ⓓ Ⓔ	9 Ⓐ Ⓑ Ⓒ Ⓓ Ⓔ	9 Ⓐ Ⓑ Ⓒ Ⓓ Ⓔ	9 Ⓐ Ⓑ Ⓒ Ⓓ Ⓔ	9 Ⓐ Ⓑ Ⓒ Ⓓ Ⓔ
10 Ⓐ Ⓑ Ⓒ Ⓓ Ⓔ	10 Ⓐ Ⓑ Ⓒ Ⓓ Ⓔ	10 Ⓐ Ⓑ Ⓒ Ⓓ Ⓔ	10 Ⓐ Ⓑ Ⓒ Ⓓ Ⓔ	10 Ⓐ Ⓑ Ⓒ Ⓓ Ⓔ
11 Ⓐ Ⓑ Ⓒ Ⓓ Ⓔ	11 Ⓐ Ⓑ Ⓒ Ⓓ Ⓔ	11 Ⓐ Ⓑ Ⓒ Ⓓ Ⓔ	11 Ⓐ Ⓑ Ⓒ Ⓓ Ⓔ	11 Ⓐ Ⓑ Ⓒ Ⓓ Ⓔ
12 Ⓐ Ⓑ Ⓒ Ⓓ Ⓔ	12 Ⓐ Ⓑ Ⓒ Ⓓ Ⓔ	12 Ⓐ Ⓑ Ⓒ Ⓓ Ⓔ	12 Ⓐ Ⓑ Ⓒ Ⓓ Ⓔ	12 Ⓐ Ⓑ Ⓒ Ⓓ Ⓔ
13 Ⓐ Ⓑ Ⓒ Ⓓ Ⓔ	13 Ⓐ Ⓑ Ⓒ Ⓓ Ⓔ	13 Ⓐ Ⓑ Ⓒ Ⓓ Ⓔ	13 Ⓐ Ⓑ Ⓒ Ⓓ Ⓔ	13 Ⓐ Ⓑ Ⓒ Ⓓ Ⓔ
14 Ⓐ Ⓑ Ⓒ Ⓓ Ⓔ	14 Ⓐ Ⓑ Ⓒ Ⓓ Ⓔ	14 Ⓐ Ⓑ Ⓒ Ⓓ Ⓔ	14 Ⓐ Ⓑ Ⓒ Ⓓ Ⓔ	14 Ⓐ Ⓑ Ⓒ Ⓓ Ⓔ
15 Ⓐ Ⓑ Ⓒ Ⓓ Ⓔ	15 Ⓐ Ⓑ Ⓒ Ⓓ Ⓔ	15 Ⓐ Ⓑ Ⓒ Ⓓ Ⓔ	15 Ⓐ Ⓑ Ⓒ Ⓓ Ⓔ	15 Ⓐ Ⓑ Ⓒ Ⓓ Ⓔ
16 Ⓐ Ⓑ Ⓒ Ⓓ Ⓔ	16 Ⓐ Ⓑ Ⓒ Ⓓ Ⓔ	16 Ⓐ Ⓑ Ⓒ Ⓓ Ⓔ	16 Ⓐ Ⓑ Ⓒ Ⓓ Ⓔ	16 Ⓐ Ⓑ Ⓒ Ⓓ Ⓔ
17 Ⓐ Ⓑ Ⓒ Ⓓ Ⓔ	17 Ⓐ Ⓑ Ⓒ Ⓓ Ⓔ	17 Ⓐ Ⓑ Ⓒ Ⓓ Ⓔ	17 Ⓐ Ⓑ Ⓒ Ⓓ Ⓔ	17 Ⓐ Ⓑ Ⓒ Ⓓ Ⓔ
18 Ⓐ Ⓑ Ⓒ Ⓓ Ⓔ	18 Ⓐ Ⓑ Ⓒ Ⓓ Ⓔ	18 Ⓐ Ⓑ Ⓒ Ⓓ Ⓔ	18 Ⓐ Ⓑ Ⓒ Ⓓ Ⓔ	18 Ⓐ Ⓑ Ⓒ Ⓓ Ⓔ
19 Ⓐ Ⓑ Ⓒ Ⓓ Ⓔ	19 Ⓐ Ⓑ Ⓒ Ⓓ Ⓔ	19 Ⓐ Ⓑ Ⓒ Ⓓ Ⓔ	19 Ⓐ Ⓑ Ⓒ Ⓓ Ⓔ	19 Ⓐ Ⓑ Ⓒ Ⓓ Ⓔ
20 Ⓐ Ⓑ Ⓒ Ⓓ Ⓔ	20 Ⓐ Ⓑ Ⓒ Ⓓ Ⓔ	20 Ⓐ Ⓑ Ⓒ Ⓓ Ⓔ	20 Ⓐ Ⓑ Ⓒ Ⓓ Ⓔ	20 Ⓐ Ⓑ Ⓒ Ⓓ Ⓔ
21 Ⓐ Ⓑ Ⓒ Ⓓ Ⓔ	21 Ⓐ Ⓑ Ⓒ Ⓓ Ⓔ	21 Ⓐ Ⓑ Ⓒ Ⓓ Ⓔ	21 Ⓐ Ⓑ Ⓒ Ⓓ Ⓔ	21 Ⓐ Ⓑ Ⓒ Ⓓ Ⓔ
22 Ⓐ Ⓑ Ⓒ Ⓓ Ⓔ	22 Ⓐ Ⓑ Ⓒ Ⓓ Ⓔ	22 Ⓐ Ⓑ Ⓒ Ⓓ Ⓔ	22 Ⓐ Ⓑ Ⓒ Ⓓ Ⓔ	22 Ⓐ Ⓑ Ⓒ Ⓓ Ⓔ
23 Ⓐ Ⓑ Ⓒ Ⓓ Ⓔ	23 Ⓐ Ⓑ Ⓒ Ⓓ Ⓔ	23 Ⓐ Ⓑ Ⓒ Ⓓ Ⓔ	23 Ⓐ Ⓑ Ⓒ Ⓓ Ⓔ	23 Ⓐ Ⓑ Ⓒ Ⓓ Ⓔ
24 Ⓐ Ⓑ Ⓒ Ⓓ Ⓔ	24 Ⓐ Ⓑ Ⓒ Ⓓ Ⓔ	24 Ⓐ Ⓑ Ⓒ Ⓓ Ⓔ	24 Ⓐ Ⓑ Ⓒ Ⓓ Ⓔ	24 Ⓐ Ⓑ Ⓒ Ⓓ Ⓔ
25 Ⓐ Ⓑ Ⓒ Ⓓ Ⓔ	25 Ⓐ Ⓑ Ⓒ Ⓓ Ⓔ	25 Ⓐ Ⓑ Ⓒ Ⓓ Ⓔ	25 Ⓐ Ⓑ Ⓒ Ⓓ Ⓔ	25 Ⓐ Ⓑ Ⓒ Ⓓ Ⓔ
26 Ⓐ Ⓑ Ⓒ Ⓓ Ⓔ	26 Ⓐ Ⓑ Ⓒ Ⓓ Ⓔ	26 Ⓐ Ⓑ Ⓒ Ⓓ Ⓔ	26 Ⓐ Ⓑ Ⓒ Ⓓ Ⓔ	26 Ⓐ Ⓑ Ⓒ Ⓓ Ⓔ
27 Ⓐ Ⓑ Ⓒ Ⓓ Ⓔ	27 Ⓐ Ⓑ Ⓒ Ⓓ Ⓔ	27 Ⓐ Ⓑ Ⓒ Ⓓ Ⓔ	27 Ⓐ Ⓑ Ⓒ Ⓓ Ⓔ	27 Ⓐ Ⓑ Ⓒ Ⓓ Ⓔ
28 Ⓐ Ⓑ Ⓒ Ⓓ Ⓔ	28 Ⓐ Ⓑ Ⓒ Ⓓ Ⓔ	28 Ⓐ Ⓑ Ⓒ Ⓓ Ⓔ	28 Ⓐ Ⓑ Ⓒ Ⓓ Ⓔ	28 Ⓐ Ⓑ Ⓒ Ⓓ Ⓔ
29 Ⓐ Ⓑ Ⓒ Ⓓ Ⓔ	29 Ⓐ Ⓑ Ⓒ Ⓓ Ⓔ	29 Ⓐ Ⓑ Ⓒ Ⓓ Ⓔ	29 Ⓐ Ⓑ Ⓒ Ⓓ Ⓔ	29 Ⓐ Ⓑ Ⓒ Ⓓ Ⓔ
30 Ⓐ Ⓑ Ⓒ Ⓓ Ⓔ	30 Ⓐ Ⓑ Ⓒ Ⓓ Ⓔ	30 Ⓐ Ⓑ Ⓒ Ⓓ Ⓔ	30 Ⓐ Ⓑ Ⓒ Ⓓ Ⓔ	30 Ⓐ Ⓑ Ⓒ Ⓓ Ⓔ

SCANTRON® EliteView™ EM-295665-1:654321

INSTRUCTIONS FOR COMPLETING THE BIOGRAPHICAL AREA ARE ON THE BACK COVER OF YOUR TEST BOOKLET.
USE ONLY A NO. 2 OR HB PENCIL TO COMPLETE THIS ANSWER SHEET. DO NOT USE INK.

1 LAST NAME   FIRST NAME   MI

(letter grids A–Z)

2 LAST 4 DIGITS OF SOCIAL SECURITY/ SOCIAL INSURANCE NO.

L

3 LSAC ACCOUNT NUMBER

4 CENTER NUMBER

5 DATE OF BIRTH

MONTH	DAY	YEAR
Jan		
Feb		
Mar		
Apr		
May		
June		
July		
Aug		
Sept		
Oct		
Nov		
Dec		

6 TEST FORM CODE

7 RACIAL/ETHNIC DESCRIPTION
Mark one or more
- 1 Amer. Indian/Alaska Native
- 2 Asian
- 3 Black/African American
- 4 Canadian Aboriginal
- 5 Caucasian/White
- 6 Hispanic/Latino
- 7 Native Hawaiian/ Other Pacific Islander
- 8 Puerto Rican
- 9 TSI/Aboriginal Australian

8 SEX
- Male
- Female

9 DOMINANT LANGUAGE
- English
- Other

10 ENGLISH FLUENCY
- Yes
- No

11 TEST DATE
MONTH / DAY / YEAR

12 TEST FORM

13 TEST BOOK SERIAL NO.

Law School Admission Test

Mark one and only one answer to each question. Be sure to fill in completely the space for your intended answer choice. If you erase, do so completely. Make no stray marks.

SECTION 1	SECTION 2	SECTION 3	SECTION 4	SECTION 5
1 A B C D E	1 A B C D E	1 A B C D E	1 A B C D E	1 A B C D E
2 A B C D E	2 A B C D E	2 A B C D E	2 A B C D E	2 A B C D E
3 A B C D E	3 A B C D E	3 A B C D E	3 A B C D E	3 A B C D E
4 A B C D E	4 A B C D E	4 A B C D E	4 A B C D E	4 A B C D E
5 A B C D E	5 A B C D E	5 A B C D E	5 A B C D E	5 A B C D E
6 A B C D E	6 A B C D E	6 A B C D E	6 A B C D E	6 A B C D E
7 A B C D E	7 A B C D E	7 A B C D E	7 A B C D E	7 A B C D E
8 A B C D E	8 A B C D E	8 A B C D E	8 A B C D E	8 A B C D E
9 A B C D E	9 A B C D E	9 A B C D E	9 A B C D E	9 A B C D E
10 A B C D E	10 A B C D E	10 A B C D E	10 A B C D E	10 A B C D E
11 A B C D E	11 A B C D E	11 A B C D E	11 A B C D E	11 A B C D E
12 A B C D E	12 A B C D E	12 A B C D E	12 A B C D E	12 A B C D E
13 A B C D E	13 A B C D E	13 A B C D E	13 A B C D E	13 A B C D E
14 A B C D E	14 A B C D E	14 A B C D E	14 A B C D E	14 A B C D E
15 A B C D E	15 A B C D E	15 A B C D E	15 A B C D E	15 A B C D E
16 A B C D E	16 A B C D E	16 A B C D E	16 A B C D E	16 A B C D E
17 A B C D E	17 A B C D E	17 A B C D E	17 A B C D E	17 A B C D E
18 A B C D E	18 A B C D E	18 A B C D E	18 A B C D E	18 A B C D E
19 A B C D E	19 A B C D E	19 A B C D E	19 A B C D E	19 A B C D E
20 A B C D E	20 A B C D E	20 A B C D E	20 A B C D E	20 A B C D E
21 A B C D E	21 A B C D E	21 A B C D E	21 A B C D E	21 A B C D E
22 A B C D E	22 A B C D E	22 A B C D E	22 A B C D E	22 A B C D E
23 A B C D E	23 A B C D E	23 A B C D E	23 A B C D E	23 A B C D E
24 A B C D E	24 A B C D E	24 A B C D E	24 A B C D E	24 A B C D E
25 A B C D E	25 A B C D E	25 A B C D E	25 A B C D E	25 A B C D E
26 A B C D E	26 A B C D E	26 A B C D E	26 A B C D E	26 A B C D E
27 A B C D E	27 A B C D E	27 A B C D E	27 A B C D E	27 A B C D E
28 A B C D E	28 A B C D E	28 A B C D E	28 A B C D E	28 A B C D E
29 A B C D E	29 A B C D E	29 A B C D E	29 A B C D E	29 A B C D E
30 A B C D E	30 A B C D E	30 A B C D E	30 A B C D E	30 A B C D E

14 PLEASE PRINT INFORMATION

LAST NAME

FIRST NAME

DATE OF BIRTH

A

INSTRUCTIONS FOR COMPLETING THE BIOGRAPHICAL AREA ARE ON THE BACK COVER OF YOUR TEST BOOKLET.
USE ONLY A NO. 2 OR HB PENCIL TO COMPLETE THIS ANSWER SHEET. DO NOT USE INK.

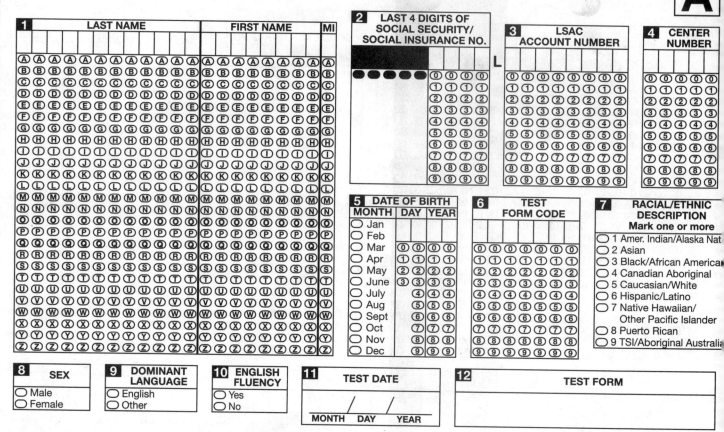

8 SEX
○ Male
○ Female

9 DOMINANT LANGUAGE
○ English
○ Other

10 ENGLISH FLUENCY
○ Yes
○ No

11 TEST DATE
MONTH / DAY / YEAR

12 TEST FORM

Law School Admission Test

Mark one and only one answer to each question. Be sure to fill in completely the space for your intended answer choice. If you erase, do so completely. Make no stray marks.

SECTION 1

1 (A) (B) (C) (D) (E)
2 (A) (B) (C) (D) (E)
3 (A) (B) (C) (D) (E)
4 (A) (B) (C) (D) (E)
5 (A) (B) (C) (D) (E)
6 (A) (B) (C) (D) (E)
7 (A) (B) (C) (D) (E)
8 (A) (B) (C) (D) (E)
9 (A) (B) (C) (D) (E)
10 (A) (B) (C) (D) (E)
11 (A) (B) (C) (D) (E)
12 (A) (B) (C) (D) (E)
13 (A) (B) (C) (D) (E)
14 (A) (B) (C) (D) (E)
15 (A) (B) (C) (D) (E)
16 (A) (B) (C) (D) (E)
17 (A) (B) (C) (D) (E)
18 (A) (B) (C) (D) (E)
19 (A) (B) (C) (D) (E)
20 (A) (B) (C) (D) (E)
21 (A) (B) (C) (D) (E)
22 (A) (B) (C) (D) (E)
23 (A) (B) (C) (D) (E)
24 (A) (B) (C) (D) (E)
25 (A) (B) (C) (D) (E)
26 (A) (B) (C) (D) (E)
27 (A) (B) (C) (D) (E)
28 (A) (B) (C) (D) (E)
29 (A) (B) (C) (D) (E)
30 (A) (B) (C) (D) (E)

SECTION 2

1 (A) (B) (C) (D) (E)
2 (A) (B) (C) (D) (E)
3 (A) (B) (C) (D) (E)
4 (A) (B) (C) (D) (E)
5 (A) (B) (C) (D) (E)
6 (A) (B) (C) (D) (E)
7 (A) (B) (C) (D) (E)
8 (A) (B) (C) (D) (E)
9 (A) (B) (C) (D) (E)
10 (A) (B) (C) (D) (E)
11 (A) (B) (C) (D) (E)
12 (A) (B) (C) (D) (E)
13 (A) (B) (C) (D) (E)
14 (A) (B) (C) (D) (E)
15 (A) (B) (C) (D) (E)
16 (A) (B) (C) (D) (E)
17 (A) (B) (C) (D) (E)
18 (A) (B) (C) (D) (E)
19 (A) (B) (C) (D) (E)
20 (A) (B) (C) (D) (E)
21 (A) (B) (C) (D) (E)
22 (A) (B) (C) (D) (E)
23 (A) (B) (C) (D) (E)
24 (A) (B) (C) (D) (E)
25 (A) (B) (C) (D) (E)
26 (A) (B) (C) (D) (E)
27 (A) (B) (C) (D) (E)
28 (A) (B) (C) (D) (E)
29 (A) (B) (C) (D) (E)
30 (A) (B) (C) (D) (E)

SECTION 3

1 (A) (B) (C) (D) (E)
2 (A) (B) (C) (D) (E)
3 (A) (B) (C) (D) (E)
4 (A) (B) (C) (D) (E)
5 (A) (B) (C) (D) (E)
6 (A) (B) (C) (D) (E)
7 (A) (B) (C) (D) (E)
8 (A) (B) (C) (D) (E)
9 (A) (B) (C) (D) (E)
10 (A) (B) (C) (D) (E)
11 (A) (B) (C) (D) (E)
12 (A) (B) (C) (D) (E)
13 (A) (B) (C) (D) (E)
14 (A) (B) (C) (D) (E)
15 (A) (B) (C) (D) (E)
16 (A) (B) (C) (D) (E)
17 (A) (B) (C) (D) (E)
18 (A) (B) (C) (D) (E)
19 (A) (B) (C) (D) (E)
20 (A) (B) (C) (D) (E)
21 (A) (B) (C) (D) (E)
22 (A) (B) (C) (D) (E)
23 (A) (B) (C) (D) (E)
24 (A) (B) (C) (D) (E)
25 (A) (B) (C) (D) (E)
26 (A) (B) (C) (D) (E)
27 (A) (B) (C) (D) (E)
28 (A) (B) (C) (D) (E)
29 (A) (B) (C) (D) (E)
30 (A) (B) (C) (D) (E)

SECTION 4

1 (A) (B) (C) (D) (E)
2 (A) (B) (C) (D) (E)
3 (A) (B) (C) (D) (E)
4 (A) (B) (C) (D) (E)
5 (A) (B) (C) (D) (E)
6 (A) (B) (C) (D) (E)
7 (A) (B) (C) (D) (E)
8 (A) (B) (C) (D) (E)
9 (A) (B) (C) (D) (E)
10 (A) (B) (C) (D) (E)
11 (A) (B) (C) (D) (E)
12 (A) (B) (C) (D) (E)
13 (A) (B) (C) (D) (E)
14 (A) (B) (C) (D) (E)
15 (A) (B) (C) (D) (E)
16 (A) (B) (C) (D) (E)
17 (A) (B) (C) (D) (E)
18 (A) (B) (C) (D) (E)
19 (A) (B) (C) (D) (E)
20 (A) (B) (C) (D) (E)
21 (A) (B) (C) (D) (E)
22 (A) (B) (C) (D) (E)
23 (A) (B) (C) (D) (E)
24 (A) (B) (C) (D) (E)
25 (A) (B) (C) (D) (E)
26 (A) (B) (C) (D) (E)
27 (A) (B) (C) (D) (E)
28 (A) (B) (C) (D) (E)
29 (A) (B) (C) (D) (E)
30 (A) (B) (C) (D) (E)

SECTION 5

1 (A) (B) (C) (D) (E)
2 (A) (B) (C) (D) (E)
3 (A) (B) (C) (D) (E)
4 (A) (B) (C) (D) (E)
5 (A) (B) (C) (D) (E)
6 (A) (B) (C) (D) (E)
7 (A) (B) (C) (D) (E)
8 (A) (B) (C) (D) (E)
9 (A) (B) (C) (D) (E)
10 (A) (B) (C) (D) (E)
11 (A) (B) (C) (D) (E)
12 (A) (B) (C) (D) (E)
13 (A) (B) (C) (D) (E)
14 (A) (B) (C) (D) (E)
15 (A) (B) (C) (D) (E)
16 (A) (B) (C) (D) (E)
17 (A) (B) (C) (D) (E)
18 (A) (B) (C) (D) (E)
19 (A) (B) (C) (D) (E)
20 (A) (B) (C) (D) (E)
21 (A) (B) (C) (D) (E)
22 (A) (B) (C) (D) (E)
23 (A) (B) (C) (D) (E)
24 (A) (B) (C) (D) (E)
25 (A) (B) (C) (D) (E)
26 (A) (B) (C) (D) (E)
27 (A) (B) (C) (D) (E)
28 (A) (B) (C) (D) (E)
29 (A) (B) (C) (D) (E)
30 (A) (B) (C) (D) (E)

13 TEST BOOK SERIAL NO.

14 PLEASE PRINT INFORMATION

LAST NAME

FIRST NAME

DATE OF BIRTH